Optimizing DAX

Improving DAX performance in Microsoft Power BI and Analysis Services

Second Edition

Alberto Ferrari and Marco Russo

Publisher / Editorial Production: SQLBI Corp., Las Vegas, NV, Unites States

Revision: 2 (April 30, 2024)

Authors: Alberto Ferrari, Marco Russo
Copy Editor: Claire Costa
Cover Designer: Daniele Perilli

ISBN: 978-1-7353652-2-0
Library of Congress Control Number: 2024903659

Contents at a Glance

SECTION 1	**CORE CONCEPTS**	
CHAPTER 1	Introduction (S01.M01)	**3**
CHAPTER 2	Introducing optimization with examples (S01.M02)	**11**
CHAPTER 3	Introducing the Tabular query architecture (S01.M03)	**33**
CHAPTER 4	Using the Power BI Desktop performance analyzer (S01.M04)	**51**
CHAPTER 5	Using DAX Studio (S01.M05)	**61**
CHAPTER 6	Introducing query plans (S01.M06)	**73**
SECTION 2	**THE FORMULA ENGINE**	
CHAPTER 7	Understanding the DAX Formula Engine (S02.M01)	**83**
CHAPTER 8	Understanding query plans (S02.M02)	**128**
CHAPTER 9	Optimizing the formula engine (S02.M03)	**167**
SECTION 3	**VERTIPAQ**	
CHAPTER 10	Understanding the VertiPaq engine (S03.M01)	**203**
CHAPTER 11	Understanding VertiPaq relationships (S03.M02)	**261**
CHAPTER 12	Analyzing VertiPaq storage engine queries (S03.M03)	**287**
CHAPTER 13	Optimizing common DAX constructs (S03.M04)	**337**
CHAPTER 14	Moving and applying filters to tables (S03.M05)	**409**
CHAPTER 15	Optimization examples for VertiPaq (S03.M06)	**465**
CHAPTER 16	Understanding security optimization (S03.M07)	**523**
SECTION 4	**DIRECTQUERY OVER SQL**	
CHAPTER 17	Understanding DirectQuery over SQL (S04.M01)	**565**
CHAPTER 18	Optimizing DirectQuery over SQL (S04.M02)	**597**
CHAPTER 19	Optimization examples for DirectQuery (S04.M03)	**673**
SECTION 5	**COMPOSITE MODELS**	
CHAPTER 20	Understanding composite models (S05.M01)	**703**
CHAPTER 21	Composite models optimization examples (S05.M02)	**733**
CHAPTER 22	Understanding complex models (S05.M03)	**769**

Contents

SECTION 1   **CORE CONCEPTS**

CHAPTER 1   Introduction (S01.M01) **3**

Prerequisites.. 3
Overview of the Tabular architecture.. 4
Structure of the training 5
Coding conventions 7
Companion content 8
      Software prerequisites.. 8
      Hardware prerequisites 9
      Download demos... 9
      Sample code references.. 10

CHAPTER 2   Introducing optimization with examples (S01.M02)..................... **11**

Optimizing DAX 11
Optimizing the model 18
Optimizing composite models 26
Conclusions 32

CHAPTER 3   Introducing the Tabular query architecture (S01.M03)................. **33**

Introducing the formula engine 33
Introducing VertiPaq and DirectQuery architectures 35
Introducing the VertiPaq storage engine 36
Introducing the DirectQuery over SQL storage engine 38
Introducing DirectQuery over AS 40
Introducing data islands and cross-island query resolution..............................42
Different types of models 47
Conclusions 49

CHAPTER 4   Using the Power BI Desktop performance analyzer (S01.M04) **51**

Running Performance Analyzer..51
Understanding the numbers reported by Performance Analyzer 54
Optimizing queries or measures?..56
What can be optimized 57
Saving performance data...60
Conclusions 60

CHAPTER 5   Using DAX Studio (S01.M05).. **61**

Installing DAX Studio...61

Introducing the metrics of a database 62
Introducing All Queries 65
Capturing Excel queries (MDX) 66
Introducing Load Performance Data 68
Introducing Query Plan and Server Timings 70
Conclusions 71

CHAPTER 6   **Introducing query plans (S01.M06)** **73**

Introducing the logical query plan 75
Introducing the physical query plan 75
Introducing storage engine queries 77
Query plans in DirectQuery 78
Conclusions 80

SECTION 2   **THE FORMULA ENGINE**

CHAPTER 7   **Understanding the DAX Formula Engine (S02.M01)** **83**

Understanding datacaches 83
Understanding materialization 90
Understanding callbacks 96
Formula engine with different storage engines 100
Understanding vertical fusion 100
Understanding horizontal fusion 105
Examples of formula engine calculations 110
    Sales of best products *110*
    Top three colors *115*
Measuring performance 118
Gathering important timings from the query plan 119
Analyzing query plans and timings 120
    Year-to-date calculation of an additive measure *120*
    Year-to-date calculation of a non-additive measure *123*
Conclusions 127

CHAPTER 8   **Understanding query plans (S02.M02)** **128**

Query plan structure 128
Query plan operator types 130
    Properties of ScaLogOp *130*
    Properties of RelLogOp *131*
    Properties of LookupPhyOp *132*
    Properties of IterPhyOp *132*
    Properties of SpoolPhyOp *133*
Interactions between the formula engine and the storage engine 133
Common query plan operators 137
Examples of query plans 139

Comparing SUM versus SUMX 139
Comparing IF versus IF.EAGER 142
Filtering with DAX versus using relationships 151
Understanding SWITCH optimization 156
Conclusions 165

CHAPTER 9   Optimizing the formula engine (S02.M03) **167**

Optimizing datacache use 167
Sales of best products 173
Running total of sales and ABC analysis 180
Year-over-year customer growth as a percentage 189
Conclusions 199

SECTION 3   **VERTIPAQ**

CHAPTER 10   Understanding the VertiPaq engine (S03.M01) **203**

Using VertiPaq Analyzer 203
Gathering vpax information with DAX Studio 203
Analyzing a vpax with VertiPaq Analyzer 205
Tabular data types 206
Introduction to the VertiPaq columnar database 207
Understanding VertiPaq compression 211
Understanding value encoding 211
Understanding hash encoding 213
Understanding run-length encoding 214
Using VertiPaq Analyzer to understand VertiPaq compression 216
Understanding re-encoding 219
Understanding segmentation and partitioning 221
Understanding the importance of sorting 229
Understanding VertiPaq relationships 234
Understanding attribute hierarchies 239
Optimizing VertiPaq models: examples 242
Sales amount versus quantity and net price 242
Storing currency conversion data 247
Date time versus date and time 256
Conclusions 260

CHAPTER 11   Understanding VertiPaq relationships (S03.M02) **261**

Regular, unidirectional one-to-many relationships 262
Regular, bidirectional one-to-many relationships 267
Regular, one-to-one relationships 275
Limited, many-to-many cardinality relationships 278
Conclusions 285

CHAPTER 12   Analyzing VertiPaq storage engine queries (S03.M03)............................**287**

Analyzing simple xmSQL queries 287
Introducing basic VertiPaq functionalities 290
Introducing batches 291
Understanding internal and external SE queries.................................... 294
Understanding distinct count in xmSQL.. 297
Understanding VertiPaq joins and filters 298
    Introducing VertiPaq joins... *298*
    Introducing bitmap indexes *299*
    Introducing reverse joins *304*
Understanding VertiCalc and callbacks 308
    Understanding CallbackDataID *309*
    Understanding EncodeCallback *314*
    Understanding LogAbsValueCallback.. *319*
    Understanding RoundValueCallback *321*
    Understanding MinMaxColumnPositionCallback *324*
    Understanding Cond *327*
Understanding the VertiPaq cache 329
Choosing the correct data type for VertiPaq calculations..................... 332
Conclusions 335

CHAPTER 13   Optimizing common DAX constructs (S03.M04) **337**

Optimizing nested iterations... 337
Understanding the effect of context transition 349
Different ways of performing a distinct count 353
Optimizing LASTDATE calculations.. 365
Avoid using SUMMARIZE and clustering 373
Optimizing division by checking for zeroes 379
Reducing the extent of the search by removing blanks......................... 386
Optimizing time intelligence calculations... 395
Distinct count over large cardinality columns....................................... 401
Conclusions 408

CHAPTER 14   Moving and applying filters to tables (S03.M05)............................**409**

Different filters in CALCULATE... 409
    Analyzing single-column filters.. *410*
    Analyzing multiple-column filters... *422*
    Analyzing filters over multiple tables.. *427*
Understanding sparse or dense filters 428
Filter columns, not tables 431
Modeling many-to-many relationships 435
    Testing the bidirectional model.. *438*
    Testing the star model.. *444*

Testing the snake model 447

Testing the advanced snake model 457

Conclusions 463

CHAPTER 15   **Optimization examples for VertiPaq (S03.M06)** **465**

Reducing nested iterations 465

Optimizing complex filters in CALCULATE 472

Optimizing Fusion Optimization 476

Currency conversion 478

Optimizing cumulative totals 486

Average price variation of products over stores 494

Optimizing the number of days with no sales 503

Computing open orders 510

Optimizing SWITCH and nested measures 516

Conclusions 521

CHAPTER 16   **Understanding security optimization (S03.M07)** **523**

Testing security conditions and their performance impact 523

Understanding when and where security is enforced 524

Understanding cached bitmap indexes and embedded filters 528

Optimizing dynamic security 536

Optimizing static security on the fact table 544

Optimizing dynamic security on the fact table 552

Conclusions 562

SECTION 4   **DIRECTQUERY OVER SQL**

CHAPTER 17   **Understanding DirectQuery over SQL (S04.M01)** **565**

Working with DirectQuery...565

Reading SQL code in this book 566

Reading the numbers in DAX Studio 568

Callback operations 570

Calculated tables 574

Calculated columns 574

How caching works in DirectQuery over SQL 576

Understanding latency to send queries to the remote server 577

Max number of rows in a data cache 577

Different types of relationships 578

Regular one-to-many relationships 578

Limited many-to-many relationships 582

One-to-one relationships 583

DirectQuery over SQL max parallel queries 583

Using different data islands 592

Introducing aggregations and hybrid tables 596
Conclusions 596

CHAPTER 18   Optimizing DirectQuery over SQL (S04.M02) **597**

Building an SQL data model for Analysis Services 597
    Designing indexes *598*
    Using columnstore indexes *601*
    Choosing column data types *603*
    Do not use Power Query transformations *607*
Optimizing relationships 607
    Choosing the best data type for relationships *608*
    Relying on referential integrity *610*
    Using COMBINEVALUES to implement multi-column relationships ... *615*
Using aggregations 623
    Introducing aggregations *623*
    Introducing VertiPaq aggregation and Dual storage mode *631*
    Designing aggregations for simple calculations *635*
    Designing aggregations for row-level calculations *638*
    Designing aggregations for distinct counts *642*
    Aggregations are not VertiPaq aliases of DirectQuery tables *646*
    Manually activating aggregations in DAX *652*
    Using automatic aggregations *659*
Using hybrid tables 659
    Introducing hybrid tables *660*
    Reducing partition queries with DataCoverageDefinition *668*
    Hybrid tables and distinct counts *668*
    Creating hybrid tables with incremental refresh *670*
Conclusions 672

CHAPTER 19   Optimization examples for DirectQuery (S04.M03) **673**

Optimizing LASTDATE calculations 673
Optimizing division by checking for zeroes 681
Optimizing time intelligence calculations 687
Computing distinct counts 695
Conclusions 700

SECTION 5   COMPOSITE MODELS

CHAPTER 20   Understanding composite models (S05.M01) **703**

Introducing composite models 703
Understanding wholesale and retail calculations 705
Calculated tables 712
Calculated columns 712
Tracing remote queries 714

Understanding relationships between tables 716
Understanding special DAX functions for composite models 720
    Understanding GROUPCROSSAPPLY and GROUPCROSSAPPLYTABLE.....*721*
    Understanding DEPENDON *723*
Splitting calculations between wholesale and retail 726
Conclusions 732

CHAPTER 21   Composite models optimization examples (S05.M02) **............................733**

Static segmentation 733
Budget and time intelligence calculations 748
Dynamic ABC analysis 759

CHAPTER 22   Understanding complex models (S05.M03) **..769**

Understanding the role of the formula engine in complex models 769
Calculated tables 773
Calculated columns 773
Relationships in complex models 780
Using SQL Server features to avoid multiple data islands.............................790
Using VertiPaq to snapshot expensive DirectQuery queries 794
Conclusions 803

Section 1
CORE CONCEPTS

Introduction

This book is the written version of the Optimizing DAX video course (second edition) published by SQLBI. While the PDF version is available to video course students, we decided to publish a printed version for those who want a printed version or do not want to get the entire video course and prefer to study books.

Several years ago, we recorded and published the first edition of the Optimizing DAX video course. At the time, Tabular was much simpler than it is today, and the DAX optimization was described in a few chapters of "The Definitive Guide to DAX" book, including some details about the VertiPaq model. In the first edition of that training, we did not cover – on purpose – DirectQuery optimizations. Indeed, DirectQuery was not a real option at that time.

Over the years, Tabular has evolved, and its complexity is now much more significant. Microsoft introduced a more usable version of DirectQuery, released composite models, and improved the DAX engine by adding new optimization techniques. Moreover, as teachers, we increased our knowledge and experience about the engine in the same period. When it was time to create a new training version, we quickly discovered the amount of materials to teach was massive. Therefore, despite this being the second edition of the Optimizing DAX video course, it is – in reality – a brand new training (and book) about the state of the art of optimizing Tabular models.

An important note is that we wrote this content using Analysis Services 2022 and Power BI versions available in 2023. Different engine versions might show different behaviors, for the better or the worse. We will say this for the first time now and repeat it multiple times during the training: you must test any of the optimization techniques we teach on your models and the version of the engine you are currently using.

Prerequisites

The content of this book is advanced. As such, it certainly does not start from scratch. We take for granted that the reader has an excellent knowledge of several topics:

- **The DAX language**. In the training, we never teach DAX concepts. Here, the goal is how to produce efficient DAX code. We will write a lot of DAX code together, taking it for granted that you will quickly understand the different formulas. If you are unfamiliar with DAX, we strongly suggest the Mastering DAX video course, "The Definitive Guide to DAX" book, and practicing the DAX language in your daily job for at least one year. **Being proficient with DAX is an absolute requirement**. The book also uses query columns and query tables described in these articles:

    - **Introducing DEFINE COLUMN in DAX queries**
      https://www.sqlbi.com/articles/introducing-define-column-in-dax-queries/

- **Introducing DEFINE TABLE in DAX queries**
  https://www.sqlbi.com/articles/introducing-define-table-in-dax-queries/

- **The SQL language**. The modules about DirectQuery use quite some SQL code. You do not need to master all the details about SQL. Still, you must be able to read and understand SQL code quickly and how indexes, column stores, and other relational database technologies may affect your query's results and performance. We use Microsoft SQL Server in the book examples. You can apply the same concepts to other relational databases – even though you cannot use the same specific techniques described for Microsoft SQL Server.

- **The Tabular architecture**. Tabular is a complex engine that includes different technologies. We will use but do not explain many features of Tabular. Even though you can read and learn most of the content of this book without a deep understanding of the Tabular engine, we strongly suggest our students attend the Mastering Tabular video course first. Unfortunately, we do not have a corresponding book for that content.

- **DAX Studio**. DAX Studio is the primary tool used throughout the entire training. We introduce some basic concepts about DAX Studio but do not go in-depth on all the tool features. If you are unfamiliar with DAX Studio, we suggest you attend the free DAX Tools training first at https://www.sqlbi.com/p/dax-tools-video-course/.

Overview of the Tabular architecture

The architecture of a modern Tabular solution can be rather complex. To perform any optimization, we must understand many technical details about a Tabular solution. Indeed, when there are performance issues, users typically report that "the dashboard is slow" or "it takes too long to produce the report". However, the report is only the tip of the iceberg of a performance issue hidden in any place of the architecture.

The following figure shows a very high-level overview of what happens when rendering a report:

Overview of a Tabular Architecture

The report sends a query to the Tabular model, which runs the query and might need to access an SQL database if the model uses DirectQuery, scan a VertiPaq storage if the model is in import mode, or connect to another Tabular model if we are using a composite model. Worse, it might be a mix of all these technologies together in a complex model.

The optimization techniques to use strongly depend on the architecture. We might face a simple DAX issue: poor code leads to bad performance. However, the same DAX code might work well with VertiPaq, and it might be a severe issue in a composite model. It might be the case that the code itself works fine, but the amount of materialization is excessive because the model uses DirectQuery.

In other words, providing guidelines about authoring good DAX code and building a performant model is nearly impossible unless we clearly understand all the pieces connected in a Tabular model.

Structure of the training

The book has five sections:

- **Section 1: Core concepts**. This introductory section starts with some optimization examples to provide an overview of the steps needed to optimize DAX code or Tabular models. Then, it covers the main topics about the Tabular architecture, includes information about the tools to use, and introduces the query plan concept.
- **Section 2: The formula engine**. This section is no longer an introduction. We go as deep as possible into the details of the formula engine, discover its operators, understand the datacaches, read the query plan, and then start optimizing code.
- **Section 3: VertiPaq**. Time for the main course. VertiPaq is the most critical section. We dive into the details of the VertiPaq engine through seven dense chapters packed with technical

information. The number of scenarios we optimize increases significantly, along with our knowledge.

- **Section 4: DirectQuery over SQL**. This section explores all the details about the DirectQuery over SQL storage engine. Please do not skip the previous sections of the book; they are required to understand how DirectQuery works.
- **Section 5: Composite models**. Composite models are a recent architectural addition to Tabular, and they prove to be more challenging because they share all the complexity of VertiPaq and DirectQuery.

A first read of the book from cover to cover reveals a long journey in DAX optimizations. Once you finish the book, you can use it as a reference to refresh your mind about specific topics.

We advise readers not to jump directly to the more advanced sessions until they are familiar with the previous topics. We build knowledge in steps and never repeat a topic multiple times. If you fast-forward to an advanced chapter, it is unlikely you will be able to appreciate several of the nuances.

Coding conventions

The book has many code samples in three languages: DAX, SQL, and xmSQL. You will learn xmSQL in this book, whereas you should already know DAX and SQL. Every language has a different style for code snippets that we present here to familiarize ourselves with.

Here is a sample code in DAX:

```
EVALUATE
SUMMARIZECOLUMNS (
    ROLLUPADDISSUBTOTAL (
        'Date'[Year],
        "IsGrandTotalRowTotal",
        ROLLUPGROUP ( 'Date'[Month], 'Date'[Month Number] ),
        "IsDM1Total"
    ),
    "Sales_Amount", 'Sales'[Sales Amount]
)
```

The following is SQL:

```
SELECT TOP (1000001) *
FROM (
    SELECT [t1_Year], SUM([a0]) AS [a0]
    FROM (
        SELECT [t1].[Year] AS [t1_Year],
            ([t3].[Quantity] * [t3].[Net Price]) AS [a0]
        FROM (
            [Data].[Sales] AS [t3]
                LEFT JOIN [dbo].[Date] AS [t1] ON ([t3].[Order Date] = [t1].[Date])
            )
        ) AS [t0]
    GROUP BY [t1_Year]
    ) AS [MainTable]
WHERE (NOT (([a0] IS NULL)))
```

And the last example is xmSQL:

```
WITH
    $Expr0 := ( PFCAST ( 'Sales'[Quantity] AS  INT ) * PFCAST ( 'Sales'[Net Price] AS  INT )  )
SELECT
    'Product'[Brand],
    SUM ( @$Expr0 )
FROM 'Sales'
    LEFT OUTER JOIN 'Product'
        ON 'Sales'[ProductKey]='Product'[ProductKey];
```

Companion content

All the examples included in the book can be downloaded and reproduced on your computer. You might see different absolute results because of differences in CPU, RAM, and software versions. However, most of the time, you will see the same relative differences between different optimization steps. Keep in mind the different baselines between your computers and ours. Because we used different hardware in different parts of the book, you will always find a reference to the CPU used in the initial comments of the DAX queries you can download.

You can download all the files following the link to **Companion content** on the https://sql.bi/optdaxdemo page.

In the following sections, we provide software and hardware prerequisites to use the demo files, how to download them, and how to find the demo files corresponding to each book chapter.

Software prerequisites

You should have the following software to practice using the book demos. If you want to know more about the optional tools, you can find more information in the Mastering Tabular video course from SQLBI at https://www.sqlbi.com/p/mastering-tabular-video-course/.

- **Power BI Desktop**
  https://powerbi.microsoft.com/downloads/

- **DAX Studio**
  https://daxstudio.org/

- **Excel** (optional)
  https://www.microsoft.com/microsoft-365/excel

- **SQL Server 2022** (optional)
  https://www.microsoft.com/sql-server/

- **SQL Server 2022 latest cumulative updates** (optional)
  https://www.microsoft.com/en-us/download/details.aspx?id=105013

- **SQL Server Analysis Services Tabular** (optional)
  https://learn.microsoft.com/analysis-services/tabular-models/tabular-models-ssas

- **SQL Server Management Studio** (optional)
  https://learn.microsoft.com/sql/ssms/download-sql-server-management-studio-ssms

- **Tabular Editor 2 or 3** (optional)
  https://www.tabulareditor.com/

Hardware prerequisites

To practice the demos with the largest PBIX demo file (Contoso 100M.pbix, 2GB), you need a computer with **at least 16GB of RAM**. If you do not have enough RAM, you can use the smaller Contoso 10M.pbix, which should run on any computer running Power BI Desktop, even though the metrics obtained can be significantly different from the ones shown in the book.

If you want to create the largest database for Analysis Services (Contoso 100M x 10), we suggest a computer with at least 64GB of RAM. This model is used in a few demos: you do not need to repeat those same demos, as you can see similar effects on smaller models, even though the results will be at a different order of magnitude.

Download demos

The demos are files we use in the book to illustrate how to measure performance and optimize code. You need Power BI Desktop and DAX Studio to repeat the same demos on your PC. For a few demos that require very large databases, you need SQL Server and Analysis Services: if you do not have enough RAM to install those databases, repeat the demos on the smaller Power BI Desktop files.

To practice the concepts learned, we suggest looking for patterns you have seen in each section by repeating the same analyses with the sample demo files provided and then on your models.

All the Contoso sample databases have the same structure; the only difference is their size. For example, Contoso 10K contains around 10,000 orders, while Contoso 1M contains around 1 million orders. Most of the demos run on Contoso 100M, and few run on a larger or smaller Contoso database: you find the reference to the Contoso version in the comments at the beginning of each DAX demo file.

The **PBIX files** contain the sample database for Power BI Desktop. You do not need to refresh these databases. Still, if you want, you should download the SQL Server backup (.bak files), restore them with the same database name (without the .bak extension) on a local SQL Server database, and create an alias named Demo that points to the SQL Server instance where you restored the bak files. Read the Creating database aliases on SQL Server 2022 article to create the Demo aliases on both 32-bit and 64-bit configurations of SQL Server: https://sql.bi/creating-aliases/.

The **Optimizing DAX - Demo files.ZIP** archive contains all the files used in the demos of the book. Download the file and unzip the content in a local folder on your computer. Most of the demos run on a Contoso sample database; only a limited number of demos have separated PBIX files that you find in the same module folder of the demo files.

The **BAK files** are SQL Server backups you can restore on SQL Server 2019 or 2022 to refresh the PBIX file and/or to populate corresponding Analysis Services databases. Read the Creating database aliases on SQL Server 2022 article to create the Demo aliases on both 32-bit and 64-bit configurations of SQL Server: https://sql.bi/creating-aliases/. The Contoso 100M.bak file is stored in two files, Contoso 100M.7z.001 and Contoso100M.7z.002: you can extract the Contoso 100M.bak using 7-Zip (https://www.7-zip.org/).

The **AS BIM - Contoso 100M X 10.ZIP** archive contains the Tabular project (BIM file) to generate the

Analysis Services database "Contoso 100M x 10" used with the demos with the largest database. You need a large server with at least 64GB of RAM to process this database. However, you can use the Contoso 100M PBIX file to run the same demos executed on "Contoso 100M x 10" (see the reference database in the comments of the DAX code): you will see similar effects at a smaller order of magnitude.

Sample code references

At the beginning of each book chapter, there is a reference to the sample code. This reference is the corresponding section and module of the Optimizing DAX video course on SQLBI. For example, SAMPLE S02.M03 means that the sample code for the chapter is in the folder starting with "S02.M03" within the Demo folder. Such a reference also corresponds to Section 02 and Module 03 of the video course.

Introducing optimization with examples

The amount of knowledge required to optimize any measure is massive. The architecture of Tabular is rather complex, and we will dive into extremely technical details to appreciate the effect of any change.

It is easy to lose sight of the overall reason why certain specifics are important when diving into details. Therefore, if we were to follow an academic approach, and explain all the details before starting to use the concepts, the training would be extremely hard to follow, somewhat boring, and you would have to constantly go back to previous chapters to refresh your memory about topics that did not seem relevant the first time around.

We chose a different approach. This first set of introductory content shows the complete process of optimization through examples. We neither explain each step in full nor do we explain why we perform certain actions. The goal of this first set of optimizations is not that of learning how to optimize. Instead, we want to show the reasoning required to perform optimizations in different architectures.

Do not consider these first optimizations as best practices, and do not try to derive complete knowledge from these examples. These are just simple examples to show the overall process. Later on, we shall start to dive into the details. Then, hopefully, having seen the complete process will help you focus on the details without losing sight of the big picture.

During the process of optimizing the code, we also use several tools. Again, we do not provide a complete reference of those tools, because the goal is to show you when the tools are used rather than explain how to use them. We provide a much greater level of detail in the following chapters. In the entire description, we are deliberately concise. If the description seems cloudy to you, this is to be expected. Our promise is that you will be able to perform the same operations once you complete the training and have some more experience under your belt.

Optimizing DAX

We start by analyzing a simple measure that contains a DAX issue. The code is poorly written, and in the process of trying to optimize it, we will also make it worse before finally reaching the optimized version. The example is not relevant, despite being quite common. The critical detail to focus on is the entire optimization process.

It all starts with a report that users describe as slow. It contains a simple measure that computes sales for only transactions whose amount is greater than 200.00 USD.

Year	Sales Gt 200
□ 2010	5,966,043,126.80
May	303,911,689.67
June	666,241,293.46
July	638,715,185.11
August	676,336,337.95
September	759,106,437.86
October	785,281,421.80
November	782,639,825.22
December	1,353,810,935.74
⊞ 2011	10,691,471,516.63
⊞ 2012	12,627,251,409.30
⊞ 2013	20,443,916,137.00
⊞ 2014	29,136,505,467.53
⊞ 2015	23,549,371,252.73
⊞ 2016	17,946,710,230.43
⊞ 2017	30,342,774,851.17
Total	223,259,265,362.06

The code of the measure is the following:

```
--------------------------
-- Measure in Sales table
--------------------------
Sales Gt 200 =
SUMX (
    Sales,
    IF (
        Sales[Quantity] * Sales[Net Price] >= 200,
        Sales[Quantity] * Sales[Net Price]
    )
)
```

If you are a seasoned DAX developer, you know where the problem is right off the bat. Nonetheless, in this section we work on the full performance analysis of the measure.

The report is on a Power BI Desktop file, using Import mode. The *Sales* table contains 200M rows, spanning around 10 years of data. We use the Performance Analyzer tool in Power BI Desktop to retrieve the DAX query executed for the visual. Before analyzing the query, Performance Analyzer already provides us with some rather interesting numbers: the query took 1.2 seconds to run on a quite powerful server with 64 virtual cores.

The code of the query is verbose, because it is automatically generated by Power BI:

```
// DAX Query
DEFINE
    VAR __DM3FilterTable =
        TREATAS ( { 2010 }, 'Date'[Year] )
    VAR __DS0Core =
        SUMMARIZECOLUMNS (
            ROLLUPADDISSUBTOTAL (
                'Date'[Year],
                "IsGrandTotalRowTotal",
                ROLLUPGROUP ( 'Date'[Month], 'Date'[Month Number] ),
                "IsDM1Total",
                NONVISUAL ( __DM3FilterTable )
            ),
            "Sales_Gt_200", 'Sales'[Sales Gt 200]
        )
    VAR __DS0PrimaryWindowed =
        TOPN (
            502,
            __DS0Core,
            [IsGrandTotalRowTotal], 0,
            'Date'[Year], 1,
            [IsDM1Total], 0,
            'Date'[Month Number], 1,
            'Date'[Month], 1
        )

EVALUATE
__DS0PrimaryWindowed
ORDER BY
    [IsGrandTotalRowTotal] DESC,
    'Date'[Year],
    [IsDM1Total] DESC,
    'Date'[Month Number],
    'Date'[Month]
```

We want to simplify the query, to make it easier to understand. In the process of simplifying the query, we need to pay attention not to get rid of the problem. The first thing to do is to execute the query in DAX Studio with Server Timings enabled to obtain the first baseline. Later on, we will check that the simplified query did not change the timings in such a way that the issue seems resolved. Here is the DAX Studio timings report.

Total	SE CPU	Line	Subclass	Duration	CPU	Par.	Rows	KB	Timeline
1,083 ms	50,360 ms								
	x47.3	2	Scan	71	391	x5.5	225	4	
FE	**SE**	4	Scan	490	25,141	x51.3	14	1	
19 ms	1,064 ms	6	Scan	503	24,828	x49.4	1	1	
1.8%	98.2%								

SE Queries	SE Cache
3	0
	0.0%

Then, we simplify the query by removing the TOPN function, the final sorting, and other lines to make it shorter. We also add the definition of the measure, so we can change it later. Here is the shorter version we are going to work with:

```
DEFINE
    MEASURE Sales[Sales Gt 200] =
        SUMX (
            Sales,
            IF (
                Sales[Quantity] * Sales[Net Price] >= 200,
                Sales[Quantity] * Sales[Net Price]
            )
        )

EVALUATE
SUMMARIZECOLUMNS (
    ROLLUPADDISSUBTOTAL (
        'Date'[Year],
        "IsGrandTotalRowTotal",
        ROLLUPGROUP ( 'Date'[Month], 'Date'[Month Number] ),
        "IsDM1Total"
    ),
    "Sales_Gt_200", 'Sales'[Sales Gt 200]
)
```

The timings of this query are close to those of the previous one.

Total	SE CPU		Line	Subclass	Duration	CPU	Par.	Rows	KB	Timeline
1,433 ms	72,265 ms									
	x51.0		2	Scan	493	24,203	x49.1	3,150	50	
FE	**SE**		4	Scan	457	23,828	x52.1	14	1	
16 ms	1,417 ms		6	Scan	467	24,234	x51.9	1	1	
1.1%	98.9%									

SE Queries	SE Cache
3	0
	0.0%

```
SET DC_KIND="AUTO";
WITH
    $Expr0 := [CallbackDataID ( IF (
            Sales[Quantity] * Sales[Net Price] >= 200,
            Sales[Quantity] * Sales[Net Price]
    ) ) ] ( PFDATAID ( 'Sales'[Quantity] ), PFDATAID ( 'Sales'[Net Price] ) )
SELECT
```

Since the numbers are similar, we know that the problem is still there and we can start the optimization process. Despite the size of the *Sales* table being relatively large (200M is not huge, but it already is a significant number), the time required to compute the result seems excessive. The degree of parallelism is exceptional (on 64 cores, we obtained x51.0). Though the entire execution time is reported as storage engine CPU, we can clearly see a CallbackDataID, indicating that the formula engine is required to kick in to compute expressions that cannot be pushed down to the storage engine.

We know that a CallbackDataID is often a source of performance issues. It is nearly impossible to remove all CallbackDataIDs from a query, but we can remove it in this situation. The problem is the IF statement inside the iteration carried on by SUMX, because the VertiPaq storage engine does not support conditional logic. We must rephrase the measure to avoid the IF statement; we replace it with a condition set by CALCULATE to rely on filtering rather than IF. A first (wrong) attempt in this direction is the following:

```
DEFINE
    MEASURE Sales[Sales Gt 200] =
        CALCULATE (
            SUMX ( Sales, Sales[Quantity] * Sales[Net Price] ),
            FILTER ( Sales, Sales[Quantity] * Sales[Net Price] >= 200 )
        )

EVALUATE
SUMMARIZECOLUMNS (
    ROLLUPADDISSUBTOTAL (
        'Date'[Year],
        "IsGrandTotalRowTotal",
        ROLLUPGROUP ( 'Date'[Month], 'Date'[Month Number] ),
        "IsDM1Total"
    ),
    "Sales_Gt_200", 'Sales'[Sales Gt 200]
)
```

The idea is to remove the requirement to compute IF by replacing it with a table filter computed by FILTER and applied by CALCULATE. It turns out to be an awful idea: the server timings are much worse than before.

Total	SE CPU	Line	Subclass	Duration	CPU	Par.	Rows	KB	Timeline
23,169 ms	58,689 ms	2	Scan	4,361	15,969	x3.7	5,150,659	60,360	
	x6.0	4	Scan	2,860	16,641	x5.8	5,150,659	20,120	
FE	**SE**	6	Scan	1,445	13,188	x9.1	735,448	8,619	
13,424 ms	9,745 ms	8	Scan	949	10,813	x11.4	735,448	2,873	
57.9%	42.1%	10	Scan	130	2,078	x16.0	1	1	

SE Queries	SE Cache
5	0
	0.0%

```
SET DC_KIND="AUTO";
WITH
    $Expr0 := ( PFCAST ( 'Sales'[Quantity] AS INT ) * PFCAST ( 'Sales'[Net Price] AS INT ) )
SELECT
    'Sales'[Quantity],
    'Sales'[Net Price],
    'Date'[Year],
    'Date'[Month],
    'Date'[Month Number],
    SUM ( @$Expr0 )
```

The storage engine CPU is a bit lower than the previous version of the measure, but the degree of parallelism is much lower this time (x6.0). Moreover, the formula engine executes a significant portion of code, making the overall performance much worse than the previous one. Overall, the execution time went from 1.5 to 23 seconds.

A deeper analysis of the xmSQL queries shows that the storage engine is not actually computing the result. Although we have removed the CallbackDataID and replaced it with an xmSQL filter, the VertiPaq engine retrieves way too much data. The following is the first xmSQL query in the previous screenshot:

```
WITH
    $Expr0 := ( PFCAST ( 'Sales'[Quantity] AS INT ) * PFCAST ( 'Sales'[Net Price] AS INT ) )
SELECT
    'Sales'[Quantity],
    'Sales'[Net Price],
    'Date'[Year],
    'Date'[Month],
    'Date'[Month Number],
    SUM ( @$Expr0 )
FROM 'Sales'
    LEFT OUTER JOIN 'Date'
        ON 'Sales'[Order Date]='Date'[Date]
WHERE
    ( COALESCE ( ( PFCAST ( 'Sales'[Quantity] AS INT ) * PFCAST ( 'Sales'[Net Price] AS INT ) ) ) >= COALESCE ( 2000000 ) ) ;
```

Even though the query groups by *Date[Year]*, *Date[Year Month]* (and *Date[Year Month Number]* because of the sort-by-column property), the xmSQL query also groups by *Sales[Quantity]* and *Sales[Net*

Price]. The reduced degree of parallelism is mainly due to the large size of the datacaches returned by the storage engine to the formula engine. Moreover, the formula engine must carry out the calculation because the VertiPaq result in the datacache does not contain the result. Hence the exaggerated time required from the formula engine. The problem is the large datacache size, resulting in extreme materialization. The technique in itself is smart. The problem is the way we expressed the query.

Indeed, we used a filter over *Sales* as a filter argument in CALCULATE. A table filter is a very bad practice that newbies oftentimes use. A seasoned DAX developer knows that a filter in CALCULATE should work on the minimum number of columns required to obtain its effect. The filter over *Sales* in CALCULATE is for sure the issue in this measure. Therefore, we move forward and replace it with a filter over the only two columns required to apply their effect, which are *Sales[Quantity]* and *Sales[Net Price]*:

```
DEFINE
    MEASURE Sales[Sales Gt 200] =
        CALCULATE (
            SUMX ( Sales, Sales[Quantity] * Sales[Net Price] ),
            FILTER (
                ALL ( Sales[Quantity], Sales[Net Price] ),
                Sales[Quantity] * Sales[Net Price] >= 200
            )
        )

EVALUATE
SUMMARIZECOLUMNS (
    ROLLUPADDISSUBTOTAL (
        'Date'[Year],
        "IsGrandTotalRowTotal",
        ROLLUPGROUP ( 'Date'[Month], 'Date'[Month Number] ),
        "IsDM1Total"
    ),
    "Sales_Gt_200", 'Sales'[Sales Gt 200]
)
```

The result is exactly what we were searching for.

Total	SE CPU		Line	Subclass	Duration	CPU	Par.	Rows	KB	Timeline
197 ms	4,984 ms		2	Scan	183	4,984	x27.2	3,150	50	
	x27.5									

FE	SE
16 ms	181 ms
8.1%	92.9%

SE Queries	SE Cache
1	0
	0.0%

```
SET DC_KIND="AUTO";
WITH
    $Expr0 := ( PFCAST ( 'Sales'[Quantity] AS INT ) * PFCAST ( 'Sales'[Net Price] AS INT ) )
SELECT
    'Date'[Year],
    'Date'[Month],
    'Date'[Month Number],
    SUM ( @$Expr0 )
FROM 'Sales'
    LEFT OUTER JOIN 'Date'
        ON 'Sales'[Order Date]='Date'[Date]
```

All the indicators are just perfect. The storage engine CPU is massively reduced, the degree of parallelism is back to being exceptional, there is virtually no formula engine involved in the query and no CallbackDataIDs anywhere. Materialization is reduced from 5 million rows to only 3,150 rows. Overall, the execution went from 1.5 seconds to a bit less than 200 hundreds milliseconds – which given the size of the *Sales* table, was expected.

Job done; the code is now good enough to go into production and replace the previous measure. In order to complete our task we had to leverage on our DAX knowledge to rephrase the code, we had to discover what is being computed by the formula engine and the storage engine, we had to check that the degree of parallelism was the one expected, and we used the size of the datacaches as an indicator of the materialization level. We used Performance Analyzer and DAX Studio to obtain our goal. We will learn all these details. For now, let us move on to the next example.

Optimizing the model

In the previous example, we optimized a piece of DAX code: The goal was to reduce the execution time of a query. We started from a measure because it is likely to be the most common optimization requirement. Nonetheless, other types of optimization are equally important. For example, reducing the size of a model improves both the execution time and the memory usage of a data model.

As in the previous example, we are not interested in providing detailed information about our considerations to optimize a model. Rather, we want to share the steps of optimizing a model by showing the reasoning behind a choice. In this example, we must choose between a calculated column and a calculation at query time.

The *Sales* table contains two columns – *Sales[Quantity]* and *Sales[Net Price]* – used to compute the sales amount by summing the quantity multiplied by the net price. This calculation is widely used in reports, along with other columns like *Quantity*, *Net Price*, and *Unit Cost*.

This is the code of the *Sales Amount* measure:

```
-----------------------------
-- Measure in Sales table
-----------------------------
Sales Amount = SUMX ( Sales, Sales[Quantity] * Sales[Net Price] )
```

The question is rather simple. Is it better to perform the multiplication at query time – using an iterator like we are doing in *Sales Amount* – or is it better to create a calculated column containing the multiplication result and then sum the calculated column at query time?

Creating a calculated column comes with several consequences:

- The model size grows because the calculated column is stored in RAM;

- The model processing time increases because the calculated column is computed sequentially at process time.

The price to pay for a calculated column is a larger model that takes more time to process. At the same time, we expect that computing the value in advance will reduce the execution time of queries. To make an educated decision, we evaluate the different impacts.

Let us start by creating the calculated column:

```
-----------------------------------
-- Calculated column in Sales table
-----------------------------------
Line Amount (USD) = Sales[Quantity] * Sales[Net Price]
```

We must evaluate the impact on both process time and size. Before measuring the time required to compute this calculated column, we note that the column will be used only in DAX calculations: therefore, we do not need to store its hierarchy. The hierarchy would consume processing time and space in memory, so we clear the *AvailableInMDX* property of the column.

Once we have created the column in the model, we process the model, triggering this way the calculation of only this column. We cannot easily measure the time required to compute only this new column. Nonetheless, because right after its creation the column is the only unprocessed entity in the entire model, measuring the default process of the model provides a good approximation of the actual cost.

Before starting the process default, we open SQL Server Profiler and trace the Progress Report events. Then, we run a refresh by using the following TMSL script in SQL Server Management Studio:

```
{
  "refresh": {
    "type": "automatic",
    "objects": [
      {
        "database": "Contoso 100M x 10"
      }
    ]
  }
}
```

Because we monitor the process and the profiler gathers all progress report events, we should avoid using the server for anything else until the process finishes. The model is quite large; the *Sales* table contains 1.4B rows, so we do not need to measure timings in an extremely precise way.

Once the processing is finished, we can look at the events to discover the time required to compute the column.

EventClass	TextData	Current Time
Progress Report Begin		2023-03-13 17:18:40.000
Progress Report End		2023-03-13 17:18:40.000
Progress Report Begin	Started sequence point algorithm.	2023-03-13 17:18:40.000
Progress Report Begin	Started processing calculated column 'Line Amount (USD)' of table 'Sales'.	2023-03-13 17:18:40.000
Progress Report End	Finished processing calculated column 'Line Amount (USD)' of table 'Sales'.	2023-03-13 17:20:22.000
Progress Report Begin	Started processing hierarchy 'Line Amount (USD)' of table 'Sales'.	2023-03-13 17:20:22.000
Progress Report End	Finished processing hierarchy 'Line Amount (USD)' of table 'Sales'.	2023-03-13 17:20:22.000
Progress Report End	Finished sequence point algorithm.	2023-03-13 17:20:22.000
Progress Report Begin		2023-03-13 17:20:22.000
Progress Report Begin	Started Phase 1 of the Commit operation in a Tabular transaction.	2023-03-13 17:20:22.000
Progress Report End	Finished Phase 1 of the Commit operation in a Tabular transaction.	2023-03-13 17:20:23.000
Progress Report Begin	Started Phase 2 of the Commit operation in a Tabular transaction.	2023-03-13 17:20:23.000
Progress Report End	Finished Phase 2 of the Commit operation in a Tabular transaction.	2023-03-13 17:20:23.000
Progress Report End		2023-03-13 17:20:23.000

The processing started at 17:18:40 and finished at 17:20:22, meaning that the calculated column took 1 minutes and 42 seconds to compute. It is also worth noting that the server used a single core during the entire calculation. This is a known limitation of AS, which computes calculated columns sequentially. The time spent to compute a calculated column cannot be reduced by increasing the number of cores. Nonetheless, we also know that if the result is good we can compute this column as a calculated column in the view that feeds the table – so that instead of being a calculated column, the *Line Amount* column becomes a regular imported column.

We perform the tests with a calculated column because we do not want to process 1.4B rows every time we run a test. The results with a calculated column are slightly imprecise, but the time required to gather them is so tiny that it is worth proceeding this way.

We can now use the VertiPaq Analyzer information to assess the size of the column.

Name	Cardinality	Total Size ↓	Data	Dictionary	Hier Size
▲ **Sales**	**1,405,546,659**	**27,321,446,296**	**22,168,420,224**	**5,126,682,000**	**16,372,000**
Order Number	94,138,244	10,696,887,352	5,617,629,840	5,079,257,512	0
CustomerKey	1,868,002	3,804,096,344	3,748,125,560	41,026,752	14,944,032
Line Amount (USD)	172,618	3,466,022,136	3,459,708,952	4,932,224	1,380,960
Net Price	24,754	2,811,721,664	2,811,094,736	626,928	0
ProductKey	2,517	2,248,971,852	2,248,875,792	75,916	20,144
Unit Cost	1,956	1,920,667,096	1,920,625,464	41,632	0
Unit Price	1,761	1,920,661,660	1,920,621,304	40,356	0
Line Number	20	385,448,264	385,446,848	1,416	0
StoreKey	74	38,664,984	38,661,720	2,656	608
Delivery Date	3,389	8,793,568	8,615,664	177,904	0
Quantity	10	7,827,232	7,825,856	1,376	0
Order Date	3,281	924,296	722,360	175,680	26,256
Exchange Rate	5,071	765,328	460,944	304,384	0
Currency Code	5	22,312	5,184	17,128	0

The entire *Sales* table uses 27GB of RAM, with the *Line Amount (USD)* column alone using 3.4GB. In other words, the calculated column alone uses around 14% of the total size of the database. The impact is quite significant in terms of RAM.

Now that the column is in place, we can measure the benefits – if any – in terms of performance. Because we are interested in an overall measure, we do not slice by any column and just compute the sales amount with either the new calculated column or the iteration. We author the following query and compute first the Calc Column row alone, and then the Measure row, alone again:

```
EVALUATE
SUMMARIZECOLUMNS (
    "Calc column", SUM ( Sales[Line Amount (USD)] )
)
```

Here is the result with the calculated column.

Total	SE CPU		Line	Subclass	Duration	CPU	Par.	Rows	KB	Timeline
90 ms	1,781 ms									
	x19.8		2	Scan	90	1,781	x19.8	1	1	

FE	SE
0 ms	90 ms
0.0%	100.0%

SE Queries	SE Cache
1	0
	0.0%

The important number is the SE CPU, which is not dependent on the number of cores. Indeed, we use a server with a very large number of cores, reaching a very high degree of parallelism. SE CPU is a better indicator of the raw power consumed to produce the result when evaluating performance.

Next, the result using the measure, therefore performing the multiplication for every row:

```
EVALUATE
SUMMARIZECOLUMNS (
    "Measure", SUMX ( Sales, Sales[Quantity] * Sales[Net Price] )
)
```

Total	SE CPU		Line	Subclass	Duration	CPU	Par.	Rows	KB	Timeline
210 ms	4,016 ms									
	x19.1		2	Scan	210	4,016	x19.1	1	1	

FE	SE
0 ms	210 ms
0.0%	100.0%

SE Queries	SE Cache
1	0
	0.0%

As expected, the calculated column is beneficial to performance. The calculated column takes 1,781 milliseconds to aggregate its values, whereas the multiplication at query time produces the same result using 4,016 milliseconds of SE CPU.

The question is whether the benefit is worth the increase in size. Before making up our mind, we want to look at further considerations. The test focuses strictly on the *Line Amount* calculated column. Nonetheless, we have other calculations following the same pattern: cost and margin. Therefore, we create two more calculated columns and measures:

```
----------------------------------------
-- Calculated column in Sales table
----------------------------------------
Line Cost (USD) = Sales[Quantity] * Sales[Unit Cost]


----------------------------------------
-- Calculated column in Sales table
----------------------------------------
Line Margin (USD) = Sales[Quantity] * ( Sales[Net Price] - Sales[Unit Cost] )


----------------------------------------
-- Measure in Sales table
----------------------------------------
Cost Amount = SUMX ( Sales, Sales[Quantity] * Sales[Unit Cost] )


----------------------------------------
-- Measure in Sales table
----------------------------------------
Margin Amount = SUMX ( Sales, Sales[Quantity] * ( Sales[Net Price] - Sales[Unit Cost] ) )
```

Then, we repeat the measurement process in a more complex query that uses the three columns and measures. First, we run this query to measure the time required to compute the values in the calculated columns:

```
EVALUATE
SUMMARIZECOLUMNS (
    "Sales Amount", SUM ( Sales[Line Amount (USD)] ),
    "Cost Amount", SUM ( Sales[Line Cost (USD)] ),
    "Margin Amount", SUM ( Sales[Line Margin (USD)] )
)
```

The timing is in line with what we expect; the time required to compute three measures is around three times the time required to compute one measure.

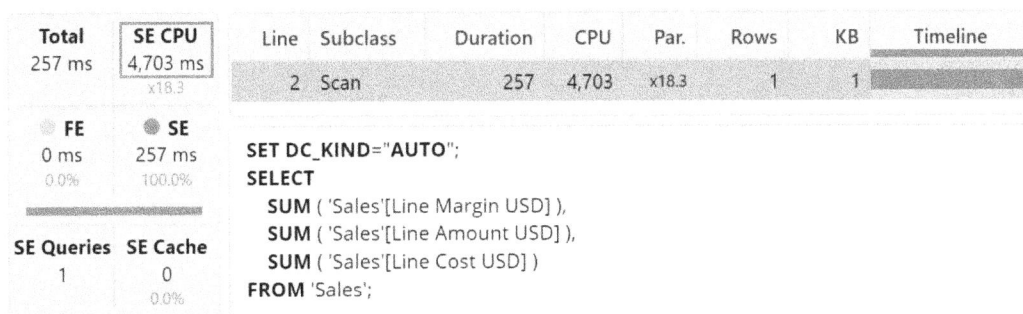

Total	SE CPU		Line	Subclass	Duration	CPU	Par.	Rows	KB	Timeline
257 ms	4,703 ms									
	x18.3		2	Scan	257	4,703	x18.3	1	1	

FE	SE
0 ms	257 ms
0.0%	100.0%

SE Queries	SE Cache
1	0
	0.0%

```
SET DC_KIND="AUTO";
SELECT
    SUM ( 'Sales'[Line Margin USD] ),
    SUM ( 'Sales'[Line Amount USD] ),
    SUM ( 'Sales'[Line Cost USD] )
FROM 'Sales';
```

Then, we execute the following query to evaluate the time required to compute the values at query time:

```
EVALUATE
SUMMARIZECOLUMNS (
    "Sales Amount", [Sales Amount],
    "Cost Amount", [Cost Amount],
    "Margin Amount", [Margin Amount]
)
```

This time, the results are worse than expected, because of the larger time in the SE CPU.

Total	SE CPU		Line	Subclass	Duration	CPU	Par.	Rows	KB	Timeline
783 ms	15,953 ms									
	x20.5		2	Scan	780	15,953	x20.5	1	1	

FE	SE
3 ms	780 ms
0.4%	99.6%

SE Queries	SE Cache
1	0
	0.0%

SET DC_KIND="AUTO";
WITH
    $Expr0 := (**PFCAST** ('Sales'[Quantity] **AS INT**) * (**PFCAST** ('Sales'[Net Price] **AS INT**)
    $Expr1 := (**PFCAST** ('Sales'[Quantity] **AS INT**) * **PFCAST** ('Sales'[Net Price] **AS INT**))
    $Expr2 := (**PFCAST** ('Sales'[Quantity] **AS INT**) * **PFCAST** ('Sales'[Unit Cost] **AS INT**))
SELECT
    SUM (@$Expr0),
    SUM (@$Expr1),
    SUM (@$Expr2)
FROM 'Sales';

Indeed, gathering three columns using calculated columns increased the time required by a factor of around three. On the other hand, the same results computed by using measures are slower: 16 seconds against 4 seconds – four times more expensive. The reason is that *Line Margin* requires multiple columns in the same expression: *Quantity*, *Net Price*, and *Unit Cost*. Increasing the expression's complexity makes the solution with the calculated column preferable.

Nonetheless, we should also evaluate the increase in terms of RAM. Here is the VertiPaq Analyzer report with the three calculated columns.

Name	Cardinality	Total Size ↓	Data	Dictionary	Hier Size
▲ **Sales**	**1,405,546,659**	**33,588,398,696**	**28,427,946,...**	**5,132,227,3...**	**18,252,448**
Order Number	94,138,244	10,696,887,352	5,617,629,840	5,079,257,512	0
CustomerKey	1,868,002	3,804,096,344	3,748,125,560	41,026,752	14,944,032
Line Amount (USD)	172,618	3,466,022,136	3,459,708,952	4,932,224	1,380,960
Line Margin (USD)	219,718	3,455,498,696	3,448,524,152	5,216,784	1,757,760
Net Price	24,754	2,811,721,664	2,811,094,736	626,928	0
Line Cost (USD)	15,334	2,811,453,704	2,811,002,488	328,528	122,688
ProductKey	2,517	2,248,971,852	2,248,875,792	75,916	20,144
Unit Cost	1,956	1,920,667,096	1,920,625,464	41,632	0
Unit Price	1,761	1,920,661,660	1,920,621,304	40,356	0
Line Number	20	385,448,264	385,446,848	1,416	0
StoreKey	74	38,664,984	38,661,720	2,656	608
Delivery Date	3,389	8,793,568	8,615,664	177,904	0
Quantity	10	7,827,232	7,825,856	1,376	0
Order Date	3,281	924,296	722,360	175,680	26,256
Exchange Rate	5,071	765,328	460,944	304,384	0
Currency Code	5	22,312	5,184	17,128	0

The three columns use 9.6GB of RAM, massively increasing the model size.

Though it is undoubtedly true that a calculated column brings good benefits to the model performance, at the same time, the price in terms of RAM consumption seems excessive. Creating one calculated column for each calculation would make the model too large.

Here is where a conclusion is hard to make without considering further details. If this were a general-purpose model, it would not make much sense to consolidate all the possible calculations in calculated columns, because the price in terms of space used would definitely be too large. On the other hand, if you have a complex calculation that involves multiple columns and intricate logic, and this calculation is at the core of most of your reports, then a calculated column to consolidate those results would make sense.

In the particular case of Contoso, with *Sales Amount*, *Cost Amount*, and *Margin Amount*, it is likely better to avoid the calculated columns to save memory, thus paying the price of working with slower queries – even though in smaller models the difference might not measurable.

As you have seen, a simple decision about whether to compute a calculated column or not requires quite a few considerations and measurements. Besides, just knowing the details of why we made a choice already has a lot of value. We did not choose randomly. We performed measurements and made decisions based on solid numbers. If at any point we need to change our mind, we already know the consequences of making any choice.

Optimizing composite models

The first optimization example we saw in this chapter was related to a simple DAX optimization. For the sake of simplicity, we used an example using a regular import model, therefore handling only xmSQL queries to the VertiPaq engine. Nonetheless, it is important to note that optimizing DAX requires a deep understanding of the entire model architecture.

As an example, we see how the composite model feature affects the process of DAX optimization. We use as an example the dynamic segmentation pattern. We will experience bad performance: the reason is not the DAX code, but rather the interaction between the local and remote engines.

This example aims to demonstrate that optimizing DAX requires more than just DAX knowledge. The same DAX code performs very differently if executed in a regular VertiPaq model, or in a composite model. In order to optimize DAX for a composite model, you need to have a profound understanding of the architecture and how the queries are split between the remote and the local servers.

We use a variation of the pattern available at Dynamic segmentation – DAX Patterns (https://www.daxpatterns.com/dynamic-segmentation/) We implement dynamic clustering on a model hosted in the Power BI Service by extending it with a composite model. Based on a configuration table, we want to dynamically cluster the customers by *Sales Amount*. The following is the configuration table created in the composite model.

Segment	MinValue	MaxValue
Low Sales	0	1,000
Medium Sales	1,000	10,000
High Sales	10,000	999,999,999

We create a measure using a slightly simplified version of the code published on www.daxpatterns.com:

```
---------------------------
-- Measure in Sales table
---------------------------
Customer in segment :=
SUMX (
    'Sales Segment',
    VAR MinSale = 'Sales Segment'[MinValue]
    VAR MaxSale = 'Sales Segment'[MaxValue]
    VAR CustInSeg =
        FILTER (
            Customer,
            VAR CustSales = [Sales Amount]
            RETURN
                CustSales > MinSale && CustSales <= MaxSale
        )
    RETURN
        COUNTROWS ( CustInSeg )
)
```

The measure mixes the *Sales Segment* table stored in the local VertiPaq model with the *Customer* table stored in the remote model. It works just fine: you can generate the following report showing the number of customers in each segment, sliced by year.

Segment	2017	2018	2019	2020	**Total**
High Sales	45	56	38	7	**152**
Low Sales	459	1,071	854	213	**2,478**
Medium Sales	656	1,236	903	205	**2,955**
Total	**1,160**	**2,363**	**1,795**	**425**	**5,585**

Although the numbers are correct, there is a performance issue. The measure would work very well in a regular VertiPaq model, but it is extremely slow in a composite model. The query that populates the matrix (somewhat simplified here) is the following:

```
--
-- Query executed on the local model
--
EVALUATE
SUMMARIZECOLUMNS (
    ROLLUPADDISSUBTOTAL ( 'Sales Segment'[Segment], "IsGrandTotalRowTotal" ),
    ROLLUPADDISSUBTOTAL ( 'Date'[Year], "IsGrandTotalColumnTotal" ),
    "Customer_in_segment", 'Sales Segment'[Customer in segment]
)
```

Looking at the server timings, we discover that this simple query runs in around three seconds on a rather small model with a few thousand sales:

Total	SE CPU		Line	Subclass	Duration	CPU	Par.	Rows	KB	Timeline	Query
2,721 ms	4,486 ms		1	DAX	554	554	x1.0				EVALUATE S
	x1.7		2	DAX	1,893	1,891	x1.0				DEFINE VAR
FE ⚠	● SE		3	DAX	1,987	1,987	x1.0				DEFINE VAR
123 ms	2,598 ms		5	Scan	1	0		3	1		SELECT 'Sale
	(2,598 ms)		6	DAX	54	54	x1.0				EVALUATE S
4.5%	95.5%		8	Scan	0	0		3	1		SELECT 'Sale
SE Queries	SE Cache		10	Scan	0	0		3	1		SELECT 'Sale
10	0										
	0.0%										

Further analysis shows that the complexity is hidden in the storage engine DAX queries sent to the remote server. If we analyze those queries, we find a first query that is already suspicious:

```
--
--  DAX DirectQuery query executed on the remote model
--
EVALUATE
SELECTCOLUMNS (
    'Customer',
    "__RN", blank(),
    "'Customer'[CustomerKey]", 'Customer'[CustomerKey],
    "'Customer'[Gender]", 'Customer'[Gender],
    "'Customer'[Name]", 'Customer'[Name],
    "'Customer'[Address]", 'Customer'[Address],
    "'Customer'[City]", 'Customer'[City],
    "'Customer'[State Code]", 'Customer'[State Code],
    "'Customer'[State]", 'Customer'[State],
    "'Customer'[Zip Code]", 'Customer'[Zip Code],
    "'Customer'[Country Code]", 'Customer'[Country Code],
    "'Customer'[Country]", 'Customer'[Country],
    "'Customer'[Continent]", 'Customer'[Continent],
    "'Customer'[Birthday]", 'Customer'[Birthday],
    "'Customer'[Age]", 'Customer'[Age]
)
```

This query retrieves all the columns of the *Customer* table. In our example, there are just a few thousand customers. In a more realistic scenario, you could have millions of customers. Therefore, the query is simple, but the datacache returned is potentially huge. Besides, it seems like neither the measure nor the report require any of those columns.

The next two queries are even worse, and they provide an explanation about why the previous query retrieved the entire *Customer* table. The first query retrieves the sales amount for each customer and year, using as a filter the entire customer table. In other words, the customer table that the local DAX engine has retrieved from the remote model is used as a filter in a subsequent query sent to the remote engine:

```
--
--  DAX DirectQuery query executed on the remote model
```

```
--
DEFINE
    VAR _Var0 =
        VALUES ( 'Date'[Year] )
    VAR _Var1 =
        SUMMARIZE (
            'Customer',
            'Customer'[CustomerKey],
            'Customer'[Gender],
            'Customer'[Name],
            'Customer'[Address],
            'Customer'[City],
            'Customer'[State Code],
            'Customer'[State],
            'Customer'[Zip Code],
            'Customer'[Country Code],
            'Customer'[Country],
            'Customer'[Continent],
            'Customer'[Birthday],
            'Customer'[Age]
        )
    VAR _Var2 = {
        ( 1212508, "Male", "David Puente", "189 Koontz Lane", "Los Angeles", "CA",
          "California", "90017", "US", "United States", "North America", DT"1992-1-4", 29 ),
        ( 1200226, "Male", "William Gaughan", "4384 Euclid Avenue", "Guadalupe", "CA",
          "California", "93434", "US", "United States", "North America", DT"1942-6-26", 78 ),
        --
        --    Several thousands of rows here, one for each customer
        --
        ( 1200334, "Male", "Micheal Boyers", "655 Carriage Court", "Los Angeles", "CA",
          "California", "90017", "US", "United States", "North America", DT"1989-9-30", 31 ),
        ( 1201225, "Male", "John Lally", "3886 Kerry Way", "Irvine", "CA",
          "California", "92614", "US", "United States", "North America", DT"1996-2-6", 24 ),
        ( 395073, "Male", "Michael Vandermark", "386 Dufferin Street", "Toronto", "ON",
          "Ontario", "M6H 4B6", "CA", "Canada", "North America", DT"1983-1-3", 38 )
    }
EVALUATE
GROUPCROSSAPPLYTABLE (
    'Date'[Year],
    _Var0,
    _Var1,
    "L1",
        GROUPCROSSAPPLY (
            'Customer'[CustomerKey],
            'Customer'[Gender],
            'Customer'[Name],
            'Customer'[Address],
            'Customer'[City],
            'Customer'[State Code],
            'Customer'[State],
            'Customer'[Zip Code],
            'Customer'[Country Code],
            'Customer'[Country],
            'Customer'[Continent],
            'Customer'[Birthday],
```

```
            'Customer'[Age],
            KEEPFILTERS (
                TREATAS (
                    _Var2,
                    'Customer'[CustomerKey],
                    'Customer'[Gender],
                    'Customer'[Name],
                    'Customer'[Address],
                    'Customer'[City],
                    'Customer'[State Code],
                    'Customer'[State],
                    'Customer'[Zip Code],
                    'Customer'[Country Code],
                    'Customer'[Country],
                    'Customer'[Continent],
                    'Customer'[Birthday],
                    'Customer'[Age]
                )
            ),
            "__Agg0", [Sales Amount]
        )
    )
)
```

Not only is this query huge, but so is its resulting data cache. Indeed, the query result is – again – the entire *Customer* table along with the *Sales Amount* result. Therefore, this is a large query with a large result… Definitely an issue.

A third query is very similar to the previous one, where the only noticeable difference is that the year is no longer part of the group by section. Still, the query includes the entire *Customer* table, and the resulting datacache contains the entire *Customer* table.

In other words, the entire *Customer* table is passed back and forth between the local and the remote servers multiple times. The number of customers in each segment is later computed in the formula engine based on the data retrieved from the remote server.

Now that the reason why the query is slow is somewhat clear, it is time to fix the problem. One of the few golden rules of DAX is to never use a table to apply a filter. A filter over a table requires scanning the entire table. The VertiPaq engine contains several optimizations and patterns that reduce the number of columns scanned. However, the DirectQuery over AS engine has a reduced set of optimizations. Therefore, Tabular ends up scanning the entire table, just because this is what we required in the DAX code.

More specifically, the problem is the reference to *Customer* in the FILTER part of the measure. It turns out that we do not need to count the rows in the *Customer* table; it is enough to retrieve only the *Customer[CustomerKey]* column to obtain a semantically equivalent measure:

```
----------------------------
-- Measure in Sales table
----------------------------
Customer in segment =
SUMX (
    'Sales Segment',
    VAR MinSale = 'Sales Segment'[MinValue]
    VAR MaxSale = 'Sales Segment'[MaxValue]
    VAR CustInSeg =
        FILTER (
            DISTINCT ( Customer[CustomerKey] ),
            VAR CustSales = [Sales Amount]
            RETURN
                CustSales > MinSale && CustSales <= MaxSale
        )
    RETURN
        COUNTROWS ( CustInSeg )
)
```

By operating this small change in the formula, we obtain the very same result, but the DAX queries sent to the remote engine are much simpler, hence the timings.

Total	SE CPU	Line	Subclass	Duration	CPU	Par.	Rows	KB	Timeline	Query
603 ms	661 ms									
	x1.2	1	DAX	102	102	x1.0				DEFINE VA
FE	**SE**	2	DAX	109	109	x1.0				DEFINE VA
37 ms	566 ms	3	DAX	93	93	x1.0				EVALUATE
	(566 ms)	5	Scan	3	0		3	1		SELECT 'Sa
6.1%	93.9%	6	DAX	53	52	x1.0				EVALUATE
		7	DAX	95	95	x1.0				EVALUATE
SE Queries	**SE Cache**	9	Scan	0	0		3	1		SELECT 'Sa
13	0									
	0.0%									

The DirectQuery query executed is way simpler than before:

```
--
--  DAX DirectQuery query executed on the remote model
--
DEFINE
    VAR _Var0 = VALUES ( 'Date'[Year] )
    VAR _Var1 = VALUES ( 'Customer'[CustomerKey] )
    VAR _Var2 = VALUES ( 'Customer'[CustomerKey] )
EVALUATE
GROUPCROSSAPPLYTABLE (
    'Date'[Year],
    _Var0,
    _Var1,
    "L1",
        GROUPCROSSAPPLY (
            'Customer'[CustomerKey],
            KEEPFILTERS ( _Var2 ),
            "__Agg0", [Sales Amount]
        )
)
```

This query retrieves the value of *Sales Amount* for each customer and year, exactly as the previous query did. The big difference is that we no longer have the ridiculous filter – instead, we obtain a smaller query, and the result set contains only the customer key, the year, and the sales amount. Consequently, the resulting data cache is smaller.

As you have seen, we updated the DAX code specifically for a composite model in this example. A measure that works just fine on a regular VertiPaq model might show performance issues with a composite model. A similar scenario applies with DirectQuery models: VertiPaq and a relational database like SQL Server are very different engines, so the DAX code optimization depends on the storage engine(s) used.

Conclusions

The goal of this chapter was not to teach any technique. We optimized DAX code, processing, and models without describing the rationale behind each decision in detail. The important part was to show that optimizing a Tabular model requires knowing several details and using many different tools. Without proper knowledge about the internals, it is nearly impossible to produce efficient code. A good DAX developer should master each of these techniques and tools.

Starting from the next chapters, we go into the details and build the knowledge needed to optimize your Tabular models. It will take some time before we can put the learning into practice. Even though at some point you might feel that all the details we provide are not so relevant... Take a deep breath and continue ingesting knowledge. As soon as we start to optimize, you will see that each detail is helpful.

Introducing the Tabular query architecture

After the introduction in the previous chapter, we now dive into the details. First, we need to introduce several important concepts that will help us understand the scope and complexity of a Tabular solution.

A Tabular solution is designed to answer queries. A client tool, like Power BI Desktop, generates DAX queries and sends them to the Tabular engine to produce reports and dashboards. Excel is another client tool that generates MDX queries, still sent to a Tabular database to produce the result shown in a pivot table.

In this chapter, we start introducing the different elements involved in answering a query, either DAX or MDX, along with considerations about their role in the optimization of a Tabular model. Indeed, when optimizing DAX, it is important to understand where the bottleneck is: it can be in the formula engine, in VertiPaq, or in DirectQuery, and the optimization process will depend on that. Here, we start to introduce the main actors in the entire discussion about optimization.

Introducing the formula engine

When Tabular receives a query, it parses its content and transforms it into a tree of operators that are executed by the formula engine. The formula engine (often shortened as **FE**) is the most powerful engine available in Tabular. The set of operators that it can execute is vast, covering the entirety of the DAX formula language.

Formula engine operators include mathematical operations, table scans, joins, and filters. Any operator in the formula engine is designed to work on datasets operating some kind of transformation. Any FE operator requires a dataset to work on; yet, the formula engine is not capable of retrieving data by itself.

Whenever the formula engine requires accessing data, it asks a proper storage engine to perform the operation. For example, if you want to retrieve the names of customers and convert them into uppercase, you author a DAX query like the following:

```
EVALUATE
SELECTCOLUMNS (
    VALUES ( Customer[Name] ),
    "Customer Name", UPPER ( Customer[Name] )
)
```

The process of solving the query looks like this:

- The formula engine asks a storage engine to retrieve the *Customer[Name]* column values from the database. The storage engine answers, producing a dataset with the requested values.

- The formula engine scans the dataset generated by the storage engine, converting each value into uppercase.

- The result is sent to the caller.

The entire flow can be summarized in the following figure.

Introducing the formula engine

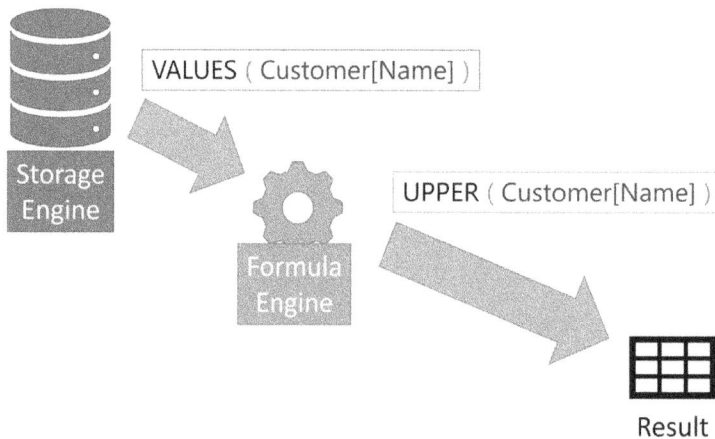

In such a simple case, the formula engine only scans the result produced by the storage engine and converts its content in uppercase. Nonetheless, despite how simple it is, this process already shows a few important details:

- The formula engine cannot access the database. Whenever the formula engine requires any data, it needs to ask the proper storage engine for that data.

- The storage engine is responsible for the data access. The transformations happen in either the formula engine or the storage engine, depending on the capabilities of the storage engine. In this example, the conversion from lowercase to uppercase happens in the formula engine because the VertiPaq storage engine cannot perform the conversion to uppercase. The storage engine only retrieved the data as it is stored in the database.

This separation of roles is very important. The entire architecture of a Tabular query resolution is based on the coordination of the formula engine with the storage engine(s) used in the data model. Besides, it also allows a DAX query to be executed against different storage engines.

The engine that executes the DAX query is the formula engine. The formula engine can work with different storage engines, depending on how developers created the solution. You can think about the formula engine as being the orchestrator of the main query. The formula engine communicates with one or more storage engines, it retrieves the datasets, and then it applies operators to produce the result.

Despite being extremely powerful, the formula engine suffers from one big limitation: it is single-threaded. No matter how powerful the server running Tabular is, the formula engine uses only one core. Therefore, it is powerful but it does not have the option of scaling its execution over different CPUs. This characteristic of the formula engine will drive many choices in the process of optimizing DAX code, because the formula engine is typically slower than the storage engines.

In later chapters, we will cover the details of the operators available in the formula engine and we will discover many more details about the formula engine. Here, we are still at a very introductory level, therefore it is time to talk about the other engines in Tabular: the storage engines. There are multiple storage engines, depending on how the data is being stored by the Tabular solution: VertiPaq, DirectQuery over SQL, and DirectQuery over AS.

Introducing VertiPaq and DirectQuery architectures

VertiPaq is the native storage engine of Tabular. When a Tabular model works in Import mode, it uses its internal VertiPaq database and storage engine. Whenever data resides in a different storage, Tabular uses a DirectQuery storage engine. We distinguish between DirectQuery over SQL and DirectQuery over AS, though there are other DirectQuery engines. We decided to group all the relational databases under "DirectQuery over SQL".

Tabular uses the DirectQuery technology whenever the data is stored outside of the model. The DirectQuery storage engine sends queries to the external data store to retrieve information. The language used by the DirectQuery storage engine to communicate with the remote storage depends on the type of DirectQuery engine. There are various options for the external data store, roughly divided into two categories:

- The external storage can be a relational database, in which case the official name of the DirectQuery technology is **DirectQuery for relational data sources**. DirectQuery for relational data sources supports many different database servers and SQL dialects. Moreover, DirectQuery for relational data sources uses a Power Query connection, therefore it works with any Power Query connector that supports DirectQuery. Power Query also supports certain non-relational data sources, therefore the technology works with both relational and non-relational data sources. Because most sources supporting DirectQuery use the SQL language, we shorten the name to **DirectQuery over SQL**. The name is not entirely precise; it also makes brilliant use of the ambiguity in the term SQL: it can be read both as the storage technology or as the language used for queries. As strange as it might seem, this ambiguity makes the name more attractive.

- Instead of being in a relational database, the external storage can be another Tabular model. In this case, the Tabular model uses a different version of DirectQuery officially named **DirectQuery for Power BI datasets and Azure Analysis Services** while in preview. Despite being accurate, the official name does not help, because it is too long to remember and use. We shorten the name to **DirectQuery over AS**, to mean that the external source is another Analysis Services (AS) database. Again, the name is not perfect, because the external database cannot be just any AS model: for example it cannot be a multidimensional model and there might be different limitations depending on the version of Tabular you are using. Still, the name is short and sweet.

When speaking about DirectQuery, we should always specify whether we are talking about DirectQuery over SQL or DirectQuery over AS. With that said, we omit the full specification if it is obvious from the context. In a chapter covering specifically DirectQuery over SQL, we use DirectQuery to mean DirectQuery over SQL, whereas in a chapter or section covering DirectQuery over AS, then DirectQuery would mean DirectQuery over AS.

It is important to note that – despite sharing the DirectQuery name – the two technologies are very different in their implementation and in the techniques needed to optimize them. Moreover, different storage engines can co-exist in the same model, generating mixed models that prove to be even more challenging. Before diving into the details, let us start by introducing the main features of the basic storage engines.

Conditions imposed by security roles are always executed in the storage engine, so that no sensitive data leaves the storage engine. Consequently, storage engines queries can include additional filters to implement security. These filters may impact performance, with different effects depending on the storage engine.

However, the presence of security roles does not impact in a direct way how we analyze the query plans and find bottlenecks. Security conditions are an additional element to consider when optimizing DAX: their presence requires additional tests and evaluations to make sure that the optimization works in all security contexts.

Introducing the VertiPaq storage engine

VertiPaq is the most frequently used storage engine. VertiPaq is the in-memory columnar database used when you create an Import model. In Import mode, data is read during refresh from the data sources and used to populate the internal VertiPaq database. When the formula engine needs to read data from the VertiPaq database, it uses the VertiPaq storage engine.

VertiPaq is an in-memory columnar database. It is designed to scan massive amounts of data stored in RAM and it implements sophisticated compression techniques to reduce memory usage to a minimum, hence increasing the speed of the queries.

The communication between the VertiPaq storage engine and the formula engine happens through binary structures that are passed back and forth between the formula engine and VertiPaq. The queries executed by the VertiPaq storage engine can also be represented in a human-readable format by using xmSQL.

xmSQL is not the language of VertiPaq. xmSQL is a human-readable representation of queries that are implemented through a proprietary communication system between the formula engine and the VertiPaq storage engine. With that said, we will analyze xmSQL quite deeply in the next chapters, because reading xmSQL queries is extremely useful to understand which part of the code is being executed by VertiPaq, and which part is being executed by the formula engine.

VertiPaq is designed to be fast and scalable. It can scan massive amounts of data using all the cores available in the server. The price for this incredible scalability lies in its flexibility: VertiPaq can perform only very simple operations: the four basic mathematical operations, basic aggregation of columns and joins between tables. Any other feature requires the intervention of the formula engine.

One big advantage of VertiPaq is that is has been designed along with Tabular. The formula engine and VertiPaq share several unique communication methods and synergies that are available only for VertiPaq, such as the capability to execute callbacks for example. We will cover these features extensively in later chapters, even though a first example helps in learning what a callback is.

Let us see how a simple DAX query involving only the *Customer* table is resolved in a VertiPaq model:

```
DEFINE
    COLUMN Customer[ContinentCountry] = Customer[Continent] & " - " & Customer[Country]
EVALUATE
SUMMARIZECOLUMNS (
    Customer[ContinentCountry],
    "#Customers", COUNTROWS ( Customer )
)
```

The query is rather simple; it retrieves the number of customers and groups them by a newly introduced column that concatenates *Customer[Continent]* and *Customer[Country]*.

ContinentCountry	#Customers
North America - United States	801,359
North America - Canada	178,104
Australia - Australia	176,945
Europe - France	88,559
Europe - Netherlands	88,734
Europe - Italy	89,103
Europe - Germany	177,960
Europe - United Kingdom	267,320

The VertiPaq storage engine can perform the grouping operation, but it cannot perform the string concatenation required by the query. Therefore, it would be impossible for the formula engine to send a single query to the VertiPaq storage engine to gather the result. Because of this limitation in VertiPaq, the formula engine would need to acquire a large table and then perform the grouping on its own, which would in turn result in poor performance. In this scenario, the formula engine uses what is called a callback operation. The formula engine asks the VertiPaq storage engine to group by a column that will be computed by the formula engine. This is the xmSQL query executed by the formula engine against the VertiPaq storage engine:

```
SELECT
    COLUMN ( ASDATAID ( [EncodeCallback ( Customer[Continent] & " - " & Customer[Country] ) ]
        ( PFDATAID ( 'Customer'[Country] ) , PFDATAID ( 'Customer'[Continent] ) ) ) ),
    COUNT ( )
FROM 'Customer';
```

The highlighted EncodeCallback is a callback operation. It is not time yet to understand the details of this query. The important thing to note is that the formula engine and the storage engine communicate very closely through an EncodeCallback, which contains a DAX expression that the VertiPaq engine cannot compute. The storage engine will call back the formula engine for each row scanned, asking it to concatenate the two strings so that the grouping can still happen inside the VertiPaq storage engine. This communication mechanism reduces the number of rows returned by the storage engine.

In the next sections, we test the same query using different storage engines to start appreciating the differences among the storage engines.

Introducing the DirectQuery over SQL storage engine

If the data of the Tabular model is not stored in its internal VertiPaq database, it can be stored in an external relational data source like for example SQL Server. In this scenario, whenever the formula engine requires data, it needs to request it from the DirectQuery over SQL storage engine. There are different DirectQuery storage engines, one for each relational data source which Tabular may be connected to. In this book, for the sake of simplicity, we cover only DirectQuery over SQL Server.

When working with DirectQuery, the storage engine is the SQL Server database. Therefore, the SQL database needs to be optimized to quickly answer the type of queries generated by the formula engine. The structure of the database is different between Import mode and DirectQuery mode. When you use Import mode, the data is loaded in VertiPaq at process time: the SQL database thus needs to be optimized for one massive, single scan of the source. On the other hand, when you use DirectQuery mode, the SQL database should be optimized for very frequent access to the data – usually on a smaller volume of data.

As an example, think about what happens if you use DirectQuery over an Azure SQL Server database with a Power BI Desktop file running on your local PC. In this case, the Tabular model is running inside Power BI Desktop; whenever the formula engine requires any data, it sends a query to the cloud service and retrieves the results using the web. This introduces some level of latency as well as a slower transportation of the data. Latency becomes relevant when many queries are being sent from the formula engine to the DirectQuery storage engine, whereas the speed of the connection becomes an important factor when the amount of data being exchanged grows.

Another important consideration about using DirectQuery is that the SQL language – used as the storage engine query language in DirectQuery – is more powerful than xmSQL. The xmSQL used in VertiPaq is not a general-purpose query language. The only purpose of xmSQL is to act as the interface between the formula engine and VertiPaq. On the other hand, SQL includes many advanced features, because it is the de-facto standard query language for databases. Because SQL is more powerful, the formula engine can push more calculations down to the storage engine query, thereby reducing the number of operations needed in the formula engine.

Let us further analyze this behavior by testing the query executed earlier against VertiPaq: this time we execute it against DirectQuery over SQL. Here is the query:

```
DEFINE
    COLUMN Customer[ContinentCountry] = Customer[Continent] & " - " & Customer[Country]
EVALUATE
SUMMARIZECOLUMNS (
    Customer[ContinentCountry],
    "#Customers", COUNTROWS ( Customer )
)
```

Unlike VertiPaq, SQL Server can perform a string concatenation. Therefore, there is no need to implement callback techniques for such a simple operation. Indeed, the formula engine sends this SQL query to the SQL Server database:

```
SELECT TOP (1000001) [t0].[ContinentCountry],
    COUNT_BIG(*) AS [a0]
FROM (
        SELECT (
                COALESCE([t0].[Continent], '') + (N' - ' + COALESCE([t0].[Country], ''))
            ) AS [ContinentCountry]
        FROM (
                (
                    select [$Table].[CustomerKey] as [CustomerKey],
                        [$Table].[Gender] as [Gender],
                        [$Table].[Name] as [Name],
                        [$Table].[Address] as [Address],
                        [$Table].[City] as [City],
                        [$Table].[State Code] as [State Code],
                        [$Table].[State] as [State],
                        [$Table].[Zip Code] as [Zip Code],
                        [$Table].[Country Code] as [Country Code],
                        [$Table].[Country] as [Country],
                        [$Table].[Continent] as [Continent],
                        [$Table].[Birthday] as [Birthday],
                        [$Table].[Age] as [Age]
                    from [dbo].[Customer] as [$Table]
                )
            ) AS [t0]
    ) AS [t0]
GROUP BY [t0].[ContinentCountry]
```

As we did with xmSQL, we shall ignore most of the details of the query – although there are a lot of important considerations we are saving for later. The relevant thing here, is that the string concatenation between the two columns happens directly inside SQL. The reason is that SQL can perform the operation, so no callback is needed. In this scenario, DirectQuery over SQL has an advantage because of the power of SQL. There will be scenarios where VertiPaq is better, because of the flexibility of callbacks. Each engine has its own strengths and weaknesses, and we are just scratching the surface for now.

Introducing DirectQuery over AS

The latest storage engine introduced in Tabular is DirectQuery over Power BI and Azure Analysis Services. As we mentioned earlier, the official name in preview was too long. The Tabular community first adopted the name, "***composite models***" as the de-facto standard name for models based on DirectQuery over Power BI and Azure Analysis Services. We have decided to use the same terminology in this book, and Microsoft made the same decision, eventually. The term, "composite model" describes the model architecture. The name of the storage engine used by a composite model is DirectQuery over AS.

In a composite model, the formula engine uses another instance of Tabular as a storage engine, which oftentimes resides on the cloud. This time, the storage engine is a full Tabular engine that is capable of understanding and executing DAX. Consequently, if a query uses only tables that are stored in the remote model, the query can be passed through to the remote Tabular engine that produces the result. In that scenario, the formula engine acts as a pass-through and it does not need to further operate on the results. Nonetheless, in a composite model there are both local and remote tables. Local tables are processed by the local VertiPaq storage engine, whereas remote tables are processed by the remote storage engine. Please note that we are not making any assumptions about the storage engine used by the remote server. It could be VertiPaq, it could be another DirectQuery over SQL, or any other structure. From the point of view of the local model, the remote model can be queried with DAX, with no assumptions on the technical details of the remote implementation.

Composite models are among the most complex models to understand well and optimize, because they share some characteristics of DirectQuery models (there is a remote server hosting data) and they also have a local VertiPaq model that can interact with the remote tables. Therefore, a query can be resolved by mixing VertiPaq queries to the local database, with remote DAX queries executed by the remote server.

On the one hand, the remote storage engine can execute any DAX statement, so the local formula engine does not need a callback mechanism to solve DAX functionalities. On the other hand, composite models often mix both local and remote tables within the same query, which requires the transfer of large amounts of data back and forth between the local and remote servers. Moreover, when data needs to be exchanged with the remote server, the DAX query tends to be extremely long and complex to analyze. Hence, it becomes harder to optimize.

In our example, the communication between the formula engine and the remote storage engine in the composite model is the simplest possible. Indeed, this is the query we are using as a test:

```
DEFINE
    COLUMN Customer[ContinentCountry] =
        Customer[Continent] & " - " & Customer[Country]
EVALUATE
SUMMARIZECOLUMNS (
    Customer[ContinentCountry],
    "#Customers", COUNTROWS ( Customer )
)
```

And this is the query that the local formula engine sends to the remote storage engine:

```
DEFINE
    COLUMN 'Customer'[ASDQ_ContinentCountry] =
        Customer[Continent] & " - " & Customer[Country]
EVALUATE
SUMMARIZECOLUMNS (
    Customer[ASDQ_ContinentCountry],
    "#Customers", COUNTROWS ( Customer )
)
```

As you can see, the queries are nearly identical – the only difference being in the name of the column defined, which is prefixed with ASDQ_ (Analysis Services DirectQuery) by the local formula engine before being sent to the storage engine.

Do not be fooled by the simplicity of this example. Composite models are complex to use and understand. We are saving this complexity for later.

Introducing data islands and cross-island query resolution

Now that we have introduced the three main storage engines, we can start talking about data islands. A data island is a set of tables and relationships that is handled by one storage engine. A single Tabular model can include multiple data islands in the same model, therefore requiring the formula engine to interact with and coordinate different storage engines in the same DAX query.

Let us use as an example the following model, where we used three different data islands, identified by the colors on the top of the table rectangle. The text describes the storage engine used for each data island.

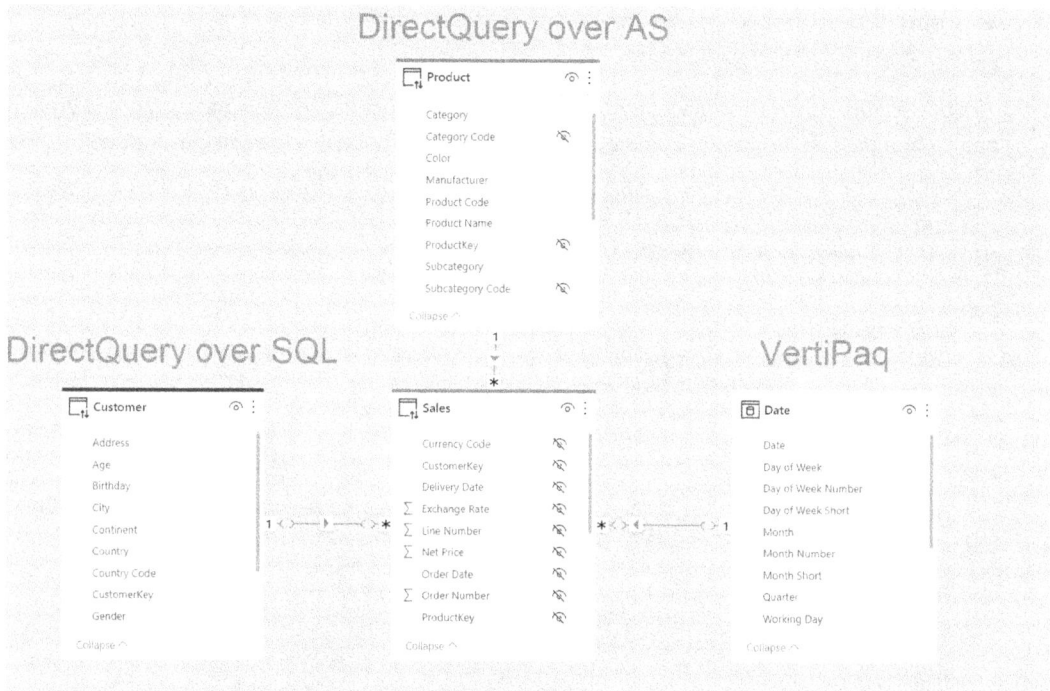

Customer is a table connected with DirectQuery over SQL, *Sales* and *Product* are tables stored in a remote Analysis Services model, therefore using DirectQuery over AS, whereas *Date* is stored in the local VertiPaq database. There are three data islands in this model. Even though we usually call each island just an island, we often refer to the local VertiPaq island as the VertiPaq continent. The VertiPaq continent is just another island; we use the name continent for it because of its unique nature of being local to the

Tabular model.

A DAX query that mixes the four tables in our example would require the local formula engine to execute queries against the different storage engines and coordinate their results.

Let us look at an example using this query as a test:

```
EVALUATE
SUMMARIZECOLUMNS (
    Customer[Continent],
    'Date'[Year],
    TREATAS ( { "Audio" }, 'Product'[Category] ),
    "Amt", [Sales Amount]
)
```

The query is grouping by *Customer[Continent]* (DirectQuery over SQL) and *Date[Year]* (VertiPaq continent). It then sums values in *Sales*, which is queried by using DirectQuery over AS. There is also a filter being placed on *Product*, again in DirectQuery over AS.

Solving the query requires a scan of *Sales* with a filter on *Product[Category]*. Because both *Sales* and *Product* belong to the same island, this filter can be applied by the remote storage engine. But the result must be grouped by columns in *Customer* (DirectQuery over SQL) and *Date* (VertiPaq continent). Because the remote AS engine does not know about the existence of either *Customer* or *Date*, it cannot perform the grouping. As a consequence, the formula engine needs to retrieve the value of *Sales Amount* grouped by *Sales[CustomerKey]* and *Date[Date]* and then perform said grouping. Despite the fact that it works well, this technique would require large amounts of data to be moved back and forth between the servers – indeed, *CustomerKey* contains many more values than *Continent* – and it would not work with non-additive measures.

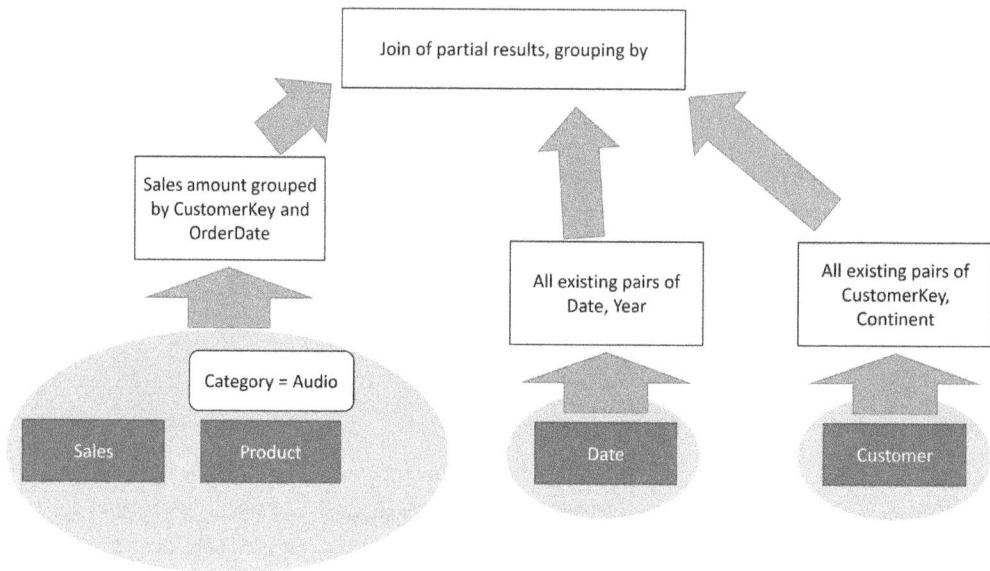

In order to reduce the amount of data being retrieved from the remote AS engine, the local formula engine chooses a different technique: it builds a very complex DAX query that actually specifies the association between *Customer[CustomerKey]* and *Customer[Continent]* as well as between *Date[Date]* and *Date[Year]*. These associations are defined in variables that are part of the query sent to the remote AS engine, which uses their content to perform the grouping and produce the result.

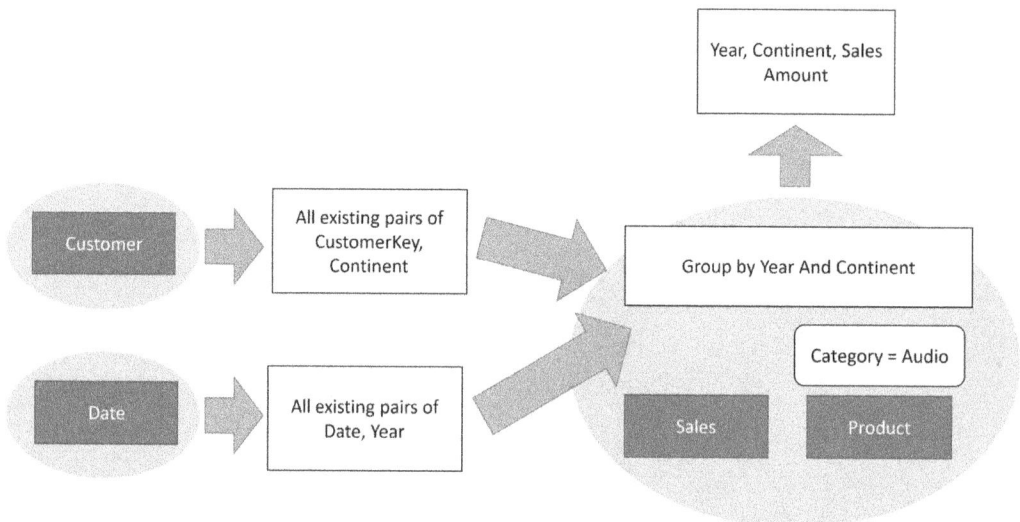

We are not going to show the details of the various queries, because they would be overwhelming at this stage. For now, it is enough to briefly highlight the algorithm after having explained the challenges.

First, the formula engine retrieves all the pairs of (*Customer[CustomerKey]*, *Customer[Continent]*) from DirectQuery over SQL:

```
SELECT TOP (1000001)
    [t2].[CustomerKey],
    [t2].[Continent]
FROM (
        (
            select [$Table].[CustomerKey] as [CustomerKey],
                [$Table].[Gender] as [Gender],
                [$Table].[Name] as [Name],
                [$Table].[Address] as [Address],
                [$Table].[City] as [City],
                [$Table].[State Code] as [State Code],
                [$Table].[State] as [State],
                [$Table].[Zip Code] as [Zip Code],
                [$Table].[Country Code] as [Country Code],
                [$Table].[Country] as [Country],
                [$Table].[Continent] as [Continent],
                [$Table].[Birthday] as [Birthday],
                [$Table].[Age] as [Age]
            from [dbo].[Customer] as [$Table]
        )
    ) AS [t2]
GROUP BY [t2].[CustomerKey],
    [t2].[Continent]
```

Then, the formula engine retrieves all the pairs of (*Date[Date]*, *Date[Year]*) from the local VertiPaq model, using an xmSQL query:

```
SELECT
    'Date'[Date],
    'Date'[Year]
FROM 'Date';
```

At this point, the formula engine knows the associations between the keys in the *Sales* table and the columns used to perform the grouping by. Therefore, it builds a rather complex query containing variables that store the association between *CustomerKey* and *Continent*, and between *Date* and *Year*, and it then asks the remote model to use those variables to perform the grouping. The query is more than 7,000 rows long. Here we show just an excerpt:

```
DEFINE
    TABLE _T40 =
        UNION (
            SELECTCOLUMNS ( _Var1, "Value", [Value] ),
            SELECTCOLUMNS ( _Var3, "Value", [Value1] )
        )
    TABLE _T45 =
        UNION (
            SELECTCOLUMNS ( _Var2, "Value", [Value] ),
            SELECTCOLUMNS ( _Var4, "Value", [Value1] )
        )
    VAR _Var0 = { "Audio" }
    VAR _Var1 = { 3, 4, 5 }
    VAR _Var2 = { 3, 4, 5, 6 }
    VAR _Var3 = {
        ( 3, 1212508 ),
        ( 3, 1200226 ),
        ( 3, 1200334 ),
                            -- Around 5,000 similar rows
        ( 3, 388173 ),
        ( 3, 395073 )
    }
    VAR _Var4 = {
        ( 3, dt"2017-01-01" ),
        ( 3, dt"2017-01-02" ),
                            -- Around 1,500 similar rows
        ( 6, dt"2020-12-30" ),
        ( 6, dt"2020-12-31" )
    }


EVALUATE
GROUPCROSSAPPLYTABLE (
    _T40[Value],
    _T45[Value],
    TREATAS ( _Var0' 'Product'[Category] ),
    TREATAS ( _Var1, _T40[Value] ),
    TREATAS ( _Var2, _T45[Value] ),
    "1",
        CALCULATETABLE (
            GROUPCROSSAPPLY (
                TREATAS (
                    DEPENDON ( _Var3, EARLIER ( _T40[Value], 2 ) ),
                    'Sales'[CustomerKey]
                ),
                TREATAS (
                    DEPENDON ( _Var4, EARLIER ( _T45[Value], 2 ) ).
                    'Sales'[Order Date]
                ),
                "__Agg0", [Sales Amount]
            ),
            ALL ( _T40[Value] ),
            ALL ( _T45[Value] )
        )
)
```

The result of the last remote query is the table returned by the formula engine as the result of the entire query.

In other words, the formula engine must take care of retrieving from each storage engine the information that the storage engine can retrieve. The formula engine coordinates the queries of the different storage engines, taking advantage of their capabilities and compensating for the gaps. Remember when we said that the formula engine orchestrates the different storage engines? Despite being basic, this is an excellent example of this orchestration.

This level of complexity appears whenever there are multiple data islands, and makes it extremely difficult to author optimal DAX code and build optimal models. Moreover, complex models like the one we have used for this example require the developer to know the details of the formula engine, all the storage engines used in the model, and how the different storage engines interact.

We will be able to tackle this complexity only towards the end. Before that, we will focus on individual storage engines to build the knowledge required to optimize models with a single data island. Once the behavior of each individual storage engine is understood, only then do we start to dive into their interaction in mixed models.

Different types of models

In the previous descriptions we focused on the storage engines. We have also seen that storage engines can be combined in the same model, leading to more complex architectures. For example, in a composite model there is a local VertiPaq model and a remote model, which has its own formula engine, and in turn can use different storage engines.

Depending on the types of storage engines used in a model, we use this classification of model types:

Model type	Storage engine	Description
Import model	VertiPaq	A model that uses only the VertiPaq storage engine. Data is loaded from one or more data sources during data refresh and stored in the local VertiPaq database.
DirectQuery model	DirectQuery over SQL	A model that uses only one DirectQuery over SQL storage engine. There is no local database, all the data is gathered from the relational data source.
Composite model	DirectQuery over AS VertiPaq	A model that uses a local VertiPaq storage and mixes this model with another Tabular model connected using DirectQuery over AS. In this type of model there are always two data islands: the VertiPaq continent and the remote Tabular island. Please note that we do not make any assumption on how the remote Tabular model is built: it could be another composite model, an Import model, or a mixed one.
Mixed models	Any combination of storage engines	Any model with multiple islands that does not fall in one of the first two categories. For example, a model that mixes DirectQuery over SQL and VertiPaq is a mixed model. In a similar way, a DirectQuery model that uses two different SQL Servers (that is, it contains two islands) is a mixed model. Composite models are mixed models. We created a category dedicated to composite models because of their popularity.

In the description of the content, we start by describing the details of Import models, then we cover DirectQuery over SQL models, and then composite models using DirectQuery over AS. Import models are the most widely used models, and this is the reason we start with them. Understanding import models requires understanding how the VertiPaq engine works. DirectQuery over SQL models are quite popular, and yet they use a single storage engine. Therefore, we describe them next.

Composite models are the first type of models that use multiple data islands. We cover them after the first two types of models because – in order to understand how composite models work – you need to have a very solid understanding of how VertiPaq models work.

Mixed models are the most challenging. In addition to the complexity of each individual storage engine, we must understand better how to optimize the transfer of data between different storage engines. Although they are the most complex models, they will be simple to understand once you have a solid understanding of composite models. Indeed, the challenges in optimizing mixed models are almost the same as the ones you face with composite models.

With all that said, before starting to work with the details of the formula engine and storage engines, we still need to introduce some basic concepts. We need to introduce the tools that we are going to use to inspect the behavior of Tabular and its queries, and we need to introduce what a query plan is. We start this process right from the next chapter.

Conclusions

In this chapter, we introduced the basic architecture of Tabular. Each of these topics requires an extensive description, which we provide in the remaining part of the book. For now, the critical factor is to start seeing the big picture because optimizing a Tabular model involves tasks in the different parts of the solution by looking at the interactions between the several layers.

Using the Power BI Desktop performance analyzer

In the previous chapters, we introduced the architecture of the Tabular models and the query engines. In this chapter, we introduce the tools we use to analyze the performance of queries. When preparing to optimize a model or a measure, most of the time is usually spent investigating the issue and measuring performance. The optimization itself often involves changing a few lines of DAX code, but the investigation is needed to understand what to change and how.

The most complex task of a developer involved in optimizing a model is to gather the correct set of measurements, interpret the data and finally apply the changes required to speed up the calculations. Remember that the most important skill of a good DAX developer lies not in being able to modify a few lines of DAX; it is knowing which lines to modify to obtain the desired result. In our case, the result is an improvement in the speed of the query.

Because Power BI Desktop is the most widely used client for Tabular, the first tool we introduce to analyze performance is Performance Analyzer as it is integrated into Power BI Desktop. We use a slow Power BI Desktop dashboard as an example. We will not spend time optimizing the report. We chose a slow report because it provides a clear picture of the numbers to search for.

Running Performance Analyzer

Performance analyzer is a tool in Power BI Desktop that records the events in the integrated Tabular server. Its main advantage is its ease of use: it can be activated directly in Power BI Desktop, and it can measure the performance of either an individual visual or an entire report page.

You activate the performance analyzer using the Performance Analyzer button in the View panel of the Power BI Desktop ribbon.

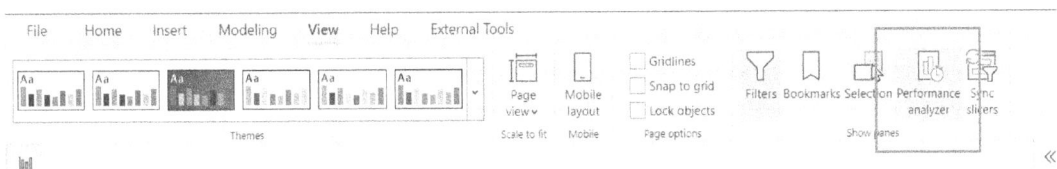

Once activated, the performance analyzer opens a new panel, in-between Filters and Visualizations.

As you see, the only active button – at first – is *Start recording*. You activate the recording of query events by clicking the *Start recording* button. Moreover, when the recording is active, each visual has an additional icon that lets you refresh just that visual, recording the time required to execute the refresh.

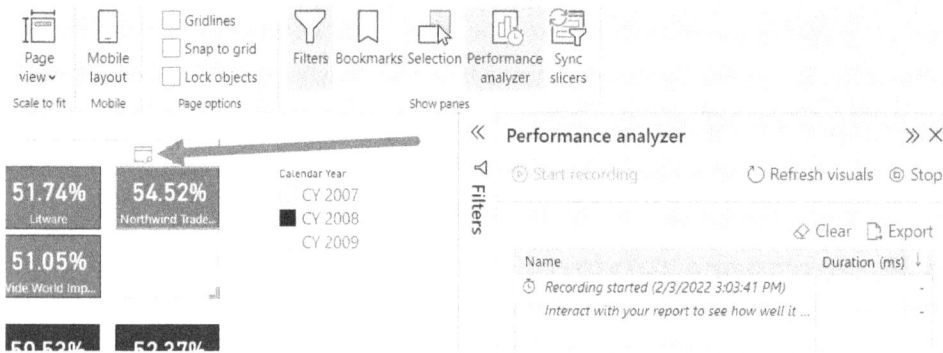

Every interaction with the report generates new events logged in Performance Analyzer when recording is active. If at any point you need to clear the log, you can do so by using the *Clear* button to start with an empty list of measurements.

In a regular Power BI Desktop report, each visual executes one or more queries against the Tabular model. In the example we are using, there are many card visuals and a slicer. Each visual shows the value of one measure in the model.

Red Products

(Blank) A. Datum	**52.86%** Adventure Works	**49.87%** Contoso	**45.64%** Fabrikam	**51.74%** Litware	**54.52%** Northwind Trade…
47.78% Proseware	**49.54%** Southridge Video	**52.64%** Tailspin Toys	**(Blank)** The Phone Com…	**51.05%** Wide World Imp…	

Black Products

55.70% A. Datum	**50.99%** Adventure Works	**52.53%** Contoso	**55.09%** Fabrikam	**50.53%** Litware	**52.37%** Northwind Trade…
53.95% Proseware	**50.26%** Southridge Video	**50.30%** Tailspin Toys	**53.25%** The Phone Com…	**52.41%** Wide World Imp…	

Blue Products

56.06% A. Datum	**54.59%** Adventure Works	**50.86%** Contoso	**55.49%** Fabrikam	**52.13%** Litware	**53.54%** Northwind Trade…
52.63% Proseware	**45.96%** Southridge Video	**48.46%** Tailspin Toys	**(Blank)** The Phone Com…	**55.62%** Wide World Imp…	

Calendar Year
- CY 2007
- ■ CY 2008
- CY 2009

Once Performance Analyzer is recording events, you can use the *Refresh visuals* button to force all visuals on the current page to refresh their content. Once the refresh takes place, the performance analyzer log is filled with information about each query.

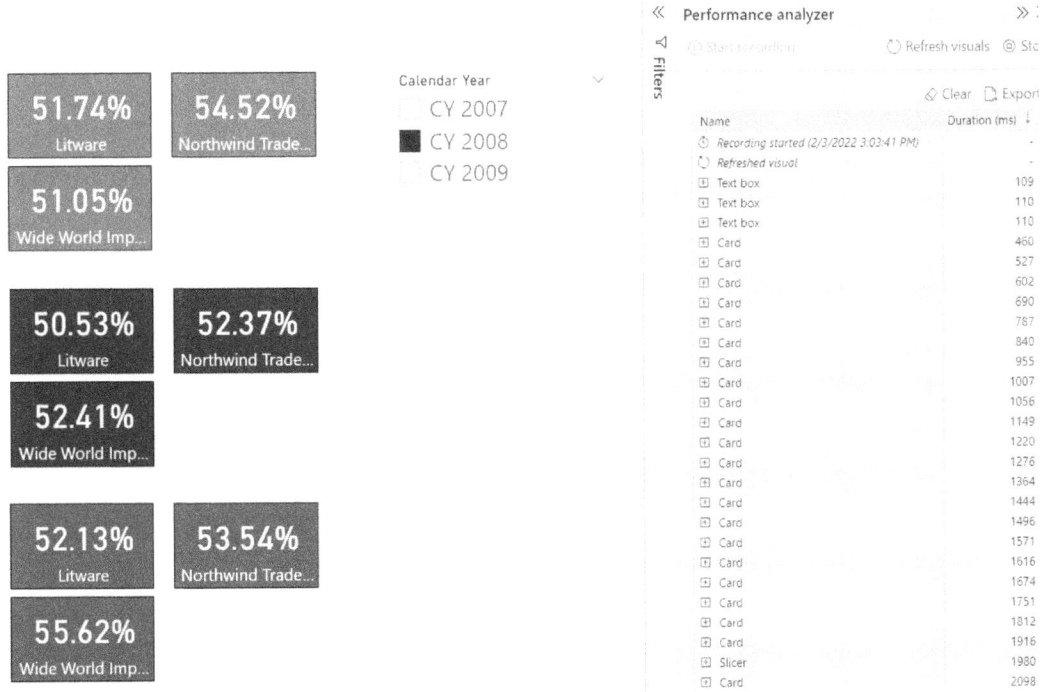

Each row shows the time required to render the visual. You can note that there are three text boxes, clearly very fast, and then all the individual cards. Selecting a node is how you can get the corresponding visual to be highlighted so you know what you are looking at. Expanding each node of the list provides more information about the steps required to gather the values for that visual.

Three numbers are recorded for each query: the time required to execute the DAX code, the time required to render the visual, and Other, which accounts for the time the visual had to wait before being executed. In that same area, you see a button to copy the content of the DAX query for that visual. Copying the query proves to be useful to execute the query in different, more advanced tools like DAX Studio.

During the process of debugging a slower report, the first step is almost always to gather information about the timings of queries by using Performance Analyzer to find out where to focus your attention.

Understanding the numbers reported by Performance Analyzer

As we have seen in the previous section, Performance Analyzer reports three numbers for each visual:

- **DAX query**: this is the time required to execute the DAX query.

- **Visual display**: indicates the time required to render the visual. On more complex visuals, the rendering time might be significant.

- **Other**: this is the time the visual had to wait before Power BI Desktop could execute the DAX query to populate the visual.

The first two are simple and easy to understand. The third one, Other, is somewhat misleading because of its name and meaning. Hence, it requires a more detailed description.

When a report contains dozens of visuals, Power BI does not execute all the DAX queries in parallel. There is a limit in Power BI, on the number of queries that are executed in parallel. The exact number of queries executed in parallel is subject to change over time. The consequence of this limit is that Power BI creates a queue of queries to send to the server; it sends the first few queries and then waits for some to be completed before submitting the next query in the queue. The time spent by a DAX query in the queue is waiting time, accounted for as Other in the performance analyzer log. *Other* can account for other small amounts of time, but we do not examine them because their absolute value is very small.

For example, let us examine the log of the report we showed in the first part of this chapter. Keep in mind that the report contains three text boxes, one slicer (not visible in the report as it is far down the list), and 33 card visuals. Here is the log, with the first few entries expanded.

The first three text boxes took around 22 milliseconds to render, with a small wait time due to internal calculations Power BI Desktop had to perform before starting the render. These visuals do not show any DAX query time because their content is static.

The first visual was executed in 372 milliseconds. Out of these 372, only 11 milliseconds were spent to execute the DAX query. Eight milliseconds were needed to render the visual, and the wait time was a whopping 353 milliseconds. The next queries (there are 33 of them) show an increasing value for their wait time. Here you can see the last few queries in the log.

Name	Duration (ms) ↓
⊞ Card	2449
⊟ Card	2476
DAX query	15
Visual display	20
Other	2440
📋 Copy query	
⊟ Card	2517
DAX query	40
Visual display	19
Other	2458
📋 Copy query	
⊟ Card	2579
DAX query	15
Visual display	8
Other	2556
📋 Copy query	

As you see, the wait time keeps increasing query after query, and for the last one it went up to 2,556 milliseconds. On the other hand, the DAX query time and the Visual display values remained fairly constant. If when looking at the log, you focus only on the duration shown in the list, you might make erroneous assumptions. For example, the last card took the same amount of time as the first card to be computed; it was rendered two and half a second later because it had to wait for other visuals to be completed, not because it is inherently slow.

In other words, the problem behind this report being slow is not to be found anywhere in the DAX code or in the model. This report is slow because there are too many card visuals. In that scenario, the solution would be to use small multiples rather than focusing on the DAX code of the measures. As you see, reading and interpreting correctly the numbers reported by Performance Analyzer is of paramount importance to then make the right decisions on how to optimize your report.

Be mindful that the technical details about the different operations required to render a Power BI report are a bit more intricate than what we have shown. That said, the description we gave in this section is adequate for most developers: it is the level of detail we use all the time when optimizing DAX code. If you are interested in a more complete description of the steps, you can refer to this document: Power BI Desktop Performance Analyzer (https://sql.bi/performance-analyzer/), which describes in a much more complete manner how and when queries are sent to the server.

Optimizing queries or measures?

By using Performance Analyzer you can copy into the clipboard the DAX query executed to produce a visual. The query can then be pasted into DAX Studio to further analyze its performance. Many developers think about optimizing a measure when they focus on performance. Instead, what can (and should) be optimized is always a query.

A Tabular server does not execute a measure. Tabular executes queries. It is important to always think about this separation for a few reasons:

- A report is built through queries, not through measures. While it is true that a fast measure is probably better than a slow measure, what really matters is how the measure behaves in a specific query.

- The same measure may act differently depending on the query being executed. It is not uncommon to author measures that work fine on small subsets of data but may have issues if they need to scan massive sets of rows. Knowing which visual (thus which query) uses the measure is often important information to support your choice between different versions of the same code.

- A query includes filters, subtotals, and joins between tables that affect the behavior of the DAX code being executed. When evaluating the performance of your code, you must consider these aspects too.

We start with Performance Analyzer logging the entire report whenever we optimize a report. Then we narrow the analysis to the slowest visual, investigating why the query generating the visual is slow – it might be the query, one of the many measures used, or the interaction between them. Finally, we start the real optimization process.

However, there are situations in which we focus on a measure without having a clear picture of the queries that will use that measure. In that case, we will need to manually author a query to test the performance and make sure that the query used for the tests is somewhat close to how users will use the measure.

What can be optimized

As explained earlier, the numbers reported by Performance Analyzer are important because they are the first indication of the path to follow to perform our optimization.

If the rendering time is the main reason a query is slow, then you know that the problem is inside the visual. Each visual is different. Therefore, we cannot provide a detailed description of how to improve their performance. But in most cases, the speed of a visual strictly depends on the number of points it renders. For example, suppose you are producing a line chart at the day level and spanning a full year. In that case, it might be useful to reduce the granularity of the chart down to the month or week level, to reduce the number of data points analyzed by the visual.

Be mindful that reducing the number of data points in many scenarios also requires adjusting the DAX formulas. Let us see the concept with an example. The following line chart shows the value of Sales Amount by Date.

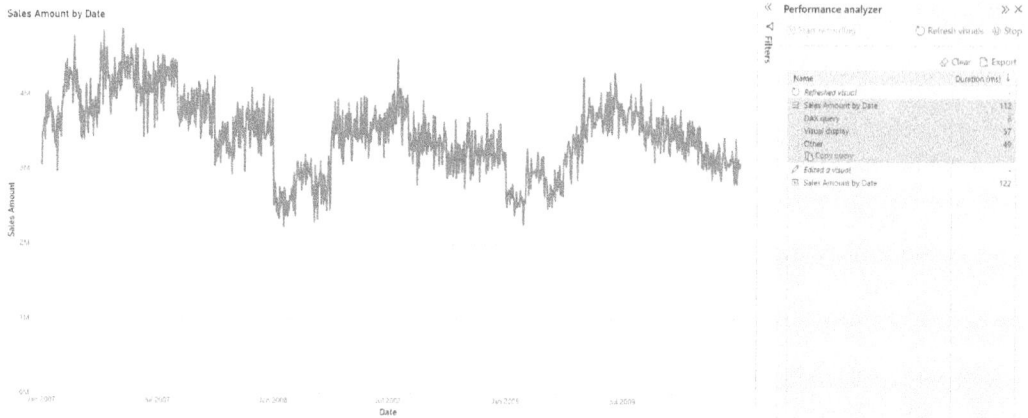

Sales Amount by Date

It takes 57 milliseconds to render the visual and only 6 milliseconds to execute the DAX query. The chart is not optimal from a usability point of view because the lines are so close that they overlap. What is more, our focus is on performance, not usability. We can create a calculated column that stores the first date of the month as each actual date, and we use that column for the x-axis instead of the date. The number of points is around 1/30th of the original:

```
-------------------------------------
-- Calculated column in Date table
-------------------------------------
BOM = DATE ( YEAR ( 'Date'[Date] ), MONTH ( 'Date'[Date] ), 1 )
-- Format String expression
"yyyy-mm"
```

Because there are fewer data points to show, the render time is reduced to 11 milliseconds.

Sales Amount by BOM

If you pay close attention to the latter two figures, you notice that the y-axis has changed. In the daily line chart, the range is 0-4M, whereas in the monthly line chart, the range is now 0-120M. The reason is that the monthly chart shows the monthly aggregate of the sales amount, no longer its daily value.

Therefore, if we want to maintain the same scale as the previous chart, we need a different aggregation. The choice of aggregation depends on the business rules: in this scenario, using an average makes sense. Therefore, we create a new measure that returns the daily average of sales:

```
---------------------------
-- Measure in Sales table
---------------------------
Daily Avg Sales = AVERAGEX ( VALUES ( 'Date'[Date] ), [Sales Amount] )
```

The result is that the chart uses the correct range of values, with a neglectable increase in terms of DAX code and a smaller number of milliseconds for the render time.

In this example, the performance improvement is not very noticeable. Getting from 57 to 11 milliseconds is not a major win. With that said, if the chart is used in a crowded dashboard, even these small savings might help improve the overall user experience.

If the query is slow because of the *Other* timing, then – as we indicated earlier – the solution requires you to reduce the number of visuals on the page. The limited availability of parallelism forces Power BI to create a queue of visuals, and the last in the queue experience a large waiting time.

Among the numbers reported by Performance Analyzer, DAX query is the most interesting one. Indeed, if your DAX code is slow, there are many options to make it faster. Unfortunately, the most interesting topic is also the more complex one. This entire book is dedicated to measuring, analyzing, changing, and optimizing your Tabular model and your DAX code, aiming at reducing the DAX query time. This is why we do not elaborate further on the topic here: many chapters are waiting to be read to describe in detail how to improve your DAX code.

Saving performance data

Before we leave this introductory chapter on Performance Analyzer, it is important to mention one last feature of the tool: the option to save the log in a file. Performance Analyzer offers you the *Export* button that lets you save the entire log in a JSON file, which external tools can later analyze.

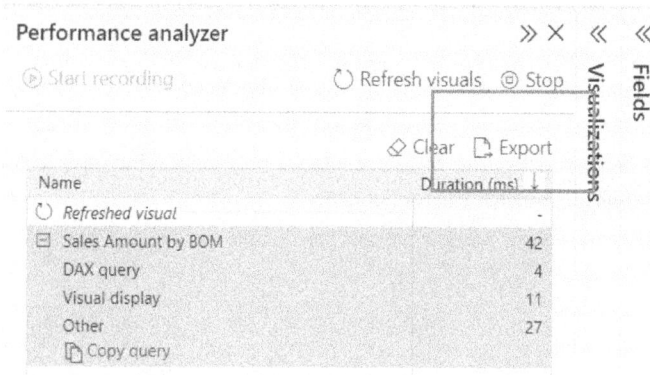

The JSON file contains the code of the queries executed and the time required to execute them. It is especially useful when analyzed with DAX Studio, the tool we introduce in the next chapter. Indeed, DAX Studio provides more powerful tools to analyze the log of Performance Analyzer, sort its content in different ways, execute individual queries, and then dive into the details of how much time was spent in the storage engine, how much time was spent in the formula engine, the query plan, and all the important information that will allow us to find out how a query is resolved under the hood. This will enable us to search for a better version of the query.

Conclusions

The Performance Analyzer feature in Power BI Desktop is usually the starting point when investigating a slower Power BI report. This tool helps find report bottlenecks in terms of identifying the slower visuals. Performance Analyzer allows you to capture the DAX query used by the visual, so you can execute and investigate it in DAX Studio to find out how to improve and optimize the DAX code of the measures in your model.

Using DAX Studio

DAX Studio is our primary tool to optimize DAX and Tabular models. If you are not experienced with DAX Studio yet, you will surely become more familiar with it before the end of this book. DAX Studio offers a rich set of features to analyze the size of a model, execute DAX queries and inspect their query plans. It also offers other sets of features and utilities that are not strictly related to optimization.

In this chapter, we do not want to provide a complete reference to DAX Studio's functionalities. We have made recorded video training pieces available and published articles about the different features. Therefore, there is no use in increasing the length of this book by repeating concepts described elsewhere.

That said, because we will be using DAX Studio extensively starting from the next chapter, it is helpful to remind our reader of its main features and to briefly describe how to activate and use them.

If you want more information about DAX Studio and the connected VertiPaq Analyzer structure, you can refer to the free video training provided here: DAX Tools Video Course (https://www.sqlbi.com/p/dax-tools-video-course/).

Installing DAX Studio

You can install DAX Studio by visiting www.daxstudio.org and downloading the version that fits your needs. You can install the complete product or download the portable version that does not require installation. The portable version can be helpful if you need DAX Studio on a computer where you cannot install the software. In contrast, we suggest installing the full version on your workstation, where you probably perform most of your DAX wizardry.

If you install the full version, DAX studio can be executed as an add-in for Excel (to connect to a Power Pivot model), as a standalone application (by just launching the app), or as an add-in for Power BI Desktop. Most developers use DAX Studio connected to their Power BI Desktop file: therefore, the latter option is more common.

Once installed, DAX Studio is visible among the External tools of Power BI Desktop.

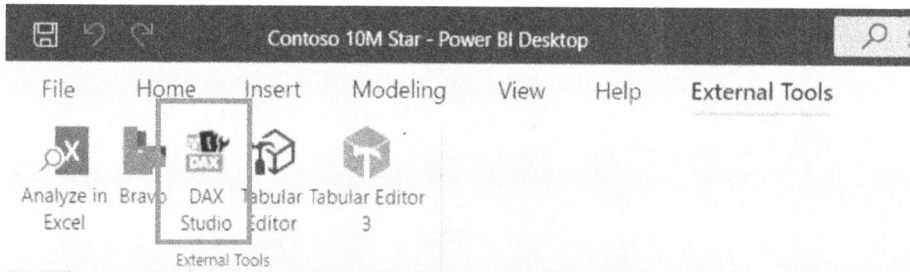

Launching DAX Studio from inside Power BI Desktop opens an instance of DAX Studio that is already connected to the Tabular server running inside Power BI Desktop. This saves us from using the *Connect* button and searching for the correct server to connect to.

Introducing the metrics of a database

VertiPaq Analyzer Metrics is the feature we use extensively during model optimizations or when we want to gather information about a model. Tabular can provide a lot of helpful information about the VertiPaq database stored in the model; in particular, the size and density of tables and columns, the types of relationships, the type of compression used for each column, table partitioning, and so on. We are not going to describe here the detailed information you can obtain. We offer a lot more detail in the chapters about VertiPaq.

To see the VertiPaq Analyzer metrics of a database, you use the *View Metrics* button in the Advanced panel of the DAX Studio ribbon.

Clicking on View Metrics opens a new panel titled VertiPaq Analyzer, which displays detailed information about your model.

Tables	Name	Cardinality	Total Size ↓	Data	Dictionary	Hier Size	Encoding	Data Type
Columns	⊿ **Sales**	**1,405,546,659**	**24,002,529,040**	**18,860,151,...**	**5,122,395,7...**	**14,991,040**	**Many**	**-**
Relationships	Order Number	94,138,244	10,688,320,720	5,609,063,208	5,079,257,512	0	HASH	Int64
Partitions	CustomerKey	1,868,002	3,804,096,344	3,748,125,560	41,026,752	14,944,032	HASH	Int64
	Net Price	24,754	2,812,365,672	2,811,092,744	1,272,928	0	HASH	Double
Summary	ProductKey	2,517	2,248,971,852	2,248,875,792	75,916	20,144	HASH	Int64
	Unit Cost	1,956	2,000,590,608	2,000,548,976	41,632	0	HASH	Decimal
	Unit Price	1,761	2,000,583,564	2,000,543,208	40,356	0	HASH	Decimal
	Line Number	20	399,264,296	399,262,880	1,416	0	HASH	Int64
	StoreKey	74	22,751,352	22,748,088	2,656	608	HASH	Int64
	Delivery Date	3,389	10,142,072	9,964,176	177,896	0	HASH	DateTime
	Quantity	10	8,191,440	8,190,064	1,376	0	HASH	Int64
	Order Date	3,281	1,172,912	970,984	175,672	26,256	HASH	DateTime
	Exchange Rate	5,071	1,060,264	755,888	304,376	0	HASH	Double
	Currency Code	5	27,104	9,984	17,120	0	HASH	String

The different tabs offer different views for the same set of data. You can inspect tables and columns, see a detailed view of the relationships in the model and the partitions of each table, or obtain a quick summary of the entire model.

You may save the metrics by using the *Export Metrics* button. Exporting the metrics generates a .vpax file that contains valuable information about your database. It does not contain any sensitive information – that is, data is not shared. The .vpax file contains the database structure, the DAX code of the model, and all the size and structural information about your tables. In other words, it contains the table statistics, and the TOM model as an option.

Exporting these metrics enables you to share information about your model with partners, consultants, and coworkers when collaborating on the development of a model. The .vpax file is a small structure that can be shared very easily. However, you might be worried about sharing the entire TOM structure of your model with external partners. So you can control whether to include the TOM structure in the .vpax file or not, by accessing the advanced options of DAX Studio.

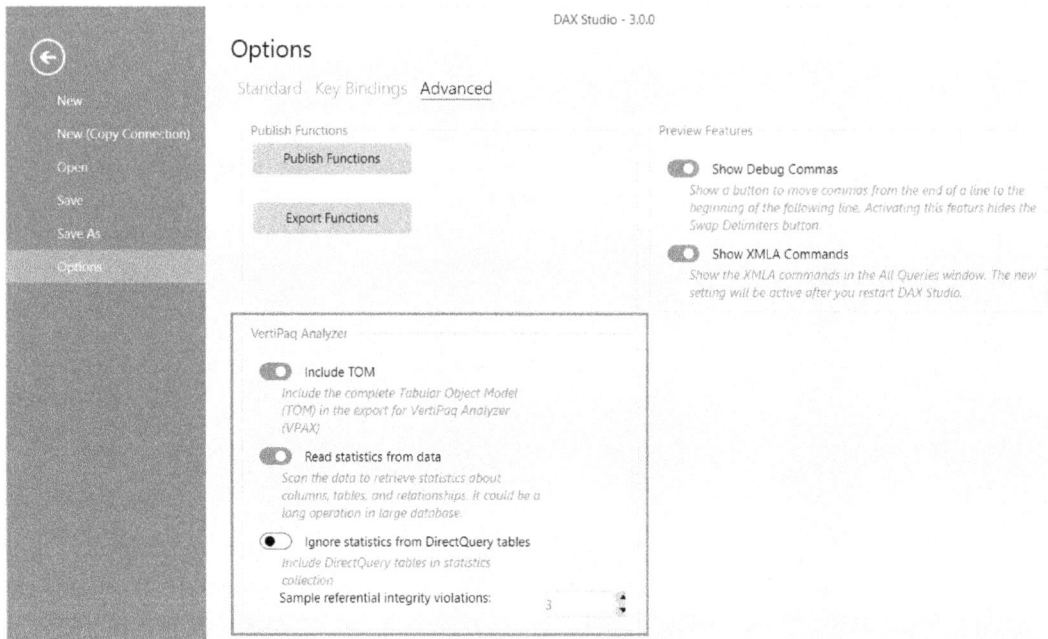

In the options, you can choose to include or exclude the TOM structure and whether you want to read statistics from the data by running a DAX query or just by executing DMV queries – the latter are faster but less accurate. Finally, when working with large DirectQuery models, it may be helpful to avoid reading detailed statistics, as each request potentially executes heavy queries against your relational model.

Once you have generated a .vpax file, you can later import it in DAX Studio, and thus obtain detailed information without being connected to the database. Whenever we at SQLBI need to work with a customer's model, the .vpax file is the first thing we request. Analyzing the .vpax file already provides us with an excellent overview of the model and it highlights possible issues, which allows us to focus on the problems if any.

In this book, we provide a lot of information about how to read, interpret, and use the detailed information available in VertiPaq Analyzer. The chapters about the VertiPaq engine cover most of the details. A less-detailed version of that information is also available in the VertiPaq Analyzer section of DAX Tools, the video training mentioned earlier in the introduction.

Introducing All Queries

In DAX Studio you will find the *Query Plan* and *Server Timings* buttons, which we will be using an incredible lot starting from the next chapter. As such, we do not talk about these two magic buttons here. However, DAX Studio also offers you the capability to capture all the queries executed by a Tabular server using a third button, *All Queries*.

DAX Studio - 3.0.0

When you activate All Queries, DAX Studio collects all the queries executed by the server. This collection is useful when you must catch queries executed by tools other than Power BI Desktop. Indeed, Power BI Desktop works with Performance Analyzer, which lets you read the queries executed in a more straightforward manner. However, different tools might require you to grab the queries executed using DAX Studio.

Once activated, All Queries opens a new panel (All Queries) that initially shows only the connection made by DAX Studio, which is shown as a subscription to the query events.

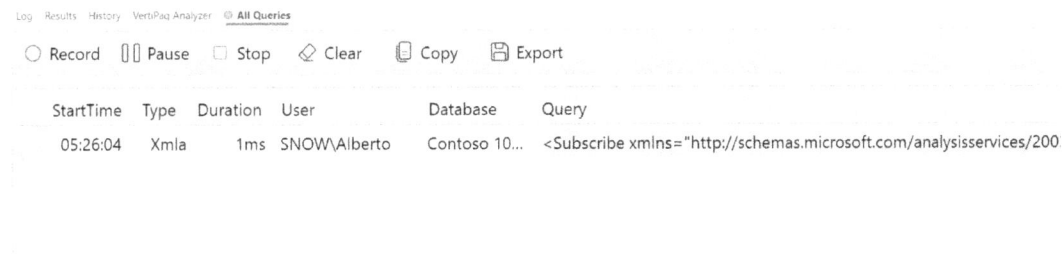

At this point, when the client tool starts to execute queries, these are logged by DAX Studio. As an example, here is what happens when we switch pages in the Power BI Desktop report that is currently open.

As you see, DAX Studio retrieved a set of two DAX queries. The queries are sorted in descending order by StartTime, so the last query is shown first.

By double-clicking on a query, its content is copied in the query editor so that you can further inspect it or start to modify it when attempting to optimize the execution of said query.

```
1 DEFINE
2   VAR __DS0FilterTable =
3     TREATAS({"Touch Screen Phones"}, 'Product'[Subcategory])
4
5   VAR __DS0Core =
6     SUMMARIZECOLUMNS(
7       ROLLUPADDISSUBTOTAL('Date'[Year], "IsGrandTotalRowTotal"),
8       ROLLUPADDISSUBTOTAL('Product'[Color], "IsGrandTotalColumnTotal"),
9       __DS0FilterTable,
10      "Sales_Amount", 'Sales'[Sales Amount]
11    )
12
13  VAR __DS0PrimaryWindowed =
14    TOPN(
15      102,
16      SUMMARIZE(__DS0Core, 'Date'[Year], [IsGrandTotalRowTotal]),
17      [IsGrandTotalRowTotal],
18      0,
19      'Date'[Year],
```

Log   Results   History   VertiPaq Analyzer   ● **All Queries**

○ Record   ⏸ Pause   ☐ Stop   ⬚ Clear   📋 Copy   💾 Export

StartTime	Type	Duration	User	Database	Query
05:26:57	DAX	229ms	SNOW\Alberto	Contoso 10...	DEFINE VAR __DS0FilterTable = TREATAS({'
05:26:57	DAX	6ms	SNOW\Alberto	Contoso 10...	DEFINE VAR __DS0Core = VALUES('Produc
05:26:04	Xmla	1ms	SNOW\Alberto	Contoso 10...	<Subscribe xmlns="http://schemas.micros

You also have the option of pausing, stopping the tracing, and saving the list of executed queries in a JSON file for consumption in other tools.

Capturing Excel queries (MDX)

An interesting example of using the *All Queries* button is to capture MDX queries executed by Excel. To demonstrate this, we use Analyze in Excel to open an instance of Excel connected to a Power BI Desktop file and build a simple Pivot Table.

	A	B	C	D	E
1					
2		**Row Labels**	**Sales Amount**		
3		**Australia**			
4		Australia	13,346,014,219.09		
5		**Europe**			
6		France	6,691,672,942.67		
7		Germany	23,893,497,017.97		
8		Italy	7,094,273,595.35		
9		Netherlands	9,422,546,135.56		
10		United Kingdom	25,469,633,054.41		
11		**North America**			
12		Canada	23,529,625,418.68		
13		United States	119,622,385,294.28		
14		**Grand Total**	**229,069,647,678.00**		
15					

Because we kept the *All Queries* feature active in DAX Studio, all the queries executed by Excel were saved.

Log   Results   History   VertiPaq Analyzer   ⊚ **All Queries**

○ Record   ⏸ Pause   ☐ Stop   ◇ Clear   🗐 Copy   🖫 Export

StartTime	Type	Duration	User	Database	Query
05:46:40	MDX	139ms	SNOW\Alberto	Contoso 10...	SELECT NON EMPTY Hierarchize(DrilldownMember(CrossJoin(
05:46:37	MDX	7ms	SNOW\Alberto	Contoso 10...	SELECT NON EMPTY Hierarchize(DrilldownMember(CrossJoin(
05:46:31	MDX	8ms	SNOW\Alberto	Contoso 10...	SELECT NON EMPTY Hierarchize({DrilldownLevel({[Customer].[
05:46:18	DMX	5ms	SNOW\Alberto	Contoso 10...	select CUBE_NAME from $SYSTEM.MDSCHEMA_CUBES

The query type is MDX this time, because Excel uses MDX – not DAX – to query Tabular. It is important to note that DAX Studio can execute both DAX and MDX queries. Therefore, double-clicking on the query pushes the query definition in the query editor. From there, you can execute the MDX query.

```
 1 SELECT
 2     NON EMPTY
 3         Hierarchize
 4         (
 5             DrillDownMember
 6             (
 7                 CrossJoin
 8                 (
 9                     {
10                         [Customer].[Continent].[All],
11                         [Customer].[Continent].[Continent].MEMBERS
12                     },
13                     {[Customer].[Country].[All]}
14                 ),
15                 [Customer].[Continent].[Continent].MEMBERS,
16                 [Customer].[Country]
17             )
18         )
19     DIMENSION PROPERTIES
```

Log   Results   History   VertiPaq Analyzer   ● All Queries

○ Record   ⏸ Pause   ☐ Stop   ⊘ Clear   ⬚ Copy   💾 Export

StartTime	Type	Duration	User	Database	Query
05:46:40	MDX	139ms	SNOW\Alberto	Contoso 10...	SELECT NON EMPTY Hierarchize(DrilldownMember(
05:46:37	MDX	7ms	SNOW\Alberto	Contoso 10...	SELECT NON EMPTY Hierarchize(DrilldownMember(

There are scenarios where the performance of a measure presents certain issues when used in MDX rather than in DAX. Each of the two languages has its own peculiarities. If a developer needs to optimize a measure specifically when used in Excel, being able to retrieve and execute an MDX query is invaluable.

Introducing Load Performance Data

In the previous chapter, we introduced the Power BI Desktop Performance Analyzer and mentioned that you have the option of saving the performance data gathered by Performance Analyzer in a JSON file. You can then use DAX Studio to read the content of that JSON file and perform further analysis with more advanced tools.

You can load performance data saved by the Performance Analyzer using the *Load Perf Data* button.

DAX Studio - 3.0.0

Q Find
⚏ Replace

Load Perf Data   All Queries   Query Plan   Server Timings   Connect   Refresh Metadata

Find   Power BI   Traces   Connection

For this example, we load the performance data saved in the previous chapter with the report containing multiple cards. Once loaded, DAX Studio shows the PBI Performance panel with the list of all the queries executed.

Export

#	Visual	QueryStart	QueryEnd	Rows	Query Ms	Render Ms	Total Ms	Query
1	Card	05:55:25	05:55:25	1	5	12	17	DEFINE VAR __DS0FilterTable = TREATAS(
2	Card	05:55:25	05:55:25	1	19	18	37	DEFINE VAR __DS0FilterTable = TREATAS(
3	Card	05:55:25	05:55:25	1	18	23	41	DEFINE VAR __DS0FilterTable = TREATAS(
4	Card	05:55:25	05:55:25	1	19	7	26	DEFINE VAR __DS0FilterTable = TREATAS(
5	Card	05:55:25	05:55:25	1	19	24	43	DEFINE VAR __DS0FilterTable = TREATAS(
6	Card	05:55:25	05:55:25	1	28	14	42	DEFINE VAR __DS0FilterTable = TREATAS(
7	Card	05:55:25	05:55:25	1	21	14	35	DEFINE VAR __DS0FilterTable = TREATAS(
8	Card	05:55:25	05:55:25	1	21	15	36	DEFINE VAR __DS0FilterTable = TREATAS(

The visualization in DAX Studio is better than the one provided by the Performance Analyzer because DAX Studio does not show the Others time, but only the Query, Render, and Total milliseconds. The Others time is not relevant to find the slowest query and is helpful only to identify a report that has too many visuals in Performance Analyzer. Once in DAX Studio, we only focus on finding the slowest DAX query. By simply sorting by one of these three columns, you can easily spot the slowest query in the report and start focusing on the issue.

As with the All Queries panel, double-clicking on the text of a query copies it into the query editor so that you can optimize the code. In the same panel, you may filter the queries in case the list is too large, and you are searching for a specific behavior – for example, queries that took more than 500 milliseconds to run.

Introducing Query Plan and Server Timings

The two buttons we use more often are *Query Plan* and *Server Timings*.

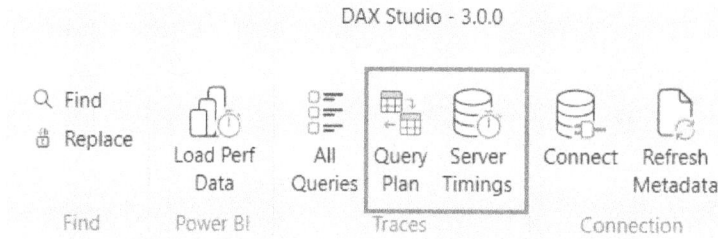

DAX Studio - 3.0.0

Activating Query Plan lets DAX Studio retrieve both the logical and the physical query plan during the execution of a query. Server Timings retrieves the storage engine queries executed by the formula engine, along with several measurements about the overall query execution time.

The query plan panel shows the physical query plan at the top and the logical query plan at the bottom.

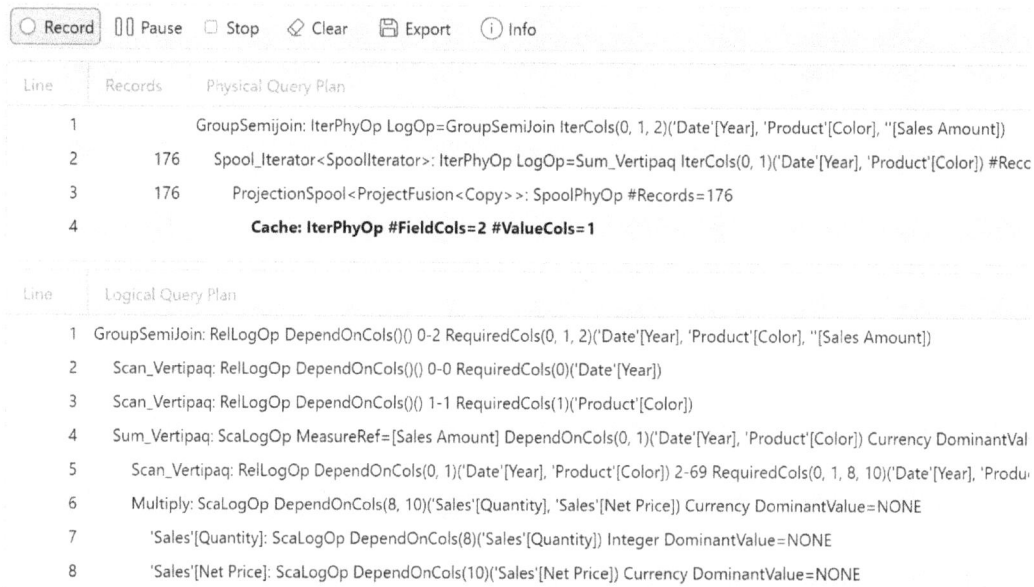

Line	Records	Physical Query Plan
1		GroupSemijoin: IterPhyOp LogOp=GroupSemiJoin IterCols(0, 1, 2)('Date'[Year], 'Product'[Color], ''[Sales Amount])
2	176	Spool_Iterator<SpoolIterator>: IterPhyOp LogOp=Sum_Vertipaq IterCols(0, 1)('Date'[Year], 'Product'[Color]) #Recc
3	176	ProjectionSpool<ProjectFusion<Copy>>: SpoolPhyOp #Records=176
4		**Cache: IterPhyOp #FieldCols=2 #ValueCols=1**

Line	Logical Query Plan
1	GroupSemiJoin: RelLogOp DependOnCols()() 0-2 RequiredCols(0, 1, 2)('Date'[Year], 'Product'[Color], ''[Sales Amount])
2	Scan_Vertipaq: RelLogOp DependOnCols()() 0-0 RequiredCols(0)('Date'[Year])
3	Scan_Vertipaq: RelLogOp DependOnCols()() 1-1 RequiredCols(1)('Product'[Color])
4	Sum_Vertipaq: ScaLogOp MeasureRef=[Sales Amount] DependOnCols(0, 1)('Date'[Year], 'Product'[Color]) Currency DominantVal
5	Scan_Vertipaq: RelLogOp DependOnCols(0, 1)('Date'[Year], 'Product'[Color]) 2-69 RequiredCols(0, 1, 8, 10)('Date'[Year], 'Produ'
6	Multiply: ScaLogOp DependOnCols(8, 10)('Sales'[Quantity], 'Sales'[Net Price]) Currency DominantValue=NONE
7	'Sales'[Quantity]: ScaLogOp DependOnCols(8)('Sales'[Quantity]) Integer DominantValue=NONE
8	'Sales'[Net Price]: ScaLogOp DependOnCols(10)('Sales'[Net Price]) Currency DominantValue=NONE

Reading a query plan is a complex operation which we have dedicated the next chapter to. Similarly, Server Timings displays in a separate panel the list of all the storage engine queries executed to answer the DAX query.

◯ Record   ❚❚ Pause   ☐ Stop   ✏ Clear   ▢ Copy   🖫 Export   ⓘ Info

Total	SE CPU	Line	Subclass	Duration	CPU	Par.	Rows	KB	Timeline	Query
484 ms	10,422 ms x21.7	2	Scan	480	10,422	x21.7	266	5		WITH $Expr0 :=

FE	SE
4 ms	480 ms
0.8%	99.2%

SE Queries	SE Cache
1	0
	0.0%

```
SET DC_KIND="AUTO";
WITH
  $Expr0 := ( PFCAST ( 'Sales'[Quantity] AS INT ) * PFCAST ( 'Sales'[Net Price] AS INT ) )
SELECT
  'Date'[Year],
  'Product'[Color],
  SUM ( @$Expr0 )
FROM 'Sales'
  LEFT OUTER JOIN 'Date'
    ON 'Sales'[Order Date]='Date'[Date]
  LEFT OUTER JOIN 'Product'
    ON 'Sales'[ProductKey]='Product'[ProductKey]
WHERE
  'Product'[Subcategory] = 'Touch Screen Phones';
```

Estimated size: rows = 266 bytes = 4,256

There are different types of storage engine queries, and each of the numbers shown is relevant. Again, an introductory chapter cannot address the complexity of reading storage engine queries. We start reading and understanding storage engine queries when introducing and describing the formula engine. What is more, you will be able to fully understand storage engine queries, how they work, and how to find issues in the code only towards the end of the VertiPaq section.

Conclusions

In this chapter, we did not talk about all the features of DAX Studio. Here, the goal was only to show some of the interesting optimization-related features we use. One of the more used capabilities of DAX Studio is its ability to show detailed information about a query's execution plan, and timings and code of related storage engine queries.

We start using these relevant features in the next chapter when introducing the concept of DAX query plans.

Introducing query plans

During the execution of a DAX query, the Tabular engine provides information about the code executed by both the storage engine and the formula engine. The formula engine algorithm is documented through the query plans: the logical query plan and the physical query plan. Both query plans describe the same algorithm in different ways. The code executed by the storage engine is documented through the storage engine queries, which are the set of queries sent from the formula engine to the storage engine(s) to retrieve the data, over which the formula engine is going to produce the results.

We do not dedicate too much time to the detailed description of the query plans. There are several reasons for this choice:

- Both query plans are tough to read and understand. A real-world query with a couple of measures generates query plans that are thousands of lines long. Despite being somewhat informative, the relevant information is too hard to retrieve. Besides, we can gather critical pieces of information by using more straightforward techniques.

- A query plan can dramatically change because of a slight variation in the DAX code. Consequently, spending hours trying to catch helpful information from a query plan results in wasting time as soon as the query plan changes because of a minor modification to the code.

- Despite being very detailed, the information in the query plan can be inferred by looking at the storage engine queries. This inference process might seem strange to newbies, but it is an important skill nonetheless. The most efficient method to distinguish between what takes place in the storage engine versus in the formula engine is to read and understand the storage engine queries, knowing that everything else is happening in the formula engine.

Regarding the storage engine queries, the level of attention required is very different. A DAX developer needs to learn every detail about the storage engine queries because these are the primary source of information about the internals of the query execution. Still, there are two reasons why we are not going into too much detail for now. First, this is still an introductory chapter. Therefore, we want our students to focus on the big picture rather than diving into the geeky details of a storage engine query. Second, there are multiple types of storage engines. A storage engine query can be executed by VertiPaq in an Import model, by SQL Server in a DirectQuery over SQL model, or by another Tabular engine if it happens to be a composite model.

Each storage engine has its own peculiarities and is worth a detailed description. Therefore, in this chapter, we are still somewhat cloudy on the details, but we focus on learning the differences between the query plans and the storage engine queries.

To introduce the various concepts, we use a relatively simple test query. The query is neither too simple nor too complex. It is just at the appropriate level of complexity for us to introduce the basic concepts without requiring too much attention to details:

```
EVALUATE
SUMMARIZECOLUMNS (
    'Product'[Brand],
    "Avg Prod Sales",
        DIVIDE (
            SUMX (
                Sales,
                Sales[Quantity] * Sales[Net Price]
            ),
            DISTINCTCOUNT ( Sales[ProductKey] )
        )
)
```

For each brand, the query produces the average sales per product.

Brand	Avg Prod Sales
Contoso	3,496.46
Wide World Importers	12,059.94
Northwind Traders	3,239.40
Adventure Works	16,835.72
Southridge Video	4,154.05
Litware	2,735.70
Fabrikam	4,324.35
Proseware	4,366.83
A. Datum	1,380.26
The Phone Company	13,001.18
Tailspin Toys	553.56

The resulting calculation divides the sales amount by the distinct count of products. The engine performs the division by using the DIVIDE function. Therefore, it requires the intervention of the formula engine because the VertiPaq storage engine cannot perform a safe division. In other words, DIVIDE must be computed by the formula engine.

This is an excellent exercise to figure out how the Tabular engine resolves the query. At this stage, it is unlikely that our readers can determine the query plan. Nonetheless, there is value in just trying to figure it out. In the remaining part of this chapter, we perform a deeper analysis of the query plans, and we figure out the algorithm. We urge our motivated readers to think about it for a while before they move on to reading.

Introducing the logical query plan

The logical query plan is the first translation of the DAX code into a query plan. The logical query plan comprises logical operators working on their arguments. We can see the query plan as text, where each operator is in a line by itself and has its arguments indented two spaces in the lines below.

The following figure shows the logical query plan of our test query, where we used red lines to group arguments of the same operator.

```
Line    Logical Query Plan
   1    GroupSemiJoin: RelLogOp DependOnCols()() 0-1 RequiredCols(0, 1)('Product'[Brand], "[Avg Prod Sales])
   2      Scan_Vertipaq: RelLogOp DependOnCols()() 0-0 RequiredCols(0)('Product'[Brand])
   3      Divide: ScaLogOp DependOnCols(0)('Product'[Brand]) Currency DominantValue=BLANK
   4        Sum_Vertipaq: ScaLogOp DependOnCols(0)('Product'[Brand]) Currency DominantValue=BLANK
   5          Scan_Vertipaq: RelLogOp DependOnCols(0)('Product'[Brand]) 1-71 RequiredCols(0, 56, 58)('Product'[Brand], 'Sales'[Quantity], 'Sales'[Net Price])
   6          Multiply: ScaLogOp DependOnCols(56, 58)('Sales'[Quantity], 'Sales'[Net Price]) Currency DominantValue=NONE
   7            'Sales'[Quantity]: ScaLogOp DependOnCols(56)('Sales'[Quantity]) Integer DominantValue=NONE
   8            'Sales'[Net Price]: ScaLogOp DependOnCols(58)('Sales'[Net Price]) Currency DominantValue=NONE
   9        DistinctCount_Vertipaq: ScaLogOp DependOnCols(0)('Product'[Brand]) Integer DominantValue=BLANK
  10          Scan_Vertipaq: RelLogOp DependOnCols(0)('Product'[Brand]) 1-1 RequiredCols(0)('Product'[Brand])
```

Both the logical and the physical query plans are readable only when they are of smaller size, as is the case for this example.

The top operator is **GroupSemiJoin**, which performs the join of two tables: its two arguments. The first argument is **Scan_Vertipaq**, an operator that scans the database through the VertiPaq storage engine and returns the column indicated: in our case, the *Product[Brand]* column, cited at the end of line two. The second argument of GroupSemiJon is **Divide** (line three).

The Divide operator has two arguments: **Sum_Vertipaq** and **DistinctCount_Vertipaq**. Sum_Vertipaq produces the sum of the multiplication of *Quantity* times *Net Price*, whereas DistinctCount_Vertipaq computes the distinct count of the product key.

The logical query plan contains a lot more information: column dependencies, required columns, and dominant value. Unfortunately, this information is very detailed but not that useful. The logical query plan looks more like a debugging tool to understand what the DAX engine is about to perform rather than a piece of information that helps figure out bottlenecks in the code.

Introducing the physical query plan

The logical query plan is not particularly interesting when looking to optimize DAX code. The physical query plan, on the other hand, provides valuable information. Be mindful that even though the information is helpful, the physical query plan is still too complex to analyze.

Here is the physical query plan of our test query.

Line	Records	Physical Query Plan
1		GroupSemijoin: IterPhyOp LogOp=GroupSemiJoin IterCols(0, 1)('Product'[Brand], "[Avg Prod Sales])
2		Extend_Lookup: IterPhyOp LogOp=Divide IterCols(0)('Product'[Brand])
3	11	Spool_Iterator<SpoolIterator>: IterPhyOp LogOp=Sum_Vertipaq IterCols(0)('Product'[Brand]) #Records=11 #KeyCols=114 #ValueCols=1
4	11	ProjectionSpool<ProjectFusion<Copy>>: SpoolPhyOp #Records=11
5		**Cache: IterPhyOp #FieldCols=1 #ValueCols=1**
6	11	SpoolLookup: LookupPhyOp LogOp=DistinctCount_Vertipaq LookupCols(0)('Product'[Brand]) Integer #Records=11 #KeyCols=114 #Value
7	11	ProjectionSpool<ProjectFusion<Copy>>: SpoolPhyOp #Records=11
8		**Cache: IterPhyOp #FieldCols=1 #ValueCols=1**

The overall structure is like the logical query plan, despite the operators being different. Moreover, there is an additional column: *Records*. The Records value indicates the number of rows processed by each operator.

The physical query plan has both advantages and disadvantages. It is a bit less verbose than the logical query plan. As you can see, there is no longer detailed information about any division and multiplication executed by the storage engine. The operators are different from the ones in the logical query plan. Finally, there is a clear distinction between what happens in the formula engine and what happens in the storage engine.

Remember that the communication between the storage engines and the formula engine is performed through datacaches, which are datasets kept in memory resulting from a storage engine query. Whenever the formula engine requires a data cache from the storage engine, there is a highlighted Cache or DirectQueryResult operator. The Cache operator is used with Vertipaq, whereas the DirectQueryResult operator is used for other storage engines. In the query plan shown in the picture, you see that we have two Cache operators: one is executing a Sum_Vertipaq operation, and the other is executing a DistinctCount_Vertipaq operation. We know this because the logical query plan shows the two operators.

Unfortunately, the physical query plan does not show the VertiPaq queries being executed. It only indicates that some datacaches are being used without clearly indicating which storage engine query generated each datacache. We can easily match the storage engine queries with the physical query plan in a simple query like the one we are analyzing. As we describe in the next section, there are only two storage engine queries: one computing a sum, and the second computing a distinct count. In a more realistic scenario, you can end up with tens or hundreds of storage engine queries, and at that point the matching becomes an impossible exercise.

The number of records of ProjectionSpool operators that consume a datacache corresponds to the number of rows processed. In other words, it indicates the size of the datacache returned by the storage engine. That number helps you to estimate the size of the internal structures processed by the formula engine operators.

As we did for the logical query plan, we do not go into too many details about the physical query plan. Instead, we want to use the small amount of information gathered to dive into the storage engine queries. Then, we shall try to derive the complete algorithm from the storage engine queries alone. It is not an academic exercise. In the real world, you always want to look at the storage engine queries first when trying to optimize DAX code. Indeed, storage engine queries are the quickest way to obtain an idea about the execution path.

Introducing storage engine queries

During the evaluation of the physical query plan, the engine needs to retrieve datacaches from the storage engine by running storage engine queries. As we have previously noted, the information about which storage engine query is used in which part of the query plan is missing. But still, with enough experience, DAX developers start to identify this information on their own.

By using DAX Studio, you can retrieve the set of storage engine queries executed, along with some helpful information about the size of the datacache returned and the time required to execute the query. The sample query in this chapter executes two storage engine queries. The first query retrieves the value of *Sales[Quantity]* times *Sales[Net Price]* grouped by *Product[Brand]*:

```
WITH
    $Expr0 := ( PFCAST ( 'Sales'[Quantity] AS INT ) * PFCAST ( 'Sales'[Net Price] AS INT ) )
SELECT
    'Product'[Brand],
    SUM ( @$Expr0 )
FROM 'Sales'
    LEFT OUTER JOIN 'Product'
        ON 'Sales'[ProductKey]='Product'[ProductKey];
```

The query is in xmSQL because we use the VertiPaq storage engine with an Import model. Later in this chapter, we show the same DAX query executed against a DirectQuery model, where the storage engine queries use SQL.

The query retrieves the sales amount for each brand. You can easily recognize in the query the numerator of the division. The second storage engine query is similar, though it retrieves a different number:

```
SELECT
    'Product'[Brand],
    DCOUNT ( 'Sales'[ProductKey] )
FROM 'Sales'
    LEFT OUTER JOIN 'Product'
        ON 'Sales'[ProductKey]='Product'[ProductKey];
```

This second xmSQL query retrieves the distinct count of *Sales[ProductKey]* grouped by brand.

The two queries produce the two operands of the DIVIDE function, both grouped by brand. Knowing this, you can now deduce that the formula engine merges the two tables joining them by *Product[Brand]*, and eventually performs the division of the numeric columns to produce the required result.

It is interesting to note that a single DAX query generated two different VertiPaq queries: one for each operand of DIVIDE. This difference depends on the kind of calculations executed. The VertiPaq storage engine can sometimes retrieve both operands in the same query. Other times (as is the case here), this is not possible, and the formula engine retrieves two datacaches to then merge them later on.

Query plans in DirectQuery

We are still in an introductory chapter: we do not want to enter the many details of the differences between VertiPaq and DirectQuery. At this stage though, it is helpful to analyze the query plans and the storage engine queries of the same test query executed against a DirectQuery model. To show the example, we duplicated both *Sales* and *Product* as DirectQuery tables, naming them *Sales DQ* and *Product DQ* respectively. Then we changed the query to reference the DirectQuery tables instead of the VertiPaq tables:

```
EVALUATE
SUMMARIZECOLUMNS (
    'Product DQ'[Brand],
    "Avg Prod Sales",
        DIVIDE (
            SUMX (
                'Sales DQ',
                'Sales DQ'[Quantity] * 'Sales DQ'[Net Price]
            ),
            DISTINCTCOUNT ( 'Sales DQ'[ProductKey] )
        )
)
```

The logical and physical query plans for DirectQuery are nearly identical to the VertiPaq query plans. This similarity is not always the case. There might be scenarios where the query plans are different because of differences in the capabilities of the storage engines. In this simple query, Tabular uses an identical logical query plan and a slightly different physical query plan.

Line	Records	Physical Query Plan
1		GroupSemijoin: IterPhyOp LogOp=GroupSemiJoin IterCols(0, 1)('Product DQ'[Brand], "[Avg Prod Sales])
2		Extend_Lookup: IterPhyOp LogOp=Divide IterCols(0)('Product DQ'[Brand])
3	11	Spool_Iterator<SpoolIterator>: IterPhyOp LogOp=Sum_Vertipaq IterCols(0)('Product DQ'[Brand]) #Records=11 #KeyCols=105 #ValueCols=2
4	11	ProjectionSpool<ProjectFusion<Copy, Copy>>: SpoolPhyOp #Records=11
5		**DirectQueryResult : IterPhyOp #FieldCols=1 #ValueCols=2 Fields('Product DQ'[Brand])**
6	11	SpoolLookup: LookupPhyOp LogOp=DistinctCount_Vertipaq LookupCols(0)('Product DQ'[Brand]) Integer #Records=11 #KeyCols=105 #ValueCols=2
7	11	ProjectionSpool<ProjectFusion<Copy, Copy>>: SpoolPhyOp #Records=11
8		**DirectQueryResult : IterPhyOp #FieldCols=1 #ValueCols=2 Fields('Product DQ'[Brand])**

The most significant difference lies in the storage engine queries produced by DirectQuery. Although the physical query plan shows two nodes consuming a datacache, they reference the same storage engine datacache that uses SQL as the query language:

```
SELECT TOP (1000001) [c95],
    (
        COUNT_BIG(DISTINCT [a0]) + MAX(
            CASE
                WHEN [a0] IS NULL THEN 1
                ELSE 0
            END
        )
    ) AS [a0],
    SUM([a1]) AS [a1]
FROM (
        SELECT [t6].[ProductKey] AS [c83],
            [t6].[Quantity] AS [c84],
            [t6].[Net Price] AS [c86],
            [t7].[Brand] AS [c95],
            [t6].[ProductKey] AS [a0],
            ([t6].[Quantity] * [t6].[Net Price]) AS [a1]
        FROM (
                (
                    select [$Table].[Order Number] as [Order Number],
                        [$Table].[Line Number] as [Line Number],
                        [$Table].[Order Date] as [Order Date],
                        [$Table].[Delivery Date] as [Delivery Date],
                        [$Table].[CustomerKey] as [CustomerKey],
                        [$Table].[StoreKey] as [StoreKey],
                        [$Table].[ProductKey] as [ProductKey],
                        [$Table].[Quantity] as [Quantity],
                        [$Table].[Unit Price] as [Unit Price],
                        [$Table].[Net Price] as [Net Price],
                        [$Table].[Unit Cost] as [Unit Cost],
                        [$Table].[Currency Code] as [Currency Code],
                        [$Table].[Exchange Rate] as [Exchange Rate]
                    from [dbo].[Sales] as [$Table]
                ) AS [t6]
                INNER JOIN (
                    select [$Table].[ProductKey] as [ProductKey],
                        [$Table].[Product Code] as [Product Code],
                        [$Table].[Product Name] as [Product Name],
                        [$Table].[Manufacturer] as [Manufacturer],
                        [$Table].[Brand] as [Brand],
                        [$Table].[Color] as [Color],
                        [$Table].[Weight Unit Measure] as [Weight Unit Measure],
                        [$Table].[Weight] as [Weight],
                        [$Table].[Unit Cost] as [Unit Cost],
                        [$Table].[Unit Price] as [Unit Price],
                        [$Table].[Subcategory Code] as [Subcategory Code],
                        [$Table].[Subcategory] as [Subcategory],
                        [$Table].[Category Code] as [Category Code],
                        [$Table].[Category] as [Category]
                    from [dbo].[Product] as [$Table]
                ) AS [t7] on ([t6].[ProductKey] = [t7].[ProductKey])
            )
    ) AS [t0]
GROUP BY [c95]
```

The query is much more verbose than its xmSQL counterpart. Nonetheless, it is pretty efficient. Due to the nature of SQL, it is possible to retrieve both the distinct count of *Sales[ProductKey]* and the sales amount with a single storage engine query. In this scenario, the formula engine does not need to join two datacaches: it can iterate a single datacache containing both the numerator and the denominator of the expression, to perform the division in the formula engine.

Conclusions

This chapter introduced query plans and storage engine queries. We deliberately used a relatively simple query to introduce query plans. Even so, you might have appreciated that the most interesting information about how the Tabular engine resolves the query is in the storage engine queries.

From time to time, we use the physical query plan to check whether there are large scans of either datacaches or temporarily-built data structures. Regardless, most of our work should focus on storage engine queries.

Section 2
THE FORMULA ENGINE

Understanding the DAX Formula Engine

In previous chapters we introduced the formula engine, with a focus on the different tasks that the formula engine and the storage engine perform. In this chapter, we dive into the formula engine's details, introducing important concepts like datacaches, materialization, and callbacks.

We are not going to describe all the details of the formula engine for two reasons: it would be too long and complex to do so, and it would not be very useful. Indeed, it is not vital to understand every formula engine operator. What is important is to obtain a good understanding of the interaction between the formula engine and the storage engine and to start picturing how the formula engine solves queries.

For this reason, at the end of this chapter, we start analyzing queries to understand the algorithm used by the formula engine to solve the request.

For now, performance is still not on the radar. We will start analyzing execution time and performance in the next chapter. This chapter is still about the fundamentals, so you obtain a good picture of the different parts of the engine involved in the resolution of a query.

Understanding datacaches

In previous chapters, we mentioned on several occasions the concept of datacache. This is where we start going deeper, and we begin with a recap of what a datacache is.

The formula engine produces the result of any DAX query and must access data to do so. Data is stored in the storage engine, which returns datasets on demand, as the result of a storage engine query. Therefore, whenever the formula engine needs any data, it asks the proper storage engine to retrieve the required dataset. The formula engine sends a query to the storage engine, which answers with the result known as a datacache. A datacache is just a table containing the result of a VertiPaq storage engine query.

Please note that – despite the term *datacache* originating from VertiPaq – in this book we use the term *datacache* more broadly. We name *datacache* any result generated by a storage engine query, either VertiPaq, DirectQuery over SQL, or DirectQuery over Analysis Services.

With a simple DAX query, the result is entirely computed by the storage engine. In this case, the formula engine only acts as a pass-through: it sends the query to the storage engine, retrieves the result, and sends it back to the caller. But when the query is no longer trivial, the formula engine retrieves one or more datacaches and manipulates them to produce the final result.

Let us see examples of a very simple query and a few more complex ones. The following DAX query retrieves the sales amount sliced by brand:

```
EVALUATE
SUMMARIZECOLUMNS (
    'Product'[Brand],
    "Sales Amount",
        SUMX (
            Sales,
            Sales[Quantity] * Sales[Net Price]
        )
)
```

The result includes two columns.

Brand	Sales Amount
Contoso	38,709,399,869.35
Wide World Importers	38,787,760,909.12
Northwind Traders	2,642,956,845.20
Adventure Works	51,700,050,318.50
Southridge Video	10,564,018,331.68
Litware	7,224,600,321.71
Fabrikam	21,736,712,371.51
Proseware	18,594,259,995.23
A. Datum	4,875,288,726.60
The Phone Company	32,496,793,282.86
Tailspin Toys	1,737,806,706.26

The physical query plan is extremely simple. You can see that all the formula engine performs is just the retrieval of the datacache from the storage engine to return it to the caller.

Line	Records	Physical Query Plan
1		GroupSemijoin: IterPhyOp LogOp=GroupSemiJoin IterCols(0, 1)('Product'[Brand], ''[Sales Amount])
2	11	Spool_Iterator<SpoolIterator>: IterPhyOp LogOp=Sum_Vertipaq IterCols(0)('Product'[Brand]) #Records=11 #KeyCols=128 #ValueCols=1
3	11	ProjectionSpool<ProjectFusion<Copy>>: SpoolPhyOp #Records=11
4		**Cache: IterPhyOp #FieldCols=1 #ValueCols=1**

The cache used in line 4 is the result of the only storage engine query executed:

```
SET DC_KIND="AUTO";
WITH
    $Expr0 := ( PFCAST ( 'Sales'[Quantity] AS    INT ) * PFCAST ( 'Sales'[Net Price] AS    INT )   )
SELECT
    'Product'[Brand],
    SUM ( @$Expr0 )
FROM 'Sales'
    LEFT OUTER JOIN 'Product'
        ON 'Sales'[ProductKey]='Product'[ProductKey];

Estimated size: rows = 14    bytes = 224
```

You might notice that for the first time, the storage engine query shows two additional lines: the first and the last. The first line (SET DC_KIND="AUTO") indicates the type of datacache required. The last line estimates the datacache size in terms of number of rows and size in bytes.

While the first line is not very interesting, the last line is. The larger the number of rows, the slower the process of transferring data from the storage engine to the formula engine. The number shown in the storage engine query is an estimate. You can easily check this by looking at the number of rows. When executing the query, the formula engine expects 14 rows. The actual number of rows is available only when the storage engine query execution is complete. The final number of rows is reported in the physical query plan. There, you can see that 11 rows were returned, not 14.

Focusing on the details of the query, the storage engine query retrieves both the *Product[Brand]* column and the aggregated value of the sales amount. The result of the storage engine query is left in a datacache containing 11 rows, which is then read by the formula engine and processed.

The simplest way to force the formula engine to execute any further operation on the datacache is to add an ORDER BY clause to the query. The result of a storage engine query is not sorted. Therefore, it is the formula engine that oversees the sorting operation:

```
EVALUATE
SUMMARIZECOLUMNS (
    'Product'[Brand],
    "Sales Amount",
        SUMX (
            Sales,
            Sales[Quantity] * Sales[Net Price]
        )
)
ORDER BY Product[Brand]
```

The only difference between the previous and the current physical query plans is that further operators are now applied to the result. These operators are required to provide the sorting. In the following figure, we highlighted the part of the query plan that is identical to the previous query's plan. The other three lines (1, 2, and 7) are required for the sorting.

Line	Records	Physical Query Plan
1		PartitionIntoGroups: IterPhyOp LogOp=Order IterCols(0, 1)('Product'[Brand], "[Sales Amount]) #Groups=1 #Rows=11
2	1	AggregationSpool<Order>: SpoolPhyOp #Records=1
3		GroupSemijoin: IterPhyOp LogOp=GroupSemiJoin IterCols(0, 1)('Product'[Brand], "[Sales Amount])
4	11	Spool_Iterator<SpoolIterator>: IterPhyOp LogOp=Sum_Vertipaq IterCols(0)('Product'[Brand]) #Records=11 #K
5	11	ProjectionSpool<ProjectFusion<Copy>>: SpoolPhyOp #Records=11
6		**Cache: IterPhyOp #FieldCols=1 #ValueCols=1**
7		ColPosition<'Product'[Brand]>: LookupPhyOp LogOp=ColPosition<'Product'[Brand]>ColPosition<'Product'[Bran

Let us now increase the complexity of the query by adding a subtotal row. Since the query is grouping by *Product[Brand]*, we can add the total by product brand:

```
EVALUATE
SUMMARIZECOLUMNS (
    ROLLUPADDISSUBTOTAL ( 'Product'[Brand], "BrandSubtotal" ),
    "Sales Amount",
        SUMX (
            Sales,
            Sales[Quantity] * Sales[Net Price]
        )
)
ORDER BY Product[Brand]
```

There is now a new row at the beginning with *BrandSubtotal* set to True; that row contains the total.

Brand	BrandSubtotal	Sales Amount
	True	229,069,647,678.00
A. Datum	False	4,875,288,726.60
Adventure Works	False	51,700,050,318.50
Contoso	False	38,709,399,869.35
Fabrikam	False	21,736,712,371.51
Litware	False	7,224,600,321.71
Northwind Traders	False	2,642,956,845.20
Proseware	False	18,594,259,995.23
Southridge Video	False	10,564,018,331.68
Tailspin Toys	False	1,737,806,706.26
The Phone Company	False	32,496,793,282.86
Wide World Importers	False	38,787,760,909.12

Adding the subtotal might have one of two effects: either Tabular chooses to compute the grand total in the formula engine by summing the individual rows in the datacache, or it performs a new storage engine query strictly for the total. The behavior changes based on the additivity of the calculation. Indeed, the formula engine can compute the subtotal by summing individual rows only for additive calculations. The formula we are computing right now is additive; therefore, the summarization takes place in the formula engine.

Line	Records	Physical Query Plan
1		PartitionIntoGroups: IterPhyOp LogOp=Order IterCols(0, 1, 2, 3)('Product'[Brand], ''[BrandSubtotal], ''[Sales Amount], ''[]) #Groups=1 #Rows=12
2	1	AggregationSpool<Order>: SpoolPhyOp #Records=1
3		Union: IterPhyOp LogOp=Union IterCols(0, 1, 2, 3)('Product'[Brand], ''[BrandSubtotal], ''[Sales Amount], ''[])
4		GroupSemijoin: IterPhyOp LogOp=GroupSemiJoin IterCols(0, 1, 2)('Product'[Brand], ''[BrandSubtotal], ''[Sales Amount])
5	11	Spool_Iterator<SpoolIterator>: IterPhyOp LogOp=Sum_Vertipaq IterCols(0)('Product'[Brand]) #Records=11 #KeyCols=121 #ValueCols
6	11	ProjectionSpool<ProjectFusion<Copy>>: SpoolPhyOp #Records=11
7		**Cache: IterPhyOp #FieldCols=1 #ValueCols=1**
8		GroupSemijoin: IterPhyOp LogOp=GroupSemiJoin IterCols(0, 1, 2)('Product'[Brand], ''[BrandSubtotal], ''[Sales Amount])
9	1	Spool_Iterator<SpoolIterator>: IterPhyOp LogOp=Sum_Vertipaq #Records=1 #KeyCols=0 #ValueCols=1
10	1	AggregationSpool<AggFusion<Sum>>: SpoolPhyOp #Records=1
11	11	Spool_Iterator<SpoolIterator>: IterPhyOp LogOp=Sum_Vertipaq IterCols(0)('Product'[Brand]) #Records=11 #KeyCols=121 #Valu
12	11	ProjectionSpool<ProjectFusion<Copy>>: SpoolPhyOp #Records=11
13		**Cache: IterPhyOp #FieldCols=1 #ValueCols=1**
14		ColPosition<'Product'[Brand]>: LookupPhyOp LogOp=ColPosition<'Product'[Brand]> ColPosition<'Product'[Brand]> LookupCols(0)('Produ

The highlighted part is computing the grand total. You can see that it is consuming 11 rows and producing only one, which is the only row with the total. Its output is then used by UNION (line 3) to merge the 11 rows or the storage engine result with the one containing the subtotal.

Moreover, there are now two lines in the query plan where the formula engine reads a datacache: at line 7 and line 13. This does not mean that there will be two storage engine queries. The formula engine reads the same datacache twice: once to produce the rows and once to compute the subtotal.

By slowly increasing the complexity of the query, we are increasing the amount of work that the formula engine is carrying on to transform the raw result produced by the storage engine into the real result generated by the DAX query.

So far, the formula engine has had to send only one storage engine query. Therefore, the query resolution process required only one datacache. We can increase the complexity a bit by turning the calculation into a non-additive one, such as a distinct count:

```
EVALUATE
SUMMARIZECOLUMNS (
    ROLLUPADDISSUBTOTAL ( 'Product'[Brand], "BrandSubtotal" ),
    "# Products",
        DISTINCTCOUNT ( Sales[ProductKey] )
)
ORDER BY Product[Brand]
```

The VertiPaq storage engine can produce distinct counts. Nonetheless, once the formula engine retrieves the distinct count by brand, it cannot simply compute the result by summing individual rows because the result would be inaccurate. Computing the aggregation of a non-additive measure requires another scan of the *Sales* table. The DAX optimizer kicks in, choosing a rather surprising query plan.

Line	Records	Physical Query Plan
1		PartitionIntoGroups: IterPhyOp LogOp=Order IterCols(0, 1, 2, 3)('Product'[Brand], "[BrandSubtotal], "[# Products], "[]) #Grou
2	1	AggregationSpool<Order>: SpoolPhyOp #Records=1
3		Union: IterPhyOp LogOp=Union IterCols(0, 1, 2, 3)('Product'[Brand], "[BrandSubtotal], "[# Products], "[])
4		GroupSemijoin: IterPhyOp LogOp=GroupSemiJoin IterCols(0, 1, 2)('Product'[Brand], "[BrandSubtotal], "[# Products])
5	11	Spool_Iterator<SpoolIterator>: IterPhyOp LogOp=DistinctCount_Vertipaq IterCols(0)('Product'[Brand]) #Records=
6	11	ProjectionSpool<ProjectFusion<Copy>>: SpoolPhyOp #Records=11
7		**Cache: IterPhyOp #FieldCols=1 #ValueCols=1**
8		GroupSemijoin: IterPhyOp LogOp=GroupSemiJoin IterCols(0, 1, 2)('Product'[Brand], "[BrandSubtotal], "[# Products])
9		Extend_Lookup: IterPhyOp LogOp=Constant
10		SingletonTable: IterPhyOp LogOp=Constant
11		Constant: LookupPhyOp LogOp=Constant Integer 2517
12		ColPosition<'Product'[Brand]>: LookupPhyOp LogOp=ColPosition<'Product'[Brand]>ColPosition<'Product'[Brand]> Lo

The highlighted part of this query plan contains the grand total calculation. Surprisingly, it does not consume any datacache. Instead, it is returning the constant value 2,517. How come the formula engine knows the result without sending a query to the storage engine? The answer is in the statistical information that VertiPaq keeps for any column in the model. For each column, VertiPaq stores its cardinality, which is the number of distinct values used for that column. Because the query does not apply any filter, the formula engine does not need to scan the *Sales* table to know the exact number of distinct values.

To force Tabular to proceed with a scan, we can add a filter to the *Product[Color]* column, like the Red filter included in the following query:

```
EVALUATE
SUMMARIZECOLUMNS (
    ROLLUPADDISSUBTOTAL ( 'Product'[Brand], "BrandSubtotal" ),
    TREATAS ( { "Red" }, Product[Color] ),
    "# Products",
        DISTINCTCOUNT ( Sales[ProductKey] )
)
ORDER BY Product[Brand]
```

The query plan is now more complex because it must include the filter on the *Product[Color]* column, using TREATAS.

Line	Records	Physical Query Plan
1		PartitionIntoGroups: IterPhyOp LogOp=Order IterCols(0, 1, 2, 3)('Product'[Brand], ''[BrandSubtotal], ''[# Products], ''[]) #Group
2	1	AggregationSpool<Order>: SpoolPhyOp #Records=1
3		Union: IterPhyOp LogOp=Union IterCols(0, 1, 2, 3)('Product'[Brand], ''[BrandSubtotal], ''[# Products], ''[])
4		GroupSemijoin: IterPhyOp LogOp=GroupSemiJoin IterCols(0, 1, 2)('Product'[Brand], ''[BrandSubtotal], ''[# Products])
5	9	Spool_Iterator<SpoolIterator>: IterPhyOp LogOp=DistinctCount_Vertipaq IterCols(1)('Product'[Brand]) #Records=9
6	9	ProjectionSpool<ProjectFusion<Copy>>: SpoolPhyOp #Records=9
7		**Cache: IterPhyOp #FieldCols=1 #ValueCols=1**
8	1	Spool_Iterator<SpoolIterator>: IterPhyOp LogOp=TreatAs IterCols(0)('Product'[Color]) #Records=1 #KeyCo
9	1	AggregationSpool<GroupBy>: SpoolPhyOp #Records=1
10		TreatAs: IterPhyOp LogOp=TreatAs IterCols(0)('Product'[Color])
11		TableCtor: IterPhyOp LogOp=TableCtor IterCols(0)(''[Value])
12		GroupSemijoin: IterPhyOp LogOp=GroupSemiJoin IterCols(0, 1, 2)('Product'[Brand], ''[BrandSubtotal], ''[# Products])
13	1	Spool_Iterator<SpoolIterator>: IterPhyOp LogOp=DistinctCount_Vertipaq #Records=1 #KeyCols=128 #ValueCols=
14	1	ProjectionSpool<ProjectFusion<Copy>>: SpoolPhyOp #Records=1
15		**Cache: IterPhyOp #FieldCols=0 #ValueCols=1**
16	1	Spool_Iterator<SpoolIterator>: IterPhyOp LogOp=TreatAs IterCols(0)('Product'[Color]) #Records=1 #KeyCo
17	1	AggregationSpool<GroupBy>: SpoolPhyOp #Records=1
18		TreatAs: IterPhyOp LogOp=TreatAs IterCols(0)('Product'[Color])
19		TableCtor: IterPhyOp LogOp=TableCtor IterCols(0)(''[Value])
20		ColPosition<'Product'[Brand]>: LookupPhyOp LogOp=ColPosition<'Product'[Brand]>ColPosition<'Product'[Brand]> Lo

The highlighted part is the additional scan of the fact table to compute the number of distinct counts of the *Product[Brand]* column for the grand total.

There are now two Cache operators, one at line 7 and one at line 15. By inspecting the storage engine queries, we find two of them: one for the distinct count sliced by brand and another for the grand total. Here is the first query:

```
SELECT
    'Product'[Brand],
    DCOUNT ( 'Sales'[ProductKey] )
FROM 'Sales'
    LEFT OUTER JOIN 'Product'
        ON 'Sales'[ProductKey]='Product'[ProductKey]
WHERE
    'Product'[Color] = 'Red';

Estimated size: rows = 9    bytes = 108
```

This first query retrieves an estimated nine rows grouping by *Product[Brand]*. The second storage engine query produces the distinct count for the grand total:

```
SELECT
    DCOUNT ( 'Sales'[ProductKey] )
FROM 'Sales'
    LEFT OUTER JOIN 'Product'
        ON 'Sales'[ProductKey]='Product'[ProductKey]
WHERE
    'Product'[Color] = 'Red';

Estimated size: rows = 1    bytes = 12
```

The two datacaches are then merged by the formula engine (Union operation at line 3 of the physical query plan) to produce the table that is eventually being sorted to produce the result.

As you have seen from this example, the work required to resolve a DAX query is split between the formula engine and the storage engine. Small variations to a query can produce quite different query plans. In our example, if a formula is additive then the grand total is computed by the formula engine; if the formula is non-additive, then the values are computed by the storage engine through an additional query.

The formula engine never accesses data directly. The formula engine works only on datacaches. The execution speed of a query is strongly tied to the size of a datacache: the smaller the datacache, the faster the query. The number of rows present in a datacache depends on the complexity of the query. There are scenarios in which the size of a datacache is the smallest possible, leading to optimal execution. However, there are scenarios where the size of the datacache is larger than required. For this latter case, we will learn how to reduce the size of datacaches to reduce the amount of work needed to move datacaches back and forth between the two engines.

Note   The formula engine generally sends one query at a time to the VertiPaq storage engine. DirectQuery for SQL can execute more than one storage engine query in parallel. However, the number of storage engine queries that can run in parallel is always limited to a small, single-digit number. There is a huge difference between a single complex storage engine request that can be parallelized within the storage engine and the same result obtained through tens of storage engine queries that need to be sequential or with reduced parallelism in the best-case scenario. Regardless of the storage engine, the best algorithm is almost always composed of a small number of complex storage engine queries with some final elaboration carried on by the formula engine. This approach reduces the communication overhead of the two engines to a minimum. We will see examples of these kinds of optimizations later.

Understanding materialization

The creation of a memory structure containing the result of a storage engine query is called *materialization*. Data resides in the data source: either VertiPaq, SQL, or other sources. A subset of data, potentially aggregated and with some calculations executed, is sent to the formula engine. The formula engine receives a physical copy of the data that needs to be temporarily stored in memory for the time required to consume it. Therefore, materialization is an expensive process because data is not only consumed: it needs to be stored before consumption.

Let us see a sample scenario by analyzing a query that generates excessive materialization in VertiPaq:

```
DEFINE
    MEASURE Sales[Big Sales Amount (slow)] =
        CALCULATE (
            [Sales Amount],
            FILTER ( Sales, Sales[Quantity] * Sales[Net Price] > 1000 )
        )

EVALUATE
SUMMARIZECOLUMNS (
    'Product'[Brand],
    "Big_Sales_Amount", 'Sales'[Big Sales Amount (slow)]
)
```

The query retrieves the sales amount, sliced by *Product[Brand]*, only for the transactions where *Quantity* times *Net Price* is greater than 1,000. The DAX query result contains 11 rows.

Brand	Big_Sales_Amount
Adventure Works	46,718,366,336.76
Proseware	14,924,825,974.41
Contoso	27,766,768,312.54
Wide World Importers	32,271,758,160.70
Litware	5,996,482,985.38
Fabrikam	19,372,914,734.66
Northwind Traders	1,728,172,433.27
A. Datum	3,252,756,088.14
Southridge Video	4,674,871,950.75
The Phone Company	23,224,137,335.25
Tailspin Toys	123,115,707.29

Because the result contains 11 rows and the calculation performed is a simple multiplication, an optimal query plan should materialize only 11 rows. Nonetheless, the query plan shows a materialization of 192,049 rows in a datacache.

Line	Records	Physical Query Plan
1		GroupSemijoin: IterPhyOp LogOp=GroupSemiJoin IterCols(0, 1)('Product'[Brand], ''[Big_Sales_Amount])
2	11	Spool_Iterator<SpoolIterator>: IterPhyOp LogOp=Sum_Vertipaq IterCols(0)('Product'[Brand]) #Records=11 #KeyCols=1
3	11	AggregationSpool<AggFusion<Sum>>: SpoolPhyOp #Records=11
4		CrossApply: IterPhyOp LogOp=Sum_Vertipaq IterCols(0)('Product'[Brand])
5	192,049	Spool_MultiValuedHashLookup: IterPhyOp LogOp=Filter_Vertipaq LookupCols(7, 9, 49)('Sales'[Quantity], 'Sales'[I
6	192,049	ProjectionSpool<ProjectFusion<>>: SpoolPhyOp #Records=192049
7		**Cache: IterPhyOp #FieldCols=3 #ValueCols=0**
8		**Cache: IterPhyOp #FieldCols=3 #ValueCols=1**

Moreover, there are two datacaches being generated: one at line 7, and one at line 8. To better understand the query plan, we need to investigate further by looking at the two storage engine queries. The first query retrieves the combinations of *Product[Brand]*, *Sales[Quantity]*, and *Sales[Net Price]* that satisfy the condition:

```
WITH
    $Expr0 := ( PFCAST ( 'Sales'[Quantity] AS   INT ) * PFCAST ( 'Sales'[Net Price] AS   INT )   )
SELECT
    'Sales'[Quantity],
    'Sales'[Net Price],
    'Product'[Brand],
    SUM ( @$Expr0 )
FROM 'Sales'
    LEFT OUTER JOIN 'Product'
        ON 'Sales'[ProductKey]='Product'[ProductKey]
WHERE
    ( COALESCE ( ( PFCAST ( 'Sales'[Quantity] AS INT ) * PFCAST ( 'Sales'[Net Price] AS INT ) ) ) > COALESCE ( 10000000 ) ) ;
```

You might wonder why the test in the WHERE condition checks for 10,000,000 – instead of 1,000 as requested in the DAX code. This is because *Sales[Net Price]* is a currency data type, therefore its value is an integer containing the original number multiplied by 10,000.

The second storage engine query is the following:

```
SELECT
    'Sales'[Quantity],
    'Sales'[Net Price],
    'Product'[Brand]
FROM 'Sales'
    LEFT OUTER JOIN 'Product'
        ON 'Sales'[ProductKey]='Product'[ProductKey]
WHERE
    ( COALESCE ( ( PFCAST ( 'Sales'[Quantity] AS INT ) * PFCAST ( 'Sales'[Net Price] AS INT ) ) ) > COALESCE ( 10000000 ) ) ;
```

The only difference between the two queries is the calculation of the sales amount, which is computed by the latter query and not by the former. In the end, we obtain two datacaches with 192,049 rows each, which are then joined by the formula engine to produce 11 rows. Indeed, at line 3 of the query plan we find an aggregation performed by the formula engine on the join of the two datacaches.

The reason for the excessive materialization is that the DAX code performs a filter on the *Sales* table. The optimizer found that out of the entire expanded *Sales* table, only three columns were required: *Brand*, *Quantity*, and *Net Price*. Nonetheless, the filter on the table forced a suboptimal query plan.

Optimizing this query is as simple as avoiding the filter on the table. By removing FILTER, DAX uses a FILTER over the two columns instead of the full table. We need to add KEEPFILTERS to maintain the semantics of the previous formula:

```
DEFINE
    MEASURE Sales[Big Sales Amount (fast)] =
        CALCULATE (
            [Sales Amount],
            KEEPFILTERS ( Sales[Quantity] * Sales[Net Price] > 1000 )
        )

EVALUATE
SUMMARIZECOLUMNS (
    'Product'[Brand],
    "Big_Sales_Amount", 'Sales'[Big Sales Amount (fast)]
)
```

The query plan is now much simpler than the one before, and also shows an optimal materialization of 11 rows.

Line	Records	Physical Query Plan
1		GroupSemijoin: IterPhyOp LogOp=GroupSemiJoin IterCols(0, 1)('Product'[Brand], ''[Big_Sales_Amount])
2	11	Spool_Iterator<SpoolIterator>: IterPhyOp LogOp=Sum_Vertipaq IterCols(0)('Product'[Brand]) #Records=11 #KeyCols=121
3	11	ProjectionSpool<ProjectFusion<Copy>>: SpoolPhyOp #Records=11
4		**Cache: IterPhyOp #FieldCols=1 #ValueCols=1**

We can look at the storage engine query, where we find a confirmation of the optimal materialization level. There is only one storage engine query that computes the entire result:

```
WITH
    $Expr0 := ( PFCAST ( 'Sales'[Quantity] AS   INT ) * PFCAST ( 'Sales'[Net Price] AS   INT )   )
SELECT
    'Product'[Brand],
    SUM ( @$Expr0 )
FROM 'Sales'
    LEFT OUTER JOIN 'Product'
        ON 'Sales'[ProductKey]='Product'[ProductKey]
WHERE
    ( COALESCE ( ( PFCAST ( 'Sales'[Quantity] AS INT ) * PFCAST ( 'Sales'[Net Price] AS INT ) ) ) > COALESCE ( 10000000 ) );
```

This latter query plan requires fewer storage engine queries because the entire calculation is pushed down to the storage engine, which materializes exactly the rows needed to produce the result.

It is not always possible to obtain such a perfect level of materialization. Most of the times, the complexity of the query is so large that some level of suboptimal materialization is expected. Nonetheless, the presence of excessive materialization in a query is easy to spot and drives major improvements in the speed of the query.

Let us see another example of poor materialization, this time with a query that simply uses the wrong aggregation function: it uses GROUPBY instead of SUMMARIZE. GROUPBY is a DAX function that is computed in the formula engine. Despite being somewhat more flexible than SUMMARIZE, its drawback is that it is not pushed down to the storage engine. Here is the query:

```
EVALUATE
GROUPBY (
    Sales,
    'Product'[Brand],
    "# Transactions", SUMX ( CURRENTGROUP (), 1 )
)
```

The result of the query contains 11 rows: one per brand.

Brand	# Transactions
The Phone Company	29,412,998
Contoso	59,718,160
Proseware	13,035,632
Adventure Works	22,972,804
Wide World Importers	24,987,197
Tailspin Toys	17,186,912
Fabrikam	10,559,982
Southridge Video	31,596,548
Litware	5,526,701
Northwind Traders	5,599,372
A. Datum	5,020,642

We observe that the query plan shows a very different level of materialization.

Line	Records	Physical Query Plan
1		AddColumns: IterPhyOp LogOp=SelectColumns IterCols(0, 1)('Product'[Brand], "[# Transactions])
2		AddColumnsValueEncoder: IterPhyOp LogOp=GroupByAgg IterCols(0, 1)('Product'[Brand], "[])
3	11	Spool_Iterator<SpoolIterator>: IterPhyOp LogOp=GroupByAgg IterCols(0, 1)('Product'[Brand], "[]) #Records=11
4	11	AggregationSpool<AggFusion<Sum>>: SpoolPhyOp #Records=11
5		AddColumnsByValue: IterPhyOp LogOp=GroupByAgg IterCols(0, 1)('Product'[Brand], "[])
6	225,616,948	Spool_Iterator<SpoolIterator>: IterPhyOp LogOp=Scan_Vertipaq IterCols(0, 48)('Sales'[RowNumber-266
7	225,616,948	ProjectionSpool<ProjectFusion<>>: SpoolPhyOp #Records=225616948
8		**Cache: IterPhyOp #FieldCols=2 #ValueCols=0**
9		Constant: LookupPhyOp LogOp=Constant Integer 1
10		ColValue<"[]>: LookupPhyOp LogOp=ColValue<"[]>"[] LookupCols(1)("[]) Integer

The highlighted section of the query plan consumes 225,616,948 rows. Moreover, 225,616,948 is the exact number of rows in the *Sales* table. Therefore, the query is materializing all the rows in *Sales*. Be mindful of the fact that the engine is not materializing all the columns in *Sales*. The optimizer determined that only some of the columns are needed: the brand is the only important column. However, it is not performing any grouping: it is materializing a datacache grouped by *Product[Brand]* and *Sales[RowNumber]*. *RowNumber* is a special column that uniquely identifies a row in VertiPaq through its physical position. The *RowNumber* column is used whenever the engine does not want any grouping:

```
SELECT
    'Sales'[RowNumber],
    'Product'[Brand]
FROM 'Sales'
    LEFT OUTER JOIN 'Product'
        ON 'Sales'[ProductKey]='Product'[ProductKey];

Estimated size: rows = 225,616,948    bytes = 902,467,792
```

As we introduced earlier, this query is deliberately inefficient. The usage of GROUPBY forces DAX to use the formula engine. We can change the behavior just by slightly changing the code. By using SUMMARIZECOLUMNS instead of GROUPBY, the optimizer pushes the entire calculation down to the storage engine, producing an optimal materialization:

```
EVALUATE
SUMMARIZECOLUMNS (
    'Product'[Brand],
    "# Transactions", COUNTROWS ( Sales )
)
```

The query plan shows that the datacache contains only 11 rows.

Line	Records	Physical Query Plan
1		GroupSemijoin: IterPhyOp LogOp=GroupSemiJoin IterCols(0, 1)('Product'[Brand], ''[# Transactions])
2	11	Spool_Iterator<SpoolIterator>: IterPhyOp LogOp=Count_Vertipaq IterCols(0)('Product'[Brand]) #Records=11
3	11	ProjectionSpool<ProjectFusion<Copy>>: SpoolPhyOp #Records=11
4		**Cache: IterPhyOp #FieldCols=1 #ValueCols=1**

The only storage engine query being generated contains an estimated 14 rows (instead of the 11 rows returned), and it already computes the result:

```
SELECT
    'Product'[Brand],
    COUNT ( )
FROM 'Sales'
    LEFT OUTER JOIN 'Product'
        ON 'Sales'[ProductKey]='Product'[ProductKey];
```

Estimated size: rows = 14   bytes = 112

Understanding callbacks

In the last example we analyzed, Tabular had to materialize all the rows in *Sales* to produce its result. We used an example with a few thousand rows; therefore, performance is still great. However, materializing an entire table on large models would result in terrible performance. The following demo runs on the Contoso 10K database, because running it on our regular model with 100M rows would result in an error.

It is important to remember that any functionality not directly supported by the storage engine requires the intervention of the formula engine. Therefore, depending on the capabilities of the storage engine used, the same query can provide different levels of materialization. The designers of Tabular took great care in creating a language that does not require large materialization. Therefore, for educational purposes, our demo must use rather unusual calculations.

To force the materialization of an entire table, we need to use functions not supported by the storage engine. For example, the BITRSHIFT function is not available in SQL Server. Therefore, the formula engine cannot rely on SQL Server to perform that type of calculation. In the following query, the formula engine is forced to retrieve from the storage engine a result containing all the values of the *Quantity* column, to perform the BITRSHIFT calculation:

```
EVALUATE
SUMMARIZECOLUMNS (
    'Product DQ'[Brand],
    "# Transactions",
        SUMX (
            'Sales DQ',
            BITRSHIFT ( 'Sales DQ'[Quantity], 2 )
        )
)
```

You can spot in the query plan that the result generated by DirectQuery contains 13,915 rows (see line 6).

Line	Records	Physical Query Plan
1		GroupSemijoin: IterPhyOp LogOp=GroupSemiJoin IterCols(0, 1)('Product DQ'[Brand], "[# Transactions])
2	15	Spool_Iterator<SpoolIterator>: IterPhyOp LogOp=SumX IterCols(0)('Product DQ'[Brand]) #Records=15 #KeyCols=1 #ValueCols=1
3	15	AggregationSpool<Sum>: SpoolPhyOp #Records=15
4		Extend_Lookup: IterPhyOp LogOp=BITRSHIFT IterCols(9)('Sales DQ'[Quantity])
5	13,915	Spool_Iterator<SpoolIterator>: IterPhyOp LogOp=Scan_Vertipaq IterCols(0, 1, 9)('Product DQ'[Brand], 'Sales DQ'[RowNum
6	13,915	ProjectionSpool<ProjectFusion<>>: SpoolPhyOp #Records=13915
7		**DirectQueryResult : IterPhyOp #FieldCols=3 #ValueCols=0 Fields('Sales DQ'[RowNumber-2662979B-1795-4F7**
8		BITRSHIFT: LookupPhyOp LogOp=BITRSHIFT LookupCols(9)('Sales DQ'[Quantity]) Integer
9		ColValue<'Sales DQ'[Quantity]>: LookupPhyOp LogOp=ColValue<'Sales DQ'[Quantity]>'Sales DQ'[Quantity] LookupCo
10		Constant: LookupPhyOp LogOp=Constant Integer 2

It is not useful to show here the code of the SQL query being executed. It is enough to say that it is a simple SELECT that retrieves all the values for *Brand* and *Quantity* from *Sales*.

This level of materialization rarely happens. To see that, you need to use functionalities that cannot be translated to the storage engine language. Because SQL Server is a very rich language, most DAX functions can be translated to SQL. As a result, you seldom end up with query plans like this. This is the reason why we needed an exotic function like BITRSHIFT.

When using more common functions, like IF, the DAX code is translated to SQL which produces a much more efficient query plan. For example, the following query does not produce any unusual level of materialization:

```
EVALUATE
SUMMARIZECOLUMNS (
    'Product DQ'[Brand],
    "Quantity GT 1",
        SUMX (
            'Sales DQ',
            IF ( 'Sales DQ'[Quantity] > 1, 'Sales DQ'[Quantity] )
        )
)
```

The SQL query generated to answer this DAX query contains a translation of the IF function with a CASE statement in SQL, as you can see from the following excerpt from the SQL storage engine query:

```
SELECT TOP (1000001) *
FROM (
        SELECT [c95],
            SUM([a0]) AS [a0]
        FROM (
                SELECT [t6].[Quantity] AS [c84],
                    [t7].[Brand] AS [c95],
                    (
                        CASE
                            WHEN (
                                NOT(([t6].[Quantity] IS NULL))
                                AND ([t6].[Quantity] > 1)
                            ) THEN [t6].[Quantity]
                            ELSE null
                        END
                    ) AS [a0]
                FROM (
                    (
...  ..  ..  ..  ..  ..  ..
                    )
                ) AS [t0]
            GROUP BY [c95]
        ) AS [MainTable]
WHERE (NOT(([a0] IS NULL)))
```

Although excessive materialization is not common when using DirectQuery over SQL Server, the same scenario is more frequent when using VertiPaq. Indeed, the VertiPaq engine offers an extremely limited set of functionalities. The xmSQL language offered by the VertiPaq storage engine can perform only very basic operations. For example, the simple IF statement shown earlier is already too complex to handle by the VertiPaq storage engine.

The following DAX query is identical to the previous one, the only difference being that it runs on VertiPaq instead of DirectQuery:

```
EVALUATE
SUMMARIZECOLUMNS (
    'Product'[Brand],
    "Quantity GT 1",
        SUMX (
            'Sales',
            IF ( 'Sales'[Quantity] > 1, 'Sales'[Quantity] )
        )
)
```

Because the VertiPaq storage engine cannot handle IF, this query would require materializing all the rows in *Sales*. To avoid this problem, the formula engine can use a callback. Callback is a feature available only with VertiPaq, because both the VertiPaq engine and the formula engine run as part of the same software.

A callback is the option of the storage engine to perform a request from the formula engine, to compute an expression that the storage engine itself can not compute. You can notice the presence of a callback already from the query plan, looking at lines 5 to 10 that are below the Cache node at line 4.

Line	Records	Physical Query Plan
1		GroupSemijoin: IterPhyOp LogOp=GroupSemiJoin IterCols(0, 1)('Product'[Brand], ' '[Quantity GT 1])
2	11	Spool_Iterator<Spooliterator>: IterPhyOp LogOp=Sum_Vertipaq IterCols(0)('Product'[Brand]) #Records=11 #KeyCols=121 #ValueCols=1
3	11	ProjectionSpool<ProjectFusion<Copy>>: SpoolPhyOp #Records=11
4		**Cache: IterPhyOp #FieldCols=1 #ValueCols=1**
5		If: LookupPhyOp LogOp=If LookupCols(56)('Sales'[Quantity]) Integer
6		GreaterThan: LookupPhyOp LogOp=GreaterThan LookupCols(56)('Sales'[Quantity]) Boolean
7		ColValue<'Sales'[Quantity]>: LookupPhyOp LogOp=ColValue<'Sales'[Quantity]>'Sales'[Quantity] LookupCols(56)('Sales'[Quantity])
8		Constant: LookupPhyOp LogOp=Constant Integer 1
9		ColValue<'Sales'[Quantity]>: LookupPhyOp LogOp=ColValue<'Sales'[Quantity]>'Sales'[Quantity] LookupCols(56)('Sales'[Quantity]) Int
10		Constant: LookupPhyOp LogOp=Constant Integer BLANK

The Cache operator at line 4 is not at the leaf level, as was the case in all the query plans analyzed so far. When a Cache statement is at the leaf level, its content is consumed by surrounding formula engine operators. In this case, the Cache operator produces the result of other formula engine operators: the IF at line 5, the GreaterThan at line 6, and so on. This means that the datacache generated at line 4 contains calculations that still require the intervention of the formula engine.

By inspecting the corresponding xmSQL query, we can better appreciate the execution flow:

```
SET DC_KIND="AUTO";
WITH
    $Expr0 := [CallbackDataID ( IF ( 'Sales'[Quantity] > 1, 'Sales'[Quantity] )   ) ] ( PFDATAID ( 'Sales'[Quantity] )   )
SELECT
    'Product'[Brand],
    SUM ( @$Expr0 )
FROM 'Sales'
    LEFT OUTER JOIN 'Product'
        ON 'Sales'[ProductKey]='Product'[ProductKey];

Estimated size: rows = 14    bytes = 224
```

The expression summed by the SELECT statement contains a CallbackDataID. CallbackDataID includes the entire DAX expression that is used inside SUMX, in the DAX query. VertiPaq scans the *Sales* table, and for each row in *Sales*, it calls back the formula engine asking it to compute the IF statement. The formula engine returns the result of the expression that is finally used by the storage engine to perform the sum.

A callback requires a lot of communication between the storage engine and the formula engine. And still, that is much better than if the storage engine had to materialize a large amount of data to pass back to the formula engine. Besides, despite the formula engine being single-threaded, when the storage engine calls back the formula engine, there is one instance of the formula engine for each VertiPaq thread. Therefore, the performance penalty is caused by the communication overhead rather than by the absence of parallelism.

Callbacks are a unique feature of the VertiPaq storage engine. It would not be possible to use a callback with an external storage engine like SQL Server. There are several important considerations to make about the performance of callbacks. But here, we only wanted to introduce the concept. We will cover callbacks in more detail in the chapter about the VertiPaq engine, as callbacks are present only with the VertiPaq storage engine.

Formula engine with different storage engines

As we have seen in the previous sections, the query plan executed by the formula engine depends on the storage engines available in the model. The same query can produce different query plans depending on several factors.

The important details to consider are:

- **Capabilities of the storage engine(s)**. VertiPaq is faster than an external engine like SQL Server but offers a more limited set of operators. VertiPaq permits callbacks, whereas a SQL query does not. If you use a composite model, then the storage engine runs DAX, offering an even more powerful set of operators. Tabular considers all these factors when building the query plan, pushing most of the calculations down to the storage engine to reduce the size of the datacaches exchanged between the formula and the storage engines.

- **Different data islands.** Whenever a query joins tables belonging to different data islands, the join cannot be pushed down to the storage engine. In that scenario, the formula engine oversees the join operation, retrieving data from the different storage engines and joining them together. So far, we have always used queries that use a single data island; later on, we will dive into the complexities of models with multiple data islands.

Understanding vertical fusion

Vertical fusion is an optimization technique implemented at the formula engine level that aims to reduce the number of storage engine queries executed. If the DAX optimizer detects that multiple aggregations can be executed within a single query, then vertical fusion reduces the number of queries sent to the storage engine. There is also another fusion optimization called *horizontal fusion*, which we will discuss later.

Let us see vertical fusion with an example. Consider the following DAX query:

```
EVALUATE
SUMMARIZECOLUMNS (
    Product[Brand],
    "Sales Quantity", SUM ( Sales[Quantity] ),
    "Max Price", MAX ( Sales[Net Price] ),
    "Min Price", MIN ( Sales[Net Price] )
)
```

The result includes three columns, which are aggregations over columns in *Sales*.

Brand	Sales Quantity	Max Price	Min Price
Contoso	187,810,357	6,247.50	2.53
Wide World Importers	78,594,313	6,247.50	19.34
Northwind Traders	17,617,376	2,652.90	16.57
Adventure Works	72,260,582	3,247.50	19.34
Southridge Video	99,402,003	999.00	0.82
Litware	17,379,762	3,199.99	3.22
Fabrikam	33,225,159	3,199.99	61.27
Proseware	41,004,762	6,247.50	19.34
A. Datum	15,795,831	1,003.20	110.94
The Phone Company	92,502,646	1,060.20	110.94
Tailspin Toys	54,058,135	598.80	3.00

Theoretically, the three calculations are separate, as shown in the physical query plan.

Line	Records	Physical Query Plan
1	11	Spool_Iterator<SpoolIterator>: IterPhyOp LogOp=GroupSemiJoin IterCols(0, 1, 2, 3)('Product'[Brand], "[Sales Qu
2	11	AggregationSpool<GroupSemiJoin>: SpoolPhyOp #Records=11
3	11	Spool_Iterator<SpoolIterator>: IterPhyOp LogOp=Sum_Vertipaq IterCols(0)('Product'[Brand]) #Records=11
4	11	ProjectionSpool<ProjectFusion<Copy, Copy, Copy>>: SpoolPhyOp #Records=11
5		**Cache: IterPhyOp #FieldCols=1 #ValueCols=3**
6	11	Spool_Iterator<SpoolIterator>: IterPhyOp LogOp=Max_Vertipaq IterCols(0)('Product'[Brand]) #Records=11
7	11	ProjectionSpool<ProjectFusion<Copy, Copy, Copy>>: SpoolPhyOp #Records=11
8		**Cache: IterPhyOp #FieldCols=1 #ValueCols=3**
9	11	Spool_Iterator<SpoolIterator>: IterPhyOp LogOp=Min_Vertipaq IterCols(0)('Product'[Brand]) #Records=11
10	11	ProjectionSpool<ProjectFusion<Copy, Copy, Copy>>: SpoolPhyOp #Records=11
11		**Cache: IterPhyOp #FieldCols=1 #ValueCols=3**

Normally, the formula engine would execute one storage engine query for each of the three values. But with vertical fusion, the three columns are queried in the same storage engine query. Indeed, the DAX query executes a single storage engine query consumed in each of the Cache nodes of the query plan:

```
SELECT
    'Product'[Brand],
    MIN ( 'Sales'[Net Price] ),
    SUM ( 'Sales'[Quantity] ),
    MAX ( 'Sales'[Net Price] )
FROM 'Sales'
    LEFT OUTER JOIN 'Product'
        ON 'Sales'[ProductKey]='Product'[ProductKey];
```

This storage engine query retrieves the brands and then three columns with the aggregated value. The datacache is not used as is. The datacache contains several values consumed by three operators and later joined together inside the formula engine, as shown in the physical query plan above.

One important detail missing in the physical query plan is which column is being retrieved by each *ProjectionSpool*. We know that there are three columns, but we do not know which column is consumed in the first, second, and third of the *Spool_Iterator* operators that are fed in *AggregationSpool* to produce the result.

Fusion also works on more complex expressions than simple aggregations. Oftentimes, the DAX code includes more complex aggregations and/or temporary results that still must be processed by the formula engine. For example, look at the following query:

```
EVALUATE
SUMMARIZECOLUMNS (
    Product[Brand],
    "Sales", [Sales Amount],
    "Cost",
        SUMX ( Sales, Sales[Quantity] * ( Sales[Unit Cost] - Sales[Net Price] ) ),
    "Margin %",
        DIVIDE (
            SUMX ( Sales, Sales[Quantity] * ( Sales[Unit Cost] - Sales[Net Price] ) ),
            SUMX ( Sales, Sales[Quantity] * Sales[Net Price] )
        )
)
```

We are using a measure and three SUMX iterators. Moreover, we also added a DIVIDE function that uses temporary results computed by the storage engine and later fed to the formula engine. Nonetheless, fusion is still active here, and the entire query produces a single storage engine query:

```
WITH
    $Expr0 := ( PFCAST ( 'Sales'[Quantity] AS INT ) * PFCAST ( 'Sales'[Net Price] AS INT ) ) ,
    $Expr1 := ( PFCAST ( 'Sales'[Quantity] AS INT ) * ( PFCAST ( 'Sales'[Unit Cost] AS INT ) - PFCAST ( 'Sales'[Net Price] AS INT ) )
)
SELECT
    'Product'[Brand],
    SUM ( @$Expr0 ),
    SUM ( @$Expr1 )
FROM 'Sales'
    LEFT OUTER JOIN 'Product'
        ON 'Sales'[ProductKey]='Product'[ProductKey];
```

Vertical fusion is also active in case there are callbacks. A callback changes the aggregated expression without impacting the ability of Tabular to execute vertical fusion. The following query uses an IF function inside the iteration over *Sales*:

```
EVALUATE
SUMMARIZECOLUMNS (
    Product[Brand],
    "Sales", [Sales Amount],
    "Sales > 1",
        SUMX (
            Sales,
            IF (
                Sales[Quantity] > 1,
                Sales[Quantity] * Sales[Net Price]
            )
        )
)
```

The presence of IF means that the storage engine requires a callback to the formula engine to compute the conditional logic. Yet we still see a single storage engine query:

```
WITH
    $Expr0 := [CallbackDataID ( IF ( Sales[Quantity] > 1, Sales[Quantity] * Sales[Net Price] )   ) ]
        ( PFDATAID ( 'Sales'[Quantity] ) , PFDATAID ( 'Sales'[Net Price] )   ),
    $Expr1 := ( PFCAST ( 'Sales'[Quantity] AS   INT ) * PFCAST ( 'Sales'[Net Price] AS   INT )   )
SELECT
    'Product'[Brand],
    SUM ( @$Expr0 ),
    SUM ( @$Expr1 )
FROM 'Sales'
    LEFT OUTER JOIN 'Product'
        ON 'Sales'[ProductKey]='Product'[ProductKey];
```

Vertical fusion is used to merge multiple requests that share the same filtering condition, into a single storage engine query with that same condition. Only the requests with the same filters are grouped together. For example, for the following DAX query, the formula engine creates two storage engine queries:

```
EVALUATE
SUMMARIZECOLUMNS (
    Product[Brand],
    "Sales", [Sales Amount],
    "Margin", [Margin],
    "Sales > 1",
        CALCULATE (
            [Sales Amount],
            Sales[Quantity] > 1
        )
)
```

One storage engine query retrieves the data for the *Sales Amount* and *Margin* measures:

```
WITH
    $Expr0 := ( PFCAST ( 'Sales'[Quantity] AS   INT ) * PFCAST ( 'Sales'[Unit Cost] AS   INT )  ),
    $Expr1 := ( PFCAST ( 'Sales'[Quantity] AS   INT ) * PFCAST ( 'Sales'[Net Price] AS   INT )  )
SELECT
    'Product'[Brand],
    SUM ( @$Expr0 ),
    SUM ( @$Expr1 )
FROM 'Sales'
    LEFT OUTER JOIN 'Product'
        ON 'Sales'[ProductKey]='Product'[ProductKey];
```

A second storage engine query computes *Sales Amount* where *Sales[Quantity]* is greater than one:

```
WITH
    $Expr0 := ( PFCAST ( 'Sales'[Quantity] AS   INT ) * PFCAST ( 'Sales'[Net Price] AS   INT )  )
SELECT
    'Product'[Brand],
    SUM ( @$Expr0 )
FROM 'Sales'
    LEFT OUTER JOIN 'Product'
        ON 'Sales'[ProductKey]='Product'[ProductKey]
WHERE
    ( PFCASTCOALESCE ( 'Sales'[Quantity] AS   INT ) > COALESCE ( 1 )  );
```

Vertical fusion is particularly useful with the DirectQuery storage engine. VertiPaq is a columnar database on the actual server running the formula engine, so the performance benefit is less evident. With DirectQuery, each query comes at an associated cost due to the communication between servers, and the SQL language. In DirectQuery, sending multiple queries to retrieve multiple columns might be very expensive. Moreover, vertical fusion becomes more useful when the storage engine can execute the expression being aggregated. SQL is more expressive than xmSQL (used by VertiPaq); therefore, DirectQuery offers more room for fusion to be efficient.

Understanding horizontal fusion

As we learned, vertical fusion reduces the number of storage engine queries when multiple measures are to be computed inside the same filter context. Horizontal fusion is an optimization that is useful the other way around: it reduces the number of storage engine queries when one same measure must be computed in different filter contexts.

Horizontal fusion is a more recent optimization technique compared to vertical fusion, so we can expect more incremental improvements over time. At the time of writing, the feature is brand new and the requirements for the optimization to kick in are very strict. It works when multiple requests to the storage engine are found with the same shape – that is, with the same aggregated columns and filters.

Here is an example, with a query that computes the ratio between blue and red products for each brand:

```
EVALUATE
SUMMARIZECOLUMNS (
    'Product'[Brand],
    "Test",
        DIVIDE (
            CALCULATE (
                [Sales Amount],
                'Product'[Color] = "Blue"
            ),
            CALCULATE (
                [Sales Amount],
                'Product'[Color] = "Red"
            )
        )
    )
)
```

The value of *Sales Amount* is computed twice: once for the red products and once for the blue products. Tabular could execute two storage engine queries – one grouping the sales of red products by brand, and one grouping the sales of blue products by brand – and then merge the two datacaches in the formula engine to divide the partial results.

However, there is another option to compute our sample query. Because the two CALCULATE functions over *Sales Amount* require the same columns and compute the same aggregation, Tabular could execute a single storage engine query by retrieving the sales amount grouped by brand and color, and then extract from a single datacache the values for red and blue. By using this technique, Tabular would execute a single storage engine query instead of two. With horizontal fusion, the number of storage engine queries is reduced and Tabular shows a different operator to retrieve the values in the physical query plan: **DataPostFilter**.

So the DAX query generates a single xmSQL query:

```
WITH
    $Expr0 := ( PFCAST ( 'Sales'[Quantity] AS    INT ) * PFCAST ( 'Sales'[Net Price] AS    INT )   ),
    $Expr1 := ( PFCAST ( 'Sales'[Quantity] AS    INT ) * PFCAST ( 'Sales'[Net Price] AS    INT )   )
SELECT
    'Product'[Brand],
    'Product'[Color],
    SUM ( @$Expr0 ),
    SUM ( @$Expr1 )
FROM 'Sales'
    LEFT OUTER JOIN 'Product'
        ON 'Sales'[ProductKey]='Product'[ProductKey]
WHERE
    'Product'[Color] IN ( 'Blue', 'Red' ) ;
```

The datacache generated contains 4 columns and 19 rows, 10 for brands with blue products and 9 for brands with red products.

Brand	Color	$Expr0	$Expr1
Contoso	Blue	177,371.91	177,371.91
Wide World Importers	Blue	90,336.87	90,336.87
Northwind Traders	Blue	4,447.10	4,447.10
Adventure Works	Blue	73,651.28	73,651.28
Southridge Video	Blue	6,770.07	6,770.07
Litware	Blue	99,526.87	99,526.87
Fabrikam	Blue	111,322.40	111,322.40
Proseware	Blue	2,859.02	2,859.02
A. Datum	Blue	6,572.98	6,572.98
Tailspin Toys	Blue	22,882.84	22,882.84
Contoso	Red	169,266.67	169,266.67
Wide World Importers	Red	33,112.30	33,112.30
Northwind Traders	Red	6,669.86	6,669.86
Adventure Works	Red	80,090.42	80,090.42
Southridge Video	Red	11,985.40	11,985.40
Litware	Red	15,945.55	15,945.55
Fabrikam	Red	53,228.82	53,228.82
Proseware	Red	9,732.21	9,732.21
Tailspin Toys	Red	2,570.08	2,570.08

The formula engine reads the same datacache twice: a first time to retrieve the values of the *Brand* column for blue products with the corresponding *Sales Amount*, and a second time to retrieve the Sales Amount value of the corresponding brand but only for red products. The operator that extracts columns from the datacache is a **DataPostFilter**.

Line	Records	Physical Query Plan
1		GroupSemijoin: IterPhyOp LogOp=GroupSemiJoin IterCols(0, 1)('Product'[Brand], ''[Test])
2		Extend_Lookup: IterPhyOp LogOp=Divide IterCols(0)('Product'[Brand])
3	10	Spool_Iterator<SpoolIterator>: IterPhyOp LogOp=Sum_Vertipaq IterCols(0)('Product'[Brand]) #Records=10 #KeyCols=121 #ValueCols=1
4	10	ProjectionSpool<ProjectFusion<Copy>>: SpoolPhyOp #Records=10
5		**DataPostFilter: IterPhyOp #FieldCols=1 #ValueCols=1**
6	9	SpoolLookup: LookupPhyOp LogOp=Sum_Vertipaq LookupCols(0)('Product'[Brand]) Currency #Records=9 #KeyCols=121 #ValueCols=1
7	9	ProjectionSpool<ProjectFusion<Copy>>: SpoolPhyOp #Records=9
8		**DataPostFilter: IterPhyOp #FieldCols=1 #ValueCols=1**

The highlighted row in the query plan is the Extend_Lookup operator performing the division between two expressions. Between lines 3 and 5 the formula engine retrieves the sales amount of blue products; between lines 6 and 8 it retrieves the sales amount of red products. We know which color is computed where because only nine brands are selling red products, whereas 10 brands sell blue products.

Horizontal fusion works with both VertiPaq and DirectQuery. It is more relevant in DirectQuery models. Indeed, it reduces the number of SQL queries executed, which is an important optimization specific to DirectQuery models.

Finally, horizontal fusion does not require the measure in the different filter contexts to be the same. The analysis performed by the horizontal fusion algorithm requires a set of common columns to be used. If we use *Total Cost* in the red color filter of the DAX query for example, horizontal fusion still takes place:

```
EVALUATE
SUMMARIZECOLUMNS (
    'Product'[Brand],
    "Test",
        DIVIDE (
            CALCULATE (
                [Sales Amount],
                'Product'[Color] = "Blue"
            ),
            CALCULATE (
                [Total Cost],
                'Product'[Color] = "Red"
            )
        )
)
```

Indeed, this DAX query is resolved with a single storage engine query:

```
WITH
    $Expr0 := ( PFCAST ( 'Sales'[Quantity] AS   INT ) * PFCAST ( 'Sales'[Net Price] AS   INT )  ),
    $Expr1 := ( PFCAST ( 'Sales'[Quantity] AS   INT ) * PFCAST ( 'Sales'[Unit Cost] AS   INT )  )
SELECT
    'Product'[Brand],
    'Product'[Color],
    SUM ( @$Expr0 ),
    SUM ( @$Expr1 )
FROM 'Sales'
    LEFT OUTER JOIN 'Product'
        ON 'Sales'[ProductKey]='Product'[ProductKey]
WHERE
    'Product'[Color] IN ( 'Blue', 'Red' ) ;
```

The datacache generated by this VertiPaq query contains both *Sales Amount* and *Total Cost*, computed with a single storage engine query.

What is needed for horizontal fusion to occur is that the filter contexts of the two calculations differ only by one column that can be added as a group-by column. As we can see, the following query still benefits from horizontal fusion, because the two filter contexts differ only by the *Product[Color]* column:

```
EVALUATE
SUMMARIZECOLUMNS (
    'Product'[Brand],
    "Test",
        DIVIDE (
            CALCULATE (
                [Sales Amount],
                'Product'[Color] = "Blue",
                'Product'[Category] = "Audio"

            ),
            CALCULATE (
                [Total Cost],
                'Product'[Color] = "Red",
                'Product'[Category] = "Audio"

            )
        )
)
```

On the other hand, if we use Computers instead of Audio in one of the two calculations, then horizontal fusion does not occur anymore, regardless of the *Sales Amount* measure being the same in both expressions:

```
EVALUATE
SUMMARIZECOLUMNS (
    'Product'[Brand],
    "Test",
        DIVIDE (
            CALCULATE (
                [Sales Amount],
                'Product'[Color] = "Blue",
                'Product'[Category] = "Computers"

            ),
            CALCULATE (
                [Sales Amount],
                'Product'[Color] = "Red",
                'Product'[Category] = "Audio"

            )
        )
)
```

This latter DAX query generates two storage engine queries: one for the numerator of DIVIDE and a second for the denominator. In this case, the Tabular engine did not evaluate that horizontal fusion was going to provide a performance advantage and chose to use two storage engine queries instead.

Examples of formula engine calculations

You might have noticed that so far, we have not been concerned with performance. Indeed, the goal of this chapter is not to talk about optimizations. Not yet. Before optimizing the code, we need to practice the fine art of understanding what is executed by the storage engine, and what is executed by the formula engine.

In the next chapter we will introduce performance considerations. However, before we leave this chapter, it is useful that we practice with a few queries. Therefore, in this section we show queries, and this time instead of explaining what is happening, we follow an approach that is more practical. We first look at the code and make educated guesses about how the engine might execute the query. Then, we investigate the storage engine queries, trying to validate our first understanding. Finally, we analyze the query plan, searching for confirmation of our analysis.

The reason why we follow this process is mainly educational. Once you are on your own trying to optimize your code, you should follow this process.

Sales of best products

In this example we want to compute for each combination of year and color, the sales amount of only the products that sold more than the average sales for all the products in all the years. The query itself does not have any particular business value, it was designed to study the behavior of the formula engine:

```
EVALUATE
VAR AverageSales =
    [Sales Amount] / COUNTROWS ( 'Product' )
RETURN
    ADDCOLUMNS (
        CROSSJOIN ( VALUES ( 'Date'[Year] ), VALUES ( 'Product'[Color] ) ),
        "@Sales",
            CALCULATE (
                SUMX (
                    'Product',
                    VAR SalesOfProduct = [Sales Amount]
                    RETURN
                        IF ( SalesOfProduct >= AverageSales, SalesOfProduct )
                )
            )
    )
```

The result produced by the query is a table with one row for each value.

Year	Color	@Sales
2010	Silver	
2011	Silver	192,840,376.65
2012	Silver	284,876,995.90
2013	Silver	1,109,059,017.49
2014	Silver	2,434,075,067.98
2015	Silver	1,319,099,285.08
2016	Silver	745,577,564.23

The analysis of a DAX query always starts with the DAX code itself. It is extremely useful to have a mental picture of the requirements before diving into the details of both the storage engine queries and the query plan. Here are the first considerations:

- The *AverageSales* variable requires the total number of products and the sales amount. The total number of products is known without requiring a storage engine query, whereas the total for *Sales Amount* requires a storage engine query to be computed.

- ADDCOLUMNS operates on the CROSSJOIN of two tables. The storage engine cannot execute a crossjoin, therefore we expect two storage engine queries: one for the values of *Date[Year]* and one for the values or *Product[Color]*. The crossjoin is likely to be computed in the formula engine.

- The *@Sales* column in ADDCOLUMNS requires a context transition over *Date[Year]* and *Product*. Because there is a primary key in *Product*, the context transition will happen by filtering (or grouping) by *Product[ProductKey]*. For each product, Tabular needs to compute the sales of that product. Nonetheless, the outer grouping – the one in ADDCOLUMNS – requires a group by *Product[Color]*. Therefore, the engine needs to gather data at the granularity of the individual product and then group it by *Product[Color]*. To achieve this, it needs a remapping table containing the *Product[ProductKey]* column and the *Product[Color]* column. Therefore, we expect to see one datacache with the sales amount grouped by *ProductKey* and *Year*, and one datacache with the association between *ProductKey* and *Color*.

- The VertiPaq storage engine cannot execute the IF statement. Therefore, it will be executed either as a callback or inside the formula engine. Indeed, Tabular can decide to gather the sales amount for all the products and then choose which ones to use inside the formula engine; or, it can inject the IF function inside the storage engine through a callback.

Now that we know what to expect, we can start looking at the storage engine queries. The first two VertiPaq queries return the values of *Date[Year]* and *Product[Color]* required for the cross-join:

```
SELECT
    'Date'[Year]
FROM 'Date';


SELECT
    'Product'[Color]
FROM 'Product';
```

As expected, the third query retrieves the sales amount grouped by *Product[ProductKey]* and *Date[Year]*:

```
WITH
    $Expr0 := ( PFCAST ( 'Sales'[Quantity] AS    INT ) * PFCAST ( 'Sales'[Net Price] AS    INT )   )
SELECT
    'Date'[Year],
    'Product'[ProductKey],
    SUM ( @$Expr0 )
FROM 'Sales'
    LEFT OUTER JOIN 'Date'
        ON 'Sales'[Order Date]='Date'[Date]
    LEFT OUTER JOIN 'Product'
        ON 'Sales'[ProductKey]='Product'[ProductKey];
```

It is worth noting that this latter query is missing the *Product[Color]* column. Therefore, we expect to find another query to associate the product key with its color so that the final grouping takes place in the formula engine. Indeed, this is exactly what we find in the next storage engine query:

```
SELECT
    'Product'[RowNumber],
    'Product'[ProductKey],
    'Product'[Color]
FROM 'Product';
```

The last storage engine query returns the missing value: the total sales amount, used to compute the *AverageSales* variable:

```
WITH
    $Expr0 := ( PFCAST ( 'Sales'[Quantity] AS    INT ) * PFCAST ( 'Sales'[Net Price] AS    INT )   )
SELECT
    SUM ( @$Expr0 )
FROM 'Sales';
```

The DAX query is resolved with a total of five storage engine queries. The formula engine executes the remaining part of the code. Hence, here is what the formula engine performs:

- It retrieves the grand total of *Sales Amount* from the storage engine and divides it by the number of products – which is known without executing any query – to obtain the average sales amount.

- It retrieves the values of *Product[Color]* and *Date[Year]*, to perform the cross-join.

- It retrieves the sales amount by *Product[ProductKey]* and *Date[Year]*.

- It scans the *Sales Amount* obtained by product and year, executing the IF statement on each row to remove values where the sales amount is less than the average sales amount computed during the first step.

- It groups the last result by *Product[Color]* by associating each product key to its corresponding color. The formula engine would have already retrieved a remapping table for this purpose.

- At this point, the formula engine has a table containing the value to return for each existing combination of color and year. But because ADDCOLUMNS operates on the crossjoin of year and color, the final result might need to include non-existing combinations present only in the crossjoin table. Therefore, the formula engine performs a final join between the crossjoin and the computed table to prepare the result.

Be mindful that all the reasoning so far is speculations. So far, we have not spent any time looking at the details of the query plan executed by the formula engine. Nonetheless, now when we look at the query plan, we will be doing so with certain expectations. We might have guessed right or wrong. In either case, we do not infer the behavior by reading the query plan. We first make educated guesses and only later search for confirmation in the query plan. The reason is simple: the query plan is extremely complex to read. Searching for confirmation is much simpler than inferring the complete behavior.

We show here, just as an example, what the physical query plan looks like.

Line	Records	Physical Query Plan
1		AddColumns: IterPhyOp LogOp=AddColumns IterCols(0, 1, 2)('Year', 'Product'[Color], '[@Sales])
2		ApplyRemap: IterPhyOp LogOp=Crossjoin IterCols(0, 1)('Date'[Year], 'Product'[Color])
3	192	CrossApply: IterPhyOp LogOp=Crossjoin IterCols(0, 1)('Date'[Year], 'Product'[Color])
4	12	Spool_Iterator<SpoolIterator>: IterPhyOp LogOp=Scan_Vertipaq IterCols(0)('Date'[Year]) #Records=12 #KeyCols=138 #ValueCols=0
5	12	ProjectionSpool<ProjectFusion<>>: SpoolPhyOp #Records=12
6		Cache: IterPhyOp #FieldCols=1 #ValueCols=0
7	16	Spool_Iterator<SpoolIterator>: IterPhyOp LogOp=Scan_Vertipaq IterCols(1)('Product'[Color]) #Records=16 #KeyCols=138 #ValueCols=0
8	16	ProjectionSpool<ProjectFusion<>>: SpoolPhyOp #Records=16
9		Cache: IterPhyOp #FieldCols=1 #ValueCols=0
10	45	Spool_Lookup: LookupPhyOp LogOp=SumX LookupCols(0, 1)('Year', 'Product'[Color]) Currency #Records=45 #KeyCols=2 #ValueCols=1 DominantValue=BLANK
11	45	AggregationSpool<Sum>: SpoolPhyOp #Records=45
12		CrossApply: IterPhyOp LogOp=VarScope IterCols(0, 3)('Date'[Year], 'Product'[ProductKey])
13	2,517	Spool_MultiValuedHashLookup: IterPhyOp LogOp=Scan_Vertipaq IterCols(3)('Product'[ProductKey]) IterCols(1, 2)('Product'[Color], 'Product'[Product]) [RowNumber-2662B79B-1795-4F74-8F37-6A1BA60...
14	2,517	ProjectionSpool<ProjectFusion<>>: SpoolPhyOp #Records=2517
15		Cache: IterPhyOp #FieldCols=3 #ValueCols=0
16	12	Spool_Iterator<SpoolIterator>: IterPhyOp LogOp=Scan_Vertipaq IterCols(0)('Date'[Year]) #Records=12 #KeyCols=138 #ValueCols=0
17	12	ProjectionSpool<ProjectFusion<>>: SpoolPhyOp #Records=12
18		Cache: IterPhyOp #FieldCols=1 #ValueCols=0
19		CrossApply: IterPhyOp LogOp=ScalarProxy IterCols(0, 3)('Date'[Year], 'Product'[ProductKey])
20	12	Spool_UniqueHashLookup: IterPhyOp LogOp=Crossjoin LookupCols(0)('Date'[Year]) #Records=12 #KeyCols=1 #ValueCols=0
21	12	AggregationSpool<GroupBy>: SpoolPhyOp #Records=12
22		ApplyRemap: IterPhyOp LogOp=Crossjoin IterCols(0, 1)('Date'[Year], 'Product'[Color])
23	192	CrossApply: IterPhyOp LogOp=Crossjoin IterCols(0, 1)('Date'[Year], 'Product'[Color])
24	12	Spool_Iterator<SpoolIterator>: IterPhyOp LogOp=Scan_Vertipaq IterCols(0)('Date'[Year]) #Records=12 #KeyCols=138 #ValueCols=0
25	12	ProjectionSpool<ProjectFusion<>>: SpoolPhyOp #Records=12
26		Cache: IterPhyOp #FieldCols=1 #ValueCols=0
27	16	Spool_Iterator<SpoolIterator>: IterPhyOp LogOp=Scan_Vertipaq IterCols(1)('Product'[Color]) #Records=16 #KeyCols=138 #ValueCols=0
28	16	ProjectionSpool<ProjectFusion<>>: SpoolPhyOp #Records=16
29		Cache: IterPhyOp #FieldCols=1 #ValueCols=0
30	2,517	Spool_UniqueHashLookup: IterPhyOp LogOp=Scan_Vertipaq LookupCols(3)('Product'[ProductKey]) #Records=2517 #KeyCols=1 #ValueCols=0
31	2,517	AggregationSpool<GroupBy>: SpoolPhyOp #Records=2517
32	2,517	Spool_Iterator<SpoolIterator>: IterPhyOp LogOp=Scan_Vertipaq IterCols(1, 2, 3)('Product'[Color], 'Product'[Product] [RowNumber-2662B79B-1795-4F74-8F37-6A1BA6059861], 'Product'[ProductKey]
33	2,517	ProjectionSpool<ProjectFusion<>>: SpoolPhyOp #Records=2517
34		Cache: IterPhyOp #FieldCols=3 #ValueCols=0
35	12	Spool_Iterator<SpoolIterator>: IterPhyOp LogOp=Scan_Vertipaq IterCols(0)('Date'[Year]) #Records=12 #KeyCols=138 #ValueCols=0
36	12	ProjectionSpool<ProjectFusion<>>: SpoolPhyOp #Records=12
37		Cache: IterPhyOp #FieldCols=1 #ValueCols=0
38	286	Spool_UniqueHashLookup: IterPhyOp LogOp=PredicateCheck LookupCols(0, 3)('Date'[Year], 'Product'[ProductKey]) #Records=286 #KeyCols=2 #ValueCols=0
39	286	AggregationSpool<GroupBy>: SpoolPhyOp #Records=286
40		PredicateCheck: IterPhyOp LogOp=PredicateCheck IterCols(0, 3)('Date'[Year], 'Product'[ProductKey])
41		Extend_Lookup: IterPhyOp LogOp=ScalarVarProxy IterCols(0, 3)('Date'[Year], 'Product'[ProductKey])
42		CrossApply: IterPhyOp LogOp=ScalarProxy IterCols(0, 3)('Date'[Year], 'Product'[ProductKey])
43	12	Spool_Iterator<SpoolIterator>: IterPhyOp LogOp=Crossjoin IterCols(0)('Date'[Year]) #Records=12 #KeyCols=1 #ValueCols=0
44	12	AggregationSpool<GroupBy>: SpoolPhyOp #Records=12
45		ApplyRemap: IterPhyOp LogOp=Crossjoin IterCols(0, 1)('Date'[Year], 'Product'[Color])
46	192	CrossApply: IterPhyOp LogOp=Crossjoin IterCols(0, 1)('Date'[Year], 'Product'[Color])
47	12	Spool_Iterator<SpoolIterator>: IterPhyOp LogOp=Scan_Vertipaq IterCols(0)('Date'[Year]) #Records=12 #KeyCols=138 #ValueCols=0
48	12	ProjectionSpool<ProjectFusion<>>: SpoolPhyOp #Records=12
49		Cache: IterPhyOp #FieldCols=1 #ValueCols=0
50	16	Spool_Iterator<SpoolIterator>: IterPhyOp LogOp=Scan_Vertipaq IterCols(1)('Product'[Color]) #Records=16 #KeyCols=138 #ValueCols=0
51	16	ProjectionSpool<ProjectFusion<>>: SpoolPhyOp #Records=16
52		Cache: IterPhyOp #FieldCols=1 #ValueCols=0
53	2,517	Spool_Iterator<SpoolIterator>: IterPhyOp LogOp=Scan_Vertipaq IterCols(3)('Product'[ProductKey]) #Records=2517 #KeyCols=1 #ValueCols=0
54	2,517	AggregationSpool<GroupBy>: SpoolPhyOp #Records=2517
55	2,517	Spool_Iterator<SpoolIterator>: IterPhyOp LogOp=Scan_Vertipaq IterCols(1, 2, 3)('Product'[Color], 'Product'[Product] [RowNumber-2662B79B-1795-4F74-8F37-6A1BA6059861], 'Product'...
56	2,517	ProjectionSpool<ProjectFusion<>>: SpoolPhyOp #Records=2517
57		Cache: IterPhyOp #FieldCols=3 #ValueCols=0
58	12	Spool_Iterator<SpoolIterator>: IterPhyOp LogOp=Scan_Vertipaq IterCols(0)('Date'[Year]) #Records=12 #KeyCols=138 #ValueCols=0
59	12	ProjectionSpool<ProjectFusion<>>: SpoolPhyOp #Records=12
60		Cache: IterPhyOp #FieldCols=1 #ValueCols=0
61		GreaterThanOrEqualTo: LookupPhyOp LogOp=GreaterThanOrEqualTo LookupCols(0, 3)('Date'[Year], 'Product'[ProductKey]) Boolean
62	27,687	SpoolLookup: LookupPhyOp LogOp=Sum_Vertipaq LookupCols(0, 3)('Date'[Year], 'Product'[ProductKey]) Currency #Records=27687 #KeyCols=138 #ValueCols=1 DominantValue=...
63	27,687	ProjectionSpool<ProjectFusion<Copy>>: SpoolPhyOp #Records=27687
64		Cache: IterPhyOp #FieldCols=2 #ValueCols=1
65	16	Spool_Iterator<SpoolIterator>: IterPhyOp LogOp=Scan_Vertipaq IterCols(1)('Product'[Color]) #Records=16 #KeyCols=138 #ValueCols=0
66	16	ProjectionSpool<ProjectFusion<>>: SpoolPhyOp #Records=16
67		Cache: IterPhyOp #FieldCols=1 #ValueCols=0
68	1	SpoolLookup: LookupPhyOp LogOp=Divide Currency #Records=1 #KeyCols=0 #ValueCols=0 DominantValue=BLANK
69	1	AggregationSpool<Copy>: SpoolPhyOp #Records=1
70		Extend_Lookup: IterPhyOp LogOp=Divide
71	1	Spool_Iterator<SpoolIterator>: IterPhyOp LogOp=Sum_Vertipaq #Records=1 #KeyCols=138 #ValueCols=1
72	1	ProjectionSpool<ProjectFusion<Copy>>: SpoolPhyOp #Records=1
73		Cache: IterPhyOp #FieldCols=0 #ValueCols=1
74		Constant: LookupPhyOp LogOp=Constant Integer 2517
75	27,687	Spool_Iterator<SpoolIterator>: IterPhyOp LogOp=ScalarVarProxy IterCols(0, 3)('Date'[Year], 'Product'[ProductKey]) #Records=27687 #KeyCols=138 #ValueCols=1
76	27,687	ProjectionSpool<ProjectFusion<Copy>>: SpoolPhyOp #Records=27687
77		Cache: IterPhyOp #FieldCols=2 #ValueCols=1
78	16	Spool_Iterator<SpoolIterator>: IterPhyOp LogOp=Scan_Vertipaq IterCols(1)('Product'[Color]) #Records=16 #KeyCols=138 #ValueCols=0
79	16	ProjectionSpool<ProjectFusion<>>: SpoolPhyOp #Records=16
80		Cache: IterPhyOp #FieldCols=1 #ValueCols=0

The physical query plan is only 80 lines; yet, that is already overwhelming. The interested reader may want to scan the physical query plan searching for the details; but despite being somewhat educational, it is not an enjoyable experience. When figuring out what the formula engine computes, your best option is to focus on what happens in the storage engine and then conclude that the formula engine needs to execute any other operation needed to compute the result.

Top three colors

Let us now study a simple execution plan: a query that retrieves the top three product colors sold in Europe, along with their sales amount:

```
EVALUATE
CALCULATETABLE (
    ADDCOLUMNS (
        TOPN ( 3, ALL ( 'Product'[Color] ), [Sales Amount] ),
        "@Sales", [Sales Amount]
    ),
    Customer[Continent] = "Europe"
)
```

The result contains three rows, along with their respective sales.

Color	@Sales
Silver	13,585,003,244.71
Black	19,762,945,774.44
White	16,363,490,279.94

The outer CALCULATETABLE filters customers in Europe. This filter can be pushed down to the storage engine as a WHERE condition. TOPN retrieves only three colors; but in order to find the top three, it needs to evaluate the sales amount for every color. ADDCOLUMNS computes *Sales Amount* and includes it as a new column (*@Sales*) in the result.

We would expect DAX to retrieve a datacache with all the colors and the sales amount. It can then use that first to find the top three colors and next to add the result to the output containing three rows. Therefore, it seems reasonable that only one storage engine query is needed for the entire query.

This time, our guess is too optimistic. Running the query shows three storage engine queries being executed. As expected, the first retrieves a datacache with the sales amount grouped by *Product[Color]* where *Customer[Continent]* is Europe:

```
WITH
    $Expr0 := ( PFCAST ( 'Sales'[Quantity] AS    INT ) * PFCAST ( 'Sales'[Net Price] AS    INT )   )
SELECT
    'Product'[Color],
    SUM ( @$Expr0 )
FROM 'Sales'
    LEFT OUTER JOIN 'Customer'
        ON 'Sales'[CustomerKey]='Customer'[CustomerKey]
    LEFT OUTER JOIN 'Product'
        ON 'Sales'[ProductKey]='Product'[ProductKey]
WHERE
    'Customer'[Continent] = 'Europe';
```

Next, there is a second query, retrieving the product colors:

```
SELECT
    'Product'[Color]
FROM 'Product';
```

Finally, a third query retrieves the sales amount for only the three colors returned by the TOPN function:

```
WITH
    $Expr0 := ( PFCAST ( 'Sales'[Quantity] AS INT ) * PFCAST ( 'Sales'[Net Price] AS INT ) )
SELECT
    'Product'[Color],
    SUM ( @$Expr0 )
FROM 'Sales'
    LEFT OUTER JOIN 'Customer'
        ON 'Sales'[CustomerKey]='Customer'[CustomerKey]
    LEFT OUTER JOIN 'Product'
        ON 'Sales'[ProductKey]='Product'[ProductKey]
WHERE
    'Customer'[Continent] = 'Europe' VAND
    'Product'[Color] IN ( 'Silver', 'White', 'Black' ) ;
```

The execution path, at this point, is clear – and it is different from what we expected. It looks like the formula engine computes the sales amount grouped by color, the list of colors, and then filters the top three. Finally, it computes the sales amount again, only for the top three colors.

Obtaining the same information from the query plan would have been much more complex. Here is the query plan of the query.

Line	Records	Physical Query Plan
1		AddColumns: IterPhyOp LogOp=AddColumns IterCols(1, 2)('Product'[Color], ''[@Sales])
2	3	Spool_Iterator<SpoolIterator>: IterPhyOp LogOp=TopN IterCols(1)('Product'[Color]) #Records=3 #KeyCols=1 #ValueCols=0
3	3	AggregationSpool<GroupBy>: SpoolPhyOp #Records=3
4		PartitionIntoGroups: IterPhyOp LogOp=TopN IterCols(1)('Product'[Color]) #Groups=1 #Rows=3
5	1	AggregationSpool<Top>: SpoolPhyOp #Records=1
6	16	Spool_Iterator<SpoolIterator>: IterPhyOp LogOp=Scan_Vertipaq IterCols(1)('Product'[Color]) #Records=16 #KeyCols=138 #ValueCols=0
7	16	ProjectionSpool<ProjectFusion<>>: SpoolPhyOp #Records=16
8		**Cache: IterPhyOp #FieldCols=1 #ValueCols=0**
9	16	SpoolLookup: LookupPhyOp LogOp=Sum_Vertipaq LookupCols(1)('Product'[Color]) Currency #Records=16 #KeyCols=138 #ValueCols=1
10	16	ProjectionSpool<ProjectFusion<Copy>>: SpoolPhyOp #Records=16
11		**Cache: IterPhyOp #FieldCols=1 #ValueCols=1**
12		Constant: LookupPhyOp LogOp=Constant Integer 3
13	3	SpoolLookup: LookupPhyOp LogOp=Sum_Vertipaq LookupCols(1)('Product'[Color]) Currency #Records=3 #KeyCols=138 #ValueCols=1 DominantV.
14	3	ProjectionSpool<ProjectFusion<Copy>>: SpoolPhyOp #Records=3
15		**Cache: IterPhyOp #FieldCols=1 #ValueCols=1**
16	3	Spool_Iterator<SpoolIterator>: IterPhyOp LogOp=TopN IterCols(1)('Product'[Color]) #Records=3 #KeyCols=1 #ValueCols=0
17	3	AggregationSpool<GroupBy>: SpoolPhyOp #Records=3
18		PartitionIntoGroups: IterPhyOp LogOp=TopN IterCols(1)('Product'[Color]) #Groups=1 #Rows=3
19	1	AggregationSpool<Top>: SpoolPhyOp #Records=1
20	16	Spool_Iterator<SpoolIterator>: IterPhyOp LogOp=Scan_Vertipaq IterCols(1)('Product'[Color]) #Records=16 #KeyCols=138 #Value
21	16	ProjectionSpool<ProjectFusion<>>: SpoolPhyOp #Records=16
22		**Cache: IterPhyOp #FieldCols=1 #ValueCols=0**
23	16	SpoolLookup: LookupPhyOp LogOp=Sum_Vertipaq LookupCols(1)('Product'[Color]) Currency #Records=16 #KeyCols=138 #Value
24	16	ProjectionSpool<ProjectFusion<Copy>>: SpoolPhyOp #Records=16
25		**Cache: IterPhyOp #FieldCols=1 #ValueCols=1**
26		Constant: LookupPhyOp LogOp=Constant Integer 3

The query plan is split in two sections: from line 2 to 12 is the retrieval of the top three colors, whereas from line 13 to 26 is the calculation of the sales amount by color for only the top three colors. You might notice that lines 2 to 12 are identical to lines 16 to 26. Indeed, these sections compute the top three colors, which are needed as a filter for calculating the @*Sales* column, and as values for ADDCOLUMNS.

At the risk of sounding repetitive, please note that the query plan, albeit very precise, is too complex to analyze. We obtained a better picture of the algorithm by guessing the flow by just reading the storage engine queries.

The analysis is complete, and we could leave it at that. But since this is a book about optimization, we should perform further considerations and edit the query to reduce the number of storage engine queries.

The algorithm chosen by Tabular makes perfect sense in case the measure added by ADDCOLUMNS is different from the measure used by RANKX. In that scenario, the engine would limit the number of calculations performed by ADDCOLUMNS. But we know we are using the same measure for the ranking and for ADDCOLUMNS. Therefore, the algorithm chosen looks unfortunate. It would be better to change the query so that the sales amount is computed only once.

We can achieve this goal by changing the query. We should push ADDCOLUMNS inside TOPN, instead of outside as it was before:

```
EVALUATE
CALCULATETABLE (
    TOPN (
        3,
        ADDCOLUMNS ( ALL ( 'Product'[Color] ), "@Sales", [Sales Amount] ),
        [@Sales]
    ),
    Customer[Continent] = "Europe"
)
```

There is no need to analyze this new query plan comprehensively. It is enough to say that this latter query executes only two storage engine queries: one to compute the colors and one to compute the sales amount grouped by color.

The query plan reflects the increased simplicity we have achieved: it is only 11 lines long compared to the 26 lines of the previous query plan.

Line	Records	Physical Query Plan
1		PartitionIntoGroups: IterPhyOp LogOp=TopN IterCols(1, 2)('Product'[Color], ''[@Sales]) #Groups=1 #Rows=3
2	1	AggregationSpool<Top>: SpoolPhyOp #Records=1
3		AddColumns: IterPhyOp LogOp=AddColumns IterCols(1, 2)('Product'[Color], ''[@Sales])
4	16	Spool_Iterator<SpoolIterator>: IterPhyOp LogOp=Scan_Vertipaq IterCols(1)('Product'[Color]) #Records=16 #KeyCols=121 #ValueCols=0
5	16	ProjectionSpool<ProjectFusion<>>: SpoolPhyOp #Records=16
6		**Cache: IterPhyOp #FieldCols=1 #ValueCols=0**
7	16	SpoolLookup: LookupPhyOp LogOp=Sum_Vertipaq LookupCols(1)('Product'[Color]) Currency #Records=16 #KeyCols=121 #ValueCols=1
8	16	ProjectionSpool<ProjectFusion<Copy>>: SpoolPhyOp #Records=16
9		**Cache: IterPhyOp #FieldCols=1 #ValueCols=1**
10		ColValue<''[@Sales]>: LookupPhyOp LogOp=ColValue<''[@Sales]>''[@Sales] LookupCols(2)(''[@Sales]) Currency
11		Constant: LookupPhyOp LogOp=Constant Integer 3

From a performance point of view, this latter query runs faster than the previous one. However, as we anticipated earlier, we are still not worried about performance here. The goal is to start to figure out the algorithm carried on by the formula engine to answer queries. Once we have a better picture of the algorithm and the reasons for the choices made by the Tabular engine, we can operate changes in the query to turn the suboptimal algorithm into a better one.

Measuring performance

A query plan consists of two separate parts: the physical query plan, executed by the formula engine, and the storage engine queries, executed by the storage engine. Optimizing a query or a measure requires us to optimize both the formula engine part and the storage engine queries. Optimizing the storage engine queries is something we will study later, after we introduce the details of the different storage engines. Here we start understanding how to measure the time spent in the formula engine and how the DAX code affects the formula engine.

There are several important things to take into account when working with formula engine optimizations:

- **The formula engine is single-threaded**. No matter how many cores are available, the formula engine runs on a single thread. Therefore, reducing the formula engine use to a minimum is important because the formula engine part of a query is usually the most critical (that is, the slowest).

- **The formula engine runs storage engine queries mostly sequentially**. As part of its execution, the formula engine runs several storage engine queries. Queries are queued and usually executed sequentially: while multiple storage queries may be executed in parallel, this is not possible when there are dependencies, and a storage engine query uses the result of a previous one. When the formula engine runs thousands of small queries, we will face performance issues because none of the storage engine queries can benefit from the full power of the machine, and parallelism is highly reduced. Therefore, writing a query in a way that executes a small number of complex storage engine queries is preferable to writing it in a way that requires many simple storage engine queries.

- **The formula engine does not cache results.** A DAX query can greatly benefit from using cached data. Once a storage engine query is executed, its results can be used multiple times without executing the same storage engine query again. Not all storage engines provide a cache system, but when available, it can significantly reduce the execution time. Nonetheless, the steps executed by the formula engine are never cached. The formula engine portion of a query plan is executed every time the query runs. This includes any datacache generated with a callback, which involves the formula engine.

Finally, be mindful that the separation of tasks between the formula engine and the storage engine depends on the storage engine being used. When you work with a DirectQuery model, the storage engine offers you the full power of the SQL language. When you work with a VertiPaq model, the storage engine query language (xmSQL) is extremely limited, albeit being amazingly fast.

Gathering important timings from the query plan

During the execution of a query, the Tabular engine records several events. These events include the query plan, the storage engine queries executed and – most relevant to us – the time spent executing each step. DAX Studio can collect these events and provide detailed information about the time spent on each step.

DAX Studio is the most convenient tool to obtain this type of information. Indeed, DAX Studio filters the most useful pieces of information, and it performs several useful calculations over the values retrieved. For example, Tabular sends an event when a storage engine query starts and another event when the storage engine query ends. The execution time is available only in the query end event. DAX Studio automatically filters out the query begin events, because they do not contain the most useful piece of information: the execution time.

However, pieces of information are missing from the Tabular set of events. Namely, Tabular does not provide the time spent in the formula engine. DAX Studio computes this value by subtracting the time spent in the storage engine from the total execution time. Because there could be hundreds of storage engine queries, this calculation represents a huge time saving. The formula engine time computed by DAX Studio corresponds to the time when no storage engine queries are running. Technically, there could be formula engine code executed while other storage engine queries are running; but this time is ignored in the calculation provided by DAX Studio, making it simpler to understand the metrics provided.

Because of the way timings are computed inside the Tabular engine, the values provided are accurate if and only if they are collected on a server that is dedicated to Tabular. On a busy server, working on many other processes, these numbers might fluctuate, making it very difficult to evaluate the benefit of any changes in the DAX code. The numbers measured make little sense if you are running Tabular on a busy server. It would be better, in that case, to perform the tests on your personal workstation or laptop to have better control over the hardware.

Analyzing query plans and timings

Let us start analyzing some query plans, this time focusing on the time spent in the formula engine versus the time spent in the storage engine. We will still analyze the details of the algorithm, but with fewer details compared to what we did in previous examples.

Year-to-date calculation of an additive measure

The first query we analyze produces the year-to-date value of *Sales Amount*, sliced by *Date[Date]* and *Product[Color]*:

```
EVALUATE
SUMMARIZECOLUMNS (
    'Date'[Date],
    'Product'[Color],
    "Sales YTD",
        CALCULATE (
            [Sales Amount],
            DATESYTD ( 'Date'[Date] )
        )
)
```

The result is large: it contains around 62,000 rows.

Date	Color	Sales YTD
08/22/2018	Black	6,964,133,920.56
08/23/2018	Black	7,003,796,871.16
08/24/2018	Black	7,030,109,224.38
08/25/2018	Black	7,077,202,035.30
08/26/2018	Black	7,082,411,901.72
08/27/2018	Black	7,102,857,069.60
08/28/2018	Black	7,128,877,932.80
08/29/2018	Black	7,164,756,004.71

First, we focus on the execution time panel, which reveals several interesting pieces of information.

Total	SE CPU
1,437 ms	3,750 ms
	x19.5

FE	SE
1,245 ms	192 ms
86.6%	13.4%

SE Queries	SE Cache
4	2
	50.0%

Let us start from the first row: the query ran in 1,437 milliseconds (Total). This time is divided between the storage engine and the formula engine. The first important detail is that the storage engine CPU time (SE CPU) is much larger: 3,750 milliseconds. The storage engine CPU sums the amount of time spent in every single CPU core used by the service. The reason why the total execution time is smaller than the storage engine CPU time is that the storage engine ran with a high degree of parallelism. As indicated, the parallelism factor is 19.5, meaning that on average a bit less than 20 cores were running the storage engine query in parallel.

The second row shows the same information, but from a different angle: it indicates that 1,245 milliseconds were spent in the formula engine (FE), and 192 milliseconds were spent in the storage engine (SE). Again, focus on the huge difference between the formula engine and the storage engine, due to the presence of parallelism in the storage engine. The storage engine used a lot more CPU power, still its execution time is way smaller than the formula engine's.

Still looking at the execution time panel, the bar chart shows a graphical representation of the ratio between the formula engine and the storage engine. The yellow part is the formula engine, whereas the blue section is the storage engine. Reading that chart is utterly simple: the more blue, the better. The more yellow, the worse. Clearly, there are other considerations to make. We will see examples where pushing calculations into the formula engine is a better choice. Nonetheless, as a rule of thumb, the more blue, the better.

Then the last line is a synthesis of the number of storage engine queries executed (SE Queries), along with the number of storage engine queries that hit the cache (SE Cache) – meaning that the formula engine requested them to the storage engine which instead of running the query, found that the result was already available and returned it straightaway.

A quick inspection of this section of the server timings already tells us that this query is bound to the formula engine. If we wanted to reduce the total execution time, we would need to work on the formula engine algorithm because most of the time is spent in the formula engine.

There are four storage engine queries, three of which are identical (indeed, two have been served by the cache). The first of the two distinct queries just gathers the dates from the *Date* table:

```
SELECT
    'Date'[Date]
FROM 'Date';
```

The second query is also simple, though somewhat verbose:

```
WITH
    $Expr0 := ( PFCAST ( 'Sales'[Quantity] AS   INT ) * PFCAST ( 'Sales'[Net Price] AS   INT )   )
SELECT
    'Date'[Date],
    'Product'[Color],
    SUM ( @$Expr0 )
FROM 'Sales'
    LEFT OUTER JOIN 'Date'
        ON 'Sales'[Order Date]='Date'[Date]
    LEFT OUTER JOIN 'Product'
        ON 'Sales'[ProductKey]='Product'[ProductKey]
WHERE
    'Date'[Date] IN ( 41133.000000, 42090.000000, 42131.000000, 43088.000000, 43129.000000, 44086.000000,
            44127.000000, 41051.000000, 41092.000000, 42049.000000..[4,018 total values, not all displayed] ) ;
```

This second query retrieves the sales amount sliced by *Date[Date]* and *Product[Color]*. The WHERE condition includes the list of dates, expressed as their floating-point value.

Hence, we know that the entire algorithm works by using just two datacaches: one containing the dates, and one containing the sales amount by date. You might already have noticed that there are no references to the year-to-date calculation that we requested in the storage engine queries.

We can conclude that the entire year-to-date calculation occurs in the formula engine. Tabular analyzed the code and determined that the formula requested is additive. Therefore, the formula engine can compute the totals without other requests to the storage engine. Consequently, the formula engine requested the sales amount by date, overseeing the year-to-date calculation.

The physical query plan is too long to be reported here. Nonetheless, a deeper analysis of the query plan shows that even though the two datacaches are relatively small, the total number of rows the formula engine needs to process is quite large. Here is the beginning of the physical query plan.

Line	Records	Physical Query Plan
1		GroupSemijoin: IterPhyOp LogOp=GroupSemiJoin IterCols(0, 1, 2)('Date'[Date], 'Product'[Color], ''[Sales YTD])
2	62,096	Spool_Iterator<SpoolIterator>: IterPhyOp LogOp=Sum_Vertipaq IterCols(0, 1)('Date'[Date], 'Product'[Color]) #Records=62096 #KeyCols=2 #ValueCols=1
3	62,096	AggregationSpool<AggFusion<Sum>>: SpoolPhyOp #Records=62096
4		CrossApply: IterPhyOp LogOp=Sum_Vertipaq IterCols(0, 1)('Date'[Date], 'Product'[Color])
5	735,843	Spool_MultiValuedHashLookup: IterPhyOp LogOp=DatesBetween LookupCols(2)('Date'[Date]) IterCols(0)('Date'[Date]) #Records=735843 #KeyCol
6	735,843	AggregationSpool<GroupBy>: SpoolPhyOp #Records=735843
7		DatesBetween: IterPhyOp LogOp=DatesBetween IterCols(0, 2)('Date'[Date], 'Date'[Date])
8		Extend_Lookup: IterPhyOp LogOp=TableToScalar IterCols(0)('Date'[Date])
9	4,018	Spool_Iterator<SpoolIterator>: IterPhyOp LogOp=Scan_Vertipaq IterCols(0)('Date'[Date]) #Records=4018 #KeyCols=68 #ValueCols=0
10	4,018	ProjectionSpool<ProjectFusion<>>: SpoolPhyOp #Records=4018
11		Cache: IterPhyOp #FieldCols=1 #ValueCols=0
12	4,018	TableToScalar: LookupPhyOp LogOp=TableToScalar LookupCols(0)('Date'[Date]) DateTime #Records=4018
13	4,018	AggregationSpool<TableToScalar>: SpoolPhyOp #Records=4018
14		StartOfYear: IterPhyOp LogOp=StartOfYear IterCols(0, 2)('Date'[Date], 'Date'[Date])
15	4,018	Spool_Iterator<SpoolIterator>: IterPhyOp LogOp=LastDate IterCols(0)('Date'[Date]) #Records=4018 #KeyCols=1 #ValueCols=0

You can see at line 5 that the formula engine needs to process 735,843 rows generated by the operators that follow. The most relevant operator is at line 7: DatesBetween generates the set of dates between two boundaries: the beginning of the year and the last visible date.

Trying to make this code faster is not our main goal for now. Our goal was to perform another query plan analysis to continue our understanding of how Tabular solves queries. This time, we started to add the execution timings to the equation.

We can conclude that calculations involving year-to-date are usually very heavy on the formula engine because the determination of which dates to use to compute a year-to-date happens in the formula engine.

Year-to-date calculation of a non-additive measure

It is interesting to perform a similar analysis on a non-additive calculation. Indeed, as soon as we use a calculation that is non-additive, we force the formula engine to run a separate query on the storage engine for each subset of data. Because the resultset contains 62,000 rows, the number of storage engine queries that need to be executed could be rather large.

We test the scenario by replacing the sales amount measure of the previous example, which is additive, with a simple distinct count of the product key:

```
EVALUATE
SUMMARIZECOLUMNS (
    'Date'[Date],
    'Product'[Color],
    "Sales YTD",
        CALCULATE (
            DISTINCTCOUNT ( Sales[ProductKey] ),
            DATESYTD ( 'Date'[Date] )
        )
)
```

A small change, like removing the additivity from the formula, results in a completely different timing – much worse than the previous one.

Total	SE CPU
267,020 ms	292,377 ms
	x1.4

FE	SE
59,186 ms	207,834 ms
22.2%	77.9%

SE Queries	SE Cache
4,021	2
	0.0%

We can make several considerations just by looking at the timings:

- The overall execution time is extremely large compared to the previous one: 267,020 milliseconds, around four minutes and half.

- There is a huge number of storage engine queries: 4,021 storage engine queries. Namely, one for each date in the result.

- The time spent in the storage engine is now very large.

The analysis of the storage engine queries is rather simple. While it is true that there are thousands, they all have the same format. Here is one of the many:

```
SELECT
    'Product'[Color],
    DCOUNT ( 'Sales'[ProductKey] )
FROM 'Sales'
    LEFT OUTER JOIN 'Date'
        ON 'Sales'[Order Date]='Date'[Date]
    LEFT OUTER JOIN 'Product'
        ON 'Sales'[ProductKey]='Product'[ProductKey]
WHERE
    'Date'[Date] IN ( 41133.000000, 42090.000000, 42131.000000, 43088.000000, 43129.000000, 44086.000000,
44127.000000, 41051.000000, 41092.000000, 42049.000000..[4,018 total values, not all displayed] ) VAND
    'Date'[Date] IN ( 40190.000000, 40231.000000, 40272.000000, 40313.000000, 40354.000000, 40395.000000,
40436.000000, 40477.000000, 40518.000000, 40286.000000..[365 total values, not all displayed] ) ;
```

The query retrieves the distinct count of *Sales[ProductKey]* sliced by *Product[Color]* for a set of dates. There are two filters on the *Date[Date]* column: the first one is the global filter of the query (it is actually not filtering anything), whereas the second represents the set of dates that create the year-to-date of a specific date.

There is one such query for each date of the result. Each datacache contains a small number of rows, one per color. Therefore, in this scenario, the formula engine first retrieves the dates, then builds the set of year-to-date dates for each date, and finally executes one storage engine query per date. This algorithm results in a huge number of storage engine queries. Each storage engine query is very fast – VertiPaq still uses parallelism for each storage engine query – but they are executed sequentially. Therefore, with so many storage engine queries, the execution time is poor.

Please note that for now, we are not interested in optimizing the code or in finding the best way to author the DAX code. Our goal is to gather information from the timings, the physical query plan, and most relevant from the storage engine queries to obtain information about the algorithm followed by Tabular to solve a query.

For these reasons, we want to perform another step, pushing more calculations to the formula engine. Indeed, we can perform a distinct count either by using the DISTINCTCOUNT function, which is pushed down to the storage engine, or by using SUMX over DISTINCT – in that latter case we obtain a pattern that is more likely solved by the formula engine:

```
EVALUATE
SUMMARIZECOLUMNS (
    'Date'[Date],
    'Product'[Color],
    "Sales YTD",
        CALCULATE (
            SUMX ( DISTINCT ( Sales[ProductKey] ), 1 ),
            DATESYTD ( 'Date'[Date] )
        )
)
```

This time, the formula engine is quite entirely in charge of resolving the query, as we can see from the timings.

Total	SE CPU
249,675 ms	40,406 ms
	x7.1

FE	SE
243,966 ms	5,709 ms
97.7%	2.3%

SE Queries	SE Cache
4	2
	50.0%

Please note that – despite the bar being entirely yellow – the total execution time is not very different from that of the previous query: it was 267,020 milliseconds before, it is 249,675 now. What changed dramatically is the ratio between formula engine and storage engine: now there are only four storage engine queries, compared to the 4,021 of the previous code.

Three of the storage engine queries still gather the dates, the fourth is the most interesting one:

```
SELECT
        'Sales'[ProductKey],
        'Date'[Date],
        'Product'[Color]
FROM 'Sales'
        LEFT OUTER JOIN 'Date'
                ON 'Sales'[Order Date]='Date'[Date]
        LEFT OUTER JOIN 'Product'
                ON 'Sales'[ProductKey]='Product'[ProductKey]
WHERE
        'Date'[Date] IN ( 41133.000000, 42090.000000, 42131.000000, 43088.000000, 43129.000000, 44086.000000,
        44127.000000, 41051.000000, 41092.000000, 42049.000000..[4,018 total values, not all displayed] ) ;

Estimated size: rows = 7,874,898    bytes = 31,499,592
```

This query materializes a datacache with 7,874,898 rows by grouping the *Sales* table by *Sales[ProductKey]*, *Date[Date]*, and *Product[Color]*. The storage engine is computing nothing else.

This means that the formula engine is responsible for further grouping by date and color, generating a table with the distinct values of the product key, and finally iterating over it to sum the constant value of 1. By changing a DAX expression, we can alter how the query plan is generated, and thus obtain different levels of performance in the execution.

Conclusions

In this chapter, we started to dive into more details about the formula engine. We learned what the formula engine is and how it splits a query into smaller pieces, uses storage engine queries to gather data, and finally processes the datacaches generated by the storage engine(s) to produce the result.

The formula engine orchestrates the full query. Despite being slow, it is powerful. Its power lies in its capacity to process datacaches with a very rich set of operators. The query plan is the main tool to investigate the formula engine's behavior. Nonetheless, the query plan is not often used as an investigation tool because of its complexity. Inferring the algorithm by inspecting the storage engine queries is a more efficient approach.

We have not covered the storage engine's details so far. We did spend some time describing some of the storage engine queries, but we still must learn a lot more before we can fully understand the behavior of Tabular. However, we are not yet done with the formula engine. In the next chapter, we dive into some more details about query plans.

Understanding query plans

In the previous chapters, we first introduced query plans, and then we started to understand the algorithm executed by the formula engine while executing a query plan. Even though we already said (and demonstrated) that the physical and logical query plans are too complex to analyze, it is helpful to know more about some of the information in query plans. In this chapter, we present further details about physical and logical query plans.

We do not provide a complete reference for all the operators used in query plans. Instead, we describe the more common ones, along with some of the information each operator provides. The full list would be overwhelming, to say the least.

We first introduce in more detail the basic structure of query plans. Then, to show the different operators, we analyze several query plans in depth. We describe how the operators interact to produce the result. In some way, this chapter is a logical continuation of the previous one. The angle is slightly different, however. In other chapters of this book, we focus mainly on storage engine queries. Here, for educational purposes, we will analyze DAX queries starting from the query plan, searching for confirmation of our analyses in the storage engine queries.

As you learn in this chapter, a detailed query plan analysis allows for a profound understanding of the execution details. Unfortunately, this kind of analysis is mostly overkill because of the level of detail provided. But still, reading and understanding a logical or physical query plan is helpful. Not to mention that – when learning about the internals of DAX – understanding the details provides insights on how to derive the formula engine's behavior from the storage engine queries.

Query plan structure

A query plan is a tree where each node represents an operator, and the children are the operands on which the operator works. Each operator provides a set of information. Let us start by looking at a straightforward query plan with an example that computes *Sales Amount* sliced by *Product[Color]*:

```
EVALUATE
ADDCOLUMNS (
    VALUES ( 'Product'[Color] ),
    "Amount", [Sales Amount]
)
```

Here is the physical query plan.

1		AddColumns: IterPhyOp LogOp=AddColumns IterCols(0, 1)('Product'[Color], ''[Amount])
2	16	Spool_Iterator<SpoolIterator>: IterPhyOp LogOp=Scan_Vertipaq IterCols(0)('Product'[Color]) #Records=16 #KeyCols=138 #ValueCols=0
3	16	ProjectionSpool<ProjectFusion<>>: SpoolPhyOp #Records=16
4		**Cache: IterPhyOp #FieldCols=1 #ValueCols=0**
5	16	SpoolLookup: LookupPhyOp LogOp=Sum_Vertipaq LookupCols(0)('Product'[Color]) Currency #Records=16 #KeyCols=138 #ValueCols=1 DominantValue=BLANK
6	16	ProjectionSpool<ProjectFusion<Copy>>: SpoolPhyOp #Records=16
7		**Cache: IterPhyOp #FieldCols=1 #ValueCols=1**

Each line is an operator, and two spaces indent the operator's arguments. In the figure, the top operator at line 1 is AddColumns, with two operands: Spool_Iterator at line 2 and SpoolLookup at line 5.

Each operator includes several details about its behavior. Let us analyze these further:

- **AddColumns** is the operator's name. There are many operators, and we do not want to explain all of them. Instead, we focus on the more frequently used ones.

- **IterPhyOp** is the operator type. There are several operator types: the most important ones are **ScaLogOp** and **RelLogOp** in the logical query plan and **LookupPhyOp**, **IterPhyOp**, and **SpoolPhyOp** in the physical query plan. We will describe these different types later in this section.

- The remaining part of the line contains the operator properties. Each operator type has a set of predefined properties. In addition to that, some operators might provide further information.

The logical query plan for the same query is the following.

1	AddColumns: RelLogOp DependOnCols()() 0-1 RequiredCols(0, 1)('Product'[Color], ''[Amount])
2	Scan_Vertipaq: RelLogOp DependOnCols()() 0-0 RequiredCols(0)('Product'[Color])
3	Sum_Vertipaq: ScaLogOp MeasureRef=[Sales Amount] DependOnCols(0)('Product'[Color]) Currency DominantValue=BLANK
4	Scan_Vertipaq: RelLogOp DependOnCols(0)('Product'[Color]) 1-68 RequiredCols(0, 7, 9)('Product'[Color], 'Sales'[Quantity], 'Sales'[Net Price])
5	Multiply: ScaLogOp DependOnCols(7, 9)('Sales'[Quantity], 'Sales'[Net Price]) Currency DominantValue=NONE
6	'Sales'[Quantity]: ScaLogOp DependOnCols(7)('Sales'[Quantity]) Integer DominantValue=NONE
7	'Sales'[Net Price]: ScaLogOp DependOnCols(9)('Sales'[Net Price]) Currency DominantValue=NONE

The format of the logical query plan is like the format of the physical query plan: each line is an operator with the operands in the following lines, indented by two spaces. However, the operators are different, and the operator properties provide different pieces of information.

Query plan operator types

As we introduced earlier, there are several operator types – the more important are the following:

Query plan	Operator type	Description
Logical plan	ScaLogOp	Scalar Logical Operator Outputs a scalar value of type numeric, string, Boolean, etc.
	RelLogOp	Relation Logical Operator Outputs a table of columns and rows.
Physical plan	LookupPhyOp	Lookup Physical Operator Given a current row as input, it calculates and returns a scalar value.
	IterPhyOp	Iterator Physical Operator Given a current row as an optional input, it returns a sequence of rows.
	SpoolPhyOp	Spool Physical Operator Reads a datacache and makes it available for the next steps in the query plan.

The result of an operator can be a scalar value (a number, a string, or another single value) or a table. Each operator type has a set of predefined properties.

Properties of ScaLogOp

The ScaLogOp operator type belongs to the logical query plan, and it provides three important pieces of information: DependsOnCols, data type, and DominantValue.

- **DependsOnCols** tracks the columns the operator depends on. For example, focus on the Sum_Vertipaq operator at line 3 in the highlighted part of this query plan:

Line	Logical Query Plan
1	AddColumns: RelLogOp DependOnCols()() 0-1 RequiredCols(0, 1)('Product'[Color], ''[Amount])
2	Scan_Vertipaq: RelLogOp DependOnCols()() 0-0 RequiredCols(0)('Product'[Color])
3	Sum_Vertipaq: ScaLogOp MeasureRef=[Sales Amount] DependOnCols(0)('Product'[Color]) Currency DominantValue=BLANK
4	Scan_Vertipaq: RelLogOp DependOnCols(0)('Product'[Color]) 1-68 RequiredCols(0, 7, 9)('Product'[Color], 'Sales'[Quantity], 'Sales'[Net Price])
5	Multiply: ScaLogOp DependOnCols(7, 9)('Sales'[Quantity], 'Sales'[Net Price]) Currency DominantValue=NONE
6	'Sales'[Quantity]: ScaLogOp DependOnCols(7)('Sales'[Quantity]) Integer DominantValue=NONE
7	'Sales'[Net Price]: ScaLogOp DependOnCols(9)('Sales'[Net Price]) Currency DominantValue=NONE

The top operator is *AddColumns*. *AddColumns* reads the content of its first operator (*Scan_Vertipaq*, at line 2). The operator at line 2 returns a table containing product colors. The second argument of *AddColumns* is the *Sum_Vertipaq* operator at line 3. *Sum_Vertipaq* is a scalar operator (meaning that it returns a number) whose value depends on the color currently being iterated by *AddColumns*. In other words, the result of line 3 depends on the color iterated by *AddColumns* while scanning the result of the operator at line 2. Dependencies are created at the leaf level of the query plan and then brought up until they are no longer needed.

- **Data type** is just the data type of the result, like Integer at line 6 and Currency at lines 3, 5, and 7.

- **DominantValue** captures the sparsity of the operator. When DominantValue is NONE, then the operator is dense. Any other value indicates a sparse operator. When the operator is sparse, the engine can avoid computing large chunks of combinations because it already knows the result.

Properties of RelLogOp

RelLogOp is a logical query plan operator that returns a table. The name RelLogOp comes from how tables are called in the internal DAX engines. Even though "table" is a commonly used name for a table, the theoretical description of DAX calls a table *relation*. Even though "relation" captures the essence of a table as a relation between the values of their columns, we prefer to stick to the more commonly used name: table. Nonetheless, it is useful to know that Rel in RelLogOp stands for *relation*, which is a *table*.

In the figure, we have three RelLogOp lines. Let us focus on the one highlighted in line 4:

Line	Logical Query Plan
1	AddColumns: RelLogOp DependOnCols()() 0-1 RequiredCols(0, 1)('Product'[Color], ''[Amount])
2	Scan_Vertipaq: RelLogOp DependOnCols()() 0-0 RequiredCols(0)('Product'[Color])
3	Sum_Vertipaq: ScaLogOp MeasureRef=[Sales Amount] DependOnCols(0)('Product'[Color]) Currency DominantValue=BLANK
4	Scan_Vertipaq: RelLogOp DependOnCols(0)('Product'[Color]) 1-68 RequiredCols(0, 7, 9)('Product'[Color], 'Sales'[Quantity], 'Sales'[Net Price])
5	Multiply: ScaLogOp DependOnCols(7, 9)('Sales'[Quantity], 'Sales'[Net Price]) Currency DominantValue=NONE
6	'Sales'[Quantity]: ScaLogOp DependOnCols(7)('Sales'[Quantity]) Integer DominantValue=NONE
7	'Sales'[Net Price]: ScaLogOp DependOnCols(9)('Sales'[Net Price]) Currency DominantValue=NONE

Scan_Vertipaq is an operator that, in this case, returns a table containing the three columns *Product[Color]*, *Sales[Quantity]*, and *Sales[Net Price]*. For each row in *Sales*, the values of *Sales[Quantity]* (line 6) and *Sales[Net Price]* (line 7) are fed into the Multiply operator (line 5), which performs the actual multiplication. Sum_Vertipaq iterates the result of Scan_Vertipaq at line 3.

The common properties are:

- **DependsOnCols**, with the same meaning as the DependsOnCol property of a ScaLogOp operator.

- **Range of columns**: in line 4, this is represented as 1-68. This property indicates the column numbers required to produce the result. The DAX engine assigns a unique, increasing number to each column in a table. Furthermore, to save space in the operator's text, this property reports the range of column numbers instead of showing the column names. You might notice that in the example, there are 68 columns in the range even though the *Sales* table does not contain so many columns. The reason is that the columns listed in the range are from the *Sales* expanded table.

- **RequiredCols**: Even though the expanded table contains 68 columns, only three of these columns are required to answer the query. The DAX engine determines the minimum set of columns required and provides their numbers and names. In the example, out of the 68 columns, only columns 0, 7, and 9 are required. These three columns are *Product[Color]*, *Sales[Quantity]*, and

Sales[Net Price], respectively.

Properties of LookupPhyOp

LookupPhyOp is a physical query plan operator that outputs a scalar value. The input of LookupPhyOp is still a table because all physical query plan operators read tables generated at the leaf level and moved up on the query plan tree. LookupPhyOp returns one value from a table, whereas IterPhyOp returns a table. In our example, there is only one LookupPhyOp at line 5:

Line	Records	Physical Query Plan
1		AddColumns: IterPhyOp LogOp=AddColumns IterCols(0, 1)('Product'[Color], ''[Amount])
2	16	Spool_Iterator<SpoolIterator>: IterPhyOp LogOp=Scan_Vertipaq IterCols(0)('Product'[Color]) #Records=16 #KeyCols=138 #ValueCols=0
3	16	ProjectionSpool<ProjectFusion<>>: SpoolPhyOp #Records=16
4		**Cache: IterPhyOp #FieldCols=1 #ValueCols=0**
5	16	SpoolLookup: LookupPhyOp LogOp=Sum_Vertipaq LookupCols(0)('Product'[Color]) Currency #Records=16 #KeyCols=138 #ValueCols=1 DominantValue=BLANK
6	16	ProjectionSpool<ProjectFusion<Copy>>: SpoolPhyOp #Records=16
7		**Cache: IterPhyOp #FieldCols=1 #ValueCols=1**

The most relevant property of the SpoolLookup operator is the **LookupCols** property. The SpoolLookup operator provides a value to its parent for each combination of the columns provided in the LookupCols property. In the example, SpoolLookup provides one value for each color to its caller. The output data type is also stated: Currency in line 5.

Other properties specific to the SpoolLookup operator are the number of rows returned (**#Records** – DAX Studio also reports it in the Records column), the number of key columns (**KeyCols**), and the number of value columns (**ValueCols**). The key columns are retrieved from the original data, whereas the value columns result from a calculation.

Properties of IterPhyOp

IterPhyOp is a physical query plan operator that outputs a table. In the example, there are two IterPhyOp: AddColumns at line 1 and Spool_Iterator at line 2.

Line	Records	Physical Query Plan
1		AddColumns: IterPhyOp LogOp=AddColumns IterCols(0, 1)('Product'[Color], ''[Amount])
2	16	Spool_Iterator<SpoolIterator>: IterPhyOp LogOp=Scan_Vertipaq IterCols(0)('Product'[Color]) #Records=16 #KeyCols=138 #ValueCols=0
3	16	ProjectionSpool<ProjectFusion<>>: SpoolPhyOp #Records=16
4		**Cache: IterPhyOp #FieldCols=1 #ValueCols=0**
5	16	SpoolLookup: LookupPhyOp LogOp=Sum_Vertipaq LookupCols(0)('Product'[Color]) Currency #Records=16 #KeyCols=138 #ValueCols=1 DominantValue=BLANK
6	16	ProjectionSpool<ProjectFusion<Copy>>: SpoolPhyOp #Records=16
7		**Cache: IterPhyOp #FieldCols=1 #ValueCols=1**

There are also two other IterPhyOp operators at line 4 and line 7. They are reading the output of a VertiPaq datacache; therefore, they are somewhat less interesting.

The **LookupCols** property indicates which columns are required to produce the output. The **IterCols** property indicates which columns are included in the output. It is important to note that the same operator can display very different behaviors depending on which combinations of LookupCols and IterCols are provided.

An IterPhyOp with only the IterCols columns is a pure iterator that returns a table. If both IterCols and LookupCols are present, the operator behaves as a table-valued function, much like the GENERATE function does in DAX. In case an IterPhyOp contains only the LookupCols property, it acts like a pure row-checker: for example, to remove unwanted rows from a spool.

Properties of SpoolPhyOp

SpoolPhyOp is a physical query plan operator that reads a datacache and makes it available for the next steps in the query plan. For example, the IterPhyOp operator at line 2 consumes the LookupPhyOp operator at line 3, and the LookupPhyOp at line 5 consumes the output of the SpoolPhyOp operator at line 6.

Line	Records	Physical Query Plan
1		AddColumns: IterPhyOp LogOp=AddColumns IterCols(0, 1)('Product'[Color], ''[Amount])
2	16	Spool_Iterator<SpoolIterator>: IterPhyOp LogOp=Scan_Vertipaq IterCols(0)('Product'[Color]) #Records=16 #KeyCols=138 #ValueCols=0
3	16	ProjectionSpool<ProjectFusion<>>: SpoolPhyOp #Records=16
4		**Cache: IterPhyOp #FieldCols=1 #ValueCols=0**
5	16	SpoolLookup: LookupPhyOp LogOp=Sum_Vertipaq LookupCols(0)('Product'[Color]) Currency #Records=16 #KeyCols=138 #ValueCols=1 DominantValue=BLANK
6	16	ProjectionSpool<ProjectFusion<Copy>>: SpoolPhyOp #Records=16
7		**Cache: IterPhyOp #FieldCols=1 #ValueCols=1**

Because the SpoolPhyOp is usually an intermediate step to provide data to another operator, we usually do not spend time looking at this operator. However, this is the first step where you can see the exact number of rows extracted from a datacache (**#Records** – DAX Studio also reports it in the Records column), which is not reported in the datacache node of the query plan. In this example, the number of records is 16 for both SpoolPhyOp operators, and the same number is also displayed for the operators consuming the result of SpoolPhyOp.

Interactions between the formula engine and the storage engine

As we already know, the formula engine executes the query plan, and its operators are using datacaches generated by the storage engine. Therefore, the query plan usually shows a set of operators that ultimately retrieve the data from Cache operators. A Cache operator reads the information in a datacache previously created by the storage engine.

For example, the following query requires the formula engine to use the TRUNC operator on the result of *Sales Amount* grouped by *Date[Year Month]*:

```
EVALUATE
SUMMARIZECOLUMNS (
    'Date'[Year Month],
    "Sales", TRUNC ( [Sales Amount] )
)
```

The query plan shows that the tree's leaf is a Cache operator, and TRUNC is executed by the formula engine iterating on the storage engine datacache.

Line	Records	Physical Query Plan
1		GroupSemijoin: IterPhyOp LogOp=GroupSemiJoin IterCols(0, 1)('Date'[Year Month], ''[Sales])
2		TRUNC: IterPhyOp LogOp=TRUNC IterCols(0)('Date'[Year Month])
3		Currency->Double: IterPhyOp LogOp=Currency->DoubleCurrency->Double IterCols(0)('Date'[Year Month])
4	119	Spool_Iterator<SpoolIterator>: IterPhyOp LogOp=Sum_Vertipaq IterCols(0)('Date'[Year Month]) #Records=
5	119	ProjectionSpool<ProjectFusion<Copy>>: SpoolPhyOp #Records=119
6		**Cache: IterPhyOp #FieldCols=1 #ValueCols=1**

There are scenarios where the formula engine and the storage engine work together to produce a result:

- When there is a callback in the storage engine request.

- When the formula engine computes a filter that is used later in a storage engine query.

In both these scenarios, the storage engine query depends on the code executed by the formula engine. To show the dependency and provide a better picture of the flow of data in these scenarios, a Cache operator is not a leaf-level node, but instead it appears in the middle of the plan.

An example of a callback is the following:

```
EVALUATE
SUMMARIZECOLUMNS (
    'Date'[Year Month],
    "Sales",
        SUMX (
            Sales,
            TRUNC ( Sales[Quantity] * Sales[Net Price] )
        )
)
```

The TRUNC operator must be executed on a row-by-row basis while scanning *Sales*. In this scenario, a callback is a perfect tool, and we can check for its presence in the xmSQL query:

```
WITH
    $Expr0 :=
        [CallbackDataID ( TRUNC ( Sales[Quantity] * Sales[Net Price] )    ) ] (
            PFDATAID ( 'Sales'[Quantity] ) ,
            PFDATAID ( 'Sales'[Net Price] )
        )
SELECT
    'Date'[Year Month],
    SUM ( @$Expr0 )
FROM 'Sales'
    LEFT OUTER JOIN 'Date'
        ON 'Sales'[Order Date]='Date'[Date];
```

The callback executes the TRUNC function and the multiplication of the two columns. Therefore, the datacache generated by the storage engine requires the execution of formula engine code. This is evident by looking at the query plan, where the Cache operator appears in the middle of the plan (at line 4), followed by the code executed by the formula engine during the callback.

Line	Records	Physical Query Plan
1		GroupSemijoin: IterPhyOp LogOp=GroupSemiJoin IterCols(0, 1)('Date'[Year Month], ''[Sales])
2	119	Spool_Iterator<SpoolIterator>: IterPhyOp LogOp=Sum_Vertipaq IterCols(0)('Date'[Year Month]) #Records=119 #Key
3	119	ProjectionSpool<ProjectFusion<Copy>>: SpoolPhyOp #Records=119
4		**Cache: IterPhyOp #FieldCols=1 #ValueCols=1**
5		TRUNC: LookupPhyOp LogOp=TRUNC LookupCols(7, 9)('Sales'[Quantity], 'Sales'[Net Price]) Currency
6		Currency->Double: LookupPhyOp LogOp=Currency->DoubleCurrency->Double LookupCols(7, 9)('Sales'[(
7		Multiply: LookupPhyOp LogOp=Multiply LookupCols(7, 9)('Sales'[Quantity], 'Sales'[Net Price]) Currency
8		ColValue<'Sales'[Quantity]>: LookupPhyOp LogOp=ColValue<'Sales'[Quantity]>'Sales'[Quantity] Loc
9		ColValue<'Sales'[Net Price]>: LookupPhyOp LogOp=ColValue<'Sales'[Net Price]>'Sales'[Net Price] Lc

In lines 5-9, the algorithm computes both the multiplication and the TRUNC function.

A similar scenario happens when the formula engine computes a filter, which is then applied to a storage engine query. As an example, let us analyze the following code:

```
EVALUATE
SUMMARIZECOLUMNS (
    Product[Color],
    "Sales",
        CALCULATE (
            [Sales Amount],
            KEEPFILTERS ( LEFT ( Product[Color], 1 ) = "R" )
        )
)
```

The filter in CALCULATE uses the LEFT function, which the storage engine cannot execute. Therefore, the formula engine needs to retrieve all product colors, search for the ones starting with an R, and finally use the list of those colors in a storage engine query that computes the sales amount.

Therefore, we expect to see two storage engine queries: one retrieving all the colors and one retrieving the sales amount of only the colors starting with an R. This is the first xmSQL query:

```
SELECT
    'Product'[Color]
FROM 'Product';
```

And here is the second xmSQL query:

```
WITH
    $Expr0 := ( PFCAST ( 'Sales'[Quantity] AS INT ) * PFCAST ( 'Sales'[Net Price] AS INT )   )
SELECT
    SUM ( @$Expr0 )
FROM 'Sales'
    LEFT OUTER JOIN 'Product'
        ON 'Sales'[ProductKey]='Product'[ProductKey]
WHERE
    'Product'[Color] = 'Red';
```

The second query includes the filter for *Product[Color]* = *"Red"* computed by the formula engine. Therefore, the second xmSQL query depends on the code executed by the formula engine. Again, this is visible in the query plan because the Cache operator is not at the leaf level, but rather it appears in the middle of the plan at line 4.

1		GroupSemijoin: IterPhyOp LogOp=GroupSemiJoin IterCols(0, 1)('Product'[Color], ''[Sales])
2	1	Spool_Iterator<SpoolIterator>: IterPhyOp LogOp=Sum_Vertipaq IterCols(0)('Product'[Color]) #Records=1 #KeyCols=
3	1	ProjectionSpool<ProjectFusion<Copy>>: SpoolPhyOp #Records=1
4		**Cache: IterPhyOp #FieldCols=0 #ValueCols=1**
5	1	Spool_Iterator<SpoolIterator>: IterPhyOp LogOp=Filter IterCols(1)('Product'[Color]) #Records=1 #KeyCols=
6	1	AggregationSpool<GroupBy>: SpoolPhyOp #Records=1
7		Filter: IterPhyOp LogOp=Filter IterCols(1)('Product'[Color])
8		Extend_Lookup: IterPhyOp LogOp=EqualTo IterCols(1)('Product'[Color])
9	16	Spool_Iterator<SpoolIterator>: IterPhyOp LogOp=Scan_Vertipaq IterCols(1)('Product'[Color]) #Rec
10	16	ProjectionSpool<ProjectFusion<>>: SpoolPhyOp #Records=16
11		**Cache: IterPhyOp #FieldCols=1 #ValueCols=0**
12		EqualTo: LookupPhyOp LogOp=EqualTo LookupCols(1)('Product'[Color]) Boolean
13		LEFT: LookupPhyOp LogOp=LEFT LookupCols(1)('Product'[Color]) String
14		ColValue<'Product'[Color]>: LookupPhyOp LogOp=ColValue<'Product'[Color]>'Product'[Col
15		Constant: LookupPhyOp LogOp=Constant Integer 1
16		Constant: LookupPhyOp LogOp=Constant String R

Whenever a Cache operator is not at the leaf level, we know that there are some interactions between the two engines. The result is always a datacache created by the storage engine. However, the datacache depends on the code the formula engine computed through a callback or by computing filters passed to the storage engine.

Common query plan operators

As we said in the introduction, we will not describe each query plan operator. You may find a more up-to-date list of query plan operators at https://docs.sqlbi.com/dax-internals/vertipaq/. However, there are several operators that you will often encounter during your analysis. In this section, we list the ones that – in our opinion – are more likely to be found and used:

Query plan	Operator	Description
Logical plan	AddColumns	Adds columns to a table.
	Calculate	Calculates a scalar expression by applying specific filters. It corresponds to the CALCULATE function in DAX.
	CalculateTable	Calculates a table expression by applying specific filters. It corresponds to the CALCULATETABLE function in DAX.
	Filter_VertiPaq	Returns a table usually applied as a filter to a Calculate operator.
	GroupBy_VertiPaq	Performs a group by of the table using the specified columns.

	GroupSemiJoin	Joins the result of two operators, returning all the rows in the first table if there is a match with the result of the second operator.
	ScalarVarProxy	Returns the value of a scalar variable computed inside a variable scope introduced with the VarScope operator.
	Scan_Vertipaq	Performs the scan of a table using the VertiPaq storage engine.
	Sum_Vertipaq	Performs a SUM aggregation using the VertiPaq storage engine. Similar operators are available for MIN, MAX, and COUNT aggregations.
	TableVarProxy	Returns the value of a table variable computed inside a variable scope introduced with the VarScope operator.
	VarScope	Opens a variable scope. It contains a list of variable definitions defined with the VarName property. The result of the VarScope operator is the last operator in the scope.
Physical plan	AggregationSpool	Aggregates the result of a Cache operator, by aggregating some of the columns contained in the datacache.
	Cache	Identifies the use of a datacache. Retrieves the content of a datacache returned by a storage engine query. In a single query plan, there might be several Cache operators reading the same datacache. In this scenario, there will be a single storage engine query generating the datacache, which is then consumed in different parts of the query plan.
	CrossApply	Performs the Cartesian product (cross-join) between two tables. The cardinality of the resulting table is not exposed directly. If the result is immediately consumed by a Spool operator, then the resulting number of records is visible. However, if a Filter operator is executed before any spool, the number of records produced by the CrossApply and then filtered is not visible and you can see only the number of filtered rows.
	DataPostFilter	Retrieves a subset of rows from a datacache resulting from a vertical fusion operation. While Cache retrieves the entire datacache, DataPostFilter retrieves some of the values based on a filter condition.
	Filter	Filters one table thus reducing the number of rows.
	GroupSemiJoin	Groups two tables by performing a semi-join.
	InnerHashJoin	Performs an inner join between two tables.

ProjectionSpool	Projects the result of a Cache operator; selects some of the columns contained in the datacache.
SpoolIterator	Summarizes a table by performing one aggregation (sum/count/distinct count/min/max/average) over a value obtained from an expression (or a column in simpler cases) and grouping by one or more columns of the original table.
SpoolLookup	Summarizes a table by performing an aggregation (sum/count/distinct count/min/max/average) over a value obtained from an expression (or a column in simpler cases). Returns a single value.
TableCtor	Builds a table from a table constructor syntax.
TreatAs	Changes the data lineage of a table (like TREATAS in DAX).

Examples of query plans

Now that we have described the structure of a query plan in more detail, we can use this information to perform a deep analysis of a few queries. Here, the goal is still educational and foundational. We are not interested in optimizing the DAX code. Therefore, we will deliberately write suboptimal code.

Comparing SUM versus SUMX

We start with a straightforward query plan to demonstrate a well-known fact: there are no performance differences between SUM and SUMX. SUM is just syntax sugar for SUMX. To clarify this, we analyze a query aggregating a column with SUM and compare it with the same query that uses SUMX:

```
EVALUATE
SUMMARIZECOLUMNS (
    'Product'[Color],
    "Quantity", SUM ( Sales[Quantity] )
)
```

The logical query plan suggests that there will be two different storage engine queries: one for the product colors and one to compute the sum.

Line	Logical Query Plan
1	GroupSemiJoin: RelLogOp DependOnCols()() 0-1 RequiredCols(0, 1)('Product'[Color], ''[Quantity])
2	Scan_Vertipaq: RelLogOp DependOnCols()() 0-0 RequiredCols(0)('Product'[Color])
3	Sum_Vertipaq: ScaLogOp DependOnCols(0)('Product'[Color]) Integer DominantValue=BLANK
4	Scan_Vertipaq: RelLogOp DependOnCols(0)('Product'[Color]) 1-68 RequiredCols(0, 7)('Product'[Color], 'Sales'[Quantity])
5	'Sales'[Quantity]: ScaLogOp DependOnCols(7)('Sales'[Quantity]) Integer DominantValue=NONE

Indeed, at line 2 and line 3, we see the two Scan_VertiPaq operators: one to get the values in *Product[Color]* and one to produce a datacache containing the sum of *Sales[Quantity]* grouped by *Product[Color]*. The two datacaches are then joined together to produce the result.

The operator at line 1 is a GroupSemiJoin. A semi-join returns the rows from the first table (line 2) only if there is a match with the second argument (line 3). Therefore, if a specific color has no matches in *Sales*, that color is removed from the output.

The logical query plan can be further optimized by removing the first scan. Indeed, it is enough to read the product colors present in the scan at line 3 to obtain the full list of colors to return. Hence, in the physical query plan, we find only one storage engine query instead of the two we would have expected.

Line	Records	Physical Query Plan
1		GroupSemijoin: IterPhyOp LogOp=GroupSemiJoin IterCols(0, 1)('Product'[Color], ''[Quantity])
2	16	Spool_Iterator<SpoolIterator>: IterPhyOp LogOp=Sum_Vertipaq IterCols(0)('Product'[Color]) #Records=16 #KeyCols=138 #ValueCols=1
3	16	ProjectionSpool<ProjectFusion<Copy>>: SpoolPhyOp #Records=16
4		**Cache: IterPhyOp #FieldCols=1 #ValueCols=1**

The absence of a second query is confirmed by the server timings, which show a single storage engine query.

Total	SE CPU		Line	Subclass	Duration	CPU	Par.	Rows	KB	Timeline
28 ms	141 ms		2	Scan	24	141	x5.9	19	1	
	x5.9									

FE	SE
4 ms	24 ms
14.3%	85.7%

SE Queries	SE Cache
1	0
	0.0%

Here is the storage engine query executed:

```
SELECT
    'Product'[Color],
    SUM ( 'Sales'[Quantity] )
FROM 'Sales'
    LEFT OUTER JOIN 'Product'
        ON 'Sales'[ProductKey]='Product'[ProductKey];
```

If we replace SUM with SUMX as mentioned earlier, we obtain the following query:

```
EVALUATE
SUMMARIZECOLUMNS (
    'Product'[Color],
    "Quantity", SUMX ( Sales, Sales[Quantity] )
)
```

Even though we changed the function (SUMX instead of SUM) the result is identical to the previous one. Here is the physical query plan.

Line	Records	Physical Query Plan
1		GroupSemijoin: IterPhyOp LogOp=GroupSemiJoin IterCols(0, 1)('Product'[Color], ''[Quantity])
2	16	Spool_Iterator<SpoolIterator>: IterPhyOp LogOp=Sum_Vertipaq IterCols(0)('Product'[Color]) #Records=16 #KeyCols=138 #ValueCols=1
3	16	ProjectionSpool<ProjectFusion<Copy>>: SpoolPhyOp #Records=16
4		**Cache: IterPhyOp #FieldCols=1 #ValueCols=1**

There are no differences between using SUM or SUMX if we compute the aggregation of a single column.

Moreover, before we leave this topic to rest, it is helpful to see how the query plan changes if, instead of using SUMMARIZECOLUMNS, we use ADDCOLUMNS and CALCULATE to obtain the same result:

```
EVALUATE
ADDCOLUMNS (
    VALUES ( 'Product'[Color] ),
    "Quantity", CALCULATE ( SUMX ( Sales, Sales[Quantity] ) )
)
```

Because ADDCOLUMNS returns colors with no corresponding rows in *Sales*, the engine cannot use a GroupSemiJon operator; it needs to use AddColumns, as we can see from the logical query plan at line 1.

Line	Logical Query Plan
1	AddColumns: RelLogOp DependOnCols()() 0-1 RequiredCols(0, 1)('Product'[Color], ''[Quantity])
2	Scan_Vertipaq: RelLogOp DependOnCols()() 0-0 RequiredCols(0)('Product'[Color])
3	Sum_Vertipaq: ScaLogOp DependOnCols(0)('Product'[Color]) Integer DominantValue=BLANK
4	Scan_Vertipaq: RelLogOp DependOnCols(0)('Product'[Color]) 1-68 RequiredCols(0, 7)('Product'[Color], 'Sales'[Quantity])
5	'Sales'[Quantity]: ScaLogOp DependOnCols(7)('Sales'[Quantity]) Integer DominantValue=NONE

The optimizer cannot reduce the number of storage engine queries this time. Indeed, the physical query plan shows two different Cache operators, one at line 4 and one at line 7.

Line	Records	Physical Query Plan
1		AddColumns: IterPhyOp LogOp=AddColumns IterCols(0, 1)('Product'[Color], ''[Quantity])
2	16	Spool_Iterator<SpoolIterator>: IterPhyOp LogOp=Scan_Vertipaq IterCols(0)('Product'[Color]) #Records=16 #KeyCols=138 #ValueCols=0
3	16	ProjectionSpool<ProjectFusion<>>: SpoolPhyOp #Records=16
4		**Cache: IterPhyOp #FieldCols=1 #ValueCols=0**
5	16	SpoolLookup: LookupPhyOp LogOp=Sum_Vertipaq LookupCols(0)('Product'[Color]) Integer #Records=16 #KeyCols=138 #ValueCols=1 D
6	16	ProjectionSpool<ProjectFusion<Copy>>: SpoolPhyOp #Records=16
7		**Cache: IterPhyOp #FieldCols=1 #ValueCols=1**

Finally, we obtain confirmation by analyzing the server timings panel, which shows two storage engine queries.

Total	SE CPU	Line	Subclass	Duration	CPU	Par.	Rows	KB	Timeline
27 ms	16 ms x0.7	2	Scan	21	16	x0.8	19	1	
		4	Scan	3	0		19	1	
FE 3 ms 11.1%	**SE** 24 ms 88.9%								

SE Queries	SE Cache
2	0 0.0%

From the execution time point of view, there are small differences in the query plan without a performance impact. The only query being added is a straightforward storage engine query that retrieves the values of the colors. At the risk of sounding repetitive, our goal for now is not to optimize code but instead to analyze together different queries and start to understand how to use the different pieces of information to then understand the algorithm executed by Tabular.

Comparing IF versus IF.EAGER

DAX offers two conditional statements: IF and IF.EAGER. The two operators provide the same result; the difference is in how the query plan is generated. Indeed, there are two ways to solve the same conditional logic. Let us elaborate with an example.

The following query computes two different measures based on the value of *Sales Amount* for each *Product[Color]*:

```
EVALUATE
ADDCOLUMNS (
    VALUES ( 'Product'[Color] ),
    "Test",
        IF (
            [Sales Amount] < 1E7,
            [Margin],
            [Total Cost]
        )
)
```

We know (just because we are experts of Contoso) that the only color whose sales amount is less than 10 million is Transparent. But Tabular is not aware of this. From the DAX point of view, there are two ways to answer the query. It can use either strict or eager evaluation.

Using strict evaluation, DAX asks the storage engine to create a datacache containing the value of *Sales Amount* for each color. Then, the formula engine scans this datacache to determine which colors satisfy the condition, and it splits the colors into two sets. Finally, it executes two storage engine queries: one computing the *Margin* measure for the colors satisfying the condition, and a second computing the Total Cost measure for the colors where the condition yields false. Strict evaluation is the default behavior of an IF statement. Strict evaluation requires the generation of three datacaches.

There is another way to compute the same query. The storage engine can produce a single datacache containing the three measures for each color: *Sales Amount*, *Margin*, and *Total Cost*. Then, the formula engine scans the datacache and chooses which of the two results to use depending on the sales value. Eager evaluation creates a single datacache with all the required values, delaying the choice of which ones will be useful later.

Strict evaluation reduces the number of calculations at the cost of a more complex algorithm and more storage engine queries. Eager evaluation computes useless values using fewer storage engine queries. It is not that eager evaluation is better than strict evaluation. There are scenarios where strict evaluation is preferable, and there are scenarios where eager evaluation is preferable. It depends on the number of rows in the datacache, the distribution of true/false values for the condition, and the complexity of the calculations involved.

Let us see how we can better understand the algorithm by analyzing the query plan first, the storage engine queries next, and the server timings last. We start with the query using a regular IF. Here is the logical query plan.

Line	Logical Query Plan
1	AddColumns: RelLogOp DependOnCols()() 0-1 RequiredCols(0, 1)('Product'[Color], ''[Sales])
2	Scan_Vertipaq: RelLogOp DependOnCols()() 0-0 RequiredCols(0)('Product'[Color])
3	If: ScaLogOp DependOnCols(0)('Product'[Color]) Currency DominantValue=BLANK
4	LessThan: ScaLogOp DependOnCols(0)('Product'[Color]) Boolean DominantValue=true
5	Currency->Double: ScaLogOp DependOnCols(0)('Product'[Color]) Double DominantValue=BLANK
6	Sum_Vertipaq: ScaLogOp MeasureRef=[Sales Amount] DependOnCols(0)('Product'[Color]) Currency DominantValue=BLANK
7	Scan_Vertipaq: RelLogOp DependOnCols(0)('Product'[Color]) 1-68 RequiredCols(0, 7, 9)('Product'[Color], 'Sales'[Quantity], 'Sales'[Net Price])
8	Multiply: ScaLogOp DependOnCols(7, 9)('Sales'[Quantity], 'Sales'[Net Price]) Currency DominantValue=NONE
9	'Sales'[Quantity]: ScaLogOp DependOnCols(7)('Sales'[Quantity]) Integer DominantValue=NONE
10	'Sales'[Net Price]: ScaLogOp DependOnCols(9)('Sales'[Net Price]) Currency DominantValue=NONE
11	Constant: ScaLogOp DependOnCols()() Double DominantValue=10000000
12	PredicateCheck: RelLogOp DependOnCols(0)('Product'[Color]) RequiredCols(0)('Product'[Color])
13	ScalarVarProxy: ScaLogOp DependOnCols(0)('Product'[Color]) Boolean DominantValue=true
14	PredicateCheck: RelLogOp DependOnCols(0)('Product'[Color]) RequiredCols(0)('Product'[Color])
15	ScalarVarProxy: ScaLogOp DependOnCols(0)('Product'[Color]) Boolean DominantValue=true
16	Subtract: ScaLogOp MeasureRef=[Margin] DependOnCols(0)('Product'[Color]) Currency DominantValue=BLANK
17	Sum_Vertipaq: ScaLogOp MeasureRef=[Sales Amount] DependOnCols(0)('Product'[Color]) Currency DominantValue=BLANK
18	Scan_Vertipaq: RelLogOp DependOnCols(0)('Product'[Color]) 1-68 RequiredCols(0, 7, 9)('Product'[Color], 'Sales'[Quantity], 'Sales'[Net Price])
19	Multiply: ScaLogOp DependOnCols(7, 9)('Sales'[Quantity], 'Sales'[Net Price]) Currency DominantValue=NONE
20	'Sales'[Quantity]: ScaLogOp DependOnCols(7)('Sales'[Quantity]) Integer DominantValue=NONE
21	'Sales'[Net Price]: ScaLogOp DependOnCols(9)('Sales'[Net Price]) Currency DominantValue=NONE
22	Sum_Vertipaq: ScaLogOp MeasureRef=[Total Cost] DependOnCols(0)('Product'[Color]) Currency DominantValue=BLANK
23	Scan_Vertipaq: RelLogOp DependOnCols(0)('Product'[Color]) 1-68 RequiredCols(0, 7, 10)('Product'[Color], 'Sales'[Quantity], 'Sales'[Unit Cost])
24	Multiply: ScaLogOp DependOnCols(7, 10)('Sales'[Quantity], 'Sales'[Unit Cost]) Currency DominantValue=NONE
25	'Sales'[Quantity]: ScaLogOp DependOnCols(7)('Sales'[Quantity]) Integer DominantValue=NONE
26	'Sales'[Unit Cost]: ScaLogOp DependOnCols(10)('Sales'[Unit Cost]) Currency DominantValue=NONE
27	Sum_Vertipaq: ScaLogOp MeasureRef=[Total Cost] DependOnCols(0)('Product'[Color]) Currency DominantValue=BLANK
28	Scan_Vertipaq: RelLogOp DependOnCols(0)('Product'[Color]) 1-68 RequiredCols(0, 7, 10)('Product'[Color], 'Sales'[Quantity], 'Sales'[Unit Cost])
29	Multiply: ScaLogOp DependOnCols(7, 10)('Sales'[Quantity], 'Sales'[Unit Cost]) Currency DominantValue=NONE
30	'Sales'[Quantity]: ScaLogOp DependOnCols(7)('Sales'[Quantity]) Integer DominantValue=NONE
31	'Sales'[Unit Cost]: ScaLogOp DependOnCols(10)('Sales'[Unit Cost]) Currency DominantValue=NONE

The main operator is an If operator at line 3. Between lines 4 and 11, there is the condition that *Sales Amount* should be less than 10 million. You can see a Scan_Vertipaq operator at line 7, indicating the generation of a datacache with the sales amount. Lines 12 to 15 verify the predicate value. This is where the set of colors is split into two buckets, the colors where the condition holds true versus the colors with a false condition – just ignore the DominantValue, which does not correspond to the result of the true/false condition of the IF predicate in the DAX expression.

Finally, lines 16 to 26 compute *Margin* by subtracting *Total Cost* from *Sales Amount*; it is worth noting the MeasureRef property in lines 16 and 22, which helps understand the code. Lines 27 to 31 compute *Total Cost* for the bucket where the condition holds false.

The physical query plan is quite long: 56 lines. The useful detail, nonetheless, is that If is the outermost operator, working on different datacaches. We highlighted two datacaches that identify the different queries generated, one with one row and one with 15 rows.

Line	Records	Physical Query Plan
1		AddColumns: IterPhyOp LogOp=AddColumns IterCols(0, 1)('Product'[Color], ''[Sales])
2	16	Spool_Iterator<SpoolIterator>: IterPhyOp LogOp=Scan_Vertipaq IterCols(0)('Product'[Color]) #Records=16 #KeyCols=138 #ValueCols=0
3	16	ProjectionSpool<ProjectFusion<>>: SpoolPhyOp #Records=16
4		**Cache: IterPhyOp #FieldCols=1 #ValueCols=0**
5		If: LookupPhyOp LogOp=If LookupCols(0)('Product'[Color]) Currency
6		LessThan: LookupPhyOp LogOp=LessThan LookupCols(0)('Product'[Color]) Boolean
7		Currency->Double: LookupPhyOp LogOp=Currency->DoubleCurrency->Double LookupCols(0)('Product'[Color]) Double
8	16	SpoolLookup: LookupPhyOp LogOp=Sum_Vertipaq LookupCols(0)('Product'[Color]) Currency #Records=16 #KeyCols=138 #ValueCols=1 DominantValue=BLANK
9	16	ProjectionSpool<ProjectFusion<Copy>>: SpoolPhyOp #Records=16
10		**Cache: IterPhyOp #FieldCols=1 #ValueCols=1**
11		Constant: LookupPhyOp LogOp=Constant Double 10000000
12		Subtract: LookupPhyOp LogOp=Subtract LookupCols(0)('Product'[Color]) Currency
13	1	SpoolLookup: LookupPhyOp LogOp=Sum_Vertipaq LookupCols(0)('Product'[Color]) Currency #Records=1 #KeyCols=138 #ValueCols=2 DominantValue=BLANK
14	1	ProjectionSpool<ProjectFusion<Copy, Copy>>: SpoolPhyOp #Records=1
15		**Cache: IterPhyOp #FieldCols=0 #ValueCols=2**
16	1	Spool_Iterator<SpoolIterator>: IterPhyOp LogOp=PredicateCheck IterCols(0)('Product'[Color]) #Records=1 #KeyCols=1 #ValueCols=0
17	1	AggregationSpool<GroupBy>: SpoolPhyOp #Records=1
18		PredicateCheck: IterPhyOp LogOp=PredicateCheck IterCols(0)('Product'[Color])
19		Extend_Lookup: IterPhyOp LogOp=ScalarVarProxy IterCols(0)('Product'[Color])
20	16	Spool_Iterator<SpoolIterator>: IterPhyOp LogOp=Scan_Vertipaq IterCols(0)('Product'[Color]) #Records=16 #KeyCols=138 #ValueCols=0
21	16	ProjectionSpool<ProjectFusion<>>: SpoolPhyOp #Records=16
22		**Cache: IterPhyOp #FieldCols=1 #ValueCols=0**
23		LessThan: LookupPhyOp LogOp=LessThan LookupCols(0)('Product'[Color]) Boolean
24		Currency->Double: LookupPhyOp LogOp=Currency->DoubleCurrency->Double LookupCols(0)('Product'[Color]) Double
25	16	SpoolLookup: LookupPhyOp LogOp=Sum_Vertipaq LookupCols(0)('Product'[Color]) Currency #Records=16 #KeyCols=138 #ValueCols=1 D
26	16	ProjectionSpool<ProjectFusion<Copy>>: SpoolPhyOp #Records=16
27		**Cache: IterPhyOp #FieldCols=1 #ValueCols=1**
28		Constant: LookupPhyOp LogOp=Constant Double 10000000
29	1	SpoolLookup: LookupPhyOp LogOp=Sum_Vertipaq LookupCols(0)('Product'[Color]) Currency #Records=1 #KeyCols=138 #ValueCols=2 DominantValue=BLANK
30	1	ProjectionSpool<ProjectFusion<Copy, Copy>>: SpoolPhyOp #Records=1
31		**Cache: IterPhyOp #FieldCols=0 #ValueCols=2**
32	1	Spool_Iterator<SpoolIterator>: IterPhyOp LogOp=PredicateCheck IterCols(0)('Product'[Color]) #Records=1 #KeyCols=1 #ValueCols=0
33	1	AggregationSpool<GroupBy>: SpoolPhyOp #Records=1
34		PredicateCheck: IterPhyOp LogOp=PredicateCheck IterCols(0)('Product'[Color])
35		Extend_Lookup: IterPhyOp LogOp=ScalarVarProxy IterCols(0)('Product'[Color])
36	16	Spool_Iterator<SpoolIterator>: IterPhyOp LogOp=Scan_Vertipaq IterCols(0)('Product'[Color]) #Records=16 #KeyCols=138 #ValueCols=0
37	16	ProjectionSpool<ProjectFusion<>>: SpoolPhyOp #Records=16
38		**Cache: IterPhyOp #FieldCols=1 #ValueCols=0**
39		LessThan: LookupPhyOp LogOp=LessThan LookupCols(0)('Product'[Color]) Boolean
40		Currency->Double: LookupPhyOp LogOp=Currency->DoubleCurrency->Double LookupCols(0)('Product'[Color]) Double
41	16	SpoolLookup: LookupPhyOp LogOp=Sum_Vertipaq LookupCols(0)('Product'[Color]) Currency #Records=16 #KeyCols=138 #ValueCols=1 D
42	16	ProjectionSpool<ProjectFusion<Copy>>: SpoolPhyOp #Records=16
43		**Cache: IterPhyOp #FieldCols=1 #ValueCols=1**
44		Constant: LookupPhyOp LogOp=Constant Double 10000000
45	15	SpoolLookup: LookupPhyOp LogOp=Sum_Vertipaq LookupCols(0)('Product'[Color]) Currency #Records=15 #KeyCols=138 #ValueCols=1 DominantValue=BLANK
46	15	ProjectionSpool<ProjectFusion<Copy>>: SpoolPhyOp #Records=15
47		**Cache: IterPhyOp #FieldCols=1 #ValueCols=1**
48	15	Spool_Iterator<SpoolIterator>: IterPhyOp LogOp=PredicateCheck IterCols(0)('Product'[Color]) #Records=15 #KeyCols=1 #ValueCols=0
49	15	AggregationSpool<GroupBy>: SpoolPhyOp #Records=15
50		PredicateCheck: IterPhyOp LogOp=PredicateCheck IterCols(0)('Product'[Color])
51		Extend_Lookup: IterPhyOp LogOp=LessThan IterCols(0)('Product'[Color])
52		Currency->Double: IterPhyOp LogOp=Currency->DoubleCurrency->Double IterCols(0)('Product'[Color])
53	16	Spool_Iterator<SpoolIterator>: IterPhyOp LogOp=Sum_Vertipaq IterCols(0)('Product'[Color]) #Records=16 #KeyCols=138 #ValueCols=1
54	16	ProjectionSpool<ProjectFusion<Copy>>: SpoolPhyOp #Records=16
55		**Cache: IterPhyOp #FieldCols=1 #ValueCols=1**
56		Constant: LookupPhyOp LogOp=Constant Double 10000000

The scenario becomes even clearer when we analyze the storage engine queries. This plan generates four storage engine queries. The first computes *Sales Amount* sliced by *Product[Color]* for all the colors:

```
WITH
    $Expr0 := ( PFCAST ( 'Sales'[Quantity] AS   INT ) * PFCAST ( 'Sales'[Net Price] AS   INT )   )
SELECT
    'Product'[Color],
    SUM ( @$Expr0 )
FROM 'Sales'
    LEFT OUTER JOIN 'Product'
        ON 'Sales'[ProductKey]='Product'[ProductKey];
```

A second storage engine query retrieves just the product colors:

```
SELECT
    'Product'[Color]
FROM 'Product';
```

The last two queries are the most interesting ones. The third query computes *Sales Amount* and *Total Cost* – needed to compute *Margin* – only for the Transparent color:

```
WITH
    $Expr0 := ( PFCAST ( 'Sales'[Quantity] AS   INT ) * PFCAST ( 'Sales'[Unit Cost] AS   INT )   ),
    $Expr1 := ( PFCAST ( 'Sales'[Quantity] AS   INT ) * PFCAST ( 'Sales'[Net Price] AS   INT )   )
SELECT
    SUM ( @$Expr0 ),
    SUM ( @$Expr1 )
FROM 'Sales'
    LEFT OUTER JOIN 'Product'
        ON 'Sales'[ProductKey]='Product'[ProductKey]
WHERE
    'Product'[Color] = 'Transparent';
```

The last query retrieves the total cost for all the remaining colors:

```
WITH
    $Expr0 := ( PFCAST ( 'Sales'[Quantity] AS   INT ) * PFCAST ( 'Sales'[Unit Cost] AS   INT )   )
SELECT
    'Product'[Color],
    SUM ( @$Expr0 )
FROM 'Sales'
    LEFT OUTER JOIN 'Product'
        ON 'Sales'[ProductKey]='Product'[ProductKey]
WHERE
    'Product'[Color] IN (
        'Grey', 'Gold', 'Azure', 'Silver', 'Silver Grey', 'Blue', 'White',
        'Red', 'Black', 'Green'..[15 total values, not all displayed] ) ;
```

The storage engine queries confirm the previous findings. The last item we check is the server timings panel.

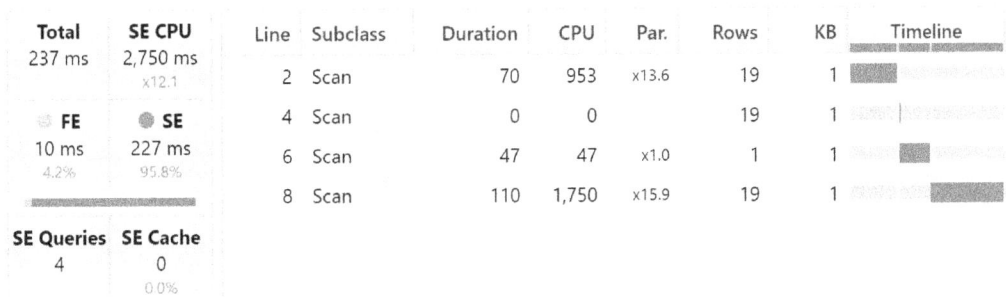

Total	SE CPU	Line	Subclass	Duration	CPU	Par.	Rows	KB	Timeline
237 ms	2,750 ms	2	Scan	70	953	x13.6	19	1	
	x12.1								
FE	SE	4	Scan	0	0		19	1	
10 ms	227 ms	6	Scan	47	47	x1.0	1	1	
4.2%	95.8%	8	Scan	110	1,750	x15.9	19	1	

SE Queries	SE Cache
4	0
	0.0%

The query is fast: 237 milliseconds. Most of the time is spent in the storage engine, and the degree of parallelism is rather good.

So far, we have double-checked how a regular IF statement is solved in the formula engine. After all this work, we might have already forgotten the original question: how is IF doing compared to IF.EAGER? Based on our DAX knowledge, IF.EAGER should show a different query plan, with a single datacache containing all the measures and an outer If to choose which measure to use based on the value of the condition.

Here is the query; the only difference with the previous one is the use of IF.EAGER instead of IF:

```
EVALUATE
ADDCOLUMNS (
    VALUES ( 'Product'[Color] ),
    "Test",
        IF.EAGER (
            [Sales Amount] < 1E7,
            [Margin],
            [Total Cost]
        )
)
```

As usual, let us start by looking at the logical query plan and follow the same process we performed with the previous query.

Line	Logical Query Plan
1	AddColumns: RelLogOp DependOnCols()() 0-1 RequiredCols(0, 1)('Product'[Color], ''[Sales])
2	Scan_Vertipaq: RelLogOp DependOnCols()() 0-0 RequiredCols(0)('Product'[Color])
3	VarScope: ScaLogOp DependOnCols(0)('Product'[Color]) Currency DominantValue=BLANK
4	Subtract: ScaLogOp VarName=<000002946709A800> MeasureRef=[Margin] DependOnCols(0)('Product'[Color]) Currency DominantValue=BLANK
5	ScalarVarProxy: ScaLogOp MeasureRef=[Sales Amount] DependOnCols(0)('Product'[Color]) Currency DominantValue=BLANK
6	Sum_Vertipaq: ScaLogOp MeasureRef=[Total Cost] DependOnCols(0)('Product'[Color]) Currency DominantValue=BLANK
7	Scan_Vertipaq: RelLogOp DependOnCols(0)('Product'[Color]) 1-68 RequiredCols(0, 7, 10)('Product'[Color], 'Sales'[Quantity], 'Sales'[Unit Cost])
8	Multiply: ScaLogOp DependOnCols(7, 10)('Sales'[Quantity], 'Sales'[Unit Cost]) Currency DominantValue=NONE
9	'Sales'[Quantity]: ScaLogOp DependOnCols(7)('Sales'[Quantity]) Integer DominantValue=NONE
10	'Sales'[Unit Cost]: ScaLogOp DependOnCols(10)('Sales'[Unit Cost]) Currency DominantValue=NONE
11	ScalarVarProxy: ScaLogOp VarName=<0000029467099180> MeasureRef=[Total Cost] DependOnCols(0)('Product'[Color]) Currency DominantValue=BL
12	If: ScaLogOp DependOnCols(0)('Product'[Color]) Currency DominantValue=BLANK
13	LessThan: ScaLogOp DependOnCols(0)('Product'[Color]) Boolean DominantValue=true
14	Currency->Double: ScaLogOp DependOnCols(0)('Product'[Color]) Double DominantValue=BLANK
15	Sum_Vertipaq: ScaLogOp MeasureRef=[Sales Amount] DependOnCols(0)('Product'[Color]) Currency DominantValue=BLANK
16	Scan_Vertipaq: RelLogOp DependOnCols(0)('Product'[Color]) 1-68 RequiredCols(0, 7, 9)('Product'[Color], 'Sales'[Quantity], 'Sales'[Net Price])
17	Multiply: ScaLogOp DependOnCols(7, 9)('Sales'[Quantity], 'Sales'[Net Price]) Currency DominantValue=NONE
18	'Sales'[Quantity]: ScaLogOp DependOnCols(7)('Sales'[Quantity]) Integer DominantValue=NONE
19	'Sales'[Net Price]: ScaLogOp DependOnCols(9)('Sales'[Net Price]) Currency DominantValue=NONE
20	Constant: ScaLogOp DependOnCols()() Double DominantValue=10000000
21	PredicateCheck: RelLogOp DependOnCols(0)('Product'[Color]) RequiredCols(0)('Product'[Color])
22	ScalarVarProxy: ScaLogOp DependOnCols(0)('Product'[Color]) Boolean DominantValue=true
23	PredicateCheck: RelLogOp DependOnCols(0)('Product'[Color]) RequiredCols(0)('Product'[Color])
24	ScalarVarProxy: ScaLogOp DependOnCols(0)('Product'[Color]) Boolean DominantValue=true
25	ScalarVarProxy: ScaLogOp DependOnCols(0)('Product'[Color]) Currency DominantValue=BLANK RefVarName=<000002946709A800>
26	ScalarVarProxy: ScaLogOp DependOnCols(0)('Product'[Color]) Currency DominantValue=BLANK RefVarName=<0000029467099180>

The logical query plan is a bit shorter than the previous one, which is already a good sign. Moreover, it shows an interesting behavior: variables are defined automatically inside the query plan in the ScalarVarProxy lines, despite no variable being used in our original DAX code. Let us jump right in!

The outer operator is AddColumns in line 1, which adds to the datacache produced in line 2 (this contains the colors) the result of the entire block starting at line 3 and going to the end of the query. Quite surprisingly, this is a VarScope block, which introduces a set of variables.

The DAX optimizer automatically creates these variables to store temporary structures. You can tell that from their names: *000002946709A800* defined at line 4, and *0000029467099180* defined at line 11. The first variable (line 4) contains a table containing *Margin* sliced by *Product[Color]*. The second variable (line 11) contains *Total Cost* sliced by *Product[Color]*. The *If* operator, this time, is no longer the top operator. Instead, *If* is executed after the variables have already been computed. This shows the behavior of eager computation: first, the engine computes all the values, and only later does it choose which one to use.

The *If* operator starts at line 12. Between lines 13 and 20, we see the check that the *Sales Amount* is less than 10 million; between lines 21 and 24 is a split of colors into buckets. And finally, lines 25 and 26 retrieve the value to use from the variables computed previously.

As expected, the logical query plan shows a different behavior than the previous DAX query using IF. The physical query plan is even more surprising because it is much shorter than the previous one. It consists of just 21 lines.

Line	Records	Physical Query Plan
1		AddColumns: IterPhyOp LogOp=AddColumns IterCols(0, 1)('Product'[Color], ''[Sales])
2	16	Spool_Iterator<SpoolIterator>: IterPhyOp LogOp=Scan_Vertipaq IterCols(0)('Product'[Color]) #Records=16 #KeyCols=138 #ValueCols=0
3	16	ProjectionSpool<ProjectFusion<>>: SpoolPhyOp #Records=16
4		**Cache: IterPhyOp #FieldCols=1 #ValueCols=0**
5		If: LookupPhyOp LogOp=If LookupCols(0)('Product'[Color]) Currency
6		LessThan: LookupPhyOp LogOp=LessThan LookupCols(0)('Product'[Color]) Boolean
7		Currency->Double: LookupPhyOp LogOp=Currency->DoubleCurrency->Double LookupCols(0)('Product'[Color]) Double
8	16	SpoolLookup: LookupPhyOp LogOp=Sum_Vertipaq LookupCols(0)('Product'[Color]) Currency #Records=16 #KeyCols=138 #ValueCols=2
9	16	ProjectionSpool<ProjectFusion<Copy, Copy>>: SpoolPhyOp #Records=16
10		**Cache: IterPhyOp #FieldCols=1 #ValueCols=2**
11		Constant: LookupPhyOp LogOp=Constant Double 10000000
12		Subtract: LookupPhyOp LogOp=Subtract LookupCols(0)('Product'[Color]) Currency
13	16	SpoolLookup: LookupPhyOp LogOp=Sum_Vertipaq LookupCols(0)('Product'[Color]) Currency #Records=16 #KeyCols=138 #ValueCols=2 Do
14	16	ProjectionSpool<ProjectFusion<Copy, Copy>>: SpoolPhyOp #Records=16
15		**Cache: IterPhyOp #FieldCols=1 #ValueCols=2**
16	16	SpoolLookup: LookupPhyOp LogOp=Sum_Vertipaq LookupCols(0)('Product'[Color]) Currency #Records=16 #KeyCols=138 #ValueCols=2 Do
17	16	ProjectionSpool<ProjectFusion<Copy, Copy>>: SpoolPhyOp #Records=16
18		**Cache: IterPhyOp #FieldCols=1 #ValueCols=2**
19	16	SpoolLookup: LookupPhyOp LogOp=Sum_Vertipaq LookupCols(0)('Product'[Color]) Currency #Records=16 #KeyCols=138 #ValueCols=2 Domi
20	16	ProjectionSpool<ProjectFusion<Copy, Copy>>: SpoolPhyOp #Records=16
21		**Cache: IterPhyOp #FieldCols=1 #ValueCols=2**

By just looking at the physical query plan, we would erroneously conclude that several storage engine queries are being executed. Indeed, we have a Cache operator at lines 4, 10, 15, 18, and 21. However, upon inspection of the storage engine queries, we discover that the same datacache is being used in multiple places. Indeed, there are only two storage engine queries being executed this time. One, as expected, retrieves the product colors:

```
SELECT
    'Product'[Color]
FROM 'Product';
```

The second query, the most interesting one, is retrieving *Sales Amount* and the *Total Cost* sliced by *Product[Color]*, for all the colors. This query is consumed in four different Cache operators in the query plan. Please note that there is no WHERE condition:

```
WITH
    $Expr0 := ( PFCAST ( 'Sales'[Quantity] AS    INT ) * PFCAST ( 'Sales'[Net Price] AS    INT )   ),
    $Expr1 := ( PFCAST ( 'Sales'[Quantity] AS    INT ) * PFCAST ( 'Sales'[Unit Cost] AS    INT )   )
SELECT
    'Product'[Color],
    SUM ( @$Expr0 ),
    SUM ( @$Expr1 )
FROM 'Sales'
    LEFT OUTER JOIN 'Product'
        ON 'Sales'[ProductKey]='Product'[ProductKey];
```

Be mindful that this datacache does not contain the values that need to be returned. Indeed, the result should contain *Margin*, which is produced by subtracting *Total Cost* from *Sales Amount*. If we look back at the physical query plan, we discover at line 12 the subtraction required to produce *Margin* out of *Sales Amount* and *Total Cost*. In other words, the DAX optimizer figured out that a single datacache with *Sales Amount* and *Total Cost* is enough to produce the result only if it leaves the subtraction operation up to the formula engine.

Finally, when it comes to the server timings pane, the simplicity of the query plan is reflected in a shorter execution time. Please note that the first query executed is the more complex one.

Total	SE CPU	Line	Subclass	Duration	CPU	Par.	Rows	KB	Timeline
112 ms	1,500 ms								
	x13.9	2	Scan	107	1,500	x14.0	19	1	
FE	**SE**	4	Scan	1	0		19	1	
4 ms	108 ms								
3.6%	96.4%								

SE Queries	SE Cache
2	0
	0.0%

The version of the query with IF.EAGER performs much better than the version with IF. The version with IF.EAGER runs in about half the time that the version with IF took. The ratio between formula and storage engines favors the storage engine, which consumes 96.4% of the total execution time.

However, it would be wrong to assume that IF.EAGER is always faster than a regular IF with strict evaluation. There are scenarios where IF performs better and scenarios where IF.EAGER is the better choice. Once you understand the difference in the query plan, you can make an educated choice based on the complexity of the formulas, the size of datacaches being generated, and the sparsity of the calculation.

For example, if one of the two branches of the conditional logic is traversed a tiny number of times and the formula to be computed in that case is very expensive, then the regular IF with strict logic is your best option. The goal of this demo is to show the different query plans generated in the two scenarios. The choice of whether to use IF or IF.EAGER depends on you and must be based on further reasoning. Do not just choose randomly: by default, IF uses strict evaluation, and it is a good default behavior. If you notice poor performance, measuring improvements with eager evaluation might drive you to choose IF.EAGER instead. However, using IF.EAGER as the default choice, is not a winning strategy.

You might also have noted that IF.EAGER artificially introduces variables in the query plan to force eager evaluation. This means that by introducing variables in your DAX code, you are making the same choice: you clearly state that you prefer eager evaluation over strict evaluation.

Filtering with DAX versus using relationships

As a further analysis of any query plan, it is interesting to see the huge difference between filtering a table through DAX code versus using a relationship. We already know – based on experience – that using a relationship is our best option. It is helpful to see the details by analyzing the query plan.

Here is the code we want to test:

```
EVALUATE
ADDCOLUMNS (
    VALUES ( 'Product'[Color] ),
    "Sales",
        VAR ProductKeys =
            CALCULATETABLE ( VALUES ( 'Product'[ProductKey] ) )
        VAR SalesOfProds =
            FILTER ( Sales, Sales[ProductKey] IN ProductKeys )
        VAR Result =
            SUMX ( SalesOfProds, Sales[Quantity] * Sales[Net Price] )
        RETURN
            Result
)
```

The outer ADDCOLUMNS iterates over *Product[Color]*. For each color, we retrieve the list of product keys of the products of that color and create a variable with the sales of those products. Finally, we iterate over those sales and compute the sales amount. In the code, we deliberately avoid using CALCULATE, apart from the computation of *ProductKeys*, to prevent triggering a context transition and a consequent automatic filter of *Sales*. In other words, we needed to prevent DAX from relying on the relationship.

The physical query plan is 42 lines long, already a bit too long to be adequately analyzed without some understanding of the underlying algorithm.

Line	Records	Physical Query Plan
1		AddColumns: IterPhyOp LogOp=AddColumns IterCols(0, 1)('Product'[Color], ''[Sales])
2	16	Spool_Iterator<SpoolIterator>: IterPhyOp LogOp=Scan_Vertipaq IterCols(0)('Product'[Color]) #Records=16 #KeyCols=138 #ValueCols=0
3	16	ProjectionSpool<ProjectFusion<>>: SpoolPhyOp #Records=16
4		**Cache: IterPhyOp #FieldCols=1 #ValueCols=0**
5	16	SpoolLookup: LookupPhyOp LogOp=SumX LookupCols(0)('Product'[Color]) Currency #Records=16 #KeyCols=1 #ValueCols=1 DominantValue=BLANK
6	16	AggregationSpool<Sum>: SpoolPhyOp #Records=16
7		Extend_Lookup: IterPhyOp LogOp=Multiply IterCols(7, 9)('Sales'[Quantity], 'Sales'[Net Price])
8		Proxy: IterPhyOp LogOp=TableVarProxy IterCols(0, 1, 6, 7, 9)('Product'[Color], 'Sales'[RowNumber-2662979B-1795-4F74-8F37-6A1BA8059B61], 'Sales'[ProductKey
9		Filter: IterPhyOp LogOp=Filter IterCols(0, 1, 6, 7, 9)('Product'[Color], 'Sales'[RowNumber-2662979B-1795-4F74-8F37-6A1BA8059B61], 'Sales'[ProductKey], 'Sale
10		CrossApply: IterPhyOp LogOp=Not IterCols(0, 6)('Product'[Color], 'Sales'[ProductKey])
11	225,616,948	Spool_MultiValuedHashLookup: IterPhyOp LogOp=Scan_Vertipaq LookupCols(6)('Sales'[ProductKey]) IterCols(1, 7, 9)('Sales'[RowNumber-2662979B-1795
12	225,616,948	ProjectionSpool<ProjectFusion<>>: SpoolPhyOp #Records=225616948
13		**Cache: IterPhyOp #FieldCols=4 #ValueCols=0**
14		Not: IterPhyOp LogOp=Not IterCols(0, 6)('Product'[Color], 'Sales'[ProductKey])
15		Extend_Const: IterPhyOp LogOp=IsEmpty IterCols(0, 6)('Product'[Color], 'Sales'[ProcuctKey])
16	2,517	Spool_Iterator<SpoolIterator>: IterPhyOp LogOp=Filter IterCols(0, 6)('Product'[Color], 'Sales'[ProductKey]) #Records=2517 #KeyCols=2 #ValueCols=
17	2,517	AggregationSpool<GroupBy>: SpoolPhyOp #Records=2517
18		Filter: IterPhyOp LogOp=Filter IterCols(0, 6, 69)('Product'[Color], 'Sales'[ProductKey], 'Product'[ProductKey])
19		CrossApply: IterPhyOp LogOp=Is IterCols(6, 69)('Sales'[ProductKey], 'Product'[ProductKey])
20	2,517	Spool_MultiValuedHashLookup: IterPhyOp LogOp=TableVarProxy_VertiPaq LookupCols(69)('Product'[ProductKey]) IterCols(0)('Product'[C
21	2,517	ProjectionSpool<ProjectFusion<>>: SpoolPhyOp #Records=2517
22		**Cache: IterPhyOp #FieldCols=2 #ValueCols=0**
23		InnerHashJoin: IterPhyOp LogOp=Is IterCols(6, 69)('Sales'[ProductKey], 'Product'[ProductKey])
24		Extend_Lookup: IterPhyOp LogOp=Extend_Lookup'Sales'[ProductKey] IterCols(6)('Sales'[ProductKey])
25	2,517	Spool_Iterator<SpoolIterator>: IterPhyOp LogOp=Scan_Vertipaq IterCols(6)('Sales'[ProductKey]) #Records=2517 #KeyCols=1 #Valu
26	2,517	AggregationSpool<GroupBy>: SpoolPhyOp #Records=2517
27	225,616,948	Spool_Iterator<SpoolIterator>: IterPhyOp LogOp=Scan_Vertipaq IterCols(1, 6, 7, 9)('Sales'[RowNumber-2662979B-1795-4F74-
28	225,616,948	ProjectionSpool<ProjectFusion<>>: SpoolPhyOp #Records=225616948
29		**Cache: IterPhyOp #FieldCols=4 #ValueCols=0**
30		ColValue<'Sales'[ProductKey]>: LookupPhyOp LogOp=ColValue<'Sales'[ProductKey]>'Sales'[ProductKey] LookupCols(6)('Sales'[Proc
31	2,517	HashLookup: IterPhyOp LogOp=HashLookup'Product'[ProductKey] IterCols(69)('Product'[ProductKey]) #Recs=2517
32	2,517	HashByValue: SpoolPhyOp #Records=2517
33		Extend_Lookup: IterPhyOp LogOp=Extend_Lookup'Product'[ProductKey] IterCols(69)('Product'[ProductKey])
34	2,517	Spool_Iterator<SpoolIterator>: IterPhyOp LogOp=TableVarProxy_VertiPaq IterCols(69)('Product'[ProductKey]) #Records=2517
35	2,517	AggregationSpool<GroupBy>: SpoolPhyOp #Records=2517
36	2,517	Spool_Iterator<SpoolIterator>: IterPhyOp LogOp=TableVarProxy_VertiPaq IterCols(0, 69)('Product'[Color], 'Product'[Produ
37	2,517	ProjectionSpool<ProjectFusion<>>: SpoolPhyOp #Records=2517
38		**Cache: IterPhyOp #FieldCols=2 #ValueCols=0**
39		ColValue<'Product'[ProductKey]>: LookupPhyOp LogOp=ColValue<'Product'[ProductKey]>'Product'[ProductKey] LookupCols
40		Multiply: LookupPhyOp LogOp=Multiply LookupCols(7, 9)('Sales'[Quantity], 'Sales'[Net Price]) Currency
41		ColValue<'Sales'[Quantity]>: LookupPhyOp LogOp=ColValue<'Sales'[Quantity]>'Sales'[Quantity] LookupCols(7)('Sales'[Quantity]) Integer
42		ColValue<'Sales'[Net Price]>: LookupPhyOp LogOp=ColValue<'Sales'[Net Price]>'Sales'[Net Price] LookupCols(9)('Sales'[Net Price]) Currency

Because of the complexity of the physical query plan, it is better to look at the logical query plan in order to start getting an idea of what the query executes. Indeed, the logical query plan is somewhat simpler.

1	AddColumns: RelLogOp DependOnCols()() 0-1 RequiredCols(0, 1)('Product'[Color], ''[Sales])
2	Scan_Vertipaq: RelLogOp DependOnCols()() 0-0 RequiredCols(0)('Product'[Color])
3	VarScope: ScaLogOp DependOnCols(0)('Product'[Color]) Currency DominantValue=BLANK
4	Scan_Vertipaq: RelLogOp VarName=ProductKeys DependOnCols(0)('Product'[Color]) 1-1 RequiredCols(0, 1)('Product'[Color], 'Product'[ProductKey])
5	Filter: RelLogOp VarName=SalesOfProds DependOnCols(0)('Product'[Color]) 1-68 RequiredCols(0, 1, 6, 7, 9)('Product'[Color], 'Sales'[RowNumber-266
6	Scan_Vertipaq: RelLogOp DependOnCols()() 1-68 RequiredCols(1, 6, 7, 9)('Sales'[RowNumber-2662979B-1795-4F74-8F37-6A1BA8059B61], 'Sales'[
7	Not: ScaLogOp DependOnCols(0, 6)('Product'[Color], 'Sales'[ProductKey]) Boolean DominantValue=false
8	IsEmpty: ScaLogOp DependOnCols(0, 6)('Product'[Color], 'Sales'[ProductKey]) Boolean DominantValue=true
9	Filter: RelLogOp DependOnCols(0, 6)('Product'[Color], 'Sales'[ProductKey]) 69-69 RequiredCols(0, 6, 69)('Product'[Color], 'Sales'[ProductKey],
10	TableVarProxy_VertiPaq: RelLogOp DependOnCols(0)('Product'[Color]) 69-69 RequiredCols(0, 69)('Product'[Color], 'Product'[ProductKey]) F
11	Is: ScaLogOp DependOnCols(6, 69)('Sales'[ProductKey], 'Product'[ProductKey]) Boolean DominantValue=false
12	'Product'[ProductKey]: ScaLogOp DependOnCols(69)('Product'[ProductKey]) Integer DominantValue=NONE
13	'Sales'[ProductKey]: ScaLogOp DependOnCols(6)('Sales'[ProductKey]) Integer DominantValue=NONE
14	SumX: ScaLogOp VarName=Result DependOnCols(0)('Product'[Color]) Currency DominantValue=BLANK
15	TableVarProxy: RelLogOp DependOnCols(0)('Product'[Color]) 1-68 RequiredCols(0, 1, 6, 7, 9)('Product'[Color], 'Sales'[RowNumber-2662979B-1795-
16	Multiply: ScaLogOp DependOnCols(7, 9)('Sales'[Quantity], 'Sales'[Net Price]) Currency DominantValue=NONE
17	'Sales'[Quantity]: ScaLogOp DependOnCols(7)('Sales'[Quantity]) Integer DominantValue=NONE
18	'Sales'[Net Price]: ScaLogOp DependOnCols(9)('Sales'[Net Price]) Currency DominantValue=NONE
19	ScalarVarProxy: ScaLogOp DependOnCols(0)('Product'[Color]) Currency DominantValue=BLANK RefVarName=Result

We added a couple of vertical lines to make it easier to follow the indentation of arguments.

As expected, the outer operator at line 1 is AddColumns. The first argument of AddColumns – the table to iterate – is a Scan_Vertipaq that retrieves the values of *Product[Color]*. The second argument of AddColumns is VarScope. VarScope introduces a scope for variables.

Please note that the entire VarScope depends on the *Product[Color]* column. Indeed, all three variables depend on the color currently being iterated . The first variable definition (*SalesOfProds*, line 5) is truncated in the figure. The full operator is the following:

```
RelLogOp VarName=SalesOfProds
DependOnCols(0)('Product'[Color])
1-68 RequiredCols(0, 1, 6, 7, 9)
('Product'[Color], 'Sales'[RowNumber-2662979B-1795-4F74-8F37-6A1BA8059B61], 'Sales'[ProductKey], 'Sales'[Quantity],
'Sales'[Net Price])
```

This operator corresponds to a VertiPaq scan that retrieves the columns from *Sales* that are needed to compute *Sales Amount* grouped by *Product[Color]*. The presence of *RowNumber* is required to retrieve all the rows from the table without any grouping.

The second variable goes from lines 5 to 13, which is pretty interesting, as the entire algorithm is there. Spend some time looking at that section; you will notice two Filter operators. This is somewhat weird, as the variable defined in DAX contains only one filter. You should consider that the variable depends on *Product[Color]*, as it is declared and used in a row context created by ADDCOLUMNS. Indeed, the definition of *SalesOfProds* retrieves the combinations of columns from *Sales*. For each row, it checks if that row belongs to the list of product keys present in the *ProductKeys* variable (see line 10). *ProductKeys* (which is defined in line 4) contains both *Product[ProductKey]* and *Product[Color]* columns.

Finally, it is worth noting that the IN operator in DAX was translated into a pair of Not and IsEmpty operators. Even though the two techniques achieve the same goal, it is interesting to see how different the implementation is, when compared with the DAX code.

From line 14 to 18, a SumX scans the *SalesOfProd* variable (line 15) and performs the multiplication.

Now that we have an idea about the algorithm, we can elaborate farther. The entire algorithm is quite linear, and we would expect problems mainly in the retrieval of the *SalesOfProds* variable. Indeed, this variable needs to contain all the rows from *Sales* (because it is grouping by the row number), producing a huge materialization.

A deeper look at the physical query plan confirms our fears. At line 11 and line 27, some operators consume a datacache containing 225 million rows – the size of the *Sales* table in our demo model.

Line	Records	Physical Query Plan
1		AddColumns: IterPhyOp LogOp=AddColumns IterCols(0, 1)('Product'[Color], ''[Sales])
2	16	Spool_Iterator<SpoolIterator>: IterPhyOp LogOp=Scan_Vertipaq IterCols(0)('Product'[Color]) #Rec
3	16	ProjectionSpool<ProjectFusion<>>: SpoolPhyOp #Records=16
4		**Cache: IterPhyOp #FieldCols=1 #ValueCols=0**
5	16	SpoolLookup: LookupPhyOp LogOp=SumX LookupCols(0)('Product'[Color]) Currency #Records=1
6	16	AggregationSpool<Sum>: SpoolPhyOp #Records=16
7		Extend_Lookup: IterPhyOp LogOp=Multiply IterCols(7, 9)('Sales'[Quantity], 'Sales'[Net Price])
8		Proxy: IterPhyOp LogOp=TableVarProxy IterCols(0, 1, 6, 7, 9)('Product'[Color], 'Sales'[RowN
9		Filter: IterPhyOp LogOp=Filter IterCols(0, 1, 6, 7, 9)('Product'[Color], 'Sales'[RowNumber
10		CrossApply: IterPhyOp LogOp=Not IterCols(0, 6)('Product'[Color], 'Sales'[ProductKey
11	225,616,948	Spool_MultiValuedHashLookup: IterPhyOp LogOp=Scan_Vertipaq LookupCols(6)('
12	225,616,948	ProjectionSpool<ProjectFusion<>>: SpoolPhyOp #Records=225616948
13		**Cache: IterPhyOp #FieldCols=4 #ValueCols=0**

It is important to note that the same datacache is used twice. There is a price to generate and materialize the datacache, but there is also a price to consume it due to its size. The more operators scanning the datacache, the more pressure on the formula engine.

The final check to perform to confirm our understanding of the algorithm is to verify the execution time.

Total	SE CPU	Line	Subclass	Duration	CPU	Par.	Rows	KB	Timeline	Query
122,793 ms	136,219 ms									
	x2.3	2	Scan	58,860	136,219	x2.3	225,616,948	1,762,633		SELECT 'Sales'[R
FE	● **SE**	4	Scan	1	0		2,517	10		SELECT 'Product
63,932 ms	58,861 ms	6	Scan	0	0		19	1		SELECT 'Product
52.1%	47.9%									

SE Queries	SE Cache
3	0
	0.0%

The execution time is split half and half between the formula engine and the storage engine. The degree of parallelism of the storage engine is extremely low (considering there are 64 cores in the machine used for the tests), and there is a storage engine query generating 225 million rows. The reduced degree of parallelism is because the process of materialization – that is, the generation of the datacache – is sequential. It takes so long to materialize the datacache that this operation adversely affects the overall degree of parallelism.

We knew in advance that the query would be a terrible choice. Nonetheless, it is helpful to learn the details to understand exactly what the DAX engine needs to do when we force it to resolve relationships through the formula engine.

The very same query can be executed relying on the existing relationship between *Sales* and *Product*:

```
EVALUATE
ADDCOLUMNS (
    VALUES ( 'Product'[Color] ),
    "Sales", [Sales Amount]
)
```

The physical query plan is straightforward. It clearly indicates that most of the work was pushed down to the storage engine, thus reducing the work of the formula engine to scanning a couple of datacaches with only 16 rows.

Line	Records	Physical Query Plan
1		AddColumns: IterPhyOp LogOp=AddColumns IterCols(0, 1)('Product'[Color], "[Sales])
2	16	Spool_Iterator<SpoolIterator>: IterPhyOp LogOp=Scan_Vertipaq IterCols(0)('Product'[Color]) #Records=16 #KeyCols=68 #ValueCols=0
3	16	ProjectionSpool<ProjectFusion<>>: SpoolPhyOp #Records=16
4		Cache: IterPhyOp #FieldCols=1 #ValueCols=0
5	16	SpoolLookup: LookupPhyOp LogOp=Sum_Vertipaq LookupCols(0)('Product'[Color]) Currency #Records=16 #KeyCols=68 #ValueCols=1
6	16	ProjectionSpool<ProjectFusion<Copy>>: SpoolPhyOp #Records=16
7		Cache: IterPhyOp #FieldCols=1 #ValueCols=1

And as expected, the performance is strikingly better.

Total	SE CPU	Line	Subclass	Duration	CPU	Par.	Rows	KB	Timeline	Query
80 ms	813 ms									
	x11.0	2	Scan	71	813	x11.5	19	1		WITH $Expr
FE	SE	4	Scan	3	0		19	1		SELECT 'Pro
6 ms	74 ms									
7.5%	92.5%									

SE Queries	SE Cache
2	0
	0.0%

We have a reasonable degree of parallelism, a highly-reduced materialization, and a query that runs several orders of magnitude faster than the previous one.

This is not to say that we performed an excellent optimization. What we did in this example was to deliberately write bad DAX code to highly increase the usage of the formula engine. A seasoned DAX developer would never write a query like the one we started with. Nonetheless, the takeaway of this demo is not how to avoid bad DAX code. Instead, it is to understand the differences between using a relationship, which is an object that the storage engine can use, versus using DAX to move a filter between tables, which requires multiple requests to the storage engine and a following computation performed by the formula engine.

Using DAX to move a filter increases the use of the formula engine. As we have seen, it results in a more complex query plan, larger materialization, and a largely-decreased use of parallelism. In other words, if you ever had to choose between using a regular one-to-many relationship or moving a filter between tables using DAX, this demo clearly showed that a relationship is by far your best option.

Understanding SWITCH optimization

As we have already discussed, the presence of conditional logic in a DAX expression requires considerable effort from both the formula engine and the storage engine. When the value of an expression depends on a condition, the formula engine splits the dataset into different buckets and evaluates the results based on the value of the condition. IF.EAGER or a smart use of variables can provide some benefits, as it reduces the number of storage engine queries executed and simplifies the overall query plan.

A common use of conditional logic is that of using a SWITCH statement to check for the value of a parameter and then performing different calculations based on that parameter. Users can often select the parameter with a slicer to change the content of the report based on their needs. The parameter is almost always stored in a table disconnected from the remaining part of the model.

As an example, we add to our Contoso model a parameter table containing three columns: *Scenario*, *Multiplier*, and *Sort Order*. The goal of the table is to multiply the sales amount by the multiplier to let our users perform a what-if analysis. Here is the code for the additional table:

```
Scenario =
    SELECTCOLUMNS (
        {
            ( "Low",    0.9, 1 ),
            ( "Medium", 1.0, 2 ),
            ( "High",   1.1, 3 )
        },
        "Scenario", [Value1],
        "Multiplier", [Value2],
        "Sort Order", [Value3]
    )
```

We then author a measure that uses the selection of the *Scenario[Scenario]* column to change the *Sales Amount* value. We can do that in different ways: by using a hard-coded value in the formula or by relying on the SELECTEDVALUE of the *Scenario[Multiplier]* column, thus obtaining a data-driven measure:

```
DEFINE
    MEASURE Sales[Amount Corrected Data Driven] =
        [Sales Amount] * SELECTEDVALUE ( Scenario[Multiplier] )

    MEASURE Sales[Amount Corrected Hardcoded] =
        [Sales Amount] *
        SWITCH (
            SELECTEDVALUE ( Scenario[Scenario] ),
            "Low", 0.9,
            "Medium", 1.0,
            "High", 1.1,
            1
        )

EVALUATE
SUMMARIZECOLUMNS (
    Scenario[Scenario],
    "Amount Corrected", [Amount Corrected Hardcoded]
)
```

As a rule of thumb, the data-driven version of the code is a better option. As it doesn't contain any conditional logic, it generally produces a better query plan. In this section, we are interested in describing the behavior of conditional logic in DAX. Therefore, we analyze only the hardcoded version.

The result of the query contains the sales amount by using the *Amount Corrected Hardcoded* measure in the three different scenarios (low, medium, and high).

Scenario	Amount Corrected
Low	206,162,682,910.20
Medium	229,069,647,678.00
High	251,976,612,445.80

We used the hard-coded version of the formula because it makes it easier to understand the query plan.

SWITCH is converted internally into a set of nested IF statements. The measure compares the current value of the *Scenario[Scenario]* column against the three values. If there is no match, the default value is 1. Therefore, we expect four possible multipliers controlled by three IF statements. Here is what we find in the query plan.

Line	Records	Physical Query Plan
1		GroupSemijoin: IterPhyOp LogOp=GroupSemiJoin IterCols(0, 1)('Scenario'[Scenario], ''[Amount Corrected])
2		Extend_Lookup: IterPhyOp LogOp=Multiply IterCols(0)('Scenario'[Scenario])
3		CrossApply: IterPhyOp LogOp=Sum_Vertipaq
4	3	Spool_Iterator<SpoolIterator>: IterPhyOp LogOp=Scan_Vertipaq IterCols(0)('Scenario'[Scenario]) #Records=3 #KeyCols=82 #Valu
5	3	ProjectionSpool<ProjectFusion<>>: SpoolPhyOp #Records=3
6		**Cache: IterPhyOp #FieldCols=1 #ValueCols=0**
7	1	Spool_Iterator<SpoolIterator>: IterPhyOp LogOp=Sum_Vertipaq #Records=1 #KeyCols=82 #ValueCols=1
8	1	ProjectionSpool<ProjectFusion<Copy>>: SpoolPhyOp #Records=1
9		**Cache: IterPhyOp #FieldCols=0 #ValueCols=1**
10		If: LookupPhyOp LogOp=Switch LookupCols(0)('Scenario'[Scenario]) Double
11		'Scenario'[Scenario] IS Low: LookupPhyOp LogOp='Scenario'[Scenario] IS Low'Scenario'[Scenario] IS Low LookupCols(0)('Scenaric
12		Constant: LookupPhyOp LogOp=Constant Double 0.9
13		If: LookupPhyOp LogOp=Switch LookupCols(0)('Scenario'[Scenario]) Double
14		'Scenario'[Scenario] IS Medium: LookupPhyOp LogOp='Scenario'[Scenario] IS Medium'Scenario'[Scenario] IS Medium Lookup(
15		Constant: LookupPhyOp LogOp=Constant Double 1
16		If: LookupPhyOp LogOp=Switch LookupCols(0)('Scenario'[Scenario]) Double
17		'Scenario'[Scenario] IS High: LookupPhyOp LogOp='Scenario'[Scenario] IS High'Scenario'[Scenario] IS High LookupCols(0)('!
18		Constant: LookupPhyOp LogOp=Constant Double 1.1
19		Constant: LookupPhyOp LogOp=Constant Double 1

Line 9 retrieves the value of *Sales Amount*, and line 6 retrieves the values of *Scenario[Scenario]*. The two tables are cross-joined at line 3, and then the Extend_Lookup operator at line 2 creates the new column based on the set of nested IF statements between lines 10 and 19. You can check that lines 12, 15, 18, and 19 show the value of the different multipliers.

The complexity of this query plan depends on the number of rows generated at line 3. The more rows there are, the more effort the formula engine puts into computing the result. Moreover, it also depends on the number of possible parameter values. Indeed, for each row, the formula engine checks the value of the parameter to perform the multiplication.

Right now, the query is extremely fast, as it only scans three rows.

Total	SE CPU		Line	Subclass	Duration	CPU	Par.	Rows	KB	Timeline	Query
48 ms	47 ms x1.1		2	Scan	43	47	x1.1	1	1		WITH $Ex
FE 5 ms 10.4%	**SE** 43 ms 89.6%		4	Scan	0	0		6	1		SELECT 'T

SE Queries 2   SE Cache 0   0.0%

```
SET DC_KIND="AUTO";
WITH
    $Expr0 := ( PFCAST ( 'Sales'[Quantity] AS INT ) * PFCAST ( 'Sales'[Net Price] AS INT ) )
SELECT
    SUM ( @$Expr0 )
FROM 'Sales';
```

The formula engine uses only five milliseconds of CPU. We increase the complexity of the query by adding a grouping by *Customer[City]*, in order to increase the number of rows to 74,311, which – multiplied by the three possible scenarios – requires the formula engine to perform 222,933 iterations:

```
EVALUATE
SUMMARIZECOLUMNS (
    Scenario[Scenario],
    Customer[City],
    "Amount Corrected", [Amount Corrected Hardcoded]
)
```

The server timings panel clearly shows a noticeable growth in the formula engine time.

Total	SE CPU		Line	Subclass	Duration	CPU	Par.	Rows	KB	Timeline	Query
820 ms	5,063 ms x17.1		2	Scan	293	5,063	x17.3	74,311	871		WITH
FE 524 ms 63.9%	**SE** 296 ms 36.1%		4	Scan	3	0		6	1		SELECT

SE Queries 2   SE Cache 0   0.0%

```
SET DC_KIND="AUTO";
WITH
    $Expr0 := ( PFCAST ( 'Sales'[Quantity] AS INT ) * PFCAST ( 'Sales'[Net Price] AS INT ) )
SELECT
    'Customer'[City],
    SUM ( @$Expr0 )
FROM 'Sales'
    LEFT OUTER JOIN 'Customer'
        ON 'Sales'[CustomerKey]='Customer'[CustomerKey];
```

Mostly, these parameters are placed as slicers in a report, and the user chooses one of the possible values. In that scenario, testing for all the possible values is a tremendous waste of time. It would be way better if the Tabular engine could check once and for all the parameter values – then if it finds only one possible value, it would prune the set of IF operators, replacing them with one. That is the exact operation that the SWITCH optimization performs.

Let us change the query by adding a condition that filters only one out of all the possible scenarios:

```
DEFINE
    MEASURE Sales[Amount Corrected Hardcoded] =
        [Sales Amount] *
        SWITCH (
            SELECTEDVALUE ( Scenario[Scenario] ),
            "Low", 0.9,
            "Medium", 1.0,
            "High", 1.1,
            1
        )

EVALUATE
SUMMARIZECOLUMNS (
    Scenario[Scenario],
    Customer[City],
    TREATAS ( { "Low" }, Scenario[Scenario] ),
    "Amount Corrected", [Amount Corrected Hardcoded]
)
```

Because of the filter placed with TREATAS, Tabular knows that only one possible value can be selected. This analysis is performed statically by looking at the code, even before the query starts to be executed. Indeed, the query plan of this latter query is much more simplified.

Line	Records	Physical Query Plan
1		GroupSemijoin: IterPhyOp LogOp=GroupSemiJoin IterCols(0, 1, 2)('Scenario'[Scenario], 'Customer'[City], "[Amount Corr
2		CrossApply: IterPhyOp LogOp=Multiply IterCols(1)('Customer'[City])
3	1	Spool_Iterator<SpoolIterator>: IterPhyOp LogOp=TreatAs IterCols(0)('Scenario'[Scenario]) #Records=1 #KeyCols=
4	1	AggregationSpool<GroupBy>: SpoolPhyOp #Records=1
5		TreatAs: IterPhyOp LogOp=TreatAs IterCols(0)('Scenario'[Scenario])
6		TableCtor: IterPhyOp LogOp=TableCtor IterCols(0)("[Value])
7		Extend_Lookup: IterPhyOp LogOp=Multiply IterCols(1)('Customer'[City])
8	74,311	Spool_Iterator<SpoolIterator>: IterPhyOp LogOp=Sum_Vertipaq IterCols(1)('Customer'[City]) #Records=74311
9	74,311	ProjectionSpool<ProjectFusion<Copy>>: SpoolPhyOp #Records=74311
10		**Cache: IterPhyOp #FieldCols=1 #ValueCols=1**
11		Constant: LookupPhyOp LogOp=Constant Double 0.9

The entire set of IF statements is no longer present. The engine knows in advance that the only valid multiplier is 0.9, shown in line 11. Also, the formula engine no longer scans the *Scenario* table. Because the condition is set with a static value, there is no need to scan the data model to search for values in the *Scenario* table.

The optimization is specific to conditional logic, and the engine needs to understand in a static way that there will be only one row. Depending on how developers express the filter, it might not be possible to determine the parameter's value statically.

For example, developers might prefer the *Scenario[Sort Order]* column instead of the *Scenario[Scenario]* column, as developers prefer to use code instead of strings that can change over time. Therefore, the code of *Amount Corrected Hardcoded* might look like this:

```
DEFINE
    MEASURE Sales[Amount Corrected Hardcoded] =
        [Sales Amount] *
        SWITCH (
            SELECTEDVALUE ( Scenario[Sort Order] ),
            1, 0.9,
            2, 1.0,
            3, 1.1,
            1
        )

EVALUATE
SUMMARIZECOLUMNS (
    Scenario[Scenario],
    Customer[City],
    TREATAS ( { "Low" }, Scenario[Scenario] ),
    "Amount Corrected", [Amount Corrected Hardcoded]
)
```

In this scenario, there is a single value for *Scenario[Sort Order]*. Still, the engine cannot detect it because the filter is on the *Scenario[Scenario]* column, whereas the condition is on the *Scenario[Sort Order]* column.

The query plan is now much more complex, and the set of nested Ifs appears again.

1		GroupSemijoin: IterPhyOp LogOp=GroupSemiJoin IterCols(0, 1, 2)('Scenario'[Scenario], 'Customer'[City], ''[Amount Corrected])
2		Extend_Lookup: IterPhyOp LogOp=Multiply IterCols(0, 1)('Scenario'[Scenario], 'Customer'[City])
3		CrossApply: IterPhyOp LogOp=Sum_Vertipaq IterCols(1)('Customer'[City])
4	1	Spool_Iterator<SpoolIterator>: IterPhyOp LogOp=TreatAs IterCols(0)('Scenario'[Scenario]) #Records=1 #KeyCols=1 #ValueCols=0
5	1	AggregationSpool<GroupBy>: SpoolPhyOp #Records=1
6		TreatAs: IterPhyOp LogOp=TreatAs IterCols(0)('Scenario'[Scenario])
7		TableCtor: IterPhyOp LogOp=TableCtor IterCols(0)(''[Value])
8	74,311	Spool_Iterator<SpoolIterator>: IterPhyOp LogOp=Sum_Vertipaq IterCols(1)('Customer'[City]) #Records=74311 #KeyCols=142 #ValueCols=1
9	74,311	ProjectionSpool<ProjectFusion<Copy>>: SpoolPhyOp #Records=74311
10		**Cache: IterPhyOp #FieldCols=1 #ValueCols=1**
11		If: LookupPhyOp LogOp=Switch LookupCols(0)('Scenario'[Scenario]) Double
12		Is: LookupPhyOp LogOp=Is LookupCols(0)('Scenario'[Scenario]) Boolean
13	1	SpoolLookup: LookupPhyOp LogOp=TableToScalar LookupCols(0)('Scenario'[Scenario]) Integer #Records=1 #KeyCols=1 #ValueCols=1 DominantValue=BLANK
14	1	AggregationSpool<Copy>: SpoolPhyOp #Records=1
15	1	Spool_Iterator<Spool_TableToScalar>: IterPhyOp LogOp=TableToScalar IterCols(0)('Scenario'[Scenario]) #Records=1 #KeyCols=142 #ValueCols=4
16	1	ProjectionSpool<ProjectFusion<Copy, Copy, Copy, Copy>>: SpoolPhyOp #Records=1
17		**Cache: IterPhyOp #FieldCols=0 #ValueCols=4**
18	1	Spool_Iterator<SpoolIterator>: IterPhyOp LogOp=TreatAs IterCols(0)('Scenario'[Scenario]) #Records=1 #KeyCols=1 #ValueCols=0
19	1	AggregationSpool<GroupBy>: SpoolPhyOp #Records=1
20		TreatAs: IterPhyOp LogOp=TreatAs IterCols(0)('Scenario'[Scenario])
21		TableCtor: IterPhyOp LogOp=TableCtor IterCols(0)(''[Value])
22		Constant: LookupPhyOp LogOp=Constant Integer 1
23		Constant: LookupPhyOp LogOp=Constant Double 0.9
24		If: LookupPhyOp LogOp=Switch LookupCols(0)('Scenario'[Scenario]) Double
25		Is: LookupPhyOp LogOp=Is LookupCols(0)('Scenario'[Scenario]) Boolean
26	1	SpoolLookup: LookupPhyOp LogOp=TableToScalar LookupCols(0)('Scenario'[Scenario]) Integer #Records=1 #KeyCols=1 #ValueCols=1 DominantValue=BLAN
27	1	AggregationSpool<Copy>: SpoolPhyOp #Records=1
28	1	Spool_Iterator<Spool_TableToScalar>: IterPhyOp LogOp=TableToScalar IterCols(0)('Scenario'[Scenario]) #Records=1 #KeyCols=142 #ValueCols=4
29	1	ProjectionSpool<ProjectFusion<Copy, Copy, Copy, Copy>>: SpoolPhyOp #Records=1
30		**Cache: IterPhyOp #FieldCols=0 #ValueCols=4**
31	1	Spool_Iterator<SpoolIterator>: IterPhyOp LogOp=TreatAs IterCols(0)('Scenario'[Scenario]) #Records=1 #KeyCols=1 #ValueCols=0
32	1	AggregationSpool<GroupBy>: SpoolPhyOp #Records=1
33		TreatAs: IterPhyOp LogOp=TreatAs IterCols(0)('Scenario'[Scenario])
34		TableCtor: IterPhyOp LogOp=TableCtor IterCols(0)(''[Value])
35		Constant: LookupPhyOp LogOp=Constant Integer 2
36		Constant: LookupPhyOp LogOp=Constant Double 1
37		If: LookupPhyOp LogOp=Switch LookupCols(0)('Scenario'[Scenario]) Double
38		Is: LookupPhyOp LogOp=Is LookupCols(0)('Scenario'[Scenario]) Boolean
39	1	SpoolLookup: LookupPhyOp LogOp=TableToScalar LookupCols(0)('Scenario'[Scenario]) Integer #Records=1 #KeyCols=1 #ValueCols=1 DominantValue=Bl
40	1	AggregationSpool<Copy>: SpoolPhyOp #Records=1
41	1	Spool_Iterator<Spool_TableToScalar>: IterPhyOp LogOp=TableToScalar IterCols(0)('Scenario'[Scenario]) #Records=1 #KeyCols=142 #ValueCols=4
42	1	ProjectionSpool<ProjectFusion<Copy, Copy, Copy, Copy>>: SpoolPhyOp #Records=1
43		**Cache: IterPhyOp #FieldCols=0 #ValueCols=4**
44	1	Spool_Iterator<SpoolIterator>: IterPhyOp LogOp=TreatAs IterCols(0)('Scenario'[Scenario]) #Records=1 #KeyCols=1 #ValueCols=0
45	1	AggregationSpool<GroupBy>: SpoolPhyOp #Records=1
46		TreatAs: IterPhyOp LogOp=TreatAs IterCols(0)('Scenario'[Scenario])
47		TableCtor: IterPhyOp LogOp=TableCtor IterCols(0)(''[Value])
48		Constant: LookupPhyOp LogOp=Constant Integer 3
49		Constant: LookupPhyOp LogOp=Constant Double 1.1
50		Constant: LookupPhyOp LogOp=Constant Double 1

At lines 17, 30 and 43, the IF statement is consuming a datacache that checks whether there is a single value for the *Scenario[Scenario]* column:

```
SELECT
    SUM (    ( PFDATAID ( 'Table'[Sort Order] ) <> 2 )    ),
    MIN ( 'Table'[Sort Order] ),
    MAX ( 'Table'[Sort Order] ),
    COUNT (    )
FROM 'Table'
WHERE
    'Table'[Scenario] = 'Low';
```

This xmSQL code checks that there is only one value for the *Scenario[Sort Order]* column by retrieving the min and max values given by the filter, and ignores blanks. If both values are the same, there is a single value and SELECTEDVALUE can thus return a non-blank result.

The relevant detail here is not the technical information about having a single value computed. What is important is the fact that the SWITCH optimization is not carried on if the engine cannot statically determine that only a defined number of branches of the conditional logic will be executed.

When developers write queries, they need to pay attention to the column tested in the SWITCH statement to ensure that the SWITCH optimization is used. When the model is browsed by a client tool, like Power BI, developers do not have control over the query.

In that scenario, a good solution is to use the TOM GroupByColumns property. Indeed, by grouping *Scenario[Scenario]* by *Scenario[Sort Order]*, Power BI generates a query that places the filter over *Scenario[Sort Order]*, making it possible to check the value of the *Sort Order* column in the DAX code. Unfortunately, the GroupByColumns property is only available in Power BI and not in Analysis Services. Moreover, GroupByColumns is not supported by MDX queries, so it is not compatible with Excel pivot tables connected to a Power BI dataset.

DAX developers need to make sure that the filter is placed on the same column they are using in the DAX SWITCH expression to let the SWITCH optimization kick in.

Be mindful that the SWITCH optimization is present even when multiple values are selected. In the following query, the filter evaluates two possible values for the *Scenario[Scenario]* column:

```
DEFINE
    MEASURE Sales[Amount Corrected Hardcoded] =
        [Sales Amount] *
        SWITCH (
            SELECTEDVALUE ( Scenario[Scenario] ),
            "Low", 0.9,
            "Medium", 1.0,
            "High", 1.1,
            1
        )

EVALUATE
SUMMARIZECOLUMNS (
    Scenario[Scenario],
    Customer[City],
    TREATAS ( { "Low", "Medium" }, Scenario[Scenario] ),
    "Amount Corrected", [Amount Corrected Hardcoded]
)
```

As you can see from the query plan, only two of the three If operators are present.

Line	Records	Physical Query Plan
1		GroupSemijoin: IterPhyOp LogOp=GroupSemiJoin IterCols(0, 1, 2)('Scenario'[Scenario], 'Customer'[City], ''[Amount Corrected])
2		Extend_Lookup: IterPhyOp LogOp=Multiply IterCols(0, 2)('Scenario'[Scenario], 'Customer'[City])
3		CrossApply: IterPhyOp LogOp=Sum_Vertipaq IterCols(2)('Customer'[City])
4	2	Spool_Iterator<SpoolIterator>: IterPhyOp LogOp=TreatAs IterCols(0)('Scenario'[Scenario]) #Records=2 #KeyCols=1 #V
5	2	AggregationSpool<GroupBy>: SpoolPhyOp #Records=2
6		TreatAs: IterPhyOp LogOp=TreatAs IterCols(0)('Scenario'[Scenario])
7		TableCtor: IterPhyOp LogOp=TableCtor IterCols(0, 1)(''[Value], ''[])
8	74,309	Spool_Iterator<SpoolIterator>: IterPhyOp LogOp=Sum_Vertipaq IterCols(2)('Customer'[City]) #Records=74309 #KeyCc
9	74,309	ProjectionSpool<ProjectFusion<Copy>>: SpoolPhyOp #Records=74309
10		**Cache: IterPhyOp #FieldCols=1 #ValueCols=1**
11		If: LookupPhyOp LogOp=Switch LookupCols(0)('Scenario'[Scenario]) Double
12		'Scenario'[Scenario] IS Low: LookupPhyOp LogOp='Scenario'[Scenario] IS Low'Scenario'[Scenario] IS Low LookupCols((
13		Constant: LookupPhyOp LogOp=Constant Double 0.9
14		If: LookupPhyOp LogOp=Switch LookupCols(0)('Scenario'[Scenario]) Double
15		'Scenario'[Scenario] IS Medium: LookupPhyOp LogOp='Scenario'[Scenario] IS Medium'Scenario'[Scenario] IS Mediu
16		Constant: LookupPhyOp LogOp=Constant Double 1
17		Constant: LookupPhyOp LogOp=Constant Double 1

In the scenario we have used to demonstrate the SWITCH optimization, the difference in performance is relatively low. Nonetheless, it is a critical optimization because it dramatically simplifies the query plan, pruning in advance entire subtrees that would not produce any result.

In more complex scenarios, this pruning operation is of paramount importance. Remember that the most optimized code is the one that does not exist. Removing branches in advance can only bring benefits to your DAX code.

Conclusions

In this chapter, we dug into some details for logical and physical query plans. As a DAX developer aiming to optimize DAX, you do not need to know each detail about the query plans. Therefore, we neither listed all the operators nor described all the internal information. You only need to be able to quickly read a query plan, searching for operators that work on large datasets to spot excessive materialization.

In our day-to-day work, we seldom analyze the query plans in depth when optimizing DAX code. Instead, we read the storage engine queries, guessing what the formula engine does from the datacaches it generates. We do perform a deeper analysis only in rare circumstances.

Nonetheless, you can efficiently guess what the formula engine does only after spending a reasonable amount of time analyzing its behavior in depth. You can start predicting the formula engine's actions once you get acquainted with its behavior.

We showed several examples with a deep analysis. We suggest our readers perform similar analyses on their models and measures. The time spent analyzing the query plans is not likely to provide ideas to improve your code, but it helps create the proficiency needed to perform optimizations.

Optimizing the formula engine

In the previous chapters, we learned how to read a query plan: the logical query plan, the physical query plan, and – most importantly – the storage engine queries. We are still at the beginning of learning the fine art of DAX optimization. Still, it is helpful to start introducing some optimization techniques.

Before performing hardcore optimizations, there is a lot we must learn about storage engines. Indeed, optimizing a DirectQuery model is different from optimizing a VertiPaq model. Still, there are several valuable techniques we can already introduce at this stage.

If we were to wait for the whole theory to be well established before starting to optimize, our readers would be overwhelmed by concepts before having fun with DAX optimizations. Therefore, let us get our hands dirty and see what we can achieve with the knowledge gained so far. No theory here, just optimization examples.

One last word of warning about these examples is that they are exactly that: examples. Please, do not use them as patterns. Some of the optimizations we show may have a broader adoption, but our goal here is not to provide generic patterns. Instead, we want to show the entire optimization process of a few queries, and focus on the formula engine tasks.

There is a pattern – a meta-pattern, to tell the truth. During the optimization, we will uncover new ideas that were not evident at the beginning of the process. The reason we spend time studying query plans and DAX's behavior is not only to find problems and possible optimizations. Another important reason is to learn about how the engine solves queries. At each step, we learn more about what DAX is doing; by understanding this, we will be able to write the code differently to drive DAX in the right direction.

Optimizing datacache use

Optimizing DAX code means finding the perfect balance between the use of the storage engine and the use of the formula engine. Sometimes, small changes in the formula can lead to significant differences, and the DAX developer oversees the finding of these changes.

Let us analyze a straightforward example that computes the aggregated difference between two columns:

```
EVALUATE
{
    SUM ( Sales[Unit Price] ) - SUM ( Sales[Net Price] )
}
```

In this first example, the server timing is not interesting, as it shows an extremely fast calculation.

Total	SE CPU
33 ms	94 ms
	x3.5

◔ FE	● SE
6 ms	27 ms
18.2%	87.9%

SE Queries	SE Cache
1	0
	0.0%

The interesting detail we want to focus on is how the optimizer computed the result. The entire expression is nothing but the subtraction of two values, which the storage engine can compute by scanning the *Sales* table. Because of vertical fusion, there is a single storage engine query retrieving at the same time both the sum of *Sales[Net Price]* and the sum of *Sales[Unit Price]*, generating a datacache with one row and two columns. Indeed, here is the only xmSQL query executed:

```
SELECT
    SUM ( 'Sales'[Net Price] ),
    SUM ( 'Sales'[Unit Price] )
FROM 'Sales';

Estimated size: rows = 1   bytes = 24
```

Because this is all that the storage engine performs, we can conclude that the subtraction between the two numbers takes place in the formula engine. We can double-check this by looking at the physical query plan.

Line	Records	Physical Query Plan
1		AddColumns: IterPhyOp LogOp=AddColumns IterCols(0)(''[Value])
2		SingletonTable: IterPhyOp LogOp=AddColumns
3		Subtract: LookupPhyOp LogOp=Subtract Currency
4	1	SpoolLookup: LookupPhyOp LogOp=Sum_Vertipaq Currency #Records=1 #KeyCols=138 #ValueCols=2 DominantValue=BLANK
5	1	ProjectionSpool<ProjectFusion<Copy, Copy>>: SpoolPhyOp #Records=1
6		**Cache: IterPhyOp #FieldCols=0 #ValueCols=2**
7	1	SpoolLookup: LookupPhyOp LogOp=Sum_Vertipaq Currency #Records=1 #KeyCols=138 #ValueCols=2 DominantValue=BLANK
8	1	ProjectionSpool<ProjectFusion<Copy, Copy>>: SpoolPhyOp #Records=1
9		**Cache: IterPhyOp #FieldCols=0 #ValueCols=2**

The highlighted operator is Subtract, which subtracts two values retrieved through *SpoolLookup* operators. The two *SpoolLookup* operate on the same datacache, and extract the two columns.

Nothing strange about this query plan; it just works and performs extremely well. But it is worth noting that the very same calculation can be expressed by pushing the subtraction down to the storage engine through an iterator:

```
EVALUATE
{
    SUMX ( Sales, Sales[Unit Price] - Sales[Net Price] )
}
```

The result of this latter query is identical to the previous one, the main difference being that instead of subtracting two aggregated values, we are aggregating a subtraction. The additional effort performed by the storage engine is immediately visible in the server timings.

Total	SE CPU
67 ms	719 ms
	x11.8

FE	SE
6 ms	61 ms
9.0%	92.5%

SE Queries	SE Cache
1	0
	0.0%

The SE CPU time is a multiple of the previous one, even though the overall execution time is still very good. The storage engine query now contains the subtraction:

```
WITH
    $Expr0 := ( PFCAST ( 'Sales'[Unit Price] AS INT ) - PFCAST ( 'Sales'[Net Price] AS INT ) )
SELECT
    SUM ( @$Expr0 )
FROM 'Sales';

Estimated size: rows = 1    bytes = 16
```

And the query plan confirms that there is now a single SpoolLookup operator extracting the value from the storage engine result.

Line	Records	Physical Query Plan
1		AddColumns: IterPhyOp LogOp=AddColumns IterCols(0)(''[Value])
2		SingletonTable: IterPhyOp LogOp=AddColumns
3	1	SpoolLookup: LookupPhyOp LogOp=Sum_Vertipaq Currency #Records=1 #KeyCols=138 #ValueCols=1 DominantValue=BLANK
4	1	ProjectionSpool<ProjectFusion<Copy>>: SpoolPhyOp #Records=1
5		**Cache: IterPhyOp #FieldCols=0 #ValueCols=1**

Based on the numbers we are witnessing, pushing down the subtraction to the storage engine was not a smart idea. It would be better first to aggregate and then subtract rather than first subtract and then aggregate.

However, that assumption would be naïve. First, we are performing the tests using the VertiPaq storage engine – we might see the opposite result using DirectQuery over SQL. In this specific example, where the result only contains one value, performing the subtraction in the formula engine proves to be a better choice than in VertiPaq. However, if the calculation is part of a more complex formula, things may differ.

The datacache generated by the storage engine in this example contains only one row. If the datacache contained many more rows that should be joined together in the formula engine, then the result would be the opposite. To demonstrate this, we change the query to generate a datacache with the cardinality of *Customer*:

```
DEFINE
    MEASURE Sales[Total Discount] =
        SUM ( Sales[Unit Price] ) - SUM ( Sales[Net Price] )
EVALUATE
{
    MAXX (
        SUMMARIZECOLUMNS (
            Customer[CustomerKey],
            "@TD", [Total Discount]
        ),
        [@TD]
    )
}
```

This query does not have any business value; its goal is to perform the calculation with the subtraction of two aggregations for each customer. In the demo database, we have around 1.8 million customers which will amplify the difference in speed. Indeed, now the numbers shown in the server timings start to grow and require more than 14 seconds to execute the query.

Total	SE CPU
6,677 ms	53,734 ms
	×10.2

FE	SE
1,410 ms	5,267 ms
21.1%	78.9%

SE Queries	SE Cache
1	0
	0.0%

From the storage engine point of view, the only thing that changed is the size of the datacache. Instead of a single row, the storage engine query now returns a rather large datacache containing around 1.8 million rows:

```
SET DC_KIND="AUTO";
SELECT
    'Customer'[CustomerKey],
    SUM ( 'Sales'[Net Price] ),
    SUM ( 'Sales'[Unit Price] )
FROM 'Sales'
    LEFT OUTER JOIN 'Customer'
        ON 'Sales'[CustomerKey]='Customer'[CustomerKey];
```

Estimated size: rows = 1,868,084   bytes = 37,361,680

The formula engine oversees scanning this datacache and finding the maximum value after performing the subtraction. Here we face the central problem: subtraction.

Finding the maximum value only requires scanning a table with 1.8 million rows. At modern computer speed, this is extremely fast. But to perform the subtraction, the physical query plan shows that the engine needs to use one SpoolIterator operator to iterate the values of the first column, and another SpoolLookup operator to extract the second column.

Line	Records	Physical Query Plan
1		AddColumns: IterPhyOp LogOp=AddColumns IterCols(0)("[Value])
2		SingletonTable: IterPhyOp LogOp=AddColumns
3	1	SpoolLookup: LookupPhyOp LogOp=MaxX Currency #Records=1 #KeyCols=0 #ValueCols=1 DominantValue=BLANK
4	1	AggregationSpool<Max>: SpoolPhyOp #Records=1
5		Extend_Lookup: IterPhyOp LogOp=Extend_Lookup"[@TD] IterCols(1)("[@TD])
6		GroupSemijoin: IterPhyOp LogOp=GroupSemiJoin IterCols(0, 1)('Customer'[CustomerKey], "[@TD])
7		OuterHashJoin: IterPhyOp LogOp=Subtract IterCols(0)('Customer'[CustomerKey])
8		Extend_Lookup: IterPhyOp LogOp=Subtract IterCols(0)('Customer'[CustomerKey])
9	1,868,084	Spool_Iterator<SpoolIterator>: IterPhyOp LogOp=Sum_Vertipaq IterCols(0)('Customer'[CustomerKey]) #Records=1868084 #K
10	1,868,084	ProjectionSpool<ProjectFusion<Copy, Copy>>: SpoolPhyOp #Records=1868084
11		**Cache: IterPhyOp #FieldCols=1 #ValueCols=2**
12	1,868,084	SpoolLookup: LookupPhyOp LogOp=Sum_Vertipaq LookupCols(0)('Customer'[CustomerKey]) Currency #Records=1868084 #I
13	1,868,084	ProjectionSpool<ProjectFusion<Copy, Copy>>: SpoolPhyOp #Records=1868084
14		**Cache: IterPhyOp #FieldCols=1 #ValueCols=2**
15	1,868,084	Spool_Iterator<SpoolIterator>: IterPhyOp LogOp=Sum_Vertipaq IterCols(0)('Customer'[CustomerKey]) #Records=1868084 #Key
16	1,868,084	ProjectionSpool<ProjectFusion<Copy, Copy>>: SpoolPhyOp #Records=1868084
17		**Cache: IterPhyOp #FieldCols=1 #ValueCols=2**
18		ColValue<"[@TD]>: LookupPhyOp LogOp=ColValue<"[@TD]>"[@TD] LookupCols(1)("[@TD]) Currency

The Spool_Iterator scans 1.8 million rows. For each row it finds the corresponding row (through SpoolLookup) in the same datacache, still consisting of 1.8 million rows. Finally, GroupSemiJoin (at line 6) removes undesired values.

In other words, the formula engine identifies the values to subtract before performing the subtraction. Because the table containing those values is large, matching one value with another takes time. This matching is why we are seeing 1.4 seconds of formula engine time.

There is no need to rebuild the relationship between values in the same datacache if we push down the subtraction operator to the storage engine:

```
DEFINE
    MEASURE Sales[Total Discount] =
        SUMX ( Sales, Sales[Unit Price] - Sales[Net Price] )
EVALUATE
{
    MAXX (
        SUMMARIZECOLUMNS (
            Customer[CustomerKey],
            "@TD", [Total Discount]
        ),
        [@TD]
    )
}
```

As usual, let us start to look at the server timings.

Total	SE CPU
4,777 ms	44,375 ms
	x10.4

● FE	● SE
490 ms	4,287 ms
10.3%	89.8%

SE Queries	SE Cache
1	0
	0.0%

The formula engine time is 20% faster than the time of the previous DAX query. There is also a similar improvement in the storage engine (SE) CPU. From the storage engine point of view, the reason is that the datacache is smaller because it contains only one result column instead of two: the size is 22MB instead of 37MB, as shown in the following xmSQL query. On the other hand, the number of rows is the same (1.8 million rows). Here is the storage engine query being executed:

```
SET DC_KIND="AUTO";
WITH
    $Expr0 := ( PFCAST ( 'Sales'[Unit Price] AS   INT ) - PFCAST ( 'Sales'[Net Price] AS   INT )   )
SELECT
    'Customer'[CustomerKey],
    SUM ( @$Expr0 )
FROM 'Sales'
    LEFT OUTER JOIN 'Customer'
        ON 'Sales'[CustomerKey]='Customer'[CustomerKey];

Estimated size: rows = 1,868,084    bytes = 22,417,008
```

However, the most significant difference both in terms of timings and query plan is in the formula engine.

Line	Records	Physical Query Plan
1		AddColumns: IterPhyOp LogOp=AddColumns IterCols(0)("[Value])
2		SingletonTable: IterPhyOp LogOp=AddColumns
3	1	SpoolLookup: LookupPhyOp LogOp=MaxX Currency #Records=1 #KeyCols=0 #ValueCols=1 DominantValue=BLANK
4	1	AggregationSpool<Max>: SpoolPhyOp #Records=1
5		Extend_Lookup: IterPhyOp LogOp=Extend_Lookup"[@TD] IterCols(1)("[@TD])
6		GroupSemijoin: IterPhyOp LogOp=GroupSemiJoin IterCols(0, 1)('Customer'[CustomerKey], "[@TD])
7	1,868,084	Spool_Iterator<SpoolIterator>: IterPhyOp LogOp=Sum_Vertipaq IterCols(0)('Customer'[CustomerKey]) #Records=1868084 #
8	1,868,084	ProjectionSpool<ProjectFusion<Copy>>: SpoolPhyOp #Records=1868084
9		**Cache: IterPhyOp #FieldCols=1 #ValueCols=1**
10		ColValue<"[@TD]>: LookupPhyOp LogOp=ColValue<"[@TD]>"[@TD] LookupCols(1)("[@TD]) Currency

There are no signs of subtraction, and a single iteration is happening on the large datacache.

As you see, there is no answer to the simple question: "Which of these two formulas is better?". The answer depends on other factors, like the size of the datacache generated and the subsequent use of the columns. Despite the generic piece of advice – to push the calculation as much as possible down to the storage engine – still holding true, there are scenarios where moving calculations to the formula engine proves to be a better choice. We show several examples later in this chapter.

Sales of best products

In this example, we want to compute the sales of the best products. We consider a product among the best if its sales are higher than the average sales of all the products. We use a large database with 1.4B rows in Sales for this demo, to show more meaningful results.

Here is the initial query:

```
DEFINE
    MEASURE Sales[Sales of best products] =
        CALCULATE (
            [Sales Amount],
            FILTER (
                'Product',
                [Sales Amount] >= AVERAGEX ( 'Product', [Sales Amount] )
            )
        )

EVALUATE
SUMMARIZECOLUMNS (
    Customer[Country],
    "Sales of best products", [Sales of best products]
)
```

The measure is relatively simple. The inner AVERAGEX computes the average sales of any product. FILTER returns the list of those products, which are then used as a filter in CALCULATE to produce the desired result.

Country	Sales of best products
United States	590,648,677,872.22
United Kingdom	125,712,404,313.28
Germany	117,087,612,483.11
France	32,835,168,537.23
Netherlands	46,044,864,379.80
Australia	65,415,132,790.05
Canada	115,785,915,449.77
Italy	34,996,900,053.15

The query is not that bad in terms of performance.

Total	SE CPU		Line	Subclass	Duration	CPU	Par.	Rows	KB	Timeline
1,504 ms	78,093 ms		2	Scan	1	0		2,520	20	
	x52.8		4	Scan	1	0		11	1	
FE	SE		6	Scan	307	15,734	x51.3	27,720	434	
26 ms	1,478 ms		8	Scan	0	0		2,517	10	
1.7%	98.3%		10	Scan	1,172	62,359	x53.2	11	1	
SE Queries	SE Cache									
5	0									
	0.0%									

There are five storage engine queries. Most of the time is spent in the storage engine, and the degree of parallelism of the storage engine is rather good. But we must dive into the details to search for any areas of improvement.

Three of the five storage engine queries are simple and not worth further investigation, because they are used to gather the product keys and the customer countries. Here is the first query that retrieves the product keys:

```
SELECT
    'Product'[ProductKey]
FROM 'Product';
```

The next one retrieves the customer countries:

```
SELECT
    'Customer'[Country]
FROM 'Customer';
```

And the third one retrieves, again, the product keys:

```
SELECT
    'Product'[RowNumber],
    'Product'[ProductKey]
FROM 'Product';
```

This third query does not look helpful, as its result has the same number of rows as the first storage engine query. However, given the small size of the *Product* table, working hard to remove this query does not seem reasonable. The last two queries, where the real work happens, are heavier and more important. The fourth query retrieves the value of *Sales Amount* sliced by *Customer[Country]* and *Product[ProductKey]*:

```
WITH
    $Expr0 := ( PFCAST ( 'Sales'[Quantity] AS   INT ) * PFCAST ( 'Sales'[Net Price] AS   INT )   )
SELECT
    'Product'[ProductKey],
    'Customer'[Country],
    SUM ( @$Expr0 )
FROM 'Sales'
    LEFT OUTER JOIN 'Product'
        ON 'Sales'[ProductKey]='Product'[ProductKey]
    LEFT OUTER JOIN 'Customer'
        ON 'Sales'[CustomerKey]='Customer'[CustomerKey];
```

The fifth and last query retrieves – again – the value of *Sales Amount*. However, this time it groups only by *Customer[Country]*, and it applies a rather complex filter:

```
WITH
    $Expr0 := ( PFCAST ( 'Sales'[Quantity] AS   INT ) * PFCAST ( 'Sales'[Net Price] AS   INT )   )
SELECT
    'Customer'[Country],
    SUM ( @$Expr0 )
FROM 'Sales'
    LEFT OUTER JOIN 'Product'
        ON 'Sales'[ProductKey]='Product'[ProductKey]
    LEFT OUTER JOIN 'Customer'
        ON 'Sales'[CustomerKey]='Customer'[CustomerKey]
WHERE
        ( 'Customer'[Country], 'Product'[ProductKey] ) IN { ( 'Netherlands', 494 ) , ( 'Canada', 1180 ) , ( 'Netherlands', 1492 ) , (
    'Australia', 429 ) , ( 'United Kingdom', 554 ) , ( 'Italy', 616 ) , ( 'United Kingdom', 1053 ) , ( 'France', 1240 ) , ( 'Australia', 1427 ) , (
    'United Kingdom', 1552 ) ..[5,136 total tuples, not all displayed]};
```

Based on the storage engine queries we are seeing, the algorithm executed by the formula engine looks straightforward. It first collects basic information about products and countries. Then it builds a datacache with *Sales Amount* for each combination of *Product[ProductKey]* and *Customer[Country]*. The datacache is not very large because it contains only 27,720 rows. It then computes the average sales by product in the formula engine and uses this information to find the products that sold more than the average in each country.

Finally, it uses this information to place a filter on the model while computing *Sales Amount* again, this time grouped by *Customer[Country]* only because it is the desired result.

Now that we have a clear picture of the algorithm, we can search for areas of improvement. The first idea is relatively simple: since we need to compute *Sales Amount* grouped by country and product, we can use the value already computed to produce the result without additional storage engine requests. There is no need to scan the *Sales* table again with a filter because the information is already present in the first scan. Besides, in building the table, we can avoid grouping by *Product[ProductKey]* – which would require a join in the VertiPaq query – and use *Sales[ProductKey]* instead.

Here is the new query, rewritten by following this idea:

```
DEFINE
    MEASURE Sales[Sales of best products] =
        VAR ProductAndSales =
            ADDCOLUMNS (
                SUMMARIZE ( Sales, Sales[ProductKey] ),
                "@Sales", [Sales Amount]
            )
        VAR AvgSales =
            AVERAGEX ( ProductAndSales, [@Sales] )
        RETURN
            SUMX ( FILTER ( ProductAndSales, [@Sales] >= AvgSales ), [@Sales] )

EVALUATE
SUMMARIZECOLUMNS (
    Customer[Country],
    "Sales of best products", [Sales of best products]
)
```

The idea paid off. The server timings show a good improvement as they run in 454ms instead of 1,504ms.

Total	SE CPU		Line	Subclass	Duration	CPU	Par.	Rows	KB	Timeline
454 ms	22,610 ms		2	Scan	284	15,266	x53.8	27,720	434	
	x51.7		4	Scan	153	7,344	x48.0	27,720	217	
FE	SE									
17 ms	437 ms									
3.7%	96.3%									
SE Queries	SE Cache									
2	0									
	0.0%									

All the timings improved. The storage engine CPU moved from 78 seconds to only 22 seconds. The formula engine time is not significantly changed. Indeed, the formula engine probably spends most of the time computing the average sales amount. We know that the previous code also computed the average in the formula engine. By iterating the *ProductAndSales* variable explicitly with AVERAGEX, we are forcing the calculation to be held in the formula engine in this new version of the code. Regardless, we have not changed the algorithm.

There are now only two storage engine queries. The first retrieves *Sales Amount* grouped by *Sales[ProductKey]* and *Customer[Country]*, similar to what we saw earlier:

```
WITH
    $Expr0 := ( PFCAST ( 'Sales'[Quantity] AS   INT ) * PFCAST ( 'Sales'[Net Price] AS   INT )   )
SELECT
    'Sales'[ProductKey],
    'Customer'[Country],
    SUM ( @$Expr0 )
FROM 'Sales'
    LEFT OUTER JOIN 'Customer'
        ON 'Sales'[CustomerKey]='Customer'[CustomerKey];
```

If you look carefully at this query, you might notice that there is another slight difference indeed. The JOIN with *Product* is missing. The reason is that this query is grouping by *Sales[ProductKey]* instead of grouping by *Product* as we did earlier. This different grouping condition saves a join – and some execution time – in the storage engine query.

There is a second storage engine query being executed:

```
SELECT
    'Sales'[ProductKey],
    'Customer'[Country]
FROM 'Sales'
    LEFT OUTER JOIN 'Customer'
        ON 'Sales'[CustomerKey]='Customer'[CustomerKey];
```

This query retrieves the product keys by country, by scanning *Sales* again. The reason for this second scan is that this is the default behavior of ADDCOLUMNS. ADDCOLUMNS most frequently requires two datacaches: one to determine the axis of the calculation (the values of *Sales[ProductKey]*) and another to determine the values to be added.

This second query in itself is not a big issue. It is fast because of parallelism, but it still uses 2,203 milliseconds of storage engine CPU.

Line	Subclass	Duration	CPU	Par.	Rows	KB
2	Scan	284	15,266	x53.8	27,720	434
4	Scan	153	7,344	x48.0	27,720	217

It takes so much CPU because it determines the values of the product keys by starting the groupby operation from *Sales*. We could obtain the same values if we scanned *Product[ProductKey]*. The *Product* table is much smaller compared to *Sales*. The *Sales* table is around 200 million rows, whereas the *Product* table is only 2,500 rows.

We can thus change the tables used in ADDCOLUMNS to DISTINCT on *Product[ProductKey]* to avoid a scan of the *Sales* table. This change probably adds the join again in the storage engine query that computes the sales amount. We need to check whether the added join is more expensive than the removed scan:

```
DEFINE
    MEASURE Sales[Sales of best products] =
        VAR ProductAndSales =
            ADDCOLUMNS (
                DISTINCT ( 'Product'[ProductKey] ),
                "@Sales", [Sales Amount]
            )
        VAR AvgSales =
            AVERAGEX ( ProductAndSales, [@Sales] )
        RETURN
            SUMX ( FILTER ( ProductAndSales, [@Sales] >= AvgSales ), [@Sales] )

EVALUATE
SUMMARIZECOLUMNS (
    Customer[Country],
    "Sales of best products", [Sales of best products]
)
```

The server timings show a good improvement in terms of storage engine CPU: it is now only 14 seconds.

Total	SE CPU	Line	Subclass	Duration	CPU	Par.	Rows	KB	Timeline
317 ms	14,875 ms	2	Scan	298	14,875	x49.9	27,720	434	
	x49.7	4	Scan	0	0		2,520	20	
FE	**SE**	6	Scan	1	0		11	1	
18 ms	299 ms								
5.7%	94.3%								

SE Queries	SE Cache
3	0
	0.0%

At the same time, we have one more storage engine query. Regardless, the CPU time used by the large storage engine query did not increase significantly, while the other two queries are so fast that the CPU reported is zero. We expect the query to show the join with *Product*. Let us inspect this:

```
WITH
    $Expr0 := ( PFCAST ( 'Sales'[Quantity] AS    INT ) * PFCAST ( 'Sales'[Net Price] AS    INT )   )
SELECT
    'Product'[ProductKey],
    'Customer'[Country],
    SUM ( @$Expr0 )
FROM 'Sales'
    LEFT OUTER JOIN 'Product'
        ON 'Sales'[ProductKey]='Product'[ProductKey]
    LEFT OUTER JOIN 'Customer'
        ON 'Sales'[CustomerKey]='Customer'[CustomerKey];
```

As you see, the join with *Product* is present, but its price seems irrelevant. The remaining two queries are straightforward and fast. The second storage engine query retrieves the product keys:

```
SELECT
    'Product'[ProductKey]
FROM 'Product';
```

Whereas the third storage engine query retrieves the countries from the *Customer* table:

```
SELECT
    'Customer'[Country]
FROM 'Customer';
```

The overall execution time of the query is not significantly better. In the end, we only saved 150 milliseconds. However, these minor optimizations can make a big difference when thousands of users are querying a model. Measured in terms of storage engine CPU, we saved 1/3 of the power required. This saving means that this last code version scales out much better with many concurrent users.

Moreover, as usual, most of this demo is not about how to improve the code. The main goal of the optimization process is to learn the internals of the DAX query engine. The more you learn, the more you can make educated guesses about how the engine is solving your queries when you are authoring code. A good DAX developer already starts the optimization process when writing the formulas: you mentally picture how the code will be executed, and with that in mind you attempt to write efficient DAX code right from the start.

Running total of sales and ABC analysis

As another interesting example, let us analyze (and optimize) the performance of a running total calculation. This scenario is a typical pattern, and we provide a simplified version for educational purposes here. In descending order of sales amount, we want to compute the running total of those sales starting from the top seller. We want to see the value for the running total grow, product after product – by definition of a running total. This requirement is a standard calculation in business analysis to perform ABC analysis.

We want to build a report containing for each product, various representations of its sales along with its ABC class. The ABC class requires that we calculate the running total of sales.

ProductKey	Sales	Sales RT	Sales Pct	ABC Class
433	12,819,469,410.55	12,819,469,410.55	0.90%	A
422	12,819,362,302.14	25,638,831,712.69	1.80%	A
416	12,816,995,161.11	38,455,826,873.80	2.70%	A
428	12,804,406,344.31	51,260,233,218.12	3.59%	A
455	12,153,865,475.55	63,414,098,693.67	4.45%	A
438	12,152,049,880.77	75,566,148,574.44	5.30%	A
444	12,148,604,669.24	87,714,753,243.68	6.15%	A
450	12,144,955,867.04	99,859,709,110.72	7.00%	A
429	7,927,107,677.15	107,786,816,787.88	7.56%	A
417	7,926,123,566.29	115,712,940,354.17	8.11%	A

ProductKey and *Sales* columns are straightforward: the code of the product and its sales volume. The running total *Sales RT* starts with the bestseller on the first row, and there it displays the same amount as *Sales*. Still in *Sales RT,* the second bestseller row sums up the sales of the first two products. The third row sums up the sales of the first three products, and so on. *Sales RT* is useful to compute *Sales Pct*, which indicates the percentage of total sales that all the best products so far have generated. In other words, the bestseller alone generated 0.90% of all sales. The first two best sellers generated 1.80% together, and so on.

The query that generated the result we have analyzed so far is the following:

```
DEFINE
    MEASURE Sales[Sales RT] =
        VAR CurrentSales = [Sales Amount]        -- Sales of the current product
        VAR ProductsWithMoreSales =
            FILTER (                             -- Products with more sales than
                ALL ( 'Product'[ProductKey] ),   -- the current product
                [Sales Amount] >= CurrentSales
            )
        VAR Result =
            CALCULATE (                          -- Computes the sales of all products
                [Sales Amount],                  -- with more sales than the current
                ProductsWithMoreSales            -- one (including the current product)
            )
        RETURN
            Result
    MEASURE Sales[Sales Pct] =
        DIVIDE ( [Sales RT], CALCULATE ( [Sales Amount], ALLSELECTED () ) )
    MEASURE Sales[ABC Class] =
        VAR Pct = [Sales Pct]
        RETURN
            SWITCH ( TRUE (), Pct <= 0.7, "A", Pct <= 0.9, "B", "C" )

EVALUATE
ADDCOLUMNS (
    VALUES ( 'Product'[ProductKey] ),
    "Sales", [Sales Amount],
    "Sales RT", [Sales RT],
    "Sales Pct", [Sales Pct],
    "ABC Class", [ABC Class]
)
ORDER BY [Sales] DESC
```

The query is rather complex. It retrieves five columns, four of which are measures. As such, we are not going to optimize the entire query. A quick analysis of the formulas of the measures shows that the complexity of the entire query resides in the *Sales RT* measure. All the other measures derive directly from *Sales RT*. Therefore, we assume that optimizing *Sales RT* will benefit the entire query.

Here are the server timings of the whole query.

Total	SE CPU	Line	Subclass	Duration	CPU	Par.	Rows	KB	Timeline
1,260 ms	2,469 ms								
	×14.0	2	Scan	73	953	×13.1	2,520	40	
FE	**SE**	4	Scan	1	0		2,520	20	
1,084 ms	176 ms	6	Scan	102	1,516	×14.9	2,520	40	
86.0%	14.0%								

SE Queries	SE Cache
3	0
	0.0%

Since we do not want to optimize the entire query as we focus on only a single measure, performing a deeper analysis of the timing distribution is pointless. We change the query to return only the *Sales RT* measure, and we perform a complete analysis of the more straightforward query:

```
DEFINE
    MEASURE Sales[Sales RT] =
        VAR CurrentSales = [Sales Amount]        -- Sales of the current product
        VAR ProductsWithMoreSales =
            FILTER (                             -- Products with more sales than
                ALL ( 'Product'[ProductKey] ),  -- the current product
                [Sales Amount] >= CurrentSales
            )
        VAR Result =
            CALCULATE (                          -- Computes the sales of all products
                [Sales Amount],                  -- with more sales than the current
                ProductsWithMoreSales            -- one (including the current product)
            )
        RETURN
            Result
EVALUATE
ADDCOLUMNS (
    ALL ( 'Product'[ProductKey] ),
    "Sales RT", [Sales RT]
)
```

As you see, we removed all the measures except the one to optimize. We also removed the ORDER BY section to simplify the query plans and avoid the noise of sorting the result. The server timings show the same numbers as the complete query. This piece evidence confirms our assumption: the complexity of the entire query lies strictly in the *Sales RT* measure.

Total	SE CPU	Line	Subclass	Duration	CPU	Par.	Rows	KB	Timeline
1,212 ms	2,828 ms	2	Scan	0	0		2,520	20	
	x16.8								
FE	**SE**	4	Scan	68	875	x12.9	2,520	40	
1,044 ms	168 ms	6	Scan	100	1,953	x19.5	2,520	40	
86.1%	13.9%								

SE Queries	SE Cache
3	0
	0.0%

This time, we need to go deeper. There are three storage engine queries, producing three datacaches. The first one just retrieves the values of the product keys:

```
SELECT
    'Product'[ProductKey]
FROM 'Product';
```

The second query retrieves the value of *Sales Amount* grouped by *Product[ProductKey]*:

```
WITH
    $Expr0 := ( PFCAST ( 'Sales'[Quantity] AS    INT ) * PFCAST ( 'Sales'[Net Price] AS    INT )   )
SELECT
    'Product'[ProductKey],
    SUM ( @$Expr0 )
FROM 'Sales'
    LEFT OUTER JOIN 'Product'
        ON 'Sales'[ProductKey]='Product'[ProductKey];
```

This query is totally expected, as *Sales Amount* grouped by *Product[ProductKey]* is the foundation of the entire algorithm. The third query, however, is somewhat surprising:

```
WITH
    $Expr0 := ( PFCAST ( 'Sales'[Quantity] AS    INT ) * PFCAST ( 'Sales'[Net Price] AS    INT )   )
SELECT
    'Product'[ProductKey],
    SUM ( @$Expr0 )
FROM 'Sales'
    LEFT OUTER JOIN 'Product'
        ON 'Sales'[ProductKey]='Product'[ProductKey]
WHERE
    'Product'[ProductKey] IN ( 955, 1912, 1953, 873, 914, 1871, 791, 832, 1789, 1830..[2,517 total values, not all displayed] ) ;
```

The filter over *ProductKey* could be an optimization created by Tabular to reduce the number of products to analyze. Indeed, by reducing the analysis to only the products with sales, the engine might reduce the effort required in order to produce the result. If that were the case, it would be a vain attempt because all products in our demo database show sales.

So we can conclude that most of the calculation takes place in the formula engine by analyzing the storage engine queries. Indeed, the storage engine only computes the sales amount sliced by product. The remaining part of the algorithm happens in the formula engine. By deeply analyzing the query plan, we want to understand where the filter comes from and why Tabular decided to place the filter.

Here is the physical query plan. It contains a surprise.

Line	Records	Physical Query Plan
1		AddColumns: IterPhyOp LogOp=AddColumns IterCols(0, 1)('Product'[ProductKey], ''[Sales RT])
2	2,517	Spool_Iterator<SpoolIterator>: IterPhyOp LogOp=Scan_Vertipaq IterCols(0)('Product'[ProductKey]) #Records=2517 #K
3	2,517	ProjectionSpool<ProjectFusion<>>: SpoolPhyOp #Records=2517
4		**Cache: IterPhyOp #FieldCols=1 #ValueCols=0**
5	2,517	SpoolLookup: LookupPhyOp LogOp=Sum_Vertipaq LookupCols(0)('Product'[ProductKey]) Currency #Records=2517 #K
6	2,517	AggregationSpool<AggFusion<Sum>>: SpoolPhyOp #Records=2517
7		CrossApply: IterPhyOp LogOp=Sum_Vertipaq IterCols(0)('Product'[ProductKey])
8	3,168,903	Spool_MultiValuedHashLookup: IterPhyOp LogOp=TableVarProxy LookupCols(1)('Product'[ProductKey]) IterCol
9	3,168,903	AggregationSpool<GroupBy>: SpoolPhyOp #Records=3168903
10		Proxy: IterPhyOp LogOp=TableVarProxy IterCols(0, 1)('Product'[ProductKey], 'Product'[ProductKey])
11		Filter: IterPhyOp LogOp=Filter IterCols(0, 1)('Product'[ProductKey], 'Product'[ProductKey])
12		Extend_Lookup: IterPhyOp LogOp=GreaterThanOrEqualTo IterCols(0, 1)('Product'[ProductKey], 'Prod
13		CrossApply: IterPhyOp LogOp=GreaterThanOrEqualTo IterCols(0, 1)('Product'[ProductKey], 'Produ
14	2,517	Spool_Iterator<SpoolIterator>: IterPhyOp LogOp=Scan_Vertipaq IterCols(0)('Product'[Productk
15	2,517	ProjectionSpool<ProjectFusion<>>: SpoolPhyOp #Records=2517
16		**Cache: IterPhyOp #FieldCols=1 #ValueCols=0**
17	2,517	Spool_Iterator<SpoolIterator>: IterPhyOp LogOp=Scan_Vertipaq IterCols(1)('Product'[Productk
18	2,517	ProjectionSpool<ProjectFusion<>>: SpoolPhyOp #Records=2517
19		**Cache: IterPhyOp #FieldCols=1 #ValueCols=0**
20		GreaterThanOrEqualTo: LookupPhyOp LogOp=GreaterThanOrEqualTo LookupCols(0, 1)('Product'[
21	2,517	SpoolLookup: LookupPhyOp LogOp=Sum_Vertipaq LookupCols(1)('Product'[ProductKey]) Curr
22	2,517	ProjectionSpool<ProjectFusion<Copy>>: SpoolPhyOp #Records=2517
23		**Cache: IterPhyOp #FieldCols=1 #ValueCols=1**
24	2,517	SpoolLookup: LookupPhyOp LogOp=Sum_Vertipaq LookupCols(0)('Product'[ProductKey]) Curr
25	2,517	ProjectionSpool<ProjectFusion<Copy>>: SpoolPhyOp #Records=2517
26		**Cache: IterPhyOp #FieldCols=1 #ValueCols=1**
27		**Cache: IterPhyOp #FieldCols=1 #ValueCols=1**
28	3,168,903	Spool_Iterator<SpoolIterator>: IterPhyOp LogOp=TableVarProxy IterCols(0, 1)('Product'[ProductKey], 'Produ
29	3,168,903	AggregationSpool<GroupBy>: SpoolPhyOp #Records=3168903
30		Proxy: IterPhyOp LogOp=TableVarProxy IterCols(0, 1)('Product'[ProductKey], 'Product'[ProductKey])
31		Filter: IterPhyOp LogOp=Filter IterCols(0, 1)('Product'[ProductKey], 'Product'[ProductKey])
32		Extend_Lookup: IterPhyOp LogOp=GreaterThanOrEqualTo IterCols(0, 1)('Product'[ProductKey], 'Pr
33		CrossApply: IterPhyOp LogOp=GreaterThanOrEqualTo IterCols(0, 1)('Product'[ProductKey], 'Prc
34	2,517	Spool_Iterator<SpoolIterator>: IterPhyOp LogOp=Scan_Vertipaq IterCols(0)('Product'[Produ
35	2,517	ProjectionSpool<ProjectFusion<>>: SpoolPhyOp #Records=2517
36		**Cache: IterPhyOp #FieldCols=1 #ValueCols=0**
37	2,517	Spool_Iterator<SpoolIterator>: IterPhyOp LogOp=Scan_Vertipaq IterCols(1)('Product'[Produ
38	2,517	ProjectionSpool<ProjectFusion<>>: SpoolPhyOp #Records=2517
39		**Cache: IterPhyOp #FieldCols=1 #ValueCols=0**
40		GreaterThanOrEqualTo: LookupPhyOp LogOp=GreaterThanOrEqualTo LookupCols(0, 1)('Produ
41	2,517	SpoolLookup: LookupPhyOp LogOp=Sum_Vertipaq LookupCols(1)('Product'[ProductKey]) Cu
42	2,517	ProjectionSpool<ProjectFusion<Copy>>: SpoolPhyOp #Records=2517
43		**Cache: IterPhyOp #FieldCols=1 #ValueCols=1**
44	2,517	SpoolLookup: LookupPhyOp LogOp=Sum_Vertipaq LookupCols(0)('Product'[ProductKey]) Cu
45	2,517	ProjectionSpool<ProjectFusion<Copy>>: SpoolPhyOp #Records=2517
46		**Cache: IterPhyOp #FieldCols=1 #ValueCols=1**

The algorithm is split into two parts:

- The definition of the filter (lines 28 to 46)
- The actual calculation (lines 1 to 27)

Let us start with the definition of the filter. However, we need to review the algorithm before analyzing why the filter is in place. Let us repeat the code here:

```
DEFINE
    MEASURE Sales[Sales RT] =
        VAR CurrentSales = [Sales Amount]          -- Sales of the current product
        VAR ProductsWithMoreSales =
            FILTER (                                -- Products with more sales than
                ALL ( 'Product'[ProductKey] ),     -- the current product
                [Sales Amount] >= CurrentSales
            )
        VAR Result =
            CALCULATE (                             -- Computes the sales of all products
                [Sales Amount],                     -- with more sales than the current
                ProductsWithMoreSales               -- one (including the current product)
            )
        RETURN
            Result
EVALUATE
ADDCOLUMNS (
    ALL ( 'Product'[ProductKey] ),
    "Sales RT", [Sales RT]
)
```

ADDCOLUMNS performs the outermost scan over ALL (*Product[ProductKey]*). During this scan, DAX computes the value of *Sales RT*, which requires building the *ProductsWithMoreSales* variable. *ProductsWithMoreSales* creates a table containing all the product keys with a value for *Sales Amount* greater than or equal to the current product.

Because of the two iterations, the engine evaluates all the pairs of *ProductKey* where the sales amount of the first is less or equal than the sales amount of the second. This evaluation iterates 3,168,903 combinations. For the curious reader, the number is (2,518 * 2,517) / 2, the same order of magnitude as the number of products squared. During the calculation of *Result*, DAX uses the product keys as a filter because we used *ProductsWithMoreSales* as a filter argument in CALCULATE.

When the formula engine computes a table that is later injected in an xmSQL query, you notice the structure starting at line 28. Indeed, at line 27 of the physical query plan, there is a Cache operator that creates a datacache with *Product[ProductKey]* (the column in FieldCols) and the result of *Sales Amount* for each product (the column in ValueCols). This result is produced by using the third storage engine query we mentioned before, which filters the list of 2,517 products obtained by combining 3.2 million combinations of products. The formula engine creates this filter, which is used in the storage engine query because of the filter argument in CALCULATE.

If the measure were a non-additive measure, then the formula engine would have executed one storage engine query for each product, using a SE query for each row. But the formula is a simple sum, so it is additive. The formula engine prefers to compute the sum of the rows for *Sales RT* by itself instead of executing hundreds of storage engine queries.

Therefore, Tabular executes the second query that contains the filter over the product keys – because *ProductsWithMoreSales* is being used as a filter argument in CALCULATE – and the individual product sales. Based on this dataset, DAX can compute the value for each product.

Now that we have a better picture of the algorithm, we understand that the filter is useless. It would be necessary if the formula were not additive. In our scenario, we can rewrite the code to avoid the filter. Moreover, half of the query plan is devoted to creating that filter.

Removing it is as simple as removing the filter from CALCULATE. To do this, we need to store the sales amount of each product in a table variable, to scan that variable instead of using CALCULATE:

```
DEFINE
    MEASURE Sales[Sales RT] =
        VAR CurrentSales = [Sales Amount]
        VAR ProductsWithSales =
            ADDCOLUMNS (
                ALL ( 'Product'[ProductKey] ),
                "@Sales Amount", [Sales Amount]
            )
        VAR ProductsWithMoreSales =
            FILTER (
                ProductsWithSales,
                [@Sales Amount] >= CurrentSales
            )
        VAR Result =
            SUMX (
                ProductsWithMoreSales,
                [@Sales Amount]
            )
        RETURN
            Result
EVALUATE
ADDCOLUMNS (
    ALL ( 'Product'[ProductKey] ),
    "Sales RT", [Sales RT]
)
```

The improvement is significant by using this version of the code.

Total	SE CPU		Line	Subclass	Duration	CPU	Par.	Rows	KB	Timeline
438 ms	828 ms		2	Scan	77	828	x10.8	2,520	40	
	x10.8		4	Scan	0	0		2,520	20	
FE	**SE**									
361 ms	77 ms									
82.4%	17.6%									

SE Queries	SE Cache
2	0
	0.0%

The formula is still dependent on the formula engine. But it runs much faster. The query plan is shorter than the previous ones, and the number of iterations required in the formula engine is also reduced.

Line	Records	Physical Query Plan
1		AddColumns: IterPhyOp LogOp=AddColumns IterCols(0, 1)('Product'[ProductKey], ''[Sales RT])
2	2,517	Spool_Iterator<SpoolIterator>: IterPhyOp LogOp=Scan_Vertipaq IterCols(0)('Product'[ProductKey]) #Records=2517 #K<
3	2,517	ProjectionSpool<ProjectFusion<>>: SpoolPhyOp #Records=2517
4		**Cache: IterPhyOp #FieldCols=1 #ValueCols=0**
5	2,517	SpoolLookup: LookupPhyOp LogOp=SumX LookupCols(0)('Product'[ProductKey]) Currency #Records=2517 #KeyCols=
6	2,517	AggregationSpool<Sum>: SpoolPhyOp #Records=2517
7		Extend_Lookup: IterPhyOp LogOp=Extend_Lookup''[@Sales Amount] IterCols(2)(''[@Sales Amount])
8		Proxy: IterPhyOp LogOp=TableVarProxy IterCols(0, 1, 2)('Product'[ProductKey], 'Product'[ProductKey], ''[@Sales
9		Filter: IterPhyOp LogOp=Filter IterCols(0, 1, 2)('Product'[ProductKey], 'Product'[ProductKey], ''[@Sales Amoul
10		Extend_Lookup: IterPhyOp LogOp=GreaterThanOrEqualTo IterCols(0, 2)('Product'[ProductKey], ''[@Sales A
11		CrossApply: IterPhyOp LogOp=GreaterThanOrEqualTo IterCols(0, 2)('Product'[ProductKey], ''[@Sales Ar
12	2,517	Spool_Iterator<SpoolIterator>: IterPhyOp LogOp=Scan_Vertipaq IterCols(0)('Product'[ProductKey]) A
13	2,517	ProjectionSpool<ProjectFusion<>>: SpoolPhyOp #Records=2517
14		**Cache: IterPhyOp #FieldCols=1 #ValueCols=0**
15		Proxy: IterPhyOp LogOp=TableVarProxy IterCols(1, 2)('Product'[ProductKey], ''[@Sales Amount])
16		AddColumns: IterPhyOp LogOp=AddColumns IterCols(1, 2)('Product'[ProductKey], ''[Sales Amo
17	2,517	Spool_Iterator<SpoolIterator>: IterPhyOp LogOp=Scan_Vertipaq IterCols(1)('Product'[ProductK
18	2,517	ProjectionSpool<ProjectFusion<>>: SpoolPhyOp #Records=2517
19		**Cache: IterPhyOp #FieldCols=1 #ValueCols=0**
20	2,517	SpoolLookup: LookupPhyOp LogOp=Sum_Vertipaq LookupCols(1)('Product'[ProductKey]) Curr<
21	2,517	ProjectionSpool<ProjectFusion<Copy>>: SpoolPhyOp #Records=2517
22		**Cache: IterPhyOp #FieldCols=1 #ValueCols=1**
23		GreaterThanOrEqualTo: LookupPhyOp LogOp=GreaterThanOrEqualTo LookupCols(0, 2)('Product'[Produ
24		ColValue<''[@Sales Amount]>: LookupPhyOp LogOp=ColValue<''[@Sales Amount]>''[@Sales Amou
25	2,517	SpoolLookup: LookupPhyOp LogOp=Sum_Vertipaq LookupCols(0)('Product'[ProductKey]) Currency <
26	2,517	ProjectionSpool<ProjectFusion<Copy>>: SpoolPhyOp #Records=2517
27		**Cache: IterPhyOp #FieldCols=1 #ValueCols=1**
28		ColValue<''[@Sales Amount]>: LookupPhyOp LogOp=ColValue<''[@Sales Amount]>''[@Sales Amount] Lookup

As you see, there are no more large iterations and the entire second section of the query plan is gone.

The interesting detail in this optimization example is that it would have been almost impossible to spot the problem in the formula had we not analyzed the entire query plan. Using CALCULATE in calculating the result forced the optimizer to choose a safer – yet useless – query plan.

Year-over-year customer growth as a percentage

In this example, we analyze and optimize a poorly written query. The query contains several mistakes. Some of the errors are easy to spot; others require a bit more analysis, and in the end we rewrite the code by using somewhat creatively the knowledge we gathered during the study of the query.

The query retrieves the year-over-year growth of the number of distinct customers, as a percentage. The starting point is poorly written:

```
DEFINE
    MEASURE Sales[# Customers] =
        DISTINCTCOUNT ( Sales[CustomerKey] )
    MEASURE Sales[Growth] =
        IF (
            AND (
                [# Customers] > 0,
                CALCULATE ( [# Customers], SAMEPERIODLASTYEAR ( 'Date'[Date] ) ) > 0
            ),
            DIVIDE (
                [# Customers]
                    - CALCULATE ( [# Customers], SAMEPERIODLASTYEAR ( 'Date'[Date] ) ),
                CALCULATE ( [# Customers], SAMEPERIODLASTYEAR ( 'Date'[Date] ) )
            )
        )

EVALUATE
SUMMARIZECOLUMNS ( 'Date'[Year], "Growth %", [Growth] )
```

The result is just the growth percentage year over year. We did not sort the result on purpose to avoid making the query plan more complex due to the final sort.

Year	Growth %
2018	1.23%
2017	3.28%
2020	-20.77%
2015	-2.23%
2014	3.01%
2013	9.57%
2012	2.98%
2011	20.88%
2019	-2.79%
2016	-3.80%

The numbers by themselves are not that interesting. What matters to us is that the query is slow. Let us start by looking at the server timings.

Total	SE CPU	Line	Subclass	Duration	CPU	Par.	Rows	KB	Timeline
10,107 ms	318,015 ms x32.4	2	Scan	1	0		14	1	
FE 278 ms 2.8%	**SE** 9,829 ms 97.2%	4	Scan	0	0		4,021	32	
		6	Scan	3	0		4,018	16	
		10	Scan	257	1,906	x7.4	1	1	
SE Queries 36	**SE Cache** 20 55.6%	14	Scan	330	3,766	x11.4	1	1	
		18	Scan	299	4,578	x15.3	1	1	
		22	Scan	343	6,813	x19.9	1	1	

On our Contoso model, the query runs in 10 seconds. Besides, if we look at the timings alone, the allocation of the formula engine and the storage engine seems to suggest that the query is already optimal: 97% of the time is spent in the storage engine. Nonetheless, we can make further considerations based on the server timings alone:

- There are 36 storage engine queries. 20 of these queries hit the cache, meaning that the same code is executed multiple times. Indeed, by looking at the DAX code, we see that some subexpressions are repeated multiple times.

- The degree of parallelism is pretty good, suggesting a good use of the storage engine.

- The query does not stress the formula engine.

The analysis proceeds with the storage engine queries. The first three queries are already interesting. The first retrieves the values of *Date[Year]*, and it is needed to perform the grouping:

```
SELECT
    'Date'[Year]
FROM 'Date';
```

Next, two queries retrieve all the values of the *Date[Date]* column and then the association between *Date[Date]* and *Date[Year]*:

```
SELECT
    'Date'[Date]
FROM 'Date';

SELECT
    'Date'[Date],
    'Date'[Year]
FROM 'Date';
```

These queries compute the SAMEPERIODLASTYEAR required as part of the condition in the IF function. Indeed, the condition of IF requires a computation of the distinct count of *Sales[CusteromKey]* for the current time period and the previous year. Therefore, the formula engine needs to build for each year, the values of *Date[Date]* in the previous year. Indeed, what follows is a series of 10 queries with this format:

```
SELECT
    DCOUNT ( 'Sales'[CustomerKey] )
FROM 'Sales'
    LEFT OUTER JOIN 'Date'
        ON 'Sales'[Order Date]='Date'[Date]
WHERE
    'Date'[Date] IN ( 41133.000000, 42090.000000, 42131.000000, 43088.000000, 43129.000000, 41051.000000,
41092.000000, 42049.000000, 43047.000000, 40969.000000..[3,652 total values, not all displayed] ) VAND
    'Date'[Date] IN ( 40190.000000, 40231.000000, 40272.000000, 40313.000000, 40354.000000, 40395.000000,
40436.000000, 40477.000000, 40518.000000, 40286.000000..[365 total values, not all displayed] ) ;
```

The first set of 3,652 values is the entire *Date* table, and the second set of 365 values is – as you may have guessed – an entire year. The formula engine detected for each year the set of dates in the previous year (because of SAMEPERIODLASTYEAR) and computed the distinct count of *Sales[CustomerKey]*. There is one such query for each year.

The IF condition includes two measures: the distinct count in the current year and the distinct count in the previous year. It is interesting to note that Tabular had to run ten different queries to retrieve the value for the previous year, whereas the values for the current year are collected through a single query:

```
SELECT
    'Date'[Year],
    DCOUNT ( 'Sales'[CustomerKey] )
FROM 'Sales'
    LEFT OUTER JOIN 'Date'
        ON 'Sales'[Order Date]='Date'[Date];
```

We see one single query that gathers 10 years, instead of 10 different queries, because the engine can rely on the relationship with the date to group by year. On the other hand, when searching for the previous year, the formula engine must create a set of dates. The relationship with the *Date* table becomes useless because SAMEPERIODLASTYEAR filters the *Date[Date]* column, not the *Date[Year]* column.

So far, the formula engine has gathered the values required for the IF condition. We know, from analyses performed earlier, that IF uses a strict algorithm by default. Therefore, we can expect the formula engine to evaluate the condition for the 10 years and split it into two lists: one for the true condition and one for the false condition. In this specific case, because there is no false value, the formula engine finds only the years for which it does need to complete the calculation.

It turns out that the only year missing from the calculation is 2010. Indeed, there were no sales in the previous year. From 2011 to 2020, all remaining years require computing the true branch of IF.

The true branch requires the same values already computed. Indeed, the following query gathers the individual dates for only the required years (2011-2020):

```
SELECT
    'Date'[Date],
    'Date'[Year]
FROM 'Date'
WHERE
    'Date'[Year] IN ( 2011, 2012, 2013, 2014, 2015, 2016, 2017, 2018, 2019, 2020 ) ;
```

The subsequent queries are identical to the ones already executed to retrieve the SAMEPERIODLASTYEAR. These are the queries that hit the cache. What is relevant here is that the formula engine executes the queries again. The cache system of VertiPaq does not repeat the query execution because the queries are identical to queries already executed. Nonetheless, the formula engine does not optimize the repeated code in the condition and in the true branch of IF.

Indeed, the last query of the set retrieves the values for the current year. This query is no longer identical to the previous one. The previous query, retrieving the distinct count by year, had no filter applied. This one contains a filter for the relevant years:

```
SELECT
    'Date'[Year],
    DCOUNT ( 'Sales'[CustomerKey] )
FROM 'Sales'
    LEFT OUTER JOIN 'Date'
        ON 'Sales'[Order Date]='Date'[Date]
WHERE
    'Date'[Year] IN ( 2011, 2012, 2013, 2014, 2015, 2016, 2017, 2018, 2019, 2020 ) ;
```

Because of the presence of the filter, this query does not hit the cache and it must be executed, as it is not identical to any previous query.

The last set of queries is made of 10 other queries to retrieve, again, the values in SAMEPERIODLASTYEAR. There are two sets because one value is required at the numerator and one at the denominator. Because of the cache, both expressions are requested by the formula engine and not executed by the storage engine.

We could look at the physical query plan to confirm the algorithm. The thing is, the query plan exceeds 10,000 rows. Not only it is not shown by DAX Studio, but it is also just impossible to analyze.

Now that we have a clear picture of the algorithm and its weak points, we can test some different options. It is clear (it already was just by looking at the code) that using variables to store the current and previous year's values is a good option. Moreover, it may be a good option to use IF.EAGER here. Indeed, by using IF.EAGER we avoid the separate evaluation of the condition and the true branch of IF. This reduces the number of storage engine queries and the complexity of the query plan.

Using variables and IF.EAGER is somewhat equivalent in this scenario. By using IF.EAGER, we would rely on the optimizer to create temporary variables, and leave it the task of figuring out which ones are the best variables. By creating variables, we can have finer control over which parts of the code need to be computed upfront. The following is the version with the variables:

```
DEFINE
    MEASURE Sales[# Customers] =
        DISTINCTCOUNT ( Sales[CustomerKey] )
    MEASURE Sales[Growth] =
        VAR CY = [# Customers]
        VAR PY =
            CALCULATE ( [# Customers], SAMEPERIODLASTYEAR ( 'Date'[Date] ) )
        VAR Result =
            IF ( CY > 0 && PY > 0, DIVIDE ( CY - PY, PY ) )
        RETURN
            Result

EVALUATE
SUMMARIZECOLUMNS ( 'Date'[Year], "Growth %", [Growth] )
```

The advantage of performing such a thorough analysis of the initial DAX query is that we now have a clear picture of the algorithm the engine is executing. Therefore, we can draw a lot of interesting conclusions just by looking at the server timings.

Total	SE CPU	Line	Subclass	Duration	CPU	Par.	Rows	KB	Timeline
6,780 ms	208,844 ms								
	x31.7	2	Scan	0	0		4,021	32	
⬤ FE	⬤ SE	4	Scan	0	0		4,018	16	
184 ms	6,596 ms	8	Scan	250	2,359	x9.4	1	1	
2.7%	97.3%	12	Scan	327	4,828	x14.8	1	1	
		16	Scan	348	5,375	x15.4	1	1	
SE Queries	SE Cache	20	Scan	347	7,516	x21.7	1	1	
14	0								
	0.0%	24	Scan	360	8,141	x22.6	1	1	

The query is faster because it uses less storage engine CPU and executes fewer SE queries. The reason is quite simple: the DAX engine retrieves all the values of the current and the previous years upfront, reusing the datacaches. We would have obtained a similar behavior by using IF.EAGER, although the code that relies on variables is more readable.

It would make sense to stop at this point. However, since we now have a clear picture of why the query is slow, we can perform several more steps and completely change the algorithm.

We could avoid using the time intelligence calculations and perform an entirely different algorithm. We could:

- Gather the distinct count of *Sales[ProductKey]* sliced by year, and store it into a variable.

- Retrieve the currently-visible year.

- Search in the variable computed earlier for the previous year.

- Perform the calculation.

The goal is to reduce the number of storage engine queries and push the entire calculation to the formula engine. We mentioned multiple times that optimization aims to push most of the calculation to the storage engine. Despite that statement, in this scenario, we aim to reduce the storage engine queries: indeed, we have noticed that the queries to retrieve the previous years require a filter on the *Date[Date]* column. This results in suboptimal code.

There are multiple ways to obtain our goal. We will show two examples. Here is the first:

```
DEFINE
    MEASURE Sales[# Customers] =
        DISTINCTCOUNT ( Sales[CustomerKey] )
    MEASURE Sales[Growth] =
        VAR Vals =
            ADDCOLUMNS ( ALLSELECTED ( 'Date'[Year] ), "@CY", [# Customers] )
        VAR CurrentYear =
            SELECTEDVALUE ( 'Date'[Year] )
        VAR CY =
            MINX ( FILTER ( Vals, 'Date'[Year] = CurrentYear ), [@CY] )
        VAR PY =
            MINX ( FILTER ( Vals, 'Date'[Year] = CurrentYear - 1 ), [@CY] )
        VAR Result =
            IF ( CY > 0 && PY > 0, DIVIDE ( CY - PY, PY ) )
        RETURN
            Result

EVALUATE
SUMMARIZECOLUMNS ( 'Date'[Year], "Growth %", [Growth] )
```

As you see, this code is more convoluted than the previous code. Nonetheless, the server timings show significant improvement in terms of speed.

Total	SE CPU		Line	Subclass	Duration	CPU	Par.	Rows	KB	Timeline
3,458 ms	134,797 ms		2	Scan	0	0		14	1	
	x39.6		6	Scan	3,400	134,797	x39.6	11	1	
FE	SE									
58 ms	3,400 ms									
1.7%	98.3%									
SE Queries	SE Cache									
2	0									
	0.0%									

All numbers are way better than before. Only two storage engine queries, much less storage engine CPU. While it is true that we shifted the calculations to the formula engine, the tables generated by this algorithm are so small that the additional effort is negligible.

There are just two storage engine queries. The first retrieves the values of *Date[Year]*:

```
SET DC_KIND="AUTO";
SELECT
    'Date'[Year]
FROM 'Date';
```

And the second storage engine query retrieves the number of customers per year:

```
SELECT
    'Date'[Year],
    DCOUNT ( 'Sales'[CustomerKey] )
FROM 'Sales'
    LEFT OUTER JOIN 'Date'
        ON 'Sales'[Order Date]='Date'[Date];
```

The formula engine oversees all the remaining tasks.

For educational purposes, it is worth studying another formulation of the same algorithm. A bit less readable than the previous one, but also more flexible in case it needs to be adjusted. This time we start with the same table with the number of customers by year, but then we create another table with the next year and join them through NATURALINNERJOIN:

```
DEFINE
    MEASURE 'Sales'[# Customers] =
        DISTINCTCOUNT ( 'Sales'[CustomerKey] )
    MEASURE 'Sales'[Growth] =
        VAR Vals =
            ADDCOLUMNS ( ALLSELECTED ( 'Date'[Year] ), "@CY", [# Customers] )
        VAR ValsPrevYear =
            SELECTCOLUMNS ( Vals, "@Year", 'Date'[Year] + 1, "@PY", [@CY] )
        VAR ValsCurYear =
            SELECTCOLUMNS ( Vals, "@Year", 'Date'[Year] + 0, "@CY", [@CY] )
        VAR AllVals =
            NATURALINNERJOIN ( ValsCurYear, ValsPrevYear )
        VAR CurrentYear =
            SELECTEDVALUE ( 'Date'[Year] )
        VAR Result =
            MINX (
                FILTER ( AllVals, [@Year] = CurrentYear ),
                IF ( [@CY] > 0 && [@PY] > 0, DIVIDE ( [@CY] - [@PY], [@PY] ) )
            )
        RETURN
            Result

EVALUATE
SUMMARIZECOLUMNS ( 'Date'[Year], "Growth %", [Growth] )
```

The storage engine queries and the execution time are nearly identical to the previous query. Indeed, the timing of this algorithm is dictated by the storage engine queries. The formula engine does most of the calculation but uses a tiny fraction of the overall time.

The optimization we have seen in this example provides different benefits with different storage engines. For example, the DirectQuery over SQL storage engine is much slower than VertiPaq. Therefore, reducing the number of queries sent to SQL and relying more on the formula engine results in a much more significant increase in performance. Even though we will be covering DirectQuery over SQL in its own dedicated section, it is helpful to see the difference between the first and the last queries we wrote in this example when executed over DirectQuery over SQL. Here is the first query:

```
DEFINE
    MEASURE 'Sales DQ'[# Customers] =
        DISTINCTCOUNT ( 'Sales DQ'[CustomerKey] )
    MEASURE 'Sales DQ'[Growth] =
        IF (
            AND (
                [# Customers] > 0,
                CALCULATE ( [# Customers], SAMEPERIODLASTYEAR ( 'Date DQ'[Date] ) ) > 0
            ),
            DIVIDE (
                [# Customers]
                    - CALCULATE([# Customers], SAMEPERIODLASTYEAR ( 'Date DQ'[Date] )),
                CALCULATE ( [# Customers], SAMEPERIODLASTYEAR ( 'Date DQ'[Date] ) )
            )
        )

EVALUATE
SUMMARIZECOLUMNS ( 'Date DQ'[Year], "Growth %", [Growth] )
```

The server timings pane shows that the query runs in around 15 seconds, with nine storage engine queries executed:

Total	SE CPU	Line	Subclass	Duration	CPU	Par.	Rows	KB	Timeline
15,413 ms	14,703 ms x1.0	1	SQL	3	3	x1.0			
		2	SQL	1	1	x1.0			
FE	SE	3	SQL	0	0				
705 ms 4.6%	14,708 ms 95.4%	4	SQL	3,297	3,296	x1.0			
		5	SQL	2,387	2,387	x1.0			
SE Queries	SE Cache	6	SQL	3	1	x0.3			
9	0 0.0%	7	SQL	3,347	3,347	x1.0			
		8	SQL	2,377	2,375	x1.0			
		9	SQL	3,293	3,293	x1.0			

The number of storage engine queries is smaller because of the advanced features available in SQL and not in VertiPaq.

The last – optimized – version of the query running over DirectQuery is the following:

```
DEFINE
    MEASURE 'Sales DQ'[# Customers] =
        DISTINCTCOUNT ( 'Sales DQ'[CustomerKey] )
    MEASURE 'Sales DQ'[Growth] =
        VAR Vals =
            ADDCOLUMNS ( ALLSELECTED ( 'Date DQ'[Year] ), "@CY", [# Customers] )
        VAR ValsPrevYear =
            SELECTCOLUMNS ( Vals, "@Year", 'Date DQ'[Year] + 1, "@PY", [@CY] )
        VAR ValsCurYear =
            SELECTCOLUMNS ( Vals, "@Year", 'Date DQ'[Year] + 0, "@CY", [@CY] )
        VAR AllVals =
            NATURALINNERJOIN ( ValsCurYear, ValsPrevYear )
        VAR CurrentYear =
            SELECTEDVALUE ( 'Date DQ'[Year] )
        VAR Result =
            MINX (
                FILTER ( AllVals, [@Year] = CurrentYear ),
                IF ( [@CY] > 0 && [@PY] > 0, DIVIDE ( [@CY] - [@PY], [@PY] ) )
            )
        RETURN
            Result

EVALUATE
SUMMARIZECOLUMNS ( 'Date DQ'[Year], "Growth %", [Growth] )
```

When executed, it shows a massive improvement in terms of performance.

Total	SE CPU	Line	Subclass	Duration	CPU	Par.	Rows	KB	Timeline
2,527 ms	2,516 ms								
	x1.0	1	SQL	3	2	x0.7			
		2	SQL	2,514	2,514	x1.0			
◌ FE	◌ SE								
10 ms	2,517 ms								
0.4%	99.6%								
SE Queries	SE Cache								
2	0								
	0.0%								

The engine executes only two storage engine queries. The simpler algorithm also highly reduced the formula engine use, despite the DAX code being more complex.

As you have seen in this example, we get insights about possible optimizations by learning what Tabular performs to answer a query. The more we understand the underlying algorithm, the more new ideas become available to us.

Conclusions

In this book's first section, we focused on the formula engine. We cannot ignore the storage engine while talking about the formula engine. The two engines work very closely together. Therefore, we used the storage engine queries to deduce the behavior of the formula engine, and we measured the performance of both the formula engine and the storage engine.

You have also seen that pushing the calculation down to the storage engine is not always your best option. It is most of the time – but not always. There are scenarios where pushing calculations into the formula engine might let us reuse datacaches already computed, and in turn improve the level of performance.

Despite the topics of the following chapters being storage engines, we extensively talk about the formula engine there as well – just like we had to mention several behaviors of the storage engine when talking about the formula engine.

Indeed, starting from the next chapter, we perform a very deep analysis of the different storage engines available in Tabular: how they work and how to improve query performance by better understanding the internals of each storage engine.

Section 3
VERTIPAQ

Understanding the VertiPaq engine

VertiPaq is the native database used by Tabular when developers create import models. Data is loaded from the data sources in the in-memory columnar database, which then serves as the storage engine to execute queries. In the sections about the formula engine, we have already seen many queries executed by the VertiPaq storage engine.

However, to obtain the best results from DAX queries running on VertiPaq, you need to learn the internal details of the VertiPaq storage engine. VertiPaq is a database with several peculiarities. You should know the details to make educated choices about the architecture of your model.

Using VertiPaq Analyzer

In this chapter, the focus is on the internals of the VertiPaq engine. During the description of the theoretical topics, we provide several examples to better understand the concepts. The examples require monitoring multiple aspects of a model, like the size of individual columns, the number of segments created for each column, the effects of changing the granularity of columns, and more.

We are about to introduce each concept in a separate section. Before doing this, we must be able to monitor all the important information about a Tabular model. Therefore, the first topic we cover is how to use Vertipaq Analyzer.

VertiPaq Analyzer is a library that extracts information from a Tabular model and saves it in a compressed set of standard JSON files. We often refer to this file as vpax, from the extension of the files generated by VertiPaq Analyzer. The VertiPaq Analyzer library is used by different tools, including DAX Studio, Tabular Editor, Bravo for Power BI, and the VertiPaq Analyzer Excel file. All these tools provide the same information, although they offer different user interfaces and features. Mostly, we use DAX Studio as the interface to see the VertiPaq Analyzer information. We use the VertiPaq Analyzer Excel file to show particular details not available in DAX Studio.

The amount of information that VertiPaq Analyzer provides is massive, and it will make sense only after reading the entire chapter. Therefore, this section introduces VertiPaq Analyzer without spending time describing each aspect. For now, the focus is on letting our reader follow the demos.

Gathering vpax information with DAX Studio

Tabular enables the discovery of all the information about the data model using Dynamic Management Views (DMV). DMVs are extremely useful for exploring how a model is compressed, the space used by different columns and tables, the number of segments in a table, or the number of bits used by columns in different segments.

The most effective way to execute DMVs is by using DAX Studio. DAX Studio offers a list of all DMVs in a simple way without the need to remember them. That said, DMVs are not intended to be read and understood by humans. DMVs provide very compact, technical information: they are perfect if consumed by a software tool, but they prove to be really challenging to be interpreted by humans.

When you are interested in gathering information about a model, a more efficient way to use DMVs is first to generate a .vpax file, and then analyze its content by using Tabular Editor, DAX Studio, or VertiPaq Analyzer. A .vpax file is a compressed archive containing JSON files with all the relevant information about a data model, without including any data from the model itself. A developer can create a .vpax file by using DAX Studio. The .vpax file is self-contained, meaning that once you save the information in a .vpax file, you can analyze a model without being connected to the Tabular instance. Examining a model offline is especially useful when working with consultants or other team members: sending a .vpax file by email is enough to share the relevant information about a model so that consultants can obtain a clear picture of the model without even being connected to it.

You can import, export, or view vpax information using the Advanced tab of DAX Studio.

Export Metrics lets you create a .vpax file of the model DAX Studio is currently connected to. Import metrics lets you load the vpax information from a previously-saved file. View Metrics lets you visualize the metrics.

DAX Studio lets you view most of the valuable information in a model. On the other hand, the VertiPaq Analyzer Excel file gives you the option to view all the detailed information in a .vpax file and – being an Excel workbook – lets you save the information, rearrange the layout, and add comments.

Developers use DAX Studio to obtain a quick overview of a model. In case more details are needed, they can use the VertiPaq Analyzer Excel file to understand the model further. To quickly view the vpax information of a model, you can use the View Metrics button once DAX Studio is connected to the desired model.

Here is an example of the information retrieved for our test model.

Tables	Name	Cardinality	Total Size ↓	Data	Dictionary	Hier Size	Encoding	Data Type
Columns	◢ **Sales**	**225,616,948**	**2,602,349,424**	**2,539,730,088**	**42,341,056**	**15,287,344**	**Many**	-
Relationships	CustomerKey	1,868,084	657,618,104	601,646,344	41,027,072	14,944,688	HASH	Int64
Relationships	Net Price	24,754	442,288,816	441,463,704	627,064	198,048	HASH	Decimal
Partitions	ProductKey	2,517	356,662,420	356,566,368	75,908	20,144	HASH	Int64
Summary	Unit Cost	1,956	311,074,232	311,017,176	41,392	15,664	HASH	Decimal
	Unit Price	1,761	310,055,228	310,000,560	40,572	14,096	HASH	Decimal
	Delivery Date	3,389	209,785,884	209,591,336	167,428	27,120	HASH	DateTime
	Order Date	3,281	160,182,944	159,990,928	165,760	26,256	HASH	DateTime
	Exchange Rate	5,071	96,058,364	95,843,264	174,524	40,576	HASH	Double
	StoreKey	74	49,756,240	49,752,984	2,648	608	HASH	Int64
	Quantity	10	3,643,992	3,642,528	1,368	96	HASH	Int64
	Currency Code	5	232,128	214,896	17,184	48	HASH	String
	▷ **Customer**	**1,868,084**	**201,323,397**	**25,967,920**	**137,940,517**	**37,414,960**	**Many**	-
	▷ **CurrencyExchan...**	**202,100**	**1,280,944**	**727,584**	**396,152**	**144,264**	**Many**	-
	▷ **Product**	**2,517**	**508,816**	**38,736**	**403,728**	**66,352**	**Many**	-
	▷ **Date**	**4,018**	**420,762**	**39,544**	**333,346**	**47,872**	**Many**	-
	▷ **Store**	**74**	**81,264**	**744**	**78,064**	**2,456**	**Many**	-
	▷ Date DO	0	8 338	126	8 193	0	DO	

As we announced earlier, we will not describe all the details provided by the VertiPaq Analyzer in this short introduction. Step by step, we will discover the details by providing examples of the theoretical concepts.

Analyzing a vpax with VertiPaq Analyzer

You can save the information gathered by DAX Studio as a .vpax file by simply using the Export Metrics button. You can then load the .vpax file in the VertiPaq Analyzer Excel tool. VertiPaq Analyzer is an Excel file containing a Power Pivot model that provides the same information that DAX Studio visualizes. However, being an Excel file, VertiPaq Analyzer provides much more flexibility.

You can download VertiPaq Analyzer from the following link: https://www.sqlbi.com/tools/vertipaq-analyzer/. Once it is open, you need to load the .vpax file previously saved with DAX Studio by using the Open VPAX button in the VertiPaq Analyzer ribbon.

Once the file is loaded in the Power Pivot model, VertiPaq Analyzer provides a set of Excel worksheets with pivot tables based on the data model populated with the content of the .vpax file. The main advantage of using VertiPaq Analyzer is the ability to build your pivot tables and reports to analyze specific aspects of your model.

Row Labels	Cardinality	Table Size	Columns Total Size	Data Size	Dictionary Size
⊞ Customer	1,868,084	201,934,041	201,934,041	25,967,920	138,551,161
⊞ Date	4,018	433,338	433,338	39,544	345,922
⊞ Date DQ	0	7,496	7,496	128	7,368
⊞ Product	2,517	508,000	508,000	38,736	402,912
⊞ Product DQ	0	7,080	7,080	112	6,968
⊟ Sales	225,616,948	2,602,499,376	2,597,508,440	2,539,730,088	42,491,008
Currency Code	5		232,064	214,896	17,120
CustomerKey	1,868,084		657,618,112	601,646,344	41,027,080
Delivery Date	3,389		209,796,352	209,591,336	177,896
Exchange Rate	5,071		96,188,216	95,843,264	304,376
Net Price	24,754		442,288,680	441,463,704	626,928
Order Date	3,281		160,192,856	159,990,928	175,672
ProductKey	2,517		356,662,428	356,566,368	75,916
Quantity	10		3,644,000	3,642,528	1,376
StoreKey	74		49,756,248	49,752,984	2,656
Unit Cost	1,956		311,074,472	311,017,176	41,632
Unit Price	1,761		310,055,012	310,000,560	40,356
⊞ Sales DQ	0	5,016	5,000	104	4,896
⊞ Store	74	80,816	80,816	744	77,616
Grand Total	227,491,641	2,805,475,163	2,800,484,211	2,565,777,376	181,887,851

Being able to save an Excel workbook with the relevant information about a data model provides the option of comparing the effect of changes and updates to your model and analyzing the changes over time in terms of memory size.

Tabular data types

In this chapter, we talk about different data types. We included a table that recaps the different data types available in DAX and the names used for the same data types in different products, because these different names are often confusing. The book mainly uses the definitions included in the DAX Data Type column.

Data Types

DAX Data Type	Data type in DAX CONVERT function	Power BI Data Type	Power Pivot and Analysis Services Data Type	Corresponding Conventional Data Type (e.g., SQL Server)	Tabular Object Model (TOM) Data Type
Integer	INTEGER	Whole Number	Whole Number	Integer / INT	int64
Decimal	DOUBLE	Decimal Number	Decimal Number	Floating point / DOUBLE	double
Currency	CURRENCY	Fixed Decimal Number	Currency	Currency / MONEY	decimal
DateTime	DATETIME	DateTime, Date, Time	Date	Date / DATETIME	dateTime
Boolean	BOOLEAN	True/False	True/False	Boolean / BIT	boolean
String	STRING	Text	Text	String / NVARCHAR(MAX)	string

Introduction to the VertiPaq columnar database

VertiPaq is an in-memory columnar database. Being in-memory means that all the data of the model resides in RAM. However, VertiPaq is not only an in-memory database, but also a columnar database. A good understanding of what a columnar database is, is key to understanding VertiPaq well.

We usually think of a table as a list of rows, with each row divided into columns. For example, consider the following *Product* table.

Product

ID	Name	Color	Unit Price
1	Camcorder	Red	112.25
2	Camera	Red	97.50
3	Smartphone	White	100.00
4	Console	Black	112.25
5	TV	Blue	1,240.85
6	CD	Red	39.99
7	Touch screen	Blue	45.12
8	PDA	Black	120.25
9	Keyboard	Black	120.50

Thinking of a table as a set of rows, we use the most natural visualization of a table structure. Technically, this is known as a row store. In a row store, data is organized by rows. When the table is stored in memory, the value of the *Name* column in the first row is adjacent to the values of the *ID* and *Color* columns in the same row. On the other hand, the value in the second row of the *Name* column is slightly farther from the *Name* value in the first row because in between we find *Color* and *Unit Price* in the first row and the value of the *ID* column in the second row. As an example, the following code is a schematic representation of the physical memory layout of a row store:

```
1, Camcorder, Red, 112.25 |
2, Camera, Red, 97.50 |
3, Smartphone, White, 100.00 |
4, Console, Black, 112.25 |
5, TV, Blue,1, 240.85 |
6, CD, Red, 39.99 |
7, Touch screen, Blue, 45.12 |
8, PDA, Black, 120.25 |
9, Keyboard, Black, 120.50
```

Imagine a developer needing to compute the sum of *Unit Price*. The engine must scan the entire memory area, reading many irrelevant values in the process. Imagine scanning the database's memory sequentially: To read the first value of *Unit Price*, the engine needs to read (and skip) the first row of *ID*, *Name*, and *Color*. Only then does it find an interesting value. The same process is repeated for all the rows. Following this technique, the engine needs to read and ignore many columns to find the relevant values to sum.

Reading and ignoring values take time. If we asked someone to compute the sum of *Unit Price*, they would not follow that algorithm. Instead, human beings would probably scan the first row of the table to search for the position of *Unit Price*, then move their eyes down, reading the values one at a time and mentally accumulating them to produce the sum. This very natural behavior is because we save time by reading vertically instead of row by row. Unfortunately, reading vertically is not an option if data is arranged in memory row by row.

A columnar database organizes data to optimize the vertical scanning of table columns. To obtain this result, it needs to store the information so that the different values of a column end up adjacent. In other words, all the values of the Unit Price column must be in the same memory area, with no other column values in the middle. In the next figure, you can see the *Product* table from before, organized by a columnar database.

Product Columns

ID	Name	Color	Unit Price
1	Camcorder	Red	112.25
2	Camera	Red	97.50
3	Smartphone	White	100.00
4	Console	Black	112.25
5	TV	Blue	1,240.85
6	CD	Red	39.99
7	Touch screen	Blue	45.12
8	PDA	Black	120.25
9	Keyboard	Black	120.50

When stored in a columnar database, each column has its data structure; it is physically separated from the others. Consequently, the different values of *Unit Price* are adjacent to one another and distant from *Color*, *Name*, and *ID*. The following code is a schematic representation of the physical memory layout of a column store:

```
ID,1,2,3,4,5,6,7,8,9
Name,Camcorder,Camera,Smartphone,Console,TV,CD,Touch screen,PDA,Keyboard
Color,Red,Red,White,Black,Blue,Red,Blue,Black,Black
Unit Price,112.25,97.50,100.00,112.25,1240.85,39.99,45.12,120.25,120.50
```

With this data structure, computing the sum of *Unit Price* is faster because the engine immediately goes to the structure containing *Unit Price*. There, it finds all the values needed to perform the computation next to each other. In other words, it does not have to read and ignore other column values: In a single scan, it obtains exclusively useful numbers, and it can quickly aggregate them.

In our next scenario, we compute the sum of *Unit Price* just for the Red products instead of summing *Unit Price*. It would help if you tried this before reading on to understand the algorithm better.

This manual calculation is not so easy anymore; it is no longer possible to obtain the desired number by simply scanning the *Unit Price* column. Developers would typically scan the *Color* column, and whenever it is Red, retrieve the corresponding value in *Unit Price*. In the end, all the values would be summed up to compute the result.

Though very intuitive, this algorithm requires a constant move of the eyes from one column to the other, possibly using a finger as a guide to save the last scanned position of *Color*. It is not an optimized way of computing the value. The reason is that the engine needs to constantly jump from one memory area to another, resulting in poor performance. A better way – which only computers use – is to scan the *Color* column, find the positions where the color is Red, and then scan the *Unit Price* column, summing only the values in the positions identified in the previous step.

This last algorithm is better because it performs one scan of the first column and one scan of the second column, always accessing memory locations adjacent to one another instead of jumping between the first and the second column during the table scan. Sequential reading of memory is much faster than random access.

Things are even worse for a more complex expression, such as the sum of the prices of all products that are either Blue or Black with a price greater than US$50. This time, there is no possibility of scanning the column one at a time because the condition depends on way too many columns. As usual, trying on paper helps better understand the problem.

There are multiple options here. One can scan the *Color* column, stop when it is either Blue or Black, and then move to the corresponding row in the price column to further check whether the price is greater than 50. If that holds true, then the value must be considered in the sum; otherwise, jump back to the *Color* column and move forward. This algorithm requires a lot of jumping back and forth between columns, so it is not optimal.

Another simple algorithm producing the desired result is to scan the table on a row basis instead of a column basis. We naturally tend to scan the table row-by-row, though the storage organization is column-by-column. Although it is a very simple operation when executed on paper by a human, the same operation is extremely expensive if executed by a computer in RAM; indeed, it requires a lot of random reads of memory, leading to poorer performance than if computed doing a sequential scan.

As we learn later, Tabular uses the best option: it scans *Color* and *Unit Price* separately, marks the rows satisfying the conditions, intersects the two partial results, and finally performs a final scan to grab the values to sum. This technique requires multiple scans, but each of these scans is fast because it is completely sequential.

A columnar storage presents both pros and cons. Columnar databases provide very quick access to a single column. Still, as soon as one needs a calculation involving more columns, after having read the column content in the columnar database, one spends time reorganizing the information and computing the final expression. Even though this example was very simple, it helps to highlight the most important characteristics of column stores:

- Single-column access is very fast: Tabular sequentially reads a single block of memory and then computes whatever aggregation is needed on that memory block.

- If an expression uses several columns, the algorithm is more complex because the engine must access different memory areas at different times, keeping track of the progress in a temporary area.

- The more columns are needed to compute an expression, the harder it becomes to produce a result. At a certain point, it becomes easier to rebuild the row storage out of the column store to compute the expression.

Column stores aim to reduce the read time. However, they spend more CPU cycles rearranging the data when more columns from the same table are used. On the other hand, row stores have a more linear algorithm to scan data, but they result in many useless reads of columns not used in the calculation. As a rule, reducing reads at the cost of increasing CPU utilization is a good deal because it is easier (and cheaper) to increase the CPU speed than to reduce I/O (or memory access) time with modern computers.

Moreover, as we will see in the next sections, columnar databases offer more options to reduce the time spent scanning data. The most relevant technique used by VertiPaq is compression.

Understanding VertiPaq compression

In the previous section, you learned that VertiPaq stores each column in a separate data structure. This simple fact allows the engine to implement extremely important amounts of compression and encoding described in this section.

The actual details of the compression algorithm of VertiPaq are proprietary. Thus, we cannot publish them in a book. Yet what we explain in this chapter is a good approximation of what takes place in the engine, and we can use it, for all intents and purposes, to describe how the VertiPaq engine stores data.

VertiPaq compression algorithms aim to reduce the memory footprint of a data model. Reducing the memory size of a model is a very important task for two very good reasons:

- A smaller model makes better use of the hardware. Why spend money on 1 TB of RAM when the same model, once compressed, can be stored in 256 GB? Saving RAM is always a good option when feasible.

- A smaller model is faster to scan. As simple as this rule is, it is very important when speaking about performance. If a column is compressed, the engine scans less RAM to read its content, resulting in better performance.

Data compression uses several techniques: value encoding, hash encoding, and run-length encoding. Each type of encoding has important properties, that ultimately affect query performance.

Understanding value encoding

Value encoding is the first type of encoding that VertiPaq might use to reduce the memory cost of a column. Consider a column containing the price of products stored as integer values. The column contains many different values, and a defined number of bits is required to represent all of them. The minimum number of bits required to store a value depends on the largest value VertiPaq needs to store. Indeed, storing a value like 1,000,000 requires more bits than storing a smaller number, like 12.

In the following example, the maximum value of *Unit Price* is 216. At least 8 bits are required to store each integer value up to that number. Nevertheless, by using a simple mathematical operation, Tabular can reduce the storage to 5 bits only.

Reducing the number of bits needed

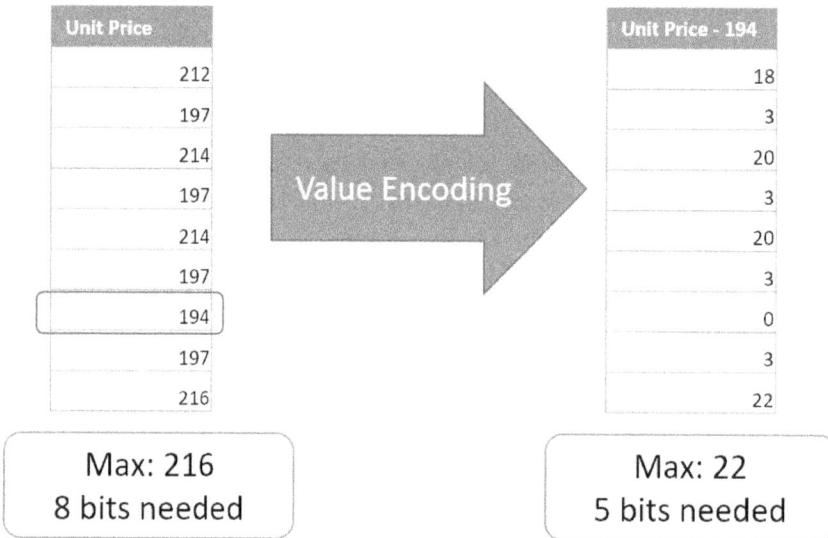

In the example, VertiPaq found out that subtracting the minimum value (194) from all the values of the column could modify the range of the values in the column, reducing it to a range from 0 to 22. Storing numbers up to 22 requires fewer bits than storing numbers up to 216. While 3 bits might seem like insignificant savings, multiplying this by a few billion rows makes it easy to see what a difference it makes.

The VertiPaq engine is more sophisticated than this. It can discover mathematical relationships between the values of a column, and when it finds them, it can use these mathematical relationships to modify the storage, reducing the memory footprint of the column as a result. Later on, when the column values are read, Tabular must apply the opposite transformation to obtain the original value. Depending on the transformation, this can happen before or after aggregating the values. Again, this increases CPU utilization and reduces the number of reads, which is a very good option.

Value encoding only takes place for numeric columns because it cannot be applied to strings. Be mindful that VertiPaq stores the *Currency* data type of DAX (also called Fixed Decimal Number in Power BI) as an integer value. However, double floating-point numbers (also known as *Decimal* in DAX and Power BI) can also be represented with value encoding. What drives the adoption of value encoding is the ability to apply mathematical operations that transform the column values into a range of integer values.

Understanding hash encoding

If value encoding is not the best option, then the engine reverts to hash encoding. Hash encoding (also known as dictionary encoding) is another technique used by VertiPaq to reduce the number of bits required to store a column. Hash encoding builds a dictionary of the distinct values of a column and then replaces the column values with indexes in the dictionary. The following figure shows the storage of the *Color* column, which uses strings and cannot be value-encoded.

Replacing datatypes with dictionary and indexes

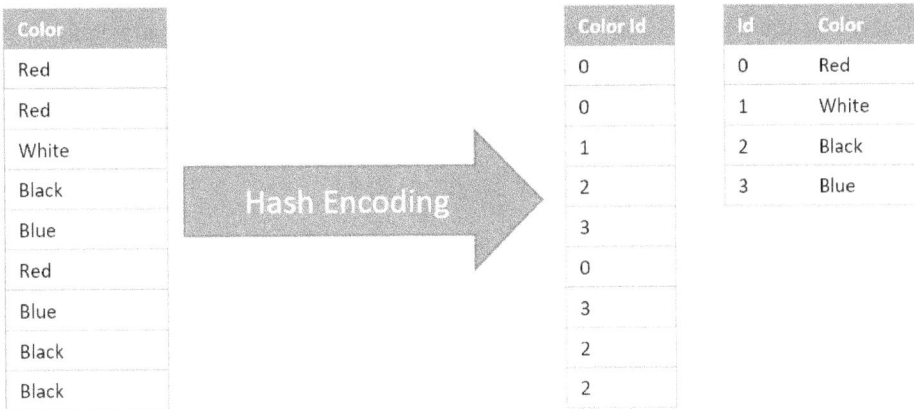

Color
Red
Red
White
Black
Blue
Red
Blue
Black
Black

Hash Encoding →

Color Id
0
0
1
2
3
0
3
2
2

Id	Color
0	Red
1	White
2	Black
3	Blue

When VertiPaq hash-encodes a column, it:

- Builds a dictionary containing the distinct values of the column;

- Replaces the values with integer numbers, where each number is the dictionary index of the original value.

There are some advantages in using hash encoding:

- All columns are represented with integer values; this makes it simpler to optimize the internal code of the engine. Moreover, it also means that VertiPaq is independent from the data type.

- The number of bits used to store a single value is the minimum number of bits necessary to store an index entry. In the example provided, 2 bits are enough because there are only four different values in the column.

These two aspects are of paramount importance for VertiPaq. It does not matter whether a column uses a string, a 64-bit integer, or a floating point to represent a value. All these data types can be hash encoded, which usually reduces the memory required and improves scanning speed.

The primary factor in determining the column size is not the data type. Instead, it is the number of distinct values of the column. We refer to the number of distinct values of a column as its *cardinality*. Repeating a concept this important is always a good thing: Of all the various aspects of an individual column, its cardinality is the most important aspect when designing a data model.

The lower the cardinality, the smaller the number of bits required to store a single value, the smaller the dictionary in case of hash encoding – and consequently, the smaller the memory footprint of the column. If a column is smaller, not only it is possible to store more data in the same amount of RAM, but it is also much faster to scan that column.

Understanding run-length encoding

Hash encoding and value encoding are two very good compression techniques. However, there is another complementary compression technique used by VertiPaq: Run Length Encoding (RLE). This technique aims to reduce the size of a column by avoiding repeated values. For example, consider a column that records in which quarter the sales took place, stored in the *Sales* table. This column might contain the string "Q1" repeated many times in contiguous rows, for all the sales in the same quarter. In that case, VertiPaq avoids storing values that are repeated. It replaces them with a slightly more complex structure that contains the value only once and the number of contiguous rows sharing the same value.

Reducing rows using Run Length Encoding (RLE)

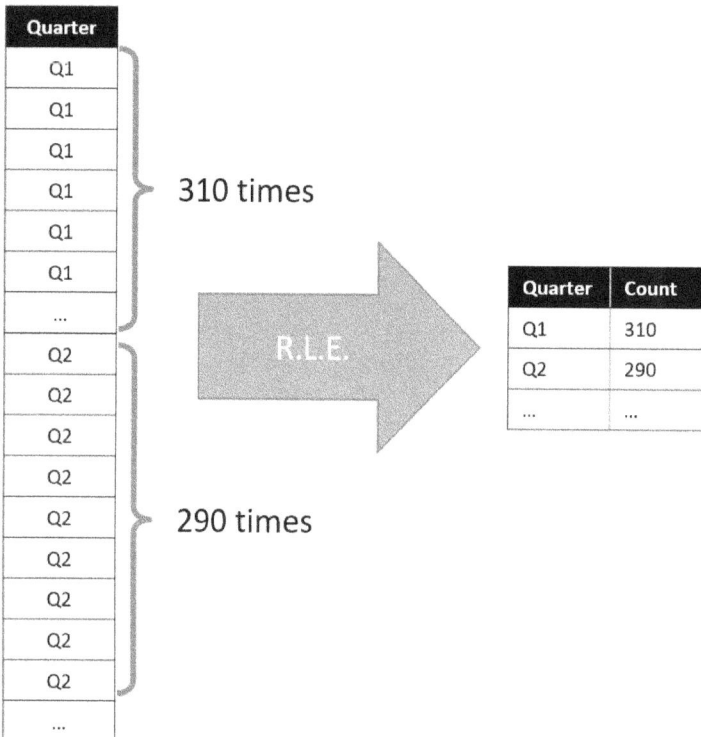

RLE's efficiency strongly depends on the repetition pattern of the column. Some columns have the same value repeated for many rows, resulting in a great compression ratio. Other columns with quickly changing values produce a lower compression ratio. Data sorting is extremely important to improve the compression ratio of RLE. The Tabular engine tries to sort data in different ways during data refresh to find an optimal sort order. When the engine chooses a sort order, it must be the same for all the columns.

Therefore, Tabular chooses a sort order to minimize the overall model size. Columns appearing first in the sort order are likely to be better compressed than those at the end of the sort order.

Finally, there could be columns in which the content changes so often that if VertiPaq tried to compress them using RLE, the compressed columns would end up using more space than the original columns. A great example of this is the primary key of a table. It shows a different value for each row, resulting in an RLE version larger than the column itself. In cases like this, VertiPaq skips the RLE compression and stores the column as is. Thus, the VertiPaq storage of a column never exceeds the original column size. Worst-case scenario, the column in VertiPaq is the same size as the source column.

In the previous example, we have shown RLE working on a *Quarter* column that contained strings. However, RLE can also process the previously hash-encoded version of a column. Each column can have both RLE and either hash or value encoding applied to it. Therefore, the VertiPaq storage for a column compressed with hash encoding consists of two distinct entities: the dictionary and the data rows. The latter is the RLE-encoded result of the hash-encoded version of the original column.

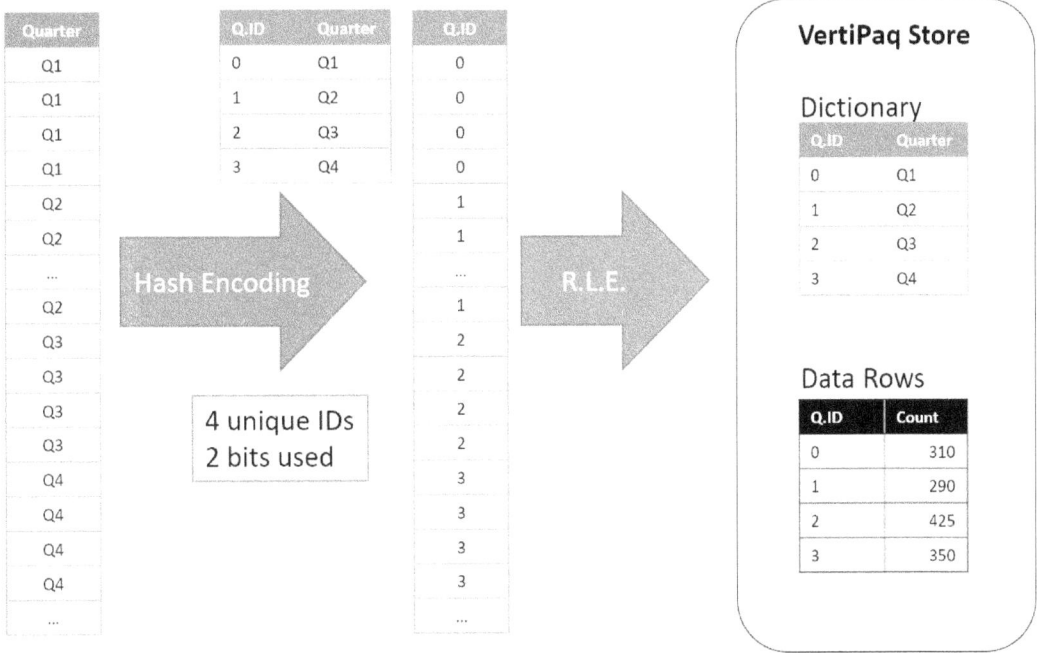

VertiPaq also applies RLE to value-encoded columns. In this case, the dictionary is missing because the column already contains value-encoded integers.

The factors influencing the compression ratio of a Tabular model are, in order of importance:

1. The cardinality of the column, which defines the number of bits used to store a value.

2. The number of repetitions, which corresponds to the distribution of data in a column. A column with many repeated values is compressed more than a column with very frequently changing

values.

3. The number of rows in the table.

4. The data type of the column, which only affects the dictionary size.

Given all these considerations, it is nearly impossible to predict the compression ratio of a table. Moreover, while a developer has full control over certain aspects of a table – they can limit the number of rows or columns, and they can change the data types – these are the least important aspects. Yet as we are about to discuss later, one can work on cardinality and repetitions too. This work improves the compression and performance of a model.

Finally, it is worth noting that reducing the cardinality of a column also increases the chances of repetitions. For example, if a time column is stored at the second granularity, then the column contains up to 86,400 distinct values. If the developer stores the same time column at the hour granularity (using 24 distinct values), they not only reduce the cardinality but also introduce repeating values. Indeed, 3,600 seconds convert to one same hour. All this results in a much better compression ratio. On the other hand, changing the data type from *DateTime* to *Integer* or even *String* offers a negligible impact on column size.

Using VertiPaq Analyzer to understand VertiPaq compression

Now that we have discussed the encoding details, we get the VertiPaq Analyzer information by using View Metrics in DAX Studio to analyze a sample data model. We use the usual Contoso database, with 1.4B rows in *Sales*. Contoso is a star schema, so the dimensions are rather small. Most of the space used by the model is in the fact table: *Sales*.

Name	Cardinality	Total Size ↓	Data	Dictionary	Hier Size
▷ Sales	1,405,546,659	31,114,066,376	25,234,204,824	5,121,572,184	753,298,720
▷ Customer	1,868,002	146,941,171	28,434,272	96,036,483	22,470,416
▷ Product	2,517	508,104	38,736	403,016	66,352
▷ Date	4,018	433,562	39,544	346,146	47,872
▷ Store	74	78,224	872	75,200	2,152

As shown in the report, *Sales* is by far the largest table in the model. At the table level, the Cardinality column indicates the number of rows. Total Size is the total size of the table, which is then divided into Data, Dictionary, hierarchies (Hier Size and User Hier Size, not shown in the screenshot), and relationships (Rel Size, not shown in the screenshot). For now, we focus on Data and Dictionary.

Dictionary indicates the size of the dictionaries created to hash-encode columns in the table. In contrast, Data shows the amount of space used for the columns, either value-encoded or hash-encoded. At the table level, the values displayed are the sum for all the columns. Investigating further, we expand *Sales* and look at the details at the column level.

Name	Cardinality	Total Size ↓	Data	Dictionary	Hier Size	Encoding	Data Type
▲ **Sales**	**1,405,546,659**	**30,933,803,284**	**25,033,930,384**	**5,121,648,004**	**768,252,824**	**Many**	-
Order Number	94,138,244	11,453,680,576	5,621,317,096	5,079,257,512	753,105,968	HASH	Int64
Net Price	24,754	5,574,565,672	5,574,466,512	136	99,024	VALUE	Decimal
Unit Price	1,761	5,445,403,768	5,445,396,584	136	7,048	VALUE	Decimal
CustomerKey	1,868,002	3,804,096,344	3,748,125,560	41,026,752	14,944,032	HASH	Int64
ProductKey	2,517	2,248,663,828	2,248,567,768	75,916	20,144	HASH	Int64
Unit Cost	1,956	1,890,937,056	1,890,879,760	41,632	15,664	HASH	Decimal
Line Number	20	446,331,456	446,331,232	136	88	VALUE	Int64
StoreKey	74	42,970,616	42,967,352	2,656	608	HASH	Int64
Delivery Date	3,389	7,192,760	7,179,064	136	13,560	VALUE	DateTime
Quantity	10	7,116,296	7,114,824	1,376	96	HASH	Int64
Order Date	3,281	1,311,648	1,109,712	175,680	26,256	HASH	DateTime
Currency Code	5	1,068,712	3,000	1,065,664	48	HASH	String
Exchange Rate	5,071	492,344	471,920	136	20,288	VALUE	Double

The sort order is based on Total Size, so the largest table columns appear at the top. When visualizing data at the column level, Cardinality indicates the cardinality of the column, which is the number of distinct values for the column. Data Type reports the column data type using the TOM naming convention.

Let us analyze in detail all the columns of the *Sales* table:

- **Order Number**: despite being an integer, it has been hash-encoded, as you can note from Encoding. Cardinality is very large (94M values), so the dictionary contains 94M entries. Indeed, you can see that Dictionary is extremely large, using 5GB of RAM. Data is around the same size.

- **Net Price, Unit Price**: these two columns have been value-encoded. Their data type is Decimal, as they are storing currencies. A Currency data type is stored as an integer, with the last four digits considered as the decimal portion. Because of Value encoding, there is no dictionary. The values stored in the data of the column are the real values; they are not entries in the dictionary. As such, the size of the dictionary shows only 136 bytes. *Net Price* has more unique values than *Unit Price* because of different discounts applied to the original price. Nonetheless, their size is very close. In this scenario, what matters is data distribution: *Net Price* and *Unit Price* change very often, so RLE is not very effective.

- **CustomerKey**: there are around 1.8M distinct customers, and the column has been hash-encoded. Again, the dictionary accounts for a large amount of RAM due to the large number of distinct values. *CustomerKey* could have been value-encoded. It was not because it was involved in a relationship. As we will see later, columns involved in relationships are hash-encoded unless we instruct Tabular otherwise.

- **ProductKey**: it shows a smaller cardinality than *CustomerKey* and has been hash-encoded, the same as *CustomerKey*. Nonetheless, its size is not smaller than *CustomerKey*. This is likely due to data distribution: the product key changes almost as frequently as the customer key, so RLE is less efficient.

- **Unit Cost**: it has a similar cardinality as *Unit Price,* and it is likely to show a similar distribution. The encoding is different: *Unit Cost* has been hash-encoded, whereas *Unit Price* has been value-encoded. In this case, hash-encoding produced a smaller column.

- **StoreKey, Quantity**: these are columns with a very limited cardinality and a very large number of repetitions; you can appreciate how efficient the encoding techniques have been on these columns, as they were stored in a small amount of memory.

- **Order Date, Delivery Date:** these two columns are interesting, as they have the same cardinality and a very similar data distribution, but they have been encoded differently. *Order Date* has been hash-encoded because it participates in a relationship; *Delivery Date* has been value-encoded (*Delivery Date* does not have a relationship to the *Date* table in the test model). In this scenario, you can appreciate the efficiency of the column size reduction through hash-encoding.

- **Exchange Rate**: a very small cardinality and a lot of repetitions produce a tiny column – it is likely to have been placed very early in the sort order.

- **Currency Code**: by far the smallest column of them all. Only five values, hash-encoded.

The information provided for each column is extremely useful to understand how VertiPaq stores data. It is worth repeating that the number of rows in a table is unimportant. Each of these columns stores 1.4B rows of data. Yet, their sizes range from 19KB to 11GB. Same number of rows, entirely different use of RAM. What matters is both the cardinality and the number of repetitions: these are the two important aspects that drive compression in VertiPaq. The smaller the cardinality, the less likely the data is to change, and the smaller the column.

The size of a column directly affects the time required to scan it. For example, let us compare the scanning of two columns we just analyzed. We execute a straightforward DAX query that requires computing the entire column, once for *Sales[Order Number]* and once for *Sales[Quantity]*.

Let us start with *Sales[Order Number]*:

```
EVALUATE { SUM ( Sales[Order Number] ) }
```

We obtain the numbers that follow.

Total	SE CPU		Line	Subclass	Duration	CPU	Par.	Rows	KB	Timeline
182 ms	3,547 ms		2	Scan	180	3,547	x19.7	1	1	
	x19.7									

FE	SE
2 ms	180 ms
1.1%	98.9%

```
SET DC_KIND="AUTO";
SELECT
    SUM ( 'Sales'[Order Number] )
FROM 'Sales';
```

SE Queries	SE Cache
1	0
	0.0%

Estimated size: rows = 1 bytes = 16

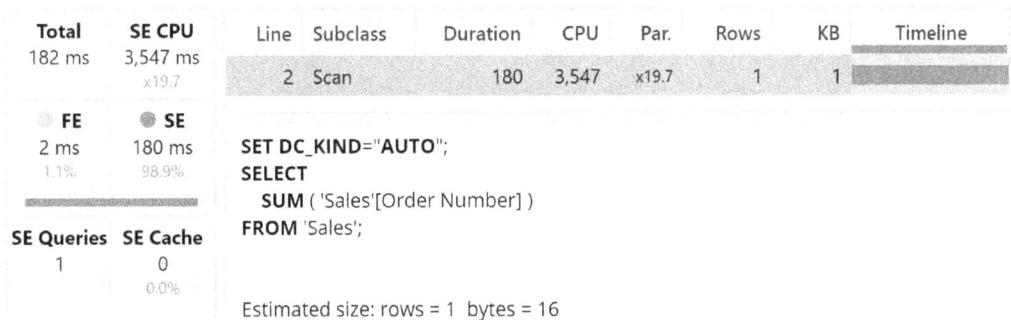

VertiPaq requires 3.5 seconds to scan the column. Let us analyze *Sales[Quantity]*:

```
EVALUATE { SUM ( Sales[Quantity] ) }
```

This results in the numbers we see below.

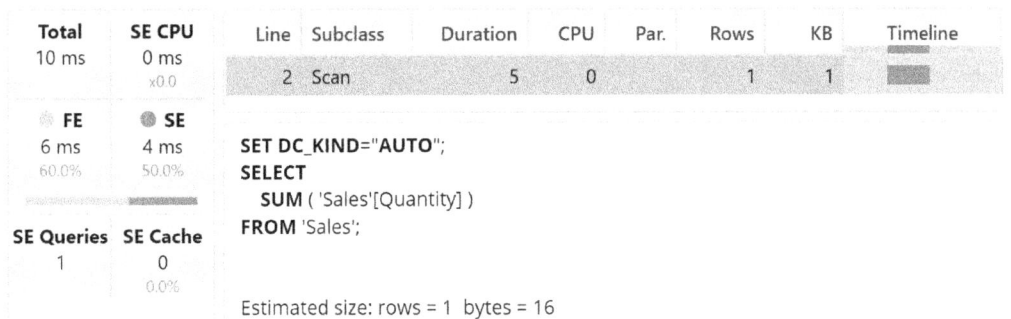

Total	SE CPU		Line	Subclass	Duration	CPU	Par.	Rows	KB	Timeline
10 ms	0 ms		2	Scan	5	0		1	1	
	x0.0									

FE	SE
6 ms	4 ms
60.0%	50.0%

```
SET DC_KIND="AUTO";
SELECT
    SUM ( 'Sales'[Quantity] )
FROM 'Sales';
```

SE Queries	SE Cache
1	0
	0.0%

Estimated size: rows = 1 bytes = 16

The difference is notably large: 16 milliseconds when we sum *Sales[Quantity]* versus 3,547 milliseconds when we sum *Sales[Order Number]*. The two columns store the very same number of rows; the difference between the two is only in the efficiency of the compression algorithms.

This is why it is important to understand how the VertiPaq engine works. Reducing the memory footprint of a column is by far your highest priority. Indeed, reducing the time required to scan a column will benefit any formula that uses that column.

Understanding re-encoding

Tabular must decide which algorithm to use to encode each column. More specifically, it needs to decide whether to use value or dictionary encoding. To make an educated decision, it reads a row sample during the first scan of the source, and it chooses a compression algorithm depending on the values found.

If the data type of the column is not numeric, or if the column participates in a relationship, then the choice is straightforward: VertiPaq goes for hash encoding. For numeric values, it uses some heuristics, for example:

- If the numbers in the column increase in a linear fashion, the column is likely a primary key, and value encoding is the best option.

- If all the numbers fall in a defined range of values within 32-bits, then value encoding is the way to go.

- If the numbers fall within a vast range of values, with values very different from one another, then hash encoding is the best choice.

Once the decision is made, Tabular starts to compress the column using the chosen algorithm. Unfortunately, Tabular sometimes makes the wrong decision and finds this out very late during processing. For example, Tabular might read a few million rows where the values are in the 100–201 range, so value encoding is the best choice. After those millions of rows, suddenly an outlier appears, such as a large number like 60,000,000. The initial choice was wrong because the number of bits needed to store such a large number is huge. What should Tabular do then? Instead of continuing with the wrong choice, Tabular can decide to re-encode the column. This decision means that the entire column is re-encoded by using hash encoding. This process might take a long time because the engine needs to reprocess the whole column.

When re-encoding occurs, you see the information in the log of the process operation.

```
Messages
Processing of the 'Sales in 2015-06' partition of the 'Sales' table started.
Reading data for the 'Sales' table 'Sales in 2015-12' partition started.
Processing of the 'Sales in 2014-01' partition of the 'Sales' table started.
Reading data for the 'Sales' table 'Sales in 2015-06' partition started.
Reading data for the 'Sales' table 'Sales in 2014-01' partition started.
Re-encoding the 'Unit Price' column of the 'Sales' table: switching to a value dictionary with updated magnitude.
Ended switching dictionary for the 'Unit Price' column of the 'Sales' table.
Re-encoding the 'Unit Cost' column of the 'Sales' table: switching to a value dictionary with updated magnitude.
Ended switching dictionary for the 'Unit Cost' column of the 'Sales' table.
Re-encoding the 'Unit Cost' column of the 'Sales' table: switching to a hash dictionary.
Ended switching dictionary for the 'Unit Cost' column of the 'Sales' table.

173 %
```

For very large datasets where processing time is important, a best practice is the following: the data distribution in the first set of rows read by Tabular should be of such quality that all types of values are represented. This in turn reduces re-encoding to a minimum. Developers do so by providing a quality sample in the first partition processed or an encoding hint parameter to the column. The encoding hint property was introduced in Analysis Services 2017 and is not available in previous versions.

You can set the Encoding Hint property of any column to one of three values: Default, Hash, or Value. The encoding hint is used as a suggestion; the engine can still force a different encoding. To provide an example, we changed the encoding hint of two columns: we provided a hint of Hash for *Sales[Exchange Rate]*, which was encoded using Value, and we suggested Value encoding for *Sales[ProductKey]*, which was encoded using Hash.

Changing the encoding hint does not invalidate a column. Therefore, a full process of the *Sales* table is required to reflect the change. Here is the VertiPaq Analyzer information after processing *Sales* with the two encoding hints.

Name	Cardinality	Total Size ↓	Data	Dictionary	Hier Size	Encoding	Data Type
◢ **Sales**	**1,405,546,659**	**30,931,483,576**	**25,031,371,992**	**5,121,876,472**	**768,263,040**	**Many**	-
Order Number	94,138,244	11,453,407,224	5,621,043,744	5,079,257,512	753,105,968	HASH	Int64
Net Price	24,754	5,573,969,680	5,573,870,520	136	99,024	VALUE	Decimal
Unit Price	1,761	5,444,064,968	5,444,057,784	136	7,048	VALUE	Decimal
CustomerKey	1,868,002	3,804,096,344	3,748,125,560	41,026,752	14,944,032	HASH	Int64
ProductKey	2,517	2,248,583,752	2,248,573,544	136	10,072	VALUE	Int64
Unit Cost	1,956	1,890,337,824	1,890,280,528	41,632	15,664	HASH	Decimal
Line Number	20	446,473,072	446,472,848	136	88	VALUE	Int64
StoreKey	74	43,202,144	43,198,880	2,656	608	HASH	Int64
Quantity	10	7,141,120	7,139,648	1,376	96	HASH	Int64
Delivery Date	3,389	7,125,864	7,112,168	136	13,560	VALUE	DateTime
Order Date	3,281	1,260,856	1,058,920	175,680	26,256	HASH	DateTime
Currency Code	5	1,068,392	2,680	1,065,664	48	HASH	String
Exchange Rate	5,071	780,128	435,168	304,384	40,576	HASH	Double

Both hints have been accepted, moving the encoding of *Sales[Exchange Rate]* to Hash and that of *Sales[ProductKey]* to Value. The size of both columns has not changed significantly: therefore, we do not obtain any benefit in this scenario. In different scenarios, it might be important to change the column encoding to optimize its storage or to avoid the re-encoding step during processing.

Understanding segmentation and partitioning

Compressing a table of several billion rows in one single step would be extremely memory-intensive and time-consuming. Therefore, a table is not processed as a single unit. During processing, Tabular splits the table into segments that contain 8 million rows each by default. When a segment is finished reading, the engine performs segment compression while reading the next segment.

It is possible to configure the segment size in Tabular using the *DefaultSegmentRowCount* entry in the configuration file of the service, or in the server properties in Management Studio. In Power BI service, these properties are set at the workspace level and must be made configurable through the Power BI Admin Portal. In Power BI Desktop and Power Pivot, the segment size is set at 1 million rows and this value cannot be changed.

Segmentation is important for several reasons, including query parallelism and compression efficiency. When querying a table, VertiPaq uses the segments as the basis for parallelism: It uses one core per segment when scanning a column. By default, VertiPaq always uses one single thread to scan a table with 8 million rows or less. We start observing parallelism in action only on much larger tables.

As a generic rule, the larger the segment, the better the compression. Having the option of analyzing more rows in a single compression step, VertiPaq can achieve better compression levels. But be mindful that this is not a strict rule. The compression level depends on the data distribution, and sometimes you might achieve better compression by reducing the segment size. On very large tables, it is important to test different segment sizes and measure the memory used to achieve optimal compression. Keep in mind that increasing the segment size can negatively affect processing time: The larger the segment, the slower the processing.

Although the dictionary is global to the table, bit-sizing occurs at the segment level. Thus, if a column has 1,000 distinct values, but only two distinct values are used in a specific segment, then that column will be compressed to a single bit for that segment.

If segments are small, then the parallelism at query time is increased, which is not always a good thing. While it is true that scanning the column is faster because more cores can do that in parallel, VertiPaq needs more time at the end of the scan to aggregate partial results computed by the different threads. If a partition is too small, then the time required for managing task switching and the final aggregation is more than the time needed to scan the data, negatively impacting the overall query performance.

During processing, the treatment of the first segment is particular if the table has only one partition. Indeed, the first segment may be larger than *DefaultSegmentRowCount*. VertiPaq reads twice the size of *DefaultSegmentRowCount* and starts to segment a table only if the table contains more rows. The first segment exception does not apply to a partitioned table. If a table is partitioned, all the segments are not larger than the default segment row count. Consequently, a nonpartitioned table with 10 million rows is stored as a single segment in Tabular. On the other hand, a table with 20 million rows uses three segments: two containing 8 million rows and one containing 4 million rows. In Power BI Desktop and Power Pivot, VertiPaq uses multiple segments for tables with more than 2 million rows.

Segments cannot exceed the partition size. If the partitioning schema of a model creates partitions of only 1 million rows, then all the segments will be smaller than 8 million rows; namely, they will be the same as the partition size. Over-partitioning a table is a mistake if the goal is to optimize performance. It obtains the opposite effect: it creates too many small partitions, which typically lowers performance.

You may inspect the details about the segment by using the View Metrics Partition page in DAX Studio. Our demo model contains 1.4B rows in *Sales*, with a partitioning scheme at the month level. We created many partitions to speed up the processing, as Tabular can process multiple partitions in parallel. The number of rows in each partition is variable. Here is the Partitions page, with data sorted by the number of rows in the partition.

Table / Partition	Rows ↓	Data	Partitions	Segments
▴ **Sales**	**1,405,546,659**	**25,001,588,944**	**144**	**258**
Sales in 2017-12	35,906,880	630,151,896	1	5
Sales in 2018-12	33,255,989	570,275,208	1	4
Sales in 2018-02	32,393,351	570,665,168	1	4
Sales in 2018-01	28,639,534	505,365,200	1	4
Sales in 2019-12	28,171,101	483,884,016	1	4
Sales in 2019-02	26,656,622	459,061,368	1	4
Sales in 2018-05	26,599,880	459,289,896	1	4
Sales in 2019-01	25,834,879	444,051,168	1	4
Sales in 2018-06	25,407,180	439,381,568	1	4
Sales in 2020-02	25,129,273	431,469,496	1	3
Sales in 2018-08	22,951,279	397,043,104	1	3
Sales in 2020-01	22,854,511	392,687,768	1	3
Sales in 2018-10	22,795,389	394,360,320	1	3

The largest partition contains around 36M rows, split into five segments. To test the effect of segment size on overall memory consumption, we process the same model once with a segment size of 1M, and then again with a segment size of 64M. The segment size needs to be a power of 2, as per Tabular specifications.

For the first test, we set the segment size to 1,048,576, which we consider roughly to be 1M rows.

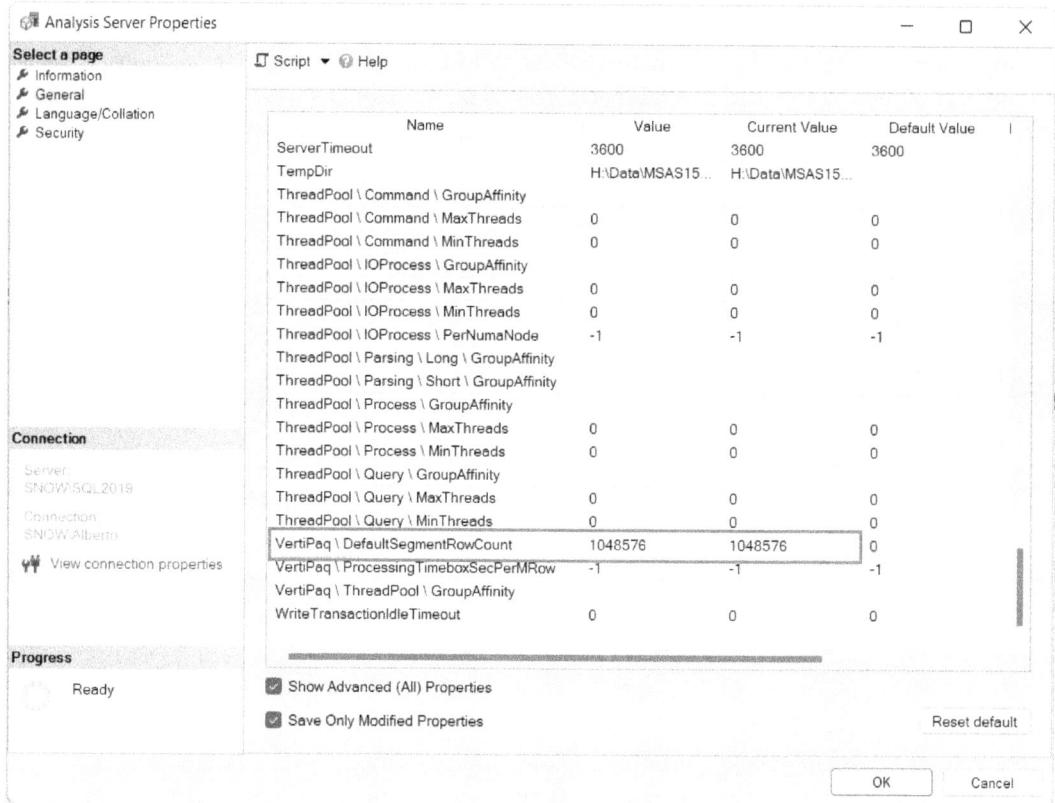

Name	Value	Current Value	Default Value	
ServerTimeout	3600	3600	3600	
TempDir	H:\Data\MSAS15...	H:\Data\MSAS15...		
ThreadPool \ Command \ GroupAffinity				
ThreadPool \ Command \ MaxThreads	0	0	0	
ThreadPool \ Command \ MinThreads	0	0	0	
ThreadPool \ IOProcess \ GroupAffinity				
ThreadPool \ IOProcess \ MaxThreads	0	0	0	
ThreadPool \ IOProcess \ MinThreads	0	0	0	
ThreadPool \ IOProcess \ PerNumaNode	-1	-1	-1	
ThreadPool \ Parsing \ Long \ GroupAffinity				
ThreadPool \ Parsing \ Short \ GroupAffinity				
ThreadPool \ Process \ GroupAffinity				
ThreadPool \ Process \ MaxThreads	0	0	0	
ThreadPool \ Process \ MinThreads	0	0	0	
ThreadPool \ Query \ GroupAffinity				
ThreadPool \ Query \ MaxThreads	0	0	0	
ThreadPool \ Query \ MinThreads	0	0	0	
VertiPaq \ DefaultSegmentRowCount	1048576	1048576	0	
VertiPaq \ ProcessingTimeboxSecPerMRow	-1	-1	-1	
VertiPaq \ ThreadPool \ GroupAffinity				
WriteTransactionIdleTimeout	0	0	0	

Using 1M rows for the segments, we hope to reduce the size of some partitions, even though the effect is irrelevant.

Table / Partition	Rows ↓	Data	Partitions	Segments
Sales	**1,405,546,6...**	**25,037,569,240**	**144**	**1,418**
Sales in 2017-12	35,906,880	625,965,520	1	35
Sales in 2018-12	33,255,989	568,488,448	1	32
Sales in 2018-02	32,393,351	565,374,672	1	31
Sales in 2018-01	28,639,534	502,517,544	1	28
Sales in 2019-12	28,171,101	483,103,392	1	27
Sales in 2019-02	26,656,622	463,120,296	1	26
Sales in 2018-05	26,599,880	462,502,336	1	26
Sales in 2019-01	25,834,879	447,191,616	1	25
Sales in 2018-06	25,407,180	441,322,952	1	25
Sales in 2020-02	25,129,273	435,708,744	1	24
Sales in 2018-08	22,951,279	400,797,336	1	22
Sales in 2020-01	22,854,511	396,843,480	1	22
Sales in 2018-10	22,795,389	395,988,296	1	22

Overall, the effect is the opposite. The total data table size is 25,037,569,240 bytes with segments of 1M rows, whereas it was 25,001,589,944 bytes with the default segment size of 8M rows. Therefore, some partitions are now smaller, and others are slightly larger. From a memory footprint point of view, the difference is not relevant. From a performance point of view, a single partition can now be scanned by as many as 35 cores simultaneously. Nonetheless, a full scan of the table requires 1,418 scan operations that will need to be merged, whereas in the previous scenario there were only 258 segments to scan. Therefore, we expect the table with segments of 8M rows to be faster to scan, even though it is a bit larger.

We cannot test a full process with a segment size larger than any partition: we use 67,108,864, which is the nearest power of 2 to 64M. Again, the difference is not particularly visible.

Table / Partition	Rows ↓	Data	Partitions	Segments
⊿ **Sales**	**1,405,546,659**	**25,012,555,944**	**144**	**144**
Sales in 2017-12	35,906,880	642,851,088	1	1
Sales in 2018-12	33,255,989	568,470,712	1	1
Sales in 2018-02	32,393,351	579,471,504	1	1
Sales in 2018-01	28,639,534	513,658,200	1	1
Sales in 2019-12	28,171,101	479,392,680	1	1
Sales in 2019-02	26,656,622	456,806,408	1	1
Sales in 2018-05	26,599,880	461,076,120	1	1
Sales in 2019-01	25,834,879	444,376,208	1	1
Sales in 2018-06	25,407,180	439,488,288	1	1
Sales in 2020-02	25,129,273	428,655,640	1	1
Sales in 2018-08	22,951,279	397,245,104	1	1
Sales in 2020-01	22,854,511	391,663,848	1	1
Sales in 2018-10	22,795,389	394,328,960	1	1

What is worth noting is that there are no segments with 64M rows. Because the size of each partition is smaller than the segment size, each partition contains only one segment.

A larger segment size can improve the query performance by reducing the overhead of task allocation (one per segment) and the number of intermediate datacaches to create for each segment and then consolidated in the final datacache returned to the formula engine. For example, we created two copies of the same Contoso database with 100M orders, processed with 1M segment size and 8M segment size, respectively.

The following picture shows the size of the *Sales* table with 1M segment size: every column has 216 segments.

Name	Cardinality	Total Size ↓	Partitions	Segments
⊿ **Sales**	**225,616,948**	**2,624,526,320**	**1**	**2,592**
CustomerKey	1,868,084	657,645,752	1	216
Net Price	24,754	442,747,184	1	216
ProductKey	2,517	356,890,516	1	216
Unit Cost	1,956	311,819,192	1	216
Unit Price	1,761	310,744,124	1	216
Delivery Date	3,389	216,249,628	1	216
Order Date	3,281	166,953,888	1	216
Exchange Rate	5,071	99,605,756	1	216
StoreKey	74	51,514,448	1	216
Quantity	10	4,920,024	1	216
Currency Code	5	417,088	1	216

We run the following DAX query that returns the average amount of *Sales[Net Price]* for the last date where there are transactions for the selected product:

```
EVALUATE
SUMMARIZECOLUMNS (
    'Product'[Product Name],
    "Last price",
        CALCULATE (
            AVERAGE ( Sales[Net Price] ),
            LASTDATE ( Sales[Order Date] )
        )
)
ORDER BY 'Product'[Product Name]
```

Here is the Server Timings result obtained by running the query on the model with 1M segment size.

Total	SE CPU		Line	Subclass	Duration	CPU	Par.	Rows	KB	Timeline
14,517 ms	62,016 ms		2	Scan	47	516	x11.0	3,284	26	
	x5.7		4	Scan	10,127	54,734	x5.4	7,874,898	30,762	
FE	SE		6	Scan	767	6,766	x8.8	2,520	40	
3,576 ms	10,941 ms									
24.6%	75.4%									

SE Queries	SE Cache
3	0
	0.0%

The different parallelism between different storage engine queries is interesting. We can ignore the xmSQL query at line 2, but looking at the other two, it doesn't seem easy to explain why line 6 has better parallelism (x8.8) than line 4 (x5.4). In later chapters, we analyze the xmSQL code. Still, at this stage, it is enough to notice the different number or rows returned by the two queries: the slowest one (line 4) generates a larger materialization (7.8 million rows) than the faster one (line 6, only 2,520 rows). Remember that every segment generates an intermediate result that must be consolidated in the result of the whole xmSQL query. In this case, this consolidation must process 216 segments, and this consolidation is likely to run in a single thread, regardless of the number of cores available. Moreover, each of these segments created an intermediate data cache of millions of rows, which is more time-consuming than reading the same amount of data to create a data cache with just a few rows.

Now, let's focus on the *Sales* table with 8M segment size: this time, every column has only 27 segments.

Name	Cardinality	Total Size ↓	Partitions	Segments
⁴ **Sales**	**225,616,948**	**2,523,716,464**	**1**	**324**
CustomerKey	1,868,084	657,620,488	1	27
Net Price	24,754	449,041,160	1	27
ProductKey	2,517	360,901,652	1	27
Unit Cost	1,956	273,302,312	1	27
Unit Price	1,761	270,638,684	1	27
Delivery Date	3,389	222,530,596	1	27
Order Date	3,281	181,112,304	1	27
Exchange Rate	5,071	96,123,636	1	27
StoreKey	74	5,787,248	1	27
Quantity	10	1,635,856	1	27
Currency Code	5	22,568	1	27

By running the same DAX query, we obtain a Server Timings result showing a much faster execution.

Total	SE CPU	Line	Subclass	Duration	CPU	Par.	Rows	KB	Timeline
9,251 ms	32,140 ms	2	Scan	33	297	x9.0	3,284	26	
	x5.5	4	Scan	5,330	25,734	x4.8	7,874,898	30,762	
FE	SE	6	Scan	484	6,109	x12.6	2,520	40	
3,404 ms	5,847 ms								
36.8%	63.2%								

SE Queries	SE Cache
3	0
	0.0%

The formula engine time does not change much – every execution produces different timings; we will never obtain exactly the same number. The big difference is the query at line 4, which runs in half the time. Even though the overall column size to scan is the same, the amount of data to write in the intermediate data cache is reduced by 87.5% – as there are 27 segments instead of 216 – and the single-thread consolidation process benefits from the same improvement.

This consolidation is not linear: indeed, we see only a 10% difference in the storage engine query at line 6, which generates a datacache of only 2,520 rows – the difference could also be smaller, because in these analyses, differences of hundreds of milliseconds are not too relevant. Remember that we made these tests on Power BI Service by changing the large dataset settings, which enables the 8M segment size for all the tables of a dataset.

The effect shown in this example can be extreme: the ratio between the table aggregated (*Sales*, 200 million rows) and the datacache generated (7.8M rows) highlights the issue. Because the performance difference depends on multiple factors (number of segments, size of segments, size of datacache, number of cores), your mileage may vary. In extreme cases, a smaller segment size for small tables could improve the query execution time by increasing the parallelism of slow callbacks to the formula engine, which will be covered in later chapters.

Understanding the importance of sorting

As we said earlier, RLE's efficiency strongly depends on the table's sort order. All the columns of the same table are sorted the same way to keep the integrity of the data at the table level. In large tables, it is important to determine the best sorting of data to improve the efficiency of RLE and to reduce the memory footprint of the model.

When Tabular reads a table, it tests different sort orders to improve the compression. In a table with many columns, this is a very time-consuming operation. Tabular sets an upper limit to the time it can spend finding the best sort order. The default can change with different versions of the engine. At printing time, the default is 10 seconds per million rows. The developer can modify its value in the *ProcessingTimeboxSecPerMRow* entry in the Analysis Services configuration. Power BI and Power Pivot do not provide access to this setting.

Note: Tabular searches for the best sort order in the data using a heuristic algorithm that certainly also considers the physical order of the rows it receives. For this reason, although one cannot force the sort order used by VertiPaq for RLE, it is possible to provide the engine with data sorted arbitrarily. The VertiPaq engine includes this sort order in the options to consider; the sort order also affects the distribution of data in different segments of the same partition.

To attain maximum compression, we can set the value of *ProcessingTimeboxSecPerMRow* to 0, which means Tabular stops searching only when it finds the best compression factor. The benefit in terms of space utilization and query speed can vary. On the other hand, processing could take much longer because the engine is being instructed to try all the possible sort orders before making a choice.

If the time configured in the *ProcessingTimeboxSecPerMRow* setting does not allow Tabular to find the optimal sort order, then the processing of the segment is timeboxed. When timeboxing happens, the segment could not be fully optimized. To demonstrate this, we reduced *ProcessingTimeboxSecPerMRow* to only one second per million rows. Consequently, many segments result in being timeboxed. You can inspect this scenario by using the VertiPaq state column of the Column Segments table in VertiPaq Analyzer – you need to use the Excel file for this detail, as the information is not visible in View Metrics in DAX Studio. Here are the numbers of segments completed, skipped, and timeboxed.

Row Labels	Partitions #	Total Segments #
COMPLETED	34	439
SKIPPED	148	265
TIMEBOXED	119	2,964
Grand Total	**148**	**3,668**

Because of timeboxing, we would expect the overall size of the database to be larger than before. Indeed, by inspecting the statistics with DAX Studio we notice that the *Sales* table is larger.

Name	Cardinality	Total Size ↓	Data	Dictionary	Hier Size	Encoding	Data Type
◢ **Sales**	**1,405,546,659**	**31,114,066,376**	**25,234,204,824**	**5,121,572,184**	**753,298,720**	**Many**	-
Order Number	94,138,244	11,446,897,280	5,614,533,784	5,079,257,528	753,105,968	HASH	Int64
Net Price	24,754	5,622,209,256	5,622,110,112	120	99,024	VALUE	Decimal
Unit Price	1,761	5,565,390,032	5,565,382,864	120	7,048	VALUE	Decimal
CustomerKey	1,868,002	3,789,152,328	3,748,125,560	41,026,768	0	HASH	Int64
ProductKey	2,517	2,248,885,984	2,248,875,792	120	10,072	VALUE	Int64
Unit Cost	1,956	1,903,845,688	1,903,788,376	41,648	15,664	HASH	Decimal
Line Number	20	393,830,840	393,830,632	120	88	VALUE	Int64
StoreKey	74	118,981,704	118,978,424	2,672	608	HASH	Int64
Quantity	10	10,022,808	10,021,320	1,392	96	HASH	Int64
Delivery Date	3,389	7,459,144	7,445,464	120	13,560	VALUE	DateTime
Currency Code	5	1,069,736	4,032	1,065,656	48	HASH	String
Order Date	3,281	1,023,632	821,696	175,680	26,256	HASH	DateTime
Exchange Rate	5,071	307,176	286,768	120	20,288	VALUE	Double

If you carefully compare the numbers in this report with the one shown before, where we allowed the default 10 seconds per million rows, you can notice that the dictionary size is identical, whereas the Data size is slightly larger in this latter report. The reason is that RLE is slightly less efficient in this example due to sorting.

The default value works for most scenarios. Nonetheless, suppose a table contains many columns (say more than a hundred). In that case, several segments will likely be timeboxed because the time required to find the optimal sort order depends on the number of columns in the table. In that scenario, increasing the limit might provide better compression and query performance.

To provide a reference, we processed the same model using zero for *ProcessingTimeboxSecPerMRow*, guaranteeing that no segments were timeboxed.

Name	Cardinality	Total Size ↓	Data	Dictionary	Hier Size	Encoding	Data Type
⊿ **Sales**	**1,405,546,659**	**30,855,326,416**	**24,975,464,864**	**5,121,572,184**	**753,298,720**	**Many**	-
Order Number	94,138,244	11,447,446,808	5,615,083,312	5,079,257,528	753,105,968	HASH	Int64
Net Price	24,754	5,558,157,176	5,558,058,032	120	99,024	VALUE	Decimal
Unit Price	1,761	5,400,491,928	5,400,484,760	120	7,048	VALUE	Decimal
CustomerKey	1,868,002	3,789,152,328	3,748,125,560	41,026,768	0	HASH	Int64
ProductKey	2,517	2,248,226,264	2,248,216,072	120	10,072	VALUE	Int64
Unit Cost	1,956	1,857,796,104	1,857,738,792	41,648	15,664	HASH	Decimal
Line Number	20	455,726,056	455,725,848	120	88	VALUE	Int64
StoreKey	74	76,468,384	76,465,104	2,672	608	HASH	Int64
Quantity	10	7,363,960	7,362,472	1,392	96	HASH	Int64
Delivery Date	3,389	6,700,584	6,686,904	120	13,560	VALUE	DateTime
Order Date	3,281	1,230,848	1,028,912	175,680	26,256	HASH	DateTime
Currency Code	5	1,067,888	2,184	1,065,656	48	HASH	String
Exchange Rate	5,071	507,320	486,912	120	20,288	VALUE	Double

The model is slightly smaller than the original model processed with the default *ProcessingTimeboxSecPerMRow* value, although there are no evident benefits in allowing for more compression – which requires a longer processing time.

To find the best sort order, developers should put the columns with the smallest number of unique values first in the sort order; indeed, these columns are likely to generate many repeating values. This way, data distribution in different segments might result in a smaller number of unique values for the first columns in the sort order, thus increasing their compression in those segments. Still, keep in mind that finding the best sort order is a very complex task. It only makes sense to spend time on this when the data model is extremely large (in the order of a few billion rows). Otherwise, the benefit obtained from these extreme optimizations is limited.

Once all the columns are compressed, Tabular completes the processing by building calculated columns, tables, hierarchies, and relationships. Hierarchies and relationships are additional data structures needed by VertiPaq to execute queries, whereas calculated columns and tables are added to the model by using DAX expressions.

Calculated columns are compressed after they are computed. However, calculated columns are not the same as standard columns. Calculated columns are created and then compressed during the final stage of processing, when all the other columns have already been compressed. Consequently, VertiPaq does not consider calculated columns when choosing the best sort order for a table.

Consider creating a calculated column that results in a *Boolean* value. There being only two values, the calculated column can be compressed very well (1 bit is enough to store a *Boolean* value), and it is a very good candidate to be first in the sort order list. By doing this, the table would show all the *TRUE* values in contiguous rows and the *FALSE* values in other contiguous rows. However, because it is a calculated column, the sort order is already defined by other columns; the calculated column may frequently change value with the sort order defined by the imported columns. In that case, the column ends up with less-than-optimal compression.

We created a new column with only four values to show this behavior by computing the order number modulus 4. The column has been created in two ways: once as a column in SQL, so that it is imported in the VertiPaq model and considered for sorting, and once as a DAX calculated column. The DAX calculated column is not part of the best sort order selection, so it results in being larger.

Here are the statistics for the imported column named *OrderMod4 Load*.

Name	Cardinality	Total Size ↓	Data	Dictionary	Hier Size	Encoding	Data Type
⊿ **Sales**	**1,405,546,659**	**31,477,880,104**	**25,599,065,...**	**5,120,525,0...**	**753,298,768**	**Many**	-
Order Number	94,138,244	11,446,575,472	5,614,211,976	5,079,257,528	753,105,968	HASH	Int64
Net Price	24,754	5,605,918,784	5,605,819,640	120	99,024	VALUE	Decimal
Unit Price	1,761	5,526,053,224	5,526,046,056	120	7,048	VALUE	Decimal
CustomerKey	1,868,002	3,789,152,328	3,748,125,560	41,026,768	0	HASH	Int64
ProductKey	2,517	2,248,835,088	2,248,824,896	120	10,072	VALUE	Int64
Unit Cost	1,956	1,915,214,080	1,915,156,768	41,648	15,664	HASH	Decimal
Line Number	20	735,461,488	735,461,280	120	88	VALUE	Int64
OrderMod4 Load	4	100,750,448	100,749,032	1,368	48	HASH	Int64
StoreKey	74	87,060,512	87,057,232	2,672	608	HASH	Int64
Delivery Date	3,389	7,785,176	7,771,496	120	13,560	VALUE	DateTime
Quantity	10	7,544,352	7,542,864	1,392	96	HASH	Int64
Order Date	3,281	2,006,624	1,804,688	175,680	26,256	HASH	DateTime
Exchange Rate	5,071	512,488	492,080	120	20,288	VALUE	Double
Currency Code	5	19,272	2,104	17,120	48	HASH	String

As you see, the column uses 100MB. The reason is that – despite it having only four values – its result changes quite often compared to other more optimized columns such as *Currency Code* and *Quantity*. Then, we remove the *OrderMod4 Load* column, create a new calculated column named *OrderMod4 Calc*, and fully reprocess the *Sales* table:

```
-------------------------------------
-- Calculated column in Sales table
-------------------------------------
OrderMod4 Calc = MOD ( Sales[Order Number], 4 )
```

The calculated column *OrderMod4 Calc* is much larger, accounting for around 350MB.

Name	Cardinality	Total Size ↓	Data	Dictionary	Hier Size	Encoding	Data Type
▲ **Sales**	**1,405,546,659**	**31,232,839,440**	**25,352,976,...**	**5,121,573,5...**	**753,298,768**	**Many**	-
Order Number	94,138,244	11,446,897,280	5,614,533,784	5,079,257,528	753,105,968	HASH	Int64
Net Price	24,754	5,580,729,352	5,580,630,208	120	99,024	VALUE	Decimal
Unit Price	1,761	5,398,598,600	5,398,591,432	120	7,048	VALUE	Decimal
CustomerKey	1,868,002	3,789,152,328	3,748,125,560	41,026,768	0	HASH	Int64
ProductKey	2,517	2,248,498,056	2,248,487,864	120	10,072	VALUE	Int64
Unit Cost	1,956	1,859,898,336	1,859,841,024	41,648	15,664	HASH	Decimal
Line Number	20	448,171,208	448,171,000	120	88	VALUE	Int64
OrderMod4 Calc	4	351,388,944	351,387,528	1,368	48	HASH	Int64
StoreKey	74	87,329,552	87,326,272	2,672	608	HASH	Int64
Quantity	10	7,513,448	7,511,960	1,392	96	HASH	Int64
Delivery Date	3,389	6,891,024	6,877,344	120	13,560	VALUE	DateTime
Order Date	3,281	1,218,568	1,016,632	175,680	26,256	HASH	DateTime
Currency Code	5	1,067,824	2,120	1,065,656	48	HASH	String
Exchange Rate	5,071	494,152	473,744	120	20,288	VALUE	Double

Be mindful that this example has been deliberately created to show the effect of sorting. In a real-world model, it is very unlikely that a calculated column use 3.5 times the space of a column loaded from the database. We created a small-cardinality column on purpose to exaggerate the effect and make it more evident. Still, developers will notice some differences, and it is always worth double-checking.

Whenever there is a chance to compute a column in DAX or in the data source (including Power Query), keep in mind that computing it in the data source results in slightly better compression. Many other factors may drive the choice of DAX instead of Power Query or SQL to calculate the column. For example, the engine automatically computes a calculated column in a large table depending on a column in a small table whenever said small table has a partial or full refresh. This happens without having to reprocess the entire large table, which would be necessary if the computation were in Power Query or SQL. This is something to consider when looking for optimal compression.

Note: A calculated table has the same compression as a regular table, without the side effects described for calculated columns. However, creating a calculated table can be quite expensive. Indeed, a calculated table requires enough memory to keep a copy of the entire uncompressed table in memory before it is compressed. Think carefully before creating a large calculated table because of the memory pressure generated at refresh time.

Understanding VertiPaq relationships

At the end of table processing, Tabular builds two additional data structures: hierarchies and relationships. Hierarchies are data structures used primarily to improve the performance of MDX queries and certain search operations in DAX. We will cover attribute hierarchies later; here, we focus on relationships.

Relationships play an essential role in the VertiPaq engine; it is important to understand how they work for extreme optimizations. There are multiple types of relationships in a Tabular model: regular one-to-many relationships, many-to-many cardinality relationships, and limited relationships. Again, we discuss more complex types of relationships in the following chapters. Here, we are only interested in defining what relationships are in terms of VertiPaq storage and behavior. Therefore, this section is dedicated to regular one-to-many relationships – the only relationship type affected during a data refresh because they create a specific memory structure in VertiPaq to improve performance at query time. For the purpose of the following explanation, a one-to-one relationship is like a one-to-many relationship and produces the same structure in VertiPaq – therefore, a VertiPaq relationship is a regular one-to-many or one-to-one relationship in the Tabular model.

A VertiPaq relationship is a data structure that maps IDs from one table, to row numbers in another table. For example, consider the columns *ProductKey* in *Sales* and *ProductKey* in *Product*. These two columns are used to build the relationship between the two tables. *Product[ProductKey]* is a primary key. *Product[ProductKey]* might have been encoded using value encoding with no compression at all because of its cardinality. Indeed, RLE could not reduce the column size in the absence of duplicated values. On the other hand, *Sales[ProductKey]* is likely to have been hash-encoded and compressed. This is because it probably contains many repetitions. Therefore, despite the columns having the same name and data type, their internal data structures are entirely different.

Moreover, because the tables are connected through a relationship, VertiPaq knows that queries are likely to place filters on *Product* and expect to filter *Sales* as a result. VertiPaq would be very slow if every time it needed to move a filter from *Product* to *Sales,* it had to perform the following: retrieve values from *Product[ProductKey]*, search for them in the dictionary of *Sales[ProductKey]*, and finally retrieve the IDs of *Sales[ProductKey]* to place the filter.

VertiPaq stores relationships as pairs of IDs and row numbers to improve query performance. Given the ID of a *Sales[ProductKey]* value, it can immediately find the corresponding row of *Product* that matches the relationship. Relationships are stored in memory, as is any other data structure of VertiPaq. The following figure shows how the relationship between *Sales* and *Product* is stored in VertiPaq.

Sales

Amount	ProductKey
25.00	1
12.50	2
2.25	3
2.50	3
14.00	4
25.00	5

Product

ProductKey	Product
1	Coffee
2	Pasta
3	Tomato
BLANK	BLANK

Row Num
1
2
3
4

Relationship

Sales[ProductKey]	Product[Row Num]
1	1
2	2
3	3
4	4
5	4

Even though the structure does not seem very intuitive, we are about to learn how VertiPaq uses relationships and why relationships have this particular structure.

When a DAX query generates requests to the VertiPaq storage engine, the presence of relationships in the data model allows for a quicker transfer of the filter context from one table to another. The internal implementation of a relationship in VertiPaq is worth knowing because relationships might affect the performance of a query even though most of the calculations happen in the storage engine.

To understand how relationships work, we start with the analysis of a query that involves only one table, *Sales*:

```
EVALUATE
{
    CALCULATE (
        COUNTROWS ( Sales ),
        Sales[Quantity] > 1
    )
}
```

A developer used to working with tables in relational databases might suppose that the engine iterates the *Sales* table, tests the value of the *Quantity* column for each row of *Sales*, and increments the returned value if the *Quantity* value is greater than 1. In fact, VertiPaq does it better: VertiPaq only scans the *Quantity* column because it already provides the number of rows for the entire table. Therefore, a single column scan is enough to solve the entire query.

This behavior is not entirely evident by analyzing the VertiPaq queries only. Indeed, the previous DAX query generated the following xmSQL query:

```
SELECT
    COUNT (   )
FROM 'Sales ( 19 )'
WHERE
        ( PFCASTCOALESCE ( 'Sales ( 19 )'[Quantity ( 87 )] AS INT ) > COALESCE ( 1 ) );
```

However, we learned that in VertiPaq there is no such thing as a table. There are only columns. The xmSQL query can be answered by just scanning the *Sales[Quantity]* column RLE structure, which contains the pairs of values and the number of rows.

If we analyze a similar query using the column of another table as a filter, then scanning a single column is no longer enough to produce the result. For example, consider the following query that counts the number of rows in *Sales* related to products of the Contoso brand:

```
EVALUATE
{
    CALCULATE (
        COUNTROWS ( Sales ),
        'Product'[Brand] = "Contoso"
    )
}
```

This time, we are using two different tables: *Sales* and *Product*. Solving this query requires more effort. Because the filter is on *Product* and the table to aggregate is *Sales*, it is impossible to scan a single column.

If you are not used to columnar databases, you probably think that to solve the query, the engine should iterate the *Sales* table, follow the relationship with *Product*, and sum either 1 if the product brand is Contoso or 0 otherwise. This would be an algorithm like the following DAX code:

```
EVALUATE
{
    SUMX (
        Sales,
        IF ( RELATED ( 'Product'[Brand] ) = "Contoso", 1, 0 )
    )
}
```

Though simple, this algorithm is much more complex than expected. Indeed, if we carefully think about the columnar nature of VertiPaq, we realize that this query involves three different columns:

- *Product[Brand]* is used to filter the *Product* table.

- *Product[ProductKey]* is used for the relationship between *Product* and *Sales*.

- *Sales[ProductKey]* is used on the *Sales* side of the relationship.

Iterating over *Sales[ProductKey]*, searching for the row number in *Product* by scanning *Product[ProductKey]*, and finally gathering the brand in *Product[Brand]* would be extremely expensive. The process requires a lot of random reads from memory, with negative consequences on performance. Therefore, VertiPaq uses an entirely different algorithm optimized for columnar databases.

First, VertiPaq scans the *Product[Brand]* column and retrieves the row numbers of the *Product* table where *Product[Brand]* is Contoso.

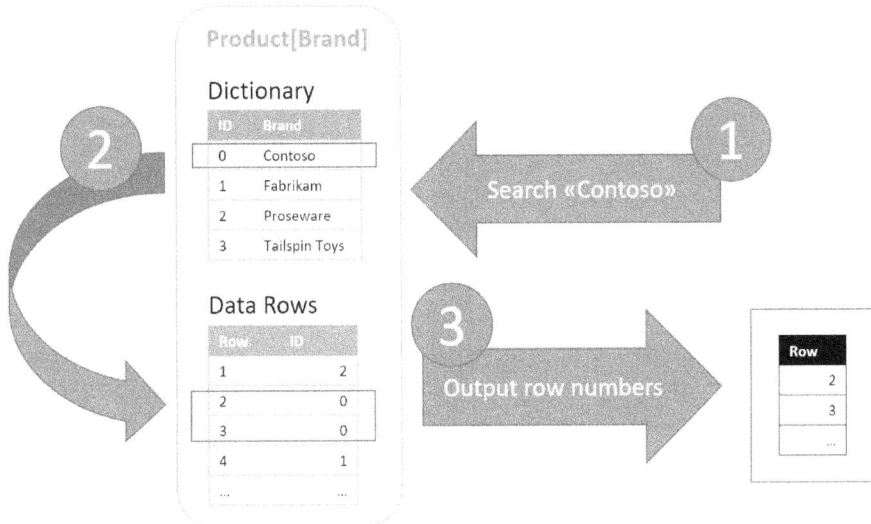

VertiPaq scans the *Brand* dictionary (1), retrieves the encoding of Contoso, and finally scans the segments of the *Brand* column (2), searching for the row numbers in the product table where the dictionary ID equals 0 (corresponding to Contoso), returning the indexes of the rows found (3). So far, the relationship structure did not come into play. This is going to happen in the next step.

At this point, VertiPaq knows which rows in the *Product* table contain the Contoso brand. The relationship between *Product* and *Sales* enables VertiPaq to translate the row numbers of *Product* in internal data IDs for *Sales[ProductKey]*. VertiPaq performs a lookup of the selected row numbers (1) to determine the values of *Sales[ProductKey]* valid for those rows (2).

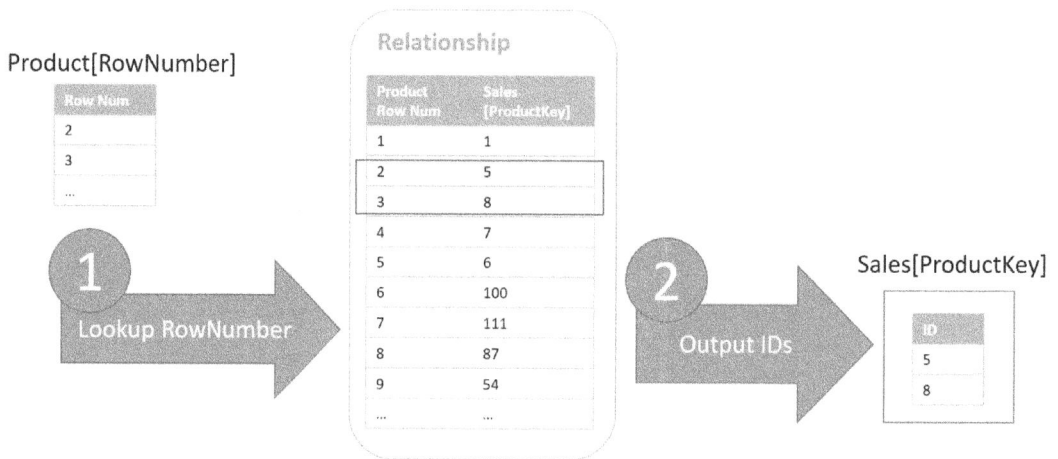

The last step is to apply the filter to the *Sales* table. Since VertiPaq already knows the list of *Sales[ProductKey]* values to filter, it is enough to scan the *Sales[ProductKey]* column to transform this list of values into row numbers and finally count them. If instead of computing *COUNTROWS*, VertiPaq had to perform *SUM* on a column, then it would perform an additional step, transforming row numbers into column values to perform the last step.

The important takeaway is that the cost of a relationship depends on the cardinality of the column that defines the relationship. Even though the previous query filtered only one brand, the cost of the relationship is the number of products for that brand. The lower the cardinality of a relationship, the better. When the cardinality of a relationship is above one million unique values, developers can experience slower performance. Performance degradation is already measurable when the relationship has 100,000 unique values. VertiPaq aggregations can mitigate the impact of high-cardinality relationships by pre-aggregating data at a different granularity, which removes the cost of traversing expensive relationships at query time.

You can use the model's statistical information to indicate the cost of traversing relationships in your model. In our sample model, three relationships are starting from *Sales* and reaching *Customer*, *Date*, and *Product*.

Table / Relationship	Size ↓	Max From Cardinality	Max To Cardinality	1:M Ratio %
◢ **Sales**	**4,990,648**	**1,868,002**	**1,868,002**	**0.13%**
Sales[CustomerKey] ∞←1 Customer[CustomerKey]	4,981,352	1,868,002	1,868,002	0.13%
Sales[Order Date] ∞←1 Date[Date]	5,256	3,281	4,018	0.00%
Sales[ProductKey] ∞←1 Product[ProductKey]	4,040	2,517	2,517	0.00%

The important pieces of information available here are:

- **Size**: the size in bytes of the relationship, indicating how large the structure is. The larger the relationship, the slower it will be to scan.
- **Max From Cardinality**: indicates the number of distinct values of the column in *Sales*. This value is usually smaller than Max To Cardinality, indicating the number of rows in *Customer*,

Product, or *Date*. The speed of a relationship depends on the number of values in *Sales*. Having both cardinalities at hand helps discover possibly heavily underused dimensions.

- **Max To Cardinality**: indicates the number of distinct values of the column on the other side of the relationship. This value corresponds to the number of rows of the table on the one-side in case of a many-to-one relationship.

- **1:M Ratio**: it is just the division of the *Max From Cardinality* by the number of rows in *Sales*. It indicates how selective a filter on a single value could be to optimize internal VertiPaq operations. Beware, this is just a big average; if you ever need to perform an analysis based on statistics, you should verify the selectivity of relationships by using different DAX queries to understand how many rows are returned based on a value in the dimension.

We can conclude from the statistical information retrieved that neither *Date* nor *Product* pose any challenge. The dimension of the relationship is tiny, and although *Date* is somewhat underused, it is still well below any warning value. On the other hand, *Customer* generates a relationship based on almost 2 million values. As such, any VertiPaq query involving *Customer* attributes pays a higher price.

Understanding attribute hierarchies

Another data structure that VertiPaq builds for columns is the attribute hierarchy. Attribute hierarchies are data structures containing the values of a column sorted properly. Before moving further, it is helpful to state why these structures are named that way.

Tabular is the youngest brother of Multidimensional, the older engine still available in Analysis Services. Several data structures in Tabular inherited their names and sometimes their functionalities from existing structures in Multidimensional. In Multidimensional, columns were named *attributes* and every attribute had a default two-level hierarchy in which the top-level contained the All member only, and the second level contained all the possible values of the column (we now call them values; in Multidimensional, values of an attribute are called *Members*). Therefore, an attribute hierarchy is nothing but a list of column values in Tabular terminology or a hierarchy of attribute members in Multidimensional terminology.

These structures were (and still are) used in Multidimensional to execute queries. Because the attribute hierarchies were always created to maintain the compatibility of Tabular models with MDX, some DAX functionalities also use attribute hierarchies to speed up calculations.

There are some details that are important to know about attribute hierarchies:

- Attribute hierarchies are mandatory if you use MDX to group by a column. MDX still requires the existence of attribute hierarchies. DAX does not.

- Attribute hierarchies are not needed in DAX or MDX for columns that are only aggregated in measures. Nonetheless, some calculations might be adversely impacted if attribute hierarchies are not created.

- If you use only DAX to query a model, then attribute hierarchies are not required to run the query.

Again, some calculations might be affected in terms of speed.

- The creation of attribute hierarchies is quite time consuming at process time. Moreover, attribute hierarchies consume a large amount of RAM for high-cardinality columns.

- When a table undergoes any processing, attribute hierarchies need to be entirely reconstructed. If you add a small partition to a gigantic table, the partition processing can be rather quick. In contrast, the construction of the attribute hierarchies might be very slow, because it needs to scan the entire table again and rebuild all attribute hierarchies.

- Developers have the option of avoiding the creation of attribute hierarchies on a column-by-column basis. Each column has an *IsAvailableInMDX* property (also called *Available in MDX* in Tabular Editor and Visual Studio) that controls whether an attribute hierarchy is created or not for that specific column.

You can use the model statistics provided by VertiPaq Analyzer to inspect in *Hier Size* the amount of space used to store attribute hierarchies.

Name	Cardinality	Total Size ↓	Data	Dictionary	Hier Size	Encoding	Data Type
▲ **Sales**	**1,405,546,659**	**30,945,822,672**	**25,065,961,120**	**5,121,572,184**	**753,298,720**	**Many**	-
Order Number	94,138,244	11,446,897,280	5,614,533,784	5,079,257,528	753,105,968	HASH	Int64
Net Price	24,754	5,592,158,440	5,592,059,296	120	99,024	VALUE	Decimal
Unit Price	1,761	5,432,050,392	5,432,043,224	120	7,048	VALUE	Decimal
CustomerKey	1,868,002	3,789,152,328	3,748,125,560	41,026,768	0	HASH	Int64
ProductKey	2,517	2,248,655,088	2,248,644,896	120	10,072	VALUE	Int64
Unit Cost	1,956	1,890,769,432	1,890,712,120	41,648	15,664	HASH	Decimal
Line Number	20	468,330,624	468,330,416	120	88	VALUE	Int64
StoreKey	74	54,913,856	54,910,576	2,672	608	HASH	Int64
Quantity	10	8,061,480	8,059,992	1,392	96	HASH	Int64
Delivery Date	3,389	7,040,360	7,026,680	120	13,560	VALUE	DateTime
Order Date	3,281	1,231,144	1,029,208	175,680	26,256	HASH	DateTime

By inspecting *Sales*, you can see that around 750MB are being used to store attribute hierarchies. Their size directly depends on the cardinality of the column. Small cardinality columns generate tiny attribute hierarchies, whereas large cardinality columns, like *Order Number*, consume quite a large amount of RAM.

You can save that space (and most relevantly, the corresponding processing time) by setting the *Available In MDX* property to False.

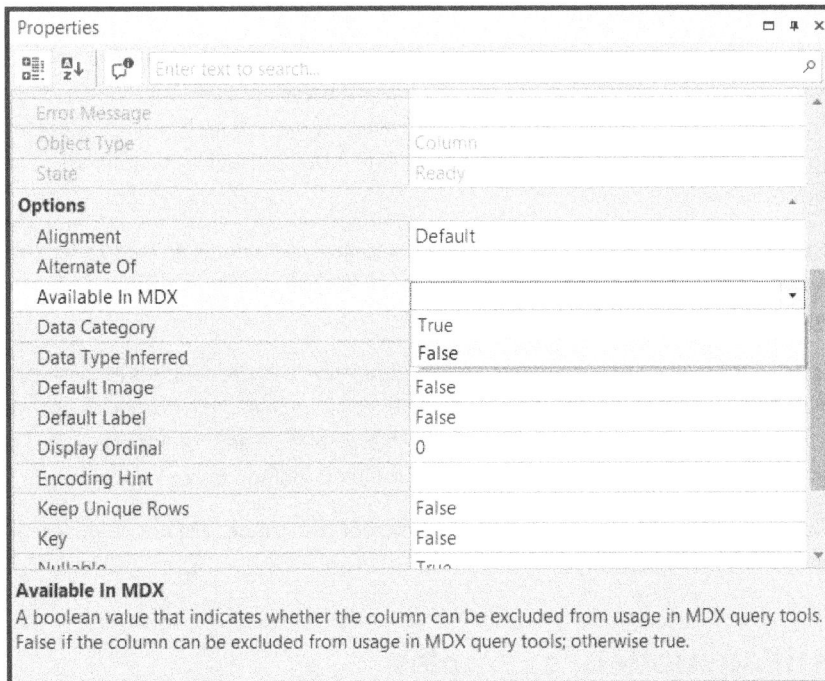

You do not need to reprocess the model after setting the *Available In MDX* property to False; the attribute hierarchies are immediately deleted and this is reflected in the VertiPaq Analyzer data, as you can see in the screenshot taken after setting the *Available In MDX* property of all the *Sales* columns to False.

Name	Cardinality	Total Size ↓	Data	Dictionary	Hier Size	Encoding	Data Type
◢ **Sales**	**1,405,546,659**	**30,134,887,512**	**25,009,373,216**	**5,120,523,648**	**0**	**Many**	**-**
Order Number	94,138,244	10,693,791,312	5,614,533,784	5,079,257,528	0	HASH	Int64
Net Price	24,754	5,584,385,992	5,584,385,872	120	0	VALUE	Decimal
Unit Price	1,761	5,400,538,712	5,400,538,592	120	0	VALUE	Decimal
CustomerKey	1,868,002	3,789,152,328	3,748,125,560	41,026,768	0	HASH	Int64
ProductKey	2,517	2,248,531,656	2,248,531,536	120	0	VALUE	Int64
Unit Cost	1,956	1,861,064,048	1,861,022,400	41,648	0	HASH	Decimal
Line Number	20	447,678,864	447,678,744	120	0	VALUE	Int64
StoreKey	74	88,188,640	88,185,968	2,672	0	HASH	Int64
Quantity	10	7,903,728	7,902,336	1,392	0	HASH	Int64
Delivery Date	3,389	6,969,320	6,969,200	120	0	VALUE	DateTime
Order Date	3,281	1,197,064	1,021,384	175,680	0	HASH	DateTime

Saving space by setting the property comes with a couple trade-offs:

- Columns can no longer be used in Excel to slice and dice. They can be used to compute values, but grouping and filtering are no longer allowed. This means that analyzing the model with Excel now comes with restrictions.

- Some DAX functionalities might end up somewhat slower. VertiPaq no longer has access to the unfiltered cardinality of columns, meaning that an expression like *COUNTROWS (ALL (table[column]))* requires a column scan. In contrast, when the attribute hierarchy is present, it is returned without executing any VertiPaq query. Similarly, MAX and MIN functions are somewhat faster with attribute hierarchies enabled.

Because the product is constantly evolving, it is not helpful to analyze in detail how and when attribute hierarchies are used in each DAX function. Moreover, your mileage might vary depending on data distribution, data types, and the kind of DAX queries involved.

We suggest keeping attribute hierarchies enabled on all dimensions, as the columns in dimensions are required both in DAX and in MDX. On fact tables, where attribute hierarchies might use a lot of space and require a long time to compute, you should disable attribute hierarchies on any column that is not directly used to slice and dice in a report, and is not used as part of a filter condition in any measure.

A double-check of performance is required to ensure that your test queries are not adversely affected by the removal of attribute hierarchies.

Optimizing VertiPaq models: examples

Now that we have completed the description of the VertiPaq peculiarities, we perform an analysis on the model, putting into practice the theory and searching for possible optimizations. Be mindful that the goal of this final section is not to provide best practices. We aim to show the method of reasoning to search for possible improvements, and more generally, the options we investigate.

Sales amount versus quantity and net price

The most widely used measure in our reports is *Sales Amount*, whose code is extremely simple:

```
--------------------------
-- Measure in Sales table
--------------------------
Sales Amount = SUMX ( Sales, Sales[Quantity] * Sales[Net Price] )
```

The measure requires scanning the *Sales* table and computing a simple multiplication. This being a simple calculation, the code is pushed down to the storage engine, and no formula engine is required. Nonetheless, it is interesting to discover what the price of the multiplication is and whether creating a calculated column containing the product of *Quantity* times *Net Price* is a smart move:

```
-------------------------------------
-- Calculated column in Sales table
-------------------------------------
Line Amount = Sales[Quantity] * Sales[Net Price]
```

Please remember that we already covered this example in the introduction. At that time, the goal was to show the process of making a choice without describing the details. Now that we better understand how VertiPaq works, we can proceed more slowly and perform several educated choices.

Before measuring the execution time of test queries, let us make several considerations:

- The cardinality of *Quantity* times *Net Price* will be much larger than the cardinality of the two source columns. It cannot be easily predicted, but in general, the cardinality of a multiplication is quite close to the multiplication of the cardinalities. Therefore, the calculated column will result in a large column.

- Being a large column, *Line Amount* will be slower to scan than *Quantity* and *Net Price*. Nonetheless, we need to figure out whether scanning a large column containing a partial result is faster than scanning two smaller columns and spending CPU cycles to perform the multiplication.

- We can compute the new column either as a calculated column or as a column computed in SQL. Given the cardinality, we do not expect a big difference between the two options because sorting will not help. Regardless, we always need to confirm our hypotheses with real numbers.

- Both the calculated and the SQL columns increase the time required to process the model. The calculated column is likely slower, as calculated columns are computed using only one core. It also has the drawback of requiring a full recalculation even if we updated only one partition.

It is important to build a list of tests and considerations before starting any test. The reason is that each test will require time to process the model, gather the result, and potentially review our considerations. Therefore, knowing in advance what to pay attention to greatly helps in scheduling the steps. For example, during the first step, we will create the calculated column. It is also a good time to collect the time required to compute the column.

It is important to obtain a baseline before performing any test. We use a straightforward query to measure just the time required to scan the columns:

```
EVALUATE
SUMMARIZECOLUMNS (
    "Result", [Sales Amount]
)
```

The baseline is around 6.5 seconds of storage engine CPU.

Total	SE CPU		Line	Subclass	Duration	CPU	Par.	Rows	KB	Timeline
142 ms	6,531 ms									
	x48.4		2	Scan	135	6,531	x48.4	1	1	

FE	SE
7 ms	135 ms
4.9%	95.1%

SE Queries	SE Cache
1	0
	0.0%

```
SET DC_KIND="AUTO";
WITH
   $Expr0 := ( PFCAST ( 'Sales'[Quantity] AS INT ) * PFCAST ( 'Sales'[Net Price] AS INT ) )
SELECT
   SUM ( @$Expr0 )
FROM 'Sales';
```

As stated, the first test is the creation of the *Line Amount* calculated column. A process default right after having created the column requires two minutes and 52 seconds. Once the process finished, we look at the result.

Name	Cardinality	Total Size ↓	Data	Dictionary	Hier Size	Encoding	Data Type
⊿ **Sales**	**1,405,546,659**	**33,635,089,672**	**28,503,262,176**	**5,125,455,888**	**1,380,960**	**Many**	-
Order Number	94,138,244	10,693,791,312	5,614,533,784	5,079,257,528	0	HASH	Int64
Net Price	24,754	5,592,059,416	5,592,059,296	120	0	VALUE	Decimal
Unit Price	1,761	5,432,043,344	5,432,043,224	120	0	VALUE	Decimal
CustomerKey	1,868,002	3,789,152,328	3,748,125,560	41,026,768	0	HASH	Int64
Line Amount	172,618	3,443,614,256	3,437,301,056	4,932,240	1,380,960	HASH	Decimal
ProductKey	2,517	2,248,645,016	2,248,644,896	120	0	VALUE	Int64
Unit Cost	1,956	1,890,753,768	1,890,712,120	41,648	0	HASH	Decimal
Line Number	20	468,330,536	468,330,416	120	0	VALUE	Int64
StoreKey	74	54,913,248	54,910,576	2,672	0	HASH	Int64
Quantity	10	8,061,384	8,059,992	1,392	0	HASH	Int64
Delivery Date	3,389	7,026,800	7,026,680	120	0	VALUE	DateTime
Order Date	3,281	1,204,888	1,029,208	175,680	0	HASH	DateTime
Exchange Rate	5,071	483,288	483,168	120	0	VALUE	Double
Currency Code	5	19,320	2,200	17,120	0	HASH	String

VertiPaq chose hash encoding for the *Line Amount* column. As you might notice, we forgot to disable the attribute hierarchy. Due to the use of the column, we would like to test value encoding, so that the column already contains the value to be summed. Therefore, we will force value encoding as the next step. However, while we have the model ready, we can execute the test query to check the time required to scan *Line Amount* with hash encoding.

The result is quite impressive. The baseline was about 6.5 seconds, the calculated column is way faster: 2.8 seconds. That is more than two times faster.

Total	SE CPU		Line	Subclass	Duration	CPU	Par.	Rows	KB	Timeline
70 ms	2,828 ms x42.2		2	Scan	67	2,828	x42.2	1	1	

FE	SE
3 ms	67 ms
4.3%	95.7%

SE Queries	SE Cache
1	0
	0.0%

```
SET DC_KIND="AUTO";
SELECT
    SUM ( 'Sales'[Line Amount] )
FROM 'Sales';
```

So far, we have tested the calculated column with hash encoding. The column is surprisingly small, smaller than the *Net Price* column on which it depends. The cardinality is quite high, yet compression works well. The next step is to force value encoding; in the meantime, we remove the attribute hierarchy that is useless for this column.

Having changed the encoding hint, we need to reprocess the full table. Here is the VertiPaq Analyzer information after the reprocess.

Name	Cardinality	Total Size ↓	Data	Dictionary	Hier Size	Encoding	Data Type
▲ **Sales**	**1,405,546,659**	**35,704,313,864**	**30,578,799,...**	**5,120,523,7...**	**0**	**Many**	**-**
Order Number	94,138,244	10,693,791,312	5,614,533,784	5,079,257,528	0	HASH	Int64
Line Amount	172,618	5,579,402,912	5,579,402,792	120	0	VALUE	Decimal
Net Price	24,754	5,579,397,088	5,579,396,968	120	0	VALUE	Decimal
Unit Price	1,761	5,398,300,536	5,398,300,416	120	0	VALUE	Decimal
CustomerKey	1,868,002	3,789,152,328	3,748,125,560	41,026,768	0	HASH	Int64
ProductKey	2,517	2,248,468,648	2,248,468,528	120	0	VALUE	Int64
Unit Cost	1,956	1,859,509,104	1,859,467,456	41,648	0	HASH	Decimal
Line Number	20	448,797,544	448,797,424	120	0	VALUE	Int64
StoreKey	74	86,521,040	86,518,368	2,672	0	HASH	Int64
Quantity	10	7,455,544	7,454,152	1,392	0	HASH	Int64
Delivery Date	3,389	6,844,600	6,844,480	120	0	VALUE	DateTime
Order Date	3,281	1,191,576	1,015,896	175,680	0	HASH	DateTime
Exchange Rate	5,071	471,624	471,504	120	0	VALUE	Double
Currency Code	5	19,240	2,120	17,120	0	HASH	String

Moving to value encoding did not produce any good results. The dictionary is gone, but the *Line Amount* column's overall size increased dramatically. Before trashing this idea, it is worth executing the test query again to check whether value encoding offers any benefits.

Total	SE CPU		Line	Subclass	Duration	CPU	Par.	Rows	KB	Timeline
103 ms	5,375 ms x55.4		2	Scan	99	5,375	x54.3	1	1	

FE	SE
6 ms	97 ms
5.8%	96.1%

SE Queries	SE Cache
1	0
	0.0%

```
SET DC_KIND="AUTO";
SELECT
    SUM ( 'Sales'[Line Amount] )
FROM 'Sales';
```

Estimated size: rows = 1 bytes = 16

Unfortunately, the timings reflect the increase in size: it is slightly better than the original *Sales Amount* but nearly twice as slow as the version with hash encoding.

Therefore, the VertiPaq choice was the correct one. Hash encoding is the way to go for this calculated column. Moving further with our list of tests, the next is to compute the same column in the data source. The column is a very simple calculation; therefore, it can be easily computed in SQL through a view, or by computing the column in Power Query. We expect compression to be better and consequently, we expect speed to be improved.

Unfortunately, none of our assumptions are correct. Despite being loaded from SQL, there are no improvements in the memory footprint this time.

Name	Cardinality	Total Size ↓	Data	Dictionary	Hier Size	Encoding	Data Type
⊿ **Sales**	**1,405,546,659**	**33,861,413,320**	**28,730,966,...**	**5,125,455,8...**	**0**	**Many**	-
Order Number	94,138,244	10,692,858,696	5,613,601,168	5,079,257,528	0	HASH	Int64
Net Price	24,754	5,581,686,448	5,581,686,328	120	0	VALUE	Decimal
Unit Price	1,761	5,408,063,888	5,408,063,768	120	0	VALUE	Decimal
CustomerKey	1,868,002	3,789,152,328	3,748,125,560	41,026,768	0	HASH	Int64
Line Amount	172,618	3,726,060,576	3,721,128,336	4,932,240	0	HASH	Decimal
ProductKey	2,517	2,248,528,848	2,248,528,728	120	0	VALUE	Int64
Unit Cost	1,956	1,862,776,000	1,862,734,352	41,648	0	HASH	Decimal
Line Number	20	456,350,560	456,350,440	120	0	VALUE	Int64
StoreKey	74	74,714,008	74,711,336	2,672	0	HASH	Int64
Quantity	10	7,627,504	7,626,112	1,392	0	HASH	Int64
Delivery Date	3,389	6,900,160	6,900,040	120	0	VALUE	DateTime
Order Date	3,281	1,202,112	1,026,432	175,680	0	HASH	DateTime
Exchange Rate	5,071	482,184	482,064	120	0	VALUE	Double
Currency Code	5	19,240	2,120	17,120	0	HASH	String

Consequently, there are no improvements in the query speed. Still, choosing a column computed at the data source level rather than a DAX calculated column offers the benefit of avoiding a full recalculation every time there is the need to process a partition. At the same time, we measured the amount of time required to compute the calculated column, which is less than three minutes. Therefore, we do not find compelling reasons in favor of one choice nor the other – unless saving three minutes from processing time is important.

Having reached this point, the analysis is complete. We now know that the price of a column containing the multiplication of *Net Price* by *Quantity* is around 3.5GB. The improvement in terms of speed is rather important. The new calculated column works better with hash encoding than with value encoding. There is a slight advantage in computing the column at the data source level rather than in DAX, mainly if we plan to partition the table.

This is the knowledge needed to make an educated choice. The final decision might consider other factors, like the amount of RAM still available in the server and how much a typical report or dashboard might benefit from the new column. Indeed, we optimized only the *Sales Amount* measure. In a report, there are many more measures, and it is hard to think about optimizing them all in the same way.

Besides, it is also important to consider the size of the model. We test performance on a medium-sized model with 1.4B rows in *Sales*. If we were to perform the tests on a smaller model (say 10-20M rows), the differences in terms of speed would be irrelevant, and the only measurable difference would be the model size increase. In small models, these optimizations are a waste of time and resources.

Another important aspect to highlight is that the theory learned in this chapter about how the VertiPaq engine works is useful to understand which tests need to be performed and how to read the numbers gathered. You cannot entirely predict the outcome of compression and query speed because they strongly depend on data distribution. Therefore, be prepared for long testing sessions to answer any questions you might have: proper testing is the only reliable tool to make educated choices.

Storing currency conversion data

All the amounts in our demo model are stored using USD as the currency. A new requirement is to build reports that show information in the original currency. The original currency is present in *Sales[Currency Code]*. The requirement is to convert the USD values into the original currency using the date of the transaction.

Here is the model diagram:

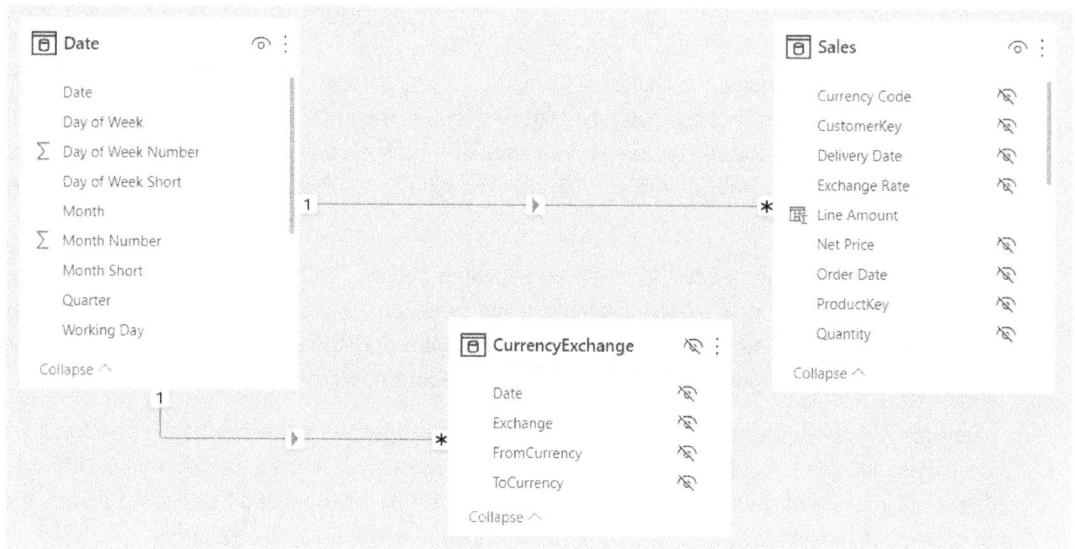

To find the exchange rate of a transaction, we need to search in the *CurrencyExchange* table a row where *FromCurrency* is USD, *ToCurrency* is the desired currency (equal to *Sales[Currency Code]*), and *Date* is the date of the transaction (equal to *Sales[Order Date]*).

There are multiple options to obtain this goal:

- Compute everything with a measure, dynamically retrieving the exchange rate through iterators and filters. Given the size of our model, this option seems too slow.
- Create a calculated column to store the value of *Net Price* converted in the desired currency, which moves the calculation's complexity at process time rather than it being found at query time.
- Build a relationship between *Sales* and *CurrencyExchange*. This option requires building a relationship based on two columns, which Tabular does not support.

It is worth remembering that – at this stage – we are not interested in optimizing everything but in choosing the best solution. Therefore, because we have several possible solutions, we will test them all and make several considerations to drive our choice.

Let us start with a measure. The measure already contains many interesting details; we will discuss them in a later chapter when looking for more advanced optimizations. For now, we just look at the code and measure its performance using a test query that slices by *Customer[Country]* and *Sales[Currency Code]*:

```
DEFINE
    MEASURE Sales[AmtLocalCurrency] =
        SUMX (
            SUMMARIZE ( Sales, Sales[Order Date], Sales[Currency Code] ),
            VAR Amount = [Sales Amount]
            VAR ExchangeRate =
                LOOKUPVALUE (
                    CurrencyExchange[Exchange],
                    CurrencyExchange[FromCurrency], "USD",
                    CurrencyExchange[ToCurrency], Sales[Currency Code],
                    CurrencyExchange[Date], Sales[Order Date]
                )
            VAR Result = Amount * ExchangeRate
            RETURN
                Result
        )
EVALUATE
SUMMARIZECOLUMNS (
    Customer[Country],
    Sales[Currency Code],
    "Amt Local", [AmtLocalCurrency]
)
ORDER BY Customer[Country], Sales[Currency Code]
```

The result shows the sales in each local currency sliced by country.

Country	Currency Code	Amt Local
Australia	AUD	16,983,533,583.74
Canada	CAD	28,718,993,030.74
France	EUR	5,645,057,011.11
Germany	EUR	20,110,340,164.21
Italy	EUR	5,780,711,365.66
Netherlands	EUR	7,949,920,737.64
United Kingdom	GBP	17,520,823,580.61
United States	USD	119,622,385,294.28

Performance-wise, the measure is not bad at all. Considering that the model contains 1.4B rows in *Sales*, the result of the query is generated in 4 seconds of CPU time which, due to parallelism, produces an output in less than one second.

Total	SE CPU	Line	Subclass	Duration	CPU	Par.	Rows	KB	Timeline
353 ms	4,156 ms	2	Scan	150	2,484	x16.6	26,248	308	
	x15.6	4	Scan	90	1,422	x15.8	26,248	103	
FE	**SE**	6	Scan	0	0		8	1	
86 ms	267 ms	8	Scan	1	0		8,087	64	
24.4%	75.6%	10	Scan	1	0		16,405	65	
SE Queries	**SE Cache**	12	Scan	24	250	x10.4	8	1	
7	0	14	Scan	1	0		11	1	
	0.0%								

Nonetheless, it would be misleading to be satisfied with this result. We are performing the test on a powerful machine that can produce a very high level of parallelism. On a less-powerful server, the experience could be worse. With that said, we have gathered the information required: the execution time of a test query with the first possible solution.

The main advantage of a solution based on a measure is that it is entirely dynamic, easy to modify, and very flexible. The disadvantage might be in terms of performance. We hope that calculated columns or relationships lead to better performance.

Here is the code for a calculated column that computes the *Sales[Net Price]* with the local currency:

```
-------------------------------------
-- Calculated column in Sales table
-------------------------------------
Net Price Local =
VAR ExchangeRate =
    LOOKUPVALUE (
        CurrencyExchange[Exchange],
        CurrencyExchange[FromCurrency], "USD",
        CurrencyExchange[ToCurrency], Sales[Currency Code],
        CurrencyExchange[Date], Sales[Order Date]
    )
VAR Result = Sales[Net Price] * ExchangeRate
RETURN
    Result
```

The calculated column is processed quite quickly. The problem is that the cardinality of the new *Net Price Local* calculated column is extremely high, resulting in a large column.

Name	Cardinality	Total Size ↓	Data	Dictionary	Hier Size	Encoding	Data Type
▲ **Sales**	**225,616,948**	**4,117,144,396**	**4,018,259,4...**	**47,271,300**	**46,622,704**	**Many**	**-**
Net Price Local	7,489,463	919,304,480	889,346,488	136	29,957,856	VALUE	Decimal
CustomerKey	1,868,084	657,645,752	601,673,992	41,027,072	14,944,688	HASH	Int64
Line Amount	172,193	573,313,644	567,005,984	4,930,108	1,377,552	HASH	Decimal
Net Price	24,754	442,747,184	441,922,072	627,064	198,048	HASH	Decimal
ProductKey	2,517	356,890,516	356,794,464	75,908	20,144	HASH	Int64
Unit Cost	1,956	311,819,192	311,762,136	41,392	15,664	HASH	Decimal
Unit Price	1,761	310,744,124	310,689,456	40,572	14,096	HASH	Decimal
Delivery Date	3,389	216,249,628	216,055,080	167,428	27,120	HASH	DateTime
Order Date	3,281	166,953,888	166,761,872	165,760	26,256	HASH	DateTime

We might save space by creating the column at the data source level. Nonetheless, *Net Price Local* depends on *Net Price*, a large column, even though it has fewer distinct values. Therefore, we already know that the column size depends not only on cardinality but also on data distribution.

Let us check the benefit in terms of performance:

```
EVALUATE
SUMMARIZECOLUMNS (
    Customer[Country],
    Sales[Currency Code],
    "Amt Local", SUMX ( Sales, Sales[Quantity] * Sales[Net Price Local] )
)
ORDER BY
    Customer[Country],
    Sales[Currency Code]
```

The query uses 1.5 seconds of storage engine CPU.

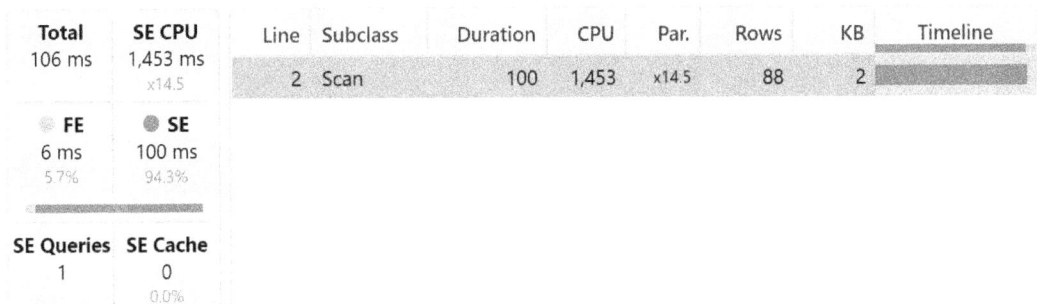

Total	SE CPU		Line	Subclass	Duration	CPU	Par.	Rows	KB	Timeline
106 ms	1,453 ms		2	Scan	100	1,453	x14.5	88	2	
	x14.5									

FE	SE
6 ms	100 ms
5.7%	94.3%

SE Queries	SE Cache
1	0
	0.0%

The advantage in terms of speed is important: it runs in less than half of the time of the measure. Nonetheless, the price is quite large in terms of memory consumption.

Besides, by storing the *Net Price* column in local currency in the *Sales* table, we can only optimize measures that depend on *Net Price*. If we needed to replicate the same for *Unit Cost*, *Unit Price*, or other currency values, the memory consumption would skyrocket. As an alternative, we could store only the exchange rate in the *Sales* table, performing the final multiplication in the measure:

```
------------------------------------
-- Calculated column in Sales table
------------------------------------
xRate =
LOOKUPVALUE (
    CurrencyExchange[Exchange],
    CurrencyExchange[FromCurrency], "USD",
    CurrencyExchange[ToCurrency], Sales[Currency Code],
    CurrencyExchange[Date], Sales[Order Date]
)
```

The *xRate* calculated column has a smaller cardinality and it changes once a day, instead of changing for nearly every row. Therefore, we expect a smaller memory footprint.

Name	Cardinality	Total Size ↓	Data	Dictionary	Hier Size	Encoding	Data Type
⊿ **Sales**	**225,616,948**	**4,117,144,396**	**4,018,259,4...**	**47,271,300**	**46,622,704**	**Many**	-
Net Price Local	7,489,463	919,304,480	889,346,488	136	29,957,856	VALUE	Decimal
CustomerKey	1,868,084	657,645,752	601,673,992	41,027,072	14,944,688	HASH	Int64
Line Amount	172,193	573,313,644	567,005,984	4,930,108	1,377,552	HASH	Decimal
Net Price	24,754	442,747,184	441,922,072	627,064	198,048	HASH	Decimal
ProductKey	2,517	356,890,516	356,794,464	75,908	20,144	HASH	Int64
Unit Cost	1,956	311,819,192	311,762,136	41,392	15,664	HASH	Decimal
Unit Price	1,761	310,744,124	310,689,456	40,572	14,096	HASH	Decimal
Delivery Date	3,389	216,249,628	216,055,080	167,428	27,120	HASH	DateTime
Order Date	3,281	166,953,888	166,761,872	165,760	26,256	HASH	DateTime
xRate	5,071	99,605,756	99,390,656	174,524	40,576	HASH	Double
StoreKey	74	51,514,448	51,511,192	2,648	608	HASH	Int64
Quantity	10	4,920,024	4,918,560	1,368	96	HASH	Int64
Currency Code	0	417,040	399,856	17,184	0	HASH	String

Indeed, the *xRate* column has a small cardinality and a minimal memory footprint.

```
EVALUATE
SUMMARIZECOLUMNS (
    Customer[Country],
    Sales[Currency Code],
    "Amt Local",
        SUMX ( Sales, Sales[Quantity] * Sales[Net Price] * Sales[xRate] )
)
```

Unfortunately, there is quite a subtle problem with this approach. *xRate* is a floating point value, *Quantity* is an integer, and *Net Price* is a currency. When handling math over currencies, if the result is not a currency, Tabular forces a CallbackDataID because math with currencies and floating point numbers can be executed only by the formula engine. Therefore, when executing the test query, performance is poor, and we notice a callback.

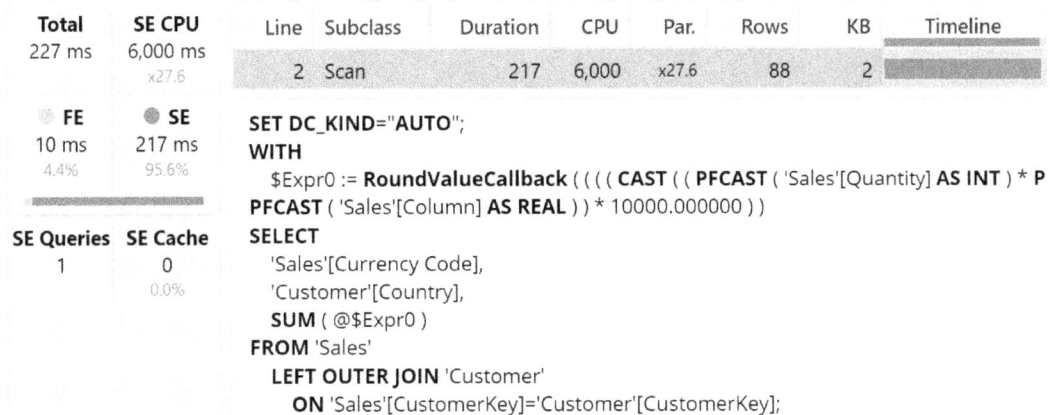

Total	SE CPU		Line	Subclass	Duration	CPU	Par.	Rows	KB	Timeline
227 ms	6,000 ms									
	x27.6		2	Scan	217	6,000	x27.6	88	2	

FE	SE
10 ms	217 ms
4.4%	95.6%

SE Queries	SE Cache
1	0
	0.0%

```
SET DC_KIND="AUTO";
WITH
    $Expr0 := RoundValueCallback ( ( ( ( CAST ( ( PFCAST ( 'Sales'[Quantity] AS INT ) * P
PFCAST ( 'Sales'[Column] AS REAL ) ) * 10000.000000 ) )
SELECT
    'Sales'[Currency Code],
    'Customer'[Country],
    SUM ( @$Expr0 )
FROM 'Sales'
    LEFT OUTER JOIN 'Customer'
        ON 'Sales'[CustomerKey]='Customer'[CustomerKey];
```

The only way to avoid the callback is to prevent mixing currency and floating point numbers. Beware that multiplying a currency by another currency also results in a callback. We will cover datatypes and callbacks in more detail in Chapter 12 (Analyzing VertiPaq storage engine queries). For now, it suffices to say that there are no ways to express the calculation without requiring a callback. The only viable option is to force the entire calculation to floating point by changing the datatype of *Sales[Net Price]* to Decimal. By doing so, the callback disappears, and we have a better picture of the advantage of storing the *xRate* column.

Total	SE CPU		Line	Subclass	Duration	CPU	Par.	Rows	KB	Timeline
145 ms	2,563 ms									
	x18.3		2	Scan	140	2,563	x18.3	88	2	

FE	SE
5 ms	140 ms
3.4%	96.6%

SE Queries	SE Cache
1	0
	0.0%

```
SET DC_KIND="AUTO";
WITH
    $Expr0 := ( ( CAST ( PFCAST ( 'Sales'[Quantity] AS INT ) AS REAL ) * PFCAST ( 'Sales'[N
SELECT
    'Sales'[Currency Code],
    'Customer'[Country],
    SUM ( @$Expr0 )
FROM 'Sales'
```

The execution is slower, but we obtain much more flexibility by storing the exchange rate. On the other hand, we need to change the datatype of *Sales[Net Price]* and any other column involved in the calculation with the exchange rate.

Remember that at this stage, we are collecting information, not making decisions. Therefore, once we investigate the second option, we can quickly analyze the third option, creating a relationship between *Sales* and *Currency Exchange*.

In Tabular, we can create relationships based on only one column. Because the relationship depends on three values, we need to create a calculated column both in *Sales* and in *CurrencyExchange* containing the concatenation of the three columns:

```
----------------------------------------
-- Calculated column in Sales table
----------------------------------------
xRateKey =
COMBINEVALUES (
    "-",
    "USD",
    Sales[Currency Code],
    Sales[Order Date]
)


-------------------------------------------------
-- Calculated column in CurrencyExchange table
-------------------------------------------------
xRateKey =
COMBINEVALUES (
    "-",
    CurrencyExchange[FromCurrency],
    CurrencyExchange[ToCurrency],
    CurrencyExchange[Date]
)
```

The newly created column acts as a primary key for *CurrencyExchange* and can be used to set up the relationship. Here is an example of its content.

xRateKey

GBP-GBP-1/4/1999

GBP-GBP-1/5/1999

GBP-GBP-1/6/1999

GBP-GBP-1/7/1999

GBP-GBP-1/8/1999

GBP-GBP-1/9/1999

GBP-GBP-1/10/1999

GBP-GBP-1/11/1999

GBP-GBP-1/12/1999

The column has a large cardinality but changes slowly, as did *xRate*. Therefore, we do not expect the column to be huge. Here is the result after having created the *xRateKey* column.

Name	Cardinality	Total Size ↓	Data	Dictionary	Hier Size	Encoding	Data Type
⊿ **Sales**	**225,616,948**	**5,134,710,477**	**4,210,578,5...**	**750,611,069**	**168,486,192**	**Many**	**-**
Net Price Local	18,948,401	1,726,001,852	873,186,568	701,228,068	151,587,216	HASH	Double
CustomerKey	1,868,084	657,645,752	601,673,992	41,027,072	14,944,688	HASH	Int64
Line Amount	185,052	575,062,048	567,704,800	5,876,816	1,480,432	HASH	Double
Net Price	24,754	443,372,768	441,922,072	1,252,648	198,048	HASH	Double
ProductKey	2,517	356,890,516	356,794,464	75,908	20,144	HASH	Int64
Unit Cost	1,956	311,819,192	311,762,136	41,392	15,664	HASH	Decimal
Unit Price	1,761	310,744,124	310,689,456	40,572	14,096	HASH	Decimal
Delivery Date	3,389	216,249,628	216,055,080	167,428	27,120	HASH	DateTime
xRateKey	16,405	208,450,961	207,780,168	539,545	131,248	HASH	String
Order Date	3,281	166,953,888	166,761,872	165,760	26,256	HASH	DateTime
xRate	5,071	99,605,756	99,390,656	174,524	40,576	HASH	Double

As expected, the column is not very large. Nonetheless, its cardinality is larger than that of *xRate*. Moreover, the calculation now needs to traverse a relationship to retrieve the value of the exchange rate. This solution does not seem to present any advantage compared to the other ones. Indeed, if we execute the code using *Net Price* as a currency, we still have the callback and poor performance.

Total	SE CPU	Line	Subclass	Duration	CPU	Par.	Rows	KB	Timeline
243 ms	6,469 ms x27.6	2	Scan	234	6,469	x27.6	88	2	

FE	SE
9 ms	234 ms
3.7%	96.3%

SE Queries	SE Cache
1	0
	0.0%

```
SET DC_KIND="AUTO";
WITH
    $Expr0 := RoundValueCallback ( ( ( ( CAST ( ( PFCAST ( 'Sales'[Quantity] AS INT ) * P
PFCAST ( 'CurrencyExchange'[Exchange] AS REAL ) ) * 10000.000000 ) )
SELECT
    'Sales'[Currency Code],
    'Customer'[Country],
    SUM ( @$Expr0 )
FROM 'Sales'
```

The result is very close to the one we obtained when we stored *xRate* in *Sales*. Testing performance with a floating point instead of a currency for the *Net Price* column is not worth it. There are no reasons why it should be faster than the *xRate* column we analyzed before.

Now that we have concluded our tests, we have a better picture of the advantages and disadvantages of our possible solutions. As usual, there are other considerations to make before deciding. If performance is not an issue, then the measure is the best solution. If seeking optimal performance, storing the exchange rate in Sales produces a good result while retaining flexibility.

Date time versus date and time

One of the critical data modeling techniques when using VertiPaq is to reduce the cardinality of columns as much as possible. Among the many columns stored in a database, date and time are important because they are almost always present.

Quite often, in SQL databases, date and time are stored in the same column, as a DateTime. Nonetheless, importing a column containing both the date and time is just wrong. The reason is – not surprisingly – cardinality.

In a DateTime column, the number of values is extremely large. There are 86,400 seconds in a day. This means that over a year, the number of distinct values can reach 365 * 86,400 = 31,536,000 distinct values. Moreover, the values change extremely often (once a second), making RLE compression useless. Therefore, using a DateTime forces VertiPaq to work with a large cardinality and a frequently-changing column: a VertiPaq nightmare.

To show the scenario, we created a *DateAndTime* column in the database that contains both the date and the time, along with two separate columns: one for the date and one for the time.

Name	Cardinality	Total Size ↓	Data	Dictionary	Hier Size	Encoding	Data Type
⊿ Sales	1,405,546,659	45,901,935,968	38,046,479,872	7,850,465,448	0	Many	-
Order Number	94,138,244	10,692,858,696	5,613,601,168	5,079,257,528	0	HASH	Int64
DateAndTime	63,376,257	8,323,874,664	5,603,817,832	2,720,056,832	0	HASH	DateTime
Net Price	24,754	5,568,894,280	5,568,894,160	120	0	VALUE	Decimal
Unit Price	1,761	5,396,075,336	5,396,075,216	120	0	VALUE	Decimal
CustomerKey	1,868,002	3,789,152,328	3,748,125,560	41,026,768	0	HASH	Int64
Time	86,400	3,753,078,288	3,748,125,560	4,952,728	0	HASH	DateTime
Line Amount	172,618	3,717,532,912	3,712,600,672	4,932,240	0	HASH	Decimal
ProductKey	2,517	2,248,347,840	2,248,347,720	120	0	VALUE	Int64
Unit Cost	1,956	1,858,043,712	1,858,002,064	41,648	0	HASH	Decimal
Line Number	20	448,664,176	448,664,056	120	0	VALUE	Int64
StoreKey	74	84,892,328	84,889,656	2,672	0	HASH	Int64
Quantity	10	7,112,200	7,110,808	1,392	0	HASH	Int64
Delivery Date	3,389	6,716,320	6,716,200	120	0	VALUE	DateTime
Order Date	3,281	1,212,808	1,037,128	175,680	0	HASH	DateTime
Exchange Rate	5,071	470,088	469,968	120	0	VALUE	Double
Currency Code	5	19,224	2,104	17,120	0	HASH	String

Let us perform some considerations about the three columns:

- *DateAndTime* is huge. The total column size is 8.3 GB and the cardinality is 63 million. As such, the column is slow to scan. The column size is due to both the cardinality and the frequency of value changes.

- *Time* has a small cardinality, but it changes very frequently. Therefore, despite it having a small number of values, RLE does not compress data very well.

- *Order Date* has a small cardinality and – at the same time – it changes very slowly: once a day. As such, the column is very well compressed and produces a small structure.

The size of a column impacts any operation on the column. This includes scanning the column to aggregate values or using filters. Indeed, a bitmap index (one bit for each row) that filters *DateAndTime* contains 64M bits, whereas a bitmap index that filters *Time* can be as small as 86,400 bits. The larger the data structures, the slower the query.

Let us perform several tests to validate our assumptions. We want to measure the time required to scan the column and perform a simple aggregation. The following query only requires one storage engine query to scan the *Sales[DateAndTime]* column:

```
EVALUATE
SUMMARIZECOLUMNS ( "Test", AVERAGE ( Sales[DateAndTime] ) )
```

Scanning *Sales[DateAndTime]* requires nearly eight seconds of storage engine CPU. Then, parallelism plays an important role in reducing the execution time. Still, it is a very expensive operation.

Total	SE CPU		Line	Subclass	Duration	CPU	Par.	Rows	KB	Timeline
141 ms	6,688 ms		2	Scan	137	6,688	x48.8	1	1	
	x48.8									

FE	SE
4 ms	137 ms
2.8%	97.2%

SE Queries	SE Cache
1	0
	0.0%

By splitting the column into two parts, we obtained *Date* and *Time*. *Time* is still relatively large; therefore, scanning the *Time* column requires some time. It is faster than *DateAndTime*, but still somewhat slow. We executed this query:

```
EVALUATE
SUMMARIZECOLUMNS ( "Test", AVERAGE ( Sales[Time] ) )
```

The query ran in a bit more than five seconds.

Total	SE CPU		Line	Subclass	Duration	CPU	Par.	Rows	KB	Timeline
114 ms	5,141 ms		2	Scan	113	5,141	x45.5	1	1	
	x45.5									

FE	SE
1 ms	113 ms
0.9%	99.1%

SE Queries	SE Cache
1	0
	0.0%

```
SET DC_KIND="AUTO";
SELECT
    SUM ( 'Sales'[Time] ),
    COUNT ()
FROM 'Sales'
WHERE
    'Sales'[Time] IS NOT NULL;
```

Date, on the other hand, is very well compressed by RLE. Therefore, we expect that scanning *Date* will be way faster. We execute this query:

```
EVALUATE
SUMMARIZECOLUMNS ( "Test", AVERAGE ( Sales[Order Date] ) )
```

That runs at the blazing speed of 7 milliseconds.

Total	SE CPU		Line	Subclass	Duration	CPU	Par.	Rows	KB	Timeline
11 ms	0 ms x0.0		2	Scan	7	0		1	1	

FE	SE
4 ms	7 ms
36.4%	63.6%

SE Queries	SE Cache
1	0
	0.0%

```
SET DC_KIND="AUTO";
SELECT
    SUM ( 'Sales'[Order Date] ),
    COUNT ( )
FROM 'Sales'
WHERE
    'Sales'[Order Date] IS NOT NULL;
```

In a typical business intelligence project, it is more frequent to slice by date attributes than by time. Therefore, obtaining an exceptional speed with date is much more relevant than super-optimizing time handling.

Moreover, if there is the need to slice by *Time*, developers can choose the granularity. So far, we used *Time* at the second level in the demo. This generates a large cardinality column and prevents RLE from working efficiently because the number of repetitions is small. By carefully analyzing their business needs, developers might choose a different grain. For example, if we use hours instead of seconds, we largely reduce the granularity and increase repetitions. Here are the *Sales* statistics using an *Hour* column.

Name	Cardinality	Total Size ↓	Data	Dictionary	Hier Size	Encoding	Data Type
⊿ Sales	1,405,546,659	34,785,000,264	29,654,552,280	5,125,457,336	0	Many	-
Order Number	94,138,244	10,693,791,312	5,614,533,784	5,079,257,528	0	HASH	Int64
Net Price	24,754	5,578,751,096	5,578,750,976	120	0	VALUE	Decimal
Unit Price	1,761	5,398,169,096	5,398,168,976	120	0	VALUE	Decimal
CustomerKey	1,868,002	3,789,152,328	3,748,125,560	41,026,768	0	HASH	Int64
Line Amount	172,618	3,724,103,800	3,719,171,560	4,932,240	0	HASH	Decimal
ProductKey	2,517	2,248,441,176	2,248,441,056	120	0	VALUE	Int64
Unit Cost	1,956	1,859,617,000	1,859,575,352	41,648	0	HASH	Decimal
Hour	24	936,263,208	936,261,760	1,448	0	HASH	Int64
Line Number	20	448,947,072	448,946,952	120	0	VALUE	Int64
StoreKey	74	86,787,896	86,785,224	2,672	0	HASH	Int64
Quantity	10	7,408,400	7,407,008	1,392	0	HASH	Int64
Delivery Date	3,389	6,877,744	6,877,624	120	0	VALUE	DateTime
Order Date	3,281	1,203,160	1,027,480	175,680	0	HASH	DateTime

When handling date and time, the choice of keeping both pieces of information in the same column is most likely the wrong choice to make. A *DateTime* column uses a huge amount of RAM because of cardinality and lack of repetition. Splitting the column into two – one for the date and one for the time – is the first step in the right direction. Next, a skilled developer should try reducing cardinality (increasing repetitions) by discussing the requirements with business users. Remember that not making a choice (that is, using the largest granularity) brings some performance issues that are most likely to be unsolved.

Conclusions

In this chapter, we learned the details of the VertiPaq engine. VertiPaq comes with important peculiarities to know to make educated choices about the data model. Understanding the different types of encoding, the relevance of cardinality and repetitions to improve compression, and the relevance of compression to performance, are important skills to acquire.

Before moving further, we suggest you spend some time reviewing your current models with VertiPaq Analyzer to understand better how your data is compressed and whether there are areas of improvement.

Starting with the next chapter, we first learn the different types of relationships. Then, we uncover the xmSQL language used by VertiPaq to communicate with the formula engine. Finally, we put all the theory into practice by performing several optimizations of VertiPaq models and queries.

Understanding VertiPaq relationships

In the previous chapter, we described the physical structure of a relationship in VertiPaq. Relationships in VertiPaq are data structures designed to speed up the process of moving a filter from the one-side of a relationship to the other side. Relationships have been carefully crafted to work with the internal representation of columns in VertiPaq.

The internal structure of relationships represents strong, regular one-to-many relationships, which is the default type of relationship in VertiPaq. Over time, Tabular evolved and developers can now create different types of relationships, like limited relationships and many-to-many cardinality relationships. Relationships can also have bidirectional filter propagation instead of the standard single-direction propagation. Even though there are now multiple types of relationships, the internal structure has not changed.

Therefore, the only type of really optimized relationships in VertiPaq are regular relationships, either one-to-many or one-to-one. All other types of relationships require more complex algorithms that can use the structure of a relationship as an aid to speed up performance. Still, these types of relationships require more effort at query time to be resolved. As such, they are slower than regular relationships.

In this chapter, we perform a first analysis of all the types of relationships available in Tabular, and we uncover details about their performance and how they are resolved using multiple storage engine queries. Moreover, in this chapter we start to look a bit more into the details of the xmSQL language used by VertiPaq to communicate with the formula engine. In the next chapter, we will go even deeper and describe the features of xmSQL and how xmSQL is used by different DAX patterns.

The goal of a relationship is ultimately to move a filter from one table to another. You filter customers and you want to compute the sales amount for those filtered customers. Therefore, you create a relationship between *Sales* and *Customers*, to let the filter propagate as wanted. Traversing a relationship comes at a cost and an important part of a model's optimization is the choice of the correct set of relationships.

We will use the large model (Contoso 100Mx10) for the first two sections (unidirectional and bidirectional relationships) to obtain measurements with meaningful values. The remaining chapter uses the regular model (Contoso 100M).

Regular, unidirectional one-to-many relationships

The most common type of relationship in any VertiPaq model is a one-to-many, regular relationship. It is also the only type of physical relationship that exists in VertiPaq. One-to-one relationships are also optimized, because they are internally implemented with two one-to-many relationships.

The first piece of information we want to gather is the cost of traversing a relationship. To measure it, we perform several tests. First, we scan the *Sales* table by applying a filter on *Sales[ProductKey]*. *Sales[ProductKey]* belongs to *Sales*, so it can be filtered without relying on the relationship:

```
EVALUATE
{
    COUNTROWS (
        FILTER ( Sales, Sales[ProductKey] >= 1 )
    )
}
```

The first query just counts the number of rows in *Sales* where *Sales[ProductKey]* is greater than or equal to one.

Total	SE CPU		Line	Subclass	Duration	CPU	Par.	Rows	KB	Timeline
119 ms	5,531 ms x47.3		2	Scan	117	5,531	x47.3	1	1	

FE	SE
2 ms	117 ms
1.7%	98.3%

SE Queries	SE Cache
1	0
	0.0%

```
SET DC_KIND="AUTO";
SELECT
    COUNT ( )
FROM 'Sales'
WHERE
    ( PFCASTCOALESCE ( 'Sales'[ProductKey] AS INT ) >= COALESCE ( 1 ) );
```

The total storage engine time is 5,531 milliseconds, and the xmSQL query did not require any join. Therefore, we are measuring the time required to scan only the *Sales[ProductKey]* column. If we slightly change the query and place the same filter on the *Product[ProductKey]* column, we can execute the following DAX code:

```
EVALUATE
{
    COUNTROWS (
        FILTER ( Sales, RELATED ( 'Product'[ProductKey] ) >= 1 )
    )
}
```

This time, the relationship comes into play and the performance is worse.

Total	SE CPU	Line	Subclass	Duration	CPU	Par.	Rows	KB	Timeline
157 ms	7,266 ms x48.1	2	Scan	151	7,266	x48.1	1	1	

FE	SE
6 ms	151 ms
3.8%	96.2%

SE Queries	SE Cache
1	0
	0.0%

```
SET DC_KIND="AUTO";
SELECT
    COUNT ( )
FROM 'Sales'
    LEFT OUTER JOIN 'Product'
        ON 'Sales'[ProductKey]='Product'[ProductKey]
    WHERE
        ( PFCASTCOALESCE ( 'Product'[ProductKey] AS INT ) >= COALESCE ( 1 ) );
```

The query consumes 7,266 milliseconds of SE CPU and it is executed with a single xmSQL query.

The relationship is used directly inside VertiPaq, with no further events occurring. Therefore, we cannot obtain more information, apart from the execution time. But based on the knowledge we have about the VertiPaq storage engine and the internal structure of relationships, we know that the algorithm is the following:

- VertiPaq scanned the *Product[ProductKey]* column to retrieve the rows where the condition holds true.

- VertiPaq used the relationship to translate *Product* row numbers into *Sales[ProductKey]* values, to move the filter from *Product[ProductKey]* to *Sales[ProductKey]*.

- At this point, there being a filter on *Sales[ProductKey]* values, VertiPaq scanned the *Sales[ProductKey]* column to count the number of rows satisfying the filter.

The additional time required to answer the query is the time required to move the filter from *Product* to *Sales* by using the physical relationship. The more relationships involved, the longer the process. As an example, let us create a filter over three columns in *Sales*:

```
EVALUATE
{
    COUNTROWS (
        FILTER (
            Sales,
            Sales[CustomerKey] >= 1
                && Sales[ProductKey] >= 1
                && Sales[StoreKey] >= 1
        )
    )
}
```

This time, VertiPaq scans the columns separately and then merges the filters before applying them to the *Sales* table. Consequently, the time required to compute the result is higher.

Total	SE CPU		Line	Subclass	Duration	CPU	Par.	Rows	KB	Timeline
313 ms	16,406 ms									
	x52.9		2	Scan	310	16,406	x52.9	1	1	

FE	SE
3 ms	310 ms
1.0%	99.0%

SE Queries	SE Cache
1	0
	0.0%

```
SET DC_KIND="AUTO";
SELECT
    COUNT ( )
FROM 'Sales'
WHERE
    ( PFCASTCOALESCE ( 'Sales'[CustomerKey] AS INT ) >= COALESCE ( 1 ) ) VAND
    ( PFCASTCOALESCE ( 'Sales'[ProductKey] AS INT ) >= COALESCE ( 1 ) ) VAND
    ( PFCASTCOALESCE ( 'Sales'[StoreKey] AS INT ) >= COALESCE ( 1 ) );
```

When expressed through relationships, the filter requires the use of the physical relationship to move the filter between tables:

```
EVALUATE
{
    COUNTROWS (
        FILTER (
            Sales,
            RELATED ( Customer[CustomerKey] ) >= 1
                && RELATED ( 'Product'[ProductKey] ) >= 1
                && RELATED ( Store[StoreKey] ) >= 1
        )
    )
}
```

This time, the engine places the filter on the three dimensions, translates them into filters over the columns of *Sales*, scans the columns in *Sales* to identify the rows satisfying the condition, and finally merges everything together. Consequently, the time required grows.

Total	SE CPU		Line	Subclass	Duration	CPU	Par.	Rows	KB	Timeline
437 ms	21,531 ms									
	x50.4		2	Scan	428	21,531	x50.3	1	1	

FE	SE
10 ms	427 ms
2.3%	97.9%

SE Queries	SE Cache
1	0
	0.0%

```
SET DC_KIND="AUTO";
SELECT
    COUNT ( )
FROM 'Sales'
    LEFT OUTER JOIN 'Product'
        ON 'Sales'[ProductKey]='Product'[ProductKey]
    LEFT OUTER JOIN 'Store'
        ON 'Sales'[StoreKey]='Store'[StoreKey]
    LEFT OUTER JOIN 'Customer'
        ON 'Sales'[CustomerKey]='Customer'[CustomerKey]
WHERE
    ( PFCASTCOALESCE ( 'Customer'[CustomerKey] AS  INT ) >= COALESCE ( 1 ) ) VAND
    ( PFCASTCOALESCE ( 'Product'[ProductKey] AS  INT ) >= COALESCE ( 1 ) ) VAND
    ( PFCASTCOALESCE ( 'Store'[StoreKey] AS  INT ) >= COALESCE ( 1 ) );
```

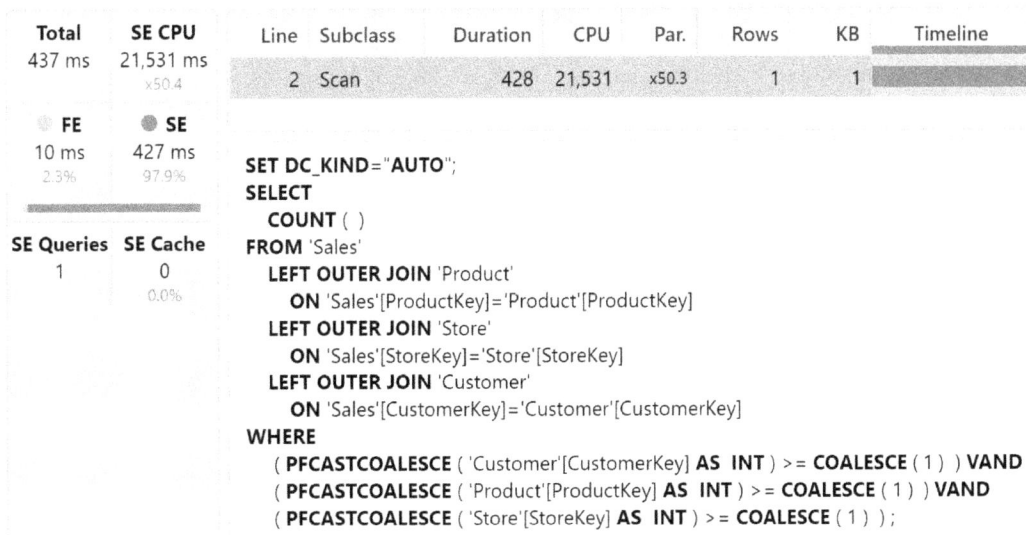

The exact time required to transfer a filter depends on its selectivity and on the size of the relationships. A relationship with millions of rows is going to be slower than a small relationship with a few hundred values. Regardless, the relevant detail here is that relationships slow down the execution of a query because the filter is moved between different tables.

It is important to measure the cost of joins in your model to know the relative cost of relationships. Each model has a different data distribution, different types of filters, and different formulas. All these factors weigh in the definition of the cost of traversing a relationship.

Be mindful that different formulations of the code might produce different query plans. Tabular chooses different ways to use relationships depending on the level of freedom left in the query. Let us see this with an example.

The previous query filtered *Sales* using RELATED inside an iterator. RELATED forced the engine to use VertiPaq relationships to apply the filter. Nonetheless, by using CALCULATE, a developer can author the code in a way that leaves to the engine the choice of how to apply different filters:

```
EVALUATE
{
    CALCULATE (
        COUNTROWS ( Sales ),
        Customer[CustomerKey] >= 1,
        'Product'[ProductKey] >= 1,
        Store[StoreKey] >= 1
    )
}
```

This code produces the same result as the previous one. Yet, the three filters are applied inside CALCULATE, leaving to Tabular the choice about how to merge the three filters. Tabular detected that two of the tables used in the filter are small: *Product* with 2,500 rows and *Store* with less than a hundred rows. Therefore, it decided to precompute a bitmap filter on the small tables, to avoid the comparison in VertiPaq and use a bitmap index instead. Here is the xmSQL code executed:

```
DEFINE TABLE '$TTable2' :=
SELECT
    SIMPLEINDEXN ('Product'[ProductKey])
FROM 'Product'
WHERE
    ( PFCASTCOALESCE ('Product'[ProductKey] AS   INT) >= COALESCE (1)   ),


DEFINE TABLE '$TTable3' :=
SELECT
    SIMPLEINDEXN ('Store'[StoreKey])
FROM 'Store'
WHERE
    ( PFCASTCOALESCE ('Store'[StoreKey] AS   INT) >= COALESCE (1)   ),


DEFINE TABLE '$TTable1' :=
SELECT
    COUNT (  )
FROM 'Sales'
    LEFT OUTER JOIN 'Product'
        ON 'Sales'[ProductKey]='Product'[ProductKey]
    LEFT OUTER JOIN 'Store'
        ON 'Sales'[StoreKey]='Store'[StoreKey]
    LEFT OUTER JOIN 'Customer'
        ON 'Sales'[CustomerKey]='Customer'[CustomerKey]
WHERE
    ( PFCASTCOALESCE ('Customer'[CustomerKey] AS   INT) >= COALESCE (1)   ) VAND
    'Product'[ProductKey] ININDEX '$TTable2'[$SemijoinProjection] VAND
    'Store'[StoreKey] ININDEX '$TTable3'[$SemijoinProjection];
```

We will describe bitmap indexes in the next chapter. Here, the important detail is only to note that this method of using relationships is faster.

Total	SE CPU		Line	Subclass	Duration	CPU	Par.	Rows	KB	Timeline
345 ms	16,938 ms		2	Scan	3	0		2,560	1	
	x52.1		4	Scan	1	0		1,000,000	123	
FE	**SE**		6	Scan	322	16,938	x52.6	1	1	
20 ms	325 ms		7	Batch	0	0				
5.8%	94.5%									

SE Queries	SE Cache
4	0
	0.0%

The query runs in 16,938 milliseconds. Compared with the 21,531 milliseconds of the previous one, there is an important gain of more than 20%.

A good DAX developer will mostly use CALCULATE to apply filters. Still, when measuring the performance of a relationship scan, it is advisable to force the engine to use a VertiPaq relationship. Then, in a real-world query, the optimizer might choose a better plan, as it did in this example.

Regular, bidirectional one-to-many relationships

Bidirectional and unidirectional one-to-many relationships have the same physical structures in VertiPaq. However, when the filter propagates from the many-side to the one-side of the relationship, there are additional subqueries executed at query time. A bidirectional relationship uses the underlying relationship in this condition, but it is not as optimized as a unidirectional relationship is.

As a first example of a bidirectional relationship filter propagation, we analyze a distinct count calculation performed with and without the bidirectional relationship involved. The following query computes the number of customers who purchased products from different brands:

```
EVALUATE
SUMMARIZECOLUMNS (
    'Product'[Brand],
    "# Customers", DISTINCTCOUNT ( Sales[CustomerKey] )
)
```

The result is the number of customers sliced by brand:

Brand	# Customers
The Phone Company	1,859,202
Adventure Works	1,863,298
Northwind Traders	1,829,641
Fabrikam	1,855,719
A. Datum	1,825,558
Proseware	1,848,844
Southridge Video	1,865,594
Tailspin Toys	1,859,533
Wide World Importers	1,863,302
Contoso	1,867,265
Litware	1,830,831

The query is resolved with a single VertiPaq query that uses the DCOUNT function in xmSQL:

Total	SE CPU		Line	Subclass	Duration	CPU	Par.	Rows	KB	Timeline
7,710 ms	345,438 ms									
	x45.0		4	Scan	7,672	345,438	x45.0	11	1	

FE	SE
40 ms	7,670 ms
0.5%	99.5%

SE Queries	SE Cache
1	0
	0.0%

```
SET DC_KIND="AUTO";
SELECT
  'Product'[Brand],
  DCOUNT ( 'Sales'[CustomerKey] )
FROM 'Sales'
  LEFT OUTER JOIN 'Product'
    ON 'Sales'[ProductKey]='Product'[ProductKey];
```

The materialization level is rather small because the VertiPaq engine uses bitmap indexes to quickly compute the distinct count aggregation (DCOUNT in xmSQL). A single storage engine query is in charge of the entire workload, with a short execution time (7,710 ms) despite the high CPU cost (345,438 ms) thanks to the high parallelism (x45.0).

A developer can perform a very similar calculation by relying on a bidirectional relationship with the following code:

```
EVALUATE
SUMMARIZECOLUMNS (
    'Product'[Brand],
    "# Customers",
        CALCULATE (
            COUNTROWS ( Customer ),
            CROSSFILTER ( Sales[CustomerKey], Customer[CustomerKey], BOTH )
        )
)
```

In the previous query, we were performing the distinct count using *Sales[CustomerKey]*. In this query, we are performing the distinct count using *Customer[CustomerKey]*, because COUNTROWS operates on *Customer*. The two results would be different in case the relationship is invalid – which is the case when values in *Sales[CustomerKey]* do not have corresponding matches in *Customer[CustomerKey]*. The query plan is different from the previous one. Now, Tabular uses a VertiPaq batch to resolve the query:

```
DEFINE TABLE '$TTable3' :=
SELECT
        'Product'[Brand],
        'Customer'[CustomerKey]
FROM 'Sales'
        LEFT OUTER JOIN 'Product'
                ON 'Sales'[ProductKey]='Product'[ProductKey]
        LEFT OUTER JOIN 'Customer'
                ON 'Sales'[CustomerKey]='Customer'[CustomerKey],


DEFINE TABLE '$TTable4' :=
SELECT
        SIMPLEINDEXN ( '$TTable3'[Customer$CustomerKey] )
FROM '$TTable3',


CREATE SHALLOW RELATION '$TRelation1'
        MANYTOMANY
        FROM 'Customer'[CustomerKey]
                TO '$TTable3'[Customer$CustomerKey],

DEFINE TABLE '$TTable1' :=
SELECT
        '$TTable3'[Product$Brand],
        SUM ( '$TTable2'[$Measure0] )
FROM '$TTable2'
        INNER JOIN '$TTable3'
                ON '$TTable2'[Customer$CustomerKey]='$TTable3'[Customer$CustomerKey]
REDUCED BY
'$TTable2' :=
SELECT
        'Customer'[CustomerKey],
        SUM ( 1 )
FROM 'Customer'
WHERE
        'Customer'[CustomerKey] ININDEX '$TTable4'[$SemijoinProjection];
```

As was the case earlier, this xmSQL query contains many structures that we will describe in the next chapters. Nonetheless, it is important here to have a generic understanding of the algorithm.

VertiPaq materializes a table (*$TTable3*) containing all the pairs of *Product[Brand]* and *Customer[CustomerKey]* by scanning *Sales*, using the relationships between *Sales*, *Customer*, and *Product*. It then builds *$TTable4*, which contains *CustomerKey* only. Later on, *$TTable4* is used as a filter in the same query to reduce the number of rows scanned. In this particular case, the filter is somewhat useless, as it does not reduce the number of rows scanned.

The last xmSQL query computes the result by scanning the $TTable2 temporary table, with another internal query that sums the number one for every customer key. Performance-wise, the result is produced after a much longer execution time.

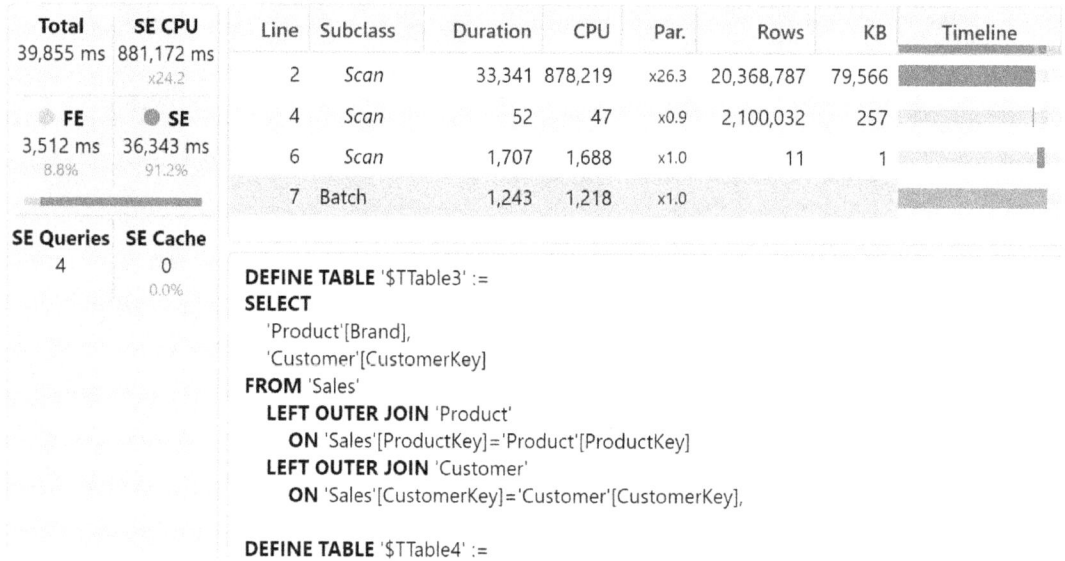

Total	SE CPU	Line	Subclass	Duration	CPU	Par.	Rows	KB	Timeline
39,855 ms	881,172 ms	2	Scan	33,341	878,219	x26.3	20,368,787	79,566	
	x24.2	4	Scan	52	47	x0.9	2,100,032	257	
FE	**SE**	6	Scan	1,707	1,688	x1.0	11	1	
3,512 ms	36,343 ms	7	Batch	1,243	1,218	x1.0			
8.8%	91.2%								

SE Queries	SE Cache
4	0
	0.0%

DEFINE TABLE '$TTable3' :=
SELECT
  'Product'[Brand],
  'Customer'[CustomerKey]
FROM 'Sales'
  LEFT OUTER JOIN 'Product'
    ON 'Sales'[ProductKey]='Product'[ProductKey]
  LEFT OUTER JOIN 'Customer'
    ON 'Sales'[CustomerKey]='Customer'[CustomerKey],

DEFINE TABLE '$TTable4' :=

The more complex storage engine operations can no longer benefit from the maximum parallelism (x26.3 vs. the previous x45.0). The storage engine CPU time doubled (881,172 ms) and the execution is five times slower (39,855 ms), whereas the formula engine still handles a fraction of the entire execution time.

The physical query plan contains only one formula engine operator, which scans just eleven rows.

Line	Records	Physical Query Plan
1		GroupSemijoin: IterPhyOp LogOp=GroupSemiJoin IterCols(0, 1)('Product'[Brand], ''[# Customers])
2	11	Spool_Iterator<SpoolIterator>: IterPhyOp LogOp=Count_Vertipaq IterCols(0)('Product'[Brand]) #Records=11
3	11	ProjectionSpool<ProjectFusion<Copy>>: SpoolPhyOp #Records=11
4		**Cache: IterPhyOp #FieldCols=1 #ValueCols=1**

The algorithm is much less straightforward than the one used with the simpler DISTINCTCOUNT function. Here are some relevant considerations:

- The materialization of 20M rows happens in the storage engine when it creates $TTable2. Even though the data does not need to be passed to the formula engine – as with most materializations – it is still considerably large.

- To move a filter from *Sales* to *Customer*, the engine had to create a temporary table and complex xmSQL queries that strongly and negatively impact performance.

- The regular relationship between *Sales* and *Customer* is used in the xmSQL code, but only to retrieve the customer key associated with the current sale.

Whenever bidirectional relationships are involved in the many-to-one direction, the engine uses a more complex pattern to move a filter from the many-side to the one-side. As we have learned in the previous chapter, the physical structure of a relationship is designed to quickly move a filter from the one-side to the many-side. Going in the opposite direction comes at a very high cost in terms of performance.

It is worth noting that the previous result can be obtained without the aid of a bidirectional relationship. Indeed, the following query produces the same result – grouping by *Customer[CustomerKey]* instead of *Sales[CustomerKey]* – with better performance:

```
EVALUATE
SUMMARIZECOLUMNS (
    'Product'[Brand],
    "# Customers",
        COUNTROWS ( SUMMARIZE ( Sales, Customer[CustomerKey] ) )
)
```

The query runs at the same speed as the one grouping by *Sales[CustomerKey]*:

Total	SE CPU		Line	Subclass	Duration	CPU	Par.	Rows	KB	Timeline
7,200 ms	358,031 ms									
	x50.0		4	Scan	7,160	358,031	x50.0	11	1	

FE	SE
40 ms	7,160 ms
0.6%	99.4%

SE Queries	SE Cache
1	0
	0.0%

```
SET DC_KIND="AUTO";
SELECT
    'Product'[Brand],
    DCOUNT ( 'Customer'[CustomerKey] )
FROM 'Sales'
    LEFT OUTER JOIN 'Product'
        ON 'Sales'[ProductKey]='Product'[ProductKey]
    LEFT OUTER JOIN 'Customer'
        ON 'Sales'[CustomerKey]='Customer'[CustomerKey];
```

The key to performance is the ability to use the DCOUNT xmSQL function over a column in a related table.

This is not to say that bidirectional relationships are to be avoided. In this specific scenario, there are better ways to express the same calculation using regular unidirectional relationships. There are scenarios where the filter needs to be transferred from the many-side to the one-side to perform more complex calculations; in that case, using a bidirectional relationship is the only way to achieve that goal.

The use of bidirectional relationships should be reduced to these complex scenarios. Relying on bidirectional relationships with the sole goal of simplifying the authoring of DAX code is not recommended, as the performance cost is huge.

With DAX, you always need to carefully evaluate the results with your own data, because data distribution and the overall query structure significantly impact the performance of any query. To demonstrate this, we complicate the previous example a bit. We want to compute the average age of customers by store country. In this example, the engine is not able to push the calculation down to the storage engine using a simple DCOUNT; instead, it generates more complex code and the difference in performance between the two options shifts in favor of bidirectional relationships.

Here is the query:

```
EVALUATE
SUMMARIZECOLUMNS (
    Store[Country],
    "Avg Age",
        CALCULATE (
            AVERAGEX ( Customer, Customer[Age] ),
            CROSSFILTER ( Sales[CustomerKey], Customer[CustomerKey], BOTH )
        )
)
```

The result contains the average age by country:

Country	Avg Age
Online	52.00
United States	52.03
Canada	52.05
Australia	51.98
United Kingdom	51.93
Germany	52.03
Netherlands	51.95
Italy	51.98
France	51.98

The pattern used by the bidirectional relationship is nearly identical to the previous one – a batch xmSQL statement creates temporary structures to simplify the transfer of filters:

```
DEFINE TABLE '$TTable3' :=
SELECT
    'Store'[Country],
    'Customer'[CustomerKey]
FROM 'Sales'
    LEFT OUTER JOIN 'Store'
        ON 'Sales'[StoreKey]='Store'[StoreKey]
    LEFT OUTER JOIN 'Customer'
        ON 'Sales'[CustomerKey]='Customer'[CustomerKey],


DEFINE TABLE '$TTable4' :=
SELECT
    SIMPLEINDEXN ( '$TTable3'[Customer$CustomerKey] )
FROM '$TTable3',


CREATE SHALLOW RELATION '$TRelation1'
    MANYTOMANY
    FROM 'Customer'[CustomerKey]
        TO '$TTable3'[Customer$CustomerKey],


DEFINE TABLE '$TTable1' :=
SELECT
    '$TTable3'[Store$Country],
    SUM ( '$TTable2'[$Measure0] ),
    SUM ( '$TTable2'[$Measure1] )
FROM '$TTable2'
    INNER JOIN '$TTable3'
        ON '$TTable2'[Customer$CustomerKey]='$TTable3'[Customer$CustomerKey]
REDUCED BY
'$TTable2' :=
SELECT
    'Customer'[CustomerKey],
    SUM ( 'Customer'[Age] ),
    SUM (   ( PFDATAID ( 'Customer'[Age] ) <> 2 )   )
FROM 'Customer'
WHERE
    'Customer'[CustomerKey] ININDEX '$TTable4'[$SemijoinProjection];
```

The query shows good performance.

Total	SE CPU		Line	Subclass	Duration	CPU	Par.	Rows	KB	Timeline
7,130 ms	144,938 ms		2	Scan	5,560	143,891	x25.9	3,678,573	14,370	
	x21.8		4	Scan	10	0		2,100,032	257	
FE	**SE**		6	Scan	743	734	x1.0	9	1	
480 ms	6,650 ms		7	Batch	338	313	x0.9			
6.7%	93.3%									

SE Queries	SE Cache
4	0
	0.0%

```
DEFINE TABLE '$TTable3' :=
SELECT
    'Store'[Country],
    'Customer'[CustomerKey]
FROM 'Sales'
    LEFT OUTER JOIN 'Store'
        ON 'Sales'[StoreKey]='Store'[StoreKey]
    LEFT OUTER JOIN 'Customer'
        ON 'Sales'[CustomerKey]='Customer'[CustomerKey],

DEFINE TABLE '$TTable4' :=
```

The most important detail, for the comparison, is that the xmSQL query at line 6 returns 9 rows. The datacache produced by VertiPaq contains three columns: the country, the sum of age, and the number of non-blank customers. In other words, the entire query has been resolved by VertiPaq, leaving to the formula engine only the division of the sum of age by the number of customers.

Writing the code without relying on bidirectional relationships requires a larger materialization. Here is the code:

```
EVALUATE
SUMMARIZECOLUMNS (
    Store[Country],
    "Avg Age",
        AVERAGEX (
            SUMMARIZE ( Sales, Customer[CustomerKey], Customer[Age] ),
            Customer[Age]
        )
)
```

Please note that SUMMARIZE must include the *Customer[CustomerKey]* column as part of the group-by columns. Failing to do so would result in an incorrect average.

The performance of this query is very close to the previous one.

Total	SE CPU	Line	Subclass	Duration	CPU	Par.	Rows	KB	Timeline
7,287 ms	164,609 ms								
	x25.6	2	Scan	6,433	164,609	x25.6	3,678,573	28,739	

FE	SE
854 ms	6,433 ms
11.7%	88.3%

SE Queries	SE Cache
1	0
	0.0%

```
SET DC_KIND="AUTO";
SELECT
    'Store'[Country],
    'Customer'[CustomerKey],
    'Customer'[Age]
FROM 'Sales'
    LEFT OUTER JOIN 'Store'
        ON 'Sales'[StoreKey]='Store'[StoreKey]
    LEFT OUTER JOIN 'Customer'
        ON 'Sales'[CustomerKey]='Customer'[CustomerKey];
```

Despite them being close in terms of performance, the amount of materialization is much larger here. The VertiPaq query generates a datacache containing 3.6M rows; indeed, the result has to include the customer key as part of the group-by columns. The same datacache was produced in the previous example, but only internally to the VertiPaq storage engine – whereas in this case this datacache is materialized for the formula engine.

The formula engine oversees grouping by country, summing customer ages, and finally the division. The larger amount of time spent in the storage engine accounts for the larger size of the datacache. Clearly, with a different data size and distribution, your mileage may vary by a lot. These tests need to be executed on your real database to gather correct measurements.

The advantage of DAX against bidirectional relationships fades away with a more complex query because the level of materialization required becomes larger. However, you should do your own evaluation, because the result may be the opposite with a different data volume, still favoring the DAX approach with smaller tables.

The point of these demos is to show you how bidirectional relationships are used by the engine. Whenever bidirectional relationships are part of the equation, Tabular relies on VertiPaq batches that materialize a filter. The level of materialization might be large, but it is usually better than the equivalent materialization if the datacache is processed by the formula engine.

Depending on the complexity of the calculation, relying on bidirectional relationships may or may not be a good idea. There are no golden rules, each model and calculation require a deeper analysis of performance.

Regular, one-to-one relationships

Tabular offers one-to-one relationships, which can be used when the column used to build the relationship is a unique key in both tables. One-to-one relationships are bidirectional by nature, and they cannot be forced to be unidirectional. Even though they are bidirectional, one-to-one relationships do not suffer from any of the issues of bidirectional relationships.

A one-to-one relationship between two tables behaves as two regular one-to-many relationships, meaning that the relationship is always resolved in the storage engine through a VertiPaq join. Therefore, even though they are quite seldom found in a data model, one-to-one relationships do not come with a performance penalty beside the cost of a regular relationship. Internally, VertiPaq creates two indexes corresponding to the two regular one-to-many relationships, using the proper relationship depending on the direction of the filter propagation used in a specific calculation.

To test performance, we duplicated the *Customer* table (1.8M rows) by loading it twice from the database. We deliberately chose not to use DAX, but rather create a calculated table to avoid differences in compression. Both *Customer* and *CustomerCopy* are created using the same data loading process and compression. Then, we created a one-to-one relationship between the two tables, based on *CustomerKey*.

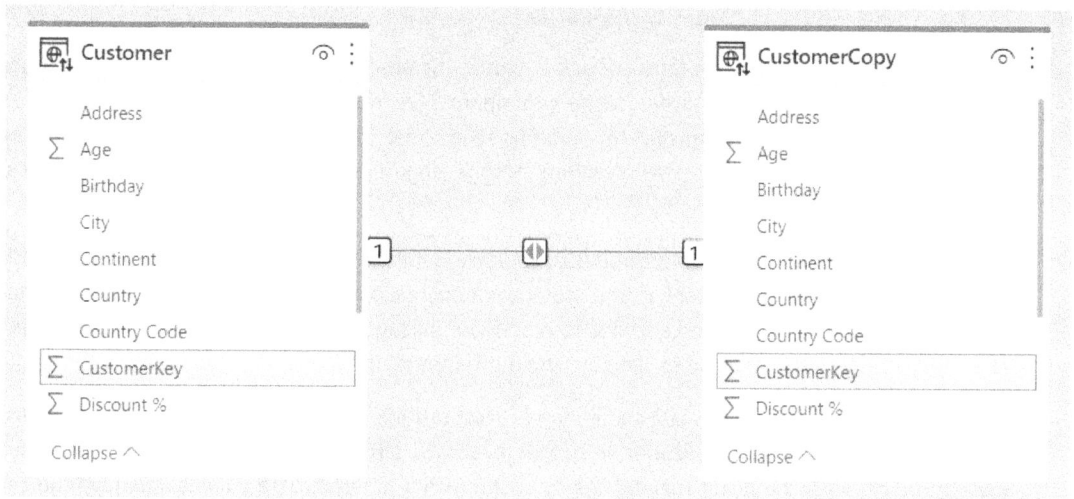

We want to measure the impact of traversing the relationship. Therefore, we do not need any complex DAX. It is enough to write a simple query that counts the customers on one table and filters the other one. The baseline is provided by this query, that uses only *Customer*:

```
EVALUATE
SUMMARIZECOLUMNS (
    Customer[Country],
    "#Customers", COUNTROWS ( Customer )
)
```

The execution is almost instantaneous, as it reports a total of two milliseconds.

Total	SE CPU		Line	Subclass	Duration	CPU	Par.	Rows	KB
2 ms	0 ms		2	Scan	1	0		11	1
	x0.0								

FE	SE
1 ms	1 ms
50.0%	50.0%

SE Queries	SE Cache
1	0
	0.0%

```
SET DC_KIND="AUTO";
SELECT
'Customer'[Country],
COUNT ( )
FROM 'Customer';
```

'Estimated size (volume, marshalling bytes) : 11, 88'

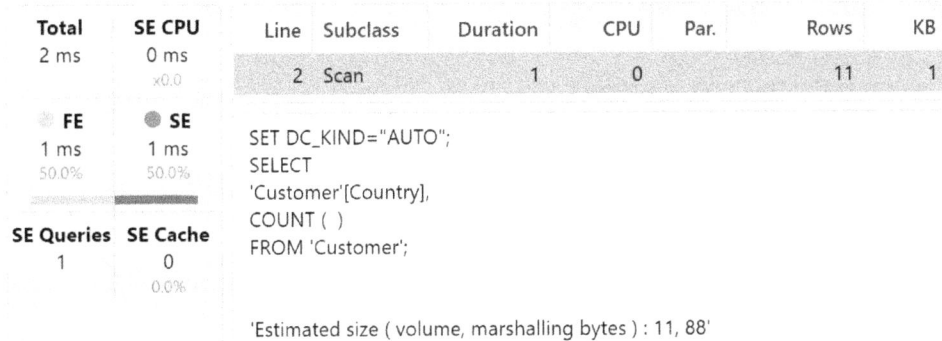

There is nothing special here. *Customer* being a small table with only 1.8M rows, it is scanned extremely fast by a single VertiPaq query.

The next step is to change the table from where we aggregate values: instead of counting the number of customers using *Customer*, we use *CustomerCopy*. This requires Tabular to move the filter from *Customer* to *CustomerCopy* by using the relationship:

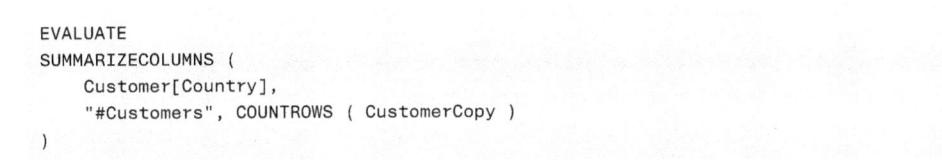

```
EVALUATE
SUMMARIZECOLUMNS (
    Customer[Country],
    "#Customers", COUNTROWS ( CustomerCopy )
)
```

This time, there is a small performance penalty, and the query includes a join.

Total	SE CPU		Line	Subclass	Duration	CPU	Par.	Rows	KB	Waterfall	Q
29 ms	31 ms		2	Scan	28	31	x1.1	11	1		SI
	x1.1										

FE	SE
1 ms	28 ms
3.4%	96.6%

SE Queries	SE Cache
1	0
	0.0%

```
SET DC_KIND="AUTO";
SELECT
'Customer'[Country],
COUNT ( )
FROM 'CustomerCopy'
        LEFT OUTER JOIN 'Customer' ON 'CustomerCopy'[CustomerKey]='Customer'[CustomerKey];
```

'Estimated size (volume, marshalling bytes) : 11, 88'

The execution time of around 30 milliseconds is entirely accounted for by the storage engine, which requires time to perform the join. To be extra cautious, we also measured the time required to move the relationship the other way around – that is, grouping by *CustomerCopy* and then counting *Customer*:

```
EVALUATE
SUMMARIZECOLUMNS (
    CustomerCopy[Country],
    "#Customers", COUNTROWS ( Customer )
)
```

Not surprisingly, the performance is almost identical. The difference is due to noise in the measurement, so the difference is very small with a reasonable variance of a few milliseconds.

Total	SE CPU	Line	Subclass	Duration	CPU	Par.	Rows	KB	Waterfall	Query
36 ms	31 ms									
	x0.9	2	Scan	35	31	x0.9	11	1		SELECT

FE	SE
1 ms	35 ms
2.8%	97.2%

```
SET DC_KIND="AUTO";
SELECT
'CustomerCopy'[Country],
COUNT ( )
FROM 'Customer'
        LEFT OUTER JOIN 'CustomerCopy' ON 'Customer'[CustomerKey]='CustomerCopy'[CustomerKey];
```

SE Queries	SE Cache
1	0
	0.0%

'Estimated size (volume, marshalling bytes) : 11, 88'

The most important part, however, is not about performance. The most relevant detail when comparing the latter two queries is that in both cases, we are witnessing a VertiPaq LEFT OUTER JOIN between the two tables. This means that it does not matter whether we filter one table or the other: in both scenarios, VertiPaq can use its internal relationship structures to optimize the filtering operation.

One-to-one relationships behave exactly as a pair of regular one-to-many relationships. One-to-one relationships are bidirectional by nature, and the cost of traversing them both ways is irrelevant – very different from a bidirectional filter over a one-to-many relationship.

Limited, many-to-many cardinality relationships

Many-to-many cardinality relationships are useful in a model whenever the column used to relate the two tables is not a primary key in both tables. In that scenario, developers can still create a limited many-to-many cardinality relationship.

Limited many-to-many cardinality relationships provide a great advantage in terms of model conciseness because they are simple to use, and because they reduce the need for technical tables. But the net result is that neither side of the relationship is the one-side. As such, the internal data structures of relationships cannot be used directly by VertiPaq to solve the relationship itself.

Limited many-to-many relationships show a performance penalty. Indeed, the relationship is resolved through a VertiPaq batch similar to the batch used with bidirectional relationships when traversing from the many-side to the one-side.

To better understand the differences between a regular one-to-many relationship and a limited many-to-many cardinality relationship, we execute the same code and we traverse the relationship between *Customer* and *Sales* with the two types of relationships. First, we measure performance with a regular relationship; then, we change the relationship to a limited many-to-many without modifying the content, and we measure the performance again.

The query is rather simple, it just counts the number of transactions by customer age:

```
EVALUATE
SUMMARIZECOLUMNS (
    Customer[Age],
    "# Transactions", COUNTROWS ( Sales )
)
```

The query is resolved with a single VertiPaq query that uses the relationship; performance is great, exactly as we would expect.

Total	SE CPU		Line	Subclass	Duration	CPU	Par.	Rows	KB	Timeline
47 ms	125 ms		2	Scan	43	125	x2.9	70	1	
	x2.9									

FE	SE
4 ms	43 ms
8.5%	91.5%

SE Queries	SE Cache
1	0
	0.0%

```
SET DC_KIND="AUTO";
SELECT
    'Customer'[Age],
    COUNT ( )
FROM 'Sales'
    LEFT OUTER JOIN 'Customer'
        ON 'Sales'[CustomerKey]='Customer'[CustomerKey];
```

Apart from performance, the important detail is the use of a LEFT OUTER JOIN in VertiPaq. This is possible because the relationship between *Customer* and *Sales* has been created during data refresh, using the internal data structures described in the previous chapter.

VertiPaq Analyzer shows the relationships in the model, and as you can see in the next figure, the relationship between *Sales* and *Customer* is a physical one-to-many relationship with a size of around 5MB.

Table / Relationship	Size ↓	Max From Cardinality	Max To Cardinality	1:M Ratio %
⊿ **Sales**	4,990,720	1,868,002	1,868,002	0.13%
Sales[CustomerKey] ∞←1 Customer[CustomerKey]	4,981,352	1,868,002	1,868,002	0.13%
Sales[Order Date] ∞←1 Date[Date]	5,256	3,281	4,018	0.00%
Sales[ProductKey] ∞←1 Product[ProductKey]	4,040	2,517	2,517	0.00%
Sales[StoreKey] ∞←1 Store[StoreKey]	72	74	74	0.00%

So far, everything is exactly as expected. The next step is to change the relationship to a limited relationship. We do not need to change anything in the data. We keep the relationship based on

Customer[CustomerKey]. We only change the relationship cardinality and we set it to be a many-to-many cardinality relationship.

Edit relationship

Select tables and columns that are related.

Sales ▾

Order Date	Delivery Date	CustomerKey	StoreKey	ProductKey	Quantity	Unit Price	Net Price	L
09/21/2019	09/23/2019	1434500	999999	1629	1	9.99	9.99	
09/21/2019	09/22/2019	1966597	999999	1629	1	9.99	9.99	
09/23/2019	09/27/2019	2012610	999999	1629	1	9.99	9.99	

⟨   ⟩

Customer ▾

CustomerKey	Gender	Name	Address	City	State Code	State	Zip Code
1901744	Male	Jukka-Pekk Heinonen	1266 Reynolds Alley	Los Angeles	CA	California	90017
2021044	Male	Jadranko Božic	2700 Brannon Street	Los Angeles	CA	California	90017
2027491	Male	Anas Walker	4487 Nickel Road	Los Angeles	CA	California	90017

⟨   ⟩

Cardinality

Many to many (*:*) ▾

Cross filter direction

Single (Customer filters Sales) ▾

☑ Make this relationship active

Apply security filter in both directions

Assume referential integrity

⚠ This relationship has cardinality Many-Many. This should only be used if it is expected that neither column (CustomerKey and CustomerKey) contains unique values, and that the significantly different behavior of Many-many relationships is understood. Learn more

[OK] [Cancel]

The change of the cardinality setting requires the execution of a process default of the model, to force Tabular to rebuild the relationship. VertiPaq Analyzer now shows that the physical structure of the relationship is no longer present, because the relationship size is now zero bytes.

Table / Relationship	Size ↓	Max From Cardinality	Max To Cardinality	1:M Ratio %
◢ **Sales**	**9,368**	**1,868,002**	**1,868,002**	**0.13%**
Sales[Order Date] ∞—1 Date[Date]	5,256	3,281	4,018	0.00%
Sales[ProductKey] ∞—1 Product[ProductKey]	4,040	2,517	2,517	0.00%
Sales[StoreKey] ∞—1 Store[StoreKey]	72	74	74	0.00%
Sales[CustomerKey] ∞—∞ Customer[CustomerKey]	0	1,868,002	1,868,002	0.13%

Because the physical relationship is no longer present, the query cannot take advantage of it. Therefore, Tabular needs to revert to a completely different query plan to move the filter from *Customer* to *Sales*. The performance impact is relevant.

		Line	Subclass	Duration	CPU	Par.	Rows	KB	Timeline
Total	**SE CPU**								
5,643 ms	99,766 ms	2	Scan	379	344	x0.9	1,868,084	7,298	
	x17.7	4	Scan	291	281	x1.0	1,868,084	7,298	
FE	**SE**	6	Scan	134	125	x0.9	1,868,096	229	
16 ms	5,627 ms	8	Scan	4,160	98,406	x23.7	67	1	
0.3%	99.7%	9	Batch	663	610	x0.9			
SE Queries	**SE Cache**								
5	0								
	0.0%								

The query that was running in a few milliseconds is now executing in 99,766 milliseconds. Moreover, with the regular relationship there was only one VertiPaq query, whereas now there are five. Actually, there is only one VertiPaq query that includes a batch; therefore, we have a set of VertiPaq queries executed together as if they were a single query. Here is the code of the batch:

```
DEFINE TABLE '$TTable3' :=
SELECT
    'Customer'[CustomerKey],
    'Customer'[Age]
FROM 'Customer',


DEFINE TABLE '$TTable4' :=
SELECT
    '$TTable3'[Customer$CustomerKey]
FROM '$TTable3',
```

```
DEFINE TABLE '$TTable5' :=
SELECT
        RJOIN ( '$TTable4'[Customer$CustomerKey] )
FROM '$TTable4'
        REVERSE BITMAP JOIN 'Sales' ON '$TTable4'[Customer$CustomerKey]='Sales'[CustomerKey],

CREATE SHALLOW RELATION '$TRelation1'
        MANYTOMANY
        FROM 'Sales'[CustomerKey]
            TO '$TTable3'[Customer$CustomerKey],


DEFINE TABLE '$TTable1' :=
SELECT
        '$TTable3'[Customer$Age],
        SUM ( '$TTable2'[$Measure0] )
FROM '$TTable2'
        INNER JOIN '$TTable3'
            ON '$TTable2'[Sales$CustomerKey]='$TTable3'[Customer$CustomerKey]
REDUCED BY
'$TTable2' :=
SELECT
        'Sales'[CustomerKey],
        SUM ( 1 )
FROM 'Sales'
WHERE
        'Sales'[CustomerKey] ININDEX '$TTable5'[$SemijoinProjection];
```

Without going into too many details, by quickly reading the xmSQL query we can observe that the pattern is extremely close to the one used by Tabular with bidirectional relationships when it moves the filter from the many-side to the one-side. It first builds a few helper tables to create the relationship between *Customer[Age]* and *Customer[CustomerKey]*, it then groups *Sales* by *Sales[CustomerKey]*, and it finally joins the tables created previously, to group by *Customer[Age]*.

The algorithm is much more complex, and therefore slower. Nonetheless, it is the price Tabular must pay for not having built the relationship during data refresh time. An additional issue is that the last two internal scan operations are not stored in the VertiPaq cache, making this approach less scalable when there are multiple requests over the same data. As you have seen, it is a very high price that needs to be paid every time the relationship is traversed.

A developer can obtain a similar behavior by creating an additional table containing all the distinct values of *Sales[CustomerKey]* and build a more canonical many-to-many pattern with the additional table.

The table can be easily created with the following code and relationships diagram:

```
---------------------------------
-- Calculated table CustomerKeys
---------------------------------
CustomerKeys = ALLNOBLANKROW ( Customer[CustomerKey] )
```

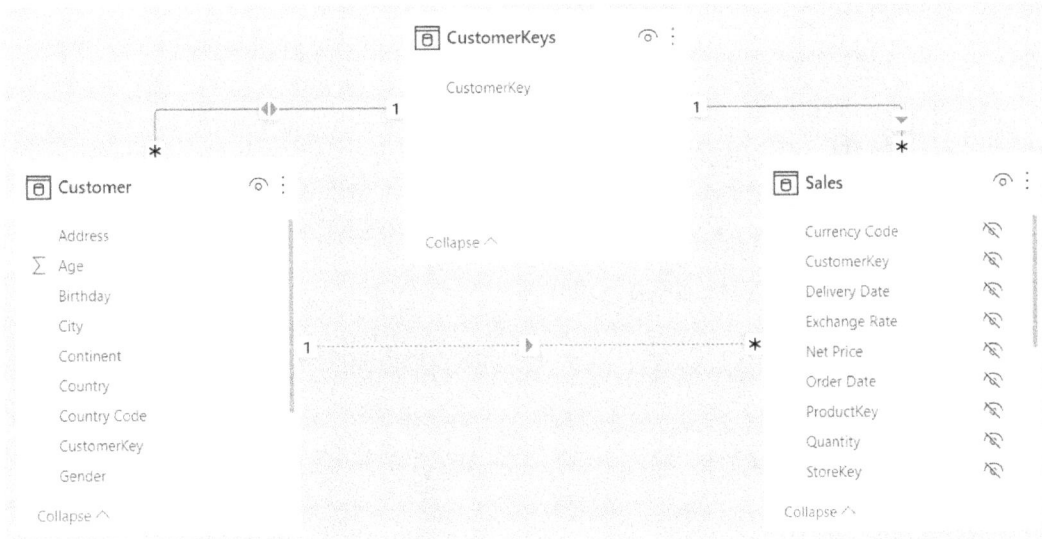

A filter on *Customer* is propagated through the bidirectional relationship to the *CustomerKeys* table, and from *CustomerKeys*, it reaches *Sales* through the unidirectional relationship. The disabled relationship in the figure is the many-to-many cardinality relationship used in the previous example.

The main advantage of this model is that it makes the filter propagation path from *Customer* to *Sales* more evident, thus providing a better understanding of the xmSQL query.

Performance-wise, the query requires a bit more storage engine CPU time, even though the batch contains fewer queries (there were five queries before) and the overall duration is similar. It might be faster or slower depending on the hardware and other conditions, but we do not observe a large difference in the execution time.

Total	SE CPU	Line	Subclass	Duration	CPU	Par.	Rows	KB	Timeline
5,090 ms	114,453 ms								
	x22.6	2	Scan	443	438	x1.0	1,868,084	7,298	
FE	**SE**	4	Scan	7	0		2,100,032	257	
17 ms	5,073 ms	6	Scan	4,573	113,969	x24.9	67	1	
0.3%	99.7%	7	Batch	50	46	x0.9			

SE Queries	SE Cache
4	0
	0.0%

The code of the batch shows a very close algorithm, compared to the one used with many-to-many cardinality relationships:

```
DEFINE TABLE '$TTable3' :=
SELECT
    'Customer'[Age],
    'Table'[CustomerKey]
FROM 'Customer'
    LEFT OUTER JOIN 'Table'
        ON 'Customer'[CustomerKey]='Table'[CustomerKey],


DEFINE TABLE '$TTable4' :=
SELECT
    SIMPLEINDEXN ( '$TTable3'[Table$CustomerKey] )
FROM '$TTable3',

CREATE SHALLOW RELATION '$TRelation1'
    MANYTOMANY
    FROM 'Table'[CustomerKey]
        TO '$TTable3'[Table$CustomerKey],


DEFINE TABLE '$TTable1' :=
SELECT
    '$TTable3'[Customer$Age],
    SUM ( '$TTable2'[$Measure0] )
FROM '$TTable2'
    INNER JOIN '$TTable3'
        ON '$TTable2'[Table$CustomerKey]='$TTable3'[Table$CustomerKey]
REDUCED BY
'$TTable2' :=
SELECT
    'Table'[CustomerKey],
    SUM ( 1 )
FROM 'Sales'
    LEFT OUTER JOIN 'Table'
        ON 'Sales'[CustomerKey]='Table'[CustomerKey]
WHERE
    'Table'[CustomerKey] ININDEX '$TTable4'[$SemijoinProjection];
```

This batch creates a table with the relationship between *Customer[Age]* and *CustomerKeys[CustomerKey]*, which is then used to create a bitmap (SIMPLEINDEXN). The core of the query is in the last table, *$TTable1*, which performs the complex set of joins needed to move the filter from *Customer* to *Sales*. Moreover, all the internal scan operations are stored in the VertiPaq cache, making this approach much more scalable when there are multiple requests for the same data. However, the query we have been using so far was too simple to show any advantage provided by physical relationships connected to the *CustomerKeys* table. We can add a filter to the query to observe something different. Consider the following query:

```
EVALUATE
SUMMARIZECOLUMNS (
    Customer[Age],
    TREATAS ( { "Canada" }, Store[Country] ),
    "# Transactions", COUNTROWS ( Sales )
)
```

If we execute the query by using the many-to-many cardinality relationship, we get a base result.

Total	SE CPU		Line	Subclass	Duration	CPU	Par.	Rows	KB	Timeline
1,763 ms	1,922 ms x1.1		2	Scan	377	359	x1.0	1,868,084	7,298	
FE	**SE**		4	Scan	304	281	x0.9	1,868,084	7,298	
16 ms 0.9%	1,747 ms 99.1%		6	Scan	140	125	x0.9	1,868,096	229	
			8	Scan	263	500	x1.9	67	1	
SE Queries	**SE Cache**		9	Batch	663	657	x1.0			
5	0 0.0%									

If we execute the query by using the two relationships connected to the *CustomerKeys* table, then we have a 50% reduction in the query execution time.

Total	SE CPU		Line	Subclass	Duration	CPU	Par.	Rows	KB	Timeline
774 ms	641 ms x0.8		2	Scan	430	422	x1.0	1,868,084	7,298	
FE	**SE**		4	Scan	6	0		2,100,032	257	
17 ms 2.2%	757 ms 97.8%		6	Scan	272	188	x0.7	67	1	
			7	Batch	49	31	x0.6			
SE Queries	**SE Cache**									
4	0 0.0%									

In our experience, the presence of the intermediate *CustomerKeys* table with the two regular relationships often provides performance benefits with large tables that are also filtered – which is a common case in many reports. However, there are many factors that affect performance, so the right choice is the one that provides more benefits in your specific scenario. Remember that you should always test and validate any optimization approach without assuming that it should work better by default.

Conclusions

In this module we analyzed the performance of different types of relationships. Each type of relationship has its own advantages and disadvantages. When using VertiPaq, regular unidirectional relationships are by far the best option. The presence of the physical representation of the relationship in VertiPaq lets Tabular push the query down to the storage engine, obtaining the best performance. One-to-one relationships behave in an identical way in both directions; therefore, they can be used in a model with confidence.

Performance starts to be troublesome as soon as the filter goes in the opposite direction. Both bidirectional relationships (where the filter flows from the many-side to the one-side) and many-to-many cardinality relationships (where the filter always flows to the many-side, as there is no one-side) show a similar behavior. The engine needs to perform grouping by and filtering in the storage engine through VertiPaq batches.

When designing a model, and when evaluating the possible optimizations of a query, you always need to account for the price of relationships. The more complex the relationship is, the more time Tabular takes to use it.

Analyzing VertiPaq storage engine queries

In all the previous chapters, we have seen many xmSQL queries. We did not spend time describing the details of xmSQL because we focused on different topics. In this chapter, we describe the details of xmSQL. We dive into syntax, performance, and how to read xmSQL code.

xmSQL is the internal language of VertiPaq. Even though we refer to xmSQL as a language, it is not really a language. xmSQL is the textual, human-readable representation of binary structures used to communicate between the formula engine and VertiPaq. These structures are represented in xmSQL to let developers understand what is happening inside a VertiPaq query. With that said, you cannot write an xmSQL query anywhere, as there is no way to execute xmSQL.

Despite its resemblance to SQL, xmSQL is different in the syntax and in the way you interpret the code. Some queries would be extremely slow if executed by an SQL engine. Yet, the same queries are fast in xmSQL because xmSQL is specifically designed to execute the code generated by the formula engine.

Moreover, a critical aspect of xmSQL is that the language itself is constantly evolving, along with Tabular and VertiPaq. Every new release of the engine may introduce new syntaxes, operators, and ways to solve a query.

Therefore, the material presented here might become obsolete quite fast. You should not be worried about this. You learn new features as we introduce them one step at a time. But this is the reason why we present the material the way we do. We are hoping that you will learn not the details of the engine but rather, the way we uncover those details. As soon as the details change, you should follow the same steps, acquire new knowledge, and adapt to the latest technology.

Analyzing simple xmSQL queries

The simplest and by far most common statement in xmSQL is SELECT. SELECT retrieves a list of column values and possibly some aggregated values. For example, let us check the xmSQL code for the following DAX query:

```
EVALUATE
SUMMARIZECOLUMNS(
    'Product'[Brand],
    "Amt", [Sales Amount],
    "Cost", [Total Cost]
)
```

A single xmSQL query resolves the entire DAX query:

```
WITH
    $Expr0 := ( PFCAST ( 'Sales'[Quantity] AS   INT ) * PFCAST ( 'Sales'[Unit Cost] AS   INT )  ),
    $Expr1 := ( PFCAST ( 'Sales'[Quantity] AS   INT ) * PFCAST ( 'Sales'[Net Price] AS   INT )  )
SELECT
    'Product'[Brand],
    SUM ( @$Expr0 ),
    SUM ( @$Expr1 )
FROM 'Sales'
    LEFT OUTER JOIN 'Product'
        ON 'Sales'[ProductKey]='Product'[ProductKey];
```

There are a few details worth noting in this simple query:

- The WITH section introduces expressions, later referenced in aggregation.
- There is no GROUP BY section in the SELECT part, as we would expect in SQL. In xmSQL, the GROUP BY is implicit when a column is referenced in a SELECT statement.
- The result contains one or more group-by columns – *Product[Brand]*, in the example – as well as one or more result columns – *SUM (@$Expr0)* and *SUM (@$Expr1)* in the example.
- The FROM section is pretty standard, with the usual JOIN operators merging multiple tables in a single query. Joins can be used in xmSQL only if there is a regular one-to-many or one-to-one relationship linking the two tables in the model – unlike SQL, where joins are created on the fly at the query level.

The result of the previous xmSQL query is a datacache with three columns: one containing the brand, the other two containing the two aggregations. You cannot inspect the result of an xmSQL query; you can only check which parts of the physical query plan consume the datacache generated by the xmSQL query, as you can see in the Cache operators in the following picture.

Line	Records	Physical Query Plan
1	11	Spool_Iterator<SpoolIterator>: IterPhyOp LogOp=GroupSemiJoin IterCols(0, 1, 2)('Product'[Brand], ''[Amt], ''[Cost])
2	11	AggregationSpool<GroupSemiJoin>: SpoolPhyOp #Records=11
3	11	Spool_Iterator<SpoolIterator>: IterPhyOp LogOp=Sum_Vertipaq IterCols(0)('Product'[Brand]) #Records=11 #K
4	11	ProjectionSpool<ProjectFusion<Copy, Copy>>: SpoolPhyOp #Records=11
5		**Cache: IterPhyOp #FieldCols=1 #ValueCols=2**
6	11	Spool_Iterator<SpoolIterator>: IterPhyOp LogOp=Sum_Vertipaq IterCols(0)('Product'[Brand]) #Records=11 #K
7	11	ProjectionSpool<ProjectFusion<Copy, Copy>>: SpoolPhyOp #Records=11
8		**Cache: IterPhyOp #FieldCols=1 #ValueCols=2**

The two Cache operators at line 5 and line 8 of the physical query plan indicate that the datacache contains one field column (the *Product[Brand]* column, in our example) and two value columns, which are aggregated values.

Because xmSQL always applies an implicit GROUP BY section with all the columns projected into the result, it is important to understand how xmSQL manages the retrieval of potentially duplicated rows. For example, the following DAX query returns the unique combinations of brand and color in the *Product* table:

```
EVALUATE
SUMMARIZECOLUMNS (
    'Product'[Brand],
    'Product'[Color]
)
```

The result comprises two columns and 111 rows corresponding to the existing combinations of brand and colors in *Product*. The physical query plan retrieves data with a single Cache operator.

Line	Records	Physical Query Plan
1		GroupSemijoin: IterPhyOp LogOp=GroupSemiJoin IterCols(0, 1)('Product'[Brand], 'Product'[Color])
2	111	Spool_Iterator<SpoolIterator>: IterPhyOp LogOp=Scan_Vertipaq IterCols(0, 1)('Product'[Brand], 'P
3	111	ProjectionSpool<ProjectFusion<>>: SpoolPhyOp #Records=111
4		**Cache: IterPhyOp #FieldCols=2 #ValueCols=0**

The corresponding xmSQL query only references *Product[Brand]* and *Product[Color]*:

```
SELECT
    'Product'[Brand],
    'Product'[Color]
FROM 'Product';
```

If we use SELECTCOLUMNS, the result is different. Indeed, SELECTCOLUMNS returns all table rows, including possible duplicated rows. The following DAX query returns all the rows in the *Product* table showing only two columns, *Brand* and *Color*:

```
EVALUATE
SELECTCOLUMNS (
    'Product',
    'Product'[Brand],
    'Product'[Color]
)
```

This time the physical query plan retrieves three columns, resulting in 2,517 rows – the exact size of the *Product* table.

Line	Records	Physical Query Plan
1	2,517	Spool_Iterator<SpoolIterator>: IterPhyOp LogOp=GroupBy_Vertipaq IterCols(0, 1, 2)('Product'[Brand], 'Product'[Color], 'Product'[RowNumber-266;
2	2,517	ProjectionSpool<ProjectFusion<>>: SpoolPhyOp #Records=2517
3		**Cache: IterPhyOp #FieldCols=3 #ValueCols=0**

The xmSQL query includes a third column (*RowNumber*) before *Product[Brand]* and *Product[Color]*:

```
SELECT
    'Product'[RowNumber],
    'Product'[Brand],
    'Product'[Color]
FROM 'Product';
```

RowNumber is a special column that is not part of the memory table. *RowNumber* represents the physical position of the row in the table stored in memory, which is not necessarily the exact position of the row in the original data source. Indeed, during compression, VertiPaq can rearrange rows at every data process. However, *RowNumber* guarantees that a row is unique. When *RowNumber* used as a group-by column, the result includes all the rows of the table. The presence of *RowNumber* "disables" the implicit GROUP BY applied to xmSQL queries.

Introducing basic VertiPaq functionalities

VertiPaq is designed to be simple and fast. The two properties go together. VertiPaq needs to be simple to be fast. As such, the set of functionalities supported by VertiPaq is quite limited. VertiPaq can:

- Compute the four mathematical operators: sum, subtraction, multiplication, and division.
- Compute simple aggregations: MIN, MAX, SUM, COUNT, DISTINCTCOUNT.
- Follow relationships between tables, provided that the relationship is stored in the model.
- Create temporary tables to store partial calculations. Those tables can be used as part of more complex expressions and filters.

- Test basic conditions to apply filters during table scans: equality, comparison (less than, greater than), and the IN operator to check that a value belongs to a list of values. Be mindful that VertiPaq cannot perform conditional logic for a column expression such as IF statements in DAX. It can only evaluate conditions while scanning a table to reduce the number of rows considered.

A simple DAX query can demonstrate the basic features of VertiPaq:

```
EVALUATE
SUMMARIZECOLUMNS (
    Customer[Continent],
    TREATAS ( { "Red", "Blue" }, 'Product'[Color] ),
    "Amt", SUMX ( Sales, Sales[Quantity] * Sales[Net Price] )
)
```

The query groups by *Customer[Continent]*, uses a filter on *Product[Color]*, and aggregates a multiplication computed row-by-row. Therefore, VertiPaq needs to scan the *Sales* table using two joins, one with *Customer* and one with *Product*:

```
WITH
    $Expr0 := ( PFCAST ( 'Sales'[Quantity] AS INT ) * PFCAST ( 'Sales'[Net Price] AS INT ) )
SELECT
    'Customer'[Continent],
    SUM ( @$Expr0 )
FROM 'Sales'
    LEFT OUTER JOIN 'Customer'
        ON 'Sales'[CustomerKey]='Customer'[CustomerKey]
    LEFT OUTER JOIN 'Product'
        ON 'Sales'[ProductKey]='Product'[ProductKey]
WHERE
    'Product'[Color] IN ( 'Blue', 'Red' ) ;
```

The entire DAX query Is resolved with a single xmSQL query, returning the required result very efficiently.

Introducing batches

VertiPaq can solve more complex queries by creating temporary tables. Creating a temporary table is one of the multiple steps in a more complex algorithm. Whenever temporary structures are needed, the formula engine executes a batch. A batch is a set of VertiPaq queries executed in sequence, where the later steps can reference data structures created in the previous steps.

From the point of view of the formula engine, a batch is a single query. From the point of view of

VertiPaq, each batch step is a separate query. The temporary structures created inside a batch are transient: they are valid only during the execution of the batch and cannot be referenced after the batch is finished. However, each step can be retrieved by the VertiPaq cache as any other xmSQL query.

A rather simple query that requires a batch is the following:

```
EVALUATE
SUMMARIZECOLUMNS (
    FILTER ( ALL ( 'Product'[Unit Price] ), 'Product'[Unit Price] >= 100 ),
    "Amt", SUMX ( Sales, Sales[Quantity] * Sales[Net Price] )
)
```

The query needs to compute the values for which the unit price is greater than or equal to 100, producing the total sales amount as the only result. The formula engine sends a batch to VertiPaq with a first step that computes the values of *Product[Unit Price]* greater than 100, and then a second query that uses the table generated during the first step as a filter:

```
DEFINE TABLE '$TTable2' :=
SELECT
    SIMPLEINDEXN ( 'Product'[Unit Price] )
FROM 'Product'
WHERE
    ( PFCASTCOALESCE ( 'Product'[Unit Price] AS INT ) >= COALESCE ( 1000000 ) ),

DEFINE TABLE '$TTable1' :=
WITH
    $Expr0 := ( PFCAST ( 'Sales'[Quantity] AS INT ) * PFCAST ( 'Sales'[Net Price] AS INT ) )
SELECT
    SUM ( @$Expr0 )
FROM 'Sales'
    LEFT OUTER JOIN 'Product'
        ON 'Sales'[ProductKey]='Product'[ProductKey]
WHERE
    'Product'[Unit Price] ININDEX '$TTable2'[$SemijoinProjection];
```

In DAX Studio, a batch is shown directly below the set of individual queries composing the batch itself – the queries that are part of a batch show the *Scan* subclass in italics to highlight that they are part of a batch.

Line	Subclass	Duration	CPU	Par.	Rows	KB	Timeline	Query
2	*Scan*	1	0		3,199,104	391		DEFINE TABLE '$TTable2' := SELECT SIMPLEINDEXN ('
4	*Scan*	107	1,813	x16.9	1	1		DEFINE TABLE '$TTable1' := WITH $Expr0 := (PFCAST
5	Batch	0	0					DEFINE TABLE '$TTable2' := SELECT SIMPLEINDEXN ('

When analyzing the performance of a batch, it is important to spend time investigating the individual steps. For example, in the figure shown, nearly all the time of the batch is spent in the query scanning

Sales (line 4): it uses 1,813 milliseconds, despite computing a single row. The previous step (line 2) is extremely fast, even though it generates a temporary table that is quite large (more than 3M rows).

Another scenario where batches play an important role is with complex relationships. Bidirectional relationships and many-to-many cardinality relationships almost always require a batch. Let us see a query that enables the bidirectional cross-filter on a relationship to count the number of products sold. Beware, this DAX code is not efficient. We wrote this only for educational purposes:

```
EVALUATE
SUMMARIZECOLUMNS (
    Customer[Continent],
    "Amt",
        CALCULATE (
            DIVIDE (
                SUMX ( Sales, Sales[Quantity] * Sales[Net Price] ),
                COUNTROWS ( 'Product' )
            ),
            CROSSFILTER ( Sales[ProductKey], 'Product'[ProductKey], BOTH )
        )
)
```

Despite being quite complex, almost the entire query can be resolved through a single VertiPaq batch:

```
DEFINE TABLE '$TTable3' :=
SELECT
    'Customer'[Continent],
    'Product'[ProductKey]
FROM 'Sales'
    LEFT OUTER JOIN 'Customer'
        ON 'Sales'[CustomerKey]='Customer'[CustomerKey]
    LEFT OUTER JOIN 'Product'
        ON 'Sales'[ProductKey]='Product'[ProductKey],


DEFINE TABLE '$TTable4' :=
SELECT
    SIMPLEINDEXN ( '$TTable3'[Product$ProductKey] )
FROM '$TTable3',


CREATE SHALLOW RELATION '$TRelation1'
    MANYTOMANY
    FROM 'Product'[ProductKey]
        TO '$TTable3'[Product$ProductKey],
```

```
DEFINE TABLE '$TTable1' :=
SELECT
    '$TTable3'[Customer$Continent],
    SUM ( '$TTable2'[$Measure0] )
FROM '$TTable2'
    INNER JOIN '$TTable3'
        ON '$TTable2'[Product$ProductKey]='$TTable3'[Product$ProductKey]
REDUCED BY
'$TTable2' :=
SELECT
    'Product'[ProductKey],
    SUM ( 1 )
FROM 'Product'
WHERE
    'Product'[ProductKey] ININDEX '$TTable4'[$SemijoinProjection];
```

This batch is somewhat complex. Let us analyze it in detail. There are four steps. The first DEFINE TABLE (*$TTable3*) creates a temporary table containing the relationship between *Product[ProductKey]* and *Customer[Continent]*. The second step defines *$TTable4*, a bitmap index containing the products referenced in *$TTable3*. It will be useful later as a filter to reduce the products to consider. In this query, the optimization introduced with $TTable4 is ineffective. Still, the engine used it as part of the query pattern. The third statement, CREATE SHALLOW RELATION, creates a relationship between the temporary table *$TTable3* (the first table computed, which contains *ProductKey* and *Continent*) and the *Product* table. This relationship is useful in the last query. It is worth remembering that a JOIN can be executed in VertiPaq only if the relationship is part of the model. Temporary relationships are useful for joining temporary tables.

Indeed, the relationship is used in the last xmSQL query, the one computing *$TTable1*. The join between *$TTable2* and *$TTable3* is possible because *$TTable2* is defined in the last REDUCED BY section as a SELECT of *Product[ProductKey]*. The shallow relationship links *Product[ProductKey]* to *Table3[Product$ProductKey]*, which are the columns used in the JOIN clause.

Understanding internal and external SE queries

Every time the formula engine sends a query to VertiPaq, Tabular sends two notifications: the external query, and the internal queries. The external query is the query sent from the formula engine to VertiPaq, or the query generated by a batch query. The internal queries are the actual queries executed by VertiPaq. Mostly, there is a single internal query identical to the external one, which is why DAX Studio hides internal queries by default.

Note The internal queries can be skipped if an external query is solved by the VertiPaq cache, as we shall describe later on in this chapter. By now, we run every DAX query by clearing the cache before every run – this way, the internal queries are never skipped in the Server Timings pane because the cache is always empty.

In certain scenarios, a noticeable difference can be observed between the internal and external queries. One single external query can create multiple internal queries, as is the case for distinct counts that we will see later. For example, let us focus on the following DAX query:

```
EVALUATE
SUMMARIZECOLUMNS (
    'Product'[Brand],
    "Amt", [Sales Amount]
)
```

The Server Timings pane shows only one query, at line number 2.

Total	SE CPU		Line	Subclass	Duration	CPU	Par.	Rows	KB	Timeline	Query
72 ms	859 ms		2	Scan	68	859	x12.6	14	1		WITH $Expr0 := (P
	x12.6										

FE	SE
4 ms	68 ms
5.6%	94.4%

```
SET DC_KIND="AUTO";
WITH
    $Expr0 := ( PFCAST ( 'Sales'[Quantity] AS INT ) * PFCAST ( 'Sales'[Net Price] AS INT ) )
SELECT
    'Product'[Brand],
    SUM ( @$Expr0 )
```

SE Queries	SE Cache
1	0
	0.0%

Line number 1 contains the internal query, which is hidden by default. You may activate the visualization of internal queries with the Internal button.

Once activated, DAX Studio shows both the internal and the external queries.

Total	SE CPU		Line	Subclass	Duration	CPU	Par.	Rows	KB	Timeline	Query
72 ms	859 ms		1	Internal	68	859	x12.6				WITH $Expr0 := (F
	x12.6		2	Scan	68	859	x12.6	14	1		WITH $Expr0 := (F

FE	SE
4 ms	68 ms
5.6%	94.4%

```
SET DC_KIND="AUTO";
WITH
    $Expr0 := ( PFCAST ( 'Sales'[Quantity] AS INT ) * PFCAST ( 'Sales'[Net Price] AS INT ) )
SELECT
    'Product'[Brand],
```

SE Queries	SE Cache
1	0
	0.0%

Let us elaborate on the differences between internal and external queries. Whenever the formula engine requires data, it sends a query to the storage engine. The storage engine needs to return the result of the query, but it can change certain details of the query to generate a more efficient execution. Moreover, some details are still in charge of the VertiPaq engine, like the type of datacache to use.

For the above example, let us analyze the differences between the internal and the external storage engine queries. First, the external query:

```
SET DC_KIND="AUTO";
WITH
    $Expr0 := ( PFCAST ( 'Sales'[Quantity] AS INT ) * PFCAST ( 'Sales'[Net Price] AS INT ) )
SELECT
    'Product'[Brand],
    SUM ( @$Expr0 )
FROM 'Sales'
    LEFT OUTER JOIN 'Product'
        ON 'Sales'[ProductKey]='Product'[ProductKey];

Estimated size: rows = 14    bytes = 224
```

The first line, SET DC_KIND, indicates that the formula engine does not require a specific type of datacache. It leaves to the storage engine the choice of the size and type of datacache. Therefore, it specifies DC_KIND="AUTO". As we are about to see, the internal query has a different DC_KIND specification.

At the end of each external query, there is an indication about the expected number of rows and the size of the resulting datacache. The storage engine does not know how many rows will be returned. The information is just an estimate – it can be useful to detect when for whatever reason, the formula engine fails in estimating the number of rows in a datacache.

VertiPaq rewrites the external query, generating the internal query:

```
SET DC_KIND="DENSE";
WITH
    $Expr0 := ( PFCAST ( 'Sales'[Quantity] AS INT ) * PFCAST ( 'Sales'[Net Price] AS INT ) )
SELECT
    'Product'[Brand],
    SUM ( @$Expr0 ),
    COUNT ()
FROM 'Sales'
    LEFT OUTER JOIN 'Product'
        ON 'Sales'[ProductKey]='Product'[ProductKey];
```

VertiPaq created a DENSE datacache because it expects most rows to contain a value. If most rows contained BLANK, then VertiPaq might have chosen a different datacache type. The internal query no longer has any estimate, and eventually, VertiPaq decided to add the number of rows for each brand to the datacache by using a COUNT function.

The reason VertiPaq often chooses to add a COUNT function to many xmSQL queries is not relevant: it is part of the internal optimizations of the engine. The formula engine asked for a query, and the VertiPaq engine chose to execute a different one, still returning the same data but with a different query syntax.

As we had anticipated, most internal queries are slight variations of the external query. Therefore, spending time understanding the subtle differences between the internal and the external query is not interesting. What is interesting to us is to be able to understand the algorithm executed by Tabular to solve a DAX query. For that purpose, the content of the external query is largely enough. However, there are rare scenarios where external and internal queries are quite different: we outline some of them, knowing that there might still be scenarios that we have not encountered yet.

Understanding distinct count in xmSQL

An example where there is a noticeable difference between internal and external queries is in the case of distinct counts. Let us look at a simple query involving distinct counts:

```
EVALUATE
SUMMARIZECOLUMNS(
    'Product'[Brand],
    "Amt", DISTINCTCOUNT ( Sales[ProductKey] )
)
```

The external xmSQL code for the query is the following:

```
SET DC_KIND="AUTO";
SELECT
    'Product'[Brand],
    DCOUNT ( 'Sales'[ProductKey] )
FROM 'Sales'
    LEFT OUTER JOIN 'Product'
        ON 'Sales'[ProductKey]='Product'[ProductKey];
```

The query uses the DCOUNT function in xmSQL. The distinct count is not a native operator in xmSQL. To perform a distinct count, xmSQL materializes a larger datacache internally. That datacache contains *Product[Brand]* and *Sales[ProductKey]*, and is materialized using a particular type of datacache: the *Existing Cache*. An Existing Cache is a datacache that contains only one bit per value, indicating whether the value is present in the table. The single external query is translated into two internal queries. The first fills the Existing Cache:

```
SELECT
    'Product'[Brand],
    'Sales'[ProductKey]
FROM 'Sales'
    LEFT OUTER JOIN 'Product'
        ON 'Sales'[ProductKey]='Product'[ProductKey];
```

The second query scans the result of the first by using the $DCOUNT_DATACACHE store, where VertiPaq stored the Existing Cache:

```
SELECT
    'Product'[Brand],
    COUNT ()
FROM $DCOUNT_DATACACHE
    LEFT OUTER JOIN 'Product'
        ON 'Sales'[ProductKey]='Product'[ProductKey];
```

As we had anticipated, despite this being interesting from a theoretical point of view, developers have no option to influence how a distinct count is implemented internally in VertiPaq. For the sake of optimizing DAX code, the distinction between internal and external queries is not that relevant.

Understanding VertiPaq joins and filters

VertiPaq queries often need to move a filter between two tables. VertiPaq can use joined tables or index-based filters to perform this operation. In this section, we briefly analyze the various options available.

Introducing VertiPaq joins

VertiPaq can join tables using four different join types: LEFT OUTER JOIN, INNER JOIN, REVERSE HASH JOIN, and REVERSE BITMAP JOIN.

LEFT OUTER JOIN relies on the existence of a regular one-to-many or one-to-one relationship stored in the VertiPaq model. This type of join is heavily optimized, assuming one of the two tables is way larger than the other. VertiPaq makes this assumption because it is a database designed for business intelligence models, where there is almost always a large fact table linked to several smaller dimensions.

INNER JOIN is another type of join that is used in conjunction with REDUCED BY. In this case, the table after REDUCED BY is a temporary table defined in the same batch; it usually includes aggregations and is the larger table involved in the join. The INNER JOIN works in the presence of a relationship created with CREATE SHALLOW RELATION in the same batch: the cartesian product of the two tables involved in the join is reduced by including only the rows that satisfy the relationship. The result of INNER JOIN can have more rows than the largest table involved in the join, whereas LEFT JOIN in xmSQL will never return more rows than those in the initial table.

On the other hand, REVERSE HASH JOIN and REVERSE BITMAP JOIN join types do not require the presence of a VertiPaq relationship. The difference between the two join types is in the algorithm. Again, the VertiPaq engine chooses between the two based on data distribution. Reverse joins perform the opposite of a regular join. Indeed, a query typically scans *Sales* and joins it to *Product* to retrieve column values from *Product* and use them while scanning *Sales*, which reduces the number of rows iterated in *Sales*. A reverse join performs the opposite operation: it lets a filter move from *Sales* to *Product*.

The most common scenario where reverse joins are used is determining which dimension values are needed to perform a query. In the next sections, we analyze a scenario where a reverse join is used along with the RJOIN table function.

Introducing bitmap indexes

Depending on the filter's complexity, VertiPaq can create indexes to perform a filtering operation. The details about when a filter is better than a relationship are quite complex, and they are part of the internal optimization algorithm of VertiPaq. Nonetheless, it is useful to see an example that clarifies how VertiPaq uses bitmap indexes.

Let us analyze this query:

```
EVALUATE
CALCULATETABLE (
    { [Sales Amount] },
    'Sales'[Unit Price] >= 1000
)
```

The measure requires a scan of the *Sales* table, and the filter applies a scan condition to the *Sales[Unit Price]* column. Not surprisingly, this generates a simple VertiPaq query:

```
WITH
    $Expr0 := ( PFCAST ( 'Sales'[Quantity] AS INT ) * PFCAST ( 'Sales'[Net Price] AS INT ) )
SELECT
    SUM ( @$Expr0 )
FROM 'Sales'
WHERE
    ( PFCASTCOALESCE ( 'Sales'[Unit Price] AS INT ) >= COALESCE ( 10000000 ) );
```

The condition operates on *Sales[Unit Price]*, a rather large column. This condition generates a query that requires around 7 seconds of storage engine CPU to run.

Total	SE CPU	Line	Subclass	Duration	CPU	Par.	Rows	KB	Timeline	Query
361 ms	7,219 ms									
	x20.2	2	Scan	358	7,219	x20.2	1	1		WITH $Expr0 := (F

FE	SE
3 ms	358 ms
0.8%	99.2%

SE Queries	SE Cache
1	0
	0.0%

```
SET DC_KIND="AUTO";
WITH
    $Expr0 := ( PFCAST ( 'Sales'[Quantity] AS INT ) * PFCAST ( 'Sales'[Net Price] AS INT ) )
SELECT
    SUM ( @$Expr0 )
FROM 'Sales'
WHERE
```

The same query can be expressed by placing the filter on *Product[Unit Price]* instead of *Sales[Unit Price]*. The *Product[Unit Price]* column is much smaller, even though the query uses a join between *Sales* and *Product* to perform the calculation:

```
EVALUATE
CALCULATETABLE (
    { [Sales Amount] },
    'Product'[Unit Price] >= 1000
)
```

The *Product[Unit Price] >= 1000* condition can be evaluated as part of the scan of *Sales*, as was the case in the previous xmSQL code, or as part of a scan of the *Product[Unit Price]* column – which is much smaller. In this scenario, Tabular chooses the latter option. It scans *Product[Unit Price]*, evaluates the condition, and builds a bitmap index containing the values of *Product[Unit Price]* filtered for the column. Once created, the index provides a faster way to evaluate the condition.

Indeed, this latter DAX query generates a batch:

```
DEFINE TABLE '$TTable2' :=
SELECT
    SIMPLEINDEXN ( 'Product'[Unit Price] )
FROM 'Product'
WHERE
    ( PFCASTCOALESCE ( 'Product'[Unit Price] AS INT ) >= COALESCE ( 10000000 ) ) ,


DEFINE TABLE '$TTable1' :=
WITH
    $Expr0 := ( PFCAST ( 'Sales'[Quantity] AS INT ) * PFCAST ( 'Sales'[Net Price] AS INT ) )
SELECT
    SUM ( @$Expr0 )
FROM 'Sales'
    LEFT OUTER JOIN 'Product'
        ON 'Sales'[ProductKey]='Product'[ProductKey]
WHERE
    'Product'[Unit Price] ININDEX '$TTable2'[$SemijoinProjection];
```

$TTable2 is a temporary table containing the result of SIMPLEINDEXN. SIMPLEINDEXN creates a bitmap index of the *Product[Unit Price]* column. *$TTable2* is then used in the second xmSQL query of the batch to check if a *Product[Unit Price]* column belongs to the index by using the ININDEX operator.

In this scenario, the choice made by Tabular pays off. The query with the bitmap index runs faster than the version without it.

Total	SE CPU		Line	Subclass	Duration	CPU	Par.	Rows	KB	Timeline	Query
265 ms	5,359 ms										
	x20.5		2	Scan	1	0		3,199,104	391		DEFINE TABLE '$TTa
FE	SE		4	Scan	260	5,359	x20.6	1	1		DEFINE TABLE '$TTa
4 ms	261 ms		5	Batch	0	0					DEFINE TABLE '$TTa
1.5%	98.5%										

SE Queries	SE Cache
3	0
	0.0%

```
DEFINE TABLE '$TTable2' :=
SELECT
    SIMPLEINDEXN ( 'Product'[Unit Price] )
FROM 'Product'
```

The size of the bitmap index created depends on the type of encoding of the indexed column. If a column is compressed with hash encoding, then the size of the bitmap index is the column's cardinality because what is indexed is the data ID of the column value. If the column is value-encoded, then the bitmap index contains one bit for each possible value of the column, which may result in being larger than the strictly-required size.

The index is on the *Product[Unit Price]* column in the example provided. *Product[Unit Price]* has a minimum value of 0.95, and a maximum value of 3,199.99. The maximum number of digits on the right of the decimal point used by the values in *Product[Unit Price]* is three (there is a product with a price of 22.788). The engine automatically recognizes that the range of values of the column can be represented by an integer value obtained by subtracting the minimum value (0.95) and then multiplying the value by 1,000, so that 22.788 becomes an integer corresponding to 22,788. You can use the following DAX query to roughly evaluate the index size for a column once you identify the correct multiplication factor to represent column values as integers (see the *Factor* variable):

```
EVALUATE
VAR MinValue = MIN ( 'Product'[Unit Price] )
VAR MaxValue = MAX ( 'Product'[Unit Price] )
VAR Factor = 1000
RETURN
{
    ( "Min value", MinValue ),
    ( "Max value", MaxValue ),
    ( "Delta", MaxValue - MinValue ),
    ( "Delta x " & Factor, (MaxValue - MinValue) * Factor ),
    ( "Bitmap size (bytes)", ROUNDUP ( ( (MaxValue - MinValue) * Factor ) / 8, 0 ) )
}
```

The query produces an estimate of the bitmap index size.

Value1	Value2
Min value	0.95
Max value	3,199.99
Delta	3,199.04
Delta x 1000	3,199,040.00
Bitmap size (bytes)	399,880.00

Be mindful that the choice between a bitmap index or a WHERE condition inside the xmSQL query follows internal optimization rules that are part of the engine – changing the shape of the condition results in a completely different plan. For example, a slightly more complex condition forces Tabular to use an IN condition instead of a bitmap index:

```
EVALUATE
CALCULATETABLE (
    { [Sales Amount] },
    OR (
        'Product'[Unit Price] >= 1000,
        'Product'[Unit Cost] < 0
    )
)
```

The condition is now working on multiple columns: therefore, a bitmap index is no longer an option. As such, Tabular first retrieves the pairs of *Product[Unit Price]* and *Product[Unit Cost]* satisfying the condition, and then it injects the condition inside the next xmSQL code:

```
WITH
    $Expr0 := ( PFCAST ( 'Sales'[Quantity] AS INT ) * PFCAST ( 'Sales'[Net Price] AS INT ) )
SELECT
    SUM ( @$Expr0 )
FROM 'Sales'
    LEFT OUTER JOIN 'Product'
        ON 'Sales'[ProductKey]='Product'[ProductKey]
WHERE
    ( 'Product'[Unit Price], 'Product'[Unit Cost] ) IN
        { ( 14750000, 4887000 ) , ( 22950000, 7603800 ) , ( 18189000, 8364500 ) , ( 10990000, 3641200 ) ,
          ( 19890000, 9146700 ) , ( 24990000, 8279700 ) , ( 15999000, 8156800 ) , ( 31999900, 10602200 ) ,
          ( 26520000, 8786600 ) , ( 15800000, 5234900 ) ..[30 total tuples, not all displayed] };
```

As a result, the query is now slower – even though it returns an identical result as the previous query because we added a useless condition on *Product[Unit Cost]* that does not filter more products.

Total	SE CPU	Line	Subclass	Duration	CPU	Par.	Rows	KB	Timeline	Query
817 ms	16,828 ms									
	x20.9	2	Scan	3	0		30	1		SELECT 'Pro
		4	Scan	803	16,828	x21.0	1	1		WITH $Exp
● FE	● SE									
13 ms	804 ms									
1.6%	98.7%									

SE Queries	SE Cache
2	0
	0.0%

```
SET DC_KIND="AUTO";
WITH
    $Expr0 := ( PFCAST ( 'Sales'[Quantity] AS INT ) * PFCAST ( 'Sales'[Net Price] AS INT ) )
SELECT
```

Knowing the data distribution, the size of the filters, and the various aspects of their model, developers can choose different formulations for the same query. For example, in a scenario like this latter code, one can force the creation of a bitmap index by moving the filter from the individual columns in *Product* to the *Product[ProductKey]* column. With this version of the query, the filter is now operating only on the *Product[ProductKey]* column:

```
EVALUATE
CALCULATETABLE (
    { [Sales Amount] },
    SELECTCOLUMNS (
        FILTER (
            'Product',
            OR (
                'Product'[Unit Price] >= 1000,
                'Product'[Unit Cost] < 0
            )
        ),
        Product[ProductKey]
    )
)
```

A bitmap index is again an option because we operate over a single column. Indeed, this DAX query reverts to the use of a bitmap index, and performance is much better.

Total	SE CPU		Line	Subclass	Duration	CPU	Par.	Rows	KB	Timeline	Query
257 ms	4,938 ms		2	*Scan*	1	0		2,560	1		DEFINE TA
	×19.7										
● FE	● SE		4	*Scan*	252	4,938	×19.6	1	1		DEFINE TA
6 ms	251 ms		5	Batch	0	0					DEFINE TA
2.3%	98.4%										

SE Queries	SE Cache
3	0
	0.0%

```
SET DC_KIND="AUTO";
DEFINE TABLE '$TTable1' :=
WITH
  $Expr0 := ( PFCAST ( 'Sales'[Quantity] AS INT ) * PFCAST ( 'Sales'[Net Price] AS INT ) )
SELECT
  SUM ( @$Expr0 )
FROM 'Sales'
  LEFT OUTER JOIN 'Product'
    ON 'Sales'[ProductKey]='Product'[ProductKey]
WHERE
  'Product'[ProductKey] ININDEX '$TTable2'[$SemijoinProjection];
```

As you have seen, bitmap indexes are very fast, although they cannot be used in all scenarios. Mostly, the choices made by Tabular are correct. Still, an experienced DAX developer might know better and author less-intuitive code to force a filter or a bitmap, depending on which one performs better.

Introducing reverse joins

An important scenario where you should inspect the internal queries is when a filter on a relatively small dimension generates an internal reverse join.

When VertiPaq scans a fact table like *Sales* (the table on the many-side of a relationship) and the query places a filter on a related dimension like *Customer* (the table on the one-side of a relationship), VertiPaq optimizes the query by applying a bitmap index on the fact table, to reduce the number of rows to scan. This technique works very well when the filter is highly selective, whereas it slows down the query when it is not selective. The choice of using a reverse join or a regular join depends on the size of the filtered dimension.

The ratio between the fact table and the dimensions can be a small number on a rather small model. Using a model with 5M rows in *Sales* and 2M rows in *Customers* is not unusual. In such a scenario, the engine chooses between a reverse join or a regular join based on the tables size and the ratio between the number of rows in the two tables. The rule used to choose between the two join types might change over time; at the time of writing, the engine uses a reverse join when the following three conditions are all met: the ratio is less than 20%, the table on the many-side has at least 131,072 rows, and the column on the many-side has at least 16,384 unique values.

On larger models – the type of models where these optimizations matter – the ratio between the dimension and the fact table is always a very small number. *Sales* contains 1.4B rows in our sample model, whereas *Customer* contains only 2M rows. The ratio is 0.14%, so the reverse join is almost always used whenever there is a filter.

To notice the presence of the reverse join you need to inspect the internal queries. As an example, let us examine the following query:

```
EVALUATE
SUMMARIZECOLUMNS (
    'Date'[Year],
    'Customer'[Gender],
    "Sales", [Sales Amount]
)
```

The query groups by two columns, and it computes *Sales Amount*, which is a simple calculation. Therefore, it can be expressed using a single xmSQL query:

```
WITH
    $Expr0 := ( PFCAST ( 'Sales'[Quantity] AS INT ) * PFCAST ( 'Sales'[Net Price] AS INT ) )
SELECT
    'Date'[Year],
    'Customer'[Gender],
    SUM ( @$Expr0 )
FROM 'Sales'
    LEFT OUTER JOIN 'Date'
        ON 'Sales'[Order Date]='Date'[Date]
    LEFT OUTER JOIN 'Customer'
        ON 'Sales'[CustomerKey]='Customer'[CustomerKey];
```

The internal query is identical. Performance-wise, the query is fast: it uses only 9,875 milliseconds of storage engine CPU.

Total	SE CPU		Line	Subclass	Duration	CPU	Par.	Rows	KB	Timeline	Quer
553 ms	9,875 ms x18.4		2	Scan	539	9,875	x18.3	70	2		WITH

FE	SE
16 ms	537 ms
2.9%	97.5%

SE Queries	SE Cache
1	0
	0.0%

```
SET DC_KIND="AUTO";
WITH
    $Expr0 := ( PFCAST ( 'Sales'[Quantity] AS INT ) * PFCAST ( 'Sales'[Net Price] AS INT ) )
SELECT
    'Date'[Year],
    'Customer'[Gender],
    SUM ( @$Expr0 )
```

To see the reverse join happening, it is enough to add a dummy filter to the *Customer* table. We use a filter that does not actually filter anything to obtain a scan of the rows used in the previous query. Indeed, in the sample database, the *Customer[Gender]* column contains only "Male" and "Female":

```
EVALUATE
SUMMARIZECOLUMNS (
    'Date'[Year],
    'Customer'[Gender],
    TREATAS ( { "Male", "Female" }, Customer[Gender] ),
    "Sales", [Sales Amount]
)
```

The result is the very same as the previous query – but it takes longer.

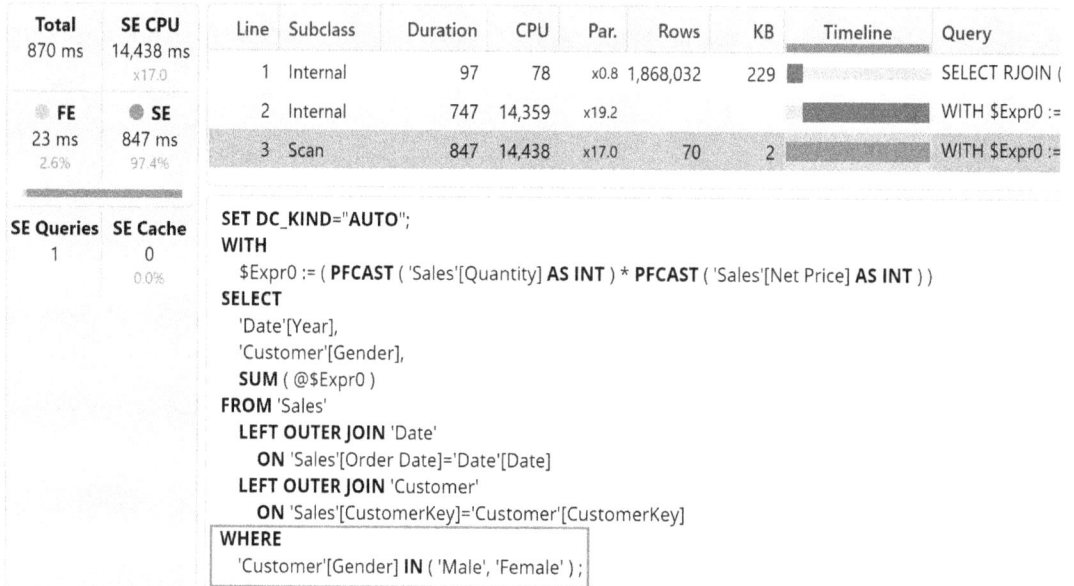

Total	SE CPU		Line	Subclass	Duration	CPU	Par.	Rows	KB	Timeline	Query
870 ms	14,438 ms		1	Internal	97	78	x0.8	1,868,032	229		SELECT RJOIN (
	x17.0		2	Internal	747	14,359	x19.2				WITH $Expr0 :=
FE	**SE**		3	Scan	847	14,438	x17.0	70	2		WITH $Expr0 :=
23 ms	847 ms										
2.6%	97.4%										

SE Queries	SE Cache
1	0
	0.0%

```
SET DC_KIND="AUTO";
WITH
  $Expr0 := ( PFCAST ( 'Sales'[Quantity] AS INT ) * PFCAST ( 'Sales'[Net Price] AS INT ) )
SELECT
  'Date'[Year],
  'Customer'[Gender],
  SUM ( @$Expr0 )
FROM 'Sales'
  LEFT OUTER JOIN 'Date'
    ON 'Sales'[Order Date]='Date'[Date]
  LEFT OUTER JOIN 'Customer'
    ON 'Sales'[CustomerKey]='Customer'[CustomerKey]
WHERE
  'Customer'[Gender] IN ( 'Male', 'Female' );
```

You can notice that the xmSQL query is nearly the same as before, with the noticeable difference that there is now a filter on *Customer[Gender]*. This time, there are two internal queries instead of one. The formula engine did not change its behavior. Based on the number of rows in the tables and the presence of a filter, VertiPaq decided to execute the query using a different algorithm. Let us further investigate the two internal queries.

The first internal query scans *Customer*, applying a filter on *Sales* to retrieve the customers that are either Male or Female, and are at the same time present in *Sales*:

```
SELECT
RJOIN ( 'Customer'[CustomerKey] )
FROM 'Customer'
    REVERSE BITMAP JOIN 'Sales' ON 'Customer'[CustomerKey]='Sales'[CustomerKey]
WHERE
    'Customer'[Gender] IN ( 'Male', 'Female' );
```

The result of this query is a bitmap index containing the customers present in the filter. The RJOIN function returns the bitmap index originated by a reverse join. This query in itself is quite fast, as it works on the dimension. The bitmap index is then used in the second xmSQL query with the INB operator:

```
SET DC_KIND="DENSE";
WITH
    $Expr0 := ( PFCAST ( 'Sales'[Quantity] AS INT ) * PFCAST ( 'Sales'[Net Price] AS INT ) )
SELECT
    'Date'[Year],
    'Customer'[Gender],
    SUM ( @$Expr0 ),
    COUNT ()
FROM 'Sales'
    LEFT OUTER JOIN 'Date'
        ON 'Sales'[Order Date]='Date'[Date]
    LEFT OUTER JOIN 'Customer'
        ON 'Sales'[CustomerKey]='Customer'[CustomerKey]
WHERE
    'Sales'[CustomerKey] INB (
        1664637, 1373204, 1346606, 2053160, 1538554, 1622418, 1482489,
        1811431, 2044862, 1236108..[1,868,002 total values, not all displayed] ) ;
```

The structure is the same as the original query; this time, there is a filter on over 1.8M customers. The reason why the query is slower is mainly because of the presence of the filter.

VertiPaq had to materialize all the values of *Customer[CustomerKey]* in a bitmap index. Be mindful that this materialization is very different from the materialization that happens when VertiPaq returns a datacache to the formula engine. In the scenario with the bitmap index, there is no communication between the formula engine and VertiPaq. The list of customers is created inside VertiPaq, used inside VertiPaq, and then destroyed. As such, the impact on performance is lower.

The technique used by VertiPaq is efficient whenever the filter applied on the dimension is restrictive. Indeed, performance is great when we change the filter so that only 178 out of 1.8M customers satisfy the condition. This query applies the filter on the *Customer[City]* column, filtering only one city:

```
EVALUATE
SUMMARIZECOLUMNS (
    'Date'[Year],
    'Customer'[Gender],
    TREATAS ( { "Rome" }, Customer[City] ),
    "Sales", [Sales Amount]
)
```

The resulting bitmap index filters only 178 customers, and it makes a real difference.

Total	SE CPU		Line	Subclass	Duration	CPU	Par.	Rows	KB	Timeline	Query
197 ms	2,922 ms		1	Internal	1	0		1,868,032	229		SELEC⌐
	x15.4										

FE	SE
7 ms	190 ms
3.6%	96.4%

SE Queries	SE Cache
1	0
	0.0%

```
LEFT OUTER JOIN 'Date'
    ON 'Sales'[Order Date]='Date'[Date]
LEFT OUTER JOIN 'Customer'
    ON 'Sales'[CustomerKey]='Customer'[CustomerKey]
WHERE
    'Sales'[CustomerKey] INB ( 1959052, 1981507, 1960431, 1685966, 1348867, 1837614, 17452
2004689, 1377836 .[178 total values, not all displayed] ) ;
```

Unfortunately, to obtain precise information about whether a regular join or a reverse join has been executed, the only option is to inspect the internal queries. Nonetheless, there are few – if any – options with DAX to force the query to be executed without a reverse join, as this is an internal VertiPaq behavior over which we do not have much control.

In a small data model, developers can still avoid the RJOIN by increasing the number of rows in the dimension with dummy rows. In a medium or large model, this is no longer an option.

Understanding VertiCalc and callbacks

When describing the formula engine earlier, we introduced the capability of the storage engine to perform callbacks. Callbacks are required whenever the VertiPaq engine needs to compute an expression that exceeds its capabilities. For example, a simple IF statement requires a callback.

Whenever VertiPaq executes a query involving callbacks, we say it executes a VertiCalc calculation. VertiCalc is a name that is not used often. We usually talk about callbacks because ultimately, a callback is always present when a VertiCalc scan is executed. Besides, in the xmSQL code the term Callback is easily identified.

There are multiple types of callbacks. We list them here in order of importance and frequency:

- **CallbackDataID**: This is the most common type of callback. VertiPaq calls back the formula engine by passing a DAX expression that is computed by the formula engine itself. VertiPaq passes to the formula embedded in the callback, the data ids of the column values fetched during the scan.

- **EncodeCallback**: This callback is used to compute the internal id of query-scoped calculated columns. It is used whenever the query requires grouping by a column that is added inside the query itself. In that case, EncodeCallback computes the id of the expression, providing to VertiPaq the option of grouping by the column.

- **LogAbsValueCallback**: This callback is used to execute the PRODUCT/PRODUCTX function by using the algorithm *SUM(LOG(ABS(<expression>)))* implemented more efficiently by the formula engine with a specific callback.

- **RoundValueCallback**: This callback executes data type conversions that the storage engine cannot perform. For example, the cast from a decimal to a currency using the CURRENCY function in DAX requires this type of callback.

- **MinMaxColumnPositionCallback**: Transforms a column value into its position in the list of all values of the column properly sorted. The transformation uses the attribute hierarchy. If the attribute hierarchy is disabled (Available in MDX=False), then this callback cannot be used, and the column must be materialized to the formula engine to find min/max values.

- **Cond**: Evaluates the conditional logic to handle scenarios where query-defined calculated columns check the presence of the blank row in case of invalid relationships.

The presence of callbacks in DAX code is inevitable – to some extent. There will be DAX expressions that can be computed only with callbacks. Nonetheless, a developer can remove callbacks with a careful analysis of the formulas in many scenarios. If this is an option, it is always worth investigating.

Finally, datacaches created using VertiCalc are not cached, as we will learn later. Before learning about the cache, let us briefly analyze the most common callbacks.

Understanding CallbackDataID

CallbackDataID is the most common type of callback available in VertiCalc. Let us examine a simple, educational formula that requires a callback:

```
EVALUATE
SUMMARIZECOLUMNS (
    'Product'[Brand],
    "Discount if greater than 3",
        SUMX (
            Sales,
            IF (
                Sales[Quantity] > 3,
                Sales[Quantity] * Sales[Net Price] * 0.8,
                Sales[Quantity] * Sales[Net Price]
            )
        )
)
```

This query discounts any sales where the quantity is greater than or equal to three. It is not a simple aggregation because it performs conditional logic during the iteration. VertiPaq does not offer conditional logic. Therefore, during the scan, VertiPaq calls back the formula engine to compute the expression to aggregate. Here is the xmSQL query executed:

```
WITH
    $Expr0 := [CallbackDataID ( IF (
                Sales[Quantity] > 3,
                Sales[Quantity] * Sales[Net Price] * 0.8,
                Sales[Quantity] * Sales[Net Price] ) ) ]
            ( PFDATAID ( 'Sales'[Quantity] ) , PFDATAID ( 'Sales'[Net Price] ) )
SELECT
    'Product'[Brand],
    SUM ( @$Expr0 )
FROM 'Sales'
    LEFT OUTER JOIN 'Product'
        ON 'Sales'[ProductKey]='Product'[ProductKey];
```

As you see, the entire IF expression is embedded in a CallbackDataID function. During the *Sales* scan, VertiPaq invokes the formula engine, asking it to compute the expression and passing the entries in the dictionary of currently-iterated values for both *Quantity* and *Net Price*. The formula engine sends back the result, which VertiPaq considers as the value to aggregate for the iterated row.

This collaboration between the formula engine and VertiPaq is of paramount importance. Because of the possibility of performing callbacks, VertiPaq can be kept fast and straightforward. VertiPaq can rely on the formula engine to compute more complex expressions if more calculation power is needed.

Callbacks do not come for free. There is a price to pay in terms of performance which is worth understanding better.

First, we repeated multiple times that the formula engine is single-threaded. Is a callback also turning the VertiPaq engine work into a single-thread operation? No. A private instance of the formula engine serves each storage engine thread. Therefore, if 20 threads are detached to compute an aggregation, each will have access to its private formula engine. Therefore, parallelism is not affected by callbacks.

There is communication occurring between VertiPaq and the formula engine for every row scanned. This communication comes at a relatively high cost. Let us analyze the performance of the scan.

Total	SE CPU		Line	Subclass	Duration	CPU	Par.	Rows	KB	Timeline	Query
3,670 ms	71,188 ms		2	Scan	3,667	71,188	x19.4	14	1		WITH $
	x19.4										

FE	SE
3 ms	3,667 ms
0.1%	99.9%

SE Queries	SE Cache
1	0
	0.0%

```
SET DC_KIND="AUTO";
WITH
    $Expr0 := [CallbackDataID ( IF (
            Sales[Quantity] > 3,
            Sales[Quantity] * Sales[Net Price] * 0.8,
            Sales[Quantity] * Sales[Net Price]
    ) ) ] ( PFDATAID ( 'Sales'[Quantity] ) , PFDATAID ( 'Sales'[Net Price] ) )
SELECT
```

The total storage engine CPU accounts for 71,188 milliseconds. Because of the level of parallelism, the engine solves the entire query in less than four seconds. But the CPU price for this query seems excessive. To compare, let us check the time required to compute a similar expression without the IF. The formula returns a different number, but we use its performance as a baseline:

```
EVALUATE
SUMMARIZECOLUMNS (
    'Product'[Brand],
    "Test",
        SUMX (
            Sales,
            Sales[Quantity] * Sales[Net Price]
        )
)
```

The query requires only 7,219 milliseconds of CPU: much faster than the previous version, but we removed the conditional logic.

Total	SE CPU	Line	Subclass	Duration	CPU	Par.	Rows	KB	Timeline	Query
394 ms	7,219 ms x18.5	2	Scan	390	7,219	x18.5	14	1		WITH $I

FE	SE
4 ms	390 ms
1.0%	99.0%

SE Queries	SE Cache
1	0
	0.0%

```
SET DC_KIND="AUTO";
WITH
    $Expr0 := ( PFCAST ( 'Sales'[Quantity] AS INT ) * PFCAST ( 'Sales'[Net Price] AS INT ) )
SELECT
    'Product'[Brand],
    SUM ( @$Expr0 )
FROM 'Sales'
    LEFT OUTER JOIN 'Product'
        ON 'Sales'[ProductKey]='Product'[ProductKey];
```

Executing the calculation in VertiCalc mode involves yet another cost. It is worth noting that the difference in performance is enormous: 7,219 milliseconds for a purely VertiPaq query against 71,188 milliseconds when the callback is involved. Sometimes, there are no ways to avoid callbacks. There are several scenarios, like this one, where simple modifications to the DAX code cannot prevent a callback.

In this scenario, given the fact that scanning the table is more than six times faster than using VertiCalc, one option is to unroll the IF statement this way:

```
EVALUATE
SUMMARIZECOLUMNS (
    'Product'[Brand],
    "Discount if greater than 3",
        CALCULATE (
            SUMX (
                Sales,
                Sales[Quantity] * Sales[Net Price]
            ),
            Sales[Quantity] <= 3
        ) +
        CALCULATE (
            SUMX (
                Sales,
                Sales[Quantity] * Sales[Net Price]
            ),
            Sales[Quantity] > 3
        ) * 0.8
)
```

Both CALCULATE functions can be computed directly by VertiPaq, because they only involve multiplication and a simple condition. Therefore, the execution requires two scans of *Sales* and because of the filter, each scan is faster than a full scan.

Total	SE CPU	Line	Subclass	Duration	CPU	Par.	Rows	KB	Timeline	Query
443 ms	7,391 ms									
	x17.2	2	Scan	154	2,703	x17.6	14	1		WITH $E>
		4	Scan	276	4,688	x17.0	14	1		WITH $E>

FE	SE
13 ms	430 ms
2.9%	97.1%

SE Queries	SE Cache
2	0
	0.0%

```
SET DC_KIND="AUTO";
WITH
    $Expr0 := ( PFCAST ( 'Sales'[Quantity] AS INT ) * PFCAST ( 'Sales'[Net Price] AS INT ) )
SELECT
    'Product'[Brand],
    SUM ( @$Expr0 )
```

The storage engine time is just 7,391 milliseconds, much shorter than the original code and slightly more expensive than our baseline. We can make it even better than this. By leveraging the property of Boolean expressions, where TRUE is treated as 1 and FALSE is treated as 0, we can author the same code this way:

```
EVALUATE
SUMMARIZECOLUMNS (
    'Product'[Brand],
    "Discount if greater than 3",
        SUMX (
            Sales,
            Sales[Quantity] * Sales[Net Price]
                * ( 0.8 + 0.2 * ( Sales[Quantity] <= 3 ) )
        )
)
```

Unfortunately, despite looking promising, this code version still requires a callback – a RoundValueCallback that we will analyze later. This time, the reason is not the code complexity but rather, the data types of the operands. The values 0.8 and 0.2 are floating point values, and the multiplication of Currency (the data type of *Net Price*) by a floating point requires a callback. Here is the xmSQL code executed:

```
WITH
    $Expr0 := RoundValueCallback ( (
        ( ( CAST ( ( PFCAST ( 'Sales'[Quantity] AS INT ) * PFCAST ( 'Sales'[Net Price] AS INT ) ) AS REAL ) / 10000.000000 )
            * ( 0.800000 + ( 0.200000 * CAST ( ( PFCASTCOALESCE ( 'Sales'[Quantity] AS INT ) <= COALESCE ( 3 ) ) AS REAL )
    ) )
        )
        * 10000.000000
    ) )
SELECT
    'Product'[Brand],
    SUM ( @$Expr0 )
FROM 'Sales'
    LEFT OUTER JOIN 'Product'
        ON 'Sales'[ProductKey]='Product'[ProductKey];
```

And the execution time is bad. Not as bad as the original IF, but still worse than the version with two scans.

Total	SE CPU		Line	Subclass	Duration	CPU	Par.	Rows	KB	Timeline	Query
1,090 ms	20,141 ms		2	Scan	1,084	20,141	x18.6	14	1		WITH $Expr
	x18.6										

FE	SE
6 ms	1,084 ms
0.6%	99.4%

SE Queries	SE Cache
1	0
	0.0%

```
SET DC_KIND="AUTO";
WITH
    $Expr0 := RoundValueCallback ( ( ( ( CAST ( ( PFCAST ( 'Sales'[Quantity] AS INT ) * PFCAST ( 'Sales
    10000.000000 ) * ( 0.800000 + ( 0.200000 * CAST ( ( PFCASTCOALESCE ( 'Sales'[Quantity] AS INT ) <=
    10000.000000 ) )
SELECT
    'Product'[Brand]
```

Luckily, there is a simple solution: instead of using decimal values like 0.8 and 0.2, we can use integer values (8 and 2) and divide the result by 10:

```
EVALUATE
SUMMARIZECOLUMNS (
    'Product'[Brand],
    "Discount if greater than 3",
        CALCULATE (
            SUMX (
                Sales,
                Sales[Quantity] * Sales[Net Price] * ( 8 + 2 * ( Sales[Quantity] < 3 ) )
            ) / 10
        )
)
```

This simple modification removes the need for the callback and produces the result with a single scan: it is not as fast as the solution with two scans, but the result between the two options could be different depending on data distribution and filter complexity.

Total	SE CPU		Line	Subclass	Duration	CPU	Par.	Rows	KB	Timeline	Query
458 ms	7,906 ms										
	x17.5		2	Scan	453	7,906	x17.5	14	1		WITH $Ex

FE	SE
5 ms	453 ms
1.1%	98.9%

SE Queries	SE Cache
1	0
	0.0%

```
SET DC_KIND="AUTO";
WITH
    $Expr0 := ( ( PFCAST ( 'Sales'[Quantity] AS INT ) * PFCAST ( 'Sales'[Net Price] AS INT ) ) * ( 8 + ( 2
    INT ) <= COALESCE ( 3 ) ) ) ) )
SELECT
    'Product'[Brand],
```

Understanding EncodeCallback

EncodeCallback is a different type of callback, required when the storage engine needs to compute the data id (that is, the entry in the dictionary) of columns added to the model inside the query. Oftentimes, EncodeCallback is present with composite models when users create calculated columns in the local model. These columns are created in the query scope; therefore, they do not have a data id in the model.

Let us consider the following query:

```
DEFINE
    COLUMN 'Product'[Price Tag] =
        IF (
            'Product'[Unit Price] >= 500,
            "Expensive",
            "Cheap"
        )

EVALUATE
SUMMARIZECOLUMNS (
    'Product'[Price Tag],
    "Amt", [Sales Amount]
)
```

The result is the sales amount grouped by the *Price Tag* calculated column created in the query.

Price Tag	Amt
Cheap	112,921,987,977.11
Expensive	116,147,659,700.89

Product[Price Tag] is not a column in the model. Nonetheless, SUMMARIZECOLUMNS groups by that column. Moreover, the expression of the column can be rather complex. In our scenario, it is a simple IF, but it might contain any DAX expression.

The calculation as it is cannot be pushed down to VertiPaq. Indeed, VertiPaq does not know about the very existence of the *Price Tag* column. Therefore, the formula engine creates the VertiPaq query using an EncodeCallback. The formula engine executes the EncodeCallback and returns the data id of the result computed by the expression passed as an argument.

Here is the single xmSQL query needed to produce the result of the previous query:

```
WITH
    $Expr0 := ( PFCAST ( 'Sales'[Quantity] AS INT ) * PFCAST ( 'Sales'[Net Price] AS INT ) )
SELECT
    COLUMN ( ASDATAID ( [EncodeCallback (
        IF (
            'Product'[Unit Price] >= 500,
            "Expensive",
            "Cheap" ) ) ]
        ( PFDATAID ( 'Product'[Unit Price] ) ) ) ),
    SUM ( @$Expr0 )
FROM 'Sales'
    LEFT OUTER JOIN 'Product'
        ON 'Sales'[ProductKey]='Product'[ProductKey];
```

Because the expression in the calculated column depends only on *Product[Unit Price]*, VertiPaq sends to EncodeCallback the data id of the *Product[Unit Price]* column. EncodeCallback calls are needed whenever the engine requires the data id of a column that does not exist in the model. The data id is needed when a column is used as part of a grouping operation. Whenever VertiPaq requires the value of a column, but not its data id, the operation can be completed with a regular callback.

As an example, let us inspect the actions required to compute the following query:

```
DEFINE
    COLUMN 'Product' [Test] = IF ( [Sales Amount] > 100, 1, 2 )

EVALUATE
SUMMARIZECOLUMNS (
    'Product'[Brand],
    "SumResult", SUM ( 'Product'[Test] )
)
```

The query groups by *Product[Brand]*, and it computes the sum of the *Product[Test]* calculated column. VertiPaq needs the value of *Product[Test]* to aggregate the individual product values. However, the query is not grouping by *Product[Test]*; it only uses the column to aggregate its values. Therefore, there is no EncodeCallback in the two xmSQL queries.

The first produces a datacache containing the *Sales Amount* value for each product:

```
WITH
    $Expr0 := ( PFCAST ( 'Sales'[Quantity] AS INT ) * PFCAST ( 'Sales'[Net Price] AS INT ) )
SELECT
    'Product'[ProductKey],
    SUM ( @$Expr0 )
FROM 'Sales'
    LEFT OUTER JOIN 'Product'
        ON 'Sales'[ProductKey]='Product'[ProductKey];
```

The second xmSQL query uses a regular CallbackDataID to compute the IF statement, which uses the datacache generated by the first xmSQL query:

```
WITH
    $Expr0 := [CallbackDataID ( IF ( [Sales Amount] > 100, 1, 2 ) ) ] ( PFDATAID ( 'Product'[ProductKey] ) )
SELECT
    'Product'[Brand],
    SUM ( @$Expr0 )
FROM 'Product';
```

However, if we use *Product[Test]* as a group by column, the VertiPaq engine needs the data id of the values produced for the calculated column. As such, we start to notice EncodeCallbacks. Let us start by looking at the modified DAX query:

```
DEFINE
    COLUMN 'Product'[Test] = IF ( [Sales Amount] > 100, 1, 2 )

EVALUATE
SUMMARIZECOLUMNS (
    'Product'[Test],
    "SumResult", SUM ( 'Product'[Test] )
)
```

We only changed the group by column in SUMMARIZECOLUMNS. This latter DAX query generates two xmSQL queries as well. The first is identical to the previous one, whereas the second xmSQL query contains both a CallbackDataID and an EncodeCallback:

```
WITH
    $Expr0 := [CallbackDataID ( IF ( [Sales Amount] > 100, 1, 2 ) ) ] ( PFDATAID ( 'Product'[ProductKey] ) )
SELECT
    COLUMN ( ASDATAID ( [EncodeCallback ( IF ( [Sales Amount] > 100, 1, 2 ) ) ] ( PFDATAID ( 'Product'[ProductKey] ) ) ) ),
    SUM ( @$Expr0 )
FROM 'Product';
```

From a performance point of view, EncodeCallback can be quite expensive. A careful rewrite of the query might often improve performance. Let us take as an example the first query we analyzed:

```
DEFINE
    COLUMN Product[Price Tag] =
        IF (
            'Product'[Unit Price] >= 500,
            "Expensive",
            "Cheap"
        )

EVALUATE
SUMMARIZECOLUMNS (
    'Product'[Price Tag],
    "Amt", [Sales Amount]
)
```

The query is resolved with a single xmSQL query, involving an EncodeCallback while iterating over *Sales*:

```
WITH
    $Expr0 := ( PFCAST ( 'Sales'[Quantity] AS INT ) * PFCAST ( 'Sales'[Net Price] AS INT ) )
SELECT
    COLUMN ( ASDATAID ( [EncodeCallback (
        IF (
            'Product'[Unit Price] >= 500,
            "Expensive",
            "Cheap" ) ) ]
        ( PFDATAID ( 'Product'[Unit Price] ) ) ) ),
    SUM ( @$Expr0 )
FROM 'Sales'
    LEFT OUTER JOIN 'Product'
        ON 'Sales'[ProductKey]='Product'[ProductKey];
```

In our model, there are around 225 million rows in *Sales*. The EncodeCallback is executed once per row during the iteration. Therefore, the query is quite expensive.

Total	SE CPU		Line	Subclass	Duration	CPU	Par.	Rows	KB	Timeline	Query
1,403 ms	27,250 ms										
	x19.6		2	Scan	1,393	27,250	x19.6	2	1		**WITH $E**

FE	SE
10 ms	1,393 ms
0.7%	99.3%

```
SET DC_KIND="AUTO";
WITH
    $Expr0 := ( PFCAST ( 'Sales'[Quantity] AS INT ) * PFCAST ( 'Sales'[Net Price] AS INT ) )
SELECT
    COLUMN ( ASDATAID ( [EncodeCallback ( IF (
        'Product'[Unit Price] >= 500,
        "Expensive".
```

SE Queries	SE Cache
1	0
	0.0%

Despite being reported as SE CPU, we know that the callback is responsible for much of the time spent in this query. The query speed is directly dependent on the number of rows in *Sales*. An important detail is that the calculated column is defined in *Product*. But the EncodeCallback is executed while iterating *Sales*. The calculated column does not depend on values of individual rows in *Sales*: its granularity is that of *Product*. Yet, by translating the calculated column into an EncodeCallback, the algorithm is now computing the column for each row in *Sales*.

These details of how the code gets translated in xmSQL are out of the developer's control. If we want to force the granularity of the calculation at the *Product* level instead of *Sales*, we need to avoid using a query calculated column and rely on DAX instead. The following query implements the very same algorithm, but it uses the GROUPBY function to perform the grouping in the formula engine:

```
EVALUATE
GROUPBY (
    ADDCOLUMNS (
        'Product',
        "@Price Tag", IF ( 'Product'[Unit Price] >= 500, "Expensive", "Cheap" ),
        "@Sales", [Sales Amount]
    ),
    [@Price Tag],
    "@Result", SUMX ( CURRENTGROUP (), [@Sales] )
)
```

By authoring the code this way, we are asking the engine to first perform the calculation of *Sales Amount* by product in @*Sales*, while also storing in the @*Price Tag* temporary calculated column the name (Expensive or Cheap) used in GROUPBY to aggregate the @*Sales* column by @*Price Tag*.

The performance of this latter query is much better.

Total	SE CPU		Line	Subclass	Duration	CPU	Par.	Rows	KB	Timeline	Query
100 ms	1,234 ms		2	Scan	89	1,234	x13.9	2,520	40		WITH $Expr
	x13.9										
FE	SE		4	Scan	0	0		2,517	20		SELECT 'Prc
11 ms	89 ms										
11.0%	89.0%										

```
SET DC_KIND="AUTO";
WITH
$Expr0 := ( PFCAST ( 'Sales'[Quantity] AS INT ) * PFCAST ( 'Sales'[Net Price] AS INT ) )
SELECT
    'Product'[ProductKey],
```

SE Queries	SE Cache
2	0
	0.0%

There are now two different storage engine queries with no callbacks, and the query runs 14 times faster than the previous one, consuming less than 5% of storage engine time (SE CPU).

The kind of optimization to choose strongly depends on the algorithm. The important detail to remember here is that calculated columns created in the scope of a query are an incredibly powerful tool to simplify the writing of DAX code. Nonetheless, if you strive for optimal performance, relying on plain DAX provides you with more opportunities to drive the engine toward a different execution strategy.

Understanding LogAbsValueCallback

LogAbsValueCallback has the very specific purpose of computing the PRODUCTX DAX function. PRODUCTX produces the aggregated result by multiplying the values of an expression. VertiPaq cannot aggregate by multiplication; it can only aggregate by SUM. Therefore, the PRODUCTX function should be resolved using the formula engine only. However, thanks to the mathematical properties of logarithms, it is possible to implement the PRODUCTX function using a SUM. Indeed, the logarithm of two multiplied values is equal to the sum of the logarithm of each value:

$$\log(ab) = \log(a) + \log(b)$$

We can check this property with the numbers 100 and 10, whose respective logarithms in base 10 are

2 and 1.

$$\log(100 * 10) = \log(100) + \log(10)$$

Indeed, log(1000) equals 3, which is the sum of 2 and 1. This mathematical property can be used to express the multiplication of two numbers using exponentials and logarithms. By using natural logarithms, the following equation holds true:

$$ab = e^{\log(a) + \log(b)}$$

Therefore, by summing the logarithms of a series of values and using an exponential function on the result, we can compute a PRODUCTX by using SUM. There is a small issue with the sign. Indeed, if any of the values in the series is a negative number, then its logarithm is undefined. Mathematically, the logarithm of a negative number does not exist. Nonetheless, regarding multiplication, the sign of a factor does not change the absolute value of the result; it only changes the sign of the result. Therefore, Tabular can compute the multiplication by computing the sum of the absolute values' logarithms and counting the number of negative values present in the series. If we express with *countneg* the number of negative values in the series, this is the formula used by Tabular:

$$ab = (e^{\log(|a|) + \log(|b|)}) * (-1^{countneg(a,b)})$$

In order to compute this equation, Tabular knows how to count negative values, but it still does not know how to compute the logarithm of an absolute value. Hence, LogAbsValueCallback is a callback that specifically computes the logarithm of the absolute value of an expression.

Using a LogAbsValueCallback, VertiPaq can aggregate large series of values without materializing large datacaches.

The database we use for demos does not contain numbers that are useful to aggregate with PRODUCTX, so we use a specific query to demonstrate just the callback:

```
EVALUATE
SUMMARIZECOLUMNS (
    CurrencyExchange[FromCurrency],
    CurrencyExchange[ToCurrency],
    "Result", PRODUCTX ( CurrencyExchange, CurrencyExchange[Exchange] )
)
```

Instead of materializing the values of the *CurrencyExchange[Exchange]* column – producing a datacache that would be virtually the same size as the entire table – VertiPaq can use the callback to reduce the materialization to only the existing combinations of the two currencies:

```
WITH
    $Expr0 := PFCAST ( 'CurrencyExchange'[Exchange] AS REAL )
SELECT
    'CurrencyExchange'[FromCurrency],
    'CurrencyExchange'[ToCurrency],
    SUM ( LogAbsValueCallback ( @$Expr0 ) ),
    SUM ( ( @$Expr0 < 0.000000 ) )
FROM 'CurrencyExchange';
```

There are both a LogAbsValueCallback call to compute the multiplication, and the condition that the SUM aggregation of the expression should be less than zero. Depending on whether the sum is odd or even, the engine knows the sign of the multiplication. It computes the absolute expression value by using an exponential over the sum of the logarithms.

Understanding RoundValueCallback

As you are probably aware, VertiPaq can perform several datatype conversions through the PFCAST function. Yet, some datatype conversions cannot be executed by the VertiPaq engine, hence requiring a callback.

To demonstrate RoundValueCallback, we changed the datatype of *Sales[Net Price]* to a floating point number (Decimal in DAX). The following query results in a single VertiPaq query because it is performing a multiplication between a floating point (*Net Price*) and an integer (*Quantity*), which is fully supported in VertiPaq:

```
EVALUATE
{
    SUMX (
        Sales,
        Sales[Quantity] * Sales[Net Price]
    )
}
```

Here is the xmSQL query executed, without any surprises:

```
WITH
    $Expr0 := ( CAST ( PFCAST ( 'Sales'[Quantity] AS INT ) AS REAL ) * PFCAST ( 'Sales'[Net Price] AS REAL ) )
SELECT
    SUM ( @$Expr0 )
FROM 'Sales';
```

The engine converted *Sales[Quantity]* to a floating point in the previous query. VertiPaq does not support the opposite conversion. Converting a floating point to an integer value requires a callback. Let us look at the following query:

```
EVALUATE
{
    SUMX (
        Sales,
        Sales[Quantity] * INT ( Sales[Net Price] )
    )
}
```

Sales[Net Price] is a floating point, and we are casting it explicitly to an integer. Because VertiPaq cannot perform the conversion, the xmSQL query includes a CallbackDataID call:

```
WITH
    $Expr0 := ( PFCAST ( 'Sales'[Quantity] AS INT )
        * [CallbackDataID ( INT ( Sales[Net Price] ) ) ]
            ( PFDATAID ( 'Sales'[Net Price] ) ) )
SELECT
    SUM ( @$Expr0 )
FROM 'Sales';
```

CallbackDataID is an expensive operation. It requires sending the data id of the columns to the formula engine. If the expression to cast is more complex than a single column, then the formula engine must compute the expression. For example, the following expression cast to integer the result of *Sales[Net Price]* minus *Sales[Unit Price]* to be cast:

```
EVALUATE
{
    SUMX (
        Sales,
        Sales[Quantity] * INT ( Sales[Unit Price] - Sales[Net Price] )
    )
}
```

Here is the corresponding xmSQL query, which includes both *Sales[Net Price]* and *Sales[Unit Price]*:

```
WITH
    $Expr0 := ( PFCAST ( 'Sales'[Quantity] AS INT )
        * [CallbackDataID ( INT ( Sales[Unit Price] - Sales[Net Price] ) ) ]
            ( PFDATAID ( 'Sales'[Unit Price] ) , PFDATAID ( 'Sales'[Net Price] ) ) )
SELECT
    SUM ( @$Expr0 )
FROM 'Sales';
```

The subtraction that could be executed by VertiPaq is instead executed inside the formula engine because of the callback. To avoid the expensive CallbackDataID and the handling of multiple parameters, in some scenarios, Tabular uses a RoundValueCallback call that performs some (but not all) of the conversions without requiring the individual arguments. At the time of writing, RoundValueCallback is used only for the CONVERT DAX function.

For example, the following query converts the currency *Sales[Unit Price]* into an integer by using RoundValueCallback instead of a regular CallbackDataID, which would be slower:

```
EVALUATE
{
    SUMX (
        Sales,
        Sales[Quantity] * CONVERT ( Sales[Unit Price], INTEGER )
    )
}
```

The xmSQL code executed is the following:

```
WITH
    $Expr0 := ( PFCAST ( 'Sales'[Quantity] AS INT )
        * RoundValueCallback ( ( CAST ( PFCAST ( 'Sales'[Unit Price] AS INT ) AS REAL ) / 10000.000000 ) ) )
SELECT
    SUM ( @$Expr0 )
FROM 'Sales';
```

RoundValueCallback is more optimized than a regular CallbackDataID; whenever possible, you should favor CONVERT over INT in your code, thus reducing the number of CallbackDataID calls. We can measure the difference by running a simple query with INT and CONVERT:

```
EVALUATE
{
    SUMX (
        Sales,
        Sales[Quantity] * INT ( Sales[Unit Price] )
    )
}
```

By using INT, the xmSQL code is using a regular CallbackDataID.

Total	SE CPU		Line	Subclass	Duration	CPU	Par.	Rows	KB	Timeline	Query
707 ms	13,484 ms		2	Scan	700	13,484	x19.3	1	1		WITH $
	x19.3										

FE	SE
7 ms	700 ms
1.0%	99.0%

```
SET DC_KIND="AUTO";
WITH
    $Expr0 := ( PFCAST ( 'Sales'[Quantity] AS INT ) * [CallbackDataID ( INT ( Sales[Unit Price] ) ) ]
SELECT
    SUM ( @$Expr0 )
FROM 'Sales';
```

SE Queries	SE Cache
1	0
	0.0%

The query ran using 13,484 milliseconds of storage engine CPU. The same query with CONVERT instead of INT uses a RoundValueCallback:

```
EVALUATE
{
    SUMX (
        Sales,
        Sales[Quantity] * CONVERT ( Sales[Unit Price], INTEGER )
    )
}
```

As you see from the server timings, the execution is almost five times faster.

Total	SE CPU		Line	Subclass	Duration	CPU	Par.	Rows	KB	Timeline	Query
149 ms	2,266 ms		2	Scan	143	2,266	x15.8	1	1		WITH $I
	x15.8										

FE	SE
6 ms	143 ms
4.0%	96.0%

```
SET DC_KIND="AUTO";
WITH
    $Expr0 := ( PFCAST ( 'Sales'[Quantity] AS INT ) * RoundValueCallback ( ( CAST ( PFCAST ( 'Sal
SELECT
    SUM ( @$Expr0 )
FROM 'Sales';
```

SE Queries	SE Cache
1	0
	0.0%

Unfortunately, it is difficult to determine exactly the scenarios in which a RoundValueCallback will be used instead of a regular Callback. We suggest checking when a callback is executed for the sole purpose of performing a datatype conversion. In that case, try to use CONVERT to force the Tabular engine to use a RoundValueCallback instead of a CallbackDataId.

Understanding MinMaxColumnPositionCallback

The only columns that Vertipaq can sort are numeric columns. Indeed, the sort order of numbers is well defined, whereas when it comes to strings, deciding whether a string needs to be sorted before or after another string is a very complex operation. Tabular supports a multitude of different alphabets, and the sort order of a string depends on the locale of the instance. Besides, the entire VertiPaq engine is designed to work strictly with numbers, treating strings as second-class citizens.

Consequently, finding the MIN or the MAX of numbers is a simple operation directly supported by VertiPaq, whereas searching for MIN or MAX of a series of strings requires the intervention of the formula engine.

Let us elaborate on the topic with a simple example. We start by searching for the minimum of a numeric column, knowing that this will be executed entirely in VertiPaq:

```
EVALUATE
{
    CALCULATE (
        MIN ( Sales[Quantity] ),
        'Product'[Brand] = "Contoso"
    )
}
```

The query is resolved with a simple xmSQL query that computes the result:

```
SELECT
    MIN ( 'Sales'[Quantity] )
FROM 'Sales'
    LEFT OUTER JOIN 'Product'
        ON 'Sales'[ProductKey]='Product'[ProductKey]
WHERE
    'Product'[Brand] = 'Contoso';
```

However, if we replace *Sales[Quantity]* with a string like *Sales[Currency Code]* in the same query, the execution is very different. In the following code, we search for the minimum of *Sales[Currency Code]*, which is a string:

```
EVALUATE
{
    CALCULATE (
        MIN ( Sales[Currency Code] ),
        'Product'[Brand] = "Contoso"
    )
}
```

Because VertiPaq does not know how to search for the minimum currency code, the only viable option is to scan the VertiPaq database to retrieve the list of all product names, then send this list to the formula engine and let it find the minimum value. Indeed, this is what we observe by looking at the xmSQL query:

```
SELECT
    'Sales'[Currency Code]
FROM 'Sales'
    LEFT OUTER JOIN 'Product'
        ON 'Sales'[ProductKey]='Product'[ProductKey]
WHERE
    'Product'[Brand] = 'Contoso';
```

As you see, VertiPaq is not searching for the minimum value because this would be out of the scope of its capabilities. Instead, it materializes the values of the currency codes in a datacache. This larger materialization can easily become excessive for a large column, thus slowing down the query.

In that scenario, Tabular can take advantage of a MinMaxColumnPositionCallback, which is a callback computed inside the formula engine, to return the position of one value in the sorted list of values of that column. For MinMaxColumnPositionCallback to perform efficiently, the VertiPaq storage must contain a data structure where the values of a column are already sorted. This way, finding the position of a data id in the list of all data ids becomes a quick operation.

It turns out that such a data structure does exist, and it is the attribute hierarchy. If a column in the VertiPaq storage has the attribute hierarchy enabled (that is, AvailableInMDX is set to True), then VertiPaq can take advantage of MinMaxColumnPositionCallback to retrieve the position of a column. In our model, we do not have AvailableInMDX set for *Sales[Currency Code]*, but we have it set for *Product[Product Name]*. Therefore, the following query is going to use a MinMaxColumnPositionCallback to compute its result:

```
EVALUATE
{
    CALCULATE (
        MIN ( 'Product'[Product Name] ),
        'Product'[Brand] = "Contoso"
    )
}
```

The xmSQL code of this query is very different from the previous queries':

```
SELECT
    MIN ( MinMaxColumnPositionCallback ( PFDATAID ( 'Product'[Product Name] ) ) )
FROM 'Product'
WHERE
    'Product'[Brand] = 'Contoso';
```

Using MinMaxColumnPositionCallback, VertiPaq can treat the strings in *Product[Product Name]* as regular numbers. And VertiPaq knows how to search for the minimum in a series of numbers.

This latter query materializes a tiny datacache, no matter how many distinct values the *Product[Product Name]* column contains. There is no need to create a large datacache because the query's result is just a number.

The presence of MinMaxColumnPositionCallback means that string columns used to search for minimum or maximum values can benefit from the attribute hierarchy. A developer should evaluate the time required to create the attribute hierarchy at process time and decide whether the benefit obtained by the capability of using a MinMaxColumnPositionCallback is worth the price.

Understanding Cond

Cond is a callback that receives three arguments, much like the IF function in DAX. Its primary use is in models with invalid relationships, where the blank row is added to a table by the VertiPaq engine to accommodate an invalid relationship.

If the column defined in the query happens to have a value even for the blank row, then Tabular needs to handle the blank row in a particular way. Its presence is extremely common with query-scoped calculated columns, even though understanding why Cond is needed requires for us to go a little deeper.

In our demo model, all the relationships are complete, meaning that each foreign key on the many-side references values present in the table on the one-side of the relationship. In other words, all *Sales[ProductKey]* values also exist in *Product[ProductKey]*. We first need to remove some of the products to show a demo where we deal with invalid relationships. Therefore, we changed the query of the *Product* table to filter out all the red products. As such, the relationship between *Sales* and *Product* becomes invalid, and Tabular creates the blank row in the *Product* table.

In that scenario, a developer can run a query like the following:

```
DEFINE
    COLUMN 'Product'[Margin %] =
        ( 'Product'[Unit Price] - 'Product'[Unit Cost] ) / 'Product'[Unit Price]

EVALUATE
SUMMARIZECOLUMNS (
    'Product'[Brand],
    "Avg Margin %", AVERAGEX ( Sales, RELATED ( 'Product'[Margin %] ) )
)
```

AVERAGEX iterates over *Sales*, and computes for each row the *Margin %* query calculated column. *Margin %* is a column created inside the query; it does not exist in the model. It is computed at query time as part of the evaluation of the query itself. The *Margin %* column has a value for each *Product* row, including the blank row.

The value of *Margin %* for the blank row is blank. Indeed, the blank row is expected to contain BLANK in each column, including the columns created in the query.

The expression used for *Margin %* satisfies this condition. If the three columns used in the expression are blank, so is the *Margin %* column. Therefore, there is no need to handle the blank row in a special way. As we see, the xmSQL query executed to answer the previous DAX query does not contain any Cond callback:

```
WITH
    $Expr0 := (
        (
            CAST (
                ( PFCAST ( 'Product'[Unit Price] AS INT ) - PFCAST ( 'Product'[Unit Cost] AS INT ) ) AS REAL
            ) / 10000.000000
        ) / (
            CAST ( PFCAST ( 'Product'[Unit Price] AS INT ) AS REAL )
            / 10000.000000
        )
    )
SELECT
    'Product'[Brand],
    SUM ( @$Expr0 ),
    COUNT ( )
FROM 'Sales'
    LEFT OUTER JOIN 'Product'
        ON 'Sales'[ProductKey]='Product'[ProductKey]
WHERE
    NOT @$Expr0 IS NULL;
```

A special behavior is required if we change the definition of our margin in a way that *Margin %* happens to have a value even in case all the columns in the row are blank. Look at the following query, where we modified the definition of *Margin %* by subtracting it from the constant value of 1:

```
DEFINE
    COLUMN 'Product'[Margin %] =
        1 - ( 'Product'[Unit Price] - 'Product'[Unit Cost] ) / 'Product'[Unit Price]

EVALUATE
SUMMARIZECOLUMNS (
    'Product'[Brand],
    "Avg Margin %", AVERAGEX ( Sales, RELATED ( 'Product'[Margin %] ) )
)
```

This simple modification means that when all the columns in *Product* are blank, *Margin %* evaluates to 1. Indeed, 1 - BLANK equals 1 in DAX. As such, *Margin %* would return a value for the blank row, violating the rules of the blank row.

To avoid this behavior, Tabular adds Cond callbacks to check the result in the special case of the blank row:

```
WITH
    $Expr0 := CAST ( 1 AS REAL ) - (
        (
            CAST (
                ( PFCAST ( 'Product'[Unit Price] AS INT ) - PFCAST ( 'Product'[Unit Cost] AS INT ) ) AS REAL
            ) / 10000.000000
        ) / (
            CAST ( PFCAST ( 'Product'[Unit Price] AS INT ) AS REAL )
            / 10000.000000
        )
    ) )
SELECT
    'Product'[Brand],
    SUM (
        Cond (
            ( PFDATAID ( 'Product'[ProductKey] ) ) = 2 ),
            -1.79769313486231571E+308,
            @$Expr0
        )
    ),
    COUNT ( )
FROM 'Sales'
    LEFT OUTER JOIN 'Product'
        ON 'Sales'[ProductKey]='Product'[ProductKey]
WHERE
    NOT Cond (
        ( PFDATAID ( 'Product'[ProductKey] ) ) = 2 ),
        -1.79769313486231571E+308,
        @$Expr0
    ) IS NULL;
```

The engine adds Cond to guarantee proper semantics for the special case of the blank row, which is identified by the data id with a value of 2.

Understanding the VertiPaq cache

VertiPaq has an internal cache system that is useful whenever the formula engine sends the same xmSQL query multiple times. It is a straightforward cache mechanism: once a query is executed, the datacache is saved. If the same query is received again, the result is returned from the cache instead of executing the query a second time.

The number of entries in the VertiPaq cache is very limited. By default, the number of entries is limited to 512 per database. The maximum value can be configured, but only under the supervision of Microsoft support – it is an advanced and potentially dangerous setting. Indeed, whenever a query is about to be executed, VertiPaq needs to scan the VertiPaq cache to check if its result is already in cache. The time required to check the presence of the result depends on the size of the cache. Increasing the limit means increasing the time required to check the presence of each query being executed. Therefore, the number of entries needs to be carefully balanced, to not harm the entire system by using a value that is too large.

An important detail to consider when reasoning about the VertiPaq cache system is that VertiCalc queries are not cached. Only pure VertiPaq queries are cached. If the result of a query involves VertiCalc, then its result is not cached. The absence of a cache is one of the most relevant reasons why a query plan including one or more callbacks requires your attention: the execution time of the VertiCalc queries needs to be accounted for at every execution, thus canceling out the advantage of the VertiPaq cache system.

The queries that hit the cache use up an execution time of zero milliseconds. The time required to search for the existence of an element in the cache is not reported – neither for queries that hit the cache, nor for the cache misses. Moreover, when there is a cache hit, the internal query is replaced with the cache hit. Cache hits, like internal queries, are hidden by default in DAX Studio and need to be enabled through the Cache button.

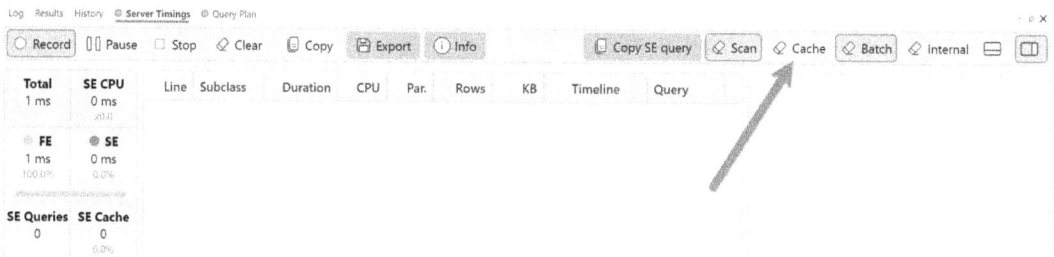

Let us see a very simple example where the cache saves a large amount of storage engine CPU. In the following query, we are performing the UNION of two identical ADDCOLUMNS results:

```
EVALUATE
UNION (
    ADDCOLUMNS (
        VALUES ( Product[Brand] ),
        "Dc1", CALCULATE ( DISTINCTCOUNT ( Sales[StoreKey] ) )
    ),
    ADDCOLUMNS (
        VALUES ( Product[Brand] ),
        "Dc2", CALCULATE ( DISTINCTCOUNT ( Sales[StoreKey] ) )
    )
)
```

For this specific query, it is interesting to activate both Internal and Cache events. Here is the list of events triggered.

Line	Subclass	Duration	CPU	Par.	Rows	KB	Timeline	Query
1	Internal	41	156	x3.8				SELECT 'Product'[Brand], 'Sales'[Sto
2	Internal	41	156	x3.8				SELECT 'Product'[Brand], 'Sales'[Sto
3	Internal	2	0					SELECT 'Product'[Brand], COUNT ()
4	Scan	43	156	x3.6	12	1		SELECT 'Product'[Brand], DCOUNT
5	Internal	0	0					SELECT 'Product'[Brand], COUNT ()
6	Scan	3	0		14	1		SELECT 'Product'[Brand] FROM 'Prc
7	Cache							SELECT 'Product'[Brand], DCOUNT
8	Scan	0	0		12	1		SELECT 'Product'[Brand], DCOUNT

There are three Scan events (lines 4, 6, and 8), four Internal events (lines 1, 2, 3, and 5), and one Cache event (line 7). The scan at line 4 computes the distinct count of stores by brand:

```
SELECT
    'Product'[Brand],
    DCOUNT ( 'Sales'[StoreKey] )
FROM 'Sales'
    LEFT OUTER JOIN 'Product'
        ON 'Sales'[ProductKey]='Product'[ProductKey];
```

As we saw earlier, the three Internal scans before line 4 are the actual implementation of the distinct count. The scan at line 6 retrieves the values of the *Product[Brand]* column, required by ADDCOLUMNS:

```
SELECT
    'Product'[Brand]
FROM 'Product';
```

The third scan, at line 8, is identical to the scan at line 4. Therefore, instead of the three internal queries, VertiPaq retrieves the result from the cache and fires a Cache event.

It is interesting to note that there are multiple optimizations happening in this simple query: not only did the cache avoid the computation of an expensive distinct count (which accounts for more than five seconds of storage engine CPU), but the formula engine also performed its own optimization. It detected that one of the two ADDCOLUMNS required the values of *Product[Brand]*, and it reused the same datacache, thus avoiding a double execution of a query identical to line 4.

As with Internal events, Cache events are disabled by default in DAX Studio. The reason is that their presence makes it harder to understand the overall execution path. Moreover, when a complex query shows zero milliseconds of execution time, it is likely a cache hit.

Choosing the correct data type for VertiPaq calculations

Despite VertiPaq being able to perform the four basic mathematical operations, some datatype combinations require the intervention of a CallbackdataId. Consequently, mixing certain datatypes comes with a performance impact derived from two aspects: first, VertiCalc is slower than a pure VertiPaq calculation; second, the datacache generated by a VertiPaq query involving a callback does not benefit from the VertiPaq cache.

Here is the conversion matrix of different operators, as defined in DAX.

Addition	Integer	Decimal	Currency
Integer	Integer	Decimal	Currency
Decimal	Decimal	Decimal	Decimal
Currency	Currency	Decimal	Currency

Subtraction	Integer	Decimal	Currency
Integer	Integer	Decimal	Currency
Decimal	Decimal	Decimal	Decimal
Currency	Currency	Decimal	Currency

Product	Integer	Decimal	Currency
Integer	Integer	Decimal	Currency
Decimal	Decimal	Decimal	Currency
Currency	Currency	Currency	Decimal

Division	Integer	Decimal	Currency
Integer	Decimal	Decimal	Decimal
Decimal	Decimal	Decimal	Decimal
Currency	Currency	Currency	Decimal

Whenever it deals with operations with different datatypes, VertiPaq performs a datatype conversion. For example, the following operation mixes two Currency datatypes:

```
EVALUATE
{
    SUMX (
        Sales,
        Sales[Net Price]           -- Currency
            + Sales[Unit Price]    -- Currency
    )
}
```

It is worth remembering that currencies are stored as integers. Because they have only four digits of precisions, a currency is stored as an integer by multiplying its value by 10,000. The xmSQL code shows the data type of the operator through an explicit PFCAST:

```
WITH
    $Expr0 := ( PFCAST ( 'Sales'[Net Price] AS INT )
        + PFCAST ( 'Sales'[Unit Price] AS INT ) )
SELECT
    SUM ( @$Expr0 )
FROM 'Sales';
```

Both operands of the + operator are cast to an integer. Therefore, VertiPaq uses integer maths. If one of the operators is Decimal, then both operands are cast to Decimal before being used with the + operator, as you can see from the following example:

```
EVALUATE
{
    SUMX (
        Sales,
        Sales[Net Price]              -- Currency
            + Sales[Exchange Rate]    -- Decimal (floating point)
    )
}
```

The xmSQL code generated for this query includes both the cast to a decimal (REAL) and the division by 10,000 to obtain the original value:

```
WITH
    $Expr0 := ( ( CAST ( PFCAST ( 'Sales'[Net Price] AS INT ) AS REAL ) / 10000.000000 )
        + PFCAST ( 'Sales'[Exchange Rate] AS REAL ) )
SELECT
    SUM ( @$Expr0 )
FROM 'Sales';
```

Most mathematical operations are executed directly inside VertiPaq, with the noticeable difference of multiplications and divisions of a Currency by a Decimal. Whenever we multiply or divide a Currency by a Decimal, VertiPaq requires using VertiCalc through either a CallbackDataId or a RoundValueCallback. Which one is used depends on several factors. For example, the following code divides a Currency by a Decimal:

```
EVALUATE
{
    SUMX (
        Sales,
        Sales[Net Price]              -- Currency
            / Sales[Exchange Rate]    -- Decimal (floating point)
    )
}
```

The xmSQL code generated includes a RoundValueCallback:

```
WITH
    $Expr0 := RoundValueCallback (
        (
            ( ( CAST ( PFCAST ( 'Sales'[Net Price] AS INT ) AS REAL ) / 10000.000000 )
            / PFCAST ( 'Sales'[Exchange Rate] AS REAL ) ) * 10000.000000
        )
    )
SELECT
    SUM ( @$Expr0 )
FROM 'Sales';
```

As stated previously, there is a high price to pay in terms of performance whenever multiplications or divisions must be performed between a Currency and a Decimal. To assess the difference in speed, we compare two calculations: one executed with a sum and another executed with a multiplication. We use the same columns so that the scan time is the same:

```
EVALUATE
{
    SUMX (
        Sales,
        Sales[Net Price]              -- Currency
            + Sales[Exchange Rate]    -- Decimal (floating point)
    )
}
```

There are no callbacks by using a simple sum, and the query uses 125 milliseconds of storage engine.

Total	SE CPU		Line	Subclass	Duration	CPU	Par.	Rows	KB	Timeline	Query
70 ms	125 ms		2	Scan	67	125	x1.9	1	1		WITH $Ex
	x1.9										

FE	SE
3 ms	67 ms
4.3%	95.7%

SE Queries	SE Cache
1	0
	0.0%

```
SET DC_KIND="AUTO";
WITH
    $Expr0 := ( ( CAST ( PFCAST ( 'Sales'[Net Price] AS INT ) AS REAL ) / 10000.000000 ) + PFCAST (
SELECT
    SUM ( @$Expr0 )
FROM 'Sales';
```

If we replace the sum with a multiplication, a callback is required:

```
EVALUATE
{
    SUMX (
        Sales,
        Sales[Net Price]              -- Currency
            * Sales[Exchange Rate]    -- Decimal (floating point)
    )
}
```

The presence of the callback makes this second query much slower.

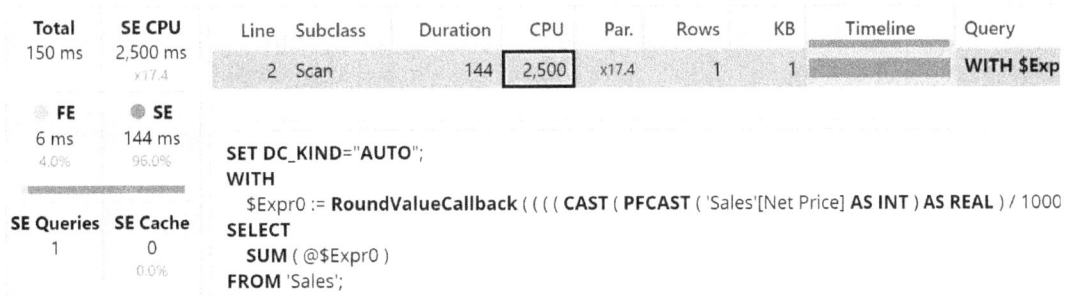

Total	SE CPU		Line	Subclass	Duration	CPU	Par.	Rows	KB	Timeline	Query
150 ms	2,500 ms										
	x17.4		2	Scan	144	2,500	x17.4	1	1		WITH $Exp

FE	SE
6 ms	144 ms
4.0%	96.0%

SE Queries	SE Cache
1	0
	0.0%

```
SET DC_KIND="AUTO";
WITH
    $Expr0 := RoundValueCallback ( ( ( ( CAST ( PFCAST ( 'Sales'[Net Price] AS INT ) AS REAL ) / 1000
SELECT
    SUM ( @$Expr0 )
FROM 'Sales';
```

The query with a callback is 20 times slower than the query without it. The difference in operator generates a minor penalty. Indeed, multiplication is around 30% times slower than addition. Nonetheless, most of the decrease in storage engine speed is due to the presence of the callback.

Moreover, because of the callback, the datacache is not cached, and any subsequent evaluation of the same query would result in more storage engine CPU being used.

On large models, if a developer foresees a lot of multiplications and divisions between Currency and Decimal datatypes, it might be helpful to convert the Currency columns to Decimal datatypes, thus pushing the calculation down to the storage engine and avoiding the callbacks altogether.

Conclusions

VertiPaq is a simple yet powerful engine that works closely with the formula engine to produce incredible performance. Despite its limited expressivity and small number of native operators, VertiPaq is designed to quickly scan a large amount of data with a great degree of parallelism.

At first sight, it might seem like VertiPaq queries are complex to read. But the language is so close to SQL that any BI professional can quickly read and understand xmSQL code.

In previous chapters, we saw several pieces of xmSQL code without going into too many details. Starting from here, and now having a better understanding of how VertiPaq works, we can perform a deeper analysis of the xmSQL code generated by DAX queries.

Optimizing common DAX constructs

In previous chapters, we showed several optimization examples. In this chapter, we provide more. This time, the focus is not on explaining a theoretical aspect of the formula engine or of VertiPaq. Instead, the focus is on the process of investigating a performance issue and then following the steps to produce better code.

> **IMPORTANT Disclaimer**: We know our readers may want to jump straight to this chapter seeking clues on how to optimize their code. Unfortunately, it is not that simple. To appreciate the content of this chapter, you need to have a solid understanding of all the previous chapters. None of the resolutions of the examples provided here are a hard and fast rule. Optimizing DAX is a complex process during which the developer makes decisions based on their specific model. **If you have jumped to this page and skipped the previous sections, we strongly advise you to go back** and proceed more slowly to acquire the knowledge required to appreciate these optimizations.

We use VertiPaq as the storage engine. Some optimizations are still valid with different storage engines, others are not. Remember that our goal – through the entire explanation process – is to show you how to optimize. Do not consider these examples as patterns because they are not. While it is true that some examples have a much broader range of applications, the extent of their relevance may vary depending on the peculiarities of your model.

Optimizing nested iterations

Most of the calculations in DAX require an iteration. When an iteration starts from inside another iteration, we say that the inner iterator is nested inside the outer iterator. An example of a nested iteration is the following:

```
EVALUATE
{
    SUMX (                          -- Outer iteration
        'Product',
        SUMX (                      -- Inner iteration
            RELATEDTABLE ( Sales ),
            Sales[Quantity] * Sales[Net Price]
        )
    )
}
```

The first SUMX starts an iteration over *Product*; inside that iteration, the second SUMX starts another iteration. The SUMX over *Sales* is nested inside the iteration over *Product*.

Despite looking simple, this query requires two iterations, as is made clear from looking at both the query plan and the storage engine queries. Here is the query plan.

Line	Records	Physical Query Plan
1		AddColumns: IterPhyOp LogOp=AddColumns IterCols(0)("[Value])
2		SingletonTable: IterPhyOp LogOp=AddColumns
3	1	SpoolLookup: LookupPhyOp LogOp=Sum_Vertipaq Currency #Records=1 #KeyCols=138 #ValueCols=1 DominantValue=BLANK
4	1	ProjectionSpool<ProjectFusion<Copy>>: SpoolPhyOp #Records=1
5		**Cache: IterPhyOp #FieldCols=0 #ValueCols=1**
6	2,517	SpoolLookup: LookupPhyOp LogOp=Sum_Vertipaq LookupCols(1)('Product'[ProductKey]) Currency #Records=2517 #Key(
7	2,517	ProjectionSpool<ProjectFusion<Copy>>: SpoolPhyOp #Records=2517
8		**Cache: IterPhyOp #FieldCols=1 #ValueCols=1**

The engine materializes 2,517 rows, which are later aggregated to produce the single result requested. 2,517 is the total number of products. Besides, you can also note that another storage engine query consumes these 2,517 rows. This pattern is the canonical shape of a query plan involving a callback. We can find confirmation by analyzing the storage engine queries, which there are two of. The first one groups the sales amount by *Product[ProductKey]*:

```
WITH
    $Expr0 := ( PFCAST ( 'Sales'[Quantity] AS INT ) * PFCAST ( 'Sales'[Net Price] AS INT ) )
SELECT
    'Product'[ProductKey],
    SUM ( @$Expr0 )
FROM 'Sales'
    LEFT OUTER JOIN 'Product'
        ON 'Sales'[ProductKey]='Product'[ProductKey];
```

This first datacache is used by the second query, which uses a callback to aggregate the temporary values computed in the first query corresponding to the outer iteration over *Product*:

```
WITH
    $Expr0 := [CallbackDataID (
        SUMX ( -- Inner iteration
            RELATEDTABLE ( Sales ),
            Sales[Quantity] * Sales[Net Price]
        )
    )] ( PFDATAID ( 'Product'[ProductKey] ) )
SELECT
    SUM ( @$Expr0 )
FROM 'Product';
```

The VertiPaq engine performed two iterations: one over *Sales* (the inner iteration) to pre-aggregate values at the granularity of the other, the iteration over *Product* (the outer iteration).

It is important to note that the inner iteration is optimized, meaning it is a pure xmSQL query involving no callbacks. VertiPaq still executes the second iteration, but this time it requires using a callback to gather values from the previous scan.

Sometimes, recognizing nested iterations is a bit trickier. For example, the code of the previous query can be authored this way:

```
EVALUATE
{
    SUMX (
        'Product',
        [Sales Amount]
    )
}
```

In this latter example, it looks like only one iteration is taking place. Nonetheless, *Sales Amount* is a measure that performs its iteration over *Sales*. Therefore, the *Sales Amount* measure starts an inner iteration nested inside the outer iteration.

Here is the code executed by expanding the *Sales Amount* measure:

```
EVALUATE
{
    SUMX (
        'Product',
        -- Expand [Sales Amount]
        CALCULATE (
            SUMX (
                Sales,
                Sales[Quantity] * Sales[Net Price]
            )
        )
        -- End of [Sales Amount]
    )
}
```

The query plan and the storage engine queries of this code version are identical to the ones analyzed earlier.

Similarly, when using grouping functions like SUMMARIZECOLUMNS, nested iterations are almost always present. For example, the following code contains a nested iteration, though – as in the previous example – it is hidden:

```
EVALUATE
SUMMARIZECOLUMNS (
    'Product'[Brand],
    "Sales Amount", [Sales Amount]
)
```

Indeed, SUMMARIZECOLUMNS groups by *Product[Brand]*, and for each brand DAX scans *Sales* to produce the sales amount. When counting the number of nested iterations of a formula, we always need to consider the expanded code of any measure to see the whole picture.

The DAX optimizer tries to avoid nested iterations as much as possible. The reason is that out of all the iterations present, only the innermost can be pushed down to the storage engine. The formula engine executes all the outer iterations. Whenever possible, the optimizer tries to reduce the number of nested iterations to push more calculations down to the storage engine.

For example, SUMMARIZECOLUMNS eliminates the double iteration by performing a grouping by *Product[Brand]* so that the final xmSQL query iterates over *Sales* and groups by *Product[Brand]* directly. Indeed, the last DAX query generates a single scan:

```
WITH
    $Expr0 := ( PFCAST ( 'Sales'[Quantity] AS INT ) * PFCAST ( 'Sales'[Net Price] AS INT ) )
SELECT
    'Product'[Brand],
    SUM ( @$Expr0 )
FROM 'Sales'
    LEFT OUTER JOIN 'Product'
        ON 'Sales'[ProductKey]='Product'[ProductKey];
```

If the optimizer determines that an iteration is intended for a grouping, it can push the iteration down to the storage engine by using a group-by-column in the xmSQL code. On the other hand, when the iteration can perform further calculations, like in the example with SUMX, the nested iteration is executed, and only the innermost iteration is pushed down to the storage engine.

When there are more than two nested iterations, the engine tries to reduce the number of iterations (that is, scans of the fact table) by creating a datacache that includes the maximum granularity – leaving it to the formula engine to perform the grouping. Let us look at an example of nested iteration with three levels and perform a full analysis of the query plans. Beware that the example is educational: it just computes the sales amount. We do not want to perform a more complex calculation because we want to focus on the DAX construct rather than on the business logic. However, we can make a few assumptions using SUMX and an additive measure that we cannot make when we use other iterators (such as AVERAGEX or MAXX) or non-additive measures. Keep that in mind before applying these considerations to other scenarios.

Here is the example we will be working on:

```
EVALUATE
{
    SUMX (
        Store,
        SUMX (
            Customer,
            [Sales Amount]
        )
    )
}
```

Two outer iterations and a third innermost iteration are hidden inside the *Sales Amount* measure. The outermost iteration is scanning *Store* (74 rows). Inside the iteration over *Store*, we start another iteration over *Customer* (almost 2M rows). We compute the *Sales Amount* measure (third iteration) for each combination of customer and store.

The query is very slow.

Total	SE CPU	Line	Subclass	Duration	CPU	Par.	Rows	KB	Timeline	Query
27,013 ms	76,313 ms x5.5	2	Scan	13,670	76,063	x5.6	20,034,751	234,783		WITH $Expr0 := (PFCAST ('
FE	SE	4	Scan	285	250	x0.9	1,868,084	14,595		SELECT 'Customer'[RowNun
13,058 ms	13,955 ms	6	Scan	0	0		1	1		**WITH $Expr0 := [Callback|**
46.3%	51.7%									

SE Queries	SE Cache
3	0
	0.0%

The large amount of time spent in the formula engine immediately comes to attention. The storage engine uses much CPU, too. Moreover, the size of the datacaches is quite large (20M for the first, almost 2M for the second), and the parallelism is too low: around 5.5 on a system with 24 cores.

Let us get more technical by inspecting the storage engine queries. When nested iterations can be grouped together, the engine tries to generate a datacache with a granularity that serves both iterators – it pushes the second of the outermost iterators back to the storage engine with a callback and executes the outermost iteration in the formula engine.

The first xmSQL retrieves the sales amount grouped by *Store[StoreKey]* and *Customer[CustomerKey]*, which are the columns iterated by the two outer iterators:

```
WITH
    $Expr0 := ( PFCAST ( 'Sales'[Quantity] AS INT ) * PFCAST ( 'Sales'[Net Price] AS INT ) )
SELECT
    'Customer'[CustomerKey],
    'Store'[StoreKey],
    SUM ( @$Expr0 )
FROM 'Sales'
    LEFT OUTER JOIN 'Customer'
        ON 'Sales'[CustomerKey]='Customer'[CustomerKey]
    LEFT OUTER JOIN 'Store'
        ON 'Sales'[StoreKey]='Store'[StoreKey];

Estimated size: rows = 20,034,751    bytes = 240,417,012
```

This query retrieves the data at the required granularity: customer and store. The datacache contains the corresponding value for *Sales Amount* for each combination of customer and store.

The second xmSQL query retrieves all the values of *Customer[CustomerKey]*. Indeed, the size of its datacache is the total number of customers:

```
SELECT
    'Customer'[RowNumber],
    'Customer'[CustomerKey]
FROM 'Customer';

Estimated size: rows = 1,868,084    bytes = 14,944,672
```

The third, most interesting query, contains a callback:

```
WITH
    $Expr0 := [CallbackDataID ( SUMX (
            Customer,
            [Sales Amount]
    ) ) ] ( PFDATAID ( 'Store'[StoreKey] ) )
SELECT
    SUM ( @$Expr0 )
FROM 'Store';

Estimated size: rows = 1    bytes = 16
```

To understand the algorithm, we need to start from this last query executed and proceed backwards. This last xmSQL query scans *Store and* executes a callback to the formula engine. Inside the callback, there is an iteration over *Customer* to compute *Sales Amount*. Therefore, the outer iteration of the algorithm is on *Store;* this iteration has been pushed down to the storage engine, which then uses a callback. The inner iteration over *Customer* is not executed by the VertiPaq engine; instead, the formula engine oversees that iteration. The formula engine iterates over the *Customer* table after it retrieves the values of

Customer[CustomerKey] with the previous query. Because the formula engine knows it needs to compute *Sales Amount* for each pair of customer and store, the first query created a datacache that contains exactly the required values: *Sales Amount* grouped by customer and store.

We can double-check the behavior by looking at the query plan.

Line	Records	Physical Query Plan
1		AddColumns: IterPhyOp LogOp=AddColumns IterCols(0)(''[Value])
2		SingletonTable: IterPhyOp LogOp=AddColumns
3	1	SpoolLookup: LookupPhyOp LogOp=Sum_Vertipaq Currency #Records=1 #KeyCols=138 #ValueCols=1 DominantValue=BLANK
4	1	ProjectionSpool<ProjectFusion<Copy>>: SpoolPhyOp #Records=1
5		**Cache: IterPhyOp #FieldCols=0 #ValueCols=1**
6	74	SpoolLookup: LookupPhyOp LogOp=SumX LookupCols(1)('Store'[StoreKey]) Currency #Records=74 #KeyCols=1 #ValueCc
7	74	AggregationSpool<Sum>: SpoolPhyOp #Records=74
8		CrossApply: IterPhyOp LogOp=Sum_Vertipaq IterCols(1, 11)('Store'[StoreKey], 'Customer'[CustomerKey])
9	1,868,084	Spool_MultiValuedHashLookup: IterPhyOp LogOp=Scan_Vertipaq LookupCols(11)('Customer'[CustomerKey]) IterC
10	1,868,084	ProjectionSpool<ProjectFusion<>>: SpoolPhyOp #Records=1868084
11		**Cache: IterPhyOp #FieldCols=2 #ValueCols=0**
12	20,034,751	Spool_Iterator<SpoolIterator>: IterPhyOp LogOp=Sum_Vertipaq IterCols(1, 11)('Store'[StoreKey], 'Customer'[Custc
13	20,034,751	ProjectionSpool<ProjectFusion<Copy>>: SpoolPhyOp #Records=20034751
14		**Cache: IterPhyOp #FieldCols=2 #ValueCols=1**

Lines 6-7 show the iteration over *Store*, whereas lines 9-10 show the iteration performed over *Customer* by the formula engine. Lines 12-13 include the materialization of *Sales Amount* grouped by customer and store.

Despite the query being slow, the analysis shows that even though the iteration was requested on the *Customer* and *Store* tables, the engine is smart enough to materialize only the table keys. Nonetheless, the important detail here is that there are three iterations: the storage engine executes the outermost iteration with a callback to run the second outermost iteration. The formula engine executes the second outermost iteration, while the VertiPaq engine executes the innermost iteration (over *Sales*) without any callback.

Because of the way we wrote the code, the outer iteration is the one on *Store*, which VertiPaq scans. During the iteration, VertiPaq invokes the formula engine through a CallbackDataID, which performs the iteration over *Customer* and grabs the results from the datacache created with the first xmSQL query.

Store is much smaller than *Customer*. There are only 74 stores, whereas there are 2M customers. Because the measure is additive and we use SUMX iterators, we can change the order of the iterators without modifying the result. Indeed, it would be better to make the storage engine perform the largest iteration and leave the small iteration to the formula engine. This goal can be accomplished by just reversing the order of the iterations:

```
EVALUATE
{
    SUMX (
        Customer,
        SUMX (
            Store,
            [Sales Amount]
        )
    )
}
```

In this latter query, the outer iteration is on *Customer* (2M rows), whereas the inner iteration is on *Store* (74 rows). The algorithm is nearly identical, although the VertiPaq engine is now scanning *Customer* instead of *Store*; consequently, the callback happens with an iteration over *Store*:

WITH
    $Expr0 := [**CallbackDataID** (SUMX (
           Store,
           [Sales Amount]
    ))](**PFDATAID** ('Customer'[CustomerKey]))
SELECT
    SUM (@$Expr0)
FROM 'Customer';

Just changing the order of the two iterations improves performance because of the massive reduction in the formula engine time.

Total	SE CPU	Line	Subclass	Duration	CPU	Par.	Rows	KB	Timeline	Query
20,110 ms	76,079 ms	2	Scan	13,600	75,766	x5.6	20,034,751	234,783		WITH $Expr0 := (PFCAST ('
	x5.5									
FE	SE	4	Scan	1	0		5,929	47		SELECT 'Store'[RowNumber]
6,192 ms	13,918 ms	6	Scan	317	313	x1.0	1	1		WITH $Expr0 := [Callback(
30.8%	69.2%									
SE Queries	SE Cache									
3	0									
	0.0%									

The time in the storage engine is nearly identical. In contrast, the time spent on the formula engine is reduced by more than 50%, which is consistent with our expectations: we reduced the number of iterations performed in the formula engine, moving the heavier calculations to VertiPaq.

It is worth noting that in this specific case, the time required for the calculation is basically the time required to materialize – and then manage – a large datacache with more than 20M rows. Reducing the number of iterations does not really help because the issue is the number of rows materialized. Indeed, the same code could be expressed by using a CROSSJOIN between *Customer* and *Store* to perform a single iteration:

```
EVALUATE
{
    SUMX (
        CROSSJOIN ( Customer, Store ),
        [Sales Amount]
    )
}
```

Despite being simpler, this code is not faster. Tabular is smart enough to recognize that it does not need to cross-join the two tables and only materializes the table keys. Nonetheless, the cross-join operation is handled in the formula engine after it retrieves the values of *Customer[CustomerKey]* and *Store[StoreKey]* with two queries:

```
SELECT
    'Store'[RowNumber],
    'Store'[StoreKey]
FROM 'Store';
```

And:

```
SELECT
    'Customer'[RowNumber],
    'Customer'[CustomerKey]
FROM 'Customer';
```

A third xmSQL query retrieves the sales amount grouped by *Customer[CustomerKey]* and *Store[StoreKey]*. Then finally the formula engine performs the cross-join, retrieves the values from the list of amounts, and performs a sum. The query speed is similar to the first one, and slower than the second we optimized by controlling the order of the nested iterators.

Total	SE CPU	Line	Subclass	Duration	CPU	Par.	Rows	KB	Timeline	Query
27,492 ms	74,719 ms x5.4	2	Scan	13,552	74,438	x5.5	20,034,751	234,783		WITH $Expr0 := (
FE	SE	4	Scan	0	0		5,929	47		SELECT 'Store'[Ro
13,620 ms 49.5%	13,872 ms 50.5%	6	Scan	320	281	x0.9	1,868,084	14,595		SELECT 'Customer

SE Queries SE Cache
3   0
             0.0%

```
SET DC_KIND="AUTO";
WITH
    $Expr0 := ( PFCAST ( 'Sales'[Quantity] AS INT ) * PFCAST ( 'Sales'[Net Price] AS INT ) )
SELECT
```

The xmSQL query does not contain any callback:

```
WITH
    $Expr0 := ( PFCAST ( 'Sales'[Quantity] AS INT ) * PFCAST ( 'Sales'[Net Price] AS INT ) )
SELECT
    'Customer'[CustomerKey],
    'Store'[StoreKey],
    SUM ( @$Expr0 )
FROM 'Sales'
    LEFT OUTER JOIN 'Customer'
        ON 'Sales'[CustomerKey]='Customer'[CustomerKey]
    LEFT OUTER JOIN 'Store'
        ON 'Sales'[StoreKey]='Store'[StoreKey];
```

By using CROSSJOIN and a single iteration, the order of the tables does not matter anymore. The reason is that the full cross-join operation is performed in the formula engine. We can find out more about the algorithm by inspecting the physical query plan.

Line	Records	Physical Query Plan
1		AddColumns: IterPhyOp LogOp=AddColumns IterCols(0)(''[Value])
2		SingletonTable: IterPhyOp LogOp=AddColumns
3	1	SpoolLookup: LookupPhyOp LogOp=SumX Currency #Records=1 #KeyCols=0 #ValueCols=1 DominantValue=BLANK
4	1	AggregationSpool<Sum>: SpoolPhyOp #Records=1
5		CrossApply: IterPhyOp LogOp=Sum_Vertipaq IterCols(1, 15)('Customer'[CustomerKey], 'Store'[StoreKey])
6		ApplyRemap: IterPhyOp LogOp=CrossJoin LookupCols(1, 15)('Customer'[CustomerKey], 'Store'[StoreKey]) IterCols
7	138,238,216	CrossApply: IterPhyOp LogOp=CrossJoin LookupCols(1, 15)('Customer'[CustomerKey], 'Store'[StoreKey]) IterCol
8	1,868,084	Spool_MultiValuedHashLookup: IterPhyOp LogOp=Scan_Vertipaq LookupCols(1)('Customer'[CustomerKey]) I
9	1,868,084	ProjectionSpool<ProjectFusion< >>: SpoolPhyOp #Records=1868084
10		**Cache: IterPhyOp #FieldCols=2 #ValueCols=0**
11	74	Spool_MultiValuedHashLookup: IterPhyOp LogOp=Scan_Vertipaq LookupCols(15)('Store'[StoreKey]) IterCols(
12	74	ProjectionSpool<ProjectFusion< >>: SpoolPhyOp #Records=74
13		**Cache: IterPhyOp #FieldCols=2 #ValueCols=0**
14	20,034,751	Spool_Iterator<SpoolIterator>: IterPhyOp LogOp=Sum_Vertipaq IterCols(1, 15)('Customer'[CustomerKey], 'Store'[S
15	20,034,751	ProjectionSpool<ProjectFusion<Copy>>: SpoolPhyOp #Records=20034751
16		**Cache: IterPhyOp #FieldCols=2 #ValueCols=1**

As you can see in the query plan, the three datacaches are used to perform the cross-join of customers and stores (lines 7-13) and to join the latter with the amounts (the CrossApply at line 5). The formula engine is in charge of the full algorithm, which translates into poor performance.

Nonetheless, the more we dive into the details of the algorithm, the more we notice that the only detail that matters here is the number of iterated rows. Reducing the number of rows is of utmost importance. The full crossjoin contains 1.8M times 74 rows, which is 138M rows. Out of those 138M rows, only 20M have a value, as we can check by the size of the datacache used at line 15. We have the option of reducing the number of iterated rows if, instead of performing a cross-join, we use SUMMARIZE to retrieve only the existing combinations of *Customer* and *Store*:

```
EVALUATE
{
    SUMX (
        SUMMARIZE ( Sales, Customer[CustomerKey], Store[StoreKey] ),
        [Sales Amount]
    )
}
```

By authoring the code using a single iteration over SUMMARIZE, there is now a single xmSQL query that retrieves the 20M-row datacache with sales amount grouped by *Customer* and *Store*:

```
WITH
    $Expr0 := ( PFCAST ( 'Sales'[Quantity] AS INT ) * PFCAST ( 'Sales'[Net Price] AS INT ) )
SELECT
    'Customer'[CustomerKey],
    'Store'[StoreKey],
    SUM ( @$Expr0 )
FROM 'Sales'
    LEFT OUTER JOIN 'Customer'
        ON 'Sales'[CustomerKey]='Customer'[CustomerKey]
    LEFT OUTER JOIN 'Store'
        ON 'Sales'[StoreKey]='Store'[StoreKey];
```

Because this is the only xmSQL query, we can assume that the formula engine remains in charge of the sum. We can double-check this condition by analyzing the query plan.

Line	Records	Physical Query Plan
1		AddColumns: IterPhyOp LogOp=AddColumns IterCols(0)(''[Value])
2		SingletonTable: IterPhyOp LogOp=AddColumns
3	1	SpoolLookup: LookupPhyOp LogOp=SumX Currency #Records=1 #KeyCols=0 #ValueCols=1 DominantValue=BLANK
4	1	AggregationSpool<Sum>: SpoolPhyOp #Records=1
5	20,034,751	Spool_Iterator<SpoolIterator>: IterPhyOp LogOp=Sum_Vertipaq IterCols(0, 1)('Customer'[CustomerKey], 'Store'[S
6	20,034,751	ProjectionSpool<ProjectFusion<Copy>>: SpoolPhyOp #Records=20034751
7		**Cache: IterPhyOp #FieldCols=2 #ValueCols=1**

The query plan is straightforward: only 7 rows to produce one datacache and then sum all the values inside it. The simplicity of the query plan is also reflected in the performance improvement.

Total	SE CPU		Line	Subclass	Duration	CPU	Par.	Rows	KB	Timeline
16,321 ms	79,094 ms		2	Scan	13,752	79,094	x5.8	20,034,751	234,783	
	x5.8									

FE	SE
2,570 ms	13,751 ms
15.7%	84.3%

SE Queries	SE Cache
1	0
	0.0%

```
SET DC_KIND="AUTO";
WITH
    $Expr0 := ( PFCAST ( 'Sales'[Quantity] AS INT ) * PFCAST ( 'Sales'[Net Price] AS INT ) )
SELECT
    'Customer'[CustomerKey],
    'Store'[StoreKey],
```

As you see, we are still reducing the time spent in the formula engine, whereas the storage engine time is the same as what we saw in the beginning of this section. This version of the code is the fastest so far. Still, we can improve it a little bit. Instead of grouping by the columns in *Customer* and *Store*, we can use the columns already present in *Sales*. The following query avoids using the relationships, and it groups by *Sales[CustomerKey]* and *Sales[StoreKey]*:

```
EVALUATE
{
    SUMX (
        SUMMARIZE ( Sales, Sales[CustomerKey], Sales[StoreKey] ),
        [Sales Amount]
    )
}
```

By avoiding relationships, we are now impacting the VertiPaq time.

Total	SE CPU		Line	Subclass	Duration	CPU	Par.	Rows	KB	Timeline
16,307 ms	72,391 ms		2	Scan	13,667	72,391	x5.3	20,034,751	234,783	
	x5.3									

FE	SE
2,640 ms	13,667 ms
16.2%	83.8%

SE Queries	SE Cache
1	0
	0.0%

```
SET DC_KIND="AUTO";
WITH
    $Expr0 := ( PFCAST ( 'Sales'[Quantity] AS INT ) * PFCAST ( 'Sales'[Net Price] AS INT ) )
SELECT
    'Sales'[CustomerKey],
    'Sales'[StoreKey],
    SUM ( @$Expr0 )
FROM 'Sales';
```

The xmSQL query clearly shows that the relationships are no longer being used, and the storage engine CPU time went down from 79,094 milliseconds to 72,391 milliseconds.

At the cost of being pedantic, we want to highlight that the time spent optimizing this query resulted in a better understanding of how the Tabular engine is resolving the query – and that is the most important outcome. We understood the difference between the outer and the inner iterations when we still had two iterators. Then we tested the same algorithm with a single iteration, producing a worse query plan but – at the same time – opening the doors to the last optimization that avoided traversing the relationships.

The more we understand the entire algorithm, the better we can modify the DAX code to drive the engine toward a faster path. Do not apply any optimizations without testing the result and the performance. For example, using MAXX or MINX as iterators, every single attempt may produce slower performance instead of providing any benefit.

Understanding the effect of context transition

We use a smaller model version in this example, with only 2M rows. The reason is that the large model would be extremely slow and memory-hungry, making it impossible to run the demo. Indeed, the performance impact is enormous when excessive materialization occurs because of context transition.

Context transition, which is the transformation of a row context into a filter context, is often responsible for slow performance. The problem mainly arises when context transition happens on the fact table due to a naïve error. As an example, let us look at the following query:

```
EVALUATE
SUMMARIZECOLUMNS (
    'Product'[Brand],
    "Sales Gt 200",
        SUMX (
            Sales,
            VAR S = [Sales Amount]
            RETURN
                IF ( S > 200, S )
        )
)
```

The code iterates over *Sales* and checks if the amount exceeds 200 for each transaction. If the condition holds, it computes the amount; otherwise, it skips that transaction. The critical detail is that we use the *Sales Amount* measure inside an iteration over *Sales*. CALCULATE always surrounds a measure reference; therefore, context transition takes place. This code has two significant issues: it is slow, and it may produce incorrect results if the *Sales* table contains duplicates. Here, the focus is only on performance, even though the accuracy of the result would be a serious issue to consider as well.

Here are the server timings. The model for this demo contains 2,237,028 rows in *Sales*. This number is going to be important in the following figure.

Total	SE CPU
1,847 ms	2,031 ms
	x1.6

FE	SE
576 ms	1,271 ms
31.2%	68.8%

SE Queries	SE Cache
2	0
	0.0%

Line	Subclass	Duration	CPU	Par.	Rows	KB	Timeline
2	Scan	944	1,375	x1.5	2,237,028	131,076	
4	Scan	327	656	x2.0	14	1	

```
SET DC_KIND="AUTO";
WITH
    $Expr0 := ( PFCAST ( 'Sales'[Quantity] AS INT ) * PFCAST ( 'Sales'[Net Price] AS INT ) )
SELECT
    'Sales'[Order Number],
    'Sales'[Line Number],
    'Sales'[Order Date],
    'Sales'[Delivery Date],
    'Sales'[CustomerKey],
    'Sales'[StoreKey],
```

The time required to scan 2.2M rows seems excessive. Moreover, there are two storage engine queries – one of which materializes exactly 2.2M rows, which is the size of the *Sales* table. Let us examine the two xmSQL queries further. The first one materializes the entire *Sales* table:

```
WITH
    $Expr0 := ( PFCAST ( 'Sales'[Quantity] AS    INT ) * PFCAST ( 'Sales'[Net Price] AS    INT )   )
SELECT
    'Sales'[Order Number],
    'Sales'[Line Number],
    'Sales'[Order Date],
    'Sales'[Delivery Date],
    'Sales'[CustomerKey],
    'Sales'[StoreKey],
    'Sales'[ProductKey],
    'Sales'[Quantity],
    'Sales'[Unit Price],
    'Sales'[Net Price],
    'Sales'[Unit Cost],
    'Sales'[Currency Code],
    'Sales'[Exchange Rate],
    SUM ( @$Expr0 )
FROM 'Sales';
```

The second query includes a callback because of the IF statement inside the loop, which receives all the columns of *Sales*:

```
WITH
    $Expr0 := [CallbackDataID ( IF ( S > 200, S )  ) ] (
            PFDATAID ( 'Sales'[Order Number]),
            PFDATAID ( 'Sales'[Line Number]),
            PFDATAID ( 'Sales'[Order Date]),
            PFDATAID ( 'Sales'[Delivery Date]),
            PFDATAID ( 'Sales'[CustomerKey]),
            PFDATAID ( 'Sales'[StoreKey]),
            PFDATAID ( 'Sales'[ProductKey]),
            PFDATAID ( 'Sales'[Quantity]),
            PFDATAID ( 'Sales'[Unit Price]),
            PFDATAID ( 'Sales'[Net Price]),
            PFDATAID ( 'Sales'[Unit Cost]),
            PFDATAID ( 'Sales'[Currency Code]),
            PFDATAID ( 'Sales'[Exchange Rate])
    )
SELECT
    'Product'[Brand],
    SUM ( @$Expr0 )
FROM 'Sales'
    LEFT OUTER JOIN 'Product'
        ON 'Sales'[ProductKey]='Product'[ProductKey];
```

This second query returns 11 rows, even though it needs to move the entire *Sales* table back and forth between the storage engine and the formula engine because of the callback that uses all the columns.

The problem with the code is the context transition happening during the assignment of the measure *Sales Amount* to the variable *S*. Because we are invoking a measure, we know CALCULATE is being added automatically by the DAX engine. CALCULATE triggers the context transition inside a loop over *Sales*.

Sales being the fact table, it does not have a primary key defined in the Tabular model. Therefore, DAX places a filter over all the table columns to perform the context transition. Context transition is an expensive operation that makes perfect sense when executed during an iteration over a dimension, but it results in terrible performance when executed against a fact table.

Solving the problem requires removing the context transition. In this example, this is as easy as replacing the reference to *Sales Amount* with the calculation happening in the row context:

```
EVALUATE
SUMMARIZECOLUMNS (
    'Product'[Brand],
    "Sales Gt 200",
        SUMX (
            Sales,
            VAR S = Sales[Quantity] * Sales[Net Price]
            RETURN
                IF ( S > 200, S )
        )
)
```

The assignment to the *S* variable now no longer includes CALCULATE; therefore, it does not execute the context transition. The server timings pane shows a significant improvement.

Total	SE CPU		Line	Subclass	Duration	CPU	Par.	Rows	KB	Timeline
254 ms	328 ms		2	Scan	53	31	x0.6	228,184	892	
	x1.6		4	Scan	150	297	x2.0	14	1	

FE	**SE**
51 ms	203 ms
20.1%	79.9%

SE Queries	**SE Cache**
2	0
	0.0%

```
SET DC_KIND="AUTO";
SELECT
    'Product'[Brand],
    'Sales'[Quantity],
    'Sales'[Net Price]
FROM 'Sales'
    LEFT OUTER JOIN 'Product'
        ON 'Sales'[ProductKey]='Product'[ProductKey];
```

The excessive materialization is now gone, and the time required to answer the query is much better. The first xmSQL query retrieves only the required columns:

```
SELECT
    'Product'[Brand],
    'Sales'[Quantity],
    'Sales'[Net Price]
FROM 'Sales'
    LEFT OUTER JOIN 'Product'
        ON 'Sales'[ProductKey]='Product'[ProductKey];
```

Because the query only retrieves three columns, the materialization level is reduced. The second query still includes a callback because of the IF statement:

```
WITH
    $Expr0 := [CallbackDataID ( IF ( S > 200, S )  )]( PFDATAID ( 'Sales'[Quantity]) , PFDATAID ( 'Sales'[Net Price])  )
SELECT
    'Product'[Brand],
    SUM ( @$Expr0 )
FROM 'Sales'
    LEFT OUTER JOIN 'Product'
        ON 'Sales'[ProductKey]='Product'[ProductKey];
```

Now that we have a solid understanding of the VertiPaq engine, we know that all the calculations in the query could be pushed down to the storage engine. The callback is not needed. Still, the optimizer did not figure out that the entire calculation could be pushed down to the VertiPaq engine.

The final step in optimizing the code is to rewrite the calculation so that the optimizer pushes the calculation to the storage engine. There are multiple ways of obtaining the same result. The simplest one is to use CALCULATE and place a filter over the two columns required:

```
EVALUATE
SUMMARIZECOLUMNS (
    'Product'[Brand],
    "Sales Gt 200",
        CALCULATE (
            [Sales Amount],
            Sales[Quantity] * Sales[Net Price] > 200
        )
)
```

This last version of the code is entirely executed in the storage engine, providing optimal performance.

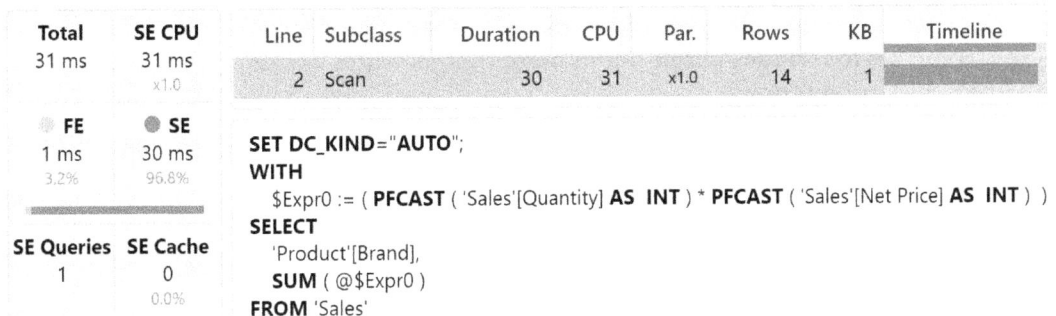

Total	SE CPU		Line	Subclass	Duration	CPU	Par.	Rows	KB	Timeline
31 ms	31 ms									
	x1.0		2	Scan	30	31	x1.0	14	1	

FE	SE
1 ms	30 ms
3.2%	96.8%

SE Queries	SE Cache
1	0
	0.0%

SET DC_KIND="AUTO";
WITH
  $Expr0 := (**PFCAST** ('Sales'[Quantity] **AS INT**) * **PFCAST** ('Sales'[Net Price] **AS INT**))
SELECT
  'Product'[Brand],
  SUM (@$Expr0)
FROM 'Sales'

There is only one xmSQL query processing the entire query and materializing only 14 rows:

```
WITH
    $Expr0 := ( PFCAST ( 'Sales'[Quantity] AS   INT ) * PFCAST ( 'Sales'[Net Price] AS   INT )  )
SELECT
    'Product'[Brand],
    SUM ( @$Expr0 )
FROM 'Sales'
    LEFT OUTER JOIN 'Product'
        ON 'Sales'[ProductKey]='Product'[ProductKey]
WHERE
    ( COALESCE (   ( PFCAST ( 'Sales'[Quantity] AS INT ) * PFCAST ( 'Sales'[Net Price] AS INT ))) > COALESCE ( 2000000 )  );
```

The entire query shifted from 1,847 milliseconds of storage engine to only 31 milliseconds.

Different ways of performing a distinct count

DAX offers the DISTINCTCOUNT function, which is optimized to compute distinct counts. As we learned, distinct counts are executed directly in VertiPaq through the DCOUNT xmSQL function, which is internally translated into an *existing datacache* bitmap.

Being executed in VertiPaq, DCOUNT uses all the cores available up to the segments used by the table to provide maximum efficiency. But despite being mostly the fastest way to compute distinct counts, DCOUNT suffers from a few drawbacks. First, during the execution of the storage engine query, the Tabular server is busy performing that calculation. Other queries received may be queued for later execution when the distinct count is completed in case the target table for DCOUNT has more segments than there are cores available. On top of that, the massive parallelism requires some coordination tasks to be completed before producing the final datacache.

There are scenarios where it is preferable to avoid using VertiPaq to compute distinct counts and rely more on the formula engine. Depending on the architecture of your server, the query could be faster or slower. From a scalability point of view, the version based on the formula engine uses a smaller fraction of the server power; this lets the same server dedicate more resources to other users, possibly producing a better overall experience.

Let us see this with an example. The following query produces the distinct count of products sliced by *Date*, *Country*, and *Color*:

```
EVALUATE
SUMMARIZECOLUMNS (
    'Date'[Date],
    Customer[Country],
    'Product'[Color],
    "# Products", DISTINCTCOUNT ( Sales[ProductKey] )
)
```

Performance-wise, the query runs pretty fast, with a good degree of parallelism.

Total	SE CPU	Line	Subclass	Duration	CPU	Par.	Rows	KB	Timeline
7,573 ms	65,781 ms	1	Internal	4,824	62,719	x13.0			
	x12.1	2	Internal	4,824	62,719	x13.0			
FE	SE	3	Internal	583	3,063	x5.3			
2,156 ms	5,417 ms	4	Scan	5,417	65,781	x12.1	411,897	6,436	
28.5%	71.5%								

SE Queries	SE Cache
1	0
	0.0%

The entire query is resolved with a single xmSQL query at line 4, involving a DCOUNT:

```
SELECT
     'Customer'[Country],
     'Date'[Date],
     'Product'[Color],
     DCOUNT ( 'Sales'[ProductKey] )
FROM 'Sales'
     LEFT OUTER JOIN 'Customer'
          ON 'Sales'[CustomerKey]='Customer'[CustomerKey]
     LEFT OUTER JOIN 'Date'
          ON 'Sales'[Order Date]='Date'[Date]
     LEFT OUTER JOIN 'Product'
          ON 'Sales'[ProductKey]='Product'[ProductKey];
```

We already know that the presence of DCOUNT means that the xmSQL query is resolved by three internal queries. Indeed, by inspecting the internal query at line 1 that computes the distinct count in an existing data cache, we notice that the scan retrieves the three grouping columns (*Date[Date]*, *Product[Color]*, and *Customer[Country]*) plus the *Sales[ProductKey]* column, required to compute the distinct count:

```
SELECT
     'Customer'[Country],
     'Date'[Date],
     'Product'[Color],
     'Sales'[ProductKey]
FROM 'Sales'
     LEFT OUTER JOIN 'Customer'
          ON 'Sales'[CustomerKey]='Customer'[CustomerKey]
     LEFT OUTER JOIN 'Date'
          ON 'Sales'[Order Date]='Date'[Date]
     LEFT OUTER JOIN 'Product'
          ON 'Sales'[ProductKey]='Product'[ProductKey];
```

It is essential to distinguish between the two storage engine queries. The datacache resulting from the xmSQL query at line 4 contains 411,897 rows, even though – internally – the VertiPaq engine had to scan the entire *Sales* table. We can check that number by using a DAX query that counts the rows produced by an equivalent DAX expression:

```
EVALUATE
{
    COUNTROWS (
        SUMMARIZE (
            Sales,
            'Date'[Date],
            'Product'[Color],
            Customer[Country],
            Sales[ProductKey]
        )
    )
}
```

The result is 37,328,683, which corresponds to the number of rows returned by the SUMMARIZE expression. Therefore, we know that the real work carried out by the VertiPaq engine is to scan 37M rows produced by the first internal storage engine query. This scan results in a smaller datacache containing 411,897 rows, each with a distinct count of products. The task of scanning all those rows, splitting the job among multiple cores, and finally consolidating the results in a single data cache is burdensome. It used 65,781 milliseconds of storage engine CPU, reduced down to 5.4 seconds thanks to parallelism.

Instead of using the DISTINCTCOUNT function, we can use a technical iterator to sum the value of 1 for each row in the DISTINCT of the *Sales[ProductKey]*, thus obtaining a version of distinct count that is mainly executed by the formula engine:

```
EVALUATE
SUMMARIZECOLUMNS (
    'Date'[Date],
    Customer[Country],
    'Product'[Color],
    "# Products", SUMX ( DISTINCT ( Sales[ProductKey] ), 1 )
)
```

Be mindful that this is not a generic replacement for distinct counts. It is a technical method to force the calculation to be executed in the formula engine rather than in the storage engine. There are scenarios where this technique has advantages and where the use of DISTINCTCOUNT is preferable. DAX developers need to be familiar with both techniques to choose the right approach for the scenario they are facing.

This last query materializes a datacache containing 57M rows, leaving the task of performing the count to the formula engine. Therefore, we expect to see a smaller amount of time in the storage engine and more time spent in the formula engine.

We look at the server timings.

Total	SE CPU		Line	Subclass	Duration	CPU	Par.	Rows	KB	Timeline
20,570 ms	65,859 ms									
	x4.4		2	Scan	14,880	65,859	x4.4	37,328,683	291,631	

FE	SE
5,690 ms	14,880 ms
27.7%	72.3%

```
SET DC_KIND="AUTO";
SELECT
    'Sales'[ProductKey],
    'Customer'[Country],
    'Date'[Date],
    'Product'[Color]
```

SE Queries	SE Cache
1	0
	0.0%

And here is the only xmSQL query executed:

```
SELECT
    'Sales'[ProductKey],
    'Customer'[Country],
    'Date'[Date],
    'Product'[Color]
FROM 'Sales'
    LEFT OUTER JOIN 'Customer'
        ON 'Sales'[CustomerKey]='Customer'[CustomerKey]
    LEFT OUTER JOIN 'Date'
        ON 'Sales'[Order Date]='Date'[Date]
    LEFT OUTER JOIN 'Product'
        ON 'Sales'[ProductKey]='Product'[ProductKey];

Estimated size: rows = 37,328,683    bytes = 298,629,464
```

The total execution time of this last version is larger (20.5 seconds instead of 7.6); however, the amount of storage engine CPU used by this latter query is very similar, even though the storage engine waiting time increased from 5.4 seconds to almost 15 seconds.

You might wonder why this latter version uses the same amount of storage engine CPU but produces a higher execution time, from the VertiPaq point of view, of 15 seconds. The reason is the size of the datacache and the related parallelism. A datacache containing 37M rows is very large, requiring time to be populated and transferred between the two engines. Indeed, the formula engine time also increased – from 2 seconds to 5.6 seconds. Overall, it does not seem like a good idea to rely on the formula engine to perform the distinct count, but for now it is just important to realize that there are different techniques to obtain one same result.

It is not that one technique is always better than the other. The two ways of calculating distinct counts use different parts of the Tabular engine. You should always double-check performance with the more common queries in your reports before choosing one against the other.

We want to really stress the fact that a DAX developer must always spend time double-checking performance. We increase the complexity of the calculation by transforming it into the year-to-date distinct count of our stores:

```
EVALUATE
SUMMARIZECOLUMNS (
    'Date'[Year Month Number],
    "# Stores",
    CALCULATE (
        DISTINCTCOUNT ( Sales[StoreKey] ),
        DATESYTD ( 'Date'[Date] )
    )
)
```

Please note that we also changed the cardinality. Instead of working at the day level, we are computing the year-to-date at the month level. The reason is that the year-to-date calculation increases the time required to perform the computation, and we do not want to handle queries that become too slow.

When using DISTINCTCOUNT, Tabular tries to push the calculation down to the storage engine. To perform this, it creates a set of filters containing the year-to-date dates of every row. For example, for March 2020, it builds a filter containing all the dates from the first of January 2020 to the end of March 2020. Once the filter is computed, the formula engine can execute a VertiPaq query to retrieve the distinct count of products in that period. Therefore, the execution requires a first set of very fast queries to retrieve the dates and their relationship with the *Date[Year Month Number]* column, which we used to perform the grouping. Later on, a set of filtered queries retrieves the actual results.

The queries in the first set are elementary, like the following:

```
SELECT
    'Date'[Date]
FROM 'Date';
```

These first three queries are extremely fast and produce tiny datacaches; therefore, they are not worth our attention. The second set of queries is more interesting. There are many of them, one for each row of the resultset. Each has the same structure, with different filters. This example is for February, so the second filter contains 59 dates (31 for January plus 28 for February):

```
SELECT
    DCOUNT ( 'Sales'[StoreKey] )
FROM 'Sales'
    LEFT OUTER JOIN 'Date'
        ON 'Sales'[Order Date]='Date'[Date]
WHERE
    'Date'[Date] IN ( 41133.000000, 42090.000000, 42131.000000, 43088.000000, 43129.000000, 44086.000000,
        44127.000000, 41051.000000, 41092.000000, 42049.000000..[4,018 total values, not all displayed] ) VAND
    'Date'[Date] IN ( 40190.000000, 40204.000000, 40231.000000, 40191.000000, 40205.000000, 40218.000000,
        40232.000000, 40192.000000, 40219.000000, 40233.000000..[59 total values, not all displayed] ) ;
```

Each of these queries is very fast, but there are many. The number of queries grows with the growth of the cardinality. It is not uncommon to witness hundreds or thousands of these small queries. As the number of queries grows, so does the time required to answer the DAX query. Moreover, there being many storage engine queries makes the VertiPaq cache almost useless. VertiPaq stores a very limited number of datacaches and when there are thousands of xmSQL queries, the cache is frequently evicted. Therefore, rerunning the same query (by the same user or by other users) would require recomputing all the xmSQL queries because their results are no longer present in the cache.

These are the server timings of the query with the year-to-date.

Total	SE CPU	Line	Subclass	Duration	CPU	Par.	Rows	KB	Timeline	Query
4,990 ms	3,896 ms									
	x0.9	2	Scan	0	0		4,021	32		SELECT 'Date'[Date
FE	SE	4	Scan	0	0		135	2		SELECT 'Date'[Year
500 ms	4,490 ms	6	Scan	1	0		4,018	16		SELECT 'Date'[Date
10.0%	50.0%	10	Scan	33	203	x6.2	0	1		SELECT DCOUNT ('
		14	Scan	33	16	x0.5	0	1		SELECT DCOUNT ('
SE Queries	SE Cache	18	Scan	33	31	x0.9	0	1		SELECT DCOUNT ('
135	0	22	C	27	70	2.4	0	1		SELECT DCOUNT ('
	0.0%									

Please note that each query returns a small number of rows. Nonetheless, we learned in the previous sections that the amount of data that needs to be scanned is much larger. The internal queries scan a lot more rows than the ones being returned.

If we execute the DAX code using the alternative formulation for the distinct count, the query looks like this:

```
EVALUATE
SUMMARIZECOLUMNS (
    'Date'[Year Month Number],
    "# Stores",
    CALCULATE (
        SUMX ( DISTINCT ( Sales[StoreKey] ), 1 ),
        DATESYTD ( 'Date'[Date] )
    )
)
```

This time, the algorithm is entirely different. In this case, we still have two sets of queries: the first one retrieves information about the dates, much like the query with DISTINCTCOUNT did. On the other hand, the second set includes a single xmSQL query that retrieves the most granular data. Here, the difference becomes relevant:

```
SELECT
    'Sales'[StoreKey],
    'Date'[Date]
FROM 'Sales'
    LEFT OUTER JOIN 'Date'
        ON 'Sales'[Order Date]='Date'[Date]
WHERE
    'Date'[Date] IN ( 41133.000000, 42090.000000, 42131.000000, 43088.000000, 43129.000000, 44086.000000,
        44127.000000, 41051.000000, 41092.000000, 42049.000000..[4,018 total values, not all displayed] ) ;
```

There are several important details to note here:

- Even though the granularity of the DAX query is at the month level, this xmSQL query retrieves data at the date granularity, which means a lot more rows than needed.

- There are no filters for individual months. The xmSQL query retrieves the entire period.

- The datacache generated by this query contains 167K rows. A considerable number compared with the few hundred rows returned by the previous queries.

The formula engine, in this scenario, materialized a table containing the data at the day level. It performs the distinct count by grouping this datacache differently to compute the year-to-date for every month. This approach is made evident by just looking at the server timings.

Total	SE CPU	Line	Subclass	Duration	CPU	Par.	Rows	KB	Timeline	Query
227 ms	1,391 ms									
	x8.3	2	Scan	0	0		4,021	32		SELECT 'Date'[D
FE	SE	4	Scan	0	0		135	2		SELECT 'Date'[Ye
60 ms	167 ms	6	Scan	0	0		4,018	16		SELECT 'Date'[D
26.4%	73.6%	8	Scan	167	1,391	x8.3	167,503	655		SELECT 'Sales'[S
SE Queries	SE Cache									
4	0									
	0.0%									

The execution time went down 95% from 5 seconds to 0.2 seconds. The saving is in both formula engine and storage engine times: Instead of 135 fast xmSQL queries, now there is a single, slower xmSQL query with a larger materialization. The great benefit we can observe by counting the distinct stores would be reduced by counting the distinct products.

We measure the year-to-date unique products by month:

```
EVALUATE
SUMMARIZECOLUMNS (
    'Date'[Year Month Number],
    "# Products",
    CALCULATE (
        DISTINCTCOUNT ( Sales[ProductKey] ),
        DATESYTD ( 'Date'[Date] )
    )
)
```

The overall execution time is 5.5 seconds.

Total	SE CPU	Line	Subclass	Duration	CPU	Par.	Rows	KB	Timeline	Query
5,588 ms	4,394 ms									
	x0.9	2	Scan	0	0		4,021	32		SELECT 'Date
FE	SE	4	Scan	1	0		135	2		SELECT 'Date
511 ms	5,077 ms	6	Scan	0	0		4,018	16		SELECT 'Date
9.1%	90.9%	10	Scan	37	250	x6.8	0	1		SELECT DCO
		14	Scan	33	63	x1.9	0	1		SELECT DCO
SE Queries	SE Cache	18	Scan	31	125	x4.0	0	1		SELECT DCO
135	0	22	Scan	33	47	x1.4	0	1		SELECT DCO
	0.0%									

Then we replace the DISTINCTCOUNT with a SUMX over DISTINCT:

```
EVALUATE
SUMMARIZECOLUMNS (
    'Date'[Year Month Number],
    "# Products",
    CALCULATE (
        SUMX ( DISTINCT ( Sales[ProductKey] ), 1 ),
        DATESYTD ( 'Date'[Date] )
    )
)
```

Instead of a 95% performance improvement, now we decreased the response time by 20%, also multiplying the storage engine CPU cost by 500%.

Total	SE CPU	Line	Subclass	Duration	CPU	Par.	Rows	KB	Timeline
6,932 ms	26,750 ms	2	Scan	0	0		4,021	32	
	x6.5	4	Scan	1	0		135	2	
● FE	● SE	6	Scan	0	0		4,018	16	
2,790 ms	4,142 ms	8	Scan	4,141	26,750	x6.5	7,874,898	30,762	
40.2%	59.8%								

SE Queries	SE Cache
4	0
	0.0%

The ratio between the formula engine and the storage engine is very different. When using a SUMX over DISTINCT, the formula engine performs a lot more work, whereas with DISTINCTCOUNT most of the work is executed by the storage engine.

As we said multiple times, these numbers are important to understand the algorithms; they do not demonstrate one version as better than the other one. The choice between the two techniques is a tradeoff between materialization, cost of the calculation in the formula engine, and number of storage engine requests.

To show another important detail, we add the *Product[Color]* column to the list of group-by columns and we modify the year-to-date calculation to a running total. The results are somewhat surprising and require further explanation.

Here is the query using DISTINCTCOUNT:

```
EVALUATE
SUMMARIZECOLUMNS (
    'Date'[Year Month Number],
    'Product'[Color],
    "# Products",
        VAR LastVisibleDate = MAX ( 'Date'[Date] )
        RETURN
            CALCULATE (
                DISTINCTCOUNT ( Sales[ProductKey] ),
                'Date'[Date] <= LastVisibleDate
            )
)
```

The execution pattern is the usual one. The query is slower because of the need to group by *Product[Color]*. We look at the server timings.

Total	SE CPU	Line	Subclass	Duration	CPU	Par.	Rows	KB	Timeline
11,743 ms	129,830 ms								
	x12.1	2	Scan	3	0		4,021	32	
FE	**SE**	4	Scan	0	0		135	2	
1,034 ms	10,709 ms	6	Scan	1	0		135	3	
8.8%	91.2%	10	Scan	42	203	x4.8	0	1	
		14	Scan	40	109	x2.7	0	1	
SE Queries	**SE Cache**	18	Scan	40	16	x0.4	0	1	
136	0	22	Scan	42	16	x0.4	0	1	
	0.0%								

The total number of storage engine queries is now 136: just one more than a similar query without *Product[Color]*. We might have expected a multiplication of the storage engine queries by the number of product colors, but this did not happen. Indeed, each storage engine query with DCOUNT now returns one value for each *Product[Color]*, like this one:

```
SELECT
    'Product'[Color],
    DCOUNT ( 'Sales'[ProductKey] )
FROM 'Sales'
    LEFT OUTER JOIN 'Date'
        ON 'Sales'[Order Date]='Date'[Date]
    LEFT OUTER JOIN 'Product'
        ON 'Sales'[ProductKey]='Product'[ProductKey]
WHERE
    'Date'[Date] IN ( 41133.000000, 42090.000000, 42131.000000, 43088.000000, 43129.000000, 44086.000000,
        44127.000000, 41051.000000, 41092.000000, 42049.000000..[4,019 total values, not all displayed] ) VAND
    'Date'[Date] IN ( 40190.000000, 40204.000000, 40231.000000, 40191.000000, 40205.000000, 40218.000000,
        40232.000000, 40192.000000, 40219.000000, 40233.000000..[60 total values, not all displayed] ) ;
```

The corresponding DAX query with the formula engine pattern (SUMX over DISTINCT) is the following:

```
EVALUATE
SUMMARIZECOLUMNS (
    'Date'[Year Month Number],
    'Product'[Color],
    "# Products",
        VAR LastVisibleDate = MAX ( 'Date'[Date] )
        RETURN
            CALCULATE (
                SUMX ( DISTINCT ( Sales[ProductKey] ), 1 ),
                'Date'[Date] <= LastVisibleDate
            )
)
```

This last version runs much more slowly than the version with DISTINCTCOUNT.

Total	SE CPU	Line	Subclass	Duration	CPU	Par.	Rows	KB	Timeline
53,467 ms	39,234 ms								
	x6.3	2	Scan	0	0		4,021	32	
FE	SE	4	Scan	1	0		135	2	
47,256 ms	6,211 ms	6	Scan	0	0		135	3	
88.4%	11.6%	8	Scan	6,210	39,234	x6.3	7,874,898	30,762	

SE Queries	SE Cache
4	0
	0.0%

The materialization produced by the xmSQL query at line 8 did not increase, despite us including *Product[Color]* in the grouping columns:

```
SELECT
        'Sales'[ProductKey],
        'Date'[Date],
        'Product'[Color]
FROM 'Sales'
    LEFT OUTER JOIN 'Date'
        ON 'Sales'[Order Date]='Date'[Date]
    LEFT OUTER JOIN 'Product'
        ON 'Sales'[ProductKey]='Product'[ProductKey]
WHERE
    'Date'[Date] IN ( 41133.000000, 42090.000000, 42131.000000, 43088.000000, 43129.000000, 44086.000000,
        44127.000000, 41051.000000, 41092.000000, 42049.000000..[4,019 total values, not all displayed] ) ;
```

Therefore, no matter which column we add to the group-by list, if the column belongs to the *Product* table – whose key in *Sales* we use for the distinct count – it does not increase the size of the materialized table, and thus does not impact performance. It is interesting that the engine is able to detect this dependency even though we used *Sales[ProductKey]* in the aggregation, because of the relationship that connects *Sales* to *Product*.

So if the materialization is similar, the version with SUMX over DISTINCT is now much slower than the version with DISTINCTCOUNT. This is because the cost in the formula engine to compute the running total is higher compared to the year-to-date we used in the previous example, when the difference between the two approaches was just 20% of execution time. The SUMX over DISTINCT version is now 530% slower – though it consumes a lower amount of CPU, 86 seconds instead of 130 seconds by summing FE and SE CPU – which would scale out better in an environment with many concurrent users.

As you have seen, the choice between the two versions depends on many factors. DAX requires for a developer to perform several tests and understand precisely how the engine behaves before making any assumptions. Choosing between DISTINCTCOUNT and SUMX over DISTINCT may profoundly impact your server's overall performance in either direction.

Optimizing LASTDATE calculations

In this example, we analyze a simple query that retrieves for each product, the last net price. The query can be written in a simple, unsophisticated way. The simplest version uses the LASTDATE function, producing a very slow query plan. By rewriting the DAX code, we obtain a much better version.

Let us start with the first query:

```
EVALUATE
SUMMARIZECOLUMNS (
    'Product'[Product Name],
    "Last price",
        CALCULATE (
            AVERAGE ( Sales[Net Price] ),
            LASTDATE ( Sales[Order Date] )
        )
)
ORDER BY 'Product'[Product Name]
```

For each product, LASTDATE returns the last order date with a row in *Sales*. Because there might be multiple sales with different net prices on that same date, we use the average net price on the last date with sales to obtain a single value. The result contains the product name and its last net price.

Product Name	Last price
A. Datum Advanced Digital Camera M300 Azure	173.21
A. Datum Advanced Digital Camera M300 Black	184.73
A. Datum Advanced Digital Camera M300 Green	178.81
A. Datum Advanced Digital Camera M300 Grey	178.29
A. Datum Advanced Digital Camera M300 Orange	173.42
A. Datum Advanced Digital Camera M300 Pink	174.36
A. Datum Advanced Digital Camera M300 Silver	178.56
A. Datum All in One Digital Camera M200 Azure	177.66
A. Datum All in One Digital Camera M200 Black	174.55
A. Datum All in One Digital Camera M200 Green	176.91

Performance is really bad when running on a *Sales* table with 200M rows. A quick look at the server timings shows a materialization of around 8M rows, which seems excessive given that there are 2,517 products in total.

Total	SE CPU		Line	Subclass	Duration	CPU	Par.	Rows	KB	Timeline
9,890 ms	45,391 ms		2	Scan	37	16	x0.4	3,284	26	
	x6.4		4	Scan	6,986	43,203	x6.2	7,874,898	30,762	
● FE	● SE		6	Scan	103	2,172	x21.1	2,520	40	
2,764 ms	7,126 ms									
27.9%	72.1%									

SE Queries	SE Cache
3	0
	0.0%

Let us investigate further by looking at the xmSQL queries. The first one retrieves the order dates, and it is not worth further investigation:

```
SELECT
    'Sales'[Order Date]
FROM 'Sales';
```

The second xmSQL query materializes 8M rows, consuming around 43 seconds of storage engine CPU:

```
SELECT
    'Sales'[Order Date],
    'Product'[Product Name]
FROM 'Sales'
    LEFT OUTER JOIN 'Product'
        ON 'Sales'[ProductKey]='Product'[ProductKey];
```

The query produces a table containing for each product the list of all the order dates. It is interesting to note that the result differs from what we asked for. Our goal was to retrieve, for each product, only the last date. The formula engine apparently oversees the search for the last date per product. A quick look at the third xmSQL query confirms our finding:

```
SELECT
     'Product'[Product Name],
     SUM ( 'Sales'[Net Price] ),
     COUNT (   )
FROM 'Sales'
     LEFT OUTER JOIN 'Product'
          ON 'Sales'[ProductKey]='Product'[ProductKey]
WHERE
     ( 'Product'[Product Name], 'Sales'[Order Date] ) IN {
          ( 'MGS Gears of War 2008 M450', 43893.000000 ) ,
          ( 'Contoso Mouse Lock Bundle E200 Grey', 43893.000000 ) ,
          ( 'MGS Bicycle Card Games2009 E166', 43893.000000 ) ,
          ( 'Contoso USB Wave Multi-media Keyboard E280 Black', 43893.000000 ) ,
          ( 'SV Hand Games men M30 Yellow', 43893.000000 ) ,
          ( 'Proseware All-In-One Photo Printer M200 Green', 43893.000000 ) ,
          ( 'Proseware Color Ink Jet Fax, Copier, Phone M250 Grey', 43893.000000 ) ,
          ( 'MGS Age of Mythology: Gold Edition M310', 43893.000000 ) ,
          ( 'Proseware Fax Machine E100 Black', 43893.000000 ) ,
          ( 'Contoso DVD 9-Inch Player Portable M300 Black', 43893.000000 )
          ..[2,517 total tuples, not all displayed]}
     VAND
          'Sales'[Net Price] IS NOT NULL;
```

This last query uses a filter over two columns to filter the last date with sales for each product. It groups by *Product[Product Name]* and computes the sum of *Sales[Net Price]* along with the count of rows. These are the ingredients needed to compute the average.

Because there is no evidence that the storage engine computes the filter, the algorithm is obvious at this point. The formula engine receives 8M rows in a datacache and searches for the max date by product. Then, it builds the filter passed to the following xmSQL query to produce the result.

It is worth noting that this last query uses 2,172 milliseconds of storage engine CPU. Hence, most of the storage engine CPU is required to build the 8M rows of datacache, and the query speed is strongly tied to the amount of time spent in the formula engine.

We can find a confirmation of our findings by quickly inspecting the query plan.

Line	Records	Physical Query Plan
1		PartitionIntoGroups: IterPhyOp LogOp=Order IterCols(0, 1)('Product'[Product Name], ''[Last price]) #Groups=1 #Rows=2
2	1	AggregationSpool<Order>: SpoolPhyOp #Records=1
3		GroupSemijoin: IterPhyOp LogOp=GroupSemiJoin IterCols(0, 1)('Product'[Product Name], ''[Last price])
4	2,517	Spool_Iterator<SpoolIterator>: IterPhyOp LogOp=Average_Vertipaq IterCols(0)('Product'[Product Name]) #Reco
5	2,517	ProjectionSpool<ProjectFusion<Average>>: SpoolPhyOp #Records=2517
6		**Cache: IterPhyOp #FieldCols=1 #ValueCols=2**
7	2,517	Spool_Iterator<SpoolIterator>: IterPhyOp LogOp=LastDate IterCols(0, 1)('Product'[Product Name], 'Sale
8	2,517	AggregationSpool<GroupBy>: SpoolPhyOp #Records=2517
9		LastDate: IterPhyOp LogOp=LastDate IterCols(0, 1)('Product'[Product Name], 'Sales'[Order Date])
10	2,517	Spool_Iterator<SpoolIterator>: IterPhyOp LogOp=Scan_Vertipaq IterCols(0)('Product'[Product N
11	2,517	AggregationSpool<GroupBy>: SpoolPhyOp #Records=2517
12	7,874,898	Spool_Iterator<SpoolIterator>: IterPhyOp LogOp=Scan_Vertipaq IterCols(0, 1)('Product'[Pr
13	7,874,898	ProjectionSpool<ProjectFusion<>>: SpoolPhyOp #Records=7874898
14		**Cache: IterPhyOp #FieldCols=2 #ValueCols=0**
15	7,874,898	Spool_MultiValuedHashLookup: IterPhyOp LogOp=Scan_Vertipaq LookupCols(0)('Product'[Prod
16	7,874,898	ProjectionSpool<ProjectFusion<>>: SpoolPhyOp #Records=7874898
17		**Cache: IterPhyOp #FieldCols=2 #ValueCols=0**
18		ColPosition<'Product'[Product Name]>: LookupPhyOp LogOp=ColPosition<'Product'[Product Name]>ColPosition

The datacache with 8M rows is consumed at lines 14 and 17. Indeed, the LastDate operator at line 9 receives the product names, grouped by the Spool_Iterator at line 10, and the list of dates returned by the Spool_MultiValuedHashLookup operator at line 15. The result contains the product name and the last date used to generate the filter for the xmSQL query at line 6.

Having reached this part of the analysis, we know we need to drive the calculation of the last order date into the storage engine. We can achieve this goal by creating a variable containing the last date for all the products by using ADDCOLUMNS. We then use the information in the variable to place a filter and compute the average. Because of the simplicity of ADDCOLUMNS, we expect the query to be sent to the storage engine directly.

These considerations lead to a new formulation which, though much more verbose, produces a better result in terms of performance. Later in this section, we show a much shorter version. Nonetheless, this code helps understand the overall algorithm:

```
EVALUATE
SUMMARIZECOLUMNS (
    'Product'[Product Name],
    "Last price",
        VAR ProdsAndDates =
            TREATAS (
                ADDCOLUMNS (
                    ALLSELECTED ( 'Product'[Product Name] ),
                    "@LastDate", CALCULATE ( MAX ( Sales[Order Date] ) )
                ),
                'Product'[Product Name],
                Sales[Order Date]
            )
        VAR Result =
            CALCULATE ( AVERAGE ( Sales[Net Price] ), KEEPFILTERS ( ProdsAndDates ) )
        RETURN
            Result
)
ORDER BY 'Product'[Product Name]
```

A first look at the server timings is already reassuring.

Total	SE CPU	Line	Subclass	Duration	CPU	Par.	Rows	KB	Timeline
163 ms	2,110 ms								
	x14.4	2	Scan	59	16	x0.3	2,520	40	
		4	Scan	1	0		2,520	20	
FE	SE	6	Scan	87	2,094	x24.1	2,520	40	
16 ms	147 ms								
9.8%	90.2%								

SE Queries	SE Cache
3	0
	0.0%

A couple of details to note: First, materialization is much lower. All the queries return 2,520 rows, which is the number of products. The large datacache with 8M rows has disappeared. Second, the time of the formula engine is nearly zero. Both pieces of information indicate that the formula engine no longer oversees the heavy calculation of the last order date per product.

Let us analyze the three storage engine queries. The first one retrieves the filter, gathering the product name and its last order date with a single xmSQL query:

```
SELECT
    'Product'[Product Name],
    MAX ( 'Sales'[Order Date] )
FROM 'Sales'
    LEFT OUTER JOIN 'Product'
        ON 'Sales'[ProductKey]='Product'[ProductKey];
```

We already know that the result of this query will be used later to compute the average. The storage engine produces the datacache in less than 4 seconds, materializing a tiny result.

The second query retrieves the product names, and it is instantaneous:

```
SELECT
    'Product'[Product Name]
FROM 'Product';
```

The third query is nearly identical to the one used in the previous version. It uses the filter on pairs of product name and order date, to compute the average net price grouped by product:

```
SELECT
    'Product'[Product Name],
    SUM ( 'Sales'[Net Price] ),
    COUNT (   )
FROM 'Sales'
    LEFT OUTER JOIN 'Product'
        ON 'Sales'[ProductKey]='Product'[ProductKey]
WHERE
    ( 'Product'[Product Name], 'Sales'[Order Date] ) IN {
        ( 'Contoso USB Wave Multi-media Keyboard E280 Black', 43893.000000 ),
        ( 'Contoso Mouse Lock Bundle E200 Grey', 43893.000000 ),
        ( 'MGS Gears of War 2008 M450', 43893.000000 ),
        ( 'MGS Bicycle Card Games2009 E166', 43893.000000 ),
        ( 'Proseware Color Ink Jet Fax, Copier, Phone M250 Grey', 43893.000000 ),
        ( 'Proseware All-In-One Photo Printer M200 Green', 43893.000000 ),
        ( 'SV Hand Games men M30 Yellow', 43893.000000 ),
        ( 'MGS Age of Mythology: Gold Edition M310', 43893.000000 ),
        ( 'Contoso Screen 106in M060 Silver', 43893.000000 ),
        ( 'Proseware Fax Machine E100 Black', 43893.000000 )
        ..[2,517 total tuples, not all displayed]}
    VAND
        'Sales'[Net Price] IS NOT NULL;
```

By using a variable, we have moved the expensive part of the calculation down to the storage engine. Again, a quick look at the query plan confirms our findings.

Line	Records	Physical Query Plan
1		PartitionIntoGroups: IterPhyOp LogOp=Order IterCols(0, 1)('Product'[Product Name], ''[Last price]) #Groups=1 #Rows=2517
2	1	AggregationSpool<Order>: SpoolPhyOp #Records=1
3		GroupSemijoin: IterPhyOp LogOp=GroupSemiJoin IterCols(0, 1)('Product'[Product Name], ''[Last price])
4	2,517	Spool_Iterator<SpoolIterator>: IterPhyOp LogOp=Average_Vertipaq IterCols(0)('Product'[Product Name]) #Records=
5	2,517	ProjectionSpool<ProjectFusion<Average>>: SpoolPhyOp #Records=2517
6		**Cache: IterPhyOp #FieldCols=1 #ValueCols=2**
7		Proxy: IterPhyOp LogOp=TableVarProxy IterCols(1, 2)('Product'[Product Name], 'Sales'[Order Date])
8	2,517	Spool_Iterator<SpoolIterator>: IterPhyOp LogOp=TreatAs IterCols(1, 2)('Product'[Product Name], 'Sales'[C
9	2,517	AggregationSpool<GroupBy>: SpoolPhyOp #Records=2517
10		TreatAs: IterPhyOp LogOp=TreatAs IterCols(1, 2)('Product'[Product Name], 'Sales'[Order Date])
11		AddColumns: IterPhyOp LogOp=AddColumns IterCols(1, 2)('Product'[Product Name], ''[@NetPrice
12	2,517	Spool_Iterator<SpoolIterator>: IterPhyOp LogOp=Scan_Vertipaq IterCols(1)('Product'[Product N
13	2,517	ProjectionSpool<ProjectFusion<>>: SpoolPhyOp #Records=2517
14		**Cache: IterPhyOp #FieldCols=1 #ValueCols=0**
15	2,517	SpoolLookup: LookupPhyOp LogOp=Max_Vertipaq LookupCols(1)('Product'[Product Name]) Da
16	2,517	ProjectionSpool<ProjectFusion<Copy>>: SpoolPhyOp #Records=2517
17		**Cache: IterPhyOp #FieldCols=1 #ValueCols=1**
18		ColPosition<'Product'[Product Name]>: LookupPhyOp LogOp=ColPosition<'Product'[Product Name]>ColPosition<'Prc

The AddColumns operator at line 11 consumes two datacaches: one with the product names (line 14) and one with the product names and last date (line 17). The result is passed to TREATAS to change the lineage, then transformed into a filter for the xmSQL query at line 6, in turn producing the result.

The DAX code we have seen here is much faster than the version using LASTDATE, and it has been helpful to focus on the algorithm. Indeed, the query plan and the xmSQL queries closely mimicked the algorithm depicted in DAX. Note that a much shorter version of the DAX code generates a similar algorithm, even though the DAX code is simpler:

```
EVALUATE
SUMMARIZECOLUMNS (
    'Product'[Product Name],
    "Last price",
        CALCULATE (
            VAR LastOrderDate =
                MAX ( Sales[Order Date] )
            VAR Result =
                CALCULATE ( AVERAGE ( Sales[Net Price] ), Sales[Order Date] = LastOrderDate
)

            RETURN
                Result
        )
)
ORDER BY 'Product'[Product Name]
```

In this version, we removed LASTDATE and replaced it with a filter over *Sales[Order Date]* in

CALCULATE, after having computed the MAX date per product.

Performance-wise, the speed of this version is very close to our optimized version.

Total	SE CPU	Line	Subclass	Duration	CPU	Par.	Rows	KB	Timeline
193 ms	2,375 ms	2	Scan	3	0		2,520	20	
	x13.6	4	Scan	62	31	x0.5	2,520	40	
FE	SE	6	Scan	30	31	x1.0	3,284	26	
18 ms	175 ms	8	Scan	80	2,313	x28.9	2,520	40	
9.3%	90.7%								
SE Queries	SE Cache								
4	0								
	0.0%								

Three of the four xmSQL queries (line 2, 4, and 8) are identical to the ones analyzed above. The fourth (line 6) retrieves the list of all order dates:

```
SELECT
    'Sales'[Order Date]
FROM 'Sales';
```

To understand why Tabular needs the list of order dates, we need to inspect the query plan.

Line	Records	Physical Query Plan
1		PartitionIntoGroups: IterPhyOp LogOp=Order IterCols(0, 1)('Product'[Product Name], ''[Last price]) #Groups=1 #Rows=2517
2	1	AggregationSpool<Order>: SpoolPhyOp #Records=1
3		GroupSemijoin: IterPhyOp LogOp=GroupSemiJoin IterCols(0, 1)('Product'[Product Name], ''[Last price])
4	2,517	Spool_Iterator<SpoolIterator>: IterPhyOp LogOp=Average_Vertipaq IterCols(0)('Product'[Product Name]) #Records=2517 #KeyCol:
5	2,517	ProjectionSpool<ProjectFusion<Average>>: SpoolPhyOp #Records=2517
6		**Cache: IterPhyOp #FieldCols=1 #ValueCols=2**
7	2,517	Spool_Iterator<SpoolIterator>: IterPhyOp LogOp=Filter IterCols(0, 1)('Product'[Product Name], 'Sales'[Order Date]) #Recor
8	2,517	AggregationSpool<GroupBy>: SpoolPhyOp #Records=2517
9		Filter: IterPhyOp LogOp=Filter IterCols(0, 1)('Product'[Product Name], 'Sales'[Order Date])
10		InnerHashJoin: IterPhyOp LogOp=EqualTo IterCols(0, 1)('Product'[Product Name], 'Sales'[Order Date])
11		Extend_Lookup: IterPhyOp LogOp=ScalarVarProxy IterCols(0)('Product'[Product Name])
12	2,517	Spool_Iterator<SpoolIterator>: IterPhyOp LogOp=Scan_Vertipaq IterCols(0)('Product'[Product Name]) #Recor
13	2,517	ProjectionSpool<ProjectFusion<>>: SpoolPhyOp #Records=2517
14		**Cache: IterPhyOp #FieldCols=1 #ValueCols=0**
15	2,517	SpoolLookup: LookupPhyOp LogOp=Max_Vertipaq LookupCols(0)('Product'[Product Name]) DateTime #Reco
16	2,517	ProjectionSpool<ProjectFusion<Copy>>: SpoolPhyOp #Records=2517
17		**Cache: IterPhyOp #FieldCols=1 #ValueCols=1**
18	3,281	HashLookup: IterPhyOp LogOp=HashLookup'Sales'[Order Date] IterCols(1)('Sales'[Order Date]) #Recs=3281
19	3,281	HashByValue: SpoolPhyOp #Records=3281
20		Extend_Lookup: IterPhyOp LogOp=Extend_Lookup'Sales'[Order Date] IterCols(1)('Sales'[Order Date])
21	3,281	Spool_Iterator<SpoolIterator>: IterPhyOp LogOp=Scan_Vertipaq IterCols(1)('Sales'[Order Date]) #Recor
22	3,281	ProjectionSpool<ProjectFusion<>>: SpoolPhyOp #Records=3281
23		**Cache: IterPhyOp #FieldCols=1 #ValueCols=0**
24		ColValue<'Sales'[Order Date]>: LookupPhyOp LogOp=ColValue<'Sales'[Order Date]>'Sales'[Order Date]
25		ColPosition<'Product'[Product Name]>: LookupPhyOp LogOp=ColPosition<'Product'[Product Name]>ColPosition<'Product'[Product

The datacache with 3,284 estimated rows is consumed at line 23, producing the list of all order dates – the actual number of rows reported in the query plan is 3,281, differing slightly from the estimated number. It is used at line 9 to match the result of *MAX (Sales[Order Date])* with actual order dates. In other words, it replaces the TREATAS used previously. In our earlier version, we changed the lineage by using TREATAS. In contrast, in this version, the matching between the *MAX (Sales[Order Date])* expression and the existing *Sales[Order Date]* values happens in the formula engine through the InnerHashJoin and the Filter operators.

We decided to leave the verbose version of the code because while learning how to optimize code, that version provides a better understanding of the various steps involved. Nonetheless, the quality of the DAX optimizer is so excellent that Tabular figured out an optimal algorithm with simpler code.

Avoid using SUMMARIZE and clustering

An interesting example of a DAX construct to avoid is SUMMARIZE to compute aggregated values. The way SUMMARIZE implements the clustering algorithm is a problem from two points of view: performance and semantics. Indeed, by using SUMMARIZE, we often build queries that have two problems: they return an incorrect result and they are extremely slow. Our goal here is not to investigate why the numbers are inaccurate, but instead why SUMMARIZE leads to slow query plans. If you are interested in learning more about SUMMARIZE and its clustering technique, you can find more information here: All the secrets of SUMMARIZEA (https://sql.bi/summarize-secrets/). In the remaining part of the demo, we assume that the reader is familiar with how SUMMARIZE applies filters.

For this demo, we use a largely reduced version of the data model because on the large model, the test query runs out of memory after consuming more than 200GB of RAM. We use the Contoso 1M Power BI Desktop file, containing around 2M rows in *Sales*.

The goal for the query is to compute the sales amount for only the brands that represent more than 10% of the overall sales volume. There are multiple ways to author the query; we chose a particularly wrong way:

```
EVALUATE
FILTER (
    SUMMARIZE (
        Sales,
        Product[Brand],
        "Sales",
            IF (
                [Sales Amount]
                    >= CALCULATE ( [Sales Amount], ALL ( Product[Brand] ) ) * 0.10,
                [Sales Amount]
            )
    ),
    NOT ( ISBLANK ( [Sales] ) )
)
```

Having reached this point of the training, you have probably already noticed several issues. IF.EAGER would be preferrable to IF, or it would be advisable to compute *Sales Amount* only once and store it into a variable. All these are reasonable remarks to make. Nonetheless, in its simplicity, the code hides a huge error.

We can quickly check that the result is wrong. In the following figure, with a sales amount of 17M, Tailspin Toys is less than 10% of the total sales.

Brand	Sales
Contoso	383,399,434.98
Southridge Video	104,914,247.44
Litware	71,784,430.83
Proseware	184,755,490.87
A. Datum	48,816,107.61
The Phone Company	322,126,193.54
Wide World Importers	382,837,404.39
Fabrikam	215,225,128.02
Tailspin Toys	17,189,218.05
Adventure Works	511,437,011.79
Northwind Traders	25,988,206.61

Being wrong is only the first of the two issues. The second problem is that the query takes an extremely long time to run.

Total	SE CPU	Line	Subclass	Duration	CPU	Par.	Rows	KB	Timeline
5,323 ms	2,047 ms x1.4	2	Scan	7	0		14	1	
FE	**SE**	4	Scan	719	1,109	x1.5	2,237,028	131,076	
3,870 ms 72.7%	1,453 ms 27.3%	6	Scan	717	938	x1.3	2,237,028	122,338	
		8	Scan	10	0		14	1	

SE Queries	SE Cache
4	0 0.0%

The problem at the root of the inaccurate numbers and the poor performance is clustering. SUMMARIZE computes new columns by placing a filter on all the columns of the expanded table being iterated. In the case of *Sales*, as in our example, the expanded table is the entire model. Because the engine detected that the remaining tables in the model were not involved, it did not use them. Nonetheless, the engine uses all the *Sales* columns as a filter.

Consequently, Tabular executes two expensive queries: one containing all the columns in *Sales* and another containing all the columns in *Sales* plus *Product[Brand]*. Because of *Sales[ProductKey]*, the two datasets have the same number of rows and almost the same columns. Finally, because all the columns in *Sales* are present in the group-by section, the datacaches contain the entire *Sales* table – uncompressed.

Here are the two xmSQL queries being executed at line 4 and 6. The query at line 4 contains all the columns in *Sales*:

```
WITH
    $Expr0 := ( PFCAST ( 'Sales'[Quantity] AS INT ) * PFCAST ( 'Sales'[Net Price] AS INT ) )
SELECT
    'Sales'[Order Number],
    'Sales'[Line Number],
    'Sales'[Order Date],
    'Sales'[Delivery Date],
    'Sales'[CustomerKey],
    'Sales'[StoreKey],
    'Sales'[ProductKey],
    'Sales'[Quantity],
    'Sales'[Unit Price],
    'Sales'[Net Price],
    'Sales'[Unit Cost],
    'Sales'[Currency Code],
    'Sales'[Exchange Rate],
    SUM ( @$Expr0 )
FROM 'Sales';
```

The query at line 6 is very similar. It does not have any aggregation; it contains *Product[Brand]* as an additional column and the join with *Product*:

```
SELECT
    'Product'[Brand],
    'Sales'[Order Number],
    'Sales'[Line Number],
    'Sales'[Order Date],
    'Sales'[Delivery Date],
    'Sales'[CustomerKey],
    'Sales'[StoreKey],
    'Sales'[ProductKey],
    'Sales'[Quantity],
    'Sales'[Unit Price],
    'Sales'[Net Price],
    'Sales'[Unit Cost],
    'Sales'[Currency Code],
    'Sales'[Exchange Rate]
FROM 'Sales'
    LEFT OUTER JOIN 'Product'
        ON 'Sales'[ProductKey]='Product'[ProductKey];
```

These two datacaches are being joined together inside the formula engine through a complex query plan that is not interesting to study further.

The problem of this query, both from the semantics and the performance points of view, is the presence of all *Sales* columns as filters. This behavior is the main characteristic of SUMMARIZE, which makes SUMMARIZE a unique and hazardous function.

We can double-check that the problem is clustering by changing how we compute the sales of all products. If instead of *ALL (Product[Brand])*, we use *ALL ()*, then we remove all the filters from the model in the inner CALCULATE. This change lets Tabular create a much better query plan and produce the correct result:

```
EVALUATE
FILTER (
    SUMMARIZE (
        Sales,
        Product[Brand],
        "Sales",
            IF (
                [Sales Amount] >= CALCULATE ( [Sales Amount], ALL () ) * 0.10,
                [Sales Amount]
            )
    ),
    NOT ( ISBLANK ( [Sales] ) )
)
```

Indeed, this version of the code now produces the expected result.

Brand	Sales
Contoso	383,399,434.98
Wide World Importers	382,837,404.39
Adventure Works	511,437,011.79
The Phone Company	322,126,193.54

Nonetheless, the best way to author this kind of query is to avoid using SUMMARIZE to compute values. If instead of SUMMARIZE we use ADDCOLUMNS, then the result becomes correct, and performance is also great with the original filters:

```
EVALUATE
FILTER (
    ADDCOLUMNS (
        SUMMARIZE ( Sales, Product[Brand] ),
        "Sales",
            IF (
                [Sales Amount] >= CALCULATE ( [Sales Amount], ALL ( Product[Brand] ) )*0.10,
                [Sales Amount]
            )
    ),
    NOT ( ISBLANK ( [Sales] ) )
)
```

ADDCOLUMNS only places a filter on *Product[Brand]*, which ALL removes. The optimizer figures out that the innermost CALCULATE is independent of any filter placed by ADDCOLUMNS, and it generates an excellent query plan with good performance.

Total	SE CPU		Line	Subclass	Duration	CPU	Par.	Rows	KB	Timeline
30 ms	31 ms		2	Scan	7	0		14	1	
	x1.0									
FE	SE		4	Scan	3	0		1	1	
0 ms	30 ms		6	Scan	3	0		14	1	
0.0%	100.0%		8	Scan	20	31	x1.6	14	1	

SE Queries	SE Cache
4	0
	0.0%

We can improve the code by using IF.EAGER instead of IF to force eager evaluation. Indeed, because the conditional logic evaluates the measure being checked, it makes sense to use IF.EAGER instead of IF. Finally, to make the code even more clear, we can use a variable to store the sales of all brands:

```
EVALUATE
VAR AllSales = [Sales Amount] * 0.10
RETURN
    FILTER (
        ADDCOLUMNS (
            SUMMARIZE ( Sales, Product[Brand] ),
            "Sales", IF.EAGER ( [Sales Amount] >= AllSales, [Sales Amount] )
        ),
        NOT ( ISBLANK ( [Sales] ) )
    )
```

The execution time of this last version of the code is even faster than the previous one, running in 16 milliseconds, with only three xmSQL queries.

Total	SE CPU		Line	Subclass	Duration	CPU	Par.	Rows	KB	Timeline
12 ms	0 ms		2	Scan	7	0		14	1	
	x0.0									
FE	SE		4	Scan	3	0		1	1	
1 ms	11 ms		6	Scan	1	0		14	1	
8.3%	91.7%									

SE Queries	SE Cache
3	0
	0.0%

You can obtain the same result (even a bit more readable) by using a variable to store *Sales Amount*. Indeed, as we learned, this is precisely what IF.EAGER performs:

```
EVALUATE
VAR AllSales = [Sales Amount] * 0.10
RETURN
    FILTER (
        ADDCOLUMNS (
            SUMMARIZE ( Sales, Product[Brand] ),
            "Sales",
                VAR SalesAmount = [Sales Amount]
                RETURN
                    IF ( SalesAmount >= AllSales, SalesAmount )
        ),
        NOT ( ISBLANK ( [Sales] ) )
    )
```

As we learned in this demonstration, using SUMMARIZE to compute aggregates is dangerous. The semantics of SUMMARIZE, based on clustering, are extraordinarily complex and likely to produce unfortunate results. Moreover, performance-wise, clustering is an extremely expensive technique that is not useful in most scenarios. Sticking to a simpler ADDCOLUMNS and increasing the use of variables reduces the execution time of the query while also producing more easy-to-understand semantics.

Optimizing division by checking for zeroes

Whenever developers need to divide one number by another, they should verify that the denominator is not zero. Failing to perform the check might result in errors propagated to the report user. There are multiple techniques to check the denominator of a division, and they are worth further analysis to choose the best one for your specific needs.

We are using a large database (1.4B rows) for this demo, because we need larger timings. The results would be the same on our regular database, however 100M rows are not enough to provide clear evidence of the findings.

The most important detail to verify before choosing the proper technique is the granularity at which the division occurs. Indeed, there are two scenarios: a division executed by the formula engine and a division executed by the storage engine. The difference is relevant because the power of the two engines is very different: the storage engine can execute neither conditional logic nor the DIVIDE function, whereas both features are available in the formula engine.

A division happens in the formula engine when it is performed over results previously aggregated by the storage engine. A simple example of such division is the following:

```
EVALUATE
SUMMARIZECOLUMNS (
    'Product'[Brand],
    "Margin %",
        [Sales Amount] / [Total Amount]
)
```

The query returns the margin as a percentage for each brand.

Brand	Margin %
Contoso	228.66%
Wide World Importers	227.29%
Northwind Traders	219.98%
Adventure Works	226.19%
Southridge Video	227.86%
Litware	224.97%

To compute the result, VertiPaq prepares a datacache containing the sales amount and the cost amount grouped by brand. The formula engine then performs the division and produces the result. Indeed, thanks to vertical fusion, a single storage engine query produces both numbers:

```
WITH
    $Expr0 := ( PFCAST ( 'Sales'[Quantity] AS INT ) * PFCAST ( 'Sales'[Unit Cost] AS INT ) ),
    $Expr1 := ( PFCAST ( 'Sales'[Quantity] AS INT ) * PFCAST ( 'Sales'[Net Price] AS INT ) )
SELECT
    'Product'[Brand],
    SUM ( @$Expr0 ),
    SUM ( @$Expr1 )
FROM 'Sales'
    LEFT OUTER JOIN 'Product'
        ON 'Sales'[ProductKey]='Product'[ProductKey];
```

The division is overseen by the formula engine, as is clearly visible in the query plan.

Line	Records	Physical Query Plan
1		GroupSemijoin: IterPhyOp LogOp=GroupSemiJoin IterCols(0, 1)('Product'[Brand], ''[Margin %])
2		Extend_Lookup: IterPhyOp LogOp=Divide IterCols(0)('Product'[Brand])
3	11	Spool_Iterator<SpoolIterator>: IterPhyOp LogOp=Sum_Vertipaq IterCols(0)('Product'[Brand]) #Records=11
4	11	ProjectionSpool<ProjectFusion<Copy, Copy>>: SpoolPhyOp #Records=11
5		**Cache: IterPhyOp #FieldCols=1 #ValueCols=2**
6	11	SpoolLookup: LookupPhyOp LogOp=Sum_Vertipaq LookupCols(0)('Product'[Brand]) Currency #Records=11
7	11	ProjectionSpool<ProjectFusion<Copy, Copy>>: SpoolPhyOp #Records=11
8		**Cache: IterPhyOp #FieldCols=1 #ValueCols=2**

In this scenario, you can safely use the DIVIDE function, which protects from division by zero. The formula engine executes DIVIDE, and because it performs only 11 divisions in this example, any further attempts to optimize the code would be a waste of time.

Things are entirely different when it is the storage engine that executes a division. The following query performs a division during the iteration over *Sales*, so the storage engine executes the division:

```
EVALUATE
SUMMARIZECOLUMNS (
    'Product'[Brand],
    "Sales with large margin",
        COUNTROWS (
            FILTER (
                Sales,
                Sales[Net Price] / Sales[Unit Cost] >= 2
            )
        )
)
```

We know that Tabular tries to push the innermost iteration down to VertiPaq. Protecting that specific division requires more attention to detail because VertiPaq cannot perform either DIVIDE or IF. To evaluate the cost of our alternatives, let us start looking at the server timings of the division without any protection against a division by zero.

Total	SE CPU		Line	Subclass	Duration	CPU	Par.	Rows	KB	Timeline
570 ms	29,438 ms x52.6		2	Scan	562	29,438	x52.4	14	1	

FE	SE
10 ms	560 ms
1.8%	98.6%

SE Queries	SE Cache
1	0
	0.0%

The query requires 30 seconds of storage engine CPU. The FILTER condition is pushed all the way down to the storage engine, resulting in the WHERE clause of the xmSQL code:

```
SELECT
    'Product'[Brand],
    COUNT ( )
FROM 'Sales'
    LEFT OUTER JOIN 'Product'
        ON 'Sales'[ProductKey]='Product'[ProductKey]
WHERE
    (
        COALESCE ( ( ( CAST ( PFCAST ( 'Sales'[Net Price] AS INT ) AS REAL ) / 10000.000000 )
            / ( CAST ( PFCAST ( 'Sales'[Unit Cost] AS INT ) AS REAL ) / 10000.000000 ) ) )
        >= COALESCE ( 2.000000 )
    );
```

By adding an IF statement to protect the division, we introduce a statement in the inner loop that requires a callback:

```
EVALUATE
SUMMARIZECOLUMNS (
    'Product'[Brand],
    "Sales with large margin",
        COUNTROWS (
            FILTER (
                Sales,
                IF (
                    Sales[Unit Cost] <> 0,
                    Sales[Net Price] / Sales[Unit Cost] >= 2
                )
            )
        )
)
```

The callback is used in the WHERE condition of the xmSQL query:

```
SELECT
    'Product'[Brand],
    COUNT ( )
FROM 'Sales'
    LEFT OUTER JOIN 'Product'
        ON 'Sales'[ProductKey]='Product'[ProductKey]
WHERE
    [CallbackDataID ( IF (
                    Sales[Unit Cost] <> 0,
                    Sales[Net Price] / Sales[Unit Cost] >= 2
    ) ) ] ( PFDATAID ( 'Sales'[Net Price] ), PFDATAID ( 'Sales'[Unit Cost] ) );
```

The callback has a dramatic impact on performance.

Total	SE CPU	Line	Subclass	Duration	CPU	Par.	Rows	KB	Timeline
2,330 ms	120,141 ms	2	Scan	2,327	120,141	x51.6	14	1	
	x51.6								

FE	SE
3 ms	2,327 ms
0.1%	99.9%

SE Queries	SE Cache
1	0
	0.0%

```
SET DC_KIND="AUTO";
SELECT
    'Product'[Brand],
    COUNT ( )
FROM 'Sales'
    LEFT OUTER JOIN 'Product'
        ON 'Sales'[ProductKey]='Product'[ProductKey]
WHERE
    [CallbackDataID ( IF (
            Sales[Unit Cost] <> 0,
            Sales[Net Price] / Sales[Unit Cost] >= 2
    ) )] ( PFDATAID ( 'Sales'[Net Price] ), PFDATAID ( 'Sales'[Unit Cost] ) );
```

The storage engine CPU time goes from 30 seconds to 120 seconds. The code is now safe, but the price to pay for this is exceptionally high. Using DIVIDE is a better option than using IF. Here is the code with DIVIDE:

```
EVALUATE
SUMMARIZECOLUMNS (
    'Product'[Brand],
    "Sales with large margin",
        COUNTROWS (
            FILTER (
                Sales,
                DIVIDE ( Sales[Net Price], Sales[Unit Cost] ) >= 2
            )
        )
)
```

DIVIDE still requires a callback, as was the case with the IF version. Nonetheless, DIVIDE is optimized to perform a division. Being so specific is how we obtain the additional advantage of better performance.

Total	SE CPU		Line	Subclass	Duration	CPU	Par.	Rows	KB	Timeline
1,401 ms	76,922 ms x55.1		2	Scan	1,397	76,922	x55.1	14	1	

FE	SE
4 ms	1,397 ms
0.3%	99.7%

SE Queries	SE Cache
1	0
	0.0%

```
SET DC_KIND="AUTO";
SELECT
  'Product'[Brand],
  COUNT ( )
FROM 'Sales'
  LEFT OUTER JOIN 'Product'
    ON 'Sales'[ProductKey]='Product'[ProductKey]
  WHERE
    ( COALESCE ( [CallbackDataID ( DIVIDE ( Sales[Net Price], Sales[Unit Cost] ) ) ] ( PFDATA
Cost] ) ) ) >= COALESCE ( 2.000000 ) ) ;
```

As you can easily see, the difference between the more generic IF and DIVIDE is firmly in favor of the latter. Nonetheless, both solutions are much slower than the base measure without any protection. Another option would be to use IFERROR to catch any division by zero and transform the error into zero or blank. However, IFERROR requires a callback:

```
EVALUATE
SUMMARIZECOLUMNS (
    'Product'[Brand],
    "Sales with large margin",
        COUNTROWS (
            FILTER (
                Sales,
                IFERROR ( Sales[Net Price] / Sales[Unit Cost], BLANK () ) > 2
            )
        )
)
```

Performance-wise, it sits half way between the previous two versions of the code.

Total	SE CPU		Line	Subclass	Duration	CPU	Par.	Rows	KB	Timeline
2,771 ms	151,656 ms x55.0		2	Scan	2,757	151,656	x55.0	14	1	

FE	SE
14 ms	2,757 ms
0.5%	99.5%

SE Queries	SE Cache
1	0
	0.0%

```
SET DC_KIND="AUTO";
SELECT
  'Product'[Brand],
  COUNT ( )
FROM 'Sales'
  LEFT OUTER JOIN 'Product'
    ON 'Sales'[ProductKey]='Product'[ProductKey]
  WHERE
    ( COALESCE ( [CallbackDataID ( IFERROR ( Sales[Net Price] / Sales[Unit Cost], BLANK () )
( 'Sales'[Unit Cost] ) ) ) > COALESCE ( 2.000000 ) ) ;
```

To obtain the best performance and still provide protection, we remove the zeros from the scan by using the *Sales[Unit Cost] <> 0* filter argument in CALCULATE:

```
EVALUATE
SUMMARIZECOLUMNS (
    'Product'[Brand],
    "Sales with large margin",
        CALCULATE (
            COUNTROWS (
                FILTER (
                    Sales,
                    Sales[Net Price] / Sales[Unit Cost] > 2
                )
            ),
            Sales[Unit Cost] <> 0
        )
)
```

This latter version with the protected division removes the problem we had in the beginning, as it requires a scan of only the values other than zero. There is no need to protect the division, thanks to the filter applied by CALCULATE outside of the scan. An inner FILTER could also apply the filter:

```
EVALUATE
SUMMARIZECOLUMNS (
    'Product'[Brand],
    "Sales with large margin",
        COUNTROWS (
            FILTER (
                FILTER (
                    Sales,
                    Sales[Unit Cost] <> 0
                ),
                Sales[Net Price] / Sales[Unit Cost] > 2
            )
        )
)
```

Both variations of the same code ensure that the code in the innermost iteration can be executed entirely by the storage engine, which removes the need for a callback. The effect on performance is excellent.

Total	SE CPU		Line	Subclass	Duration	CPU	Par.	Rows	KB	Timeline
724 ms	37,641 ms		2	Scan	720	37,641	x52.3	14	1	
	x52.3									

FE	SE
4 ms	720 ms
0.6%	99.4%

SE Queries	SE Cache
1	0
	0.0%

```
SET DC_KIND="AUTO";
SELECT
    'Product'[Brand],
    COUNT ( )
FROM 'Sales'
    LEFT OUTER JOIN 'Product'
        ON 'Sales'[ProductKey]='Product'[ProductKey]
WHERE
    'Sales'[Unit Cost] NIN ( null ) VAND
    ( COALESCE ( ( ( CAST ( PFCAST ( 'Sales'[Net Price] AS INT ) AS REAL ) / 10000.00000
    AS REAL ) / 10000.000000 ) ) ) > COALESCE ( 2.000000 ) );
```

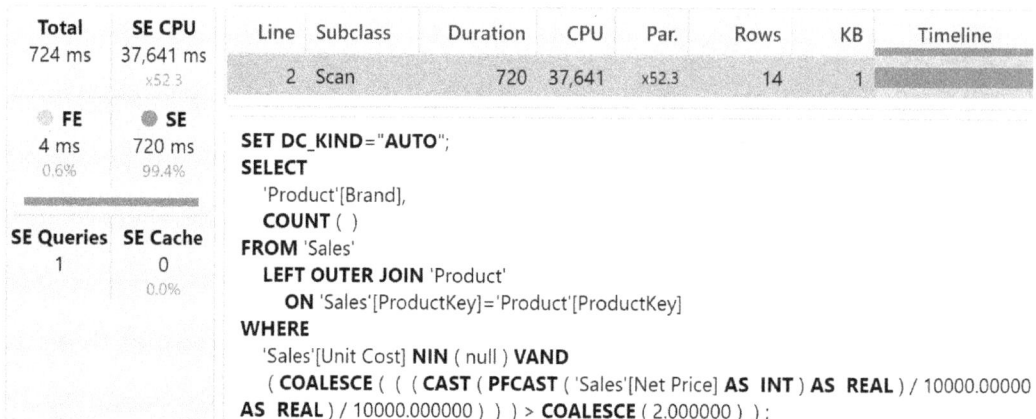

The query is executed with a single xmSQL query with no callback, with both filters being pushed down to VertiPaq:

```
SELECT
    'Product'[Brand],
    COUNT ( )
FROM 'Sales'
    LEFT OUTER JOIN 'Product'
        ON 'Sales'[ProductKey]='Product'[ProductKey]
WHERE
    'Sales'[Unit Cost] NIN ( null ) VAND
    (
        COALESCE ( ( ( CAST ( PFCAST ( 'Sales'[Net Price] AS INT ) AS REAL ) / 10000.000000 )
            / ( CAST ( PFCAST ( 'Sales'[Unit Cost] AS INT ) AS REAL ) / 10000.000000 ) ) )
        > COALESCE ( 2.000000 )
    );
```

There is a price to pay for the protection of the division, but this last version introduces 8 seconds of storage engine CPU added to the 30 seconds already needed for the simple scan and the division.

As you have learned in this demonstration, optimizing a division requires first an understanding of which of the two engines executes the division. If the formula engine executes the division, then DIVIDE is your best option, though IF is viable. If it is the storage engine that performs the division, then using CALCULATE or FILTER to remove zeros upfront proves to be the best technique, as it avoids callbacks.

Reducing the extent of the search by removing blanks

In DAX, small details are incredibly relevant. One of those details is the handling of blank values. In DAX, blank equals zero, meaning a blank value is treated much like a zero. This simple behavior might introduce inefficiencies in your DAX code. Indeed, making sure that blank values – if present – can be ignored, proves to be a powerful optimization tool.

We run the following demo on a small Power BI file because there are substantial performance differences between the optimized version and the non-optimized version.

The following query computes the sales amount for only the combinations of *Date[Date]*, *Customer[State]*, and *Product[Color]* where the sum of *Sales[Quantity]* is greater than or equal to zero. To avoid returning the entire dataset, we embedded SUMMARIZECOLUMNS inside COUNTROWS, so the result only contains one row:

```
DEFINE
    MEASURE Sales[Test] =
        IF ( SUM ( Sales[Quantity] ) >= 0, [Sales Amount] )

EVALUATE
{
    COUNTROWS (
        SUMMARIZECOLUMNS (
            'Date'[Date],          -- 4,018 values
            Customer[State],       --   605 values
            'Product'[Color],      --    16 values
            "Test", [Test]
        )
    )
}
```

Before analyzing the query plan, let us perform a static algorithm analysis. From a pure semantics point of view, SUMMARIZECOLUMNS should perform the CROSSJOIN of all the values of *Date[Date]*, *Customer[State]*, and *Product[Color]*. We added comments in the code to state the number of values of each column.

The entire CROSSJOIN contains 4,018 x 605 x 16 rows – that is, 38,894,240 combinations. Not all combinations produce a result. Indeed, *Sales* contains only 2.2M rows; therefore, most combinations produce BLANK for the sum of *Sales[Quantity]*. In such scenarios, Tabular may optimize the execution by scanning only the non-BLANK combinations.

Nonetheless, the condition in the *Test* measure checks whether *SUM (Sales[Quantity])* is **greater or equal** to zero. A combination of the three group-by columns resulting in a blank would equal zero, making the *SUM (Sales[Quantity]) >= 0* condition true. Therefore, the engine cannot ignore blanks, as they might be part of the calculation. As humans, we know that if the quantity equals zero, the sales amount is zero, too. However, Tabular needs to stay on the safe side. Therefore, it considers all possible combinations, ignoring none.

Moreover, based on the previous knowledge acquired about IF, we know that there are two queries: one to retrieve the combinations where the condition holds true and a second using the result of the first query as a filter.

With all this in mind, this is the expected algorithm:

- Retrieve the values of the three group-by columns to perform the CROSSJOIN in the formula engine.

- Build a datacache with the sum of *Sales[Quantity]* grouped by the three columns.

- Check all possible combinations against the value of *Sales[Quantity]* to determine the combinations where the condition holds true.

- Use the result of the previous step to build a filter over *Sales*.

- Execute another scan of *Sales*, which gathers the sales amount for only the combinations included in the filter.

Now that we have a basic understanding of the algorithm, we can execute the code and analyze the plans deeper. We start with the server timings.

Total	SE CPU	Line	Subclass	Duration	CPU	Par.	Rows	KB	Timeline
20,743 ms	531 ms x1.3	2	Scan	0	0		19	1	
FE 20,349 ms 98.1%	SE 394 ms 1.9%	4	Scan	0	0		608	5	
		6	Scan	1	0		4,021	32	
		8	Scan	183	234	x1.3	1,120,396	13,130	
SE Queries 5	SE Cache 0 0.0%	10	Scan	211	297	x1.4	1,120,396	13,130	

The query took only 394 milliseconds of storage engine, but a ridiculous time of 20,349 milliseconds of formula engine. Indeed, the entire query runs in 20.7 seconds.

The first three xmSQL queries retrieve the values of the three group-by columns:

```
SELECT
    'Product'[Color]
FROM 'Product';

SELECT
    'Customer'[State]
FROM 'Customer';

SELECT
    'Date'[Date]
FROM 'Date';
```

The fourth xmSQL query is needed to evaluate the condition in the IF statement. It groups by the three columns and it computes the sum of *Sales[Quantity]*:

```
SELECT
    'Customer'[State],
    'Date'[Date],
    'Product'[Color],
    SUM ( 'Sales'[Quantity] )
FROM 'Sales'
    LEFT OUTER JOIN 'Customer'
        ON 'Sales'[CustomerKey]='Customer'[CustomerKey]
    LEFT OUTER JOIN 'Date'
        ON 'Sales'[Order Date]='Date'[Date]
    LEFT OUTER JOIN 'Product'
        ON 'Sales'[ProductKey]='Product'[ProductKey];
```

The result of this query is used in the fifth query as a WHERE condition in xmSQL. Please note the number of total tuples shown: 38,903,920, the same size as the entire CROSSJOIN:

```
WITH
    $Expr0 := ( PFCAST ( 'Sales'[Quantity] AS INT ) * PFCAST ( 'Sales'[Net Price] AS INT ) )
SELECT
    'Customer'[State],
    'Date'[Date],
    'Product'[Color],
    SUM ( @$Expr0 )
FROM 'Sales'
    LEFT OUTER JOIN 'Customer'
        ON 'Sales'[CustomerKey]='Customer'[CustomerKey]
    LEFT OUTER JOIN 'Date'
        ON 'Sales'[Order Date]='Date'[Date]
    LEFT OUTER JOIN 'Product'
        ON 'Sales'[ProductKey]='Product'[ProductKey]
WHERE
    ( 'Date'[Date], 'Customer'[State], 'Product'[Color] ) IN {
        ( 40191.000000, 'Chiltern', 'Pink' ) , ( 43526.000000, 'Trafford', 'Brown' ) ,
        ( 40523.000000, 'Havering', 'Grey' ) , ( 42765.000000, 'Welwyn Hatfield', 'Azure' ) ,
        ( 43858.000000, 'Blackpool', 'Silver Grey' ) , ( 40911.000000, 'Vale of Glamorgan', 'Transparent' ) ,
        ( 42862.000000, 'Newham', 'White' ) , ( 43955.000000, 'Boston', 'Red' ) ,
        ( 42101.000000, 'Denbighshire', 'Green' ) , ( 43194.000000, 'Weymouth and Portland', 'Orange' )
        ..[38,903,920 total tuples, not all displayed]};
```

Based on our findings so far, we expect to find a complex query plan.

Line	Records	Physical Query Plan
1		AddColumns: IterPhyOp LogOp=AddColumns IterCols(0)(''[Value])
2		SingletonTable: IterPhyOp LogOp=AddColumns
3	1	SpoolLookup: LookupPhyOp LogOp=CountRows Integer #Records=1 #KeyCols=0 #ValueCols=1 DominantValue=BLANK
4	1	AggregationSpool<Count>: SpoolPhyOp #Records=1
5		GroupSemijoin: IterPhyOp LogOp=GroupSemiJoin IterCols(0, 1, 2)('Date'[Date], 'Customer'[State], 'Product'[Color])
6		CrossApply: IterPhyOp LogOp=Sum_Vertipaq IterCols(0, 1, 2)('Date'[Date], 'Customer'[State], 'Product'[Color])
7	38,903,920	Spool_UniqueHashLookup: IterPhyOp LogOp=PredicateCheck LookupCols(0, 1, 2)('Date'[Date], 'Customer'[State], 'Product'[Color]) #I
8	38,903,920	AggregationSpool<GroupBy>: SpoolPhyOp #Records=38903920
9		PredicateCheck: IterPhyOp LogOp=PredicateCheck IterCols(0, 1, 2)('Date'[Date], 'Customer'[State], 'Product'[Color])
10		Extend_Lookup: IterPhyOp LogOp=ScalarVarProxy IterCols(0, 1, 2)('Date'[Date], 'Customer'[State], 'Product'[Color])
11		CrossApply: IterPhyOp LogOp=ScalarVarProxy IterCols(0, 1, 2)('Date'[Date], 'Customer'[State], 'Product'[Color])
12	4,019	Spool_Iterator<SpoolIterator>: IterPhyOp LogOp=Scan_Vertipaq IterCols(0)('Date'[Date]) #Records=4019 #KeyCols=76
13	4,019	ProjectionSpool<ProjectFusion<>>: SpoolPhyOp #Records=4019
14		**Cache: IterPhyOp #FieldCols=1 #ValueCols=0**
15	605	Spool_Iterator<SpoolIterator>: IterPhyOp LogOp=Scan_Vertipaq IterCols(1)('Customer'[State]) #Records=605 #KeyCols
16	605	ProjectionSpool<ProjectFusion<>>: SpoolPhyOp #Records=605
17		**Cache: IterPhyOp #FieldCols=1 #ValueCols=0**
18	16	Spool_Iterator<SpoolIterator>: IterPhyOp LogOp=Scan_Vertipaq IterCols(2)('Product'[Color]) #Records=16 #KeyCols=7
19	16	ProjectionSpool<ProjectFusion<>>: SpoolPhyOp #Records=16
20		**Cache: IterPhyOp #FieldCols=1 #ValueCols=0**
21		GreaterThanOrEqualTo: LookupPhyOp LogOp=GreaterThanOrEqualTo LookupCols(0, 1, 2)('Date'[Date], 'Customer'[State], '
22	1,120,396	SpoolLookup: LookupPhyOp LogOp=Sum_Vertipaq LookupCols(0, 1, 2)('Date'[Date], 'Customer'[State], 'Product'[Color]'
23	1,120,396	ProjectionSpool<ProjectFusion<Copy>>: SpoolPhyOp #Records=1120396
24		**Cache: IterPhyOp #FieldCols=3 #ValueCols=1**
25		Constant: LookupPhyOp LogOp=Constant Integer 0
26	1,120,396	Spool_Iterator<SpoolIterator>: IterPhyOp LogOp=Sum_Vertipaq IterCols(0, 1, 2)('Date'[Date], 'Customer'[State], 'Product'[Color]) #Re
27	1,120,396	ProjectionSpool<ProjectFusion<Copy>>: SpoolPhyOp #Records=1120396
28		**Cache: IterPhyOp #FieldCols=3 #ValueCols=1**
29	38,903,920	Spool_Iterator<SpoolIterator>: IterPhyOp LogOp=PredicateCheck IterCols(0, 1, 2)('Date'[Date], 'Customer'[State], 'Product'[C
30	38,903,920	AggregationSpool<GroupBy>: SpoolPhyOp #Records=38903920
31		PredicateCheck: IterPhyOp LogOp=PredicateCheck IterCols(0, 1, 2)('Date'[Date], 'Customer'[State], 'Product'[Color])
32		Extend_Lookup: IterPhyOp LogOp=ScalarVarProxy IterCols(0, 1, 2)('Date'[Date], 'Customer'[State], 'Product'[Color])
33		CrossApply: IterPhyOp LogOp=ScalarVarProxy IterCols(0, 1, 2)('Date'[Date], 'Customer'[State], 'Product'[Color])
34	4,019	Spool_Iterator<SpoolIterator>: IterPhyOp LogOp=Scan_Vertipaq IterCols(0)('Date'[Date]) #Records=4019 #Key(
35	4,019	ProjectionSpool<ProjectFusion<>>: SpoolPhyOp #Records=4019
36		**Cache: IterPhyOp #FieldCols=1 #ValueCols=0**
37	605	Spool_Iterator<SpoolIterator>: IterPhyOp LogOp=Scan_Vertipaq IterCols(1)('Customer'[State]) #Records=605 #
38	605	ProjectionSpool<ProjectFusion<>>: SpoolPhyOp #Records=605
39		**Cache: IterPhyOp #FieldCols=1 #ValueCols=0**
40	16	Spool_Iterator<SpoolIterator>: IterPhyOp LogOp=Scan_Vertipaq IterCols(2)('Product'[Color]) #Records=16 #Ke
41	16	ProjectionSpool<ProjectFusion<>>: SpoolPhyOp #Records=16
42		**Cache: IterPhyOp #FieldCols=1 #ValueCols=0**
43		GreaterThanOrEqualTo: LookupPhyOp LogOp=GreaterThanOrEqualTo LookupCols(0, 1, 2)('Date'[Date], 'Customer'
44	1,120,396	SpoolLookup: LookupPhyOp LogOp=Sum_Vertipaq LookupCols(0, 1, 2)('Date'[Date], 'Customer'[State], 'Product
45	1,120,396	ProjectionSpool<ProjectFusion<Copy>>: SpoolPhyOp #Records=1120396
46		**Cache: IterPhyOp #FieldCols=3 #ValueCols=1**
47		Constant: LookupPhyOp LogOp=Constant Integer 0

The algorithm is split into two parts: lines 28-47 create the filter, whereas lines 3-26 use the filter to evaluate the result. The massive amount of formula engine CPU identified earlier is required to scan 38M rows multiple times.

Optimizing this code is surprisingly simple. We need to help the optimizer understand that we are not interested in blank values, so there is no need to build the full cross-join of the three group-by columns. This goal can be accomplished by simply removing zero from the interesting values. In the following query, we just replaced greater than or equal with strictly greater than:

```
DEFINE
    MEASURE Sales[Test] =
        IF ( SUM ( Sales[Quantity] ) > 0, [Sales Amount] )

EVALUATE
{
    COUNTROWS (
        SUMMARIZECOLUMNS (
            'Date'[Date],          -- 4,018 values
            Customer[State],       --   605 values
            'Product'[Color],      --    16 values
            "Test", [Test]
        )
    )
}
```

Once executed, this query performs a lot better.

Total	SE CPU	Line	Subclass	Duration	CPU	Par.	Rows	KB	Timeline
932 ms	625 ms								
	x1.5	2	Scan	187	281	x1.5	1,120,396	13,130	
FE	SE	4	Scan	235	344	x1.5	1,120,396	13,130	
510 ms	422 ms								
54.7%	45.3%								

SE Queries	SE Cache
2	0
	0.0%

As you can easily spot, the first three xmSQL queries are missing because there is no need to retrieve the values of the three group-by columns. Providing Tabular with the option of ignoring blanks helped the optimizer find a better way to compute the result.

The two remaining queries are nearly identical to the ones in the previous version of the code. The only significant difference is that the filter of the second query now contains only 1.1M tuples instead of 38M as it did before.

```
WITH
    $Expr0 := ( PFCAST ( 'Sales'[Quantity] AS INT ) * PFCAST ( 'Sales'[Net Price] AS INT ) )
SELECT
    'Customer'[State],
    'Date'[Date],
    'Product'[Color],
    SUM ( @$Expr0 )
FROM 'Sales'
    LEFT OUTER JOIN 'Customer'
        ON 'Sales'[CustomerKey]='Customer'[CustomerKey]
    LEFT OUTER JOIN 'Date'
        ON 'Sales'[Order Date]='Date'[Date]
    LEFT OUTER JOIN 'Product'
        ON 'Sales'[ProductKey]='Product'[ProductKey]
WHERE
    ( 'Date'[Date], 'Customer'[State], 'Product'[Color] ) IN {
        ( 42161.000000, 'California', 'Silver' ) , ( 42493.000000, 'Virginia', 'Black' ) ,
        ( 41568.000000, 'Huntingdonshire', 'White' ) , ( 42796.000000, 'New South Wales', 'Red' ) ,
        ( 43866.000000, 'Wisconsin', 'Black' ) , ( 40498.000000, 'Scottish Borders', 'Blue' ) ,
        ( 41475.000000, 'South Australia', 'Yellow' ) , ( 43381.000000, 'Zuid-Holland', 'Grey' ) ,
        ( 43659.000000, 'Washington', 'Silver' ) , ( 41909.000000, 'Utah', 'Gold' )
        ..[1,120,396 total tuples, not all displayed]};
```

The critical point is to understand that excluding the blank results from an aggregation like *SUM (Sales[Quantity])* is the crucial item that results in a more efficient execution. Indeed, the following code would be as fast as the one with the condition "greater than zero" although it includes the original "greater than or equal to zero". This is because the exclusion of the blank result is an explicit part of the filter condition:

```
DEFINE
    MEASURE Sales[Test] =
        IF (
            SUM ( Sales[Quantity] ) >= 0 && NOT ISBLANK ( SUM ( Sales[Quantity] ) ),
            [Sales Amount]
        )

EVALUATE
{
    COUNTROWS (
        SUMMARIZECOLUMNS (
            'Date'[Date],          -- 4,018 values
            Customer[State],       --   605 values
            'Product'[Color],      --    16 values
            "Test", [Test]
        )
    )
}
```

The code can still be improved by using IF.EAGER instead of IF. We know, based on our data, that the calculation needs to happen for all the existing combinations; therefore, there is no point in splitting the combinations of columns between true and false values:

```
DEFINE
    MEASURE Sales[Test] =
        IF.EAGER ( SUM ( Sales[Quantity] ) > 0, [Sales Amount] )

EVALUATE
{
    COUNTROWS (
        SUMMARIZECOLUMNS (
            'Date'[Date],        -- 4,018 values
            Customer[State],     --   605 values
            'Product'[Color],    --    16 values
            "Test", [Test]
        )
    )
}
```

Here are the server timings, showing again some level of improvement.

Total	SE CPU		Line	Subclass	Duration	CPU	Par.	Rows	KB	Timeline
700 ms	250 ms									
	×1.3		2	Scan	200	250	×1.3	1,120,396	21,883	
FE	SE		4	Scan	0	0		19	1	
500 ms	200 ms		6	Scan	0	0		608	5	
71.4%	28.6%		8	Scan	0	0		4,021	32	

SE Queries	SE Cache
4	0
	0.0%

As in earlier examples, a developer can obtain the same result by declaring variables rather than using IF.EAGER, with the very same query plan:

```
DEFINE
    MEASURE Sales[Test] =
        VAR SalesAmount = [Sales Amount]
        RETURN
            IF ( SUM ( Sales[Quantity] ) > 0, SalesAmount )

EVALUATE
{
    COUNTROWS (
        SUMMARIZECOLUMNS (
            'Date'[Date],        -- 4,018 values
            Customer[State],     --   605 values
            'Product'[Color],    --    16 values
            "Test", [Test]
        )
    )
}
```

With both IF.EAGER and the variables stored before the IF function, the engine executed the three queries to retrieve the values – but at the same time it removed the second query generated by IF, because we are now using IF.EAGER or the variables. Because of fusion, a single xmSQL query retrieves the sum of *Sales[Quantity]* and the sales amount in a single step:

```
WITH
    $Expr0 := ( PFCAST ( 'Sales'[Quantity] AS INT ) * PFCAST ( 'Sales'[Net Price] AS INT ) )
SELECT
    'Customer'[State],
    'Date'[Date],
    'Product'[Color],
    SUM ( 'Sales'[Quantity] ),
    SUM ( @$Expr0 )
FROM 'Sales'
    LEFT OUTER JOIN 'Customer'
        ON 'Sales'[CustomerKey]='Customer'[CustomerKey]
    LEFT OUTER JOIN 'Date'
        ON 'Sales'[Order Date]='Date'[Date]
    LEFT OUTER JOIN 'Product'
        ON 'Sales'[ProductKey]='Product'[ProductKey];
```

Replacing "less or equal" with "less than" and IF with IF.EAGER or with the variables is enough to obtain the best performance. Two tiny changes in the code improved performance from 20 seconds to less than 1 second. This impact is not unusual: tiny differences in the DAX code trigger different behaviors in the optimizer; only with experience will you find those details.

Optimizing time intelligence calculations

The standard DAX time intelligence functions based on a date column are simple and convenient to use, but they frequently generate excessive materialization because of how they are implemented. Indeed, when you use time intelligence calculations, DAX retrieves data at the day granularity and then performs the calculations inside the formula engine. This behavior helps reduce the number of storage engine queries, and the technique can be used only with additive calculations. Non-additive calculations require the execution of multiple storage engine queries anyway.

The following query computes the growth in sales against the same time period in the previous year. It groups data by *Date[Year Month]*, *Customer[State]*, and *Product[Color]*:

```
DEFINE
    MEASURE Sales[Growth] =
        VAR Cy = [Sales Amount]
        VAR Py =
            CALCULATE ( [Sales Amount], SAMEPERIODLASTYEAR ( 'Date'[Date] ) )
        VAR Result = Cy - Py
        RETURN
            Result

EVALUATE
TOPN (
    100,
    SUMMARIZECOLUMNS (
        'Date'[Year Month],
        Customer[State],
        'Product'[Color],
        "Growth", [Growth]
    ),
    [Growth], DESC
)
```

The query produces only 100 rows because of TOPN. Nonetheless, it needs to generate a larger result, with 1.2M rows out of which it retrieves the first 100. But the server timings panel shows a materialization that is much larger.

Total	SE CPU		Line	Subclass	Duration	CPU	Par.	Rows	KB	Timeline
20,700 ms	66,328 ms		2	Scan	3	0		4,021	32	
	x4.3		4	Scan	0	0		4,018	16	
FE	**SE**		6	Scan	13,731	60,531	x4.4	12,926,984	151,489	
5,196 ms	15,504 ms		8	Scan	1,770	5,797	x3.3	994,647	11,657	
25.1%	74.9%									

SE Queries	**SE Cache**
4	0
	0.0%

The row at line 6 shows the generation of a datacache with 13 million rows. As we always do, we now fully analyze the query plan to understand what is happening.

The first xmSQL query retrieves the values of the *Date[Date]* column:

```
SELECT
    'Date'[Date]
FROM 'Date';
```

The second xmSQL query retrieves the relationship between *Date[Date]* and the *Date[Year Month]* column, used in the grouping:

```
SELECT
    'Date'[Date],
    'Date'[Year Month]
FROM 'Date';
```

The fourth query starts to be more interesting:

```
WITH
    $Expr0 := ( PFCAST ( 'Sales'[Quantity] AS   INT ) * PFCAST ( 'Sales'[Net Price] AS   INT )   )
SELECT
    'Customer'[State],
    'Date'[Date],
    'Product'[Color],
    SUM ( @$Expr0 )
FROM 'Sales'
    LEFT OUTER JOIN 'Customer'
        ON 'Sales'[CustomerKey]='Customer'[CustomerKey]
    LEFT OUTER JOIN 'Date'
        ON 'Sales'[Order Date]='Date'[Date]
    LEFT OUTER JOIN 'Product'
        ON 'Sales'[ProductKey]='Product'[ProductKey]
WHERE
    'Date'[Date] IN ( 42131.000000, 41133.000000, 43088.000000, 42090.000000, 43129.000000, 41051.000000,
41092.000000, 43047.000000, 42049.000000, 41010.000000..[3,652 total values, not all displayed] ) ;

Estimated size: rows = 12,926,984    bytes = 155,123,808
```

This query returns a datacache with 13M rows. The reason is that it is grouping by *Date[Date]* instead of by *Date[Year Month]*, as required by the initial DAX query. The WHERE condition is not particularly useful in this scenario, as it includes the entire date range. Before drawing any conclusion, let us take a quick look at the fourth xmSQL query:

```
WITH
    $Expr0 := ( PFCAST ( 'Sales'[Quantity] AS   INT ) * PFCAST ( 'Sales'[Net Price] AS   INT )   )
SELECT
    'Customer'[State],
    'Date'[Year Month],
    'Product'[Color],
    SUM ( @$Expr0 )
FROM 'Sales'
    LEFT OUTER JOIN 'Customer'
        ON 'Sales'[CustomerKey]='Customer'[CustomerKey]
    LEFT OUTER JOIN 'Date'
        ON 'Sales'[Order Date]='Date'[Date]
    LEFT OUTER JOIN 'Product'
        ON 'Sales'[ProductKey]='Product'[ProductKey];

Estimated size: rows = 994,647    bytes = 11,935,764
```

This last query returns 1M rows grouping by *Date[Year Month]* as expected.

The problem in this measure is that we used a time intelligence function. When SAMEPERIODLASTYEAR needs to compute the range of dates corresponding to the current month moved back one year, it determines the individual dates corresponding to the same period in the previous year. Therefore, Tabular needs to perform these steps:

- It determines, for each month, the set of dates included in the months queried.

- It computes the set of all individual dates needed to define the same months, moved back one year.

- It executes a query that groups by date, generating the 20M row datacache.

- The formula engine uses the 20M row datacache to extract from there the sets of dates corresponding to the previous month.

Because we used SAMEPERIODLASTYEAR, DAX materialized a large dataset. As you might have noticed, the SAMEPERIODLASTYEAR logic is not pushed down to VertiPaq. Standard time intelligence calculation functions based on the *Date* column are never the best option when seeking the best performance. Implementing a custom logic by using more complex DAX code or leveraging different columns in the model makes a lot more sense.

We need to rebuild time intelligence calculations without using time intelligence functions. This requires us to be able to compute the same month in the previous year without relying on SAMEPERIODLASTYEAR.

The *Date* table includes a *Date[Year Month Number]* column that increases once per month. This detail is essential because we can go back and forth over months by subtracting/adding one to the *Date[Year Month Number]* value. To better appreciate the content of the column, we included an extract of the *Date* table, with only the first day of each month:

```
EVALUATE
SELECTCOLUMNS (
    FILTER ( Date, DAY ( 'Date'[Date] ) = 1 ),
    [Date],
    [Year],
    [Year Month],
    [Year Month Number]
)
ORDER BY 'Date'[Date]
```

Here is the result:

Date	Year	Year Month	Year Month Number
00/01/10	2,010	January 2010	24,121
00/01/10	2,010	February 2010	24,122
00/01/10	2,010	March 2010	24,123
00/01/10	2,010	April 2010	24,124
00/01/10	2,010	May 2010	24,125
00/01/10	2,010	June 2010	24,126
00/01/10	2,010	July 2010	24,127
00/01/10	2,010	August 2010	24,128
00/01/10	2,010	September 2010	24,129
00/01/10	2,010	October 2010	24,130
00/01/10	2,010	November 2010	24,131
00/01/10	2,010	December 2010	24,132
00/01/11	2,011	January 2011	24,133
00/01/11	2,011	February 2011	24,134

Please note that the value *of Date[Year Month Number]* in January 2011 is 24,133. If we need to determine the *Date[Year Month Number]* of January 2010, we can subtract 12 from the value, and we obtain 24,121. This simple mathematical property lets us rewrite the logic of SAMEPERIODLASTYEAR with a filter over the *Date[Year Month Number]* column:

```
DEFINE
    MEASURE Sales[Growth] =
        VAR Cy = [Sales Amount]
        VAR PrevYearMonthNumber =
            MAX ( 'Date'[Year Month Number] ) - 12
        VAR Py =
            CALCULATE (
                [Sales Amount],
                'Date'[Year Month Number] = PrevYearMonthNumber,
                REMOVEFILTERS ( 'Date' )
            )
        VAR Result = Cy - Py
        RETURN
            Result
EVALUATE
TOPN (
    100,
    SUMMARIZECOLUMNS (
        'Date'[Year Month],
        Customer[State],
        'Product'[Color],
        "Growth", [Growth]
    ),
    [Growth], DESC
)
```

Running this query produces a faster execution.

Total	SE CPU	Line	Subclass	Duration	CPU	Par.	Rows	KB	Timeline
4,937 ms	14,500 ms								
	x4.1	2	Scan	1	0		135	2	
FE	SE	4	Scan	3	0		135	3	
1,383 ms	3,554 ms	6	Scan	1	0		135	2	
28.0%	72.0%	8	Scan	1,733	7,250	x4.2	971,539	11,386	
		10	Scan	1,818	7,250	x4.0	994,647	11,657	
SE Queries	SE Cache								
5	0								
	0.0%								

All the relevant numbers in Server Timings are improved. There are three tiny storage engine queries, that gather the dates and the values of the *Year Month Number* column. Finally, the two most important queries materialize around 1M rows each.

The pattern we have seen in this example applies to most time intelligence calculations. Using standard time intelligence functions based on a date column for small models is fine. When models are complex or when excessive materialization is an issue, reducing the materialization by using more advanced patterns and techniques in DAX is a great opportunity for improvement.

Distinct count over large cardinality columns

The speed of distinct counts strongly depends on the cardinality of the column to count. We already know that the memory footprint of a column depends on cardinality. Consequently, large-cardinality columns use more memory and take longer to scan. While this is true for all calculations (including distinct counts), DISTINCTCOUNT suffers from another issue: the cardinality determines the size of the bitmap used to perform the distinct count. When these bitmaps exceed the size of the CPU cache, performance starts to degrade very quickly.

The exact cardinality at which the problem arises depends on several factors: the size of the CPU's cache used in the server, and other factors that developers have little or no control over. Roughly speaking, columns with cardinalities up to a few million work well, whereas cardinalities of tens of million and above are a serious issue.

To introduce the topic, we analyze the distinct count of three different columns: *Sales[ProductKey]* with 2,517 values, *Sales[CustomerKey]* with 1.8M values, and *Sales[Order Number]* with 94M values. The following query includes the three columns. Being DISTINCTCOUNT, we know that fusion cannot be applied; therefore, each column is queried separately:

```
EVALUATE
SUMMARIZECOLUMNS (
    'Product'[Brand],
    "# Products",  DISTINCTCOUNT ( Sales[ProductKey] ),
    "# Customers", DISTINCTCOUNT ( Sales[CustomerKey] ),
    "# Orders",    DISTINCTCOUNT ( Sales[Order Number] )
)
```

Indeed, there are three storage engine queries.

Total	SE CPU	Line	Subclass	Duration	CPU	Par.	Rows	KB	Timeline
21,351 ms	305,750 ms								
	x14.4	4	Scan	67	844	x12.6	11	1	
FE	SE	8	Scan	2,960	47,750	x16.1	11	1	
174 ms	21,177 ms	12	Scan	18,150	257,156	x14.2	11	1	
0.8%	99.2%								

SE Queries	SE Cache
3	0
	0.0%

The first query scans *Sales[ProductKey]*, the second query scans *Sales[CustomerKey]*, and the third one scans *Sales[Order Number]*. The timings of the three xmSQL queries are extremely different, ranging from 844 to 257,156 milliseconds. The slowest column scan is three orders of magnitude slower than the fastest. The difference in storage is not enough to justify the additional time required. Indeed *Sales[ProductKey]* is stored in 2.2GB of RAM, whereas *Sales[Order Number]* is stored in 10GB. Despite being five times larger, a distinct count of *Sales[Order Number]* uses two hundred times the time required to compute the distinct count of *Sales[ProductKey]*.

When computing distinct counts, VertiPaq creates a special datacache containing one bit for each possible value of the column. The bitmap is then populated while scanning the column and continuously updated during the scan. As such, the size of the bitmap is relevant to the speed of the distinct count calculation. If the bitmap fits in the CPU cache, then updating it does not require accessing RAM to write values. On the other hand, if the bitmap exceeds the cache size, several write operations require accessing RAM – which is a slow operation, at least from the CPU standpoint.

To provide a better picture of the relationship between size, cardinality, and speed of the distinct count calculation, we created a set of columns starting from *Sales[Order Number]* in a database with 1.4B rows in the *Sales* table. Each column divides the order number by a power of two.

Column	Cardinality	Size
Order Number	94,138,244	10,690,143,056
Order Number Div 002	47,070,167	5,766,489,168
Order Number Div 004	25,535,886	5,186,016,696
Order Number Div 008	11,768,748	4,328,128,152
Order Number Div 016	5,885,216	3,277,902,240
Order Number Div 032	2,943,417	2,988,483,344
Order Number Div 064	1,472,552	2,884,341,832
Order Number Div 128	737,924	2,753,016,320
Order Number Div 256	370,575	2,317,409,480

The column size ranges from 2.3 GB to 10 GB. Whenever we halve the number of orders, we reduce the cardinality, but compression no longer reduces the column size after a certain point. It is worth noting that these are calculated columns. Therefore, the engine cannot use them to change the sort order. The choice of a calculated column is on purpose. We want cardinality to be the only meaningful variable during these tests. If the smaller columns were better optimized, it would be harder to use these numbers for our reasoning because of there being more variables involved.

We evaluated the storage engine time required for each column to perform DISTINCTCOUNT and SUM, grouping by *Product[Brand]*. We measured the timings.

Column	Cardinality	Size	Distinct Count (ms)	SUM (ms)
Order Number	94,138,244	10,690,143,056	2,663,516	8,297
Order Number Div 002	47,070,167	5,766,489,168	1,940,391	7,125
Order Number Div 004	25,535,886	5,186,016,696	1,539,172	6,656
Order Number Div 008	11,768,748	4,328,128,152	961,469	5,969
Order Number Div 016	5,885,216	3,277,902,240	603,781	5,469
Order Number Div 032	2,943,417	2,988,483,344	380,125	5,438
Order Number Div 064	1,472,552	2,884,341,832	230,844	5,406
Order Number Div 128	737,924	2,753,016,320	138,281	5,344
Order Number Div 256	370,575	2,317,409,480	86,188	5,063

The time required to perform a sum depends solely on the size of the column. The larger the column, the more time is required to scan it. Distinct count, on the other hand, has an entirely different pattern. Despite the size of the largest column being around five times larger than the smallest one, the time required to perform the distinct count is ridiculously larger.

To give our readers a better picture of the effect, we added three columns: *Size Ratio*, *DC Ratio*, and *SUM Ratio*. Each column divides the size, distinct count, and sum by the smallest of their respective values to transform the numbers into relative values.

Column	Cardinality	Size	Distinct Count (ms)	SUM (ms)	Size Ratio	DC Ratio	SUM Ratio
Order Number	94,138,244	10,690,143,056	2,663,516	8,297	4.61	30.90	1.64
Order Number Div 002	47,070,167	5,766,489,168	1,940,391	7,125	2.49	22.51	1.41
Order Number Div 004	25,535,886	5,186,016,696	1,539,172	6,656	2.24	17.86	1.31
Order Number Div 008	11,768,748	4,328,128,152	961,469	5,969	1.87	11.16	1.18
Order Number Div 016	5,885,216	3,277,902,240	603,781	5,469	1.41	7.01	1.08
Order Number Div 032	2,943,417	2,988,483,344	380,125	5,438	1.29	4.41	1.07
Order Number Div 064	1,472,552	2,884,341,832	230,844	5,406	1.24	2.68	1.07
Order Number Div 128	737,924	2,753,016,320	138,281	5,344	1.19	1.60	1.06
Order Number Div 256	370,575	2,317,409,480	86,188	5,063	1.00	1.00	1.00

As you see by comparing *Size Ratio* with *DC Ratio*, the time required to perform a distinct count grows much faster than the column size does. As soon as *Cardinality* reaches around 2M, the growth becomes faster.

Unfortunately, this is the expected behavior of distinct counts in VertiPaq. Columns with a large cardinality are a real challenge. Your best option, if feasible, is to reduce cardinality. Despite being the best option, it is seldom a viable path. On large datasets, columns like the order number or the customer code tend to have many unique values. In scenarios like this, model changes might improve performance.

A good option is to create an *Orders* table containing the order number and the *Sales* columns that are linked to the order. We did this by using a simple SUMMARIZECOLUMNS function:

```
-- Calculated table Orders
----------------------------
Orders =
SUMMARIZECOLUMNS (
    Sales[Order Number],
    Sales[StoreKey],
    Sales[Order Date],
    Sales[CustomerKey]
)
```

The new *Orders* table contains 94M rows (one for each order), and the three foreign keys (*StoreKey*, *Order Date*, and *CustomerKey*) can be used to build relationships with the dimensions linked to the order. As you can see, there is no relationship with *Product*, because *Orders* no longer contains the product key.

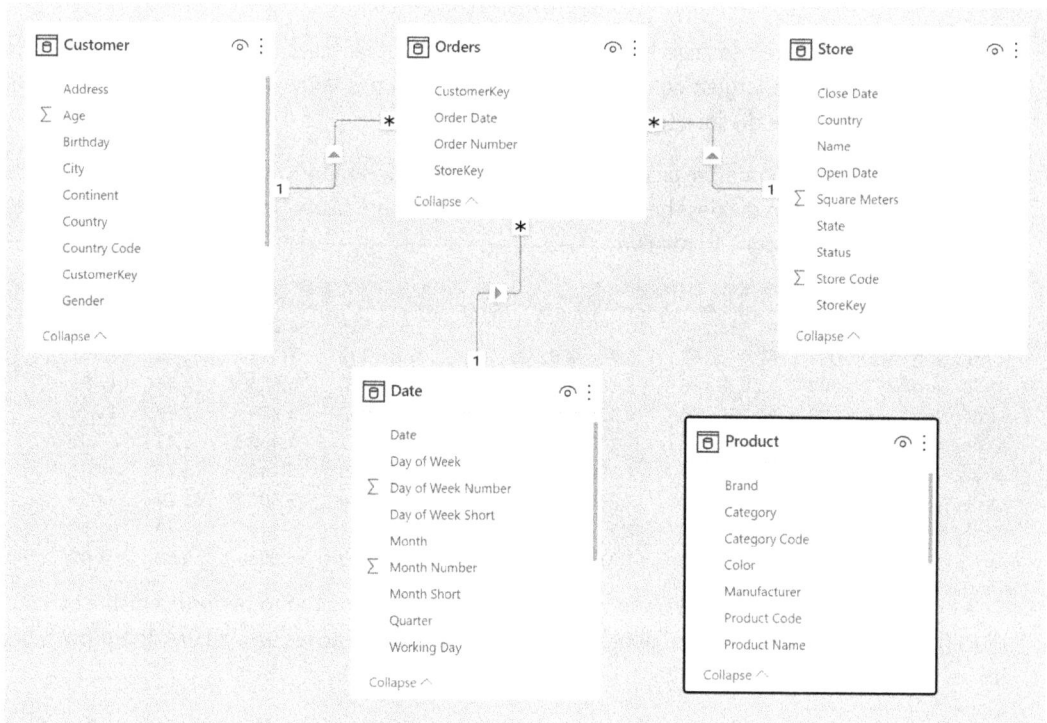

Because *Orders* contains one row per order, instead of performing a distinct count we can now use a simple COUNTROWS to gather the results. Indeed, the following query returns the very same number for both columns:

```
EVALUATE
SUMMARIZECOLUMNS (
    Customer[Continent],
    "# Orders 1", DISTINCTCOUNT ( Sales[Order Number] ),
    "# Orders 2", COUNTROWS ( Orders )
)
```

Continent	# Orders 1	# Orders 2
Europe	29,738,971	29,738,971
North America	58,755,910	58,755,910
Australia	5,599,797	5,599,797

Despite the numbers being the same, the computational effort of the two calculations is very different. Here are the server timings of the previous query.

Total	SE CPU		Line	Subclass	Duration	CPU	Par.	Rows	KB	Timeline
11,345 ms	143,625 ms		4	Scan	10,993	143,609	x13.1	3	1	
	x13.0		6	Scan	18	16	x0.9	6	1	
FE	SE									
334 ms	11,011 ms									
2.9%	97.1%									

SE Queries	SE Cache
2	0
	0.0%

COUNTROWS required 16 milliseconds for the storage engine query at line 6, whereas DISTINCTCOUNT required 143,609 milliseconds to run the storage engine query at line 4. The version with COUNTROWS is less powerful. In our model, the *Orders* table does not have a relationship with *Product*, because an individual order is related to multiple products. The relationship between orders and products is stored in *Sales*, but it is not stored in *Orders*.

Here, a good option is to use ISCROSSFILTERED to check whether there is an active filter over the *Product* table and to direct the calculation to either COUNTROWS or DISTINCTCOUNT. The measure works in any scenario, reverting to slow calculations only when needed:

```
DEFINE
    MEASURE Sales[# Orders] =
        IF (
            ISCROSSFILTERED ( 'Product' ),
            DISTINCTCOUNT ( Sales[Order Number] ),
            COUNTROWS ( Orders )
        )

EVALUATE
SUMMARIZECOLUMNS (
    Customer[Continent],
    "# Orders", [# Orders]
)
```

This query runs extremely fast because *Product* is not filtered.

Total	SE CPU		Line	Subclass	Duration	CPU	Par.	Rows	KB	Timeline
33 ms	16 ms		2	Scan	17	16	x0.9	6	1	
	x0.9									

FE	SE
16 ms	17 ms
48.5%	51.5%

SE Queries	SE Cache
1	0
	0.0%

```
SET DC_KIND="AUTO";
SELECT
    'Customer'[Continent],
    COUNT ( )
FROM 'Table'
    LEFT OUTER JOIN 'Customer'
        ON 'Table'[CustomerKey]='Customer'[CustomerKey];
```

It is worth noting that both IF and ISCROSSFILTERED are very well optimized. Indeed, Tabular detected that the ISCROSSFILTERED condition can be evaluated statically, meaning that the value is defined before running the query. As such, the query plan does not include either IF or ISCROSSFILTERED.

Line	Records	Physical Query Plan
1		GroupSemijoin: IterPhyOp LogOp=GroupSemiJoin IterCols(0, 1)('Customer'[Continent], ''[# Orders])
2	3	Spool_Iterator<SpoolIterator>: IterPhyOp LogOp=Count_Vertipaq IterCols(0)('Customer'[Contine
3	3	ProjectionSpool<ProjectFusion<Copy>>: SpoolPhyOp #Records=3
4		**Cache: IterPhyOp #FieldCols=1 #ValueCols=1**

In a more complex scenario, where there might be a filter over *Product*, things are different; the engine uses the fast calculation when feasible and reverts to the slow calculation when required. For example, the following query includes two calculations. There is one at the *Product[Brand]* level and one at the *Customer[Continent]* level because of the subtotals required:

```
DEFINE
    MEASURE Sales[# Orders] =
        IF (
            ISCROSSFILTERED ( 'Product' ),
            DISTINCTCOUNT ( Sales[Order Number] ),
            COUNTROWS ( Orders )
        )

EVALUATE
SUMMARIZECOLUMNS (
    Customer[Continent],
    ROLLUPADDISSUBTOTAL ( Product[Brand], "Brand Total" ),
    "# Orders", [# Orders]
)
```

The query is resolved by using two xmSQL queries.

Total	SE CPU	Line	Subclass	Duration	CPU	Par.	Rows	KB	Timeline
27,706 ms	260,750 ms								
	x9.7	4	Scan	26,958	260,719	x9.7	33	1	
FE	SE	6	Scan	20	31	x1.6	6	1	
728 ms	26,978 ms								
2.6%	97.4%								

SE Queries	SE Cache
2	0
	0.0%

```
SET DC_KIND="AUTO";
SELECT
    'Customer'[Continent],
    'Product'[Brand],
    DCOUNT ( 'Sales'[Order Number] )
FROM 'Sales'
    LEFT OUTER JOIN 'Customer'
        ON 'Sales'[CustomerKey]='Customer'[CustomerKey]
    LEFT OUTER JOIN 'Product'
        ON 'Sales'[ProductKey]='Product'[ProductKey];
```

The xmSQL query that includes *Product[Brand]* executes a DCOUNT. In contrast, the xmSQL query that uses only *Customer[Continent]* uses a more straightforward COUNT, which results in a much faster execution time. If we were to execute the very same DAX query by using just the DISTINCTCOUNT, the result would be worse:

```
DEFINE
    MEASURE Sales[# Orders] = DISTINCTCOUNT ( Sales[Order Number] )

EVALUATE
SUMMARIZECOLUMNS (
    Customer[Continent],
    ROLLUPADDISSUBTOTAL ( Product[Brand], "Brand Total" ),
    "# Orders", [# Orders]
)
```

The DAX query still requires two xmSQL queries; however, the xmSQL query for the subtotals using DCOUNT is way slower than the previous one using COUNT.

Total	SE CPU	Line	Subclass	Duration	CPU	Par.	Rows	KB	Timeline
36,911 ms	405,922 ms	4	Scan	25,634	261,391	x10.2	33	1	
	x11.3	8	Scan	10,270	144,531	x14.1	3	1	
FE	**SE**								
1,007 ms	35,904 ms								
2.7%	97.3%								

SE Queries	SE Cache
2	0
	0.0%

```
SET DC_KIND="AUTO";
SELECT
    'Customer'[Continent],
    DCOUNT ( 'Sales'[Order Number] )
FROM 'Sales'
    LEFT OUTER JOIN 'Customer'
        ON 'Sales'[CustomerKey]='Customer'[CustomerKey];
```

Depending on the user's requirements, a developer can use different variations of this technique. For example, they could create a snapshot table containing the distinct count of orders at the month level, reducing the size of the fact table. When implementing these techniques, it is essential to check that the conditional logic embedded in the measures can be resolved statically, as in the example provided here. Moreover, variables should be used carefully.

There are also interesting techniques to approximate the distinct count, that might be worth exploring. One of these techniques was described by Phil Seamark in the article, DAX : Approx Distinct Count (https://dax.tips/2019/12/20/dax-approx-distinct-count/).

Other interesting resources include a blog from Greg Galloway about distinct count optimizations (https://tinyurl.com/faster-distinct-count) in the special scenario where most distinct counts resolve to one. Splitting the column into two can reduce the time required because you can mix sum and distinct count to obtain the desired result.

Conclusions

This chapter presented several optimization techniques for common DAX constructs. However, you should not just apply the pattern as they are. Instead, strive to understand how we measured the performance improvement and how we analyzed the bottleneck of the original code by using query plan and server timings information.

The optimization suggested in each case does not use additional tools or techniques: we rewrite the same request by using a different DAX expression that results in a more efficient execution. Optimizing DAX often means rewriting the business logic, to reduce or remove redundant calculations.

Moving and applying filters to tables

Most of the calculations in DAX require moving a filter from one table to another. This goal is usually accomplished through relationships, although other techniques might come in handy. In this chapter, we analyze different techniques to move filters, to understand of how a filter can be propagated in VertiPaq.

Different filters in CALCULATE

From a conceptual point of view, filters in CALCULATE are tables. Therefore, whatever expression a developer uses for a filter, it is always translated into a table. Despite this being true for DAX semantics, the optimizer uses different techniques to move a filter between tables, depending on the format of the filter and on specific considerations made during the query optimization process.

Most of the choices made by the optimizer are not documented and are subject to frequent changes during product updates. However, there is great value in understanding how to gather precise measurements about how filters are propagated. You most likely will need to measure similar queries on your model with the specific version of Tabular you are using.

A filter can be operating over one or more columns, and the type of condition also matters:

- Single-column filters.
  - With an equality condition like ***Product[Unit Cost] = 10***. This is the simplest type of filter, and it is always very well optimized by using either a batch or a WHERE conditions in xmSQL.
  - With more complex conditions like ***Product[Unit Cost] >= 10***. In this case, the values selected are multiple and the filter can be expressed either as a condition in xmSQL, as a table filter, or with a batch.
  - With a table of values, using IN or TREATAS. This type of condition is always represented as a table filter.
- Filters over multiple columns from the same table.
  - With an equality condition like ***Product[Unit Cost] = 10 || Product[Unit Price] = 10***. Despite using multiple columns, these filters are optimized too.
  - With more complex conditions like ***Product[Unit Cost] >= 10 || Product[Unit Price] <= 10***. In this scenario, the values selected are multiple, and the filter can be expressed either as a condition in xmSQL or as a table filter. When using strings, callbacks might be present and should be removed.
  - With a table of values, using IN or TREATAS. This is represented as a table filter.
- Filters over multiple columns from different tables.
  - These filters need to be provided as a table expression.

The goal of this section is not to provide an extensive description of all the possible conditions. There might be filter scenarios not covered by this analysis. Nonetheless, we tested most of the possible scenarios. Reading the analysis lets you find interesting ideas for other optimization strategies and better understand the numbers you gather from your performance measurements.

Analyzing single-column filters

To test the performance of single-column filters, we need to measure a filter placed on the table containing the aggregated columns with the same filter placed on a related table. By doing this, the only difference between the two queries is the presence of the relationship.

To obtain this goal, we created a column in *Sales* containing *RELATED (Customer[Continent])*. The column is named *Sales[RelatedContinent]*. We then compute the sales amount by placing the filter first on *Customer[Continent]* and then on *Sales[RelatedContinent]* by using the following query:

```
DEFINE
    MEASURE Sales[Test] =
        CALCULATE (
            [Sales Amount],
            -- Only one of the two following filters
            -- should be used in the next tests
            Sales[RelatedContinent] = "Europe"
            Customer[Continent] = "Europe"
        )

EVALUATE
SUMMARIZECOLUMNS (
    "Amount", [Test]
)
```

Before moving further with the tests, let us make a few considerations.

When the filter is placed on the table containing the aggregated columns by using *Sales[RelatedCustomer]*, the filter needs to be pushed down to the VertiPaq storage engine through a simple WHERE condition. Evaluating the query requires filtering *Sales*, which contains 1.4B rows. The *Sales[RelatedContinent]* column contains only three values, exactly as *Customer[Continent]* does. When the filter is working on *Customer[Continent]*, the engine must apply the filter to the *Customer* table (containing only 2M rows). Still, it needs to move the filter from *Customer* to *Sales* using the *Sales[CustomerKey]* column, containing 2M values.

Therefore, we expect the filter on the table containing the aggregated columns to be faster, and the difference between the two queries represents the time required to move the filter from *Customer* to *Sales*.

First, the query filtering *Sales[RelatedContinent]*:

```
DEFINE
    MEASURE Sales[Test] =
        CALCULATE (
            [Sales Amount],
            Sales[RelatedContinent] = "Europe"
        )

EVALUATE
SUMMARIZECOLUMNS (
    "Amount", [Test]
)
```

We take a look at the server timings.

Total	SE CPU	Line	Subclass	Duration	CPU	Par.	Rows	KB	Timeline
55 ms	1,828 ms								
	x36.6	2	Scan	50	1,828	x36.6	1	1	

FE	SE
5 ms	50 ms
9.1%	90.9%

SE Queries	SE Cache
1	0
	0.0%

```
SET DC_KIND="AUTO";
WITH
    $Expr0 := ( PFCAST ( 'Sales'[Quantity] AS INT ) * PFCAST ( 'Sales'[Net Price] AS INT )
SELECT
    SUM ( @$Expr0 )
FROM 'Sales'
WHERE
    'Sales'[RelatedContinent] = 'Europe';
```

The query runs with a single xmSQL query where the filter is pushed down to VertiPaq through a WHERE condition. The storage engine time is 1,828 milliseconds. As you see, there are no relationships involved. Let us now test the second scenario:

```
DEFINE
    MEASURE Sales[Test] =
        CALCULATE (
            [Sales Amount],
            Customer[Continent] = "Europe"
        )

EVALUATE
SUMMARIZECOLUMNS (
    "Amount", [Test]
)
```

The query filtering *Customer[Continent]* shows a different timing, as expected.

Total	SE CPU	Line	Subclass	Duration	CPU	Par.	Rows	KB	Timeline
175 ms	4,906 ms								
	x29.2	3	Scan	168	4,906	x29.2	1	1	

FE	SE
7 ms	168 ms
4.0%	96.0%

SE Queries	SE Cache
1	0
	0.0%

```
SET DC_KIND="AUTO";
WITH
    $Expr0 := ( PFCAST ( 'Sales'[Quantity] AS INT ) * PFCAST ( 'Sales'[Net Price] AS INT )
SELECT
    SUM ( @$Expr0 )
FROM 'Sales'
    LEFT OUTER JOIN 'Customer'
        ON 'Sales'[CustomerKey]='Customer'[CustomerKey]
WHERE
    'Customer'[Continent] = 'Europe';
```

This time the xmSQL query contains a JOIN to *Customer*, and the condition is imposed over *Customer[Continent]* in VertiPaq. The storage engine CPU is now 4,906 milliseconds.

The increased storage engine time corresponds to the price to traverse the relationship, which is therefore around 3 seconds of storage engine CPU out of a total of 5 seconds of execution time.

The *Customer* table contains around 2M rows; therefore, the column used to move the relationship is quite large. It is useful to perform a similar test, this time using the *Product* table, which only contains 2.5K rows. As before, we created a *Sales[RelatedProductName]* calculated column to filter the same number of rows, and avoid the relationship:

```
DEFINE
    MEASURE Sales[Test] =
        CALCULATE (
            [Sales Amount],
            Sales[RelatedProductName] = "A. Datum SLR-like Digital Camera M400 Black"
        )

EVALUATE
SUMMARIZECOLUMNS (
    "Amount", [Test]
)
```

Here are the server timings.

Total	SE CPU	Line	Subclass	Duration	CPU	Par.	Rows	KB	Timeline
54 ms	1,781 ms								
	x37.1	2	Scan	48	1,781	x37.1	1	1	

FE	SE
6 ms	48 ms
11.1%	88.9%

SE Queries	SE Cache
1	0
	0.0%

```
SET DC_KIND="AUTO";
WITH
    $Expr0 := ( PFCAST ( 'Sales'[Quantity] AS INT ) * PFCAST ( 'Sales'[Net Price] AS INT )
SELECT
    SUM ( @$Expr0 )
FROM 'Sales'
WHERE
    'Sales'[RelatedProductName] = 'A. Datum SLR-like Digital Camera M400 Black';
```

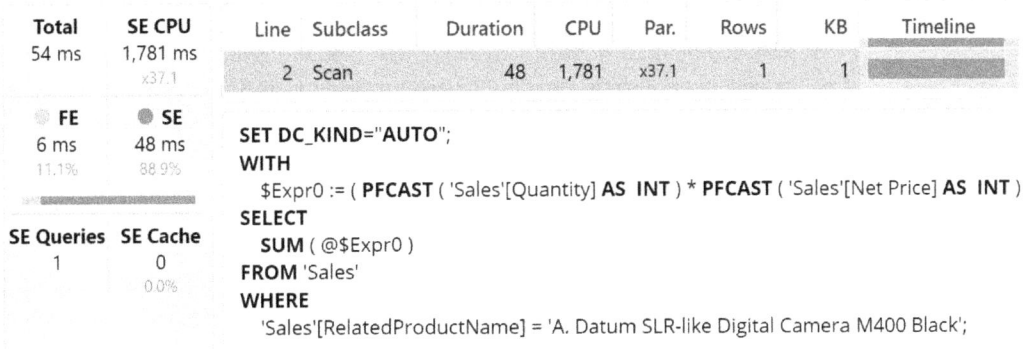

The same query, using the relationship, filters *Product[ProductName]*:

```
DEFINE
    MEASURE Sales[Test] =
        CALCULATE (
            [Sales Amount],
            Product[Product Name] = "A. Datum SLR-like Digital Camera M400 Black"
        )

EVALUATE
SUMMARIZECOLUMNS (
    "Amount", [Test]
)
```

As with the previous example, in this scenario the filter is on the *Product* table. Therefore, it needs to be moved from *Product* to *Sales*, this time using a much smaller column because *Product[ProductKey]* has only 2.5K distinct values.

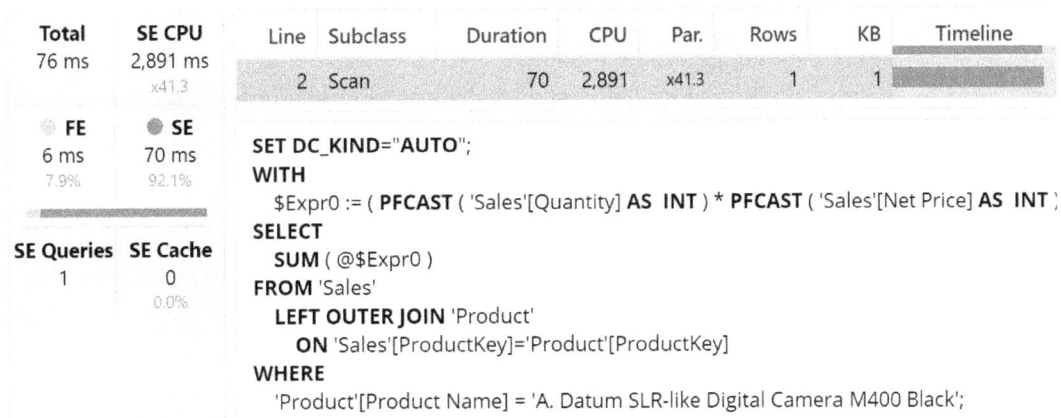

Total	SE CPU	Line	Subclass	Duration	CPU	Par.	Rows	KB	Timeline
76 ms	2,891 ms								
	x41.3	2	Scan	70	2,891	x41.3	1	1	

FE	SE
6 ms	70 ms
7.9%	92.1%

SE Queries	SE Cache
1	0
	0.0%

```
SET DC_KIND="AUTO";
WITH
    $Expr0 := ( PFCAST ( 'Sales'[Quantity] AS INT ) * PFCAST ( 'Sales'[Net Price] AS INT )
SELECT
    SUM ( @$Expr0 )
FROM 'Sales'
    LEFT OUTER JOIN 'Product'
        ON 'Sales'[ProductKey]='Product'[ProductKey]
WHERE
    'Product'[Product Name] = 'A. Datum SLR-like Digital Camera M400 Black';
```

This time, the difference between the two measurements is around 1,000 milliseconds out of 2,800 milliseconds. The performance penalty of using a relationship is still present, albeit smaller. The performance of a relationship strongly depends on the cardinality of the column used as the key. The smaller the column cardinality, the faster the relationship.

After these first tests, it would be wrong to conclude that a relationship is always slower than a filter on the same table. Indeed, relationships are more efficient as soon as the filter becomes complex. When using a relationship, the engine can move the filter using the relationship in VertiPaq, as we have demonstrated so far, or by using a batch with bitmap indexes. Bitmap indexes are an option only when the filter traverses a relationship.

Let us show this behavior with a filter, still on a single value, but with a different column: *Product[Unit Cost]*. In this scenario, Tabular chooses to use a batch to solve the relationship, obtaining better performance with the relationship than with the column in the *Sales* table. Here is the query working with *Sales[RelatedUnitCost]*:

```
DEFINE
    MEASURE Sales[Test] =
        CALCULATE (
            [Sales Amount],
            Sales[RelatedUnitCost] = 10.57
        )

EVALUATE
SUMMARIZECOLUMNS (
    "Amount", [Test]
)
```

The server timings show a large amount of storage engine CPU.

Total	SE CPU		Line	Subclass	Duration	CPU	Par.	Rows	KB	Timeline
188 ms	9,000 ms		2	Scan	181	9,000	x49.7	1	1	
	x49.7									

FE	SE
7 ms	181 ms
3.7%	96.3%

SE Queries	SE Cache
1	0
	0.0%

```
SET DC_KIND="AUTO";
WITH
    $Expr0 := ( PFCAST ( 'Sales'[Quantity] AS INT ) * PFCAST ( 'Sales'[Net Price] AS INT )
SELECT
    SUM ( @$Expr0 )
FROM 'Sales'
WHERE
    ( COALESCE ( ( CAST ( PFCAST ( 'Sales'[RelatedUnitCost] AS INT ) AS REAL ) /
10000.000000 ) ) = COALESCE ( 10.570000 ) );
```

The xmSQL query uses a WHERE condition directly on the *Sales[Unit Cost]* column, with 9,000 milliseconds of storage engine CPU being used. The same query, using *Product[Unit Cost]* is surprisingly fast:

```
DEFINE
    MEASURE Sales[Test] =
        CALCULATE (
            [Sales Amount],
            Product[Unit Cost] = 10.57
        )

EVALUATE
SUMMARIZECOLUMNS (
    "Amount", [Test]
)
```

Here are the server timings.

Total	SE CPU		Line	Subclass	Duration	CPU	Par.	Rows	KB	Timeline
115 ms	4,719 ms		2	Scan	0	0		105,984	13	
	x42.9									
FE	SE		4	Scan	104	4,719	x45.4	1	1	
5 ms	110 ms		5	Batch	6	0				
4.3%	95.7%									

SE Queries	SE Cache
3	0
	0.0%

DEFINE TABLE '$TTable2' :=
SELECT
    SIMPLEINDEXN ('Product'[Unit Cost])
FROM 'Product'

The query runs in only 4,719 milliseconds using a batch, and that is half the execution time of the companion query filtering *Sales[RelatedUnitCost]*. The reason is the efficiency of the batch that implements the relationship by using a bitmap index. Here is the complete xmSQL code:

```
DEFINE TABLE '$TTable2' :=
SELECT
    SIMPLEINDEXN ( 'Product'[Unit Cost] )
FROM 'Product'
WHERE
    ( COALESCE (   ( CAST ( PFCAST ( 'Product'[Unit Cost] AS   INT ) AS   REAL ) / 10000.000000 )   ) = COALESCE (
10.570000 )  ),

DEFINE TABLE '$TTable1' :=
WITH
    $Expr0 := ( PFCAST ( 'Sales'[Quantity] AS   INT ) * PFCAST ( 'Sales'[Net Price] AS   INT )  )
SELECT
    SUM ( @$Expr0 )
FROM 'Sales'
    LEFT OUTER JOIN 'Product'
        ON 'Sales'[ProductKey]='Product'[ProductKey]
WHERE
    'Product'[Unit Cost] ININDEX '$TTable2'[$SemijoinProjection];
```

Tabular chose to use a batch because the condition involves a currency value, so there is a need to perform a currency conversion. Because the filter requires some math, Tabular found it more convenient to perform the test on the *Product* table which contains a small number of rows compared to *Sales*. The values of *Product[Unit Cost]* satisfying the condition are stored in *$TTable2*, with a bitmap index. Consequently, when computing *$TTable1*, VertiPaq can use the bitmap index in the WHERE condition and speed up the scanning of *Sales*.

Be mindful that we can neither say that a bitmap index is always faster than a WHERE condition, nor the opposite. Tabular makes educated choices based on its internal optimization algorithms. As a developer, you always have the choice to refactor your DAX code to drive one choice versus the other, depending on which option is best.

So far, we have analyzed simple conditions with an equality operator. Therefore, pushing the filter down to the VertiPaq engine was always possible. When the filtering condition involves multiple values, pushing the condition to the storage engine might be more difficult. Tabular chooses batches or creates a temporary table with all the selected values. Let us see a few examples.

A condition that filters all the orders starting on January 1st 2015 can be expressed by either filtering *Sales[Order Date]*, or through the relationship with *Date*. If we use *Sales[Order Date]*, then the condition for greater or equal can be pushed down to the storage engine:

```
DEFINE
    MEASURE Sales[Test] =
        CALCULATE (
            [Sales Amount],
            Sales[Order Date] >= DATE ( 2015, 1, 1 )
        )

EVALUATE
SUMMARIZECOLUMNS (
    "Amount", [Test]
)
```

The query is resolved with a single xmSQL query that executes the filter directly inside VertiPaq.

Total	SE CPU		Line	Subclass	Duration	CPU	Par.	Rows	KB	Timeline
117 ms	4,531 ms		2	Scan	103	4,531	x44.0	1	1	
	x44.0									

FE	SE
14 ms	103 ms
12.0%	88.0%

SE Queries	SE Cache
1	0
	0.0%

```
SET DC_KIND="AUTO";
WITH
    $Expr0 := ( PFCAST ( 'Sales'[Quantity] AS INT ) * PFCAST ( 'Sales'[Net Price] AS INT )
SELECT
    SUM ( @$Expr0 )
FROM 'Sales'
WHERE
    ( PFCASTCOALESCE ( 'Sales'[Order Date] AS REAL ) >= COALESCE ( 42005.000000 )
```

The same query can be executed by placing a filter over the *Date* table and relying on the relationship between *Sales* and *Date*:

```
DEFINE
    MEASURE Sales[Test] =
        CALCULATE (
            [Sales Amount],
            'Date'[Date] >= DATE ( 2015, 1, 1 )
        )

EVALUATE
SUMMARIZECOLUMNS (
    "Amount", [Test]
)
```

This time, Tabular chooses a batch to solve the query.

Total	SE CPU		Line	Subclass	Duration	CPU	Par.	Rows	KB	Timeline
116 ms	4,219 ms		2	Scan	9	0		4,032	1	
	x39.4		4	Scan	97	4,219	x43.5	1	1	
			5	Batch	1	0				

FE	SE
9 ms	107 ms
7.8%	92.2%

SE Queries	SE Cache
3	0
	0.0%

```
DEFINE TABLE '$TTable2' :=
SELECT
    SIMPLEINDEXN ( 'Date'[Date] )
FROM 'Date'
WHERE
    ( PFCASTCOALESCE ( 'Date'[Date] AS REAL ) >= COALESCE ( 42005.000000 ) ) ),
```

The batch is quite standard. It builds a bitmap index over *Date[Date]*, which is the key of the relationship, and then it uses it to scan *Sales*:

```
DEFINE TABLE '$TTable2' :=
SELECT
    SIMPLEINDEXN ( 'Date'[Date] )
FROM 'Date'
WHERE
    ( PFCASTCOALESCE ( 'Date'[Date] AS   REAL ) >= COALESCE ( 42005.000000 )   ),

DEFINE TABLE '$TTable1' :=
WITH
    $Expr0 := ( PFCAST ( 'Sales'[Quantity] AS   INT ) * PFCAST ( 'Sales'[Net Price] AS   INT )   )
SELECT
    SUM ( @$Expr0 )
FROM 'Sales'
    LEFT OUTER JOIN 'Date'
        ON 'Sales'[Order Date]='Date'[Date]
WHERE
    'Date'[Date] ININDEX '$TTable2'[$SemijoinProjection];
```

Performance-wise, the cost of the relationship is relatively small due to the reduced size of the *Date* table. It is relevant to note that the performance does not depend on the column used to filter. When filtering through a relationship, the additional price depends on the key of the relationship, not on the column used to filter. Indeed, filtering the *Date[Year]* column that contains only 10 values produces the very same result in terms of performance:

```
DEFINE
    MEASURE Sales[Test] =
        CALCULATE (
            [Sales Amount],
            'Date'[Year] >= 2015
        )

EVALUATE
SUMMARIZECOLUMNS (
    "Amount", [Test]
)
```

The server timings are the same as for the previous query filtering *Date[Date]*.

		Line	Subclass	Duration	CPU	Par.	Rows	KB	Timeline
Total	**SE CPU**	2	Scan	0	0		64	1	
113 ms	4,281 ms								
	x41.6	4	Scan	103	4,281	x41.6	1	1	
FE	**SE**	5	Batch	1	0				
10 ms	103 ms								
8.8%	92.0%								

SE Queries **SE Cache**
3   0
0.0%

DEFINE TABLE '$TTable2' :=
SELECT
   SIMPLEINDEXN ('Date'[Year])
FROM 'Date'
WHERE
   (**PFCASTCOALESCE** ('Date'[Year] **AS INT**) >= **COALESCE** (2015)),

Using a batch is one possible technique used by Tabular to move a filter when the selection contains multiple values. Another technique is to retrieve the list of values in the formula engine, perform the selection there, and finally push the filter in the storage engine as a list of static values. For example, the following query generates two storage engine queries – one to retrieve the product names and one to retrieve the result:

```
DEFINE
    MEASURE Sales[Test] =
        CALCULATE (
            [Sales Amount],
            Product[Product Name] >= "A"
        )

EVALUATE
SUMMARIZECOLUMNS (
    "Amount", [Test]
)
```

As you see, this time there are two storage engine queries.

		Line	Subclass	Duration	CPU	Par.	Rows	KB	Timeline
Total	**SE CPU**	2	Scan	1	0		2,520	20	
217 ms	10,625 ms								
	x50.6	4	Scan	210	10,625	x50.6	1	1	
FE	**SE**								
7 ms	210 ms								
3.2%	96.8%								

SET DC_KIND="AUTO";
SELECT
  'Product'[Product Name]
FROM 'Product';

SE Queries **SE Cache**
2   0
0.0%

The first xmSQL query retrieves all the values of the *Product[Product Name]* column:

```
SELECT
    'Product'[Product Name]
FROM 'Product';
```

The second query includes the list of product names in the WHERE condition:

```
WITH
    $Expr0 := ( PFCAST ( 'Sales'[Quantity] AS   INT ) * PFCAST ( 'Sales'[Net Price] AS   INT )   )
SELECT
    SUM ( @$Expr0 )
FROM 'Sales'
    LEFT OUTER JOIN 'Product'
        ON 'Sales'[ProductKey]='Product'[ProductKey]
WHERE
    'Product'[Product Name] IN ( 'A. Datum SLR-like Digital Camera M400 Black', 'Fabrikam Refrigerator 4.6CuFt E2800 Silver',
'Litware Refrigerator 9.7CuFt M560 Silver', 'Contoso Wireless Laser Mouse E50 Grey', 'SV 160GB USB2.0 Portable Hard Disk M65
Grey', 'Contoso Washer & Dryer 15.5in E155 White', 'Contoso USB 2.0 Dock Station docking station M800 White', 'Contoso USB
Optical Mouse E200 Grey', 'MGS Rise of Nations: Thrones and Patriots2009 E145', 'Litware Washer & Dryer 21in E214
White'..[2,517 total values, not all displayed] ) ;
```

This latter method may be used by a developer to specify a filter over a single column is an explicit table expression. In this scenario, like in the previous ones, the optimizer may choose to inject the filter in a WHERE condition or to use a bitmap index.

When working with a single column, table expressions containing basic conditions like greater than, less than, or equal to, show the same behavior as the conditions we have just seen. Indeed, the following table expression in CALCULATE produces the same behavior as a simple condition:

```
DEFINE
    MEASURE Sales[Test] =
        CALCULATE (
            [Sales Amount],
            FILTER (
                ALL ( 'Product'[Unit Cost] ),
                'Product'[Unit Cost] >= 1000 || 'Product'[Unit Cost] <= 20
            )
        )

EVALUATE
SUMMARIZECOLUMNS (
    "Amount", [Test]
)
```

Based on the previous examples, we know that this table expression is solved using a bitmap index. Nonetheless, by using table expressions, you can create more complex scenarios like the following:

```
DEFINE
    MEASURE Sales[Test] =
        CALCULATE (
            [Sales Amount],
            TREATAS (
                GENERATESERIES ( 1, 1000, 0.5 ),
                'Product'[Unit Cost]
            )
        )

EVALUATE
SUMMARIZECOLUMNS (
    "Amount", [Test]
)
```

Here, GENERATESERIES produces a table with 2,000 values, which needs to be created inside the formula engine. Therefore, the formula engine generates the table with all the values, which are then fed into a TREATAS formula engine operator that computes the values of the column that are actually present in the database. It turns out that out of 2,000 values, only 9 are valid; none of the remaining values are present as possible values of *Product[Unit Cost]*.

Therefore, the only xmSQL query generated is the following:

```
WITH
    $Expr0 := ( PFCAST ( 'Sales'[Quantity] AS   INT ) * PFCAST ( 'Sales'[Net Price] AS   INT )  )
SELECT
    SUM ( @$Expr0 )
FROM 'Sales'
    LEFT OUTER JOIN 'Product'
        ON 'Sales'[ProductKey]='Product'[ProductKey]
WHERE
    'Product'[Unit Cost] IN ( 520000, 110000, 285000, 765000, 1375000, 15000, 160000, 130000, 115000 );
```

In scenarios like this one, where the table expression needs to be computed by the formula engine, a batch is not an option. Therefore, the formula engine computes the list of values to be used in the WHERE condition for the filter.

Here is a quick recap of how the engine can implement a single-column filter in DAX:

- Apply the same predicate to WHERE in xmSQL.

- Within the same xmSQL batch, create a table with the list of values with a first xmSQL query and then use the result in a following xmSQL query within the same batch.

- Materialize the list of values in the formula engine through a first xmSQL query and then prepare a second xmSQL query that includes a list of values to filter in the WHERE condition.

Analyzing multiple-column filters

When a condition uses multiple columns from the same table, Tabular can either push the condition down to the storage engine as a multi-column filter, or use a batch – depending on how the filter expression is written. The following query filters both the *Customer[Country]* and the *Customer[Continent]* columns:

```
DEFINE
    MEASURE Sales[Test] =
        CALCULATE (
            [Sales Amount],
            KEEPFILTERS (
                OR (
                    Customer[Country] = "Italy",
                    Customer[Continent] = "North America"
                )
            )
        )

EVALUATE
SUMMARIZECOLUMNS (
    "Amount", [Test]
)
```

Because the conditions are simple equality conditions, they can be pushed down to the storage engine in a WHERE condition.

Total	SE CPU		Line	Subclass	Duration	CPU	Par.	Rows	KB	Timeline
345 ms	17,219 ms									
	x50.6		2	Scan	340	17,219	x50.6	1	1	

FE	SE
5 ms	340 ms
1.4%	98.6%

SE Queries	SE Cache
1	0
	0.0%

```
SET DC_KIND="AUTO";
WITH
    $Expr0 := ( PFCAST ( 'Sales'[Quantity] AS INT ) * PFCAST ( 'Sales'[Net Price] AS INT )
SELECT
    SUM ( @$Expr0 )
FROM 'Sales'
    LEFT OUTER JOIN 'Customer'
        ON 'Sales'[CustomerKey]='Customer'[CustomerKey]
    WHERE
        ( COALESCE ( ( PFDATAID ( 'Customer'[Country] ) = 10 ) ) OR COALESCE ( ( PFDATA
( 'Customer'[Continent] ) = 3 ) ) );
```

With more complex conditions that select multiple values, Tabular produces a table of values to speed up the calculation. For example, by replacing "equal to" with "greater than or equal to", the query plan becomes very different:

```
DEFINE
    MEASURE Sales[Test] =
        CALCULATE (
            [Sales Amount],
            KEEPFILTERS (
                OR (
                    Customer[Country] >= "Italy",
                    Customer[Continent] >= "North America"
                )
            )
        )

EVALUATE
SUMMARIZECOLUMNS (
    "Amount", [Test]
)
```

In this scenario, Tabular must compute the pairs of *Customer[Country]* and *Customer[Continent]* that satisfy the condition. Therefore, it now executes two storage engine queries: one to find the values and one to retrieve the result.

The server timings panel shows the two storage engine queries.

Total	SE CPU		Line	Subclass	Duration	CPU	Par.	Rows	KB	Timeline
373 ms	18,422 ms x50.3		2	Scan	1	0		66	1	
			4	Scan	367	18,422	x50.2	1	1	

FE	SE
7 ms	366 ms
1.9%	98.1%

SE Queries	SE Cache
2	0
	0.0%

```
SET DC_KIND="AUTO";
SELECT
  'Customer'[Country],
  'Customer'[Continent]
FROM 'Customer'
WHERE
  ( COALESCE ( [CallbackDataID ( Customer[Country] >= "Italy" ) ] ( PFDATAID
( 'Customer'[Country] ) ) ) OR COALESCE ( [CallbackDataID ( Customer[Continent] >=
"North America" ) ] ( PFDATAID ( 'Customer'[Continent] ) ) ) );
```

The first xmSQL query retrieves the values that are later used to place the filter:

```
SELECT
    'Customer'[Country],
    'Customer'[Continent]
FROM 'Customer'
WHERE
    ( COALESCE ( [CallbackDataID ( Customer[Country] >= "Italy" ) ] ( PFDATAID ( 'Customer'[Country] )   )   )
    OR
    COALESCE ( [CallbackDataID ( Customer[Continent] >= "North America" ) ] ( PFDATAID ( 'Customer'[Continent] ) ) ) );
```

The result of this first xmSQL query is used to prepare the WHERE condition of the second xmSQL query:

```
WITH
    $Expr0 := ( PFCAST ( 'Sales'[Quantity] AS    INT ) * PFCAST ( 'Sales'[Net Price] AS    INT )   )
SELECT
    SUM ( @$Expr0 )
FROM 'Sales'
    LEFT OUTER JOIN 'Customer'
        ON 'Sales'[CustomerKey]='Customer'[CustomerKey]
WHERE
    ( 'Customer'[Country], 'Customer'[Continent] )
    IN { ( 'Canada', 'North America' ) , ( 'Netherlands', 'Europe' ) , ( 'Italy', 'Europe' ) ,
        ( 'United States', 'North America' ) , ( 'United Kingdom', 'Europe' ) };
```

The query uses 18 seconds of storage engine CPU because it pushes the condition down to the storage engine. In this scenario, it is possible to force the use of a batch with SIMPLENINDEXN by changing the shape of the filter to a table filter. Indeed, Tabular cannot use a batch because the filter involves two different columns. Nonetheless, because both columns belong to the *Customer* dimension, we can force the filter to use the *Sales[CustomerKey]* column:

```
DEFINE
    MEASURE Sales[Test] =
        CALCULATE (
            [Sales Amount],
            FILTER (
                Customer,
                OR (
                    Customer[Country] >= "Italy",
                    Customer[Continent] >= "North America"
                )
            )
        )

EVALUATE
SUMMARIZECOLUMNS (
    "Amount", [Test]
)
```

By placing the filter over the *Customer* table, Tabular can use *Sales[CustomerKey]* as the single column to test. Performance is way better than before.

Total	SE CPU	Line	Subclass	Duration	CPU	Par.	Rows	KB	Timeline
327 ms	9,266 ms	2	*Scan*	3	0		2,100,032	257	
	x29.2	5	*Scan*	314	9,266	x29.5	1	1	
FE	**SE**	6	Batch	0	0				
10 ms	317 ms								
3.1%	96.9%								

SE Queries	SE Cache
3	0
	0.0%

DEFINE TABLE '$TTable2' :=
SELECT
   SIMPLEINDEXN ('Customer'[CustomerKey])

The batch builds a bitmap index which is then used to scan *Sales*:

```
DEFINE TABLE '$TTable2' :=
SELECT
    SIMPLEINDEXN ( 'Customer'[CustomerKey] )
FROM 'Customer'
WHERE
    ( COALESCE ( [CallbackDataID ( Customer[Country] >= "Italy" ) ] ( PFDATAID ( 'Customer'[Country] )   )   )
    OR
    COALESCE ( [CallbackDataID ( Customer[Continent] >= "North America" ) ] ( PFDATAID ( 'Customer'[Continent] ) ) ) ) ,

DEFINE TABLE '$TTable1' :=
WITH
    $Expr0 := ( PFCAST ( 'Sales'[Quantity] AS   INT ) * PFCAST ( 'Sales'[Net Price] AS   INT )   )
SELECT
    SUM ( @$Expr0 )
FROM 'Sales'
    LEFT OUTER JOIN 'Customer'
        ON 'Sales'[CustomerKey]='Customer'[CustomerKey]
WHERE
    'Customer'[CustomerKey] ININDEX '$TTable2'[$SemijoinProjection];
```

The advantage of using a bitmap to scan *Sales* is clear in the server timings, which show an improvement of around 50%.

Though somewhat of an extreme approach, a developer may force the use of a bitmap index even in the case of equality operators by writing the condition in a more complex way. In the following example, we expressed an equality condition with a pair of inequality conditions:

```
DEFINE
    MEASURE Sales[Test] =
        CALCULATE (
            [Sales Amount],
            FILTER (
                Customer,
                OR (
                    AND (
                        Customer[Country] >= "Italy",
                        Customer[Country] <= "Italy"
                    ),
                    AND (
                        Customer[Continent] >= "North America",
                        Customer[Continent] <= "North America"
                    )
                )
            )
        )

EVALUATE
SUMMARIZECOLUMNS (
    "Amount", [Test]
)
```

By us forcing a more complex expression, the optimizer chose to use a batch instead of pushing the condition down to VertiPaq, producing in turn a better execution time: 7,719 milliseconds instead of the 17,219 milliseconds we had before.

Total	SE CPU	Line	Subclass	Duration	CPU	Par.	Rows	KB	Timeline
250 ms	7,719 ms	2	Scan	3	0		2,100,032	257	
	x32.2	5	Scan	239	7,719	x32.3	1	1	
FE	**SE**	6	Batch	0	0				
10 ms	240 ms								
4.0%	96.8%								

SE Queries	SE Cache
3	0
	0.0%

DEFINE TABLE '$TTable2' :=
SELECT
   SIMPLEINDEXN ('Customer'[CustomerKey])
FROM 'Customer'

Be mindful that this kind of optimization is extreme. It is not true that a batch is always faster than a condition executed by the VertiPaq engine. It depends on many factors, and it should always be evaluated with great care.

The takeaway is always the same: by changing the DAX code, you can direct the optimizer towards one solution or another. You need to carefully check the performance of your different options before making an educated choice about the best solution for your specific needs.

Here is a recap of how the Tabular engine can implement a filter with DAX conditions that involve multiple columns:

- Apply the corresponding predicate to WHERE in xmSQL.

- Materialize the possible combinations of the values of multiple columns in the formula engine through a first xmSQL query. Then, prepare a second xmSQL query with a list of the filtered combinations of values (tuples) to filter in the WHERE condition.

- Within the same xmSQL batch, create a table with a bitmap index on a single column that can uniquely identify the filtered combinations of values. Then, use that result in a subsequent xmSQL query within the same batch. This approach does not materialize the values to the formula engine.

Analyzing filters over multiple tables

Filters over multiple tables need to always be expressed as tables. VertiPaq has the option of accepting filters over multiple columns: these types of filters can oftentimes be pushed down to VertiPaq in an efficient way.

For example, the following measure places a filter on both the *Product[Brand]* and *Customer[Continent]* columns:

```
DEFINE
    MEASURE Sales[Test] =
        CALCULATE (
            [Sales Amount],
            TREATAS (
                {
                    ( "Contoso", "North America" ),
                    ( "Litware", "Europe" )
                },
                Product[Brand],
                Customer[Continent]
            )
        )

EVALUATE
SUMMARIZECOLUMNS (
    "Amount", [Test]
)
```

Despite looking complex, as a filter, it can be expressed with a single xmSQL query.

Total	SE CPU		Line	Subclass	Duration	CPU	Par.	Rows	KB	Timeline
423 ms	20,453 ms									
	x50.8		2	Scan	403	20,453	x50.8	1	1	

FE	SE
20 ms	403 ms
4.7%	95.3%

SE Queries	SE Cache
1	0
	0.0%

```
SET DC_KIND="AUTO";
WITH
    $Expr0 := ( PFCAST ( 'Sales'[Quantity] AS INT ) * PFCAST ( 'Sales'[Net Price] AS INT
SELECT
    SUM ( @$Expr0 )
FROM 'Sales'
    LEFT OUTER JOIN 'Product'
        ON 'Sales'[ProductKey]='Product'[ProductKey]
    LEFT OUTER JOIN 'Customer'
        ON 'Sales'[CustomerKey]='Customer'[CustomerKey]
    WHERE
        ( 'Product'[Brand], 'Customer'[Continent] ) IN { ( 'Litware', 'Europe' ) , ( 'Contoso',
'North America' ) };
```

The filtering condition is pushed down to the VertiPaq engine through a filter over tuples.

In general, the formula engine always prepares an arbitrary filter over columns of multiple tables, which may require additional xmSQL queries to retrieve the data to prepare the filter. The filter is applied to a storage engine request by the formula engine providing the list of tuples allowed. We never see a single filter condition involving columns of multiple tables applied directly to the xmSQL query.

Understanding sparse or dense filters

As you may have noticed in the previous sections, Tabular often creates bitmaps through SIMPLEINDEXN to propagate filters between tables. A bitmap filter is a data structure with a bit for each column id to state whether that value is selected. Developers might notice a significant difference in speed depending on the sparsity of the keys in the selection. When the bitmap contains a filter with a contiguous set of values, checking for the existence of values in the bitmap is faster because of internal optimizations executed by the VertiPaq engine.

An example might greatly help better understand this concept. The *Customer* table in our Contoso database has been loaded with fake customer names. When we generated the names, we sorted them by country. Therefore, all customers in one same country have adjacent customer keys.

The following report shows for each country, the first and last customer keys, along with the number of customers and their distribution.

Country	First CustomerKey	Last CustomerKey	Num Customers	Distribution
Australia	1	200,000	176,945	
Canada	200,001	400,000	178,104	
Germany	400,001	600,000	177,960	
France	600,001	700,000	88,559	
Italy	700,001	800,000	89,103	
Netherlands	800,001	900,000	88,734	
United Kingdom	900,001	1,199,999	267,320	
United States	1,200,001	2,100,000	801,359	

When the DAX engine builds a bitmap index or uses a relationship to move a filter from *Customer* to *Sales*, the calculation is based on the *Customer[CustomerKey]* column. When the selection contains contiguous values, the bitmap is optimized and faster. Therefore, if a filter contains contiguous values, performance is better.

Be mindful that what matters is not the values of the customer keys but their data ids. However, because the table is being loaded sorted by *CustomerKey*, the data ids were generated in a very similar order.

We can test this behavior by calculating the sales amount using two different filters: one filters customers in the United States and Canada, and the second filters female customers only. The two filters produce around the same number of customers and rows in *Sales*, so the time spent scanning the *Sales* table is very close. Nonetheless, the filter over *Customer[Country]* results in a much faster execution.

Let us start with a filter over *Customer[Country]*:

```
EVALUATE
SUMMARIZECOLUMNS (
    "Sales Amount",
        CALCULATE (
            [Sales Amount],
            Customer[Country] IN { "United States", "Canada" }
        )
)
```

The selection of the United States filter results in the filter of all customer keys between 1,200,001 and 2,100,000: a contiguous set of values in a well-defined range. Adding Canada produces two buckets, each of which is still contiguous. Hence, the filter is optimized, and performance is great.

Total	SE CPU	Line	Subclass	Duration	CPU	Par.	Rows	KB	Timeline
220 ms	6,750 ms x31.7	3	Scan	213	6,750	x31.7	1	1	

FE	SE
7 ms	213 ms
3.2%	96.8%

SE Queries	SE Cache
1	0
	0.0%

```
SET DC_KIND="AUTO";
WITH
    $Expr0 := ( PFCAST ( 'Sales'[Quantity] AS INT ) * PFCAST ( 'Sales'[Net Price] AS INT ) )
SELECT
    SUM ( @$Expr0 )
FROM 'Sales'
    LEFT OUTER JOIN 'Customer'
        ON 'Sales'[CustomerKey]='Customer'[CustomerKey]
WHERE
    'Customer'[Country] IN ( 'United States', 'Canada' ) ;
```

The same query with a filter over *Customer[Gender]* produces the very same xmSQL code and query plan:

```
EVALUATE
SUMMARIZECOLUMNS(
    "Sales Amount",
        CALCULATE (
            [Sales Amount],
            Customer[Gender] = "Male"
        )
)
```

Nonetheless, male and female customers are scattered around the *Customer* table and generate a selection of *Sales[CustomerKey]* values that include an extensive range of ids. Consequently, the filter cannot be optimized, and performance is just ok.

Total	SE CPU	Line	Subclass	Duration	CPU	Par.	Rows	KB	Timeline
530 ms	22,906 ms x44.1	3	Scan	520	22,906	x44.1	1	1	

FE	SE
10 ms	520 ms
1.9%	98.1%

SE Queries	SE Cache
1	0
	0.0%

```
SET DC_KIND="AUTO";
WITH
    $Expr0 := ( PFCAST ( 'Sales'[Quantity] AS INT ) * PFCAST ( 'Sales'[Net Price] AS INT ) )
SELECT
    SUM ( @$Expr0 )
FROM 'Sales'
    LEFT OUTER JOIN 'Customer'
        ON 'Sales'[CustomerKey]='Customer'[CustomerKey]
WHERE
    'Customer'[Gender] = 'Male';
```

You can notice the vast delta between 6,750 milliseconds and 22,906 milliseconds. The only difference between the two queries is the sparsity of the filter.

In this example, we deliberately exaggerated the effect by loading the *Customer* table sorted by *Country*. In a more real-world scenario, table filters and scans would probably hit sometimes contiguous and sometimes non-contiguous sets of values. So when wanting to squeeze the most out of your model, in case there are some very commonly used filters, it may make sense to experiment with the sorting of dimensions to optimize specific queries.

Be mindful that overly optimizing a specific filter might have the opposite effect on different filters. In our example, sorting customer keys by country makes sense if we expect most analyses involving customers to apply filters on geographical attributes.

Filter columns, not tables

One of the few golden rules in DAX is to apply filters to columns and refrain from filtering tables. When a CALCULATE filter is placed on a table, the semantics may be affected because of context transition, and the query plan is often suboptimal. The DAX optimizer has many more options when the filters work at the column level rather than at the table level. Let us see an example of this.

The following measure applies an OR filter over two columns in *Sales*. The developer decided to implement this condition as a FILTER over *Sales*:

```
DEFINE
    MEASURE Sales[Test] =
        CALCULATE (
            [Sales Amount],
            FILTER (
                Sales,
                Sales[Quantity] = 2 || Sales[Net Price] >= 20
            )
        )

EVALUATE
SUMMARIZECOLUMNS (
    'Product'[Color],
    "Test", [Test]
)
```

The result contains the sales amount filtered and grouped by color for a total of 16 rows.

Color	Test
White	321,163,828,702.05
Grey	103,038,708,535.75
Black	388,070,443,377.10
Gold	49,766,561,172.61
Silver	266,050,611,570.18
Pink	25,386,616,975.60
Brown	99,864,632,039.36

The problem with the measure is its performance. We take a look at the server timings.

Total	SE CPU		Line	Subclass		Duration	CPU	Par.	Rows	KB	Timeline
10,200 ms	253,422 ms		2	Scan		5,187	148,469	x28.6	860,708	10,087	
	x30.6		4	Scan		3,091	104,953	x34.0	860,708	3,363	

FE	SE
1,923 ms	8,277 ms
18.9%	81.2%

SE Queries	SE Cache
2	0
	0.0%

253,422 milliseconds of storage engine CPU are excessive, as it is 1.9 seconds of formula engine. Moreover, the result contains 16 rows, whereas the materialization consists of two datacaches with 860,768 rows each. As usual, we perform a deeper analysis to understand the algorithm followed by Tabular.

Let us start with the two xmSQL queries. The first computes *Sales Amount* grouped by *Product[Color]*, *Sales[Quantity]*, and *Sales[Net Price]*:

```
WITH
    $Expr0 := ( PFCAST ( 'Sales'[Quantity] AS   INT ) * PFCAST ( 'Sales'[Net Price] AS   INT )  )
SELECT
    'Product'[Color],
    'Sales'[Quantity],
    'Sales'[Net Price],
    SUM ( @$Expr0 )
FROM 'Sales'
    LEFT OUTER JOIN 'Product'
        ON 'Sales'[ProductKey]='Product'[ProductKey]
WHERE
    ( COALESCE (   ( PFDATAID ( 'Sales'[Quantity] ) = 4 )   )
    OR
    COALESCE (   ( PFCASTCOALESCE ( 'Sales'[Net Price] AS   INT ) >= COALESCE ( 200000 ) ) ) );
```

The second xmSQL query is very similar, but it retrieves only the group-by columns:

```
SELECT
    'Product'[Color],
    'Sales'[Quantity],
    'Sales'[Net Price]
FROM 'Sales'
    LEFT OUTER JOIN 'Product'
        ON 'Sales'[ProductKey]='Product'[ProductKey]
WHERE
    ( COALESCE (    ( PFDATAID ( 'Sales'[Quantity] ) = 4 )    )
    OR
    COALESCE (    ( PFCASTCOALESCE ( 'Sales'[Net Price] AS    INT ) >= COALESCE ( 200000 ) ) ) );
```

The storage engine queries themselves do not seem to retrieve a reasonable set of data. There seems to be no reason to perform the grouping by *Quantity* and *Net Price*. Therefore, we perform a deeper analysis, looking at the query plan.

Line	Records	Physical Query Plan
1		GroupSemijoin: IterPhyOp LogOp=GroupSemiJoin IterCols(0, 1)('Product'[Color], "[Test])
2	16	Spool_Iterator<SpoolIterator>: IterPhyOp LogOp=Sum_Vertipaq IterCols(0)('Product'[Color]) #Records=16
3	16	AggregationSpool<AggFusion<Sum>>: SpoolPhyOp #Records=16
4		CrossApply: IterPhyOp LogOp=Sum_Vertipaq IterCols(0)('Product'[Color])
5	860,708	Spool_MultiValuedHashLookup: IterPhyOp LogOp=Filter_Vertipaq LookupCols(24, 40, 42)('Product
6	860,708	ProjectionSpool<ProjectFusion<>>: SpoolPhyOp #Records=860708
7		Cache: IterPhyOp #FieldCols=3 #ValueCols=0
8		Cache: IterPhyOp #FieldCols=3 #ValueCols=1

Unfortunately, the query plan does not shed much light on the scenario. The algorithm is clear; still, it does not look reasonable. The two datacaches generated by VertiPaq are retrieved at lines 7 and 8. Line 7 retrieves the datacache without the sales amount, whereas line 8 reads the datacache with the result of *Sales Amount*. The two datacaches are joined inside the formula engine through the CrossApply operator at line 4. Then the result of the join is aggregated, again in the formula engine, by the AggregationSpool operator at line 3.

Most of the formula engine time is probably spent in the join operation between two datacaches containing 860,708 rows each.

The optimizer accurately detected that the filter depends on *Sales[Quantity]* and *Sales[Net Price]*, so it did not materialize the entire *Sales* table. The DAX engine also added the *Product[Color]* column to the list of columns to retrieve, as it is part of the group-by columns. But the optimizer failed to understand that the materialization of all the valid combinations of *Sales[Quantity]* and *Sales[Net Price]* is unnecessary. As such, performance is poor.

This scenario happens very frequently whenever we use entire tables as filter arguments in CALCULATE. It is possible to help the optimizer by avoiding table filters and replacing them with column filters. Not only is the syntax shorter, but performance is also largely improved. In the following DAX code, we removed the filter over *Sales*, replacing it with an equivalent filter over two columns:

```
DEFINE
    MEASURE Sales[Test] =
        CALCULATE (
            [Sales Amount],
            KEEPFILTERS ( Sales[Quantity] = 2 || Sales[Net Price] >= 20 )
        )

EVALUATE
SUMMARIZECOLUMNS (
    'Product'[Color],
    "Test", [Test]
)
```

Moving the filter over the column helped the optimizer solve the DAX query with a single xmSQL query:

```
WITH
    $Expr0 := ( PFCAST ( 'Sales'[Quantity] AS    INT ) * PFCAST ( 'Sales'[Net Price] AS    INT )  )
SELECT
    'Product'[Color],
    SUM ( @$Expr0 )
FROM 'Sales'
    LEFT OUTER JOIN 'Product'
        ON 'Sales'[ProductKey]='Product'[ProductKey]
WHERE
    ( COALESCE (    ( PFDATAID ( 'Sales'[Quantity] ) ) = 4 )   )
    OR
    COALESCE (    ( PFCASTCOALESCE ( 'Sales'[Net Price] AS    INT ) >= COALESCE ( 200000 )   )  )
    );
```

This xmSQL query computes *Sales Amount* sliced by *Product[Color]* with no reference to other group-by columns. Not only is the xmSQL code much simpler, but performance is also way better.

Total	SE CPU		Line	Subclass	Duration	CPU	Par.	Rows	KB	Timeline
520 ms	27,203 ms		2	Scan	511	27,203	x53.2	19	1	
	x53.3									

FE	SE
10 ms	510 ms
1.9%	98.3%

SE Queries	SE Cache
1	0
	0.0%

```
SET DC_KIND="AUTO";
WITH
    $Expr0 := ( PFCAST ( 'Sales'[Quantity] AS INT ) * PFCAST ( 'Sales'[Net Price] AS INT
SELECT
    'Product'[Color],
    SUM ( @$Expr0 )
FROM 'Sales'
    LEFT OUTER JOIN 'Product'
        ON 'Sales'[ProductKey]='Product'[ProductKey]
    WHERE
        ( COALESCE ( ( PFDATAID ( 'Sales'[Quantity] ) = 4 ) ) OR COALESCE
    ( ( PFCASTCOALESCE ( 'Sales'[Net Price] AS INT ) >= COALESCE ( 200000 ) ) ) );
```

The storage engine CPU went from 253,422 milliseconds down to 27,203 milliseconds, which is one less order of magnitude. The formula engine is nearly non-existent, and the VertiPaq engine materializes only 19 rows. It is worth remembering that the number of rows (19) is an estimate. A further look at the query plan shows that the engine materialized only 16 rows, the exact number of rows in the result.

Line	Records	Physical Query Plan
1		GroupSemijoin: IterPhyOp LogOp=GroupSemiJoin IterCols(0, 1)('Product'[Color], ''[Test])
2	16	Spool_Iterator<SpoolIterator>: IterPhyOp LogOp=Sum_Vertipaq IterCols(0)('Product'[
3	16	ProjectionSpool<ProjectFusion<Copy>>: SpoolPhyOp #Records=16
4		Cache: IterPhyOp #FieldCols=1 #ValueCols=1

Filtering a table is the wrong choice. Whenever a developer needs to activate a filter, using column filters is almost always the best option.

Modeling many-to-many relationships

A common scenario where filters must be moved between tables is many-to-many relationships. We analyzed different ways of modeling many-to-many relationships in a previous chapter. However, performing a deep-dive into the details of many-to-many modeling in Tabular is useful.

The Contoso database does not contain a many-to-many pattern. Therefore, we added two tables: *Sport* and *CustomerSport*. Each customer may play zero, one, or more sports, and the *CustomerSport* bridge table stores this information.

There are multiple ways to model the same scenario. One, and probably the most canonical, is to create a one-to-many and then a many-to-one chain of relationships between *Sport* and *Customer*. The solution requires the relationship between *CustomerSport* and *Customer* to use bidirectional filtering.

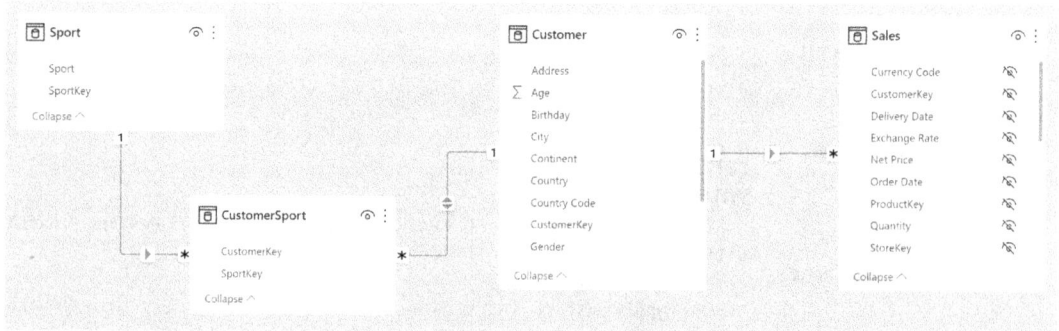

There are at least two other options to obtain the same effect. One requires the use of a many-to-many cardinality cross-filter relationship between *CustomerSport* and *Sales*.

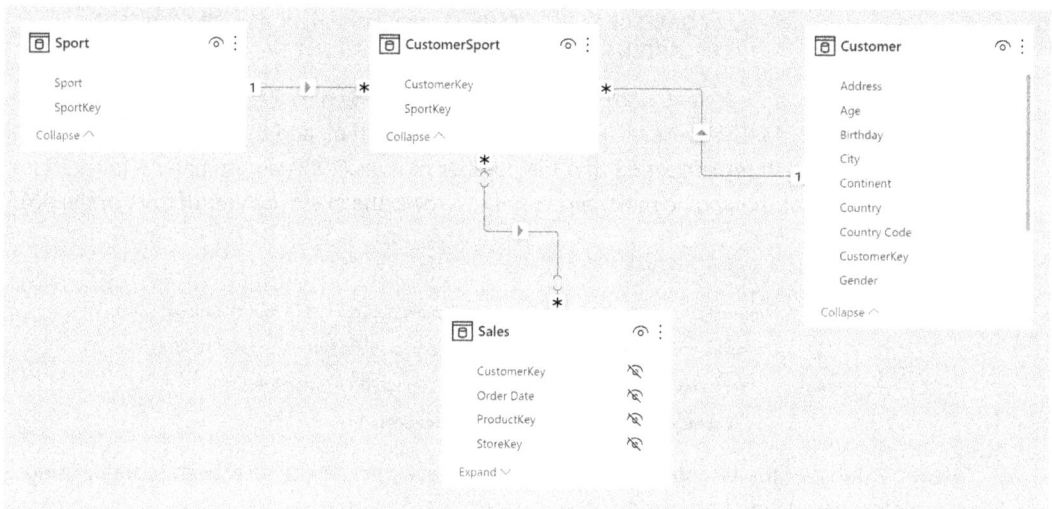

This second option has the advantage of not needing bidirectional cross-filter relationships. However, using a complex chain involving a many-to-many cardinality relationship to move the filter from *Customer* to *Sales* might create performance issues. A third option seems to get the best of both worlds. We keep the many-to-many relationship between *CustomerSport* and *Sales*, but we link *Customer* directly to *Sales*.

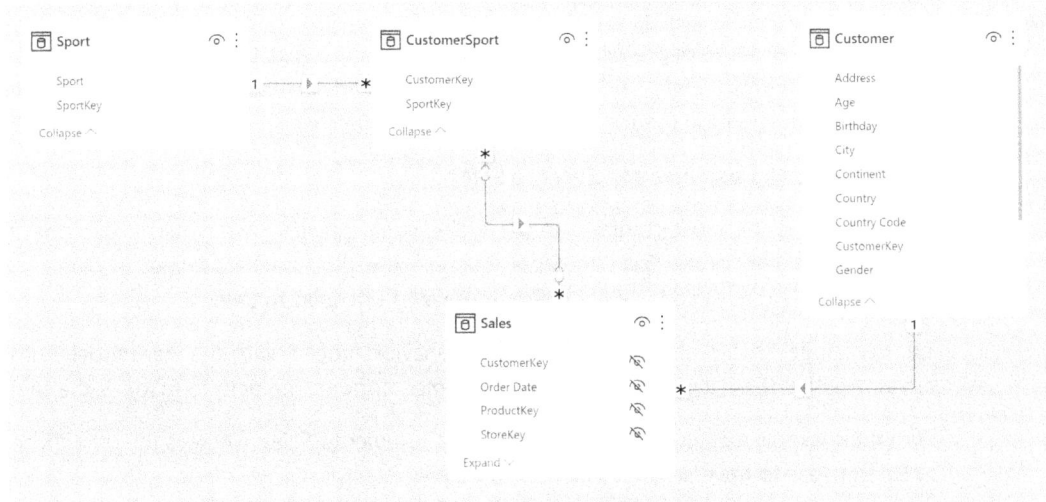

We need a name for the three models: the first is the *Bidirectional Model*, because it involves a bidirectional relationship. The other two have different shapes: the second model is the *Star Model*, and the third is the *Snake Model*.

The three models have advantages and disadvantages, depending on the type of query that is executed. Despite it looking the least intuitive, the third is often the best, especially if we reduce the size of the *CustomerSport* bridge table by merging customers with the same combinations of sports – as we show in an additional snake model called the *Advanced Snake Model*. However, our goal is not to show only the best one but to guide our readers in evaluating the performance of the various models.

For each model, we want to test three scenarios: a filter from *Customer* to *Sales*, a filter from *Sport* to *Sales*, and finally, a filter from both *Customer* and *Sport* to *Sales*.

Before starting the tests, let us perform several considerations:

- **Filter from *Customer* to *Sales***

  Customer is directly linked to *Sales* through a one-to-many regular relationship in both the bidirectional and the snake models. Therefore, we expect to see the full power of VertiPaq relationships in action and great speed in transferring the filter using a VertiPaq join.

  However, in the star model, the relationship between *Customer* and *Sales* needs to use the *CustomerSport* table as a bridge and traverse a many-to-many cardinality relationship, which requires an xmSQL batch.

  Therefore, we expect the star to be the slowest, with bidirectional and snake performing very well.

- **Filter from *Sport* to *Sales***

  In this scenario, the star and the snake models behave the same way: the filter starts from *Sport*, filters the *CustomerSport* table, and traverses a many-to-many cardinality relationship to *Sales*.

Hence, we know it will be an xmSQL batch.

The bidirectional model is probably worse because it needs to use *Customer* as an additional step. The filter starts from *Sport*, and it reaches the *CustomerSport* table. From there, it traverses a bidirectional relationship (hence, a batch) to filter *Customer*, which moves the filter to *Sales*.

- **Filter from both *Customer* and *Sport* to *Sales***

  This scenario is the most complex. In the bidirectional scenario, we would expect the filter to behave like a filter from *Sport* to *Sales*, because the filter over *Customer* is direct, and the relationship is already used when the filter is moved from *Sport* to *Sales*.

  The star model should also display the same behavior. Indeed, with the star model, it does not matter whether the filter starts from *Sales*, *Customer*, or both. The path to follow is the same.

  With the snake, one filter operates directly from *Customer* to *Sales*, whereas the other (from *Sport* to *Sales*) needs to traverse the *CustomerSport* table.

After testing a few simple queries to analyze the impact of each filter, we use the following query to compare the performance of the different models:

```
EVALUATE
SUMMARIZECOLUMNS (
    Sport[Sport],
    Customer[Continent],
    "Sales Amount", [Sales Amount]
)
```

The query computes the sales amount sliced by both the *Sport[Sport]* and *Customer[Continent]* columns. By using *Sport*, *Continent*, or both columns in the query, we can perform all the combinations of interest.

Testing the bidirectional model

We start by measuring the bidirectional model with a filter over only *Customer[Continent]*:

```
EVALUATE
SUMMARIZECOLUMNS (
    Customer[Continent],
    "Sales Amount", [Sales Amount]
)
```

This query uses a one-to-many relationship from *Customer* to *Sales*. It is going to be solved entirely by the storage engine; therefore, we expect optimal performance.

Total	SE CPU		Line	Subclass	Duration	CPU	Par.	Rows	KB	Timeline
103 ms	1,281 ms		2	Scan	97	1,281	x13.2	6	1	
	x13.2									

FE	SE
6 ms	97 ms
5.8%	94.2%

SE Queries	SE Cache
1	0
	0.0%

```
SET DC_KIND="AUTO";
WITH
    $Expr0 := ( PFCAST ( 'Sales'[Quantity] AS INT ) * PFCAST ( 'Sales'[Net Price] AS INT )
SELECT
    'Customer'[Continent],
    SUM ( @$Expr0 )
FROM 'Sales'
    LEFT OUTER JOIN 'Customer'
        ON 'Sales'[CustomerKey]='Customer'[CustomerKey];
```

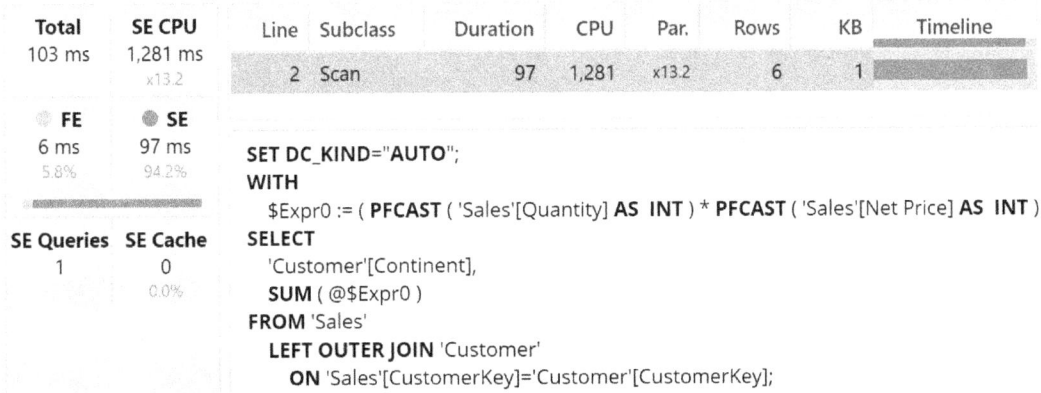

There are no surprises here: with an excellent degree of parallelism, the query is blazingly fast.

The scenario is entirely different if we filter by *Sport[Sport]*:

```
EVALUATE
SUMMARIZECOLUMNS (
    Sport[Sport],
    "Sales Amount", [Sales Amount]
)
```

The filter must move from *Sport* to *CustomerSport*, using a regular one-to-many relationship, and then from *CustomerSport* to *Customer* by using a bidirectional relationship.

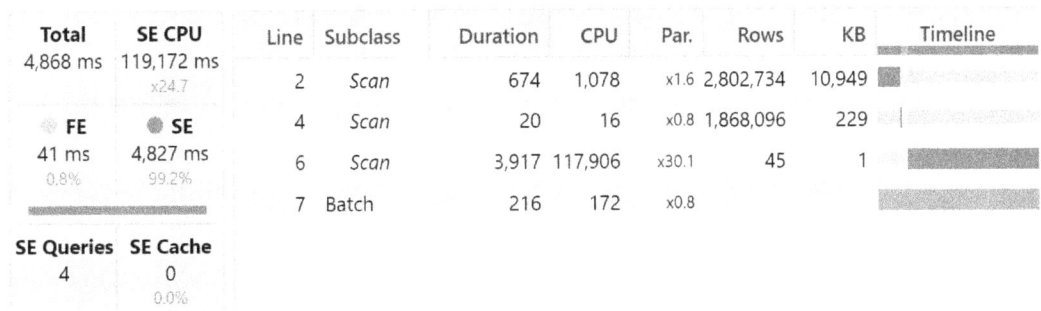

Total	SE CPU		Line	Subclass	Duration	CPU	Par.	Rows	KB	Timeline
4,868 ms	119,172 ms		2	Scan	674	1,078	x1.6	2,802,734	10,949	
	x24.7		4	Scan	20	16	x0.8	1,868,096	229	
			6	Scan	3,917	117,906	x30.1	45	1	
			7	Batch	216	172	x0.8			

FE	SE
41 ms	4,827 ms
0.8%	99.2%

SE Queries	SE Cache
4	0
	0.0%

Despite being resolved entirely in the storage engine, this time the query requires a batch to be executed. Performance-wise, moving the filter comes at a much larger price: more than 10x. Let us dive into the details of the batch:

```
DEFINE TABLE '$TTable3' :=
SELECT
    'Customer'[CustomerKey],
    'Sport'[Sport]
FROM 'CustomerSport'
    LEFT OUTER JOIN 'Customer'
        ON 'CustomerSport'[CustomerKey]='Customer'[CustomerKey]
    LEFT OUTER JOIN 'Sport'
        ON 'CustomerSport'[SportKey]='Sport'[SportKey],


DEFINE TABLE '$TTable4' :=
SELECT
    SIMPLEINDEXN ( '$TTable3'[Customer$CustomerKey] )
FROM '$TTable3',


CREATE SHALLOW RELATION '$TRelation1'
    MANYTOMANY
    FROM 'Customer'[CustomerKey]
        TO '$TTable3'[Customer$CustomerKey],


DEFINE TABLE '$TTable1' :=
SELECT
    '$TTable3'[Sport$Sport],
    SUM ( '$TTable2'[$Measure0] )
FROM '$TTable2'
    INNER JOIN '$TTable3'
        ON '$TTable2'[Customer$CustomerKey]='$TTable3'[Customer$CustomerKey]
REDUCED BY
'$TTable2' :=
WITH
    $Expr0 := ( PFCAST ( 'Sales'[Quantity] AS   INT ) * PFCAST ( 'Sales'[Net Price] AS   INT )   )
SELECT
    'Customer'[CustomerKey],
    SUM ( @$Expr0 )
FROM 'Sales'
    LEFT OUTER JOIN 'Customer'
        ON 'Sales'[CustomerKey]='Customer'[CustomerKey]
WHERE
    'Customer'[CustomerKey] ININDEX '$TTable4'[$SemijoinProjection];
```

The first three queries of the batch build a bitmap index through SIMPLEINDEXN to filter the customers related to a sport. The bitmap is stored in *$TTable4*, which is then used in the last REDUCED BY clause to filter the customers. *$TTable4* is built on *$TTable3*, which stores the relationship between customers and sports. That same *$TTable3* is used to build a many-to-many relationship between *Customer* and *Sports*.

These two data structures (the relationship and the bitmap index) are used in the most complex xmSQL query that *$TTable1* originates from.

The first table, *$TTable4*, has around 2.8M rows, the number of rows in *CustomerSport*. The second table, $TTable3$, around 1.8M rows. Actually, these are estimates. $TTable3$ contains the distinct values of *Customer[CustomerKey]*, therefore its size is 1.4M.

The speed of the query depends on the size of these two internal structures, which are central to the algorithm executed to create the result: $TTable1$. The larger these structures, the slower the query. We can quickly check this by artificially reducing the number of customers being scanned:

```
EVALUATE
SUMMARIZECOLUMNS (
    Sport[Sport],
    TREATAS ( GENERATESERIES ( 1, 10000 ), CustomerSport[CustomerKey] ),
    "Sales Amount", [Sales Amount]
)
```

By reducing the size of $TTable3$ to only 13,284 rows, the query is much faster.

Total	SE CPU	Line	Subclass	Duration	CPU	Par.	Rows	KB	Timeline
204 ms	344 ms	2	Scan	17	0		13,284	52	
	x1.9	4	Scan	1	0		1,868,096	229	
FE	**SE**	6	Scan	150	344	x2.3	45	1	
27 ms	177 ms	7	Batch	9	0				
13.2%	86.8%								

SE Queries	SE Cache
4	0
	0.0%

We have already described this effect a few times. However, it is still helpful to remind our readers of this. The real variable in bidirectional relationships is not the size of the table; it is the size of the internal structures used during the execution of the batch. A bidirectional relationship used with a very restrictive filter shows impressive performance.

However, the goal in this scenario is not to optimize the bidirectional relationships. Our goal is to obtain a clear picture of the advantages and disadvantages of the model.

Let us now check the performance when both filters are being applied:

```
EVALUATE
SUMMARIZECOLUMNS (
    Sport[Sport],
    Customer[Continent],
    "Sales Amount", [Sales Amount]
)
```

Using both tables to move the filter shows a substantial degradation in performance.

Total	SE CPU	Line	Subclass	Duration	CPU	Par.	Rows	KB	Timeline
14,887 ms	112,406 ms x11.0	2	Scan	705	1,109	x1.6	2,802,734	10,949	
FE 4,649 ms 31.2%	SE 10,238 ms 68.8%	4	Scan	9,533	111,297	x11.7	1,401,151	16,420	
SE Queries 2	SE Cache 0 0.0%								

There are several considerations to keep in mind about this plan:

- The amount of formula engine time is considerable. More than 4 seconds of formula engine is worrisome, compared to the few milliseconds of the previous examples.

- There are only two storage engine queries, with a very large materialization and a small degree of parallelism.

- The timeline shows that the formula engine works between the two xmSQL queries – which suggests that the formula engine needs to compute a filter to send to the second storage engine query.

The two storage engine queries are like the ones used in the batch when we were filtering only by *Sport*:

```
SELECT
    'Customer'[CustomerKey],
    'Customer'[Continent],
    'Sport'[Sport]
FROM 'CustomerSport'
    LEFT OUTER JOIN 'Customer'
        ON 'CustomerSport'[CustomerKey]='Customer'[CustomerKey]
    LEFT OUTER JOIN 'Sport'
        ON 'CustomerSport'[SportKey]='Sport'[SportKey];
```

This first xmSQL query retrieves the relationship between *Customer[CustomerKey]* and *Sport[Sport]*. It also includes the relationship between *Customer[CustomerKey]* and *Customer[Continent]*. This piece of information is needed to perform the grouping of sports and continents, using the *Customer[CustomerKey]* to match them.

The second xmSQL query is executed with a complex filter computed by the formula engine based on the first query:

```
WITH
    $Expr0 := ( PFCAST ( 'Sales'[Quantity] AS  INT ) * PFCAST ( 'Sales'[Net Price] AS  INT )  )
SELECT
    'Customer'[CustomerKey],
    'Customer'[Continent],
    SUM ( @$Expr0 )
FROM 'Sales'
    LEFT OUTER JOIN 'Customer'
        ON 'Sales'[CustomerKey]='Customer'[CustomerKey]
WHERE
    ( 'Customer'[Continent], 'Customer'[CustomerKey] ) IN { ( 'Europe', 618263 ) , ( 'Europe', 1076959 ) , ( 'Europe', 1152466 ) , (
    'Australia', 97161 ) , ( 'Europe', 768275 ) , ( 'North America', 1598353 ) , ( 'North America', 1623214 ) , ( 'North America', 1441251 ) ,
    ( 'Europe', 576563 ) , ( 'Australia', 130463 ) ..[1,401,151 total tuples, not all displayed]};
```

The filter only restricts the customers in a way that is very close to what we saw with the batch and the bitmap index. The resulting datacache contains the customer key and the sales amount without mentioning the sport.

At this point, it is clear that the formula engine evaluates the relationship between customers and sports. The two datacaches share the customer keys, so the formula engine can merge them using the customer keys and build the final output. This condition is also confirmed by the significant amount of time spent in the formula engine after completing the two xmSQL queries.

A quick look at the query plan confirms our findings.

Line	Records	Physical Query Plan
1		GroupSemijoin: IterPhyOp LogOp=GroupSemiJoin IterCols(0, 1, 2)('Sport'[Sport], 'Customer'[Continent],
2	135	Spool_Iterator<SpoolIterator>: IterPhyOp LogOp=Sum_Vertipaq IterCols(0, 1)('Sport'[Sport], 'Custome
3	135	AggregationSpool<AggFusion<Sum>>: SpoolPhyOp #Records=135
4		CrossApply: IterPhyOp LogOp=Sum_Vertipaq IterCols(0, 1)('Sport'[Sport], 'Customer'[Continent])
5	2,802,734	Spool_MultiValuedHashLookup: IterPhyOp LogOp=Scan_Vertipaq LookupCols(1, 2)('Customer
6	2,802,734	ProjectionSpool<ProjectFusion<>>: SpoolPhyOp #Records=2802734
7		Cache: IterPhyOp #FieldCols=3 #ValueCols=0
8		Cache: IterPhyOp #FieldCols=2 #ValueCols=1
9	2,802,734	Spool_Iterator<SpoolIterator>: IterPhyOp LogOp=Scan_Vertipaq IterCols(0, 1, 2)('Sport'[Sp
10	2,802,734	ProjectionSpool<ProjectFusion<>>: SpoolPhyOp #Records=2802734
11		Cache: IterPhyOp #FieldCols=3 #ValueCols=0

The datacache used at lines 7 and 11 is the one containing the relationship between *Customer[CustomerKey]*, *Customer[Continent]*, and *Sport[Sport]*. It is used at line 11 to restrict the customers considered by the xmSQL query consumed at line 8, and it is also used at line 7 during the merge with the datacache containing the sales amount.

The strong impact on performance depends on the fact that – with two filters – the formula engine is used to solve the relationship. The two filters produce a large materialization and require the formula engine to merge large tables.

Testing the star model

The star model has a different structure when compared to the bidirectional model. Indeed, there are no bidirectional relationships. Two regular, strong one-to-many relationships link both *Customer* and *Sport* to the bridge table, which in turn uses a many-to-many cardinality relationship to filter *Sales*.

Consequently, we expect a more consistent level of performance, regardless of whether we are filtering *Sport* or *Customer*. However, we should inspect the xmSQL code much more closely to clearly understand how the engine moves the filter from the dimensions to *Sales*.

Let us start by analyzing the sales amount sliced only by *Sport[Sport]*:

```
EVALUATE
SUMMARIZECOLUMNS (
    Sport[Sport],
    "Sales Amount", [Sales Amount]
)
```

We used *Sport[Sport]* as the first test because it can easily be compared with a similar query plan in the bidirectional model. Performance is pretty good when compared with the bidirectional model using *Sport*.

Total	SE CPU	Line	Subclass	Duration	CPU	Par.	Rows	KB	Timeline
5,997 ms	105,156 ms	2	Scan	619	859	x1.4	2,802,734	10,949	
	x17.6	4	Scan	234	219	x0.9	1,401,151	5,474	
FE	**SE**	6	Scan	100	78	x0.8	1,868,096	229	
30 ms	5,967 ms	8	Scan	3,647	102,641	x28.1	45	1	
0.5%	99.5%	9	Batch	1,367	1,359	x1.0			
SE Queries	**SE Cache**								
5	0								
	0.0%								

Moreover, the good news is that the entire query is resolved in the storage engine using a batch that includes four subqueries. Despite looking somewhat similar to the batch we observed in the bidirectional model, its behavior is very different from the internal point of view:

```
DEFINE TABLE '$TTable3' :=
SELECT
    'Sport'[Sport],
    'CustomerSport'[CustomerKey]
FROM 'CustomerSport'
    LEFT OUTER JOIN 'Sport'
        ON 'CustomerSport'[SportKey]='Sport'[SportKey],
```

```
DEFINE TABLE '$Ttable4' :=
SELECT
        '$Ttable3'[CustomerSport$CustomerKey]
FROM '$Ttable3',


DEFINE TABLE '$Ttable5' :=
SELECT
        RJOIN ( '$Ttable4'[CustomerSport$CustomerKey] )
FROM '$Ttable4'
        REVERSE BITMAP JOIN 'Sales' ON '$Ttable4'[CustomerSport$CustomerKey]='Sales'[CustomerKey],


CREATE SHALLOW RELATION '$Trelation1'
        MANYTOMANY
        FROM 'Sales'[CustomerKey]
            TO '$Ttable3'[CustomerSport$CustomerKey],


DEFINE TABLE '$Ttable1' :=
SELECT
        '$Ttable3'[Sport$Sport],
        SUM ( '$Ttable2'[$Measure0] )
FROM '$Ttable2'
        INNER JOIN '$Ttable3'
            ON '$Ttable2'[Sales$CustomerKey]='$Ttable3'[CustomerSport$CustomerKey]
REDUCED BY
'$Ttable2' :=
WITH
        $Expr0 := ( PFCAST ( 'Sales'[Quantity] AS   INT ) * PFCAST ( 'Sales'[Net Price] AS   INT )   )
SELECT
        'Sales'[CustomerKey],
        SUM ( @$Expr0 )
FROM 'Sales'
WHERE
        'Sales'[CustomerKey] ININDEX '$Ttable5'[$SemijoinProjection];
```

In the bidirectional model, the engine used the *CustomerSport* table to determine a filter over *Customer*. In this scenario, the engine still uses *CustomerSport*. Still, it no longer needs to filter *Customer*: the filter goes directly to *Sales*, even though it does so by traversing a many-to-many cardinality relationship.

The structure of *$TTable3* is the same as what we had observed in the bidirectional model: it contains all the combinations of *Sport* and *CustomerKey*. Its size is the same as the number of rows in *CustomerSport*. Based on this first table, VertiPaq builds a second table containing only the customer keys (*$TTable4*). *$TTable4* is used to build *$TTable5*, which uses a reverse bitmap join to determine which customer keys in *CustomerSport* are also present in *Sales*.

The remaining part of the algorithm is the same as what we saw in the bidirectional model, with the noticeable difference that in the calculation of *$TTable1* the code is slightly simpler: it does not require a join with *Customer* in the REDUCED BY section.

Ultimately, the overall result is that the code is somewhat slower than the version with bidirectional filters. It executes a very similar algorithm, even though it does so with a different internal architecture.

We can now test the same query, filtering this time by *Customer[Continent]*:

```
EVALUATE
SUMMARIZECOLUMNS (
    Customer[Continent],
    "Sales Amount", [Sales Amount]
)
```

The relationship architecture is the same as the one with *Sport[Sport]*, the only difference being that we are using *Customer[Continent]* instead of *Sport[Sport]*. Performance is slightly better because of the smaller number of rows returned.

Total	SE CPU	Line	Subclass	Duration	CPU	Par.	Rows	KB	Timeline
4,577 ms	71,000 ms								
	x15.6	2	Scan	350	484	x1.4	1,401,151	5,474	
FE	**SE**	4	Scan	203	188	x0.9	1,401,151	5,474	
20 ms	4,557 ms	6	Scan	103	94	x0.9	1,868,096	229	
0.4%	99.6%	8	Scan	3,430	69,766	x20.3	3	1	
		9	Batch	471	468	x1.0			
SE Queries	**SE Cache**								
5	0								
	0.0%								

Hence, the findings indicate that filtering by *Customer* is much slower because the star model requires traversing the many-to-many cardinality relationship. Filtering by *Sport* shows a comparable speed.

The real advantage of the star model is observed when we mix the two filters in the same query. The bidirectional model would revert to a formula engine-intensive calculation in that scenario. The star model shows a much more efficient behavior:

```
EVALUATE
SUMMARIZECOLUMNS (
    Sport[Sport],
    Customer[Continent],
    "Sales Amount", [Sales Amount]
)
```

By using both dimensions to filter *Sales*, the query plan is nearly identical to the two previous tests.

Total	SE CPU		Line	Subclass	Duration	CPU	Par.	Rows	KB	Timeline
5,946 ms	97,172 ms		2	Scan	660	859	x1.3	2,802,734	10,949	
	x16.4		4	Scan	257	250	x1.0	1,401,151	5,474	
FE	SE		6	Scan	91	94	x1.0	1,868,096	229	
34 ms	5,912 ms		8	Scan	3,688	94,766	x25.7	135	2	
0.6%	99.4%		9	Batch	1,216	1,203	x1.0			
SE Queries	SE Cache									
5	0									
	0.0%									

The only real difference between this set of xmSQL queries and the two previous tests is in the first scan:

```
DEFINE TABLE '$TTable3' :=
SELECT
    'Customer'[Continent],
    'Sport'[Sport],
    'CustomerSport'[CustomerKey]
FROM 'CustomerSport'
    LEFT OUTER JOIN 'Customer'
        ON 'CustomerSport'[CustomerKey]='Customer'[CustomerKey]
    LEFT OUTER JOIN 'Sport'
        ON 'CustomerSport'[SportKey]='Sport'[SportKey];
```

In its simplicity, this xmSQL query clearly explains the difference between the two models. In the bidirectional model, the engine needs to revert to a formula engine-bound algorithm when there are multiple filters. With the star model, the presence of multiple filters is pushed down to the storage engine during the first step of an algorithm that is still fully executed by the storage engine without materializing intermediate filters to the formula engine.

Still, when the filter is only on the *Customer* table, the bidirectional model works faster. Indeed, it relies on a regular one-to-many relationship which is by far, the best way to move a filter in DAX.

Testing the snake model

Now that we have performed a deep analysis of the two previous models, it is quite clear what the goal of the snake model is. In the snake model, the relationship between *Sport* and *Sales* is created by using a many-to-many cardinality relationship, as with the star model. At the same time, the relationship between *Customer* and *Sales* is built upon a regular one-to-many relationship. In other words, we use the best type of relationship from the two previous models and mix them into a single structure.

We expect to obtain great performance when filtering *Sales* by only *Customer*. We can then predict reasonable performance when filtering from *Sport* to *Sales*, as with the star model. The most interesting part will be how the two filters are merged when both dimensions are used.

Let us start with *Customer*:

```
EVALUATE
SUMMARIZECOLUMNS (
    Customer[Continent],
    "Sales Amount", [Sales Amount]
)
```

No surprises here: the filter is extremely fast.

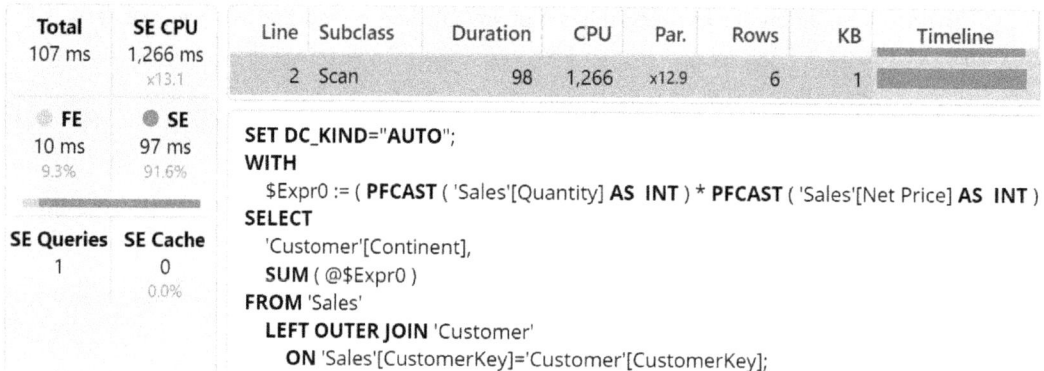

Total	SE CPU		Line	Subclass	Duration	CPU	Par.	Rows	KB	Timeline
107 ms	1,266 ms									
	x13.1		2	Scan	98	1,266	x12.9	6	1	

FE	SE
10 ms	97 ms
9.3%	91.6%

```
SET DC_KIND="AUTO";
WITH
    $Expr0 := ( PFCAST ( 'Sales'[Quantity] AS INT ) * PFCAST ( 'Sales'[Net Price] AS INT )
SELECT
    'Customer'[Continent],
    SUM ( @$Expr0 )
FROM 'Sales'
    LEFT OUTER JOIN 'Customer'
    ON 'Sales'[CustomerKey]='Customer'[CustomerKey];
```

SE Queries	SE Cache
1	0
	0.0%

When the filter starts from the *Sport* table, we expect a behavior like the star model, with a batch consisting of four different scans:

```
EVALUATE
SUMMARIZECOLUMNS (
    Sport[Sport],
    "Sales Amount", [Sales Amount]
)
```

Indeed, the result confirms our expectations.

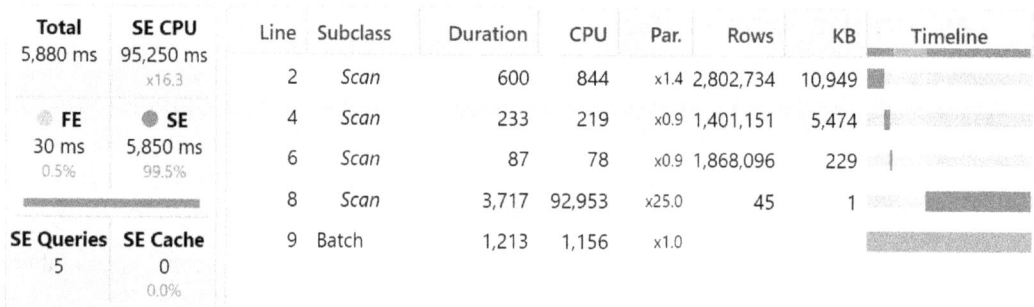

Total	SE CPU		Line	Subclass	Duration	CPU	Par.	Rows	KB	Timeline
5,880 ms	95,250 ms									
	x16.3		2	Scan	600	844	x1.4	2,802,734	10,949	
FE	SE		4	Scan	233	219	x0.9	1,401,151	5,474	
30 ms	5,850 ms		6	Scan	87	78	x0.9	1,868,096	229	
0.5%	99.5%		8	Scan	3,717	92,953	x25.0	45	1	
			9	Batch	1,213	1,156	x1.0			

SE Queries	SE Cache
5	0
	0.0%

The most interesting test is the one combining the two filters, as the algorithm is for sure different from the previous ones:

```
EVALUATE
SUMMARIZECOLUMNS (
    Sport[Sport],
    Customer[Continent],
    "Sales Amount", [Sales Amount]
)
```

The structure of the xmSQL code, as well as the timings, are surprisingly similar to the star.

Total	SE CPU	Line	Subclass	Duration	CPU	Par.	Rows	KB	Timeline
6,088 ms	110,781 ms	2	Scan	626	875	x1.4	2,802,734	10,949	
	x18.3	4	Scan	250	219	x0.9	1,401,151	5,474	
FE	**SE**	6	Scan	104	109	x1.0	1,868,096	229	
36 ms	6,052 ms	8	Scan	3,885	108,438	x27.9	135	2	
0.6%	99.4%	9	Batch	1,188	1,140	x1.0			
SE Queries	**SE Cache**								
5	0								
	0.0%								

The xmSQL batch executes this code:

DEFINE TABLE '$TTable3' :=
SELECT
    'Sport'[Sport],
    'CustomerSport'[CustomerKey]
FROM 'CustomerSport'
    LEFT OUTER JOIN 'Sport'
        ON 'CustomerSport'[SportKey]='Sport'[SportKey],

DEFINE TABLE '$TTable4' :=
SELECT
    '$TTable3'[CustomerSport$CustomerKey]
FROM '$TTable3',

DEFINE TABLE '$TTable5' :=
SELECT
    RJOIN ('$TTable4'[CustomerSport$CustomerKey])
FROM '$TTable4'
    REVERSE BITMAP JOIN 'Sales' **ON** '$TTable4'[CustomerSport$CustomerKey]='Sales'[CustomerKey],

```
CREATE SHALLOW RELATION '$TRelation1'
    MANYTOMANY
    FROM 'Sales'[CustomerKey]
        TO '$TTable3'[CustomerSport$CustomerKey],


DEFINE TABLE '$TTable1' :=
SELECT
    '$TTable2'[Customer$Continent],
    '$TTable3'[Sport$Sport],
    SUM ( '$TTable2'[$Measure0] )
FROM '$TTable2'
    INNER JOIN '$TTable3'
        ON '$TTable2'[Sales$CustomerKey]='$TTable3'[CustomerSport$CustomerKey]
REDUCED BY
'$TTable2' :=
WITH
    $Expr0 := ( PFCAST ( 'Sales'[Quantity] AS    INT ) * PFCAST ( 'Sales'[Net Price] AS    INT )    )
SELECT
    'Sales'[CustomerKey],
    'Customer'[Continent],
    SUM ( @$Expr0 )
FROM 'Sales'
    LEFT OUTER JOIN 'Customer'
        ON 'Sales'[CustomerKey]='Customer'[CustomerKey]
WHERE
    'Sales'[CustomerKey] ININDEX '$TTable5'[$SemijoinProjection];
```

The structure is a mix between the star and the bidirectional models. In the star model, *Customer* was involved in creating the first table from the beginning. This approach is not an option with the snake model: *Customer* comes into play only at the end, during the evaluation of *$TTable1*. However, it is used with a regular one-to-many relationship – therefore, with an xmSQL join.

The engine first scans *CustomerSport* to move the filter from *Sport* to *Sales* with the bitmap index. It then adds a join to the final query (*$TTable1*) using VertiPaq directly.

So far, the snake model is the best overall technique to model this many-to-many relationship. However, we are not done with our tests yet.

With previous models, we saw that the query speed is substantially bound to the selectivity of the filters. Reducing the number of customers in the bridge table improves performance significantly. In the snake model, a filter over *Customer* does not propagate to the *CustomerSport* table. The size of the internal data structures created to move the filter from *Sport* to *Sales* is not affected by a filter over *Customer*.

In the following query, we simulate what would generally happen in a query that applies a filter over *Customer*.

```
EVALUATE
SUMMARIZECOLUMNS (
    Sport[Sport],
    Customer[Continent],
    TREATAS ( { "Italy" }, Customer[Country] ),
    "Sales Amount", [Sales Amount]
)
```

The filter over Italian customers is reducing the number of customers in *Customer*, but it is not affecting *CustomerSport*, because there are no active relationships between *Customer* and *CustomerSport*. Hence, when we look at the server timings, you can see that the number of rows returned in the first set of scans is absolutely identical to the number of rows used in the previous queries.

Total	SE CPU		Line	Subclass	Duration	CPU	Par.	Rows	KB	Timeline
2,360 ms	2,906 ms		2	Scan	630	891	x1.4	2,802,734	10,949	
	x1.3		4	Scan	252	250	x1.0	1,401,151	5,474	
FE	SE		6	Scan	87	78	x0.9	1,868,096	229	
37 ms	2,323 ms		8	Scan	173	500	x2.9	45	1	
1.6%	98.4%		9	Batch	1,181	1,187	x1.0			
SE Queries	SE Cache									
5	0									
	0.0%									

The performance improvement comes only from the last scan (line 8), which benefits from the presence of a filter over *Customer*. We knew that reducing the size of the internal datacaches created during scans 2, 4, and 6 would benefit the query. Hence, it is worth testing how the performance is going to change when we move the filter from *Customer* to *CustomerSport*:

```
EVALUATE
SUMMARIZECOLUMNS (
    Sport[Sport],
    Customer[Continent],
    CALCULATETABLE (
        TREATAS (
            VALUES ( Customer[CustomerKey] ),
            CustomerSport[CustomerKey]
        ),
        TREATAS ( { "Italy" }, Customer[Country] )
    ),
    "Sales Amount", [Sales Amount]
)
```

We need a complex CALCULATETABLE to move the filter from *Customer* to *CustomerSport*, because there are no active relationships to use. Therefore, we expect at least one additional query that retrieves the customer keys from *Customer*, which are then used as a filter in the remaining part of the scans.

Indeed, the server timings confirm our speculations.

Total 291 ms	SE CPU 172 ms	Line	Subclass	Duration	CPU	Par.	Rows	KB	Timeline
	x0.7	2	Scan	7	0		89,103	349	
FE	SE	4	*Scan*	17	16	x0.9	133,536	522	
52 ms	239 ms	6	*Scan*	5	0		66,759	261	
17.9%	82.1%	8	*Scan*	5	0		1,868,096	229	
SE Queries	SE Cache	10	*Scan*	156	125	x0.8	45	1	
6	0	11	Batch	49	31	x0.6			
	0.0%								

There is a new xmSQL query at line 2, which comes before the four-scans batch. Despite the additional query, performance is greatly improved. The timeline shows that after the scan at line 2, we can find the computation of the filter over *CustomerSport*. Moreover, the size of the datacaches of the internal scans of the batch shows a significant improvement. Consequently, speed is way better.

As expected, the first scan is used to retrieve the customer keys in Italy:

```
SELECT
    'Customer'[CustomerKey]
FROM 'Customer'
WHERE
    'Customer'[Country] = 'Italy';
```

The batch includes a filter applied directly to *CustomerSport* during the creation of the first table (*$TTable3*):

```
DEFINE TABLE '$TTable3' :=
SELECT
    'Sport'[Sport],
    'CustomerSport'[CustomerKey]
FROM 'CustomerSport'
    LEFT OUTER JOIN 'Sport'
        ON 'CustomerSport'[SportKey]='Sport'[SportKey]
WHERE
    'CustomerSport'[CustomerKey] IN ( 761527, 762525, 763523, 797414, 760529, 795418, 728634, 730630, 726638,
    756537..[66,759 total values, not all displayed] ) ,


DEFINE TABLE '$TTable4' :=
SELECT
    '$TTable3'[CustomerSport$CustomerKey]
FROM '$TTable3',
```

```
DEFINE TABLE '$TTable5' :=
SELECT
    RJOIN ( '$TTable4'[CustomerSport$CustomerKey] )
FROM '$TTable4'
    REVERSE BITMAP JOIN 'Sales' ON '$TTable4'[CustomerSport$CustomerKey]='Sales'[CustomerKey],


CREATE SHALLOW RELATION '$TRelation1'
    MANYTOMANY
    FROM 'Sales'[CustomerKey]
        TO '$TTable3'[CustomerSport$CustomerKey],


DEFINE TABLE '$TTable1' :=
SELECT
    '$TTable2'[Customer$Continent],
    '$TTable3'[Sport$Sport],
    SUM ( '$TTable2'[$Measure0] )
FROM '$TTable2'
    INNER JOIN '$TTable3'
        ON '$TTable2'[Sales$CustomerKey]='$TTable3'[CustomerSport$CustomerKey]
REDUCED BY
'$TTable2' :=
WITH
    $Expr0 := ( PFCAST ( 'Sales'[Quantity] AS   INT ) * PFCAST ( 'Sales'[Net Price] AS   INT )   )
SELECT
    'Sales'[CustomerKey],
    'Customer'[Continent],
    SUM ( @$Expr0 )
FROM 'Sales'
    LEFT OUTER JOIN 'Customer'
        ON 'Sales'[CustomerKey]='Customer'[CustomerKey]
WHERE
    'Sales'[CustomerKey] ININDEX '$TTable5'[$SemijoinProjection];
```

Despite being a good optimization strategy, the technique we highlighted suffers from a serious drawback: it cannot be implemented in a measure. Let us look carefully at the code:

```
EVALUATE
SUMMARIZECOLUMNS (
    Sport[Sport],
    Customer[Continent],
    CALCULATETABLE (
        TREATAS (
            VALUES ( Customer[CustomerKey] ),
            CustomerSport[CustomerKey]
        ),
        TREATAS ( { "Italy" }, Customer[Country] )
    ),
    "Sales Amount", [Sales Amount]
)
```

The filter for Italy is specifically created inside SUMMARIZECOLUMNS through a complex CALCULATETABLE. Unfortunately, this technique is possible only when the developers fully control the query generation. When users browse the model through a client tool, the filters are placed in SUMMARIZECOLUMNS by the client tool, and developers can only work with measures. Therefore, the filter transfer must happen in the measure, like in the following example:

```
EVALUATE
SUMMARIZECOLUMNS (
    Sport[Sport],
    Customer[Continent],
    TREATAS ( { "Italy" }, Customer[Country] ),
    "Sales Amount",
        CALCULATE (
            [Sales Amount],
            TREATAS (
                VALUES ( Customer[CustomerKey] ),
                CustomerSport[CustomerKey]
            ),
            REMOVEFILTERS ( Customer )
        )
)
```

The presence of REMOVEFILTERS is beneficial to the performance. Indeed, we use the current filter from *Customer* to evaluate the filter placed on *CustomerSport*. Hence, *CustomerSport* is already using the previous filter over *Customer*, and any filter from *Customer* can be removed; indeed, it is useless. Performance-wise, this avoids using the relationship between *Customer* and *Sales*, thus speeding up the execution.

Despite this approach generating a more extended batch (it now consists of six xmSQL queries), performance is great.

Total	SE CPU	Line	Subclass	Duration	CPU	Par.	Rows	KB	Timeline
294 ms	281 ms								
	x1.0	2	Scan	7	0		89,103	349	
FE	SE	4	Scan	5	0		2,100,032	257	
20 ms	274 ms								
6.8%	93.2%	6	Scan	32	16	x0.5	133,536	522	
		8	Scan	7	0		66,759	261	
SE Queries	SE Cache	10	Scan	7	0		1,868,096	229	
7	0								
	0.0%	12	Scan	153	219	x1.4	45	1	
		13	Batch	63	46	x0.7			

Therefore, the benefits are attractive despite the DAX code being more challenging to author. Developers using many-to-many relationships on large models should consider optimizing their measures using the snake model and directly moving the filters to the bridge table through DAX code in their measures.

A possible further optimization to the snake model is to rely on an inactive physical relationship between *CustomerSport* and *Customer*, which is activated on demand only to move the filter from *Customer* to *CustomerSport*. We take a look at the model.

With this model, moving the filter just requires manipulating the active relationships:

```
EVALUATE
SUMMARIZECOLUMNS (
    Sport[Sport],
    Customer[Continent],
    TREATAS ( { "Italy" }, Customer[Country] ),
    "Sales Amount",
        CALCULATE (
            [Sales Amount],
            USERELATIONSHIP ( CustomerSport[CustomerKey], Customer[CustomerKey] ),
            CROSSFILTER ( Sales[CustomerKey], Customer[CustomerKey], NONE )
        )
)
ORDER BY
    Sport[Sport],
    Customer[Continent]
```

The query plan and the server timings are slightly better than when we were moving the filter in DAX.

Total 247 ms	SE CPU 172 ms x0.8	Line	Subclass	Duration	CPU	Par.	Rows	KB	Timeline
		3	Scan	27	0		133,536	522	
FE 20 ms 8.1%	SE 227 ms 92.3%	5	Scan	7	0		66,759	261	
		7	Scan	6	0		1,868,096	229	
		9	Scan	149	125	x0.8	45	1	
SE Queries 5	SE Cache 0 0.0%	10	Batch	39	47	x1.2			

The query is still using a batch, noticeably simpler than the previous one:

```
DEFINE TABLE '$TTable3' :=
SELECT
    'Customer'[Continent],
    'Sport'[Sport],
    'CustomerSport'[CustomerKey]
FROM 'CustomerSport'
    LEFT OUTER JOIN 'Customer'
        ON 'CustomerSport'[CustomerKey]='Customer'[CustomerKey]
    LEFT OUTER JOIN 'Sport'
        ON 'CustomerSport'[SportKey]='Sport'[SportKey]
WHERE
    'Customer'[Country] = 'Italy',


DEFINE TABLE '$TTable4' :=
SELECT
    '$TTable3'[CustomerSport$CustomerKey]
FROM '$TTable3',


DEFINE TABLE '$TTable5' :=
SELECT
    RJOIN ( '$TTable4'[CustomerSport$CustomerKey] )
FROM '$TTable4'
    REVERSE BITMAP JOIN 'Sales' ON '$TTable4'[CustomerSport$CustomerKey]='Sales'[CustomerKey],


CREATE SHALLOW RELATION '$TRelation1'
    MANYTOMANY
    FROM 'Sales'[CustomerKey]
        TO '$TTable3'[CustomerSport$CustomerKey],
```

```
DEFINE TABLE '$TTable1' :=
SELECT
    '$TTable3'[Customer$Continent],
    '$TTable3'[Sport$Sport],
    SUM ( '$TTable2'[$Measure0] )
FROM '$TTable2'
    INNER JOIN '$TTable3'
        ON '$TTable2'[Sales$CustomerKey]='$TTable3'[CustomerSport$CustomerKey]
REDUCED BY
'$TTable2' :=
WITH
    $Expr0 := ( PFCAST ( 'Sales'[Quantity] AS   INT ) * PFCAST ( 'Sales'[Net Price] AS   INT )   )
SELECT
    'Sales'[CustomerKey],
    SUM ( @$Expr0 )
FROM 'Sales'
WHERE
    'Sales'[CustomerKey] ININDEX '$TTable5'[$SemijoinProjection];
```

The relationship comes into play in the creation of the first table, which results in a better query plan.

Testing the advanced snake model

This chapter aims to focus on the cost of the relationships in a Tabular model. In many-to-many relationships, the size of the bridge table defines the cost of the relationship because it contributes to the number of unique values transferred by the filter operation. Because we have seen different approaches to solving a specific model, it is worth mentioning an additional optimization technique when we have an entity (*Customer*) that has an attribute with multiple choices (*Sport*). Although each customer can play a different combination of sports, one same combination of sports may be played by several customers. The *CustomerSport* bridge table does not reduce these combinations and transfers the filter to the *Sales* table as a list of values for *CustomerKey*, which has almost 2M values. If the number of distinct combinations is one or two orders of magnitude smaller, we can reduce the relationship cost and significantly improve the overall query execution time. As shown in the following diagram, we aim to replace the *CustomerSport* table with the *SportsCombinations* table.

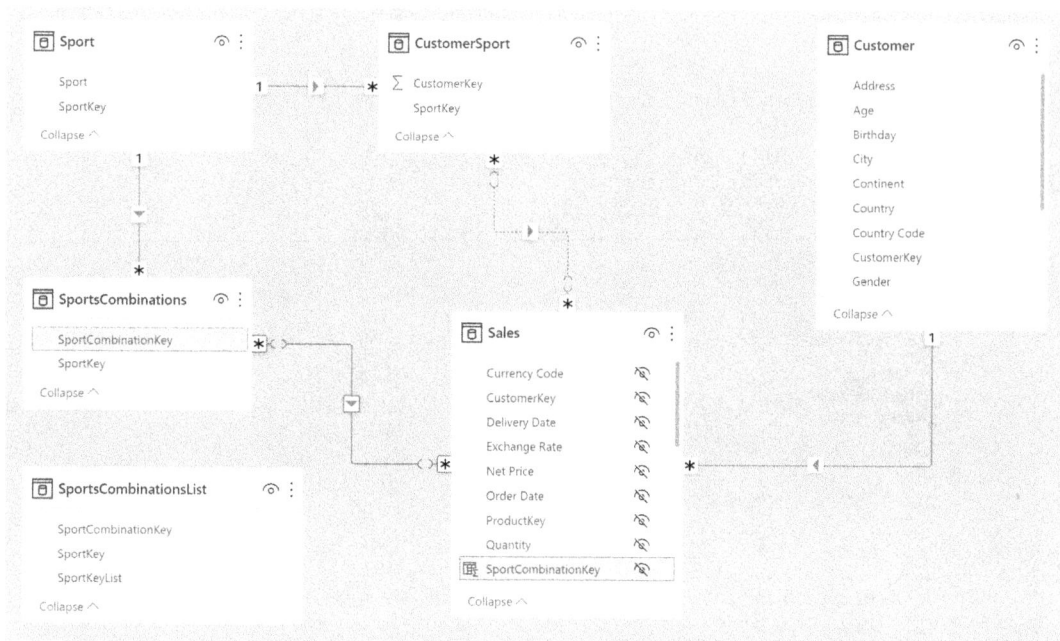

The relationship between *SportsCombinations* and *Sales* requires a *SportCombinationKey* in *Sales* that must have the same value for all customers with the same combination of sports. We can obtain the *SportsCombinations* bridge table by reducing the *CustomerSport* table, even though this requires some data pre-processing.

Ideally, data preparation should be done before importing tables in the Tabular model. In that scenario, we could import only *Sport* and *SportsCombinations*, without importing the *CustomerSport* table. However, we create the required tables and columns in DAX to show the possible optimizations in the Tabular model. For this reason, we keep the *CustomerSport* table in the model and create a *SportsCombinationsList* table as an intermediate step to obtain *SportsCombinations*. Remember that the processing time may be too high in a larger model. We keep additional tables (*CustomerSport* and *SportsCombinationsList*) in RAM, that would not be required if the data preparation was made before importing data.

First, we create a *SportKeyList* column in *Customer*, which expands the list of sports for each customer. For example, a customer playing Tennis and Golf gets a "3-5" string, whereas a customer playing only Tennis gets "3". Suppose the customer does not play any sport. We can also identify that case with a specific "0" key, making it possible to apply that selection in the future – something that would be impossible with the initial model. Because we did not add a "No sports" row in the *Sport* table with *SportKey* equal to 0, the blank value for *Sport* includes those customers without any sport selected:

```
----------------------------------------
-- Calculated column in Customer table
----------------------------------------
SportKeyList =
VAR CurrentCustomer = Customer[CustomerKey] -- 0 is "No Sport"
RETURN
    COALESCE (
        CONCATENATEX (
            CALCULATETABLE (
                CustomerSport,
                REMOVEFILTERS (),
                CustomerSport[CustomerKey] = CurrentCustomer
            ),
            CustomerSport[SportKey],
            "-",
            CustomerSport[SportKey]
        ),
        "0"
    )
```

Once we have the list of sports in *Customer[SportKeyList]*, we expand that list to one row for each sport in that combination and assign a unique integer id to each combination. The *SportsCombinationsList* calculated table we obtain is an intermediate step we use to produce the final bridge table. The *SportCombinationKey* column is the unique identifier of each combination of sports:

```
----------------------------------------------
-- Calculated table SportsCombinationsList
----------------------------------------------
SportsCombinationsList =
VAR _CustomerSports =
    GROUPBY (
        Customer,
        Customer[SportKeyList],
        "@CustomerKey", MINX ( CURRENTGROUP (), Customer[CustomerKey] )
    )
VAR _SportsCombinations =
    ADDCOLUMNS (
        _CustomerSports,
        "SportCombinationKey", RANKX ( _CustomerSports, Customer[SportKeyList],, ASC )
    )
```

```
VAR Result =
    SELECTCOLUMNS (
        NATURALLEFTOUTERJOIN (
            _SportsCombinations,
            ADDCOLUMNS ( CustomerSport, "@CustomerKey", CustomerSport[CustomerKey] + 0 )
        ),
        [SportCombinationKey],
        "SportKeyList", Customer[SportKeyList],
        "SportKey", CustomerSport[SportKey]
    )
RETURN
    Result
```

In the *Customer* table, we create an additional *SportCombinationKey* calculated column that transforms the list of sports into the corresponding identifier we obtained in *SportsCombinationsList*:

```
----------------------------------------
-- Calculated column in Customer table
----------------------------------------
SportCombinationKey =
LOOKUPVALUE (
    SportsCombinationsList[SportCombinationKey],
    SportsCombinationsList[SportKeyList],
    Customer[SportKeyList]
)
```

We use the last column to populate the corresponding *SportCombinationKey* calculated column in *Sales*, which we later use to connect *Sales* to the new bridge table. Using an integer value instead of a string saves time in later creating the calculated column in the *Sales* table. If we used the *SportKeyList* string instead of *SportCombinationKey*, the processing of the following calculated column would take longer to create and update the dictionary:

```
-------------------------------------
-- Calculated column in Sales table
-------------------------------------
SportCombinationKey =
RELATED ( Customer[SportCombinationKey] )
```

We finally create the *SportsCombinations* calculated table we use as a bridge table. These additional steps are required for performance reasons and to avoid circular dependencies once we create the relationships:

```
----------------------------------------
-- Calculated table SportsCombinations
----------------------------------------
SportsCombinations =
SUMMARIZE (
    SportsCombinationsList,
    SportsCombinationsList[SportCombinationKey],
    SportsCombinationsList[SportKey]
)
```

If we remove the tables used to create *SportsCombinations* from the diagram, we see the same snake model we had initially: we just replaced *CustomerSport* with *SportsCombinations*.

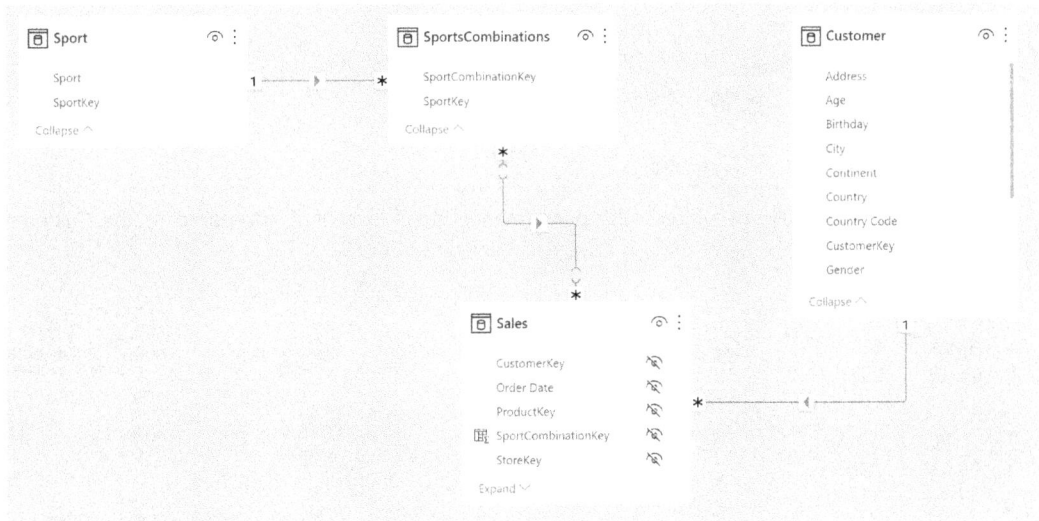

Because the query plan is identical, we focus only on the server timings, and we ignore the individual storage engine queries because they present no difference. We start by filtering only the *Sport* table:

```
EVALUATE
SUMMARIZECOLUMNS (
    Sport[Sport],
    "Sales Amount", [Sales Amount]
)
```

The query is much faster than with the *CustomerSport* bridge table.

Total	SE CPU	Line	Subclass	Duration	CPU	Par.	Rows	KB	Timeline
197 ms	3,156 ms x17.5	2	Scan	3	0		44,596	175	
		4	Scan	3	0		15,226	60	
FE 17 ms 8.6%	SE 180 ms 91.4%	6	Scan	2	0		15,232	2	
		8	Scan	167	3,156	x18.9	46	1	
SE Queries 5	SE Cache 0 0.0%	9	Batch	5	0				

We also repeat the test by combining the two filters:

```
EVALUATE
SUMMARIZECOLUMNS (
    Sport[Sport],
    Customer[Continent],
    "Sales Amount", [Sales Amount]
)
```

When combining the two filters, the performance is still excellent compared to the *CustomerSport* bridge table.

Total	SE CPU	Line	Subclass	Duration	CPU	Par.	Rows	KB	Timeline
330 ms	2,531 ms x8.2	2	Scan	3	0		44,596	175	
		4	Scan	3	0		15,226	60	
FE 20 ms 6.1%	SE 310 ms 94.5%	6	Scan	1	0		15,232	2	
		8	Scan	299	2,531	x8.5	138	2	
SE Queries 5	SE Cache 0 0.0%	9	Batch	6	0				

The further optimization of adding a relationship between *Customer* and *SportCombinations*, which worked well in the snake model, is not feasible in the advanced snake. Indeed, the *SportCombinations* table does not have the customer keys. A relationship between *Customer* and *SportCombinations* should be a many-to-many relationship based on the combinations of sports of the selected customer. In that situation, the selection of a customer would include the sales of all the customers that have the same combinations of sports as the selected customer. This would give us in a different result that is not useful because it would include sales of customers that are not selected in the *Customer* table.

The level of optimization described in this last Advanced Snake model is neither always guaranteed nor always possible. However, for the brave reader who made it to this point, having followed the entire dissertation might help generate new ideas to test their specific model: it all depends on multiple factors, and the wise developers perform several tests on actual data before making their decision.

Conclusions

Filtering tables and moving filters between tables are two of the most frequent operations that happen during the execution of DAX code. During the first authoring of measures and queries, developers often do not spend too much time optimizing the filters. However, the impact of filtering can be quite significant. Consequently, the final steps in optimizing a measure always include a deeper analysis of whether the filter is being executed at its best speed.

Understanding how filters are moved over the model becomes extremely important when creating complex models with intricate chains of relationships.

Finally, even though we know we are repeating ourselves once more, make sure to perform tests. The numbers and the clues we report are based on our model, our experience, and the current version of Tabular. Newer releases might change the way filters are processed.

Optimization examples for VertiPaq

The previous examples were targeting specific performance issues we wanted to present and solve. This chapter provides examples of optimizations of queries you may run into more often, regardless of the performance challenge. We show the entire optimization process, starting from the query and ending with the needed changes in the model or in the DAX code to produce a better query plan.

It is fine if some of these examples have already been shown before. In the previous chapters, the goal was to show an optimization without going into too many details. Here, the goal is to use the knowledge acquired so far to really understand how the optimization is performed.

Reducing nested iterations

When your code includes iterations, it is always important to reduce the number of iterations to the minimum cardinality or push them down to the storage engine as much as possible.

To demonstrate this scenario, we created a column in *Customer* with the discount percentage associated with the customer. The calculated column contains made up data, based on the customer key:

```
----------------------------------------
-- Calculated column in Customer table
----------------------------------------
Discount % = MOD ( Customer[CustomerKey], 10 ) / 100
```

Based on this column, we want to compute the total discount if we were to apply the discount percentage for each customer to their purchases. The most intuitive way to obtain this – and the way the performs the worst – is to use the following code:

```
DEFINE
    MEASURE Sales[Total Discount] =
        SUMX (
            Customer,
            [Sales Amount] * Customer[Discount %]
        )

EVALUATE
SUMMARIZECOLUMNS (
    'Date'[Year],
    "Total Discount", [Total Discount]
)
ORDER BY 'Date'[Year]
```

The result is relatively simple, it is the total discount by year.

Year	Total Discount
2010	275,022,177.29
2011	492,407,164.52
2012	580,823,462.20
2013	941,895,464.64
2014	1,342,413,806.72
2015	1,086,639,420.39

Before diving into the analysis, let us elaborate on what the algorithm could look like. Tabular must compute the sales amount by customer and month in a datacache. Next, it iterates over the customer and year-month columns to aggregate the results and produce its output.

In the model, we have 1.8M customers and 11 years worth of data. Therefore, the size of the datacache could reach 20M rows. However, not all the combinations exist, so the size will actually be smaller. However, it still is in the range of several million.

The query is extremely slow, with a massive amount of time spent in the formula engine.

Total	SE CPU		Line	Subclass	Duration	CPU	Par.	Rows	KB	Timeline
35,513 ms	83,281 ms		2	Scan	14,352	83,031	x5.8	16,936,952	198,480	
	x5.7		4	Scan	264	250	x0.9	1,868,084	14,595	
FE	**SE**									
20,897 ms	14,616 ms									
58.8%	41.2%									
SE Queries	SE Cache									
2	0									
	0.0%									

The xmSQL queries are not that complex; the problem is the size of the datacaches. Indeed, as expected, the first xmSQL query retrieves the sales amount by year-month and customer:

```
WITH
    $Expr0 := ( PFCAST ( 'Sales'[Quantity] AS INT ) * PFCAST ( 'Sales'[Net Price] AS INT ) )
SELECT
    'Customer'[CustomerKey],
    'Date'[Year],
    SUM ( @$Expr0 )
FROM 'Sales'
    LEFT OUTER JOIN 'Customer'
        ON 'Sales'[CustomerKey]='Customer'[CustomerKey]
    LEFT OUTER JOIN 'Date'
        ON 'Sales'[Order Date]='Date'[Date];
```

The generated datacache contains almost 17M rows. The second xmSQL query retrieves the customer keys and the customer discount from *Customer*:

```
SELECT
    'Customer'[RowNumber],
    'Customer'[CustomerKey],
    'Customer'[Discount %]
FROM 'Customer';
```

Because these are the only two VertiPaq queries, it is clear that the multiplication of sales amount by discount and the aggregation of all the customers together takes place in the formula engine. The formula engine must group, multiply, and sum from a rather large datacache with 17M rows. Hence the performance issues.

It would be much better if the entire calculation were moved down to VertiPaq. In the end, multiplication and grouping are the only calculations required, and they are well within the scope of VertiPaq. However, the problem here arises from the optimizer – the engine that optimizes the query plan – not being able to figure out that even though the iteration is at the customer level, data could be grouped at the *Customer[Discount %]* level. However, a simple change in the DAX code greatly helps the optimizer.

If instead of iterating over *Customer*, we iterate over the values of *Customer[Discount %]*, then we make it evident that the aggregation happens at the granularity of the *Discount %* column:

```
DEFINE
    MEASURE Sales[Total Discount] =
        SUMX (
            VALUES ( Customer[Discount %] ),
            [Sales Amount] * Customer[Discount %]
        )

EVALUATE
SUMMARIZECOLUMNS (
    'Date'[Year],
    "Total Discount", [Total Discount]
)
```

Before we look at performance, we should check the result – there are small differences.

Year	Total Discount
2010	275,022,175.66
2011	492,407,162.56
2012	580,823,460.31
2013	941,895,463.37
2014	1,342,413,805.42
2015	1,086,639,418.87

The *Total Discount* result for year 2010 was 275,022,177.29 with the previous measure, but now 2010 returns 275,022,175.66. The difference of 0.37 is caused by a different rounding of the numbers. A possible workaround could be to convert *Sales[Net Price]* to Decimal from the current Currency data type. However, similar issues are always present and depend on the different ways you express the calculation in DAX. From now on, we consider these differences irrelevant for our optimization example. In case you need to reduce the rounding issues for your model, first of all you should decide the precision of the calculation required for each iteration and arrange the data type and the DAX expressions accordingly.

Performance-wise, the boost is impressive.

Total	SE CPU	Line	Subclass	Duration	CPU	Par.	Rows	KB	Timeline
105 ms	1,078 ms x10.8	2	Scan	100	1,078	x10.8	182	3	

FE	SE
5 ms	100 ms
4.8%	95.2%

SE Queries	SE Cache
1	0
	0.0%

The entire query is resolved in 105 milliseconds, all of which is storage engine time. Therefore, we can take advantage of a remarkable degree of parallelism. The xmSQL query computes the same datacache we had in the previous query. This time, however, the materialized size is very different – less than 200 rows instead of almost 2 million:

```
WITH
    $Expr0 := ( PFCAST ( 'Sales'[Quantity] AS INT ) * PFCAST ( 'Sales'[Net Price] AS INT ))
SELECT
    'Customer'[Discount %],
    'Date'[Year],
    SUM ( @$Expr0 )
FROM 'Sales'
    LEFT OUTER JOIN 'Customer'
        ON 'Sales'[CustomerKey]='Customer'[CustomerKey]
    LEFT OUTER JOIN 'Date'
        ON 'Sales'[Order Date]='Date'[Date];
```

Another great advantage of this query plan is that the value of the customer discount is available directly in the datacache containing the sales amount. This approach reduces the need for the formula engine to merge two different datacaches, as was the case in the previous query.

In this last query, the materialization is relatively small (less than 200 rows), and the time required to multiply the sales amount by the discount is irrelevant. Indeed, if we push the entire calculation down to the storage engine by using a different formulation of the query, the code runs a bit more slowly:

```
DEFINE
    MEASURE Sales[Total Discount] =
        SUMX (
            Sales,
            Sales[Quantity] * Sales[Net Price]
                * RELATED ( Customer[Discount %] )
        )

EVALUATE
SUMMARIZECOLUMNS (
    'Date'[Year],
    "Total Discount", [Total Discount]
)
```

The storage engine uses more time to perform 225 million multiplications, one for each row in *Sales*.

Total	SE CPU	Line	Subclass	Duration	CPU	Par.	Rows	KB	Timeline
224 ms	3,672 ms								
	x16.8	2	Scan	218	3,672	x16.8	14	1	▬▬▬▬

FE	SE
6 ms	218 ms
2.7%	97.3%

SE Queries	SE Cache
1	0
	0.0%

Despite leveraging higher parallelism, the comparison between a few thousand multiplications made by the formula engine and billions made by the storage engine is in favor of the former. Moreover, pushing the calculation to the storage engine included a RoundValueCallback that does not keep the result in the storage engine cache:

```
WITH
    $Expr0 := RoundValueCallback (
        ( ( ( CAST ( ( PFCAST ( 'Sales'[Quantity] AS INT ) * PFCAST ( 'Sales'[Net Price] AS INT ) ) AS REAL ) / 10000.000000 )
            * PFCAST ( 'Customer'[Column] AS REAL ) ) * 10000.000000 ) )
SELECT
    'Date'[Year],
    SUM ( @$Expr0 )
FROM 'Sales'
    LEFT OUTER JOIN 'Customer'
        ON 'Sales'[CustomerKey]='Customer'[CustomerKey]
    LEFT OUTER JOIN 'Date'
        ON 'Sales'[Order Date]='Date'[Date];
```

If the materialization level were larger, then pushing the multiplication down to the storage engine would make sense. For example, the same query as before, grouping by *Product[Category]* and *Date[Date]* instead of *Date[Year]*, takes longer:

```
DEFINE
    MEASURE Sales[Total Discount] =
        SUMX (
            VALUES ( Customer[Discount %] ),
            [Sales Amount] * Customer[Discount %]
        )

EVALUATE
SUMMARIZECOLUMNS (
    'Product'[Category],
    'Date'[Date],
    "Total Discount", [Total Discount]
)
```

Because of the increased number of rows, the query is slower.

Total	SE CPU		Line	Subclass	Duration	CPU	Par.	Rows	KB	Timeline
540 ms	6,781 ms		2	Scan	470	6,781	x14.4	262,459	3,076	
	x14.4									

FE	SE
70 ms	470 ms
13.0%	87.0%

SE Queries	SE Cache
1	0
	0.0%

On the other hand, the version that pushes down the entire calculation to the storage engine is not sensitive to the number of rows materialized because the effort it needs to make is the same – that is, a full scan of the *Sales* table with two multiplications:

```
DEFINE
    MEASURE Sales[Total Discount] =
        SUMX (
            Sales,
            Sales[Quantity] * Sales[Net Price]
                * RELATED ( Customer[Discount %] )
        )

EVALUATE
SUMMARIZECOLUMNS (
    'Product'[Category],
    'Date'[Date],
    "Total Discount", [Total Discount]
)
```

The Server Timings pane shows that despite the grouping by *Date[Date]* and *Product[Brand]* and the generation of a larger materialization, the storage engine CPU cost increased less because of the smaller materialization required from the storage engine.

Total	SE CPU		Line	Subclass	Duration	CPU	Par.	Rows	KB	Timeline
345 ms	5,703 ms		2	Scan	300	5,703	x19.0	26,248	308	
	x19.0									

FE	SE
45 ms	300 ms
13.0%	87.0%

SE Queries	SE Cache
1	0
	0.0%

The version that pushes the entire calculation down to the VertiPaq engine runs at a constant speed for the internal calculation – despite the query's granularity – and materializes only the result required by the original DAX query. The version based on the formula engine calculation multiplies that materialization by the cardinality of the column iterated (*Customer[Discount %]*). For small materializations, the multiplication performed by the storage engine is slightly slower than the version that performs the multiplication at the formula engine level. In contrast, when the level of materialization increases, the storage engine provides a better option. However, you must constantly balance the need to keep the code easy to maintain, with more extreme optimization techniques. Keeping a common business logic in a single measure (*Sales Amount*) is important: duplicating the same code in different measures for optimization reasons must be carefully evaluated because of the long-term cost in terms of maintainability.

Optimizing complex filters in CALCULATE

One key to obtaining good DAX code is to keep it as simple as possible. Simpler DAX code provides more options for the engine to generate optimal query plans. The more complex the expression, the harder it is for the optimizer to work around a good query plan.

A simple example of this generic concept is how CALCULATE uses the filter arguments. The best way to express a filter argument is to use a simple filter on only one column. Even though the DAX syntax offers you the option of using more complex filters, these often generate slower query plans.

Let us look at the following query, computing sales in Italy and France for male customers born in October:

```
DEFINE
    MEASURE Sales[Test] =
        CALCULATE (
            [Sales Amount],
            Customer[Country] IN { "Italy", "France" }
                && Customer[Gender] = "Male"
                && MONTH ( Customer[Birthday] ) = 10
        )

EVALUATE
SUMMARIZECOLUMNS ( 'Product'[Brand], "Test", [Test] )
```

The filter in itself has no particular business meaning. It just uses multiple columns from a dimension merged in a single filter. There are three conditions in a logical AND. Two conditions are relatively simple and can be directly pushed down to the storage engine. The third involves the MONTH function, which only the formula engine can solve. Therefore, DAX must first resolve the condition by either finding the dates that satisfy the condition (gathering the *Customer[Birthday]* values and then resolving the condition in the formula engine) or using a callback during the scan.

The condition involves three columns. The condition on *Customer[Gender]* has only one value. There is the possibility of a correlation between *Customer[Country]* and *Customer[Birthday]*. If that were the case, the resulting filter would be smaller. Hoping for the best, Tabular executes a query to retrieve *Customer[Country]* and *Customer[Birthday]* combinations that satisfy the condition. Once the combinations are found, they are used as a filter to compute the filtered sales amount sliced by brand.

Performance is not bad. The query uses 9,969 milliseconds of storage engine and an insignificant amount of time in the formula engine.

Total	SE CPU	Line	Subclass	Duration	CPU	Par.	Rows	KB	Timeline
264 ms	9,969 ms x39.2	2	Scan	9	0		3,532	14	
		4	Scan	245	9,969	x40.7	14	1	

FE	SE
10 ms	254 ms
3.8%	96.2%

SE Queries	SE Cache
2	0
	0.0%

```
SET DC_KIND="AUTO";
SELECT
    'Customer'[Country],
    'Customer'[Birthday]
FROM 'Customer'
```

The first xmSQL query retrieves the combinations of *Customer[Country]* and *Customer[Birthday]*:

```
SELECT
    'Customer'[Country],
    'Customer'[Birthday]
FROM 'Customer'
WHERE
    'Customer'[Gender] = 'Male' VAND
    'Customer'[Country] IN ( 'France', 'Italy' ) VAND
      ( COALESCE ( [CallbackDataID] ( MONTH ( Customer[Birthday] ) ) ] ( PFDATAID ( 'Customer'[Birthday] ) ) )
        = COALESCE ( 10 ) );
```

There is a callback in the filtering section. However, this operation being a scan over a small table, its cost is irrelevant. The second query uses the information retrieved in the first query to build a filter pushed down to the VertiPaq engine:

```
WITH
    $Expr0 := ( PFCAST ( 'Sales'[Quantity] AS INT ) * PFCAST ( 'Sales'[Net Price] AS INT ) )
SELECT
    'Product'[Brand],
    SUM ( @$Expr0 )
FROM 'Sales'
    LEFT OUTER JOIN 'Product'
        ON 'Sales'[ProductKey]='Product'[ProductKey]
    LEFT OUTER JOIN 'Customer'
        ON 'Sales'[CustomerKey]='Customer'[CustomerKey]
WHERE
    ( 'Customer'[Country], 'Customer'[Gender], 'Customer'[Birthday] ) IN
        {
            ( 'France', 'Male', 13798.000000 ) , ( 'France', 'Male', 20367.000000 ) ,
            ( 'France', 'Male', 19660.000000 ) , ( 'France', 'Male', 17468.000000 ) ,
            ( 'France', 'Male', 15625.000000 ) , ( 'Italy', 'Male', 13445.000000 ) ,
            ( 'Italy', 'Male', 25119.000000 ) , ( 'Italy', 'Male', 35731.000000 ) ,
            ( 'Italy', 'Male', 25112.000000 ) , ( 'Italy', 'Male', 21470.000000 ) ..[3,532 total tuples, not all displayed]
        };
```

This second query is responsible for most of the execution time. Its reduced speed is mainly due to the complex filter requiring VertiPaq to check multiple columns simultaneously.

When we authored the CALCULATE expression, we used multiple columns in the same condition. Tabular used the same pattern when querying the VertiPaq engine, pushing down a complex condition to the storage engine. If we change how CALCULATE applies the filters by using a more straightforward pattern, that change will propagate to the VertiPaq filter. We can perform this change because the conditions are using a logical AND:

```
DEFINE
    MEASURE Sales[Test] =
        CALCULATE (
            [Sales Amount],
            Customer[Country] IN { "Italy", "France" },
            Customer[Gender] = "Male",
            MONTH ( Customer[Birthday] ) = 10
        )

EVALUATE
SUMMARIZECOLUMNS ( 'Product'[Brand], "Test", [Test] )
```

With this version of the code, Tabular does not try to merge the filters into one. Instead, it evaluates each filter separately, and then if possible it pushes them down to the VertiPaq engine. The Server Timings pane shows a significant improvement.

Total	SE CPU	Line	Subclass	Duration	CPU	Par.	Rows	KB	Timeline
117 ms	813 ms x7.7	2	Scan	3	0		24,496	192	
FE 11 ms 9.4%	SE 106 ms 90.6%	5	Scan	103	813	x7.9	14	1	

SE Queries 2   SE Cache 0 0.0%

```
SET DC_KIND="AUTO";
SELECT
    'Customer'[Birthday]
FROM 'Customer';
```

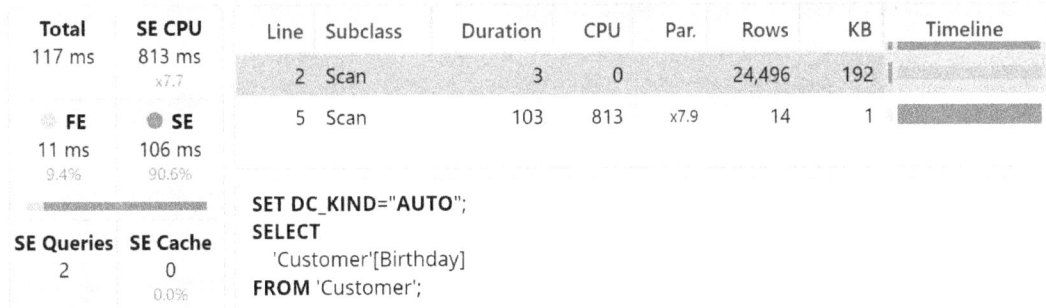

The first xmSQL query retrieves all the values of the *Customer[Birthday]* column. This datacache is then scanned by the formula engine to evaluate the MONTH condition, where the formula engine discovers the values to use as a filter in the following query.

The second xmSQL query uses only 813 milliseconds (one-third of the time spent in the previous DAX query) because its filtering section is much simpler:

```
WITH
    $Expr0 := ( PFCAST ( 'Sales'[Quantity] AS INT ) * PFCAST ( 'Sales'[Net Price] AS INT ) )
SELECT
    'Product'[Brand],
    SUM ( @$Expr0 )
FROM 'Sales'
    LEFT OUTER JOIN 'Product'
        ON 'Sales'[ProductKey]='Product'[ProductKey]
    LEFT OUTER JOIN 'Customer'
        ON 'Sales'[CustomerKey]='Customer'[CustomerKey]
WHERE
    'Customer'[Gender] = 'Male' VAND
    'Customer'[Country] IN ( 'France', 'Italy' ) VAND
    'Customer'[Birthday] IN (
        21109.000000, 37186.000000, 17082.000000, 30975.000000, 26952.000000,
        33512.000000, 37195.000000, 33522.000000, 31691.000000, 19662.000000
        ..[2,077 total values, not all displayed]
    );
```

The filters are placed on the individual columns, which results in better performance. This is not a golden rule. There are scenarios where combining multiple filters in a single condition improves your performance, mainly when the storage engine query can rely on SIMPLEINDEXN filtering.

As is always the case with DAX, you need to test different formulations of the same code to find the best combination in your specific scenario.

Optimizing Fusion Optimization

We have introduced and used Fusion multiple times. When a similar expression is evaluated in a different filter context, Fusion simplifies the execution by executing a single query. Despite being simple and powerful, Fusion is not faster than code that is correctly optimized.

A common scenario is a model with multiple measures that are summed together to produce the total of the individual measures. Each measure places a specific filter over a base calculation:

```
DEFINE
    MEASURE Sales[Sales Contoso] =
        CALCULATE ( [Sales Amount], KEEPFILTERS ( 'Product'[Brand] = "Contoso" ) )
    MEASURE Sales[Sales Fabrikam] =
        CALCULATE ( [Sales Amount], KEEPFILTERS ( 'Product'[Brand] = "Fabrikam" ) )
    MEASURE Sales[Sales Litware] =
        CALCULATE ( [Sales Amount], KEEPFILTERS ( 'Product'[Brand] = "Litware" ) )
    MEASURE Sales[Sales Fancy Brands] =
        [Sales Contoso] + [Sales Fabrikam] + [Sales Litware]

EVALUATE
SUMMARIZECOLUMNS (
    'Product'[Color],
    "Sales Fancy Brands", [Sales Fancy Brands]
)
```

Each of the three measures requires scanning *Sales* with a filter over the *Product[Brand]* column. We know that Vertical Fusion kicks in and merges the different scans. Indeed, looking at the Server Timings pane, there is only one storage engine query.

Total	SE CPU		Line	Subclass	Duration	CPU	Par.	Rows	KB	Timeline
300 ms	5,875 ms									
	x20.3		2	Scan	291	5,875	x20.2	266	9	

FE	SE
10 ms	290 ms
3.3%	97.0%

SE Queries	SE Cache
1	0
	0.0%

```
SET DC_KIND="AUTO";
WITH
    $Expr0 := ( PFCAST ( 'Sales'[Quantity] AS INT ) * PFCAST ( 'Sales'[Net Price] AS INT ) ),
    $Expr1 := ( PFCAST ( 'Sales'[Quantity] AS INT ) * PFCAST ( 'Sales'[Net Price] AS INT ) ),
    $Expr2 := ( PFCAST ( 'Sales'[Quantity] AS INT ) * PFCAST ( 'Sales'[Net Price] AS INT ) )
SELECT
    'Product'[Brand],
    'Product'[Color],
    SUM ( @$Expr0 ),
    SUM ( @$Expr1 ),
    SUM ( @$Expr2 )
FROM 'Sales'
    LEFT OUTER JOIN 'Product'
        ON 'Sales'[ProductKey]='Product'[ProductKey]
WHERE
    'Product'[Brand] IN ( 'Contoso', 'Litware', 'Fabrikam' );
```

However, the storage engine query includes three columns that compute the same expression. The datacache generated contains both the *Product[Brand]* and the *Product[Color]* columns as group-by columns. The formula engine filters the datacache and joins them using the *Product[Color]* column. In this scenario, the time spent in the formula engine is tiny because the number of rows in the datacache is so small.

However, the sales amount is computed by the storage engine three times, and this comes at a cost. If we express the same calculation with a single filter, the query runs much faster:

```
DEFINE
    MEASURE Sales[Sales Fancy Brands] =
        CALCULATE (
            [Sales Amount],
            KEEPFILTERS (
                'Product'[Brand] IN { "Contoso", "Fabrikam", "Litware" }
            )
        )

EVALUATE
SUMMARIZECOLUMNS (
    'Product'[Color],
    "Sales Fancy Brands", [Sales Fancy Brands]
)
```

By applying a single filter, VertiPaq no longer needs to group by *Product[Brand]*, as the datacache will not be read by multiple operators in the query plan. Moreover, the sales amount is computed only once.

Total 193 ms	SE CPU 3,891 ms x20.8	Line	Subclass	Duration	CPU	Par.	Rows	KB	Timeline
		2	Scan	187	3,891	x20.8	19	1	

FE 6 ms 3.1%	SE 187 ms 96.9%

SE Queries	SE Cache
1	0 0.0%

```
SET DC_KIND="AUTO";
WITH
    $Expr0 := ( PFCAST ( 'Sales'[Quantity] AS INT ) * PFCAST ( 'Sales'[Net Price] AS INT ) )
SELECT
    'Product'[Color],
    SUM ( @$Expr0 )
FROM 'Sales'
    LEFT OUTER JOIN 'Product'
        ON 'Sales'[ProductKey]='Product'[ProductKey]
WHERE
    'Product'[Brand] IN ( 'Contoso', 'Litware', 'Fabrikam' ) ;
```

The xmSQL query runs much faster, and there is a small benefit also from the formula engine point of view.

Besides, the speed of this latter measure does not depend on the number of brands selected. The price to pay is always that of a single fact table scan. On the other hand, if we rely only on Fusion, each additional calculation requires one more column to be computed and more operators in the formula engine.

Fusion is a beautiful optimization made by the Tabular engine. However, well-written code is always a better option.

Currency conversion

In Chapter 10 (Understanding the VertiPaq engine), we briefly treated the topic of currency conversion. We showed a measure with an average optimization level without analyzing it further. Indeed, the topic was different then, and we did not introduce the concepts required to perform a deeper analysis.

At this stage of your learning path, you possess all the knowledge required to perform a complete analysis of the measure, from a naïve implementation to a very well-optimized one.

The Contoso model stores data in USD. We want to build a measure (*AmtLocalCurrency*) that shows the values using the local currency in the *Amt Local* column of the following report.

Country	Currency Code	Amt Local
Australia	AUD	16,983,533,592.22
Canada	CAD	28,718,993,045.46
France	EUR	5,645,057,015.93
Germany	EUR	20,110,340,180.78
Italy	EUR	5,780,711,370.25
Netherlands	EUR	7,949,920,744.34
United Kingdom	GBP	17,520,823,596.35
United States	USD	119,622,385,294.28

Building the report requires searching in the *CurrencyExchange* table for the conversion rate on the date of the transaction. Because the *CurrencyExchange* table has no relationship with other tables in the model, we use LOOKUPVALUE to search for the conversion rate.

A first, straightforward implementation is the following:

```
DEFINE
    MEASURE Sales[AmtLocalCurrency] =
        SUMX (
            Sales,
            VAR Amount = [Sales Amount]
            VAR ExchangeRate =
                LOOKUPVALUE (
                    CurrencyExchange[Exchange],
                    CurrencyExchange[FromCurrency], "USD",
                    CurrencyExchange[ToCurrency], Sales[Currency Code],
                    CurrencyExchange[Date], Sales[Order Date]
                )
            VAR Result = Amount * ExchangeRate
            RETURN
                Result
        )


EVALUATE
SUMMARIZECOLUMNS (
    Customer[Country],
    Sales[Currency Code],
    "Amt Local", [AmtLocalCurrency]
)
ORDER BY Customer[Country], Sales[Currency Code]
```

The query takes forever to run!

Total	SE CPU	Line	Subclass	Duration	CPU	Par.	Rows	KB	Timeline
705,610 ms	1,198,578 ms	2	Scan	166,240	524,625	x3.2	225,608,216	11,456,668	
	x3.3	4	Scan	195,660	535,703	x2.7	225,608,216	10,575,386	
FE	SE	6	Scan	1	0		8	1	
341,039 ms	364,571 ms	8	Scan	1	0		8,087	64	
48.3%	51.7%	10	Scan	3	0		16,405	65	
SE Queries	SE Cache	12	Scan	2,640	138,234	x52.4	88	2	
8	0	14	Scan	23	16	x0.7	8	1	
	0.0%	16	Scan	3	0		11	1	

The problem here is quite obvious: the *Amount* variable is computed by evaluating a measure, forcing a context transition while iterating over *Sales*. Because it does not have a primary key, the entire *Sales* table (225M rows) must be materialized before performing the calculation. Materializing *Sales* requires a huge amount of memory.

This first issue is simple to solve despite being a game-stopper. Indeed, while iterating *Sales*, we can compute the value of the sales amount by simply multiplying *Sales[Quantity]* by *Sales[Net Price]*. The two columns required are present in the row context of *Sales*. The next version requires a lot less memory, even though it is still far from being optimal:

```
DEFINE
    MEASURE Sales[AmtLocalCurrency] =
        SUMX (
            Sales,
            VAR Amount = Sales[Quantity] * Sales[Net Price]
            VAR ExchangeRate =
                LOOKUPVALUE (
                    CurrencyExchange[Exchange],
                    CurrencyExchange[FromCurrency], "USD",
                    CurrencyExchange[ToCurrency], Sales[Currency Code],
                    CurrencyExchange[Date], Sales[Order Date]
                )
            VAR Result = Amount * ExchangeRate
            RETURN
                Result
        )


EVALUATE
SUMMARIZECOLUMNS (
    Customer[Country],
    Sales[Currency Code],
    "Amt Local", [AmtLocalCurrency]
)
ORDER BY Customer[Country], Sales[Currency Code]
```

The query requires around one minute to run, with an excessive level of materialization and a very low degree of parallelism.

Total	SE CPU	Line	Subclass	Duration	CPU	Par.	Rows	KB	Timeline
65,608 ms	160,141 ms x3.4	2	Scan	46,830	138,672	x3.0	117,102,770	914,866	
FE	SE	4	Scan	1	0		8	1	
18,294 ms 27.9%	47,314 ms 72.1%	6	Scan	1	0		8,087	64	
		8	Scan	3	0		16,405	65	
SE Queries	SE Cache	10	Scan	454	21,453	x47.3	88	2	
7	0 0.0%	12	Scan	24	16	x0.7	8	1	
		14	Scan	1	0		11	1	

Most of the time of the query is spent in the first storage engine query, which takes 138,672 milliseconds of storage engine CPU and materializes 117,102,770 rows. The datacache is enormous, which explains the reduced degree of parallelism.

Before changing the code, let us perform a deeper analysis of the algorithm followed by the Tabular engine. There are seven xmSQL queries, the first of which is the most interesting one:

```
SELECT
    'Sales'[Order Date],
    'Sales'[Quantity],
    'Sales'[Net Price],
    'Sales'[Currency Code],
    'Customer'[Country]
FROM 'Sales'
    LEFT OUTER JOIN 'Customer'
        ON 'Sales'[CustomerKey]='Customer'[CustomerKey];
```

This query materializes all the combinations of *Order Date*, *Quantity*, *Net Price*, *Currency Code*, and *Country*. There are no signs of the sales amount being computed: the datacache contains all the original columns without further calculation. The absence of the sales amount computation in the datacache indicates that the formula engine will execute the calculation.

Moreover, a deeper analysis shows that these are all the columns required by the expression inside SUMX, with the addition of *Customer[Country]* required by SUMMARIZECOLUMNS to perform the grouping.

The following two xmSQL queries are relatively simple. The first one retrieves the values of *CurrencyExchange[ToCurrency]*:

```
SELECT
    'CurrencyExchange'[ToCurrency]
FROM 'CurrencyExchange';
```

While the following retrieves the dates from the same table:

```
SELECT
    'CurrencyExchange'[Date]
FROM 'CurrencyExchange';
```

The dates and currency codes are used to gather another important datacache that contains the exchange rates:

```
SELECT
    'CurrencyExchange'[Date],
    'CurrencyExchange'[ToCurrency],
    'CurrencyExchange'[Exchange]
FROM 'CurrencyExchange'
WHERE
    'CurrencyExchange'[Date] IN ( 43106.000000, 41110.000000, 41069.000000, 43065.000000, 42067.000000, 42983.000000,
41985.000000, 40987.000000, 41028.000000, 43024.000000..[3,281 total values, not all displayed] ) VAND
    'CurrencyExchange'[FromCurrency] = 'USD' VAND
    'CurrencyExchange'[ToCurrency] IN ( 'AUD', 'CAD', 'EUR', 'GBP', 'USD' ) ;
```

At this point, the formula engine has two datacaches available that contain the columns required to compute the inner expression of SUMX. The fifth xmSQL query performs the real calculation, making the formula engine and the storage engine work together through a callback:

```
WITH
    $Expr2 := ( PFCAST ( 'Sales'[Quantity] AS INT ) * PFCAST ( 'Sales'[Net Price] AS INT ) ),
    $Expr1 := RoundValueCallback ( ( ( ( CAST ( @$Expr2 AS REAL ) / 10000.000000 ) * [CallbackDataID ( ExchangeRate )] (
PFDATAID ( 'Sales'[Order Date] ) , PFDATAID ( 'Sales'[Currency Code] ) ) ) * 10000.000000 ) ),
    $Expr0 := @$Expr1
SELECT
    'Sales'[Currency Code],
    'Customer'[Country],
    SUM ( @$Expr0 )
FROM 'Sales'
    LEFT OUTER JOIN 'Customer'
        ON 'Sales'[CustomerKey]='Customer'[CustomerKey];
```

This query is interesting because it shows the power of the collaboration between the formula engine and the storage engine. The formula engine has all the information required to perform the calculation, but it is single-threaded. However, the formula engine can execute code on multiple threads thanks to the callbacks. By executing an xmSQL query with callbacks, the storage engine uses many threads to split the calculation among different cores. Indeed, you can notice that the degree of parallelism is excellent (47.3x), even though callbacks to the formula engine execute most of the calculations. Every thread of the storage engine executes the callback in its own private instance of the formula engine, so that the single-threaded architecture of the formula engine is not violated.

The last two xmSQL queries are very fast and retrieve the currency code from *Sales* and the country from *Customer:*

```
SELECT
    'Sales'[Currency Code]
FROM 'Sales';

SELECT
    'Customer'[Country]
FROM 'Customer';
```

After this detailed algorithm analysis, we can start changing the code. The slowest part of the query is the materialization of 117M rows. That materialization level is required because Tabular decided to perform the calculation entirely in the formula engine. Nonetheless, we know that the algorithm does not depend on all the columns being materialized. Among the columns, *Sales[Quantity]* and *Sales[Net Price]* can be used to compute the sales amount directly in the storage engine, materializing only the currency code and the order date:

```
DEFINE
    MEASURE Sales[AmtLocalCurrency] =
        SUMX (
            SUMMARIZE (
                Sales,
                Sales[Currency Code],
                Sales[Order Date]
            ),
            VAR Amount = [Sales Amount]
            VAR ExchangeRate =
                LOOKUPVALUE (
                    CurrencyExchange[Exchange],
                    CurrencyExchange[FromCurrency], "USD",
                    CurrencyExchange[ToCurrency], Sales[Currency Code],
                    CurrencyExchange[Date], Sales[Order Date]
                )
            VAR Result = Amount * ExchangeRate
            RETURN
                Result
        )
EVALUATE
SUMMARIZECOLUMNS (
    Customer[Country],
    Sales[Currency Code],
    "Amt Local", [AmtLocalCurrency]
)
ORDER BY Customer[Country], Sales[Currency Code]
```

This slight improvement brings terrific results.

Total	SE CPU	Line	Subclass	Duration	CPU	Par.	Rows	KB	Timeline
378 ms	3,829 ms ×13.8	2	Scan	153	2,313	×15.1	26,248	308	
FE	SE	4	Scan	91	1,500	×16.5	26,248	103	
101 ms 26.7%	277 ms 73.3%	6	Scan	1	0		8	1	
		8	Scan	1	0		8,087	64	
SE Queries	SE Cache	10	Scan	2	0		16,405	65	
7	0 0.0%	12	Scan	28	16	×0.6	8	1	
		14	Scan	1	0		11	1	

The structure of the VertiPaq queries is very close to the previous execution; therefore, it is irrelevant to redo the full analysis. The main difference is that now there are no callbacks because the storage engine computes the sales amount through the first query:

```
WITH
    $Expr0 := ( PFCAST ( 'Sales'[Quantity] AS INT ) * PFCAST ( 'Sales'[Net Price] AS INT ) )
SELECT
    'Sales'[Order Date],
    'Sales'[Currency Code],
    'Customer'[Country],
    SUM ( @$Expr0 )
FROM 'Sales'
    LEFT OUTER JOIN 'Customer'
        ON 'Sales'[CustomerKey]='Customer'[CustomerKey];
```

The materialization level is much lower (26K rows versus the previous 117M). This change increases the degree of parallelism and speeds up the entire calculation.

We can go a bit further with the optimization process. Now that we have solved the problem of excessive materialization, we can make minor changes to simplify the code. Performance-wise, we will not obtain any benefit, but the code may be better in some models, so it is worth sharing.

The last version we authored uses LOOKUPVALUE to retrieve the exchange rate. We have seen that Tabular materializes a table with the *CurrencyExchange* content to operate. We can perform the same operation explicitly and use NATURALINNERJOIN rather than LOOKUPVALUE:

```
DEFINE
    MEASURE Sales[AmtLocalCurrency] =
        VAR AggregatedSales =
            ADDCOLUMNS (
                SUMMARIZE (
                    Sales,
                    Sales[Order Date],
                    Sales[Currency Code]
                ),
                "@Sales Amount", [Sales Amount]
            )
        VAR ExchangeRates =
            CALCULATETABLE (
                TREATAS (
                    SUMMARIZE (
                        'CurrencyExchange',
                        'CurrencyExchange'[Exchange],
                        'CurrencyExchange'[ToCurrency],
                        'CurrencyExchange'[Date]
                    ),
                    'CurrencyExchange'[Exchange],
                    Sales[Currency Code],
                    Sales[Order Date]
                ),
                'CurrencyExchange'[FromCurrency] = "USD"
            )


        VAR Conversion =
            NATURALINNERJOIN (
                AggregatedSales,
                ExchangeRates
            )
        VAR Result =
            SUMX (
                Conversion,
                [@Sales Amount] * 'CurrencyExchange'[Exchange]
            )
        RETURN
            Result

EVALUATE
SUMMARIZECOLUMNS (
    Customer[Country],
    Sales[Currency Code],
    "Amt Local", [AmtLocalCurrency]
)
ORDER BY
    Customer[Country],
    Sales[Currency Code]
```

The main advantage of this query is that it shows fewer storage engine queries.

Total	SE CPU	Line	Subclass	Duration	CPU	Par.	Rows	KB	Timeline
365 ms	3,141 ms	2	Scan	7	0		40,420	158	
	x11.6								
FE	**SE**	4	Scan	27	16	x0.6	8	1	
95 ms	270 ms	6	Scan	147	2,375	x16.2	26,248	308	
26.0%	74.0%	8	Scan	89	750	x8.4	26,248	103	
SE Queries	**SE Cache**								
4	0								
	0.0%								

Nonetheless, the performance of this measure depends on the two scans of *Sales* that – alone – contribute to the vast majority of the query timings.

It is worth noting that the first scan at line 2 retrieves the content of the *ExchangeRate* table without any filter. We executed the same query in the previous code version, but there was a specific filter by *Date* to reduce the number of rows. Indeed, the first datacache retrieves 40,420 rows, though only 26,248 are useful. In this last code version, NATURALINNERJOIN guarantees to use only the useful rows. But the two algorithms can provide somewhat different results depending on the data distribution, granularity of the query, and model size. It is always worth testing different versions of the same code.

Optimizing cumulative totals

Cumulative totals are an area with a lot of room for optimizations. Writing a simple running total is simple, but performance may not be good. Reducing the execution time requires some effort and understanding of the DAX internals, as we will demonstrate.

The goal is relatively simple: we want to create a running total of the sales amount in a report.

Date	Sales Amount	Running Total
05/18/2010	19,880,837.75	19,880,837.75
05/19/2010	27,857,958.41	47,738,796.17
05/20/2010	30,161,536.27	77,900,332.44
05/21/2010	21,055,657.64	98,955,990.08
05/22/2010	35,405,622.46	134,361,612.53
05/23/2010	3,973,484.99	138,335,097.52
05/24/2010	17,291,065.24	155,626,162.76
05/25/2010	21,309,684.47	176,935,847.23
05/26/2010	28,410,315.67	205,346,162.90
05/27/2010	30,093,844.32	235,440,007.22

The running total sums all the dates before the current date, with the current date. Therefore, a straightforward implementation uses CALCULATE and DATESBETWEEN to obtain our goal:

```
DEFINE
    MEASURE Sales[Running Total] =
        CALCULATE (
            [Sales Amount],
            DATESBETWEEN (
                'Date'[Date],
                BLANK (),
                MAX ( 'Date'[Date] )
            )
        )
EVALUATE
SUMMARIZECOLUMNS (
    'Date'[Date],
    "Running Total", [Running Total]
)
```

The query computes the sales amount at the granularity of *Date[Date]* for two very good reasons: SUMMARIZECOLUMNS is grouping by *Date[Date]*, and we use DATESBETWEEN – which similarly to any other standard time intelligence function based on a date column, requires data at the day level.

Moreover, we also learned that time intelligence functions are evaluated in the formula engine. Once the data has been gathered at the day level, the formula engine aggregates partial values. This holds true if the measure is additive, as is the case of *Sales Amount*. If the measure were non-additive, then the entire description (hence, optimization) would be completely different.

The Server Timings pane shows that the query runs in around 1.7 seconds.

Total	SE CPU	Line	Subclass	Duration	CPU	Par.	Rows	KB	Timeline
1,715 ms	1,125 ms x11.4	2	Scan	0	0		4,021	32	
		4	Scan	0	0		4,021	32	
FE	SE	6	Scan	1	0		4,021	63	
1,616 ms	99 ms	8	Scan	98	1,125	x11.5	4,021	63	
94.2%	5.8%								

SE Queries	SE Cache
4	1
	25.0%

The time spent in the storage engine is minuscule: this code is firmly bound to the formula engine. Indeed, there are four tiny storage engine queries. Nonetheless, the analysis of the Timeline shows that there is a gap between the first three and the fourth. Therefore, the formula engine must compute a filter to pass to the last xmSQL query. Let us dig deeper. The first three queries are elementary:

```
SELECT
    'Date'[Date]
FROM 'Date';

SELECT
    'Date'[Date]
FROM 'Date';

SELECT
    'Date'[Date],
    MAX ( 'Date'[Date] )
FROM 'Date';
```

Nothing interesting here. Still, we know that with these three datacaches the formula engine is about to build some filters used in the last query:

```
WITH
    $Expr0 := ( PFCAST ( 'Sales'[Quantity] AS INT ) * PFCAST ( 'Sales'[Net Price] AS INT ) )
SELECT
    'Date'[Date],
    SUM ( @$Expr0 )
FROM 'Sales'
    LEFT OUTER JOIN 'Date'
        ON 'Sales'[Order Date]='Date'[Date]
WHERE
    'Date'[Date] IN (
        41133.000000, 42090.000000, 42131.000000, 43088.000000, 43129.000000,
        44086.000000, 44127.000000, 41051.000000, 41092.000000, 42049.000000
        ..[4,018 total values, not all displayed] ) ;
```

Here is the first surprise. The filter is not filtering anything, and it includes only 4,018 rows. As such, it should be computed in a handful of milliseconds without any gap in the Timeline. Therefore, we expect to witness a query plan with some complexity in defining a filter that is not useful. These are all good news: with a superficial analysis of storage engine queries, we already have clues on what to search for in terms of optimization.

Here is the query plan.

Line	#Records	Physical Query Plan
1		GroupSemijoin: IterPhyOp LogOp=GroupSemiJoin IterCols(0, 1)('Date'[Date], ''[Running Total])
2	3,882	Spool_Iterator<SpoolIterator>: IterPhyOp LogOp=Sum_Vertipaq IterCols(0)('Date'[Date]) #Records=3882 #KeyCols=1 #ValueCols=1
3	3,882	AggregationSpool<AggFusion<Sum>>: SpoolPhyOp #Records=3882
4		CrossApply: IterPhyOp LogOp=Sum_Vertipaq IterCols(0)('Date'[Date])
5	8,078,189	Spool_MultiValuedHashLookup: IterPhyOp LogOp=DatesBetween LookupCols(1)('Date'[Date]) IterCols(0)('Date'[Date]) #Records=8
6	8,078,189	AggregationSpool<GroupBy>: SpoolPhyOp #Records=8078189
7		DatesBetween: IterPhyOp LogOp=DatesBetween IterCols(0, 1)('Date'[Date], 'Date'[Date])
8		Extend_Lookup: IterPhyOp LogOp=Max_Vertipaq IterCols(0)('Date'[Date])
9	4,019	Spool_Iterator<SpoolIterator>: IterPhyOp LogOp=Scan_Vertipaq IterCols(0)('Date'[Date]) #Records=4019 #KeyCols=13ξ
10	4,019	ProjectionSpool<ProjectFusion<>>: SpoolPhyOp #Records=4019
11		**Cache: IterPhyOp #FieldCols=1 #ValueCols=0**
12	4,018	SpoolLookup: LookupPhyOp LogOp=Max_Vertipaq LookupCols(0)('Date'[Date]) DateTime #Records=4018 #KeyCols=1ξ
13	4,018	ProjectionSpool<ProjectFusion<Copy>>: SpoolPhyOp #Records=4018
14		**Cache: IterPhyOp #FieldCols=1 #ValueCols=1**
15		Constant: LookupPhyOp LogOp=Constant DateTime BLANK
16		**Cache: IterPhyOp #FieldCols=1 #ValueCols=1**
17	8,078,189	Spool_Iterator<SpoolIterator>: IterPhyOp LogOp=DatesBetween IterCols(0, 1)('Date'[Date], 'Date'[Date]) #Records=8078189 #K
18	8,078,189	AggregationSpool<GroupBy>: SpoolPhyOp #Records=8078189
19		DatesBetween: IterPhyOp LogOp=DatesBetween IterCols(0, 1)('Date'[Date], 'Date'[Date])
20		Extend_Lookup: IterPhyOp LogOp=Max_Vertipaq IterCols(0)('Date'[Date])
21	4,019	Spool_Iterator<SpoolIterator>: IterPhyOp LogOp=Scan_Vertipaq IterCols(0)('Date'[Date]) #Records=4019 #KeyCols=
22	4,019	ProjectionSpool<ProjectFusion<>>: SpoolPhyOp #Records=4019
23		**Cache: IterPhyOp #FieldCols=1 #ValueCols=0**
24	4,018	SpoolLookup: LookupPhyOp LogOp=Max_Vertipaq LookupCols(0)('Date'[Date]) DateTime #Records=4018 #KeyCols=
25	4,018	ProjectionSpool<ProjectFusion<Copy>>: SpoolPhyOp #Records=4018
26		**Cache: IterPhyOp #FieldCols=1 #ValueCols=1**
27		Constant: LookupPhyOp LogOp=Constant DateTime BLANK

Please note that lines 5-15 are replicated at lines 17-27. The formula engine computes the same data structure and iterates 8 million rows twice: once to apply the filter of the VertiPaq query at line 16 and once to compute the result. This pattern is very common when CALCULATE requires complex filters.

The duplicated calculation happening in the formula engine is the main reason for the low speed of this query. We can perform the first test by removing CALCULATE, which has a complex filter and relies on an iterator with context transition. This removal is possible because of the additive nature of *Sales Amount*:

```
DEFINE
    MEASURE Sales[Running Total] =
        SUMX (
            DATESBETWEEN (
                'Date'[Date],
                BLANK (),
                MAX ( 'Date'[Date] )
            ),
            [Sales Amount]
        )
EVALUATE
SUMMARIZECOLUMNS (
    'Date'[Date],
    "Running Total", [Running Total]
)
```

Quite surprisingly, the timings are very close, and the query plan is nearly identical.

Total	SE CPU	Line	Subclass	Duration	CPU	Par.	Rows	KB	Timeline
1,661 ms	1,313 ms	2	Scan	0	0		4,021	32	
	x15.8	4	Scan	0	0		4,021	32	
FE	**SE**	6	Scan	0	0		4,021	63	
1,578 ms	83 ms	8	Scan	83	1,313	x15.8	4,021	63	
95.0%	5.0%								

SE Queries	SE Cache
4	1
	25.0%

In some cases, moving from CALCULATE and a complex filter to an iterator helps the optimizer find a better way to express the same calculation. In this specific scenario, it did not produce any benefit. When optimizing DAX, the road to success is paved with failures.

Another promising idea is to leverage window functions. The WINDOW function in DAX is explicitly designed to handle scenarios like this running total. Therefore it is for sure an option to explore:

```
DEFINE
    MEASURE Sales[Running Total] =
        SUMX (
            WINDOW (
                0, ABS,
                0, REL,
                ORDERBY ( 'Date'[Date] )
            ),
            [Sales Amount]
        )
EVALUATE
SUMMARIZECOLUMNS (
    'Date'[Date],
    "Running Total", [Running Total]
)
```

The number of storage engine queries is reduced, but the timings are basically identical to our previous trials.

Total	SE CPU	Line	Subclass	Duration	CPU	Par.	Rows	KB	Timeline
1,650 ms	1,297 ms x14.9	2	Scan	0	0		4,021	32	
FE	SE	4	Scan	87	1,297	x14.9	4,021	63	
1,563 ms	87 ms								
94.7%	5.3%								

SE Queries	SE Cache
2	0
	0.0%

The query plan uses the window operator; there are still two iterations over 8M rows, showing an algorithm that is surprisingly close to the ones we have seen. Also, the Timeline confirms our findings: between the first and the second xmSQL queries, there is a considerable formula engine effort to produce the filter used by the second xmSQL query.

This time, the key to performance is to force DAX to change the algorithm. We want to avoid the filter on the second xmSQL query by using a variable that computes the sales amount by date, and then by using a WINDOW function to scan it in a similar way to what we did in the last query. However, this time we do not use the context transition because we pre-aggregate the values in the variable:

```
DEFINE
    MEASURE Sales[Running Total] =
        VAR SourceTable =
            ADDCOLUMNS (
                ALL ( 'Date'[Date] ),
                "@Sales", [Sales Amount]
            )
        RETURN
            SUMX (
                WINDOW (
                    0, ABS,
                    0, REL,
                    SourceTable,
                    ORDERBY ( 'Date'[Date] )
                ),
                [@Sales]
            )
EVALUATE
SUMMARIZECOLUMNS (
    'Date'[Date],
    "Running Total", [Running Total]
)
```

There still are two xmSQL queries, but the execution time is now much better.

Total	SE CPU		Line	Subclass	Duration	CPU	Par.	Rows	KB	Timeline
248 ms	859 ms		2	Scan	0	0		4,021	32	
	x12.8		4	Scan	67	859	x12.8	4,021	63	
⦿ **FE**	⦿ **SE**									
181 ms	67 ms									
73.0%	27.0%									

SE Queries	SE Cache
2	0
	0.0%

The first query retrieves the dates, and it is not that interesting. The second computes the sales amount by date, and this time there is no filter:

```
WITH
    $Expr0 := ( PFCAST ( 'Sales'[Quantity] AS INT ) * PFCAST ( 'Sales'[Net Price] AS INT ) )
SELECT
    'Date'[Date],
    SUM ( @$Expr0 )
FROM 'Sales'
    LEFT OUTER JOIN 'Date'
        ON 'Sales'[Order Date]='Date'[Date];
```

The Timeline clearly indicates that the formula and storage engines are no longer interleaved.

Moreover, by looking at the query plan, you can appreciate that the Window operator is avoiding the quadratic complexity of the formula: there are no more large iterations.

Line	Records	Physical Query Plan
1		GroupSemijoin: IterPhyOp LogOp=GroupSemiJoin IterCols(0, 1)('Date'[Date], ''[Running Total])
2	3,881	Spool_Iterator<SpoolIterator>: IterPhyOp LogOp=VarScope IterCols(0)('Date'[Date]) #Records=3881 #KeyCols=1 #ValueCols=1
3	3,881	AggregationSpool<Sum>: SpoolPhyOp #Records=3881
4		Extend_Lookup: IterPhyOp LogOp=Extend_Lookup''[@Sales] IterCols(2)(''[@Sales])
5		Window: IterPhyOp LogOp=Window IterCols(0, 1, 2)('Date'[Date], 'Date'[Date], ''[@Sales])
6	1	AggregationSpool<Order>: SpoolPhyOp #Records=1
7		Proxy: IterPhyOp LogOp=TableVarProxy IterCols(1, 2)('Date'[Date], ''[@Sales])
8		AddColumns: IterPhyOp LogOp=AddColumns IterCols(1, 2)('Date'[Date], ''[@Sales])
9	4,019	Spool_Iterator<SpoolIterator>: IterPhyOp LogOp=Scan_Vertipaq IterCols(1)('Date'[Date]) #Records=4019 #KeyCols
10	4,019	ProjectionSpool<ProjectFusion<>>: SpoolPhyOp #Records=4019
11		**Cache: IterPhyOp #FieldCols=1 #ValueCols=0**
12	3,281	SpoolLookup: LookupPhyOp LogOp=Sum_Vertipaq LookupCols(1)('Date'[Date]) Currency #Records=3281 #KeyCols
13	3,281	ProjectionSpool<ProjectFusion<Copy>>: SpoolPhyOp #Records=3281
14		**Cache: IterPhyOp #FieldCols=1 #ValueCols=1**
15		ColValue<'Date'[Date]>: LookupPhyOp LogOp=ColValue<'Date'[Date]>'Date'[Date] LookupCols(1)('Date'[Date]) DateTim
16	4,019	ProjectionSpool<ProjectFusion<Copy, Copy>>: SpoolPhyOp #Records=4019
17		DataAggAll_SortedOrder: IterPhyOp LogOp=Window IterCols(0, 1, 2)('Date'[Date], 'Date'[Date], ''[@Sales]) #Groups=1 #F
18	1	AggregationSpool<Order>: SpoolPhyOp #Records=1
19		Proxy: IterPhyOp LogOp=TableVarProxy IterCols(1, 2)('Date'[Date], ''[@Sales])
20		AddColumns: IterPhyOp LogOp=AddColumns IterCols(1, 2)('Date'[Date], ''[@Sales])
21	4,019	Spool_Iterator<SpoolIterator>: IterPhyOp LogOp=Scan_Vertipaq IterCols(1)('Date'[Date]) #Records=4019 #Ke
22	4,019	ProjectionSpool<ProjectFusion<>>: SpoolPhyOp #Records=4019
23		**Cache: IterPhyOp #FieldCols=1 #ValueCols=0**
24	3,281	SpoolLookup: LookupPhyOp LogOp=Sum_Vertipaq LookupCols(1)('Date'[Date]) Currency #Records=3281 #Ke
25	3,281	ProjectionSpool<ProjectFusion<Copy>>: SpoolPhyOp #Records=3281
26		**Cache: IterPhyOp #FieldCols=1 #ValueCols=1**
27		ColValue<'Date'[Date]>: LookupPhyOp LogOp=ColValue<'Date'[Date]>'Date'[Date] LookupCols(1)('Date'[Date]) Da
28	4,019	Spool_Iterator<SpoolIterator>: IterPhyOp LogOp=Scan_Vertipaq IterCols(0)('Date'[Date]) #Records=4019 #KeyCols=138 #\
29	4,019	ProjectionSpool<ProjectFusion<>>: SpoolPhyOp #Records=4019
30		**Cache: IterPhyOp #FieldCols=1 #ValueCols=0**
31		ColValue<''[@Sales]>: LookupPhyOp LogOp=ColValue<''[@Sales]>''[@Sales] LookupCols(2)(''[@Sales]) Currency

The query running in 248 milliseconds is good enough. Nonetheless, it is interesting to check whether the improvement comes from using WINDOW or pre-aggregated variables; or maybe both ingredients are required to obtain good performance.

To double-check this, we wrote a last version of the same code that uses a variable to pre-aggregate the results, but it relies on a standard FILTER function to compute the running total:

```
DEFINE
    MEASURE Sales[Running Total] =
        VAR SourceTable =
            ADDCOLUMNS (
                ALL ( 'Date'[Date] ),
                "@Sales", [Sales Amount]
            )
        RETURN
            SUMX (
                FILTER (
                    SourceTable,
                    'Date'[Date] <= MAX ( 'Date'[Date] )
                ),
                [@Sales]
            )

EVALUATE
SUMMARIZECOLUMNS (
    'Date'[Date],
    "Running Total", [Running Total]
)
```

This last version of the code is better than the first ones but far worse than the version using WINDOW.

Total	SE CPU		Line	Subclass	Duration	CPU	Par.	Rows	KB	Timeline
797 ms	1,031 ms									
	x14.9		2	Scan	66	1,031	x15.6	4,021	63	
FE	**SE**		4	Scan	3	0		4,021	32	
728 ms	69 ms		6	Scan	0	0		4,021	63	
91.3%	8.7%									

SE Queries	SE Cache
3	0
	0.0%

This version does not apply the filter computed in the formula engine as in the initial example (hence the better performance). Still, the algorithm is not as optimized as the previous version with WINDOW: it uses four times more formula engine CPU than our best solution. However, performing these tests is of paramount importance. Whenever you author sensitive code, you should test different variations of the same algorithm to find the best. Any new idea is worth being tested, at least to be sure that it is a dead-end and not worth further investigation.

Average price variation of products over stores

In this example, we analyze a complex query that computes the average price variation of products in different stores. We gather the first and last order dates for each product and store. Then, we retrieve the net price of the product on the first and last dates to evaluate the net price variation as a percentage.

The result contains only the product name and the average variation over all selected stores.

Product Name	Avg Var%
A. Datum Advanced Digital Camera M300 Azure	-29.75%
A. Datum Advanced Digital Camera M300 Black	-29.25%
A. Datum Advanced Digital Camera M300 Green	-27.31%
A. Datum Advanced Digital Camera M300 Grey	-29.05%
A. Datum Advanced Digital Camera M300 Orange	-29.60%

The calculation requires several steps, as displayed in the following code:

```
EVALUATE
ADDCOLUMNS (
    VALUES ( 'Product'[Product Name] ),
    "Avg Var%",
        AVERAGEX (
            VAR StoresAndFirstLastDate =
                ADDCOLUMNS (
                    VALUES ( 'Store'[Name] ),
                    "@First Sale", CALCULATE ( MIN ( Sales[Order Date] ) ),
                    "@Last Sale", CALCULATE ( MAX ( Sales[Order Date] ) )
                )
            VAR StoresAndFirstLastPrice =
                ADDCOLUMNS (
                    StoresAndFirstLastDate,
                    "@First Net Price",
                        VAR FirstSale = [@First Sale]
                        RETURN
                            CALCULATE (
                                AVERAGE ( Sales[Net Price] ),
                                'Date'[Date] = FirstSale
                            ),
                    "@Last Net Price",
                        VAR LastSale = [@Last Sale]
                        RETURN
                            CALCULATE (
                                AVERAGE ( Sales[Net Price] ),
                                'Date'[Date] = LastSale
                            )
                )
```

```
        VAR StoresAndVar =
            ADDCOLUMNS (
                StoresAndFirstLastPrice,
                "@Var %",
                    DIVIDE (
                        [@Last Net Price] - [@First Net Price],
                        [@First Net Price]
                    )
                )
        RETURN
            StoresAndVar,
        [@Var %]
        )
    )
ORDER BY [Product Name]
```

The first variable (*StoresAndFirstLastDate*) computes the first and last order dates for each combination of product and store. The second variable (*StoresAndFirstLastPrice*) uses the results of the first variable to compute the net price on the first and last dates. Because there may be multiple rows in *Sales* for any given combination of product, store, and date, it computes the net price as an average. The last variable (*StoresAndVar*) computes the variation, as a percentage, between the first and the last net prices.

The query is very slow. It has a considerable amount of formula engine time (87 seconds), and despite the storage engine time not being huge (144 seconds), it shows a minimal degree of parallelism.

Total	SE CPU		Line	Subclass	Duration	CPU	Par.	Rows	KB	Timeline
131,200 ms	144,985 ms									
	x3.3		2	Scan	608	8,938	x14.7	168,639	3,294	
FE	**SE**		4	Scan	1	0		70	1	
87,518 ms	43,682 ms		6	Scan	1	0		2,520	20	
66.7%	33.3%		8	Scan	1	0		4,021	32	
SE Queries	**SE Cache**		10	Scan	24,210	70,719	x2.9	50,973,748	995,582	
6	0		12	Scan	18,863	65,328	x3.5	37,037,990	723,399	
	0.0%									

To understand why the code is slow, we need to dive into the details of xmSQL queries. The first retrieves the first and last order dates from *Sales*, grouping by product and store:

```
SELECT
    'Product'[Product Name],
    'Store'[Name],
    MAX ( 'Sales'[Order Date] ),
    MIN ( 'Sales'[Order Date] )
FROM 'Sales'
    LEFT OUTER JOIN 'Product'
        ON 'Sales'[ProductKey]='Product'[ProductKey]
    LEFT OUTER JOIN 'Store'
        ON 'Sales'[StoreKey]='Store'[StoreKey];
```

This first query is expected, as it implements the *StoresAndFirstLastDate* variable. The next three queries are elementary, as they retrieve a few columns from *Date*, *Store*, and *Product*:

```
SELECT
        'Store'[Name]
FROM 'Store';

SELECT
        'Product'[Product Name]
FROM 'Product';

SELECT
        'Date'[Date]
FROM 'Date';
```

The last two xmSQL queries are the real issue. They retrieve the sum of *Sales[Net Price]* for the dates retrieved in the first query (the first and last date). However, instead of retrieving only the useful combinations of store, date, and product, they retrieve all of them. Both queries have the same format, although the date selection is different:

```
SELECT
        'Date'[Date],
        'Product'[Product Name],
        'Store'[Name],
        SUM ( 'Sales'[Net Price] ),
        COUNT ( )
FROM 'Sales'
        LEFT OUTER JOIN 'Date'
                ON 'Sales'[Order Date]='Date'[Date]
        LEFT OUTER JOIN 'Product'
                ON 'Sales'[ProductKey]='Product'[ProductKey]
        LEFT OUTER JOIN 'Store'
                ON 'Sales'[StoreKey]='Store'[StoreKey]
WHERE
        'Date'[Date] IN ( 41051.000000, 41092.000000, 42131.000000, 41133.000000, 42049.000000, 40928.000000,
40969.000000, 42008.000000, 41885.000000, 41844.000000..[1,781 total values, not all displayed] ) VAND
        'Sales'[Net Price] IS NOT NULL;
```

After having seen the xmSQL queries, the algorithm is clear. First, Tabular generates a datacache with the first and last sales by product and store. Then it uses only the dates as a filter to generate two datacaches: one with the net prices on the first date and one with the net prices on the last date. The formula engine is in charge of finding the net price on the first and last date for each product and store, computing the average, and finally generating the variation as a percentage.

The generated datacaches are large (51 and 37 million rows), which is the reason for the reduced degree of parallelism: the materialization is a sequential process.

A first trial, which is still not the best option, is to leverage the DAX window functions. Because the code needs to retrieve the first and last sales by product and store, we can give the INDEX function a try:

```
DEFINE
    MEASURE Sales[Avg Var] =
        VAR StartPrice =
            AVERAGEX (
                INDEX (
                    1,
                    ORDERBY ( Sales[Order Date] ),
                    PARTITIONBY ( Sales[ProductKey], Sales[StoreKey] )
                ),
                CALCULATE ( AVERAGE ( Sales[Net Price] ) )
            )


        VAR EndPrice =
            AVERAGEX (
                INDEX (
                    -1,
                    ORDERBY ( Sales[Order Date] ),
                    PARTITIONBY ( Sales[ProductKey], Sales[StoreKey] )
                ),
                CALCULATE ( AVERAGE ( Sales[Net Price] ) )
            )
        RETURN
            DIVIDE ( EndPrice - StartPrice, StartPrice )

EVALUATE
ADDCOLUMNS (
    VALUES ( 'Product'[Product Name] ),
    "Avg Var%", [Avg Var]
)
ORDER BY [Product Name]
```

The algorithm, in this version of the code, is simpler. The *Avg Var* measure computes the average variation by retrieving the first and last combination of *Product, Store,* and *Date*. In this version of the code, we used the columns in *Sales* to make up a single table that will serve as the source table of the INDEX function and improve both readability and speed. Nonetheless, the result is quite disappointing. It is faster but still not optimal.

Total	SE CPU	Line	Subclass	Duration	CPU	Par.	Rows	KB	Timeline
144,397 ms	117,593 ms	2	Scan	435	2,734	x6.3	186,258	728	
	x3.2	4	Scan	35,593	105,953	x3.0	95,120,394	371,565	
FE	SE	6	Scan	353	4,875	x13.8	186,258	4,366	
107,719 ms	36,678 ms	8	Scan	297	4,031	x13.6	186,258	4,366	
74.6%	25.4%	10	Scan	0	0		2,520	20	
SE Queries	SE Cache								
5	0								
	0.0%								

Because this algorithm is very different from the previous one, it is worth performing the full analysis of the xmSQL queries. The first retrieves the combinations of *Sales[StoreKey]*, *Sales[ProductKey]*, and *Product[Product Name]* from *Sales*:

```
SELECT
    'Sales'[StoreKey],
    'Sales'[ProductKey],
    'Product'[Product Name]
FROM 'Sales'
    LEFT OUTER JOIN 'Product'
        ON 'Sales'[ProductKey]='Product'[ProductKey];
```

This first datacache is not very large, and it is helpful to map the product names – used by ADDCOLUMNS in the final query – with the combinations of *StoreKey* and *ProductKey* used in the measure. The second xmSQL query retrieves the source for the table used by both INDEX functions:

```
SELECT
    'Sales'[Order Date],
    'Sales'[StoreKey],
    'Sales'[ProductKey]
FROM 'Sales';
```

The resulting datacache is quite large: 95M rows. Again, we witness a strongly-reduced degree of parallelism due to the size of the result.

Once the source table for INDEX is ready, the formula engine must retrieve the first and last row by store and product. This formula engine time is evident in the Timeline column: there is a gap between the second and the third xmSQL queries. Once the first and last rows have been identified, they are used as filters in the third and fourth xmSQL queries. They have the very same structure, just with different filters:

```
SELECT
    'Sales'[Order Date],
    'Sales'[StoreKey],
    'Sales'[ProductKey],
    'Product'[Product Name],
    SUM ( 'Sales'[Net Price] ),
    COUNT ( )
FROM 'Sales'
    LEFT OUTER JOIN 'Product'
        ON 'Sales'[ProductKey]='Product'[ProductKey]
WHERE
        ( 'Product'[Product Name], 'Sales'[Order Date], 'Sales'[ProductKey], 'Sales'[StoreKey] ) IN { ( 'Proseware Laptop12 M210
    White', 43890.000000, 412, 670 ) , ( 'WWI Projector 1080p LCD86 White', 43888.000000, 622, 510 ) , ( 'Contoso Lens Adapter
    M450 Silver', 43890.000000, 1305, 100 ) , ( 'Proseware LCD24 X300 White', 43888.000000, 475, 440 ) , ( 'WWI Screen 125in M1611
    White', 42532.000000, 628, 20 ) , ( 'Contoso Multi-Use Terminal Cable E308 White', 43882.000000, 1261, 650 ) , ( 'MGS RalliSport
    Challenge2009 E155', 43890.000000, 1799, 510 ) , ( 'The Phone Company Smart phones 4 GB of Memory M300 Gold',
    43889.000000, 1512, 10 ) , ( 'The Phone Company Smart phones Expert M400 Black', 42129.000000, 1478, 110 ) , ( 'NT Bluetooth
    Active Headphones E202 Silver', 43892.000000, 77, 510 ) ..[186,258 total tuples, not all displayed]} VAND
    'Sales'[Net Price] IS NOT NULL;
```

You can see that this VertiPaq query retrieves the data required to compute the average net price. Despite being much longer, in terms of text, it is extremely fast. It only takes five seconds of storage engine CPU with a somewhat good degree of parallelism. Moreover, it is worth noting that these last two are the queries that retrieve useful information. The previous one, with a much larger number of rows, was useful only to build the filter of these last two. Reducing the amount of time required to generate the filters will be our next step.

The last xmSQL query retrieves the product names from *Product*, and it is not worth our attention.

This first test now looks like a waste of time because the improvement has not been great. But it is still an important step forward because it indicates that the queries that retrieve the first and the last net price are very fast. The slower part is the computation of the filter. Once the filter is ready, the actual calculation is fast and straightforward.

It turns out that computing the first and last dates by product and store can be pushed down to the VertiPaq engine using simple functions like MIN and MAX while grouping by product and store. The following definition goes in this direction. It avoids using window functions, and it relies on more basic DAX functions, intending to simplify the calculation of the filter:

```
DEFINE
    MEASURE Sales[Avg Var] =
        VAR Stores =
            VALUES ( 'Store'[Name] )
        VAR StoresAndFirstLastDate =
            ADDCOLUMNS (
                Stores,
                "First Sale", CALCULATE ( MIN ( Sales[Order Date] ) ),
                "Last Sale", CALCULATE ( MAX ( Sales[Order Date] ) )
            )
        VAR StoresAndFirstDate =
            TREATAS (
                SELECTCOLUMNS (
                    StoresAndFirstLastDate,
                    Store[Name],
                    [First Sale]
                ),
                Store[Name],
                Sales[Order Date]
            )
        VAR StoresAndLastDate =
            TREATAS (
                SELECTCOLUMNS (
                    StoresAndFirstLastDate,
                    Store[Name],
                    [Last Sale]
                ),
                Store[Name],
                Sales[Order Date]
            )


        VAR Result =
            AVERAGEX (
                Stores,
                VAR StartPrice =
                    CALCULATE (
                        AVERAGE ( Sales[Net Price] ),
                        KEEPFILTERS ( StoresAndFirstDate )
                    )
                VAR EndPrice =
                    CALCULATE (
                        AVERAGE ( Sales[Net Price] ),
                        KEEPFILTERS ( StoresAndLastDate )
                    )
                RETURN
                    ( EndPrice - StartPrice ) / StartPrice
            )
    RETURN
        Result
```

```
EVALUATE
ADDCOLUMNS (
    VALUES ( 'Product'[Product Name] ),
    "Avg Var%", [Avg Var]
)
ORDER BY [Product Name]
```

Because we wanted to speed up the filter calculation, we used a single DAX expression (*StoresAndFirstLastDate*) to retrieve both the min and max order dates. The following variables are just a combination of TREATAS and SELECTCOLUMNS to build tables that can be used as filter arguments in CALCULATE. It is worth noting that – in this calculation – we removed the product from the grouping columns. Indeed, because the product name is already in the outer query, further grouping by product proves to be pointless.

This change in the algorithm pays off.

Total	SE CPU	Line	Subclass	Duration	CPU	Par.	Rows	KB	Timeline
1,317 ms	18,532 ms								
	x19.5	2	Scan	628	8,266	x13.2	168,639	3,294	
FE	SE	4	Scan	3	0		70	1	
368 ms	949 ms	6	Scan	1	0		2,520	20	
27.9%	72.1%	8	Scan	160	5,047	x31.5	168,639	3,294	
SE Queries	SE Cache	10	Scan	157	5,219	x33.2	168,639	3,294	
5	0								
	0.0%								

There is a great improvement in terms of performance: from 140 seconds to just one second. The big difference is the first VertiPaq query:

```
SELECT
    'Product'[Product Name],
    'Store'[Name],
    MAX ( 'Sales'[Order Date] ),
    MIN ( 'Sales'[Order Date] )
FROM 'Sales'
    LEFT OUTER JOIN 'Product'
        ON 'Sales'[ProductKey]='Product'[ProductKey]
    LEFT OUTER JOIN 'Store'
        ON 'Sales'[StoreKey]='Store'[StoreKey];
```

This xmSQL query replaces the entire calculation of the first and last order dates; it materializes a much smaller number of rows and runs way faster. The other VertiPaq queries are similar to those analyzed in the previous versions of the DAX query and not worth investigating further.

Optimizing the number of days with no sales

In this example, we want to optimize a calculation that solves a common pattern known as "gaps and islands". The goal is to find gaps in dates based on a measure. Using Contoso, we define a gap as a day with no sales, and the goal is to show, for every date, the number of previous dates with no sales. A gap is nothing but a period during which there are no sales.

The report looks like this:

Product Name				Date	Sales Amount	DaysWith0
A. Datum Advanced Digital Camera M300 Azure				01/01/2011	265.41	0
				01/02/2011		1
Year		Country		01/03/2011		2
2011		Netherlands		01/04/2011		3
				01/05/2011		4
				01/06/2011	1,646.74	0
				01/07/2011		1
				01/08/2011	2,138.34	0
				01/09/2011		1
				01/10/2011		2
				01/11/2011		3
				01/12/2011		4
				01/13/2011		5
				01/14/2011		6
				01/15/2011	1,646.74	0

We highlighted one of the gaps, between the 8th of January 2011 and the 15th of January 2011. The measure shows the number of consecutive days with no sales on each date. There are multiple ways to solve one same scenario: we start with a very naïve version of the code and then optimize it one step at a time.

The last picture shows a report that filters one product, one country, and one year. We did this to generate multiple gaps and show the figure. But running the query with such a small filter does not provide a clear picture of the performance because it is too fast. Therefore, we prepared a query with fewer gaps but with a larger set of data:

```
DEFINE
    MEASURE Sales[DaysWith0] =
        VAR CurrentDate =
            MAX ( 'Date'[Date] )
        VAR FirstDateEver =
            CALCULATE ( MIN ( 'Date'[Date] ), REMOVEFILTERS () )
        VAR PrevDateWithSales =
            COALESCE (
                CALCULATE ( MAX ( 'Sales'[Order Date] ), 'Date'[Date] <= CurrentDate ),
                FirstDateEver
            )
        VAR Result =
            INT ( CurrentDate - PrevDateWithSales )
        RETURN
            Result
EVALUATE
SUMMARIZECOLUMNS (
    'Date'[Date],
    "DaysWith0", 'Sales'[DaysWith0]
)
ORDER BY 'Date'[Date]
```

This first version of the measure has a precise algorithm: it first computes the current date and the first date in the model. Then it computes the last order date (the last date with sales) that is earlier than the current date. The measure uses the first date as a default value if there is no "last date with sales".

Once the measure knows the last date with sales, subtracting the last date with sales from the current date provides the result.

Despite being simple, this algorithm is quite slow.

Total	SE CPU		Line	Subclass	Duration	CPU	Par.	Rows	KB	Timeline
2,434 ms	359 ms									
	x6.6		2	Scan	0	0		4,021	32	
FE	SE		4	Scan	0	0		4,021	63	
2,380 ms	54 ms		6	Scan	54	359	x6.6	4,021	63	
97.8%	2.2%									

SE Queries	SE Cache
3	0
	0.0%

There are only three tiny storage engine queries, and most of the time is spent in the formula engine. The first two queries retrieve two small datacaches from the *Date* table:

```
SELECT
    'Date'[Date]
FROM 'Date';

SELECT
    'Date'[Date],
    MAX ( 'Date'[Date] )
FROM 'Date';
```

After these two small queries, there is a huge gap in the Timeline, showing that the formula engine does a lot of work to create the filter used in the following VertiPaq query. Then, the last xmSQL query retrieves for every date, the *MAX(Sales[Order Date])* with a filter over *Date*:

```
SELECT
    'Date'[Date],
    MAX ( 'Sales'[Order Date] )
FROM 'Sales'
    LEFT OUTER JOIN 'Date'
        ON 'Sales'[Order Date]='Date'[Date]
WHERE
    'Date'[Date] IN (
        41133.000000, 42090.000000, 42131.000000, 43088.000000, 43129.000000,
        44086.000000, 44127.000000, 41051.000000, 41092.000000, 42049.000000
        ..[4,019 total values, not all displayed] ) ;
```

The xmSQL queries do not contain any clue about the real algorithm, which is somewhat expected as nearly all the time is spent in the formula engine. The query plan is quite long (91 lines) and does not fit here in its entirety. But by inspecting it, we quickly find iterations over millions of rows.

Line	Records	Physical Query Plan
1		PartitionIntoGroups: IterPhyOp LogOp=Order IterCols(0, 1)('Date'[Date], ''[DaysWith0]) #Groups=1 #Rows=4019
2	1	AggregationSpool<Order>: SpoolPhyOp #Records=1
3		GroupSemijoin: IterPhyOp LogOp=GroupSemiJoin IterCols(0, 1)('Date'[Date], ''[DaysWith0])
4		Extend_Lookup: IterPhyOp LogOp=VarScope IterCols(0)('Date'[Date])
5	4,019	Spool_Iterator<SpoolIterator>: IterPhyOp LogOp=Scan_Vertipaq IterCols(0)('Date'[Date]) #Records=4019 #KeyCols=138 #V&
6	4,019	ProjectionSpool<ProjectFusion<>>: SpoolPhyOp #Records=4019
7		**Cache: IterPhyOp #FieldCols=1 #ValueCols=0**
8		INT: LookupPhyOp LogOp=INT LookupCols(0)('Date'[Date]) Integer
9		DateTime->Double: LookupPhyOp LogOp=DateTime->DoubleDateTime->Double LookupCols(0)('Date'[Date]) Double
10		Subtract: LookupPhyOp LogOp=Subtract LookupCols(0)('Date'[Date]) DateTime
11	4,018	SpoolLookup: LookupPhyOp LogOp=Max_Vertipaq LookupCols(0)('Date'[Date]) DateTime #Records=4018 #KeyCols
12	4,018	ProjectionSpool<ProjectFusion<Copy>>: SpoolPhyOp #Records=4018
13		**Cache: IterPhyOp #FieldCols=1 #ValueCols=1**
14		If: LookupPhyOp LogOp=If LookupCols(0)('Date'[Date]) DateTime
15		ISBLANK: LookupPhyOp LogOp=ISBLANK LookupCols(0)('Date'[Date]) Boolean
16	3,881	SpoolLookup: LookupPhyOp LogOp=Calculate LookupCols(0)('Date'[Date]) DateTime #Records=3881 #KeyCol:
17	3,881	AggregationSpool<AggFusion<Max>>: SpoolPhyOp #Records=3881
18		CrossApply: IterPhyOp LogOp=Max_Vertipaq IterCols(0)('Date'[Date])
19	8,078,190	Spool_MultiValuedHashLookup: IterPhyOp LogOp=Filter LookupCols(1)('Date'[Date]) IterCols(0)('Date'[
20	8,078,190	AggregationSpool<GroupBy>: SpoolPhyOp #Records=8078190
21		Filter: IterPhyOp LogOp=Filter IterCols(0, 1)('Date'[Date], 'Date'[Date])
22		Extend_Lookup: IterPhyOp LogOp=LessThanOrEqualTo IterCols(0, 1)('Date'[Date], 'Date'[Date])
23		CrossApply: IterPhyOp LogOp=LessThanOrEqualTo IterCols(0, 1)('Date'[Date], 'Date'[Date])
24	4,019	Spool_Iterator<SpoolIterator>: IterPhyOp LogOp=Scan_Vertipaq IterCols(0)('Date'[Date])
25	4,019	ProjectionSpool<ProjectFusion<>>: SpoolPhyOp #Records=4019
26		**Cache: IterPhyOp #FieldCols=1 #ValueCols=0**
27	4,019	Spool_Iterator<SpoolIterator>: IterPhyOp LogOp=Scan_Vertipaq IterCols(1)('Date'[Date])
28	4,019	ProjectionSpool<ProjectFusion<>>: SpoolPhyOp #Records=4019
29		**Cache: IterPhyOp #FieldCols=1 #ValueCols=0**
30		LessThanOrEqualTo: LookupPhyOp LogOp=LessThanOrEqualTo LookupCols(0, 1)('Date'[Date
31		ColValue<'Date'[Date]>: LookupPhyOp LogOp=ColValue<'Date'[Date]>'Date'[Date] Look(
32	4,018	SpoolLookup: LookupPhyOp LogOp=Max_Vertipaq LookupCols(0)('Date'[Date]) DateTime
33	4,018	ProjectionSpool<ProjectFusion<Copy>>: SpoolPhyOp #Records=4018
34		**Cache: IterPhyOp #FieldCols=1 #ValueCols=1**
35		**Cache: IterPhyOp #FieldCols=1 #ValueCols=1**
36	8,078,190	Spool_Iterator<SpoolIterator>: IterPhyOp LogOp=Filter IterCols(0, 1)('Date'[Date], 'Date'[Date]) #Rec
37	8,078,190	AggregationSpool<GroupBy>: SpoolPhyOp #Records=8078190
38		Filter: IterPhyOp LogOp=Filter IterCols(0, 1)('Date'[Date], 'Date'[Date])
39		Extend_Lookup: IterPhyOp LogOp=LessThanOrEqualTo IterCols(0, 1)('Date'[Date], 'Date'[Dat(
40		CrossApply: IterPhyOp LogOp=LessThanOrEqualTo IterCols(0, 1)('Date'[Date], 'Date'[Date]

Despite the picture showing two of those large scans, the full query plan contains four of them. The key to understanding why there are scans of 8M rows is in the CALCULATE function inside the *PrevDateWithSales* variable:

```
        VAR PrevDateWithSales =
            COALESCE (
                CALCULATE ( MAX ( 'Sales'[Order Date] ), 'Date'[Date] <= CurrentDate ),
                FirstDateEver
            )
```

The outer SUMMARIZECOLUMNS iterates by date. For every date, the engine builds a filter with all the dates earlier than the given date. To obtain this result, the formula engine builds a datacache with all the combinations of two dates where the second date is less than or equal to the first. The number of those combinations is (4,019 x 4,018) / 2 = 8,074,171.

Those combinations are then used as a filter argument in CALCULATE, which requires computing the filter before invoking an xmSQL query – hence the huge gap in the timeline. Moreover, the same structure is likely to be used in multiple query plan steps, slowing down the entire calculation. Removing CALCULATE is of great help in this scenario. Instead of relying on CALCULATE, we can precompute the list of all the order dates (the only dates with sales) and then use that table to find the last date with sales:

```
DEFINE
    MEASURE Sales[DaysWith0] =
        VAR CurrentDate =
            MAX ( 'Date'[Date] )
        VAR FirstDateEver =
            CALCULATE ( MIN ( 'Date'[Date] ), REMOVEFILTERS () )
        VAR AllOrderDates =
            CALCULATETABLE ( VALUES ( Sales[Order Date] ), REMOVEFILTERS ( 'Date' ) )
        VAR PrevDateWithSales =
            COALESCE (
                MAXX (
                    FILTER ( AllOrderDates, Sales[Order Date] <= CurrentDate ),
                    Sales[Order Date]
                ),
                FirstDateEver
            )
        VAR Result =
            INT ( CurrentDate - PrevDateWithSales )
        RETURN
            Result
EVALUATE
SUMMARIZECOLUMNS (
    'Date'[Date],
    "DaysWith0", 'Sales'[DaysWith0]
)
ORDER BY 'Date'[Date]
```

By creating the *AllOrderDate* variable, we can use MAXX instead of *CALCULATE(MAX(…))* to find the last order date before the current date. The advantage in terms of performance is evident.

Total	SE CPU	Line	Subclass	Duration	CPU	Par.	Rows	KB	Timeline
698 ms	16 ms								
	x1.0	2	Scan	1	0		4,021	32	
FE	● **SE**	4	Scan	0	0		4,021	63	
682 ms	16 ms	6	Scan	17	16	x0.9	3,284	26	
97.7%	2.3%								

SE Queries	SE Cache
3	0
	0.0%

The three xmSQL queries are nearly the same, with the very noticeable difference that the last one is missing the filter. Indeed, you can see from the timeline that now the three storage engine queries are executed one immediately after the other; the formula engine kicks in later to perform its task.

This first optimization happens very frequently. CALCULATE is mostly good to use. However, there are scenarios like this one where the filter requires a lot of formula engine time. In such cases, it could be better to materialize the filter in a variable and use regular iterators on the variable rather than using CALCULATE, as we did in the last example.

We can move one step forward by making data distribution assumptions. In the database we are using, most of the dates do have sales. The number of gaps is relatively small. Still, the DAX code we wrote is performing the complex part of the algorithm (MAXX) also for dates that for sure, are not gaps. We could add some conditional logic to the formula to perform the calculation only when we know for sure that we are dealing with a date without sales. If there are sales on a particular date, we can immediately return 0 or BLANK. The algorithm becomes more complex because of the IF statement, and at the same time, we save time by avoiding computing a number when we already know it will be zero. Whether the optimization does any good depends on the data we are dealing with. In our scenario, it does help:

```
DEFINE
    MEASURE Sales[DaysWith0] =
        VAR CurrentDate =
            MAX ( 'Date'[Date] )
        VAR FirstDateEver =
            CALCULATE ( MIN ( 'Date'[Date] ), REMOVEFILTERS () )
        VAR AllOrderDates =
            CALCULATETABLE ( VALUES ( Sales[Order Date] ), REMOVEFILTERS ( 'Date' ) )
```

```
            RETURN
                IF (
                    NOT ( CurrentDate IN AllOrderDates ),
                    VAR PrevDateWithSales =
                        COALESCE (
                            MAXX (
                                FILTER (
                                    AllOrderDates,
                                    Sales[Order Date] <= CurrentDate
                                ),
                                Sales[Order Date]
                            ),
                            FirstDateEver
                        )
                    VAR Result =
                        INT ( CurrentDate - PrevDateWithSales )
                    RETURN
                        Result,
                    0
                )
EVALUATE
SUMMARIZECOLUMNS ( 'Date'[Date], "DaysWith0", 'Sales'[DaysWith0] )
ORDER BY 'Date'[Date]
```

Adding the IF function further reduces the execution time.

Total	SE CPU	Line	Subclass	Duration	CPU	Par.	Rows	KB	Timeline
522 ms	16 ms x0.8	2	Scan	3	0		4,021	32	
		4	Scan	0	0		4,021	63	
FE	SE	6	Scan	17	16	x0.9	3,284	26	
502 ms	20 ms								
96.2%	3.8%								

SE Queries	SE Cache
3	0
	0.0%

Using the knowledge we have gathered so far, we know this last optimization is not guaranteed to work in every scenario. If the number of gaps is small compared to the days with sales, then the optimization works. With an increasing number of gaps, this formula quickly becomes the same as the one without the conditional logic, and at some point it even becomes slower because of the increased complexity.

Computing open orders

Choosing the perfect formula to compute the number of open orders is complex. While there is a clear winner or a set of winners for different datasets in most scenarios, each formula and data model presents advantages and disadvantages in analyzing open orders.

An order is open between the day when it is placed (*Sales[Order Date]*) and the date when it is shipped (*Sales[Delivery Date]*). The goal of the formula is to compute the number of open orders on each day. When aggregated over a period that spans multiple days, the definition of open orders becomes more open to interpretation. The version we implement here considers as open any order that – during the period – has been in the open status. Our goal is to obtain a report that we slice by date.

Date	Open Orders
01/01/2015	144,904
01/02/2015	120,146
01/03/2015	157,218
01/04/2015	76,747
01/05/2015	93,632
01/06/2015	96,039
01/07/2015	101,723
01/08/2015	101,943
01/09/2015	81,587

The following formula can fulfill the requirements:

```
DEFINE MEASURE Sales[Open Orders] =
    VAR StartDate = MIN ( 'Date'[Date] )
    VAR EndDate = MAX ( 'Date'[Date] )
    VAR Result =
        CALCULATE (
            DISTINCTCOUNT ( Sales[Order Number] ),
            Sales[Order Date] <= EndDate,
            Sales[Delivery Date] >= StartDate,
            REMOVEFILTERS ( 'Date' )
        )
    RETURN
        Result
EVALUATE
    SUMMARIZECOLUMNS (
        'Date'[Date],
        TREATAS ( { 2015 }, 'Date'[Year] ),
        "Open Orders", [Open Orders]
    )
ORDER BY [Date]
```

The distinct count is not additive; consequently, the engine executes a VertiPaq query for each date. The condition defined in CALCULATE depends on the specific date and must be computed because it involves "greater than" and "less than" operators. Therefore, we expect to notice a first set of queries to retrieve the dates from *Date[Date]*, *Sales[Order Date]*, and *Sales[Delivery Date]*, followed by 365 xmSQL queries, each of which retrieves one value.

The following is the Server Timings pane for the query. There are many more rows (369 queries) in the result; we show only the first ones.

Total	SE CPU	Line	Subclass	Duration	CPU	Par.	Rows	KB	Timeline
20,543 ms	10,821 ms	2	Scan	37	16	x0.4	3,284	26	
	x0.7	4	Scan	0	0		4,021	32	
FE	**SE**	6	Scan	1	0		4,021	95	
4,182 ms	16,361 ms	8	Scan	40	0		3,392	27	
20.4%	79.6%	12	Scan	55	0		1	1	
SE Queries	**SE Cache**	16	Scan	49	16	x0.3	1	1	
369	21	20	Scan	53	16	x0.3	1	1	
	5.7%	24	Scan	53	47	x0.9	1	1	

The first four queries are elementary, confirming our assumptions:

```
SELECT
    'Sales'[Order Date]
FROM 'Sales';

SELECT
    'Date'[Date]
FROM 'Date'
WHERE
    'Date'[Year] = 2015;

SELECT
    'Date'[Date],
    MAX ( 'Date'[Date] ),
    MIN ( 'Date'[Date] )
FROM 'Date'
WHERE
    'Date'[Year] = 2015;

SELECT
    'Sales'[Delivery Date]
FROM 'Sales';
```

Based on these four tiny datacaches, the formula engine prepares 365 queries, each retrieving one of the values to return. They all have the same shape:

```
SELECT
    DCOUNT ( 'Sales'[Order Number] )
FROM 'Sales'
WHERE
    'Sales'[Order Date] IN ( 41841.000000, 41822.000000, 41779.000000, 40734.000000, 40686.000000, 40605.000000,
42021.000000, 41972.000000, 41929.000000, 41888.000000..[1,889 total values, not all displayed] ) VAND
    'Sales'[Delivery Date] IN ( 42993.000000, 42958.000000, 42913.000000, 43149.000000, 43112.000000, 43059.000000,
43018.000000, 42086.000000, 42033.000000, 43339.000000..[1,784 total values, not all displayed] ) VAND
    'Sales'[Order Date] IN ( 41841.000000, 41822.000000, 41779.000000, 40734.000000, 40686.000000, 40605.000000,
42021.000000, 41972.000000, 41929.000000, 41888.000000..[1,886 total values, not all displayed] ) VAND
    'Sales'[Delivery Date] IN ( 42993.000000, 42958.000000, 42913.000000, 43149.000000, 43112.000000, 43059.000000,
43018.000000, 43339.000000, 43300.000000, 43249.000000..[1,445 total values, not all displayed] ) ;
```

The query plan is not helpful this time. It is more than 10,000 lines long because of the massive number of filters to prepare and queries to execute.

Each xmSQL query is very fast, but they are coordinated by the formula engine – which is single-threaded – and as such they are executed sequentially. Performance-wise, the query is quite slow, accounting for a lot of time in the formula engine and a small amount of time in the storage engine, but with a strongly reduced degree of parallelism.

Unfortunately, the measure being non-additive, there are no options to make it any faster. The engine must scan the table for every date, leading to poor performance. We need a distinct count because we need to count the orders, and the order numbers are scattered over the *Sales* table.

A possible optimization is to build a separate table at the granularity of the *Sales[Order Number]*. With that table, we could rely on COUNTROWS instead of DISTINCTCOUNT, obtaining an additive calculation that can be optimized much better. We perform this by creating a calculated table:

```
----------------------------
-- Calculated Table Orders
----------------------------
Orders =
SUMMARIZECOLUMNS (
    Sales[Order Number],
    Sales[CustomerKey],
    "Order Date", MIN ( Sales[Order Date] ),
    "Delivery Date", MAX ( Sales[Delivery Date] )
)
```

The *Open Orders* measure is similar by using the *Orders* table, with the noticeable advantage that we can rely on COUNTROWS:

```
DEFINE
    MEASURE Sales[Open Orders] =
        VAR StartDate = MIN ( 'Date'[Date] )
        VAR EndDate = MAX ( 'Date'[Date] )
        VAR Result =
            CALCULATE (
                COUNTROWS( Orders ),
                Orders[Order Date] <= EndDate,
                Orders[Delivery Date] >= StartDate
            )
        RETURN
            Result
EVALUATE
    SUMMARIZECOLUMNS (
        'Date'[Date],
        TREATAS ( { 2015 }, 'Date'[Year] ),
        "Open Orders",  [Open Orders]
    )
ORDER BY [Date]
```

Performance is much better than before.

Total	SE CPU	Line	Subclass	Duration	CPU	Par.	Rows	KB	Waterfall
400 ms	16 ms								
	x0.0	2	Scan	1	0		3,284	26	
FE	SE	4	Scan	0	0		4,021	32	
400 ms	0 ms	6	Scan	0	0		4,021	95	
100.0%	1.3%								
		8	Scan	2	16	x8.0	3,392	27	
SE Queries	SE Cache	10	Scan	2	0		4,366	52	
5	0								
	0.0%								

There are only five tiny xmSQL queries, indicating that the algorithm is entirely executed inside the formula engine. The first four VertiPaq queries are the same as the previous query; the fifth retrieves all the pairs of *Order Date* and *Delivery Date*:

```
SELECT
    'Orders'[Order Date],
    'Orders'[Delivery Date],
    COUNT ()
FROM 'Orders'
WHERE
    'Orders'[Order Date] IN ( 42214.000000, 42297.000000, 40960.000000, 40945.000000, 41116.000000, 41389.000000,
40719.000000, 40677.000000, 41493.000000, 41648.000000..[1,889 total values, not all displayed] ) VAND
    'Orders'[Delivery Date] IN ( 43741.000000, 43293.000000, 42290.000000, 42884.000000, 42793.000000, 43075.000000,
43894.000000, 43853.000000, 43766.000000, 42730.000000..[1,784 total values, not all displayed] );
```

On this datacache, the formula engine prepares the filters and performs the counting. Despite being much faster, this formula requires building the calculated table (or an equivalent table created during ETL). Moreover, the formula is entirely in charge of the formula engine. As such, executing the same query multiple times requires the same amount of time: it does not benefit from the VertiPaq cache.

There is another modeling option for the open order that requires building a table that contains the order number and the dates when the order was active:

```
--------------------------------
-- Calculated Table OpenOrders
--------------------------------
OpenOrders =
SELECTCOLUMNS (
    GENERATE (
        Orders,
        DATESBETWEEN ( 'Date'[Date], Orders[Order Date], Orders[Delivery Date] )
    ),
    "Order Number", Orders[Order Number],
    "CustomerKey", Orders[CustomerKey],
    "Date", 'Date'[Date]
)
```

The table contains more rows than the *Orders* table because it contains a row for each day the order was active. Therefore, its size depends on the duration of the open status of each order. Nonetheless, it now contains a single date column; consequently, we can rely on a relationship between *OpenOrders* and *Date* and author the *Open Orders* measure with a single distinct count:

```
DEFINE
MEASURE Sales[Open Orders] =
    DISTINCTCOUNT ( OpenOrders[Order Number] )
EVALUATE
    SUMMARIZECOLUMNS (
        'Date'[Date],
        TREATAS ( { 2015 }, 'Date'[Year] ),
        "Open Orders", [Open Orders]
    )
ORDER BY [Date]
```

Because it uses a distinct count, the measure is still somewhat slow. This formula relies on a relationship to move a filter between *Date* and *OpenOrders*. Because relationships are part of the VertiPaq model, the query is resolved with a single VertiPaq query.

Total	SE CPU		Line	Subclass	Duration	CPU	Par.	Rows	KB	Timeline
3,815 ms	33,391 ms									
	x9.3		4	Scan	3,598	33,391	x9.3	343	6	

● FE	● SE	
217 ms	3,598 ms	
5.7%	94.3%	

```
SET DC_KIND="AUTO";
SELECT
    'Date'[Date],
    DCOUNT ( 'Table'[Order Number] )
FROM 'Table'
    LEFT OUTER JOIN 'Date'
        ON 'Table'[Date]='Date'[Date]
```

SE Queries	SE Cache
1	0
	0.0%

The xmSQL query is relatively simple, including both the filter on *Date* and the relationship between *OpenOrders* and *Date*:

```
SELECT
    'Date'[Date],
    DCOUNT ( 'Table'[Order Number] )
FROM 'Table'
    LEFT OUTER JOIN 'Date'
        ON 'Table'[Date]='Date'[Date]
WHERE
    'Date'[Year] = 2015;
```

Performance is not as great as it was with the *Orders* table. Moreover, the machine we use to perform the tests has many cores. Therefore, some amount of parallelism is involved (still reduced because of the cardinality of the *Order Number* column). Performance would only be worse on a server with a smaller number of cores.

However, the measure is using only the storage engine, which might be beneficial in some scenarios.

As is always the case with DAX, each solution has advantages and disadvantages. In the case of open orders, there is no one solution with only advantages. The simplest version is slow but does not require any further table. Creating an order table produces a very fast solution at the cost of there being an additional table in the model. Using the *OpenOrders* table that snapshots the order at the day level generates a solution that sits in the middle in terms of performance but uses the full power of the storage engine.

It is worth testing all these possibilities before deciding which version of the code is the most appropriate for your specific model. Always remember that because of the nature of VertiPaq compression, the unique data distribution of your model might drive you to make different decisions.

Note The open orders computation is an application of the generic "Events in progress" pattern. You can find more examples and variations in this article: https://www.daxpatterns.com/events-in-progress/

Optimizing SWITCH and nested measures

In certain scenarios, it is required to perform conditional logic and adjust parameter values depending on some conditions. For example, consider a situation where we need to multiply the sales amount by a factor that depends on the product brand.

The following code is a pattern very commonly created by DAX newbies. It starts with a measure that performs the correction based on the SELECTEDVALUE of *Product[Brand]*, which is later used inside an iteration over *Product[Brand]*:

```
DEFINE
    MEASURE Sales[Sales Brand Corrected] =
        SWITCH (
            SELECTEDVALUE ( 'Product'[Brand] ),
            "Contoso", [Sales Amount] * 1.01,
            "Fabrikam", [Sales Amount] * 1.02,
            "Litware", [Sales Amount] * 1.03,
            [Sales Amount]
        )
    MEASURE Sales[Sales Amount Corrected] =
        SUMX (
            VALUES ( 'Product'[Brand] ),
            [Sales Brand Corrected]
        )
EVALUATE
SUMMARIZECOLUMNS (
    'Product'[Color],
    "Sales Amount", [Sales Amount],
    "Sales Amount Corrected", [Sales Amount Corrected]
)
```

Despite being quite simple, this measure is shockingly slow. Understanding the details of the algorithm is extremely useful.

Total	SE CPU	Line	Subclass	Duration	CPU	Par.	Rows	KB	Timeline
1,723 ms	34,376 ms	2	Scan	1	0		266	9	
	x20.2	4	Scan	253	5,094	x20.1	266	5	
FE	SE	6	Scan	0	0		266	3	
24 ms	1,699 ms	8	Scan	0	0		19	1	
1.4%	98.6%	10	Scan	328	6,438	x19.6	266	5	
SE Queries	SE Cache	12	Scan	477	9,766	x20.5	266	5	
7	0	14	Scan	641	13,078	x20.4	266	5	
	0.0%								

There are three tiny VertiPaq queries and four rather complex queries. Let us start by looking at the tiny ones (lines 2, 6, and 8).

The first xmSQL query (line 2) is needed for the SELECTEDVALUE function. Indeed, SELECTEDVALUE needs to know whether, for a given combination of *Product[Color]* and *Product[Brand]*, there is only one value for the *Product[Brand]* column. As humans, we find the solution straightforward: if the query groups by *Product[Brand]*, there is a single value. Unfortunately, DAX is not a human, and the pattern of SELECTEDVALUE requires checking that there is a single value:

```
SELECT
    'Product'[Brand],
    'Product'[Color],
    SUM ( ( PFDATAID ( 'Product'[Brand] ) <> 2 ) ),
    MIN ( MinMaxColumnPositionCallback ( PFDATAID ( 'Product'[Brand] ) ) ),
    MAX ( MinMaxColumnPositionCallback ( PFDATAID ( 'Product'[Brand] ) ) ),
    COUNT ( )
FROM 'Product';
```

Despite being quite useless, this xmSQL query is extremely fast; therefore, we do not have to worry about it.

The second small xmSQL query (line 6) retrieves the combinations of *Brand* and *Color*:

```
SELECT
    'Product'[Brand],
    'Product'[Color]
FROM 'Product';
```

The third small xmSQL query (line 8) retrieves the product colors:

```
SELECT
    'Product'[Color]
FROM 'Product';
```

The next four xmSQL queries are the ones that perform the calculation, even though they may look surprising at first sight. The query at line 4 is the following:

```
WITH
    $Expr0 := ( PFCAST ( 'Sales'[Quantity] AS INT ) * PFCAST ( 'Sales'[Net Price] AS INT ) )
SELECT
    'Product'[Brand],
    'Product'[Color],
    SUM ( @$Expr0 )
FROM 'Sales'
    LEFT OUTER JOIN 'Product'
        ON 'Sales'[ProductKey]='Product'[ProductKey]
WHERE
    ( 'Product'[Color], 'Product'[Brand] ) IN {
        ( 'Grey', 'Contoso' ) , ( 'Gold', 'Contoso' ) ,
        ( 'Silver', 'Contoso' ) , ( 'Silver Grey', 'Contoso' ) ,
        ( 'Blue', 'Contoso' ) , ( 'Transparent', 'Contoso' ) ,
        ( 'White', 'Contoso' ) , ( 'Red', 'Contoso' ) ,
        ( 'Black', 'Contoso' ) , ( 'Green', 'Contoso' )
        ..[15 total tuples, not all displayed]};
```

This query retrieves the sales amount of products from the Contoso brand. It filters 15 rows because there are 15 different colors in the Contoso product offering. Looking at the DAX code, this looks like the dataset needed to compute the first branch of the SWITCH.

The xmSQL query at line 10 is more intricate:

```
WITH
    $Expr0 := ( PFCAST ( 'Sales'[Quantity] AS INT ) * PFCAST ( 'Sales'[Net Price] AS INT ) )
SELECT
    'Product'[Brand],
    'Product'[Color],
    SUM ( @$Expr0 )
FROM 'Sales'
    LEFT OUTER JOIN 'Product'
        ON 'Sales'[ProductKey]='Product'[ProductKey]
WHERE
    ( 'Product'[Color], 'Product'[Brand] ) IN {
        ( 'Blue', 'Litware' ) , ( 'Blue', 'A. Datum' ) , ( 'Green', 'Tailspin Toys' ) ,
        ( 'Orange', 'Wide World Importers' ) , ( 'Brown', 'Fabrikam' ) , ( 'White', 'Northwind Traders' ) ,
        ( 'White', 'Litware' ) , ( 'Pink', 'Wide World Importers' ) , ( 'Pink', 'Southridge Video' ) ,
        ( 'Grey', 'Adventure Works' )
        ..[96 total tuples, not all displayed]
    } VAND
    ( 'Product'[Color], 'Product'[Brand] ) IN {
        ( 'Brown', 'Fabrikam' ) , ( 'Grey', 'Fabrikam' ) , ( 'Gold', 'Fabrikam' ) ,
        ( 'Silver', 'Fabrikam' ) , ( 'Silver Grey', 'Fabrikam' ) , ( 'Blue', 'Fabrikam' ) ,
        ( 'White', 'Fabrikam' ) , ( 'Red', 'Fabrikam' ) , ( 'Black', 'Fabrikam' ) ,
        ( 'Green', 'Fabrikam' )
        ..[12 total tuples, not all displayed]
    };
```

There are two conditions. The second is a filter for Fabrikam products. The first, containing 96 rows, looks strange. To make sense of it, we should remember that SWITCH is internally converted into a set of nested IF statements. The second branch of the SWITCH is not just a filter for Fabrikam. It is a filter saying "Fabrikam and NOT Contoso", because Contoso has been evaluated in the previous branch.

The complexity of the filter comes from the need to express, in a filter, the combination of the current filter plus the negation of any filters evaluated previously. Now that the rules of the game are clear, the xmSQL query at line 12 is not surprising:

```
WITH
    $Expr0 := ( PFCAST ( 'Sales'[Quantity] AS INT ) * PFCAST ( 'Sales'[Net Price] AS INT ) )
SELECT
    'Product'[Brand],
    'Product'[Color],
    SUM ( @$Expr0 )
FROM 'Sales'
    LEFT OUTER JOIN 'Product'
        ON 'Sales'[ProductKey]='Product'[ProductKey]
WHERE
    ( 'Product'[Color], 'Product'[Brand] ) IN {
        ( 'Blue', 'Litware' ) , ( 'Blue', 'A. Datum' ) , ( 'Green', 'Tailspin Toys' ) ,
        ( 'Orange', 'Wide World Importers' ) , ( 'Brown', 'Fabrikam' ) , ( 'White', 'Northwind Traders' ) ,
        ( 'White', 'Litware' ) , ( 'Pink', 'Wide World Importers' ) , ( 'Pink', 'Southridge Video' ) ,
        ( 'Grey', 'Adventure Works' ) ..[96 total tuples, not all displayed]
    } VAND
    ( 'Product'[Color], 'Product'[Brand] ) IN {
        ( 'Blue', 'Litware' ) , ( 'Blue', 'A. Datum' ) , ( 'Green', 'Tailspin Toys' ) ,
        ( 'Orange', 'Wide World Importers' ) , ( 'Grey', 'Contoso' ) , ( 'White', 'Northwind Traders' ) ,
        ( 'White', 'Litware' ) , ( 'Pink', 'Wide World Importers' ) , ( 'Pink', 'Southridge Video' ) ,
        ( 'Grey', 'Adventure Works' ) ..[99 total tuples, not all displayed]
    } VAND
    ( 'Product'[Color], 'Product'[Brand] ) IN {
        ( 'Blue', 'Litware' ) , ( 'White', 'Litware' ) , ( 'Red', 'Litware' ) ,
        ( 'Black', 'Litware' ) , ( 'Green', 'Litware' ) , ( 'Orange', 'Litware' ) ,
        ( 'Pink', 'Litware' ) , ( 'Yellow', 'Litware' ) , ( 'Purple', 'Litware' ) ,
        ( 'Brown', 'Litware' ) ..[12 total tuples, not all displayed]
    };
```

The complexity of the filter increases. The xmSQL query at line 14 has the same structure with an even longer filter. By looking at the Server Timings pane, you can observe that the increasing complexity of the filter corresponds to an increasing execution time.

Line	Subclass	Duration	CPU	Par.	Rows	KB
2	Scan	3	0		266	9
4	Scan	237	4,875	x20.6	266	5
6	Scan	0	0		266	3
8	Scan	0	0		19	1
10	Scan	333	6,703	x20.1	266	5
12	Scan	470	9,688	x20.6	266	5
14	Scan	628	13,281	x21.1	266	5

All the queries retrieve the same amount of information with the same degree of parallelism. However, a more complex filter means a higher execution time. You can easily imagine that the scenario would be much worse if the number of SWITCH elements were more significant.

Having reached this point, our readers will probably recognize the scenario of strict evaluation of IF statements. The pattern we are observing is the pattern of conditional logic we have seen before. If an IF function generated this pattern of execution plan, a good option would be to use IF.EAGER. However, there is no such option with SWITCH. Yet, we can obtain an eager evaluation by using variables:

```
DEFINE
    MEASURE Sales[Sales Brand Corrected] =
        VAR SalesAmount = [Sales Amount]
        VAR Factor =
            SWITCH (
                SELECTEDVALUE ( 'Product'[Brand] ),
                "Contoso", 1.01,
                "Fabrikam", 1.02,
                "Litware", 1.03,
                1
            )
        VAR Result = SalesAmount * Factor
        RETURN
            Result
    MEASURE Sales[Sales Amount Corrected] =
        SUMX (
            VALUES ( 'Product'[Brand] ),
            [Sales Brand Corrected]
        )

EVALUATE
SUMMARIZECOLUMNS (
    'Product'[Color],
    "Sales Amount", [Sales Amount],
    "Sales Amount Corrected", [Sales Amount Corrected]
)
```

In this last version of the measure, we removed *Sales Amount* from the SWITCH statement. We computed it into the *SalesAmount* variable, which we used later to multiply by the factor computed with SWITCH. The performance gain is impressive.

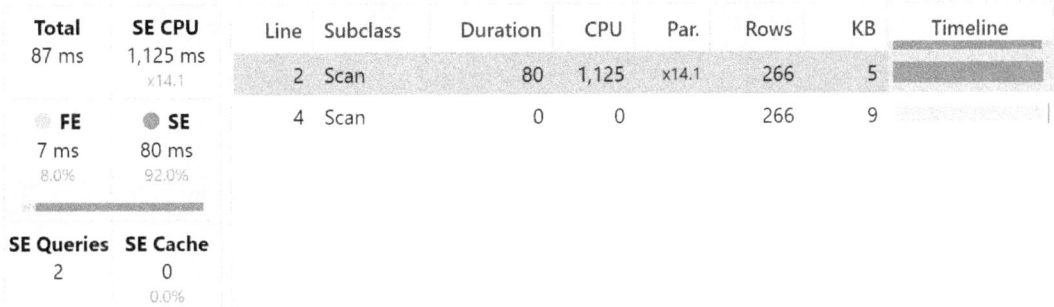

Total	SE CPU		Line	Subclass	Duration	CPU	Par.	Rows	KB	Timeline
87 ms	1,125 ms		2	Scan	80	1,125	x14.1	266	5	
	x14.1		4	Scan	0	0		266	9	
FE	SE									
7 ms	80 ms									
8.0%	92.0%									

SE Queries	SE Cache
2	0
	0.0%

The first xmSQL query retrieves the sales amount:

```
WITH
    $Expr0 := ( PFCAST ( 'Sales'[Quantity] AS INT ) * PFCAST ( 'Sales'[Net Price] AS INT ) )
SELECT
    'Product'[Brand],
    'Product'[Color],
    SUM ( @$Expr0 )
FROM 'Sales'
    LEFT OUTER JOIN 'Product'
        ON 'Sales'[ProductKey]='Product'[ProductKey];
```

There not being any filters, the scan is much faster than any of the previous four. Overall, the query produces the same result, at a tiny fraction of the time required before.

Conclusions

This chapter showed a reasonable number of examples, with the goal of demonstrating the process of optimizing code. We chose the examples based on our experience, and attempted to cover as many useful scenarios as possible.

Whenever you find a new challenge, try to treat it as one of these examples. Start gathering a baseline with the most intuitive formulation of the DAX code, then use the information provided by DAX Studio to understand better how the DAX engine solved the query. The more you learn about the internals of the engine, the more natural it will be to formulate the DAX code in a way that instructs the optimizer to find the best path.

Understanding security optimization

Among the many threats to performance, row-level security holds a very special place. Security is quite frequently added to a model towards the end of the development process because it is a complex, utterly boring step. How unfortunate this is! Security needs to be designed from the very beginning and incorporated into the development of the solution from the very early stages of the process.

Indeed, security is pervasive. It adds a layer of complexity around each and every calculation. If the security rules are simple and well-optimized, their impact is minimal. However, when security is not designed from the beginning, developers often end up with suboptimal solutions that slow down the entire model.

Optimizing conditions and filters for security is no different from optimizing any DAX formula. However, it is crucial to understand when and how security rules are enforced, and how to test security performance to guarantee a minimal impact on the overall model performance.

We are not going to cover object-level security. This book is about performance, and object-level security does not impact performance. On the other hand, row-level security may have a profound impact on the overall model performance.

Testing security conditions and their performance impact

To test your model's performance under security constraints, you must use DAX Studio and change the advanced connection properties. This change is of paramount importance. When developers work on a model, they are usually administrators of the instance of Analysis Services they are using. If a user is an administrator of the model (or of the instance), then security rules are not applied. It does not matter whether your user belongs to a specific role: as an administrator, you browse the model without any security activated.

However, administrators can impersonate any set of roles when querying a model by setting the Role property in the connection string. Using DAX Studio, developers can impersonate a role by activating the advanced options of the Connect dialog and setting the role name(s) to impersonate in the Roles connection attribute.

Impersonating a role is the simplest way to check the security settings are correct and performing. You can also impersonate a specific username by using the Effective User Name connection property when connecting to Analysis Services or use the View As feature in DAX Studio after you establish the connection to Power BI Desktop, as we will be showing later.

Understanding when and where security is enforced

Security conditions are DAX expressions evaluated in the row context of a table. Security filters are evaluated for every query executed against the database and implemented at the storage engine level. The reason for this is that by applying the filters during the VertiPaq scan of the model, no unsecured data ever leaves the storage engine.

Security conditions are evaluated for each table as soon as that table is referenced in a query. Therefore, the impact of security evaluation might be larger on the first query if the security condition is cached.

Depending on the complexity of the condition and the table size, security filters may be cached or not. If a security filter is cached, it is evaluated on the first query referencing the table and then saved for later. If a security filter is not cached, it is evaluated on every query.

Regardless of whether a security filter is cached, the security condition is evaluated for every table scan of any table that the security filter can reach.

For example, we created a CustomerEurope role that filters only customers living in Europe.

Manage security roles ✕

Create new security roles and use filters to define row-level data restrictions.

Roles	Select tables	Filter data		Switch to DAX editor

+ New

⊞ CurrencyExcha...

⊞ CurrencyExcha...

🔳 CustomerEurope ⋯

⊞ Customer ▽ ⋯

⊞ Customer DQ ⋯

▦ Select all   + Add   🗑 Delete   ▦ Group   ▦ Ungroup

Show data when...

All ⌄ of these rules are true

⠿   Continent ⌄   Equals ⌄   Europe

In the Tabular model, the security role is described as a logical condition such as:

```
ROLE CustomerEurope:

Customer[Continent] == "Europe"
```

Running a query that slices by *Product[Brand]* also involves *Customer* in the xmSQL code because of the need to add the security role condition. Indeed, the following DAX query only uses the *Product* and *Sales* tables:

```
EVALUATE
SUMMARIZECOLUMNS (
    'Product'[Brand],
    "Sales Amount", [Sales Amount]
)
```

However, *Customer* filters *Sales,* and the security condition filters *Customer*. Therefore, the xmSQL code generated to answer the query is the following:

```
WITH
    $Expr0 := ( PFCAST ( 'Sales'[Quantity] AS INT ) * PFCAST ( 'Sales'[Net Price] AS INT ) )
SELECT
    'Product'[Brand],
    SUM ( @$Expr0 )
FROM 'Sales'
    LEFT OUTER JOIN 'Customer'
        ON 'Sales'[CustomerKey]='Customer'[CustomerKey]
    LEFT OUTER JOIN 'Product'
        ON 'Sales'[ProductKey]='Product'[ProductKey]
WHERE
    COALESCE ( ( PFDATAID ( 'Customer'[Continent] ) = 4 ) );
```

There are two tables joined to *Sales*: *Product* and *Customer*. *Customer* is required because of the condition on the *Customer[Continent]* column. Every xmSQL query contains the filtering conditions defined by the active security roles. We obtain two scans if we add the calculation of the distinct count of products:

```
DEFINE
    MEASURE Sales[# Products] =
        DISTINCTCOUNT ( Sales[ProductKey] )

EVALUATE
SUMMARIZECOLUMNS (
    'Product'[Brand],
    "Sales Amount", [Sales Amount],
    "# Products", [# Products]
)
```

Here is the server timings panel.

Total	SE CPU	Line	Subclass	Duration	CPU	Par.	Rows	KB	Timeline
163 ms	344 ms x2.2	2	Scan	83	188	x2.3	14	1	
FE 10 ms 6.1%	**SE** 153 ms 93.9%	6	Scan	70	156	x2.2	11	1	

SE Queries	SE Cache
2	0 0.0%

The first xmSQL query at line 2 is identical to the previous example; the new query at line 6 is the following:

```
SELECT
    'Product'[Brand],
    DCOUNT ( 'Sales'[ProductKey] )
FROM 'Sales'
    LEFT OUTER JOIN 'Customer'
        ON 'Sales'[CustomerKey]='Customer'[CustomerKey]
    LEFT OUTER JOIN 'Product'
        ON 'Sales'[ProductKey]='Product'[ProductKey]
WHERE
    COALESCE ( ( PFDATAID ( 'Customer'[Continent] ) = 4 ) );
```

Both the JOIN with *Customer* and the condition to filter *Customer[Continent]* are added to every xmSQL query. The important detail is that the security conditions affect every xmSQL query. Therefore, a slow filter condition can significantly impact the performance of the entire model.

As an extreme example of the impact of security roles on performance, let us change the definition of the role with an equivalent (but much worse) condition that requires using the formula engine.

When you specify a condition with the DAX editor, you use the same DAX syntax applied to the security role in the Tabular model:

```
ROLE CustomerEurope:

FIND ( "Europe", Customer[Continent], 1, - 1 ) <> -1
```

Because FIND can be solved only by the formula engine, a callback is required to evaluate the condition, and the time required to answer the query skyrockets above 45 seconds.

Total	SE CPU		Line	Subclass	Duration	CPU	Par.	Rows	KB	Timeline	Query
45,922 ms	1,039,000 ms		2	Scan	22,970	518,703	x22.6	14	1		WITH $Expr0 :=
	x22.6		6	Scan	22,941	520,297	x22.7	11	1		SELECT 'Product
FE	SE										
11 ms	45,911 ms										
0.0%	100.0%										

```
SET DC_KIND="AUTO";
SELECT
    'Product'[Brand],
    DCOUNT ( 'Sales'[ProductKey] )
FROM 'Sales'
    LEFT OUTER JOIN 'Customer'
        ON 'Sales'[CustomerKey]='Customer'[CustomerKey]
    LEFT OUTER JOIN 'Product'
        ON 'Sales'[ProductKey]='Product'[ProductKey]
WHERE
    COALESCE ( ( COALESCE ( [CallbackDataID] ( FIND ( "Europe", Customer[Continent], 1, -1 ) ) ] ( PFDAT/
```

SE Queries	SE Cache
2	0
	0.0%

The callback is present in the WHERE condition of both xmSQL queries; here is the xmSQL query at line 2:

```
WITH
    $Expr0 := ( PFCAST ( 'Sales'[Quantity] AS INT ) * PFCAST ( 'Sales'[Net Price] AS INT ) )
SELECT
    'Product'[Brand],
    SUM ( @$Expr0 )
FROM 'Sales'
    LEFT OUTER JOIN 'Customer'
        ON 'Sales'[CustomerKey]='Customer'[CustomerKey]
    LEFT OUTER JOIN 'Product'
        ON 'Sales'[ProductKey]='Product'[ProductKey]
WHERE
    COALESCE ( ( COALESCE ( [CallbackDataID] ( FIND ( "Europe", Customer[Continent], 1, -1 ) ) ] ( PFDATAID (
'Customer'[Continent] ) ) ) ) <> COALESCE ( -1 ) ) ) ;
```

This example is an extreme situation. Any experienced DAX developer would quickly realize that using FIND in a security condition leads to a disaster. However, the goal was to demonstrate that the impact of security can be huge.

Understanding cached bitmap indexes and embedded filters

Evaluating security conditions can be expensive, as we showed earlier. Under certain conditions, the VertiPaq engine can cache the security conditions in bitmap indexes to make their evaluation faster. The conditions may change over time, and they are not documented. However, our tests indicate two conditions for a cache to be created:

- The filtering condition is complex, where the term "complex" is not clearly defined. Simple equality conditions are considered simple. Anything else is quite always considered complex.

- The filtered table does not exceed 131,072 (128K) rows.

The bitmap index is used only when both conditions are met.

As an example, we created two roles, CustomerEurope and ProductContoso, with a similar expression that filters *Customer[Continent]* and *Product[Brand]* by using the "greater than or equal to" operator:

```
ROLE CustomerEurope:

    Customer[Continent] >= "Europe"
```

```
ROLE ProductContoso:

    'Product'[Brand] >= "Contoso"
```

Both filters use a condition over strings that cannot be executed inside VertiPaq. *Customer* contains 1.8M rows; therefore, it exceeds 128K. *Product* contains 2,517 rows; therefore, it is well within the limit of

128K rows. Consequently, the two conditions use different techniques. For *Product*, VertiPaq creates a bitmap cache, whereas the filter over *Customer* requires a callback – with a substantial impact on performance.

We will always use the following query to test the performance and the storage engine queries in this section:

```
EVALUATE
SUMMARIZECOLUMNS (
    Store[Country],
    "Sales", [Sales Amount]
)
```

Before running the test, make sure you select both roles in the DAX Studio connection dialog box. When the two roles are active, you should see the following warning above the DAX editor.

```
Roles: CustomerEurope, ProductContoso

1 EVALUATE
2 SUMMARIZECOLUMNS (
3     Store[Country],
4     "Sales", [Sales Amount]
5 )
6
```

After running the query, the server timings pane shows 30,563 milliseconds of storage engine CPU, with two VertiPaq scans.

Total	SE CPU	Line	Subclass	Duration	CPU	Par.	Rows	KB	Timeline
657 ms	30,563 ms								
	x47.5	2	Scan	1	0		2,517	10	
FE	SE	4	Scan	643	30,563	x47.5	12	1	
14 ms	643 ms								
2.1%	97.9%								

SE Queries	SE Cache
2	0
	0.0%

The first xmSQL query retrieves the brand of each product:

```
SELECT
    'Product'[RowNumber],
    'Product'[Brand]
FROM 'Product';
```

Interestingly, this xmSQL query is not used in any of the physical query plan operators. If we look at the query plan, the only datacache consumed contains one field column and one result. Therefore, it is undoubtedly not the first xmSQL query.

Line	Records	Physical Query Plan
1		GroupSemijoin: IterPhyOp LogOp=GroupSemiJoin IterCols(0, 1)('Store'[Country], ''[Sales])
2	9	Spool_Iterator<SpoolIterator>: IterPhyOp LogOp=Sum_Vertipaq IterCols(0)('Store'[Country]) #Records=9
3	9	ProjectionSpool<ProjectFusion<Copy>>: SpoolPhyOp #Records=9
4		**Cache: IterPhyOp #FieldCols=1 #ValueCols=1**

The reason VertiPaq retrieves products and brands is to build a bitmap index of the products with a brand that is greater than or equal to Contoso. Therefore, the result of this xmSQL query is used internally to build the index. A confirmation is shown in the second xmSQL query that includes one callback to resolve the filter on *Customer* and one bitmap index to resolve the filter on *Product*:

```
WITH
    $Expr0 := ( PFCAST ( 'Sales'[Quantity] AS INT ) * PFCAST ( 'Sales'[Net Price] AS INT ) )
SELECT
    'Store'[Country],
    SUM ( @$Expr0 )
FROM 'Sales'
    LEFT OUTER JOIN 'Customer'
        ON 'Sales'[CustomerKey]='Customer'[CustomerKey]
    LEFT OUTER JOIN 'Product'
        ON 'Sales'[ProductKey]='Product'[ProductKey]
    LEFT OUTER JOIN 'Store'
        ON 'Sales'[StoreKey]='Store'[StoreKey]
WHERE
    ( COALESCE ( [CallbackDataID ( [Continent] >= "Europe" ) ] ( PFDATAID ( 'Customer'[Continent] ) ) )
    OR
    VERTICALC ( 'Product'.$ROWFILTER IN
'0xffffffffffffffffffffffffffffffffffffffffffffffff000003ffffffffffffffffffff00000000000003ffffff00000000000offffffffffffffffffffffffffffff
ffff..[40 total units, not all displayed]' ) ) ;
```

The bitmap index is used in the VERTICALC condition. The bitmap index is created once, and used whenever the *Product* table needs to be filtered. The implication is that the price of evaluating a complex security rule is paid only once per connection. Subsequent queries from the same user can take advantage of the storage engine cache. However, if you run this same query a second time without clearing the cache, only the first xmSQL query (at line 2 in the previous server timings) is retrieved by the cache. In contrast, the xmSQL query at line 4 is repeated every time because of the formula engine callback in the *Customer[Continent]* condition.

Indeed, despite having a similar filter, *Customer* is not filtered with a bitmap index, because of the large number of rows in the dimension. The performance impact of the callback required by the *Customer[Continent]* condition is huge. The callback is present because a string comparison cannot be pushed down to the storage engine. However, a comparison of integers is well within the capabilities of the storage engine. A simple and efficient way to replace the filter over the *Customer* table with a filter that can be pushed down to the storage engine is to replace the string with an integer.

We create a new *Customer[ContinentCode]* calculated column with the alphabetical sort order of *Customer[Continent]*:

```
-----------------------------------------
-- Calculated column in Customer table
-----------------------------------------
ContinentCode =
RANKX (
    ALL ( Customer[Continent] ),
    Customer[Continent],
    ,
    ASC
)
```

The new calculated column assigns numbers to the continent, using the same sort order as the original string:

```
EVALUATE
SUMMARIZECOLUMNS (
    Customer[Continent],
    Customer[ContinentCode]
)
ORDER BY Customer[Continent]
```

As you see, the numbers are assigned correctly.

Continent	ContinentCode
Australia	1
Europe	2
North America	3

We can rewrite the filtering condition over *Customer* using a number rather than a string. Knowing that Europe corresponds to number 2, we obtain the following roles:

```
ROLE CustomerEurope:

    Customer[ContinentCode] >= 2

ROLE ProductContoso:

    'Product'[Brand] >= "Contoso"
```

Our test query shows a significant improvement in terms of speed, almost one order of magnitude for the SE CPU metric.

Total	SE CPU	Line	Subclass	Duration	CPU	Par.	Rows	KB	Timeline
180 ms	3,031 ms	2	Scan	1	0		2,517	10	
	x18.0								
⬤ FE	⬤ SE	4	Scan	167	3,031	x18.1	12	1	
12 ms	168 ms								
6.7%	93.3%								
SE Queries	SE Cache								
2	0								
	0.0%								

By inspecting the second xmSQL query, we find out that the callback is no longer present:

```
WITH
    $Expr0 := ( PFCAST ( 'Sales'[Quantity] AS INT ) * PFCAST ( 'Sales'[Net Price] AS INT ) )
SELECT
    'Store'[Country],
    SUM ( @$Expr0 )
FROM 'Sales'
    LEFT OUTER JOIN 'Customer'
        ON 'Sales'[CustomerKey]='Customer'[CustomerKey]
    LEFT OUTER JOIN 'Product'
        ON 'Sales'[ProductKey]='Product'[ProductKey]
    LEFT OUTER JOIN 'Store'
        ON 'Sales'[StoreKey]='Store'[StoreKey]
WHERE
    ( COALESCE ( ( PFCASTCOALESCE ( 'Customer'[ContinentCode] AS INT ) >= COALESCE ( 2 ) ) )
    OR
    VERTICALC ( 'Product'.$ROWFILTER IN
'0xfffffffffffffffffffffffffffffffffffffffffffffffff000003ffffffffffffffffffffffff00000000000003ffffff00000000000offfffffffffffffffffffffffffffffff
ffff..[40 total units, not all displayed]' ) ) ;
```

At the cost of sounding pedantic, we want to stress further that the improvement is not only relative to this specific query. Any scan of *Sales* greatly benefits from this optimization. The impact will be impressive in a typical report that includes tens or hundreds of scans. Moreover, a second execution of the same query without clearing the cache also benefits from the storage engine cache for all the xmSQL queries, resulting in a storage engine execution time of zero second.

Total	SE CPU	Line	Subclass	Duration	CPU	Par.	Rows	KB	Timeline
7 ms	0 ms x0.0	1	Cache						
FE	SE	2	Scan	0	0		12	1	
7 ms	0 ms								
100.0%	0.0%								

SE Queries	SE Cache
1	1
	100.0%

In this example, we had to optimize the filter over *Customer[Continent]* because of the callback. The same scenario does not apply to *Product*. Indeed, suppose we create a Product[BrandCode] calculated column and use it as a filtering condition. In that case, the engine still makes a bitmap index because using "greater than or equal to" is already considered a complex operation.

Here is the expression for the *Product[BrandCode]* calculated column:

```
----------------------------------------
-- Calculated column in Product table
----------------------------------------
BrandCode =
RANKX (
    ALL ( Product[Brand] ),
    Product[Brand],
    ,
    ASC
)
```

The Contoso brand is in third position, in alphabetical order.

Brand	BrandCode
A. Datum	1
Adventure Works	2
Contoso	3
Fabrikam	4
Litware	5

We also change the filtering condition using the *Product[BrandCode]* for brands that are greater than or equal to Contoso, which is third:

```
ROLE CustomerEurope:

    Customer[ContinentCode] >= 2

ROLE ProductContoso:

    'Product'[BrandCode] >= 3
```

The resulting server timings are nearly identical to the previous execution because the bitmap index is still present.

Total	SE CPU		Line	Subclass	Duration	CPU	Par.	Rows	KB	Timeline
193 ms	3,563 ms		2	Scan	1	0		2,517	10	
	x19.8		4	Scan	180	3,563	x19.8	12	1	
FE	SE									
13 ms	180 ms									
6.7%	93.3%									

SE Queries	SE Cache
2	0
	0.0%

The first xmSQL query scans the *Product[BrandCode]* column to build the bitmap index used in the following xmSQL query. Besides, bitmap indexes are very fast. If we were able to push the condition down to VertiPaq using a WHERE condition, performance would be the same, if not worse.

Instead, it is possible to further optimize the performance of the CustomerEurope security role by using a table smaller than *Customer*. The limitation of using a bitmap index is the number of rows where the security condition is placed. If the column to be filtered is small, as is *Customer[Continent]* in our scenario, but the column belongs to a much larger table like *Customer*, then we can force the use of a bitmap index by creating a hidden calculated table to store only *Continent*:

```
-------------------------------
-- Calculated table Continent
-------------------------------
Continent = ALLNOBLANKROW ( Customer[Continent] )
```

We build a relationship between *Customer* and *Continent*.

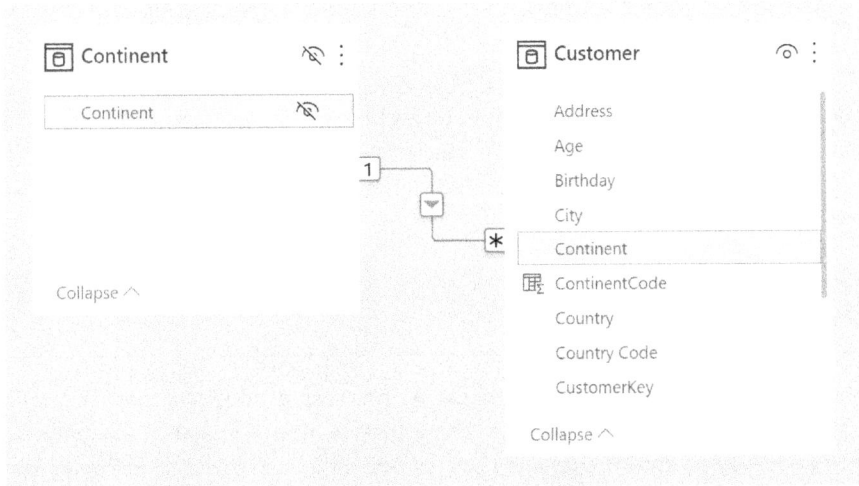

Finally, we place the filter condition on the *Continent* table instead of *Customer*:

```
ROLE CustomerEurope:

    Continent[Continent] >= "Europe"

ROLE ProductContoso:

    'Product'[BrandCode] >= 3
```

By doing this small change, we set the security condition on a table with only three rows that is certainly suitable for a bitmap index. Running our test query shows the improvement.

Total	SE CPU	Line	Subclass	Duration	CPU	Par.	Rows	KB	Timeline
170 ms	2,203 ms								
	x13.5	2	Scan	3	0		36	1	
FE	**SE**	4	Scan	1	0		2,517	10	
7 ms	163 ms	6	Scan	160	2,203	x13.8	12	1	
4.1%	95.9%								

SE Queries	SE Cache
3	0
	0.0%

There are now two small queries at the beginning to build the two bitmap indexes, and then the main query uses bitmap indexes to execute the filter.

There is a good performance improvement in the storage engine CPU. Again, be mindful that this improvement will be multiplied for every table scan because security constraints are always applied.

Suppose a security condition is simple enough to be evaluated in the storage engine, and the filtered table is not small enough. In that case, the condition test is embedded in every xmSQL query and evaluated at every scan. Performance may of may not be an issue, depending on the complexity of the condition.

As a rule of thumb, developers should try their best to use bitmap indexes for security. Bitmap indexes are the fastest way to evaluate security constraints. They also ensure that the filter evaluation happens once and for all. Once the first query has been executed, further access to the same tables will no longer require scanning the secured tables.

Optimizing dynamic security

The security constraints are quite frequently based on dynamic expressions that use the USERNAME, USERPRINCIPALNAME, or CUSTOMDATA functions. These three functions in and of themselves do not pose any threat to performance. Indeed, they are resolved as constant values. In the following examples, we create the connection from DAX Studio to Power BI Desktop by applying the CustomData parameter in the Additional Options.

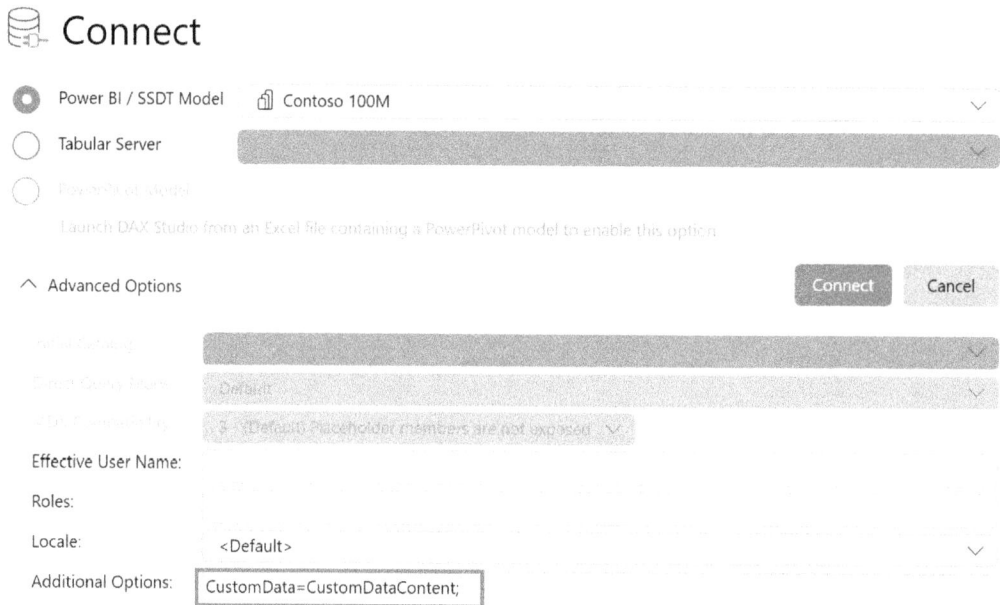

The following query does not execute any xmSQL code. It gathers its result from constant values:

```
EVALUATE
SUMMARIZECOLUMNS (
    "Username", USERNAME (),
    "PrincipalName", USERPRINCIPALNAME (),
    "CustomData", CUSTOMDATA ()
)
```

The result contains the required information when the user marco@contoso.com creates the connection by using DAX Studio.

Username	PrincipalName	CustomData
AzureAD\MarcoRusso	marco@contoso.com	CustomDataContent

However, the query plan clearly shows that all values are constant.

Line	Records	Physical Query Plan
1	1	Spool_Iterator<SpoolIterator>: IterPhyOp LogOp=GroupSemiJoin IterCols(0, 1, 2)("[Username], "[PrincipalNar
2	1	AggregationSpool<GroupSemiJoin>: SpoolPhyOp #Records=1
3		Extend_Lookup: IterPhyOp LogOp=Constant
4		SingletonTable: IterPhyOp LogOp=Constant
5		Constant: LookupPhyOp LogOp=Constant String AzureAD\MarcoRusso
6		Extend_Lookup: IterPhyOp LogOp=Constant
7		SingletonTable: IterPhyOp LogOp=Constant
8		Constant: LookupPhyOp LogOp=Constant String marco@contoso.com
9		Extend_Lookup: IterPhyOp LogOp=Constant
10		SingletonTable: IterPhyOp LogOp=Constant
11		Constant: LookupPhyOp LogOp=Constant String CustomDataContent

There are no VertiPaq queries at lines 5, 8, and 11: the information is provided as a constant value. However, these functions in and of themselves do not enforce any security. These functions are mainly used to set security dynamically through DAX expressions and bridge tables.

To test dynamic security, we must impersonate a specific user and also activate the corresponding role. After establishing a connection without impersonating any role or username, we use the View As feature in the Advanced ribbon.

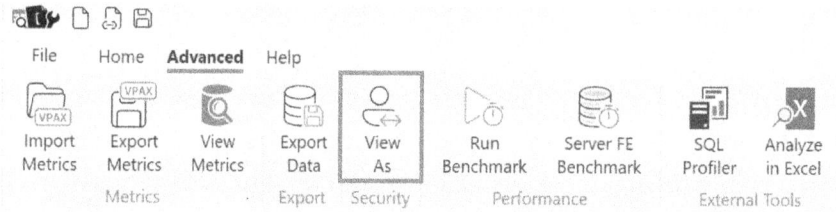

While the role activation is automatic when a non-admin user connects to a Tabular model in DAX Studio, we must specify both the username and the roles to activate. In this case, we activate only the CustomerDynamic role, which we want to test for performance, and we impersonate the alberto@contoso.com username in the following examples.

View As

You can choose to impersonate another user which will apply all the roles which that user is a member of. Or you can choose to test one or more roles directly

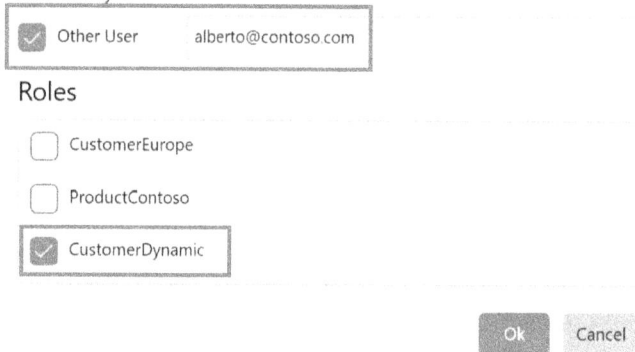

| ✓ | Other User | alberto@contoso.com |

Roles

☐ CustomerEurope

☐ ProductContoso

✓ CustomerDynamic

Ok   Cancel

When you are an administrator, you can test the security by specifying the username to impersonate. An administrator username will have full access without any security role being applied.

After we activate the View As feature, a message displays the active roles and the username impersonated above the editor in DAX Studio: both USERNAME and USERPRINCIPALNAME return the impersonated username.

```
1 EVALUATE
2 SUMMARIZECOLUMNS (
3     "Username", USERNAME (),
4     "PrincipalName", USERPRINCIPALNAME (),
5     "CustomData", CUSTOMDATA ()
6 )
7
```

Log   **Results**   History   ● Server Timings   ● Query Plan

Username	PrincipalName	CustomData
alberto@contoso.com	alberto@contoso.com	CustomDataContent

The process of optimizing a dynamic security expression is no different from the process of optimizing any DAX query. The goal is always to use the most efficient way to move a filter from one table to the target, possibly using bitmap filters. Let us elaborate on this with an example.

We want to define security based on the username by using a configuration table that maps users to continents. For the sake of our example, we create the table in DAX:

```
-------------------------------------
-- Calculated table UserContinents
-------------------------------------
UserContinents =
SELECTCOLUMNS (
    {
        ( "marco@contoso.com", "Europe" ),
        ( "marco@contoso.com", "North America" ),
        ( "alberto@contoso.com", "North America" ),
        ( "alberto@contoso.com", "Australia" )
    },
    "UserName", [Value1],
    "Continent", [Value2]
)
```

The *UserContinents* table has the following content.

UserName	Continent
marco@contoso.com	Europe
marco@contoso.com	North America
alberto@contoso.com	North America
alberto@contoso.com	Australia

Then we create a role named CustomerDynamic that filters the customers based on the username. We can achieve the result in multiple ways:

- We place a filter on the *Customer* table that filters only customers whose continent belongs to the continents visible in the configuration table for the current user.

- We place a filter on the configuration table, along with a many-to-many cardinality relationship with *Customer*.

There may be other options; however, these are the ones that we are using for the demo. There is no way we can choose one solution over another without performing some serious testing. As you have already learned, security conditions are essential for the performance of the entire model: the time spent making a perfect choice is time well spent.

We start by creating the CustomerDynamic security role with the DAX filter applied to *Customer[Continent]*.

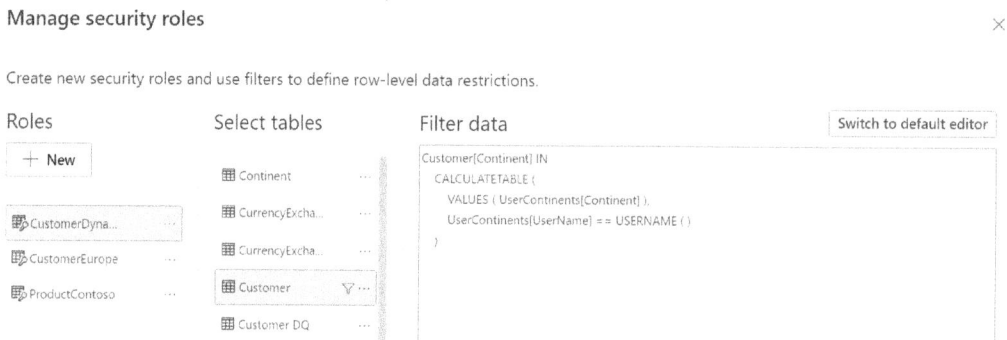

Here is the DAX expression defined in the filter on *Customer*:

```
CustomerDynamic:

Customer[Continent] IN
    CALCULATETABLE (
        VALUES ( UserContinents[Continent] ),
        UserContinents[UserName] == USERNAME ( )
    )
```

The filter on *UserContinents* shows only the continents associated with the currently logged-in user;

the DAX condition checks that the *Customer[Continent]* column belongs to that list of continents.

Based on the knowledge we have gained so far, we can already make several considerations about this technique. It filters a large table (*Customer*); therefore, no bitmap indexes will be used. The condition involves CALCULATETABLE, VALUES, and the IN operator. It is very unlikely that the DAX optimizer will find a way to express such a complex calculation in xmSQL. Therefore, we expect a callback in the WHERE condition.

To test the performance of dynamic security, we use the query from the previous sections:

```
EVALUATE
SUMMARIZECOLUMNS (
    Store[Country],
    "Amount", [Sales Amount]
)
```

Here is the server timings pane.

Total	SE CPU		Line	Subclass	Duration	CPU	Par.	Rows	KB	Timeline
523 ms	25,219 ms									
	x49.3		2	Scan	0	0		6	1	
FE	**SE**		4	Scan	0	0		6	1	
11 ms	512 ms		6	Scan	512	25,219	x49.3	12	1	
2.1%	97.9%									

SE Queries	SE Cache
3	0
	0.0%

SET DC_KIND="AUTO";

The first two xmSQL queries at lines 2 and 4 retrieve the values of *Customer[Continent]* and *UserContinents[Continent]*, respectively. The last xmSQL query at line 6 calculates *Sales Amount* by *Store[Country]* and shows a callback:

```
WITH
    $Expr0 := ( PFCAST ( 'Sales'[Quantity] AS INT ) * PFCAST ( 'Sales'[Net Price] AS INT ) )
SELECT
    'Store'[Country],
    SUM ( @$Expr0 )
FROM 'Sales'
    LEFT OUTER JOIN 'Customer'
        ON 'Sales'[CustomerKey]='Customer'[CustomerKey]
    LEFT OUTER JOIN 'Store'
        ON 'Sales'[StoreKey]='Store'[StoreKey]
WHERE
    COALESCE ( NOT COALESCE ( [CallbackDataID (
        Customer[Continent] IN
            CALCULATETABLE (
                VALUES ( UserContinents[Continent] ),
                UserContinents[UserName] == USERNAME ()
            )
    ) ] ( PFDATAID ( 'Customer'[Continent] ) ) ) ) ;
```

We have learned so far that applying security on the *Customer* table is not a good option because of the size of the table. It is way better to use a smaller table. Indeed, the *UserContinents* table can be secured with a simpler condition. We can then create a many-to-many cardinality relationship between *UserContinents* and *Customer*, based on the *Continent* column.

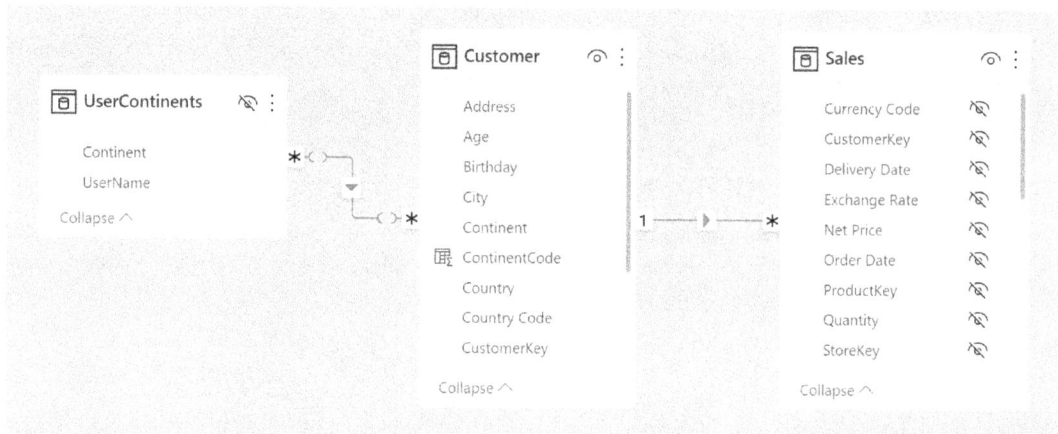

We remove the security filter from the *Customer* table and apply a condition to *UserContinents* only – the condition must be defined by using the DAX editor. Otherwise, the expression containing the USERNAME function would be considered a static string, resulting in no matches being found.

Manage security roles

×

Create new security roles and use filters to define row-level data restrictions.

Roles	Select tables	Filter data
		Switch to default editor

Roles

+ New

- CustomerDyna... ···
- CustomerEurope ···
- ProductContoso ···

Select tables

- ⊞ CurrencyExcha... ···
- ⊞ Customer ···
- ⊞ Customer DQ ···
- ⊞ Date ···
- ⊞ Date DQ ···
- ⊞ Product ···
- ⊞ Product DQ ···
- ⊞ Sales ···
- ⊞ Sales DQ ···
- ⊞ Store ···
- ⊞ UserContinents ▽···

Filter data

[UserName] == USERNAME()

[Save] [Close]

The DAX filter expression for UserContinents in the *CustomerDynamic* role is the following:

```
UserContinents:

UserContinents[UserName] == USERNAME ()
```

By using this security setup, performance is much better because the DAX engine relies on limited and regular relationships, which generates a batch request.

Total	SE CPU		Line	Subclass	Duration	CPU	Par.	Rows	KB	Timeline
189 ms	156 ms									
	x0.9		2	Scan	3	0		2	1	
FE	**SE**		4	Scan	2	0		64	1	
11 ms	178 ms		7	Scan	173	156	x0.9	4	1	
5.8%	94.2%		8	Batch	0	0				
SE Queries	**SE Cache**									
4	0									
	0.0%									

The following is the xmSQL code of the complete batch event:

```
DEFINE TABLE '$TTable2' :=
SELECT
    'UserContinents'[Continent]
FROM 'UserContinents'
WHERE
    COALESCE ( ( PFDATAID ( 'UserContinents'[UserName] ) = 4 ) ),


DEFINE TABLE '$TTable3' :=
SELECT
    RJOIN ( '$TTable2'[UserContinents$Continent] )
FROM '$TTable2'
    REVERSE BITMAP JOIN 'Customer' ON '$TTable2'[UserContinents$Continent]='Customer'[Continent],


DEFINE TABLE '$TTable1' :=
WITH
    $Expr0 := ( PFCAST ( 'Sales'[Quantity] AS INT ) * PFCAST ( 'Sales'[Net Price] AS INT ) )
SELECT
    'Store'[Country],
    SUM ( @$Expr0 )
FROM 'Sales'
    LEFT OUTER JOIN 'Customer'
        ON 'Sales'[CustomerKey]='Customer'[CustomerKey]
    LEFT OUTER JOIN 'Store'
        ON 'Sales'[StoreKey]='Store'[StoreKey]
WHERE
    'Customer'[Continent] ININDEX '$TTable3'[$SemijoinProjection];
```

The subsequent queries will take advantage of the storage engine cache by removing the callbacks. The bitmap index generated for the limited relationship is still effective, reducing the storage engine cost by more than one order of magnitude. All the other considerations are still valid for the dynamic security. By applying the security on smaller tables, we get a better execution plan with bitmap indexes and without expensive callbacks that invalidate the use of the storage engine cache for all xmSQL queries.

Optimizing static security on the fact table

Now that we have elaborated on the relevant aspects of security, let us see a practical example of security implemented in a suboptimal way, along with possible solutions.

The requirement is to create a role that filters attributes in two tables: the customer country and the product brand. These security rules may be static or dynamic. In this first example, we analyze a static scenario; we will cover the dynamic scenario in the following example.

If the security condition could be placed separately on the two tables, the solution would be straightforward: you would place one filter on *Product*, one filter on *Customer*, and the job would be done. You might need to further optimize the filter on the customer because the *Customer* table would have many rows. However, that scenario would be relatively simple.

In our example, the solution based on two separate filters is not an option because the requirement is to filter one brand in one country and two brands in a different country. Namely, we want to filter Contoso and Litware for the United States, and only Contoso for Canada. If we placed the filters separately on the two tables, we would obtain Contoso and Litware for both the United States and Canada, whereas we want to exclude Litware from Canada.

One option to model this scenario is to place the filter on *Sales*. The *Sales* table is related to both *Customer* and *Product*; therefore, it looks like the best place to set security conditions:

```
ComplexRule: Filter placed on Sales

( RELATED ( Customer[Country] ), RELATED ( Product[Brand] ) )
IN
{
    ( "United States", "Contoso" ),
    ( "United States", "Litware" ),
    ( "Canada", "Contoso" )
}
```

Based on what we have learned in this chapter, we know that every storage engine query requires a join with *Customer* and *Product* to place the security filter. To test the performance, we impersonate the ComplexRule role and use a simple query that groups by the column *Store[Country]*, which belongs to a table (*Store*) that is not part of the security conditions:

```
EVALUATE
SUMMARIZECOLUMNS ( Store[Country], "Sales", [Sales Amount] )
```

In the server timings pane, there are two xmSQL queries: one to retrieve the combinations of *Customer[Country]* and *Product[Brand]*, and the other to gather the results.

Total	SE CPU	Line	Subclass	Duration	CPU	Par.	Rows	KB	Timeline
237 ms	3,922 ms								
	x18.1	2	Scan	54	422	x7.8	154	2	
FE	SE	4	Scan	163	3,500	x21.5	12	1	
20 ms	217 ms								
8.4%	91.6%								

SE Queries	SE Cache
2	0
	0.0%

The first query is fast is very simple, but it still uses 422 milliseconds of storage engine CPU:

```
SELECT
    'Customer'[Country],
    'Product'[Brand]
FROM 'Sales'
    LEFT OUTER JOIN 'Customer'
        ON 'Sales'[CustomerKey]='Customer'[CustomerKey]
    LEFT OUTER JOIN 'Product'
        ON 'Sales'[ProductKey]='Product'[ProductKey];
```

The second query is the one computing the result. It takes longer because of the joins and the condition required by the security filter:

```
WITH
    $Expr0 := ( PFCAST ( 'Sales'[Quantity] AS INT ) * PFCAST ( 'Sales'[Net Price] AS INT ) )
SELECT
    'Store'[Country],
    SUM ( @$Expr0 )
FROM 'Sales'
    LEFT OUTER JOIN 'Customer'
        ON 'Sales'[CustomerKey]='Customer'[CustomerKey]
    LEFT OUTER JOIN 'Product'
        ON 'Sales'[ProductKey]='Product'[ProductKey]
    LEFT OUTER JOIN 'Store'
        ON 'Sales'[StoreKey]='Store'[StoreKey]
WHERE
    COALESCE ( VERTICALC ( ( 'Customer'[Country], 'Product'[Brand] )
        IN { ( 'Canada', 'Contoso' ) , ( 'United States', 'Litware' ) , ( 'United States', 'Contoso' ) } ) );
```

To optimize the security role, we can work on two sides: reducing the size of the tables involved and reducing the complexity of the filter. Because the condition works on multiple tables, we need a new table containing the allowed combinations of brands and countries. We can create a *Security* table using the following code:

```
-----------------------------
-- Calculated table Security
-----------------------------
Security =
VAR CountriesAndBrands =
    SUMMARIZE ( Sales, Customer[Country], 'Product'[Brand] )
VAR Result =
    ADDCOLUMNS (
        CountriesAndBrands,
        "SecurityKey", ROWNUMBER ( CountriesAndBrands )
    )
RETURN
    Result
```

The result contains all the existing combinations of *Customer[Country]* and *Product[Brand]*, along with an integer *SecurityKey* column that we use to set the relationship with *Sales*.

Country	Brand	SecurityKey
Australia	The Phone Company	10
Australia	Wide World Importers	11
Canada	A. Datum	12
Canada	Adventure Works	13
Canada	Contoso	14
Canada	Fabrikam	15

Once the table is in place, we can create a *SecurityKey* calculated column in *Sales* to create a relationship with the *Security* table:

```
--------------------------------------
-- Calculated column in Sales table
--------------------------------------
SecurityKey =
LOOKUPVALUE (
    Security[SecurityKey],
    Security[Brand], RELATED ( 'Product'[Brand] ),
    Security[Country], RELATED ( Customer[Country] )
)
```

The *Security* table is connected to *Sales* through the *SecurityKey* column. Usually, these elements created to implement security are hidden.

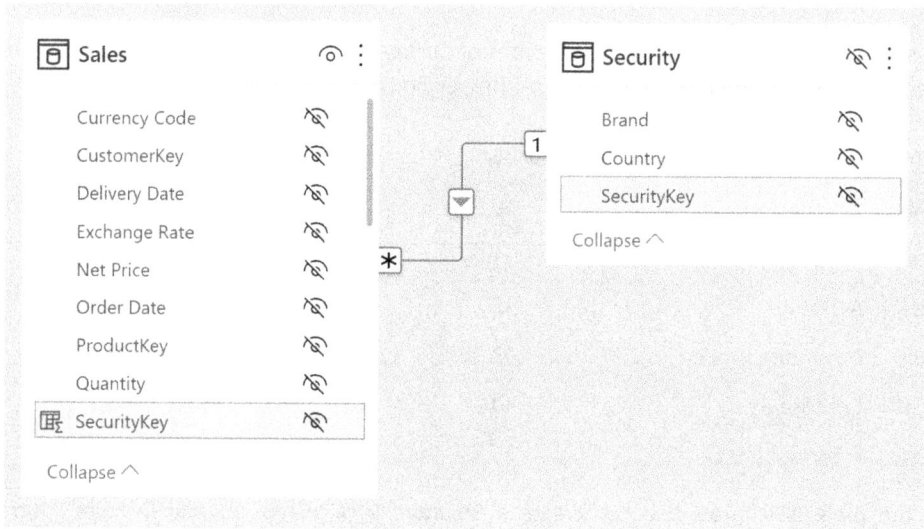

Finally, we replicate the condition required by the security role. This time, the filter is set on the *Security* table, which contains only 80 rows:

```
ComplexRuleOptimized1: Filter placed on Security

( Security[Country], Security [Brand]  )
IN
{
    ( "United States", "Contoso" ),
    ( "United States", "Litware" ),
    ( "Canada", "Contoso" )
}
```

We test the same query as before to notice a slight performance improvement.

Total	SE CPU	Line	Subclass	Duration	CPU	Par.	Rows	KB	Timeline
134 ms	2,875 ms	2	Scan	1	0		154	2	
	x23.0								
◉ FE	◉ SE	4	Scan	124	2,875	x23.2	12	1	
9 ms	125 ms								
6.7%	93.3%								

```
SELECT
  'Store'[Country],
  SUM ( @$Expr0 )
FROM 'Sales'
  LEFT OUTER JOIN 'Store'
```

SE Queries	SE Cache
2	0
	0.0%

As it did before, the first query retrieves the combinations of *Country* and *Brand*. This time, it is operating on the *Security* table instead of *Sales*. Hence, the storage engine CPU time is much lower:

```
SELECT
    Security[Country],
    Security [Brand]
FROM Security
```

The second xmSQL query is slightly faster because it has only one join with *Security*, compared with the two joins it used before with *Customer* and *Product*. Moreover, *Security* is a tiny table, so the price of the join is certainly lower:

```
WITH
    $Expr0 := ( PFCAST ( 'Sales'[Quantity] AS INT ) * PFCAST ( 'Sales'[Net Price] AS INT ) )
SELECT
    'Store'[Country],
    SUM ( @$Expr0 )
FROM 'Sales'
    LEFT OUTER JOIN 'Store'
        ON 'Sales'[StoreKey]='Store'[StoreKey]
    LEFT OUTER JOIN Security
        ON 'Sales'[SecurityKey]= Security[SecurityKey]
WHERE
    COALESCE ( VERTICALC ( ( Security[Country], Security[Brand] )
        IN { ( 'Canada', 'Contoso' ) , ( 'United States', 'Litware' ) , ( 'United States', 'Contoso' ) } ) ) ;
```

Although reducing the size of the table used for the security filter did improve performance, it is still not optimal. When dealing with security filters, we always want to obtain the best possible performance because of how pervasive the impact on any query tends to be. A good option, in this scenario, is to work on the filter condition. The condition involves two columns, and both are strings. We know that the best performance would be with a single numeric column, to push the entire calculation down to the storage engine or force the use of a bitmap index. Both solutions work here and are worth testing because the best is also the least intuitive.

To force the use of a bitmap index, we can change the security filter by using a more complex CALCULATE:

```
ComplexRuleOptimized2: Filter placed on Security

Security[SecurityKey] IN
CALCULATETABLE (
    VALUES ( Security[SecurityKey] ),
    ( Security[Country], Security[Brand] )
        IN {
            ( "United States", "Contoso" ),
            ( "United States", "Litware" ),
            ( "Canada", "Contoso" )
        }
)
```

Using this version of the security filter increases the number of storage engine queries. At the same time, the most expensive xmSQL query runs much faster, showing excellent improvement.

Total 110 ms	SE CPU 359 ms x3.6		Line	Subclass	Duration	CPU	Par.	Rows	KB	Timeline
			2	Scan	1	0		91	1	
FE 10 ms 9.1%	**SE** 100 ms 90.9%		4	Scan	0	0		88	1	
			6	Scan	99	359	x3.6	12	1	

SE Queries 3   SE Cache 0 0.0%

```
+EXPIV  (TTCAST ( Sales [Quantity] AS INT )   TTCAST ( Sales [Net Price] AS INT ))
SELECT
    'Store'[Country],
    SUM ( @$Expr0 )
FROM 'Sales'
```

The first query contains a callback to retrieve the *Security[SecurityKey]* column used to build the bitmap index:

```
SELECT
    Security[SecurityKey]
FROM Security
WHERE
    ( Security[Country], Security[Brand] ) IN { ( 'Canada', 'Contoso' ) , ( 'United States', 'Litware' ) , ( 'United States', 'Contoso' ) }
VAND
    [CallbackDataID ( CALCULATETABLE (
        VALUES ( Security[SecurityKey] ) ,
        ( Security[Country], Security[Brand] )
            IN {
                ( "United States", "Contoso" ) ,
                ( "United States", "Litware" ) ,
                ( "Canada", "Contoso" )
            }
    ) ) ] ( PFDATAID ( Security[SecurityKey] ) , PFDATAID ( Security[SecurityKey] ) ) ;
```

The second xmSQL query retrieves the columns for the bitmap index:

```
SELECT
    Security[RowNumber],
    Security[SecurityKey]
FROM Security;
```

These first two queries are used together to determine the *Security[SecurityKey]* values to include in the bitmap index. Once the index is ready, the third xmSQL query uses it to run much faster:

```
WITH
    $Expr0 := ( PFCAST ( 'Sales'[Quantity] AS INT ) * PFCAST ( 'Sales'[Net Price] AS INT ) )
SELECT
    'Store'[Country],
    SUM ( @$Expr0 )
FROM 'Sales'
    LEFT OUTER JOIN 'Store'
        ON 'Sales'[StoreKey]='Store'[StoreKey]
    LEFT OUTER JOIN Security
        ON 'Sales'[SecurityKey]=Security[SecurityKey]
WHERE
    VERTICALC ( Security.$ROWFILTER IN '0x00000100000000110000000000000000' ) ;
```

This version of the security filter consumes less storage engine CPU than the original one – depending on the clock speed and the parallelism involved, it could also generate a faster execution time that we did not observe on the hardware we tested. At the risk of being pedantic, let us remind our reader that this improvement is effective on any query that accesses the *Sales* table for every scan. A typical measure that performs several scans of the *Sales* table will benefit massively from this optimization.

We can try to push the optimization further by removing the callback. Unfortunately, despite looking very smart, this technique proves to be suboptimal. By manually scanning the *Security* table, we can identify the values of *Security[SecurityKey]* that match our requirements: 14, 80, and 82. The idea is that filtering the values directly would avoid the callback and obtain better performance, as the entire query would be pushed down to VertiPaq:

```
ComplexRuleOptimized3: Filter placed on Security

Security[SecurityKey] IN { 14, 80, 82 }
```

Performance is worse by using this version of security conditions.

Total	SE CPU	Line	Subclass	Duration	CPU	Par.	Rows	KB	Timeline
118 ms	828 ms	2	Scan	1	0		91	1	
	x7.5	4	Scan	110	828	x7.5	12	1	

FE	SE
8 ms	110 ms
6.8%	93.2%

SE Queries	SE Cache
2	0
	0.0%

```
SET DC_KIND="AUTO";
WITH
    $Expr0 := ( PFCAST ( 'Sales'[Quantity] AS INT ) * PFCAST ( 'Sales'[Net Price] AS INT ) )
SELECT
```

We achieved the goal of removing the callback. The first xmSQL query retrieves the values of the *Security[SecurityKey]* column. At the same time, the condition is pushed down to the VertiPaq engine in its entirety, as we can appreciate from the second VertiPaq query:

```
WITH
    $Expr0 := ( PFCAST ( 'Sales'[Quantity] AS INT ) * PFCAST ( 'Sales'[Net Price] AS INT ) )
SELECT
    'Store'[Country],
    SUM ( @$Expr0 )
FROM 'Sales'
    LEFT OUTER JOIN 'Store'
        ON 'Sales'[StoreKey]='Store'[StoreKey]
    LEFT OUTER JOIN Security
        ON 'Sales'[SecurityKey]=Security[SecurityKey]
WHERE
    COALESCE ( VERTICALC ( Security[SecurityKey] IN ( 14, 82, 80 ) ) ) ;
```

It turns out that checking the value of the column in VertiPaq is slower than using a bitmap index. The code is faster than the original version. Still, it is more expensive in terms of storage engine CPU than our previous attempt that creates and consumes a bitmap index. Because of the different parallelism of these approaches, the comparison in execution time can provide other winners depending on the CPU clock speed.

Regarding security conditions, it is paramount that developers spend enough time at the beginning of the project to identify the best way to implement the security restrictions. The impact on the project might be much more significant than expected.

Optimizing dynamic security on the fact table

We analyzed a complex security restriction based on a static table in the previous example. Complex security rules are created in many scenarios using dynamic conditions based on the username. As an example, we created a table to filter the pairs of *Customer[Country]* and *Product[Brand]* that should be visible based on the username:

```
UserCountriesBrands =
SELECTCOLUMNS (
    {
        ( "marco@contoso.com", "Italy", "Contoso" ),
        ( "marco@contoso.com", "Italy", "Litware" ),
        ( "marco@contoso.com", "France", "Contoso" ),
        ( "marco@contoso.com", "Germany", "Litware" ),
        ( "alberto@contoso.com", "Germany", "Litware" ),
        ( "alberto@contoso.com", "Australia", "Contoso" ),
        ( "alberto@contoso.com", "Australia", "Litware" ),
        ( "alberto@contoso.com", "Australia", "Tailspin Toys" )
    },
    "UserName", [Value1],
    "Country", [Value2],
    "Brand", [Value3]
)
```

Based on the experience of the previous example, we know that setting the filtering condition directly on *Sales* is troublesome. However, we run a test to assess the performance:

```
ComplexRuleDynamic: Filter placed on Sales

( RELATED ( Customer[Country] ), RELATED ( Product[Brand] ) )
    IN SELECTCOLUMNS (
        FILTER (
            UserCountriesBrands,
            UserCountriesBrands[UserName] == USERNAME ()
        ),
        [Country],
        [Brand]
    )
```

The condition checks whether the pairs of *Customer[Country]* and *Product[Brand]* are allowed in the *UserCountriesBrand* table, which is filtered to show only the rows of the current user. By activating the user alberto@contoso.com, we use as a test a simple query that computes the *Sales Amount* measure sliced by *Customer[Country]* and *Product[Brand]*:

```
EVALUATE
SUMMARIZECOLUMNS (
    Customer[Country],
    Product[Brand],
    "Sales", [Sales Amount]
)
```

As expected, the query is very slow.

Total	SE CPU	Line	Subclass	Duration	CPU	Par.	Rows	KB	Timeline
540 ms	23,297 ms								
	x44.5	2	Scan	53	78	x1.5	154	2	
FE	SE	4	Scan	0	0		42	1	
16 ms	524 ms	6	Scan	471	23,219	x49.3	154	3	
3.0%	97.0%								

SE Queries	SE Cache
3	0
	0.0%

The first two queries at lines 2 and 4 retrieve the *Customer[Country]* and *Product[Brand]* pairs from *Sales* and *UserCountriesBrands*. The third query at line 6 includes a callback to execute the complex filtering condition, and it is the most expensive xmSQL query:

```
WITH
    $Expr0 := ( PFCAST ( 'Sales'[Quantity] AS INT ) * PFCAST ( 'Sales'[Net Price] AS INT ) )
SELECT
    'Customer'[Country],
    'Product'[Brand],
    SUM ( @$Expr0 )
FROM 'Sales'
    LEFT OUTER JOIN 'Customer'
        ON 'Sales'[CustomerKey]='Customer'[CustomerKey]
    LEFT OUTER JOIN 'Product'
        ON 'Sales'[ProductKey]='Product'[ProductKey]
WHERE
    COALESCE ( NOT COALESCE ( [[CallbackDataID (
    ( RELATED ( Customer[Country] ) , RELATED ( Product[Brand] ) )
        IN SELECTCOLUMNS (
            FILTER (
                UserCountriesBrands,
                UserCountriesBrands[UserName] == USERNAME ()
            ) ,
            'Country",
            'Brand"
        )
    ) ' ( PFDATAID ( 'Customer'[Country] ) , PFDATAID ( 'Product'[Brand] ) ) ) ) ;
```

We know that to optimize the code, we need to let Tabular create a security bitmap filter. In the static security example, we achieved this goal by creating a relationship with the *Security* table, which contains a key and all the pairs of *Country* and *Brand* allowed.

In the dynamic scenario, we cannot create a relationship between *Sales* and the *UserCountriesBrands* table because the combinations of *Customer[Country]* and *Product[Brand]* are not unique in the configuration table. However, we can create a suitable filtering condition on the *Security* table by using an expression that moves the filter from *UserCountriesBrands* to *Security*:

```
ComplexRuleDynamicOptimized: Filter placed on Security

( Security[Country], Security[Brand] )
    IN SELECTCOLUMNS (
        FILTER (
            UserCountriesBrands,
            UserCountriesBrands[UserName] == USERNAME ()
        ),
        [Country],
        [Brand]
    )
```

By applying the security filter on the *Security* table, we then rely on the relationship between *Security* and *Sales* to execute the filter. The security flow is depicted in the following figure.

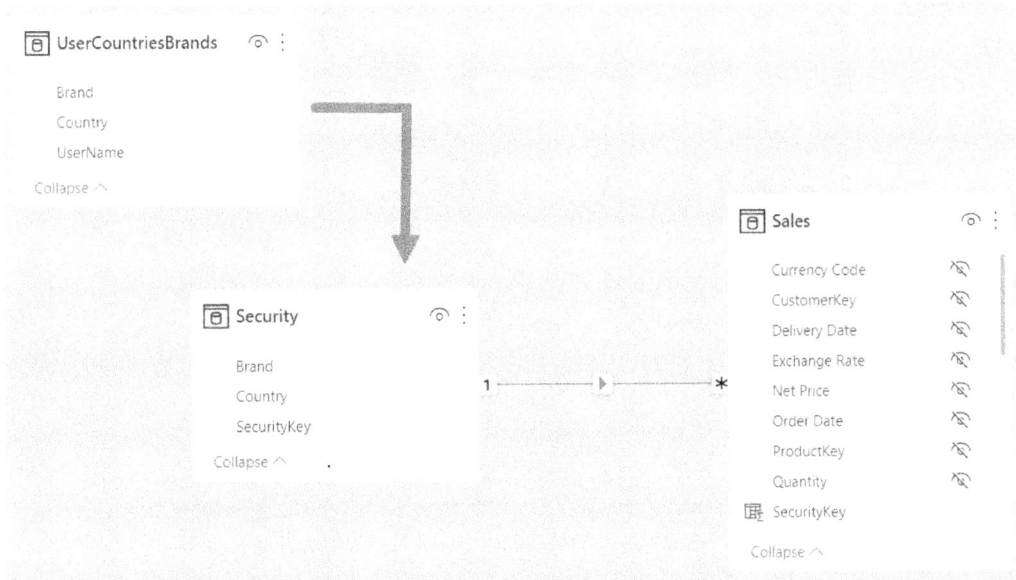

The red arrow is the filter moved by the security expression in the Security table. Once *Security* is filtered, it will filter *Sales* according to the brands and countries visible in *UserCountriesBrands*.

Performance-wise, this technique is much faster.

Total	SE CPU	Line	Subclass	Duration	CPU	Par.	Rows	KB	Timeline
107 ms	141 ms								
	x1.5	2	Scan	1	16	x16.0	88	1	
FE	**SE**	4	Scan	0	0		42	1	
12 ms	95 ms	6	Scan	94	125	x1.3	154	3	
11.2%	88.8%								

SE Queries	SE Cache
3	0
	0.0%

The last query clearly shows that the bitmap index is in place:

```
WITH
    $Expr0 := ( PFCAST ( 'Sales'[Quantity] AS INT ) * PFCAST ( 'Sales'[Net Price] AS INT ) )
SELECT
    'Customer'[Country],
    'Product'[Brand],
    SUM ( @$Expr0 )
FROM 'Sales'
    LEFT OUTER JOIN 'Customer'
        ON 'Sales'[CustomerKey]='Customer'[CustomerKey]
    LEFT OUTER JOIN 'Product'
        ON 'Sales'[ProductKey]='Product'[ProductKey]
    LEFT OUTER JOIN Security
        ON 'Sales'[SecurityKey]=Security[SecurityKey]
WHERE
    VERTICALC ( Security.$ROWFILTER IN '0x00000000000000000000000000000000' ) ;
```

Using this technique also offers us an interesting opportunity to make the system safer. Indeed, the very content of *UserCountriesBrands* should be hidden from any user. Discovering which users have access to which pairs of brands and countries is a real security issue. However, because the table is used to build the security bitmap filter and is not part of any other calculation, its content can safely be hidden by using FALSE for its row-level filter:

ComplexRuleDynamicOptimized: *Filter placed on UserCountriesBrands*

FALSE

No user will be able to explore the content of the configuration table; at the same time, the content of the table is used by Tabular to build the security bitmap filter on *Security*. The *Security* table does not contain sensitive information and is always adequately protected.

Suppose the dynamic security of this latter example does not have to be mixed to other conditions based on the Security table. In that case, an additional option can simplify the DAX code required in the filter condition. By creating *UserCountriesBrands* with an extra *SecurityKey* column, we can connect the *UserCountriesBrands* table to the *Security* table. Here is the updated code of the *UserCountriesBrands* calculated table:

```
UserCountriesBrands =
ADDCOLUMNS (
    SELECTCOLUMNS (
        {
            ( "marco@contoso.com", "Italy", "Contoso" ),
            ( "marco@contoso.com", "Italy", "Litware" ),
            ( "marco@contoso.com", "France", "Contoso" ),
            ( "marco@contoso.com", "Germany", "Litware" ),
            ( "alberto@contoso.com", "Germany", "Litware" ),
            ( "alberto@contoso.com", "Australia", "Contoso" ),
            ( "alberto@contoso.com", "Australia", "Litware" ),
            ( "alberto@contoso.com", "Australia", "Tailspin Toys" )
        },
        "UserName", [Value1],
        "Country", [Value2],
        "Brand", [Value3]
    ),
    "SecurityKey", LOOKUPVALUE (
        Security[SecurityKey],
        Security[Brand], [Brand],
        Security[Country], [Country]
    )
)
```

The regular relationship between *UserCountriesBrands* and *Security* must have a bidirectional filter that also propagates security filters.

Edit relationship

Select tables and columns that are related.

UserCountriesBrands ▾

UserName	Brand	Country	SecurityKey
marco@contoso.com	Contoso	Italy	47
marco@contoso.com	Litware	Italy	49
marco@contoso.com	Contoso	France	25

Security ▾

Country	Brand	SecurityKey
United States	Contoso	80
Germany	Contoso	36
Australia	Contoso	3

Cardinality

Many to one (*:1)

☑ Make this relationship active

Assume referential integrity

Cross filter direction

Both ▾

☑ Apply security filter in both directions

OK   Cancel

This results in a structure where we can filter *UserCountriesBrands* to filter *Sales*.

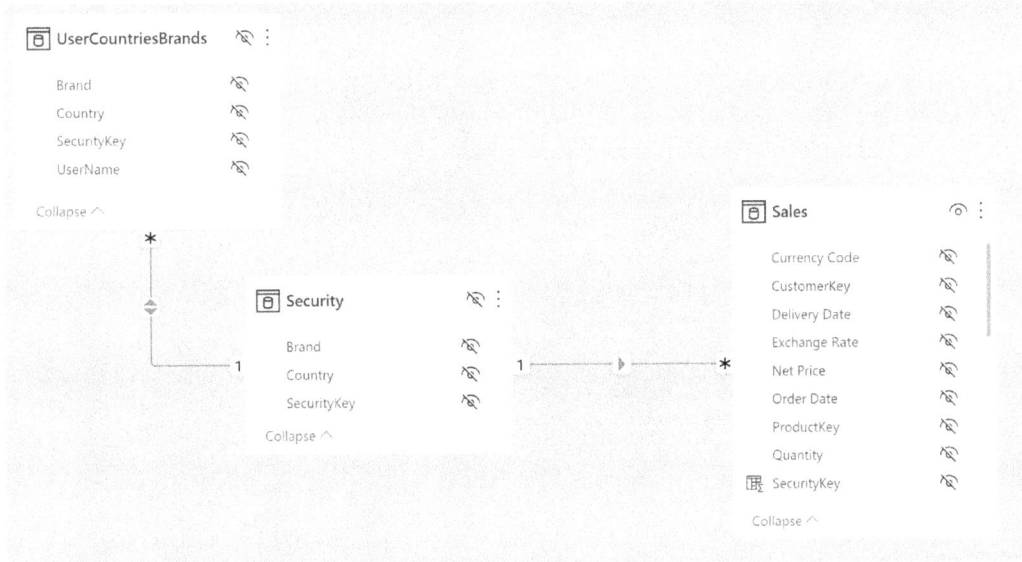

The security role is straightforward: it just filters the *UserName* column in *UserCountriesBrands*:

```
ComplexRuleDynamicSecurity: Filter placed on UserCountriesBrands

UserCountriesBrands[UserName] == USERNAME ()
```

The result of our test query by impersonating the user alberto@contoso.com is as good as the last optimized version, if not slightly better.

Total	SE CPU	Line	Subclass	Duration	CPU	Par.	Rows	KB	Timeline
70 ms	63 ms								
	x1.2	2	Scan	3	0		128	1	
FE	SE	4	Scan	51	63	x1.2	0	1	
16 ms	54 ms	5	Batch	0	0				
22.9%	77.1%								

SE Queries	SE Cache
3	0
	0.0%

This result is excellent, but it comes at the price of not being able to apply filters on the *Security* table in other roles either. In this example, it is challenging to create the *SecurityKey* column as a calculated column in *UserCountriesBrands* because of circular dependencies that could be raised by the other calculations we included in the model. While you might find an easier way to implement this pattern when you import the *Security* and *UserCountriesBrands* tables from a data source instead of using calculated tables, we can consider another approach that provides similar performance without the restrictions described.

First, we create a *SecurityKey* calculated column in *UserCountriesBrands* similar to what we have previously done on the *Sales* table. To keep a single file with all the examples, we duplicated the *UserCountriesBrands* table into *UserCountriesBrands2*:

```
-----------------------------------------------------
-- Calculated column in UserCountriesBrands2 table
-----------------------------------------------------
SecurityKey =
LOOKUPVALUE (
    Security[SecurityKey],
    Security[Brand], UserCountriesBrands2[Brand],
    Security[Country], UserCountriesBrands2[Country]
)
```

Then we create a many-to-many cardinality relationship between *UserCountriesBrands* and *Sales*: we cannot use a regular relationship because several customers are linked to the same combination of *Country* and *Brand*.

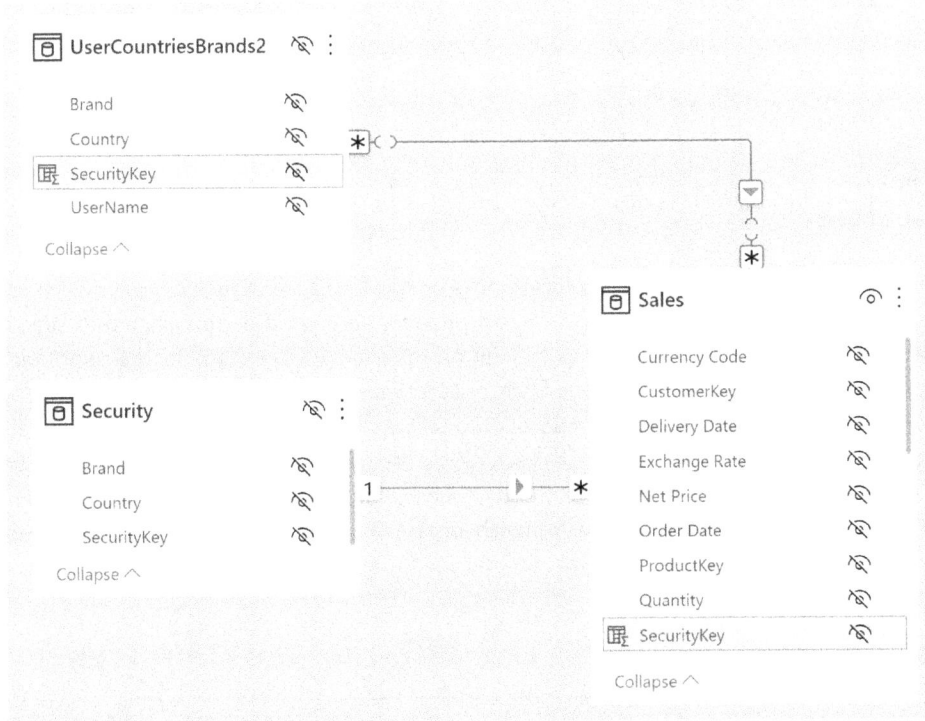

We define a security role that filters *UserCountriesBrands2[UserName]*:

```
ComplexRuleDynamicSecurity: Filter placed on UserCountriesBrands2

UserCountriesBrands2[UserName] == USERNAME ()
```

The query still performs well: there is an additional scan in the storage engine batch to implement the many-to-many cardinality relationship. As we have seen in previous chapters, this approach can be faster or slower than the two relationships we have seen before, depending on the data distribution. However, the difference is often irrelevant, as it depends on the number of unique values filtered in the relationship.

Total	SE CPU	Line	Subclass	Duration	CPU	Par.	Rows	KB	Timeline
91 ms	63 ms								
	x0.8	2	Scan	0	0		4	1	
FE	**SE**	4	Scan	0	0		128	1	
14 ms	77 ms	6	Scan	74	63	x0.9	4	1	
15.4%	84.6%	7	Batch	3	0				
SE Queries	**SE Cache**								
4	0								
	0.0%								

The main advantage of the last pattern is that it provides very good performance with simple filter conditions and without applying restrictions to filter on other tables. For example, the same role could have restrictions active on both *Security* and *UserCountriesBrands2* – something that is impossible if we propagate a security filter from *UserCountriesBrands* to *Security* through a relationship, as we have shown in the previous example. By using this last approach, a user can only see the rows in *UserCountriesBrands2* that correspond to the active combinations of *Country* and *Brands*. It is impossible to completely hide all the rows of *UserCountriesBrands2* with this approach: in case you need to, you should consider using the technique we used for the ComplexRuleDynamicOptimized role.

Conclusions

The most important takeaway of this section is that security needs to be studied and tested well in advance during project development. A poorly implemented security system can be the single source of failure in a project because of its strong negative impact on performance.

Optimizing security conditions is no different from optimizing regular DAX code. However, when implementing security filters, developers must pay special attention to squeezing the most out of the engine.

When dealing with dynamic security, the number of scenarios is impressive because every project is its own universe. However, the techniques to implement are always the same: you should place security on a small table, where bitmap indexes or simple conditions in xmSQL work at their best.

If the filter needs to be moved across different tables, rely on relationships as much as possible to let the storage engine use joins or batches to solve the query in VertiPaq.

Section 4
DIRECTQUERY OVER SQL

Understanding DirectQuery over SQL

Having reached this point in the book, you have a solid understanding of the differences between the formula engine and the storage engine, as well as a clear picture of the role of the storage engine in the execution of a query and the optimization of a data model.

It should come as no surprise that introducing a different storage engine will twist the architecture completely. DirectQuery over SQL is very different from VertiPaq in speed and expressivity. Consequently, the collaboration between the formula and storage engines goes differently.

It would be a serious mistake to assume that the same optimization techniques are valid for SQL and VertiPaq. Although several considerations are valid for both storage engines, the differences are much more remarkable than the similarities.

In this chapter, we take for granted that the reader has a good understanding of VertiPaq. Therefore, we focus on the differences between a data model using VertiPaq and a data model using DirectQuery. The goal of the chapter is to provide a solid foundation on how the DirectQuery over SQL storage engine works. In the following chapters, we will properly optimize DAX code with DirectQuery over SQL.

In this section, we cover models with a single DirectQuery connection. In other words, the model contains one data island using DirectQuery over SQL. The complexity would be much larger if the model used VertiPaq and DirectQuery – or multiple DirectQuery data islands. However, we will describe models with multiple data islands later. For now, we focus on a single DirectQuery data island.

Working with DirectQuery

Before diving into the details of DirectQuery, we need to address a critical topic that is not technical: the competencies required to work with DirectQuery. When dealing with a VertiPaq model, the Tabular developer can (and should) perform all the optimizations and design choices. The VertiPaq model is stored in Tabular; therefore, any change to the model is possible.

When working with DirectQuery, the database is stored in SQL. Tabular reads data from SQL and computes values with it, but if developers need to change the data model, they need to change the data structure in SQL. Therefore, you either have full access to the SQL database and a good knowledge of the SQL architecture – along with the ability to perform changes – or you need the help of the database administrator.

Optimizing DirectQuery means making multiple choices on the Tabular data model and the SQL database. Be prepared to perform or ask for numerous changes in the source SQL database because – ultimately – the speed of a DAX query in DirectQuery directly depends on the speed of the underlying SQL database.

Lastly, **DirectQuery is slower than VertiPaq**. As a matter of fact, it is nearly impossible to obtain the outstanding performance of a VertiPaq model with DirectQuery. The choice of DirectQuery over VertiPaq needs to be driven by solid reasons, like the requirement for real-time reporting or a huge model not fitting in RAM. If performance is on your radar, your first choice should be a VertiPaq model. **Choosing DirectQuery means accepting a compromise in terms of performance**. And you should have an excellent reason to accept that compromise.

Reading SQL code in this book

In this chapter, and all of the following chapters, we show a large amount of SQL code – namely the code executed by SQL server to answer storage engine queries. We show a simplified version of the actual SQL code executed. Indeed, DAX Studio simplifies the code to make it more readable. The rationale behind this simplification is that the goal of the SQL code is not to show the exact SQL code executed, but instead to show the structure of the query.

For example, let us focus on a straightforward DAX query like the following:

```
EVALUATE
SUMMARIZECOLUMNS (
    'Date'[Year],
    "Sales", [Sales Amount]
)
```

The raw SQL code generated to answer this query is very verbose:

```
SELECT
TOP (1000001) *
FROM
(

SELECT [c16],SUM([a0])
 AS [a0]
FROM
(

SELECT [t1].[Year] AS [c16],[t3].[Quantity] AS [c54],[t3].[Net Price] AS [c56],
([t3].[Quantity] * [t3].[Net Price])
 AS [a0]
FROM
((
```

```
select [$Table].[Order Number] as [Order Number],
    [$Table].[Line Number] as [Line Number],
    [$Table].[Order Date] as [Order Date],
    [$Table].[Delivery Date] as [Delivery Date],
    [$Table].[CustomerKey] as [CustomerKey],
    [$Table].[StoreKey] as [StoreKey],
    [$Table].[ProductKey] as [ProductKey],
    [$Table].[Quantity] as [Quantity],
    [$Table].[Unit Price] as [Unit Price],
    [$Table].[Net Price] as [Net Price],
    [$Table].[Unit Cost] as [Unit Cost],
    [$Table].[Currency Code] as [Currency Code],
    [$Table].[Exchange Rate] as [Exchange Rate],
    [$Table].[Line Amount] as [Line Amount],
    [$Table].[DateAndTime] as [DateAndTime],
    [$Table].[Time] as [Time],
    [$Table].[Hour] as [Hour]
from [Data].[Sales] as [$Table]
) AS [t3]

LEFT OUTER JOIN

(
select [$Table].[Date] as [Date],
    [$Table].[Year] as [Year],
    [$Table].[Year Quarter] as [Year Quarter],
    [$Table].[Year Quarter Number] as [Year Quarter Number],
    [$Table].[Quarter] as [Quarter],
    [$Table].[Year Month] as [Year Month],
    [$Table].[Year Month Short] as [Year Month Short],
    [$Table].[Year Month Number] as [Year Month Number],
    [$Table].[Month] as [Month],
    [$Table].[Month Short] as [Month Short],
    [$Table].[Month Number] as [Month Number],
    [$Table].[Day of Week] as [Day of Week],
    [$Table].[Day of Week Short] as [Day of Week Short],
    [$Table].[Day of Week Number] as [Day of Week Number],
    [$Table].[Working Day] as [Working Day],
    [$Table].[Working Day Number] as [Working Day Number]
from [dbo].[Date] as [$Table]
) AS [t1] on
(
[t3].[Order Date] = [t1].[Date]
)
)
)
 AS [t0]
GROUP BY [c16]
)
AS [MainTable]

WHERE
(
NOT (
```

```
(
    [a0] IS NULL
    )
  )
 )
```

That same code, simplified and properly formatted by DAX Studio, makes the structure of the query easier to understand:

```
SELECT TOP (1000001) *
FROM (
    SELECT [t1_Year],
        SUM([a0]) AS [a0]
    FROM (
        SELECT [t1].[Year] AS [t1_Year],
            [t3].[Quantity] AS [t3_Quantity],
            [t3].[Net Price] AS [t3_Net Price],
            ([t3].[Quantity] * [t3].[Net Price]) AS [a0]
        FROM (
            [Data].[Sales] AS [t3]
                LEFT JOIN [dbo].[Date] AS [t1] ON ([t3].[Order Date] = [t1].[Date])
            )
        ) AS [t0]
    GROUP BY [t1_Year]
    ) AS [MainTable]
WHERE (NOT (([a0] IS NULL)))
```

When it is relevant to inspect the original code, we shall include it in the book. However, we mostly show simplified code to focus on the critical structure of the query rather than on the implementation details.

Reading the numbers in DAX Studio

Before going any farther, we must address a critical point about the numbers reported in DAX Studio. As we learned in the previous chapters, DAX Studio reports three relevant metrics:

- **Formula engine time**: The time spent in the formula engine. This value is computed as the overall execution time minus the time spent in the storage engine.

- **Storage engine time**: The time required to answer the storage engine queries. The more cores, the lower this number because of parallelism.

- **Storage engine CPU**: The total CPU time used to answer the storage engine queries. This value is independent of the number of cores and is the primary metric for optimizing the storage engine queries.

When using VertiPaq, the only number computed by DAX Studio is the formula engine time. DAX Studio determines that value by performing a simple subtraction because the AS engine does not report the formula engine time. On the other hand, both storage engine time and CPU are reported directly by the Tabular engine and are accurate values.

When using DirectQuery, the only value reported by Tabular is the storage engine time, which is the time required to answer a SQL query. DAX Studio computes the storage engine CPU by summing all the individual storage engine times of the SQL queries. This value may be inaccurate due to parallelism; therefore, developers should use the number cautiously.

We want to show you the effect of parallelism using two figures that will be described later. For now, focus on the value of the storage engine CPU. The first timings have been gathered with no parallelism involved, from the point of view of the formula engine:

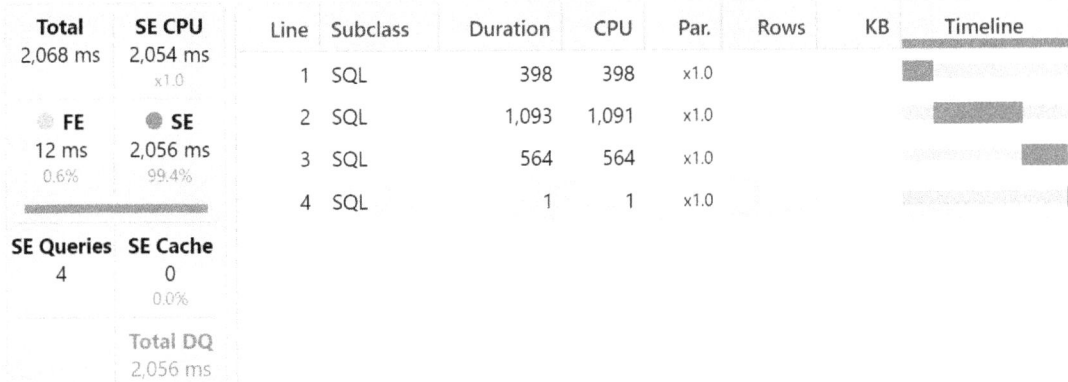

Total	SE CPU	Line	Subclass	Duration	CPU	Par.	Rows	KB	Timeline
2,068 ms	2,054 ms								
	x1.0	1	SQL	398	398	x1.0			
FE	SE	2	SQL	1,093	1,091	x1.0			
12 ms	2,056 ms	3	SQL	564	564	x1.0			
0.6%	99.4%	4	SQL	1	1	x1.0			
SE Queries	**SE Cache**								
4	0								
	0.0%								
	Total DQ								
	2,056 ms								

The total execution time is around 2 seconds, with 2 seconds of storage engine CPU. None of the SQL queries were using 100% of the CPU available.

If we execute the same DAX query running multiple SQL statements simultaneously, all the SQL queries start together, saturating the CPU power. Consequently, each SQL query takes longer to execute. However, the total execution time is lower because of parallelism.

Total	SE CPU		Line	Subclass	Duration	CPU	Par.	Rows	KB	Timeline
1,915 ms	5,336 ms		1	SQL	1,532	1,532	x1.0			
	x2.8		2	SQL	1,898	1,898	x1.0			
FE ⚠	SE		3	SQL	1,905	1,905	x1.0			
10 ms	1,905 ms		4	SQL	1	1	x1.0			
0.5%	99.5%									

SE Queries	SE Cache
4	0
	0.0%

	Total DQ
	5,336 ms

If we were to compare the SE CPU of this execution (5.3 seconds) with the previous one, we would conclude that the second execution is slower. However, this is not the case: the second execution is faster. Given the scarcity of metrics reported by the AS engine, we cannot compute the storage engine CPU precisely. DAX Studio does its best to estimate the storage engine CPU, but in the presence of parallelism, it may produce inaccurate numbers.

We will comment on these numbers in detail later. For now, the critical point is that the storage engine CPU – the primary value used to estimate the performance of storage engine queries – is no longer the primary metric for DirectQuery.

Callback operations

In VertiPaq models, whenever the storage engine needs to scan a table and compute an expression that exceeds the VertiPaq capabilities, it relies on VertiCalc and callbacks. We have highlighted several times that the presence of a callback may be a threat to performance. At the same time, callbacks are powerful tools because they rely on the strong collaboration between the DAX formula engine and the VertiPaq storage engine to compute complex expressions without depending on excessive materialization.

Callbacks are not an option in DirectQuery because the database and the Tabular engine run on different architectures, most likely on different hardware. The database engine cannot call back the formula engine to resolve a complex piece of DAX code. Despite this limitation, we should be aware that the expressivity of SQL is such that callbacks are seldom required because SQL can express much more complex queries than xmSQL. However, in the rare event that SQL cannot express the complexity of a DAX expression, the absence of callbacks may generate excessive materialization until it stops the query execution. Indeed, as we will introduce later, there is a hard limit on the number of rows materialized in a datacache: in the absence of callbacks, the query can reach this limit, albeit in rather extreme scenarios.

As an example, let us look at the following query:

```
EVALUATE
SUMMARIZECOLUMNS (
    'Product'[Brand],
    "Sales",
        SUMX (
            Sales,
            IF (
                Sales[Quantity] >= 3,
                Sales[Quantity] * Sales[Net Price]
            )
        )
)
```

If we execute this query on a VertiPaq model, there is a callback to express the IF function, which the VertiPaq engine cannot execute. However, the same query in DirectQuery generates a complex SQL statement that resolves the IF statement directly in SQL:

```
SELECT TOP (1000001) *
FROM (
    SELECT [t2_Brand],
        SUM([a0]) AS [a0]
    FROM (
        SELECT [t2].[Brand] AS [t2_Brand],
            [t3].[Quantity] AS [t3_Quantity],
            [t3].[Net Price] AS [t3_Net Price],
            (
                CASE
                    WHEN (
                            NOT (([t3].[Quantity] IS NULL))
                            AND ([t3].[Quantity] >= 3)
                            )
                        THEN ([t3].[Quantity] * [t3].[Net Price])
                    ELSE NULL
                    END
                ) AS [a0]
        FROM (
            [Data].[Sales] AS [t3]
                LEFT JOIN [dbo].[Product] AS [t2] ON ([t3].[ProductKey] = [t2].[ProductKey])
            )
        ) AS [t0]
    GROUP BY [t2_Brand]
    ) AS [MainTable]
WHERE (NOT (([a0] IS NULL)))
```

The IF statement is translated into a CASE WHEN statement in SQL. The power of SQL comes to help overcome the absence of VertiCalc and of callbacks, which are available in VertiPaq.

Another interesting example of DirectQuery using the power of SQL is with more complex functions, like CONTAINSSTRING. VertiPaq cannot execute CONTAINSSTRING, whereas SQL supports an equivalent syntax, pushing the evaluation down to SQL. The following query would result in a callback if executed in VertiPaq:

```
EVALUATE
SUMMARIZECOLUMNS (
    'Product'[Brand],
    "Sales Filtered",
        CALCULATE (
            [Sales Amount],
            KEEPFILTERS ( CONTAINSSTRING ( 'Product'[Brand], "W" ) )
        )
)
```

Because SQL offers the CHARINDEX function, DirectQuery pushes the CONTAINSSTRING evaluation down to the storage engine query:

```
SELECT TOP (1000001) *
FROM (
    SELECT [t2_Brand],
        SUM([a0]) AS [a0]
    FROM (
        SELECT [t2].[Brand] AS [t2_Brand],
            [t3].[Quantity] AS [t3_Quantity],
            [t3].[Net Price] AS [t3_Net Price],
            ([t3].[Quantity] * [t3].[Net Price]) AS [a0]
        FROM (
            [Data].[Sales] AS [t3]
                LEFT JOIN [dbo].[Product] AS [t2] ON ([t3].[ProductKey] = [t2].[ProductKey])
            )
        ) AS [t0]
    WHERE (CHARINDEX(N'W', COALESCE([t2_Brand], '')) > 0)
    GROUP BY [t2_Brand]
    ) AS [MainTable]
WHERE (NOT (([a0] IS NULL)))
```

Several DAX functions can be pushed down to SQL. However, there are DAX functions with no corresponding SQL syntax: in that case, there could be a very large materialization or multiple queries to the storage engine. For example, the BITLSHIFT DAX function cannot be represented in SQL. Therefore, the following query produces multiple storage engine queries:

```
EVALUATE
SUMMARIZECOLUMNS (
    'Product'[Brand],
    "Sales Filtered",
        CALCULATE (
            [Sales Amount],
            KEEPFILTERS ( BITLSHIFT( Customer[Age], 10 ) )
        )
)
```

The first SQL query retrieves the values of *Customer[Age]*:

```
SELECT TOP (1000001) [t0].[Age]
FROM ([dbo].[Customer]) AS [t0]
GROUP BY [t0].[Age]
```

The formula engine then evaluates the values of *Customer[Age]* for which the condition is true, and it produces the second SQL query:

```
SELECT TOP (1000001) *
FROM (
    SELECT [basetable0].[t2_Brand],
        SUM([a0]) AS [a0]
    FROM (
        (
            SELECT [t0_Age],
                [t2_Brand],
                [a0]
            FROM (
                SELECT [t0].[Age] AS [t0_Age],
                    [t2].[Brand] AS [t2_Brand],
                    [t3].[Quantity] AS [t3_Quantity],
                    [t3].[Net Price] AS [t3_Net Price],
                    ([t3].[Quantity] * [t3].[Net Price]) AS [a0]
                FROM (
                    (
                        [Data].[Sales] AS [t3]
                            INNER JOIN [dbo].[Customer] AS [t0]
                                ON ([t3].[CustomerKey] = [t0].[CustomerKey]
                                )
                    )
                    LEFT JOIN [dbo].[Product] AS [t2]
                        ON ([t3].[ProductKey] = [t2].[ProductKey])
                )
            ) AS [t0]
        ) AS [basetable0]
```

```
        INNER JOIN (
        (SELECT 33 AS [t0_Age])
        UNION ALL (SELECT 43 AS [t0_Age])
        UNION ALL (SELECT 68 AS [t0_Age])
        UNION ALL (SELECT 36 AS [t0_Age])
        ...
        UNION ALL (SELECT 57 AS [t0_Age])
        UNION ALL (SELECT 40 AS [t0_Age])
        UNION ALL (SELECT 20 AS [t0_Age])
        UNION ALL (SELECT 74 AS [t0_Age])
        ) AS [semijoin1] ON (([semijoin1].[t0_Age] = [basetable0].[t0_Age]))
    )
    GROUP BY [basetable0].[t2_Brand]
    ) AS [MainTable]
WHERE (NOT (([a0] IS NULL)))
```

The power of SQL makes up for the absence of callbacks. Using DirectQuery, most DAX functions can be pushed down to the storage engine. Therefore, despite this being a limitation, it does not strongly affect performance. However, the complexity of a SQL query strongly depends on the DAX function used.

With VertiPaq, the rules are simple: the VertiPaq engine offers minimal functionalities, and the formula engine must compute everything else. When using DirectQuery, the storage engine is much more powerful; therefore, the structure of the queries can be more complex. The formula engine executes less work, while at the same time the storage engine oversees a more extensive set of calculations.

Calculated tables

DirectQuery over SQL does not support calculated tables. This limitation is more related to the architecture than to performance. However, developers can still create materialized views or tables in SQL to obtain a behavior like calculated tables. If you create a pure DirectQuery model in Power BI Desktop, a calculated table is always created as a local table in a composite model, but the table must be refreshed and is not automatically synchronized with the data on the relational database.

If BI developers need a calculated table, they must compute and store it in the SQL database. Hence, they must alter the source database to fit their reporting needs.

Calculated columns

Calculated columns in a VertiPaq model are computed once at refresh time and stored in the database. We have seen several examples where using a calculated column improves performance by reducing the CPU power required at query time. Calculated columns can also be created in DirectQuery. However, DirectQuery does not store the values of the calculated column in the database. DirectQuery evaluates calculated columns at query time. Moreover, there are some architectural limitations in their usage.

For example, the following calculated column computes the line amount by multiplying *Sales[Quantity]* by *Sales[Net Price]*:

```
-------------------------------------
-- Calculated column in Sales table
-------------------------------------
Line Amount = Sales[Quantity] * Sales[Net Price]
```

However, the following query shows that the calculation is executed on the fly at query time:

```
EVALUATE
SUMMARIZECOLUMNS (
    Customer[Country],
    "Sales Amount", SUM ( Sales[Line Amount] )
)
```

A single SQL query resolves the DAX query:

```
SELECT TOP (1000001) *
FROM (
    SELECT [t0].[Country] AS [t0_Country],
        SUM([t3].[Line Amount]) AS [a0]
    FROM (
        (
            SELECT [t3].[CustomerKey] AS [CustomerKey],
                ([t3].[Quantity] * [t3].[Net Price]) AS [Line Amount]
            FROM ([dbo].[Sales]) AS [t3]
            ) AS [t3]
            LEFT JOIN [dbo].[Customer] AS [t0] ON ([t3].[CustomerKey] = [t0].[CustomerKey])
        )
    GROUP BY [t0].[Country]
    ) AS [MainTable]
WHERE (NOT (([a0] IS NULL)))
```

The calculation of *Quantity* multiplied by *Net Price* happens within the SQL code, as is the case for any calculated column in DirectQuery.

When working with DirectQuery over SQL, the calculation is always pushed down to the SQL engine: when you create calculated columns in DAX, the SQL code is generated by DirectQuery; when you implement the calculation in SQL directly in the data source, you have full control over the SQL code executed. As usual, you must carefully evaluate the best solution in your specific scenario.

How caching works in DirectQuery over SQL

From a scalability standpoint, it is essential to note that SQL does not have a caching system; it always queries fresh data. During the execution of a single DAX query, the datacaches retrieved by the storage engine are cached. As soon as the query completes its execution, the datacaches are cleared and must be recomputed on the next run. The absence of a cache does not substantially impact an individual query. However, in a multi-user environment, it may lower the overall performance of the system by executing some common queries multiple times.

For example, running the following query requires around 1.4 seconds of storage engine CPU:

```
EVALUATE
SUMMARIZECOLUMNS (
    'Date'[Year],
    "Sales", [Sales Amount]
)
```

Total	SE CPU	Line	Subclass	Duration	CPU	Par.	Rows	KB	Timeline
1,424 ms	1,420 ms								
	x1.0	1	SQL	1,420	1,420	x1.0			

FE	SE
4 ms	1,420 ms
0.3%	99.7%

SE Queries	SE Cache
1	0
	0.0%

Total DQ
1,420 ms

```
SELECT TOP (1000001) *
FROM (
    SELECT [t1_Year],
        SUM([a0]) AS [a0]
    FROM (
        SELECT [t1].[Year] AS [t1_Year],
            [t3].[Quantity] AS [t3_Quantity],
            [t3].[Net Price] AS [t3_Net Price],
            ([t3].[Quantity] * [t3].[Net Price]) AS [a0]
        FROM (
            [Data].[Sales] AS [t3]
                LEFT JOIN [dbo].[Date] AS [t1] ON ([t3].[Order Date] = [t1].[Date])
        )
    ) AS [t0]
    GROUP BY [t1_Year]
) AS [MainTable]
WHERE (NOT (([a0] IS NULL)))
```

Running the same query immediately after, without clearing the cache, executes the SQL query again. Because SQL does not cache its results, the execution time is nearly identical to the first execution.

Performing that same operation with VertiPaq produces a faster result because the second execution of the query hits the cache, and the result is instantaneous.

Understanding latency to send queries to the remote server

The formula engine sends one or more requests to the SQL engine to execute a DAX query in DirectQuery. The query must be sent through the network, handled by the remote SQL engine, and then the result returns to the formula engine. The mechanism is not far from the communication between the formula engine and VertiPaq; the main difference is that VertiPaq and the formula engine communicate on the same server. In contrast, communication between the SQL engine and the formula engine often takes place between different servers or between different processes when the two services run on the same server. Consequently, communication is slower than with VertiPaq, introducing some latency to execute every query.

The latency has an impact depending on the number of queries executed. The more queries, the more the latency plays a role in the performance of the DAX code. Be mindful that – because of the power of SQL – the number of queries executed in DirectQuery is typically smaller than those executed in VertiPaq for the same DAX query. Therefore, reducing the number of queries mitigates the impact of latency. We will see several examples of this in the following chapters.

Max number of rows in a data cache

A DirectQuery query has a hard limit on the number of rows that can be retrieved. The formula engine does not know how many rows will be returned by a storage engine query until the query itself is completed. A datacache with hundreds of millions of rows would create serious issues for both memory and performance. Consequently, every request sent to the DirectQuery storage engine contains a TOP clause to limit the number of rows. The default is TOP 1,000,000 (1M). If the query returns more than 1M rows, it raises an error and terminates.

There are mainly two scenarios where this can happen: when scanning a large fact table using functions that cannot be expressed in SQL, or when the model contains large dimensions used for grouping operations.

A straightforward example of this behavior is the following query:

```
EVALUATE
SUMMARIZECOLUMNS (
    Customer[Name],
    "Amt", [Sales Amount]
)
```

There are 1.8M customers in our sample model. Because the result would contain more than 1M rows, the query does not return any value but just the error:

```
The resultset of a query to external data source has exceeded the maximum allowed size of
'1000000' rows.
```

However, the same situation can happen with a smaller result, but when some internal datacaches are too large. For example, the following query generates an error because the *CustomersAndSales* variable would require a datacache created in DirectQuery that contains more than 1M rows:

```
EVALUATE
SUMMARIZECOLUMNS (
    Customer[Country],
    "# Large Customers",
        VAR CustomersAndSales =
            ADDCOLUMNS ( VALUES ( Customer[CustomerKey] ), "@Amt", [Sales Amount] )
        VAR AvgSales =
            AVERAGEX ( CustomersAndSales, [@Amt] )
        VAR LargeCustomers =
            COUNTROWS ( FILTER ( CustomersAndSales, [@Amt] > AvgSales ) )
        RETURN
            LargeCustomers
)
```

In some scenarios, developers would have the option of refactoring the code to reduce the materialization. However, in most situations, the maximum number of rows retrieved in a single query is a hard limit.

You may modify the default value of 1M at the server or capacity level with the *MaxIntermediateRowSetCount* property of the AS engine. However, be mindful that increasing the value to too large a number might let poorly designed queries use a massive amount of resources, thus affecting the stability of the server.

Different types of relationships

When discussing VertiPaq, we discussed how the VertiPaq storage engine handles different types of relationships, which strongly impacts performance. DirectQuery is different. SQL is more powerful than VertiPaq in terms of relationship handling. Therefore, the differences among the various types of relationships are less relevant. However, learning how different types of relationships are translated into different SQL constructs is helpful.

Regular one-to-many relationships

A regular one-to-many relationship generates LEFT OUTER joins in SQL. By default, Tabular considers any relationship as potentially non-valid. Therefore, it must execute LEFT OUTER joins between tables linked by regular relationships. For example, the following query groups by *Customer[Country]* and computes the sales amount, requiring a scan of *Sales*:

```
EVALUATE
SUMMARIZECOLUMNS (
    Customer[Country],
    "Sales Amount", [Sales Amount]
)
```

A single SQL query resolves this DAX query:

```
SELECT TOP (1000001) *
FROM (
    SELECT [t0_Country],
        SUM([a0]) AS [a0]
    FROM (
        SELECT [t0].[Country] AS [t0_Country],
            [t3].[Quantity] AS [t3_Quantity],
            [t3].[Net Price] AS [t3_Net Price],
            ([t3].[Quantity] * [t3].[Net Price]) AS [a0]
        FROM (
            [Data].[Sales] AS [t3]
                LEFT JOIN [dbo].[Customer] AS [t0]
                    ON ([t3].[CustomerKey] = [t0].[CustomerKey])
            )
        ) AS [t0]
    GROUP BY [t0_Country]
    ) AS [MainTable]
WHERE (NOT (([a0] IS NULL)))
```

In the innermost query, a JOIN between *Sales* and *Customer* is expressed as a LEFT JOIN (an OUTER join). We use the server timings of the query as a reference for the following comparisons.

Total	SE CPU	Line	Subclass	Duration	CPU	Par.	Rows	KB	Timeline
1,713 ms	1,707 ms x1.0	1	SQL	1,707	1,707	x1.0			

FE 6 ms 0.4%	**SE** 1,707 ms 99.6%

```
SELECT TOP (1000001) *
FROM (
    SELECT [t0_Country],
    SUM([a0]) AS [a0]
FROM (
    SELECT [t0].[Country] AS [t0_Country],
        [t3].[Quantity] AS [t3_Quantity],
        [t3].[Net Price] AS [t3_Net Price],
        ([t3].[Quantity] * [t3].[Net Price]) AS [a0]
```

SE Queries 1	**SE Cache** 0 0.0%
	Total DQ 1,707 ms

The SQL engine might perform better if it relied on referential integrity and used an INNER JOIN rather than an OUTER JOIN. However, when working with DirectQuery, Tabular cannot perform any assumption on the data because the data is stored in SQL rather than in its internal database. By default, it assumes that a relationship can be invalid. Developers can inform Tabular of the presence of referential integrity by checking the **Assume referential integrity** flag in the relationship.

Edit relationship

Select tables and columns that are related.

Sales

Order Number	Line Number	Order Date	Delivery Date	CustomerKey	StoreKey	Produc
149000977	0	Saturday, May 29, 2010	Saturday, May 29, 2010	1891556	550	
149009449	0	Saturday, May 29, 2010	Saturday, May 29, 2010	1706671	550	
149009070	0	Saturday, May 29, 2010	Saturday, May 29, 2010	1967204	550	

Customer

CustomerKey	Gender	Name	Address	City	State Code	State	Zip Code
1275812	Male	Scott Kohier	972 Brannon Street	Los Angeles	CA	California	90017
1276653	Male	Jonathan Williams	2758 Red Maple Drive	Los Angeles	CA	California	90017
1279112	Male	Thomas Wells	1181 Rainbow Road	Los Angeles	CA	California	90017

Cardinality

Many to one (*:1)

Cross filter direction

Single

☑ Make this relationship active

Apply security filter in both directions

☑ Assume referential integrity   Learn more

OK   Cancel

By enabling the flag, the query now uses an INNER JOIN rather than an OUTER JOIN:

```
SELECT TOP (1000001) *
FROM (
    SELECT [t0_Country],
        SUM([a0]) AS [a0]
    FROM (
        SELECT [t0].[Country] AS [t0_Country],
            [t3].[Quantity] AS [t3_Quantity],
            [t3].[Net Price] AS [t3_Net Price],
            ([t3].[Quantity] * [t3].[Net Price]) AS [a0]
        FROM (
            [Data].[Sales] AS [t3]
                INNER JOIN [dbo].[Customer] AS [t0]
                    ON ([t3].[CustomerKey] = [t0].[CustomerKey])
        )
    ) AS [t0]
    GROUP BY [t0_Country]
) AS [MainTable]
WHERE (NOT (([a0] IS NULL)))
```

Be mindful that using an INNER JOIN can result in either better or lower performance, depending on the structure of the SQL database. Assuming that an INNER JOIN is always the best option would be incorrect. As is always the case with Tabular, extensive testing is required before making any decision.

As a matter of fact in this specific scenario, using an INNER JOIN produces lower performance, mainly because we are using a columnstore as the source.

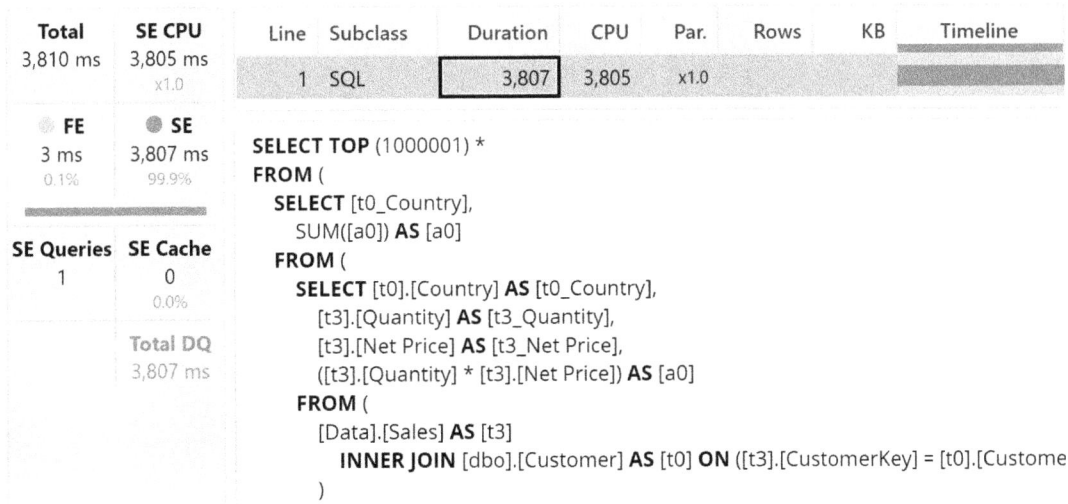

Total	SE CPU		Line	Subclass	Duration	CPU	Par.	Rows	KB	Timeline
3,810 ms	3,805 ms x1.0		1	SQL	3,807	3,805	x1.0			

FE	SE
3 ms	3,807 ms
0.1%	99.9%

SE Queries	SE Cache
1	0
	0.0%

Total DQ
3,807 ms

```
SELECT TOP (1000001) *
FROM (
    SELECT [t0_Country],
        SUM([a0]) AS [a0]
    FROM (
        SELECT [t0].[Country] AS [t0_Country],
            [t3].[Quantity] AS [t3_Quantity],
            [t3].[Net Price] AS [t3_Net Price],
            ([t3].[Quantity] * [t3].[Net Price]) AS [a0]
        FROM (
            [Data].[Sales] AS [t3]
                INNER JOIN [dbo].[Customer] AS [t0] ON ([t3].[CustomerKey] = [t0].[Custome
        )
```

The flag "Assume referential integrity" has additional side effects other than the type of join. When a relationship is valid and "assume referential integrity" is set, Tabular does not need to consider the blank row on the one-side of the relationship. This assumption simplifies certain queries and can boost performance in some scenarios. We will cover this aspect in a later chapter.

Limited many-to-many relationships

If the relationship between *Customer* and *Sales* is created as a many-to-many relationship, then the code to run the same query will be different and more complex.

As a reminder, here is the query:

```
EVALUATE
SUMMARIZECOLUMNS (
    Customer[Country],
    "Sales Amount", [Sales Amount]
)
```

The following SQL code executes the DAX query on a model where the relationship is set as many-to-many:

```
SELECT TOP (1000001) *
FROM (
    SELECT [semijoin1].[t0_Country],
        SUM([a0]) AS [a0]
    FROM (
        (
            SELECT [t3_CustomerKey],
                [a0]
            FROM (
                SELECT [t3].[CustomerKey] AS [t3_CustomerKey],
                    [t3].[Quantity] AS [t3_Quantity],
                    [t3].[Net Price] AS [t3_Net Price],
                    ([t3].[Quantity] * [t3].[Net Price]) AS [a0]
                FROM ([Data].[Sales]) AS [t3]
                ) AS [t0]
            ) AS [basetable0]
        INNER JOIN (
        SELECT [t0].[CustomerKey] AS [t3_CustomerKey],
            [t0].[Country] AS [t0_Country]
        FROM ([dbo].[Customer]) AS [t0]
        GROUP BY [t0].[CustomerKey],
            [t0].[Country]
        ) AS [semijoin1] ON (
            (
                [semijoin1].[t3_CustomerKey] = [basetable0].[t3_CustomerKey]
                OR [semijoin1].[t3_CustomerKey] IS NULL
                AND [basetable0].[t3_CustomerKey] IS NULL
                )
            )
        )
    GROUP BY [semijoin1].[t0_Country]
    ) AS [MainTable]
WHERE (NOT (([a0] IS NULL)))
```

The code is more complex than the simple JOIN executed for regular one-to-many relationships, mainly because of the need to handle blanks in both tables. However, the code is more straightforward than the batch executed by VertiPaq to obtain the same result.

A quick look at the server timings shows a performance degradation compared with a regular one-to-many relationship: in this specific scenario, it is around 40% slower.

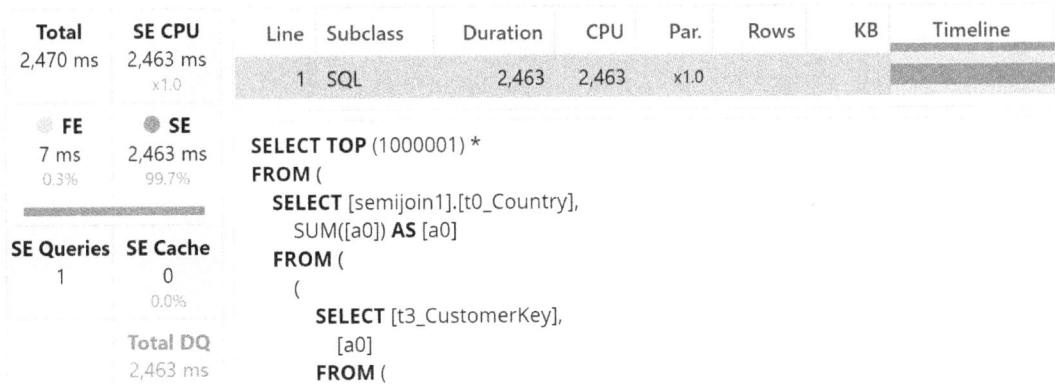

Total	SE CPU	Line	Subclass	Duration	CPU	Par.	Rows	KB	Timeline
2,470 ms	2,463 ms								
	x1.0	1	SQL	2,463	2,463	x1.0			

FE	SE
7 ms	2,463 ms
0.3%	99.7%

```
SELECT TOP (1000001) *
FROM (
    SELECT [semijoin1].[t0_Country],
        SUM([a0]) AS [a0]
    FROM (
        (
            SELECT [t3_CustomerKey],
            [a0]
            FROM (
```

SE Queries	SE Cache
1	0
	0.0%

Total DQ
2,463 ms

However, remember that we still have not covered any optimization technique with DirectQuery: these are just base findings to get a rough idea of the type of queries generated. The structure of the SQL database profoundly impacts the performance, and we have not covered that yet.

One-to-one relationships

One-to-one relationships are resolved through a regular JOIN (INNER or OUTER) and pose no threat to performance. As with VertiPaq, one-to-one relationships are bidirectional by nature but are solved using regular joins in both directions.

DirectQuery over SQL max parallel queries

The execution of a DAX query almost always results in the execution of multiple SQL statements sent to the DirectQuery storage engine. To optimize the overall execution time, Tabular can simultaneously send multiple SQL queries to the data source. Developers can fine-tune the maximum degree of parallelism: the correct setting might profoundly impact performance. The DAX code itself also plays an essential role in the parallelism involved in DirectQuery.

Let us start with a simple example. The following query computes three columns, each with a different filter created through CALCULATE:

```
EVALUATE
SUMMARIZECOLUMNS (
    'Product'[Brand],
    "Fabrikam",
        CALCULATE (
            DISTINCTCOUNT ( Sales[CustomerKey] ),
            'Product'[Brand] = "Fabrikam"
        ),
    "Contoso and Litware",
        CALCULATE (
            DISTINCTCOUNT ( Sales[CustomerKey] ),
            'Product'[Brand] IN { "Contoso", "Litware" } ),
    "Red",
        CALCULATE (
            DISTINCTCOUNT ( Sales[CustomerKey] ),
            'Product'[Color] = "Red"
        )
)
```

The DAX query generates three SQL queries, one per column. Each query groups by *Product[Brand]* and computes the expression in SQL, which is a simple DISTINCT COUNT. There is an additional SQL query to retrieve the values of *Product[Brand]*, which the formula engine needs to merge the partial results.

If no parallelism is involved, the SQL queries are executed sequentially, as shown in the timeline.

Total	SE CPU	Line	Subclass	Duration	CPU	Par.	Rows	KB	Timeline
2,068 ms	2,054 ms	1	SQL	398	398	x1.0			
	x1.0	2	SQL	1,093	1,091	x1.0			
FE	SE	3	SQL	564	564	x1.0			
12 ms	2,056 ms	4	SQL	1	1	x1.0			
0.6%	99.4%								

SE Queries	SE Cache
4	0
	0.0%

Total DQ
2,056 ms

The total execution time is around 2 seconds. SQL Server is very good at parallelism; the formula engine can send multiple queries simultaneously to reduce the overall execution time. Developers can configure the maximum number of DirectQuery queries sent in parallel through the **Model\MaxParallelismPerQuery** property in TOM. The feature is available for models starting with compatibility level 1569.

The previous screenshot shows the execution with the MaxParallelismPerQuery property set to 1. Setting the value to 64 (the number of cores in the test machine) shows a parallel execution of nearly all the queries.

Total	SE CPU		Line	Subclass	Duration	CPU	Par.	Rows	KB	Timeline
1,915 ms	5,336 ms		1	SQL	1,532	1,532	x1.0			
	x2.8									
FE ⚠	SE ●		2	SQL	1,898	1,898	x1.0			
10 ms	1,905 ms		3	SQL	1,905	1,905	x1.0			
0.5%	99.5%		4	SQL	1	1	x1.0			

SE Queries	SE Cache
4	0
	0.0%

Total DQ
5,336 ms

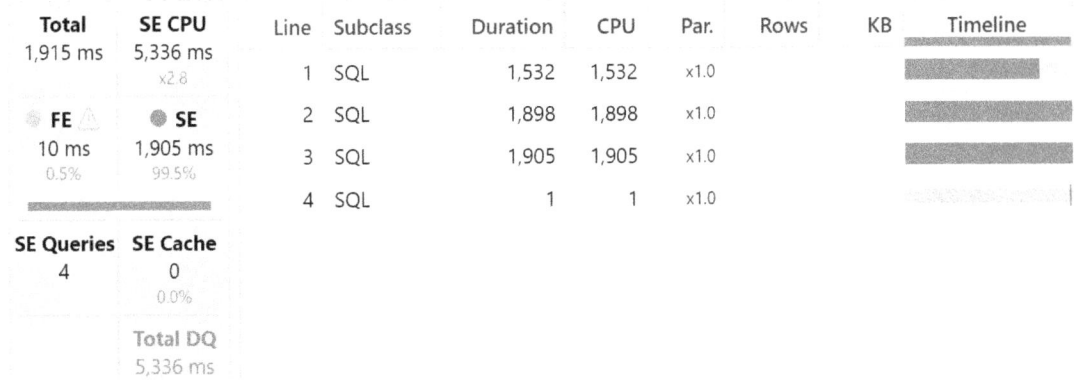

The timeline shows that all the SQL queries start at the same time. The execution time of each query is larger because its execution now overlaps with the other ones. However, the overall execution time of the DAX query is faster.

Be mindful that parallelism is a double-edged sword. There are scenarios where increasing parallelism brings good benefits; in other scenarios, the increased parallelism harms the execution time. It depends on many factors, and only intense testing can provide clues as to the value to set for the property.

Moreover, an important consideration is that the SQL database administrator might require a limit on the maximum number of queries executed in parallel. SQL Server databases are almost always shared resources, and allocating all the resources to one service would be unfair. Before changing the maximum number of parallel queries, discussing this with the database administrator is always suggested.

As we mentioned earlier, DAX plays an essential role in the benefits of parallelism. Let us elaborate on this with an example. The following query includes an IF statement:

```
EVALUATE
SUMMARIZECOLUMNS (
    'Product'[Brand],
    "IF Example",
        IF (
            [Sales Amount] > 1E3,
            [Margin],
            [Sales Amount]
        )
)
```

Based on what we analyzed in the previous chapters, we know that the IF conditional statement is resolved by first evaluating the condition and then executing two queries: one to compute *Margin* for the brands where the condition holds true, and a second to calculate *Sales Amount* for the brands where the condition is false.

Total	SE CPU	Line	Subclass	Duration	CPU	Par.	Rows	KB	Timeline
5,403 ms	8,147 ms								
	x1.5	1	SQL	1,541	1,541	x1.0			
FE ⚠	● SE	2	SQL	1	1	x1.0			
11 ms	5,392 ms	3	SQL	2,757	2,757	x1.0			
	(5,392 ms)	4	SQL	3,850	3,848	x1.0			
0.2%	99.8%								

SE Queries	SE Cache
4	0
	0.0%

Total DQ
8,149 ms

Despite some parallelism visible in the timeline, the first query must be executed before the others. Indeed, the filter in the following queries depends on the result of the first query. Let us look at more details. The first query computes *Sales Amount* by *Brand*, which is needed to evaluate the condition:

```
SELECT TOP (1000001) *
FROM (
    SELECT [t2_Brand],
        SUM([a0]) AS [a0]
    FROM (
        SELECT [t2].[Brand] AS [t2_Brand],
            [t3].[Quantity] AS [t3_Quantity],
            [t3].[Net Price] AS [t3_Net Price],
            ([t3].[Quantity] * [t3].[Net Price]) AS [a0]
        FROM (
            [Data].[Sales] AS [t3]
                LEFT JOIN [dbo].[Product] AS [t2] ON ([t3].[ProductKey] = [t2].[ProductKey])
            )
        ) AS [t0]
    GROUP BY [t2_Brand]
    ) AS [MainTable]
WHERE (NOT (([a0] IS NULL)))
```

The second query is irrelevant, as it only retrieves the values of the brands. The last two queries compute the two branches of the IF statement. One calculates *Sales Amount* for the Adventure Works brand only:

```
SELECT TOP (1000001) *
FROM (
    SELECT [t2_Brand],
        SUM([a0]) AS [a0]
    FROM (
        SELECT [t2].[Brand] AS [t2_Brand],
            [t3].[Quantity] AS [t3_Quantity],
            [t3].[Net Price] AS [t3_Net Price],
            ([t3].[Quantity] * [t3].[Net Price]) AS [a0]
        FROM (
            [Data].[Sales] AS [t3]
                LEFT JOIN [dbo].[Product] AS [t2] ON ([t3].[ProductKey] = [t2].[ProductKey])
            )
        ) AS [t0]
    WHERE (
            ([t2_Brand] IN (N'Adventure Works '))
            OR ([t2_Brand] IS NULL)
            )
    GROUP BY [t2_Brand]
    ) AS [MainTable]
WHERE (NOT (([a0] IS NULL)))
```

The other computes *Margin* for all other brands:

```
SELECT TOP (1000001) *
FROM (
    SELECT [t2_Brand],
        SUM([a0]) AS [a0],
        SUM([a1]) AS [a1]
    FROM (
        SELECT [t2].[Brand] AS [t2_Brand],
            [t3].[Quantity] AS [t3_Quantity],
            [t3].[Net Price] AS [t3_Net Price],
            [t3].[Unit Cost] AS [t3_Unit Cost],
            ([t3].[Quantity] * [t3].[Unit Cost]) AS [a0],
            ([t3].[Quantity] * [t3].[Net Price]) AS [a1]
        FROM (
            [Data].[Sales] AS [t3]
                LEFT JOIN [dbo].[Product] AS [t2] ON ([t3].[ProductKey] = [t2].[ProductKey])
            )
        ) AS [t0]
```

```
        WHERE (
                (
                        [t2_Brand] IN (
                                N'The Phone Company',
                                N'Litware',
                                N'Contoso',
                                N'Southridge Video',
                                N'Tailspin Toys',
                                N'Northwind Traders',
                                N'Adventure Works',
                                N'Wide World Importers',
                                N'A. Datum',
                                N'Proseware',
                                N'Fabrikam'
                                )
                        )
                )
        GROUP BY [t2_Brand]
        ) AS [MainTable]
WHERE (
        NOT (([a0] IS NULL))
        OR NOT (([a1] IS NULL))
        )
```

There are two issues with this DAX query: not only are there multiple SQL queries being executed, but they cannot be parallelized because some queries depend on the results of others. In this example, dependency is very easy to recognize. With more complex code, tracking and understanding the dependencies can prove to be much more difficult.

In this scenario, you can significantly improve performance by using IF.EAGER instead of IF:

```
EVALUATE
SUMMARIZECOLUMNS (
    'Product'[Brand],
    "IF Example",
        IF.EAGER (
            [Sales Amount] > 1E3,
            [Margin],
            [Sales Amount]
        )
)
```

When using IF.EAGER, the entire DAX query is resolved with two SQL queries: one to retrieve the different brands and one to compute all the required values at once.

Total	SE CPU	Line	Subclass	Duration	CPU	Par.	Rows	KB	Timeline
1,919 ms	1,905 ms	1	SQL	1,904	1,904	x1.0			
	x1.0								
		2	SQL	3	1	x0.3			
FE	SE								
12 ms	1,907 ms								
0.6%	99.4%								

SE Queries	SE Cache
2	0
	0.0%
	Total DQ
	1,907 ms

Despite being more complex, the SQL query computes all the values, and it then leaves to the formula engine the task of choosing the ones to return:

```
SELECT TOP (1000001) *
FROM (
    SELECT [t2_Brand],
        SUM([a0]) AS [a0],
        SUM([a1]) AS [a1]
    FROM (
        SELECT [t2].[Brand] AS [t2_Brand],
            [t3].[Quantity] AS [t3_Quantity],
            [t3].[Net Price] AS [t3_Net Price],
            [t3].[Unit Cost] AS [t3_Unit Cost],
            ([t3].[Quantity] * [t3].[Unit Cost]) AS [a0],
            ([t3].[Quantity] * [t3].[Net Price]) AS [a1]
        FROM (
            [Data].[Sales] AS [t3]
                LEFT JOIN [dbo].[Product] AS [t2] ON ([t3].[ProductKey] = [t2].[ProductKey])
            )
        ) AS [t0]
    GROUP BY [t2_Brand]
    ) AS [MainTable]
WHERE (
        NOT (([a0] IS NULL))
        OR NOT (([a1] IS NULL))
        )
```

As discussed in previous chapters, we can obtain the same result as IF.EAGER by using variables:

```
EVALUATE
SUMMARIZECOLUMNS (
    'Product'[Brand],
    "IF Example",
        VAR SalesAmount = [Sales Amount]
        VAR Margin = [Margin]
        RETURN
        IF (
            SalesAmount > 1E3,
            Margin,
            SalesAmount
        )
)
```

In this example, the improvement comes from reducing the number of queries, which is possible because the filter context in the two branches of the IF statement is the same. If we use CALCULATE to change the filter context of the two branches, the benefit is smaller because the engine cannot entirely merge the queries. This case is very representative of what we see in the real world:

```
EVALUATE
SUMMARIZECOLUMNS (
    'Product'[Brand],
    "IF Example",
        IF (
            [Sales Amount] > 1E3,
            CALCULATE ( [Sales Amount], Product[Color] = "Black" ),
            CALCULATE ( [Sales Amount], Customer[Gender] = "Male" )
        )
)
```

We execute this code using three different settings: first with MaxParallelismPerQuery set to 1, then with MaxParallelismPerQuery set to 64, and finally using IF.EAGER instead of IF.

The first figure shows the results when no parallelism is allowed.

Total	SE CPU		Line	Subclass	Duration	CPU	Par.	Rows	KB	Timeline
4,051 ms	4,038 ms									
	x1.0		1	SQL	1,554	1,554	x1.0			
FE	**SE**		2	SQL	530	529	x1.0			
11 ms	4,040 ms		3	SQL	1	1	x1.0			
0.3%	99.7%		4	SQL	1,957	1,954	x1.0			

SE Queries 4   **SE Cache** 0   0.0%

Total DQ 4,042 ms

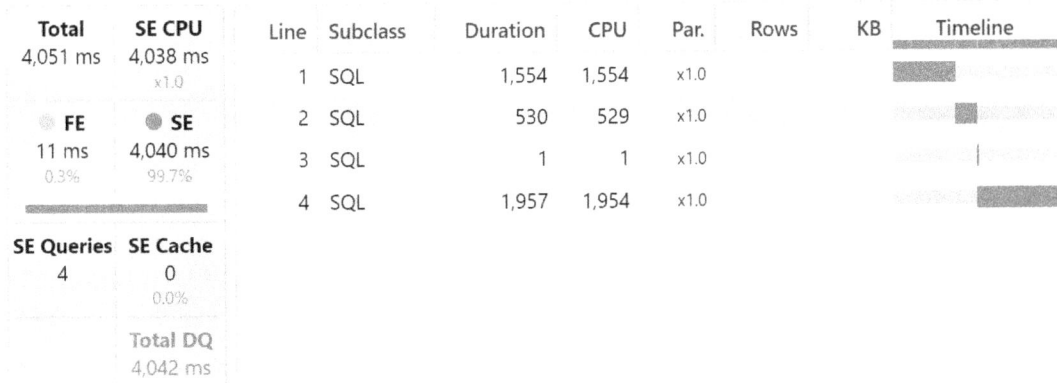

The query runs in around 4 seconds; the timeline clearly shows the sequential execution of the SQL queries. During the execution, the server CPU jumps to 100% because SQL Server uses all the available cores for each query. Therefore, the second test that allows parallelism does not improve efficiency because all the cores are already busy.

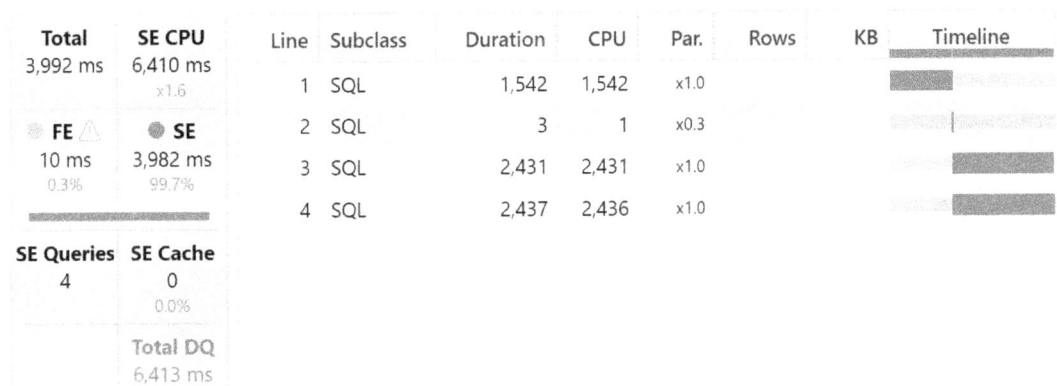

Total	SE CPU		Line	Subclass	Duration	CPU	Par.	Rows	KB	Timeline
3,992 ms	6,410 ms									
	x1.6		1	SQL	1,542	1,542	x1.0			
FE ⚠	**SE**		2	SQL	3	1	x0.3			
10 ms	3,982 ms		3	SQL	2,431	2,431	x1.0			
0.3%	99.7%		4	SQL	2,437	2,436	x1.0			

SE Queries 4   **SE Cache** 0   0.0%

Total DQ 6,413 ms

Moreover, there is still the effect of the IF function that requires some of the queries to be sequential. The last test uses IF.EAGER and provides better performance.

Total	SE CPU		Line	Subclass	Duration	CPU	Par.	Rows	KB	Timeline
3,477 ms	9,937 ms									
	x2.9		1	SQL	3,133	3,132	x1.0			
FE ⚠	**SE**		2	SQL	3,340	3,340	x1.0			
11 ms	3,466 ms		3	SQL	3,464	3,464	x1.0			
0.3%	99.7%		4	SQL	3	1	x0.3			

SE Queries 4   **SE Cache** 0   0.0%

Total DQ 9,940 ms

The total execution time is further reduced; the timeline shows that the first three SQL queries are executed in parallel. Each query is slightly slower than the corresponding one executed with IF in the previous test. However, the overall execution time is reduced thanks to parallelism.

Using different data islands

If multiple DirectQuery connections exist to different databases, we say there are multiple DirectQuery data islands. Each database is an island, regardless of whether the database is being stored on the same server or in a different server. In this section, we cover only models with a single DirectQuery connection. However, it is helpful to introduce why having multiple data islands strongly impacts performance.

When using different data islands, the data is scattered across different islands. As such, the engine cannot push a single query on the storage engine when the DAX query involves columns from tables stored on different islands. Therefore, having multiple SQL data sources is the same as having multiple storage engines: data must pass through the formula engine.

For example, we added to the model a copy of *Product* retrieved from a different SQL database. You can see in the diagram that *Product* and *Product (Island 2)* are using two different databases: Contoso 100M x 10 and Contoso 100K. Apart from the database where they are stored, the content of the two tables is the same.

When Tabular joins *Sales* with *Product*, it can inject a JOIN between the two tables in the SQL query so that the join operation happens inside SQL Server. However, the same cannot occur when *Sales* is joined with *Product (Island 2)* because the two tables are in different databases (data islands). Let us look at the following query:

```
EVALUATE
SUMMARIZECOLUMNS (
    'Product'[Brand],
    "Sales Amount", [Sales Amount]
)
```

The query generates a single SQL statement:

```
SELECT TOP (1000001) *
FROM (
    SELECT [t2_Brand],
        SUM([a0]) AS [a0]
    FROM (
        SELECT [t2].[Brand] AS [t2_Brand],
            [t3].[Quantity] AS [t3_Quantity],
            [t3].[Net Price] AS [t3_Net Price],
            ([t3].[Quantity] * [t3].[Net Price]) AS [a0]
        FROM (
            [Data].[Sales] AS [t3]
                LEFT JOIN [dbo].[Product] AS [t2] ON ([t3].[ProductKey] = [t2].[ProductKey])
            )
        ) AS [t0]
    GROUP BY [t2_Brand]
    ) AS [MainTable]
WHERE (NOT (([a0] IS NULL)))
```

The LEFT JOIN between the two tables is directly inside the query. If we replace *Product* with *Product (Island 2)*, then this query pattern is no longer viable:

```
EVALUATE
SUMMARIZECOLUMNS (
    'Product (Island 2)'[Brand],
    "Sales Amount", [Sales Amount]
)
```

By executing this DAX query, we obtain two separate SQL queries: one to retrieve the product keys and the brands to create an association between *Brand* and *ProductKey*; the second to retrieve *Sales Amount* sliced by *Brand*. Here is the first one:

```
SELECT TOP (1000001) [t6].[ProductKey],
    [t6].[Brand]
FROM ([dbo].[Product]) AS [t6]
GROUP BY [t6].[ProductKey],
    [t6].[Brand]
```

This query scans *Product* and builds a datacache that lets the formula engine know which brand is associated with each product key. The second query is much more verbose because it contains the association between brands and product keys, created through a series of UNION ALL statements:

```
SELECT TOP (1000001) *
FROM (
    SELECT [semijoin1].[c84],
        SUM([a0]) AS [a0]
    FROM (
        (
            SELECT [t3_ProductKey],
                [a0]
            FROM (
                SELECT [t3].[ProductKey] AS [t3_ProductKey],
                    [t3].[Quantity] AS [t3_Quantity],
                    [t3].[Net Price] AS [t3_Net Price],
                    ([t3].[Quantity] * [t3].[Net Price]) AS [a0]
                FROM ([Data].[Sales]) AS [t3]
                ) AS [t0]
            ) AS [basetable0]
                INNER JOIN (
                    ( SELECT 3 AS [c84],  1 AS [t3_ProductKey] )
                    UNION ALL
                    ( SELECT 3 AS [c84], 2 AS [t3_ProductKey] )

                    --
                    -- Several thousands of these SELECT statements
                    --

                    UNION ALL
                    ( SELECT 3 AS [c84], 3 AS [t3_ProductKey] )
                ) AS [semijoin1] ON (
                    (
                        [semijoin1].[t3_ProductKey] = [basetable0].[t3_ProductKey]
                    )
                )
            )
        )
    GROUP BY [semijoin1].[c84]
    ) AS [MainTable]
WHERE (NOT (([a0] IS NULL)))
```

This is only an excerpt of the whole query. The original query is 20,154 lines long. The size and complexity of these types of queries strongly depend on the content of the tables. Be mindful that *Product* contains a few thousand rows. A similar query with *Customer* would be much worse, as there are 1.8M customers.

However, the goal of this section is not to describe the details of queries in scenarios with multiple data islands. We wrote this section to explain the reasons that led us to cover complex models separately in Chapter 22. In the next few chapters about DirectQuery, we will always work with simple DirectQuery models with only one island.

Introducing aggregations and hybrid tables

Before moving on to the following chapters, we briefly introduce two technologies that we cover later in more detail: aggregations and hybrid tables.

Aggregations are summary tables stored in VertiPaq or DirectQuery containing pre-aggregated values from the main table. Tabular automatically uses aggregations whenever possible. They help reduce the number of SQL queries sent to the SQL Server.

Hybrid tables are tables that contain both VertiPaq and DirectQuery partitions. They are helpful in scenarios where real-time is among the requirements. The latest data is accessible through the DirectQuery partition, whereas historical data is stored in VertiPaq to guarantee optimal performance.

Both technologies require a much deeper discussion, which will take place in the following chapters. We introduced them here to let our readers know we did not forget about these technologies!

Conclusions

In this chapter, we introduced the most important differences between DirectQuery and VertiPaq regarding technology. SQL is more powerful than xmSQL, as it allows the formula engine to generate complex SQL queries that solve most of the common DAX code. On the other hand, the absence of callbacks may create problems with the size of datacaches. When DAX expressions cannot be pushed down to SQL, the materialization can be larger than the maximum number of rows the two engines can exchange, leading to aborted queries.

These aspects are of paramount importance when dealing with DirectQuery. As we will show in the following chapters, they affect how to optimize a query and how to design the database.

Optimizing DirectQuery over SQL

Now that we have a basic understanding of the architecture of DirectQuery, we can start analyzing details about how to build a data model for Tabular optimized to run with DirectQuery. We begin by considering the SQL model regarding tables, column data types, and indexes. Then, we talk a bit more about relationships, and finally, we cover two important aspects of optimization: aggregations and hybrid tables. These last two features aim to overcome the speed limitations of DirectQuery, letting developers mix VertiPaq data structures and DirectQuery tables within the same model. As with any technology, it is essential to understand the internals of their implementation to make the right choices at design time.

Building an SQL data model for Analysis Services

Using DirectQuery, the performance of any DAX query strongly depends on the performance of the underlying SQL database. The first and most important detail to address is that the design principles of the relational data source are entirely different between a relational model built for VertiPaq and a relational model built for DirectQuery.

If your Tabular model is VertiPaq, the data source receives a small number of queries that are basically SELECT statements for the entire table. **SELECT * FROM Sales** is the kind of query generated to populate the *Sales* table. The query may return hundreds of millions of rows, which would be fine. The query is executed, the data is processed into a VertiPaq store, and the job is done. Once the query has been executed, the SQL service is no longer responsible for any DAX query. If the SQL queries executed during the processing of the model result in a full table scan of the table, that is totally fine. Due to the large amount of data transferred from the SQL service to Tabular, a table scan is a good choice.

When using DirectQuery, the scenario is entirely different. Each DAX query executed produces multiple SQL queries that typically contain grouping, filtering, and calculations. Each of these queries is going to retrieve a small dataset that the SQL service must execute in the most efficient way possible. The SQL database should include indexes and data structures that make it easy for the SQL service to produce its answers.

We do not cover details about what index type to create or whether a column store is better than a clustered indexed table in SQL Server. If we were to start covering the details of SQL Server optimizations, we would need a whole other book. There are plenty of great books and trainings about optimizing SQL Server; they do a much better job than whatever we could write. Besides, Microsoft SQL Server is one of the many possible relational databases that can be used in DirectQuery over SQL. Covering all the different SQL engines would be impossible and useless because there would be no way to provide decent advice.

The tips we will provide are based on SQL Server; we expect the reader to translate those concepts for their specific database and to integrate our considerations with their knowledge of the domain and of the database server.

Designing indexes

As we said earlier, when working with Import mode, the queries executed are always full table scans. Therefore, there is no real need to build indexes and additional data structures to optimize queries. Conversely, when using DirectQuery, indexes can dramatically speed up calculations. However, due to the freedom users have in querying a data model, building indexes is most often impractical.

For sure, indexes in SQL are a powerful tool when you can predict the queries that will be executed. This predictability is the case of a database queried through software. When software generates the queries, you know what they will look like, the type of operations executed, and their frequency. However, when users generate the queries by creating a report in Power BI, there is no way to predict which columns will be placed on rows and columns of a Power BI visual or which measures will be used. As such, indexes cannot go very far in optimizing a database.

Let us look at this with an example. We created a copy of *Sales* (*Sales 1*) as a simple heap in SQL Server. It is very inefficient because each query requires a full table scan. Indeed, a simple DAX query like the following one requires a vast amount of time:

```
EVALUATE
SUMMARIZECOLUMNS (
    'Product'[Brand],
    "Sales", [Sales Amount]
)
```

The DAX query is resolved through this SQL code:

```
SELECT TOP (1000001) *
FROM (
    SELECT [t2_Brand],
        SUM([a0]) AS [a0]
    FROM (
        SELECT [t2].[Brand] AS [t2_Brand],
            [t3].[Quantity] AS [t3_Quantity],
            [t3].[Net Price] AS [t3_Net Price],
            ([t3].[Quantity] * [t3].[Net Price]) AS [a0]
        FROM (
            [Data].[Sales1] AS [t3]
                LEFT JOIN [dbo].[Product] AS [t2] ON ([t3].[ProductKey] = [t2].[ProductKey])
            )
        ) AS [t0]
    GROUP BY [t2_Brand]
    ) AS [MainTable]
WHERE (NOT (([a0] IS NULL)))
```

The execution time shows that the query is very inefficient.

Total	SE CPU		Line	Subclass	Duration	CPU	Par.	Rows	KB	Timeline
49,678 ms	49,664 ms									
	×1.0		1	SQL	49,664	49,664	×1.0			

FE	SE
14 ms	49,664 ms
0.0%	100.0%

SE Queries	SE Cache
1	0
	0.0%

Total DQ
49,664 ms

```
SELECT TOP (1000001) *
FROM (
    SELECT [t2_Brand],
        SUM([a0]) AS [a0]
    FROM (
        SELECT [t2].[Brand] AS [t2_Brand],
            [t3].[Quantity] AS [t3_Quantity],
            [t3].[Net Price] AS [t3_Net Price],
            ([t3].[Quantity] * [t3].[Net Price]) AS [a0]
        FROM (
            [Data].[Sales1] AS [t3]
            LEFT JOIN [dbo].[Product] AS [t2] ON ([t3].[ProductKey] = [t2].[ProductKey])
```

By looking at the SQL query plan, we can observe that the most expensive operation is the table scan. All other operations are irrelevant.

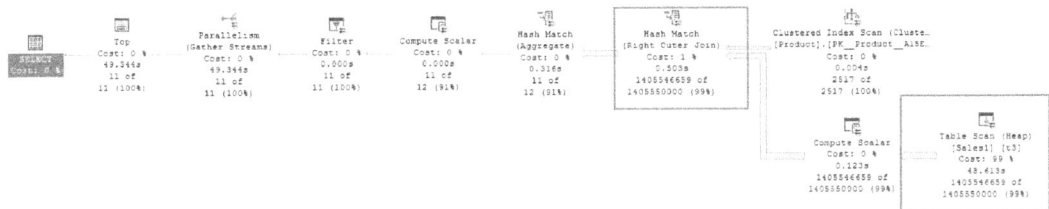

In the figure, we highlighted the Table Scan and the Hash Match operations; the latter merges *Sales* with *Product*. Despite it being a tiny percentage for now, it will become more interesting later.

To speed up the query, we can create an index that covers the required columns in *Sales*:

```
CREATE INDEX IDX_Test1 ON [Data].[Sales1] ( [ProductKey], [Quantity], [Net Price] )
```

SQL Server can scan the index rather than scanning the entire *Sales* table. The index contains the required columns and is much smaller than the original table. Once the index is in place, the query runs faster.

Total	SE CPU		Line	Subclass	Duration	CPU	Par.	Rows	KB	Timeline
5,838 ms	5,827 ms x1.0		1	SQL	5,827	5,827	x1.0			

FE 11 ms 0.2%	SE 5,827 ms 99.8%

```
SELECT TOP (1000001) *
FROM (
  SELECT [t2_Brand],
    SUM([a0]) AS [a0]
  FROM (
    SELECT [t2].[Brand] AS [t2_Brand],
      [t3].[Quantity] AS [t3_Quantity],
      [t3].[Net Price] AS [t3_Net Price],
      ([t3].[Quantity] * [t3].[Net Price]) AS [a0]
    FROM (
      [Data].[Sales1] AS [t3]
      LEFT JOIN [dbo].[Product] AS [t2] ON ([t3].[ProductKey] = [t2].[ProductKey])
```

SE Queries	SE Cache
1	0 0.0%

Total DQ
5,827 ms

The presence of the index makes the query run ten times faster. As you can see from the SQL query plan, the engine now scans the index rather than the table, resulting in a much better execution time.

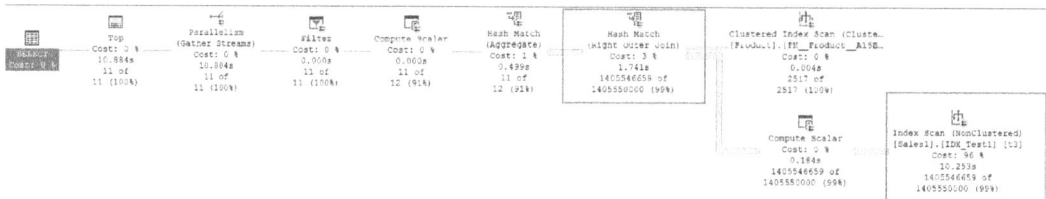

The percentage of the Hash Match is now a bit larger (from 1% to 3%). This difference does not mean that the Hash Match is slower. By reducing the time required to scan the *Sales* columns, the Hash Match operation starts to be more relevant.

Despite looking promising, this database optimization technique does not go very far. For example, changing the measure used in the query makes the index useless. If we use *Margin Amount* instead of *Sales Amount*, then the query also requires the product cost and becomes slow again because the SQL query includes columns not covered by the index:

```
EVALUATE
SUMMARIZECOLUMNS (
    'Product'[Brand],
    "Margin", [Margin]
)
```

The SQL code now includes the *Unit Cost* column, making the index useless:

```
SELECT TOP (1000001) *
FROM (
    SELECT [t2_Brand],
        SUM([a0]) AS [a0],
        SUM([a1]) AS [a1]
    FROM (
        SELECT [t2].[Brand] AS [t2_Brand],
            [t3].[Quantity] AS [t3_Quantity],
            [t3].[Net Price] AS [t3_Net Price],
            [t3].[Unit Cost] AS [t3_Unit Cost],
            ([t3].[Quantity] * [t3].[Unit Cost]) AS [a0],
            ([t3].[Quantity] * [t3].[Net Price]) AS [a1]
        FROM (
            [Data].[Sales1] AS [t3]
                LEFT JOIN [dbo].[Product] AS [t2] ON ([t3].[ProductKey] = [t2].[ProductKey])
            )
        ) AS [t0]
    GROUP BY [t2_Brand]
    ) AS [MainTable]
WHERE (
        NOT (([a0] IS NULL))
        OR NOT (([a1] IS NULL))
        )
```

We could include the *Unit Cost* column in the index. However, you may add so many columns to the index that its size becomes close to the original table. At that point, the benefit of using an index becomes minimal.

Using columnstore indexes

A great way to ensure your SQL Server database maintains flexibility and speed is to rely on columnstore indexes. A columnstore index is a technology remarkably similar to VertiPaq, implemented in SQL Server. Despite the many similarities, columnstore indexes are not identical to VertiPaq.

A columnstore index is a column-based structure, like VertiPaq. Columns are compressed and encoded, like VertiPaq. Still, there are two significant differences:

- A columnstore index is queried through SQL, not xmSQL. SQL is much more powerful than xmSQL, which is a great advantage.
- Relationships are not part of a columnstore index. Moving a filter between two tables is much more expensive in SQL than in VertiPaq.

We execute the query we used in the previous tests with indexes, this time using *Sales*, which is stored with a clustered columnstore index:

```
EVALUATE
SUMMARIZECOLUMNS (
    'Product'[Brand],
    "Sales", [Sales Amount]
)
```

Performance-wise, the improvement is enormous.

Total	SE CPU		Line	Subclass	Duration	CPU	Par.	Rows	KB	Timeline
1,810 ms	1,803 ms x1.0		1	SQL	1,803	1,803	x1.0			

FE	SE
7 ms	1,803 ms
0.4%	99.6%

SE Queries	SE Cache
1	0
	0.0%

Total DQ
1,803 ms

```
SELECT TOP (1000001) *
FROM (
  SELECT [t2_Brand],
    SUM([a0]) AS [a0]
  FROM (
    SELECT [t2].[Brand] AS [t2_Brand],
      [t3].[Quantity] AS [t3_Quantity],
      [t3].[Net Price] AS [t3_Net Price],
      ([t3].[Quantity] * [t3].[Net Price]) AS [a0]
    FROM (
      [Data].[Sales] AS [t3]
```

The same query ran in 49 seconds with no indexes and 6 seconds with a dedicated index. On the columnstore, the same query runs in 1.8 seconds. Using a columnstore is like indexing each column – with the noticeable advantage that data is highly compressed, which reduces the time required to load the tables in memory.

Columnstore indexes are extremely fast when scanning and performing group-by operations on a single table. Joins, on the other hand, are still an issue. If we look at the query plan of the SQL code, we notice an increased percentage impact of the Hash Match operator.

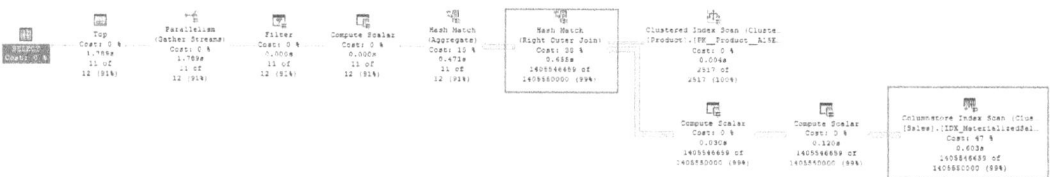

The Hash Match join operation accounts for 38% of the overall execution time. As before, the absolute time required to perform the match did not increase. What increases is the relative importance of the join operation compared to the others. Indeed, it is possible to optimize the scan operation, whereas joins are not improving at the same rate.

In more complex scenarios with increasing joins, the price of traversing relationships becomes even more relevant. When using VertiPaq, relationships are stored in an optimized structure that speeds up join operations. The physical structure of relationships in VertiPaq marks an important difference with

DirectQuery over SQL. Even though it is possible to obtain decent performance for table scans by using columnstore indexes, the absence of optimized data structures for relationships is a critical factor that makes DirectQuery slower than VertiPaq.

Choosing column data types

When we create a DirectQuery table in a Tabular model, the datatype of SQL Server columns is what drives our choice of the datatype of a Tabular column. For example, a SQL Server column of type TINYINT, INT, or BIGINT creates a column in the Tabular table of type INT (Whole Number). A SQL Server FLOAT or DOUBLE creates a Decimal Number.

Once the column has been created in the Tabular model, you can still change the datatype to a different one. For example, the *Sales[Net Price]* column in SQL Server is stored as MONEY, creating a CURRENCY column in Tabular. However, developers might later consider representing the Tabular column as a Decimal Number. This small change forces every SQL query to execute an expensive CAST, slowing down the entire query.

Let us elaborate on the concept with an example. The *Sales[Net Price]* column is stored as a MONEY datatype in SQL Server. MONEY in SQL Server corresponds to CURRENCY in Tabular. The following DAX query uses the *Sales[Net Price]* column:

```
EVALUATE
SUMMARIZECOLUMNS (
    'Product'[Brand],
    "Sales", SUMX ( Sales, Sales[Quantity] * Sales[Net Price] )
)
```

Once executed, it generates the following SQL query:

```
SELECT TOP (1000001) *
FROM (
    SELECT [t2_Brand],
        SUM([a0]) AS [a0]
    FROM (
        SELECT [t2].[Brand] AS [t2_Brand],
            [t3].[Quantity] AS [t3_Quantity],
            [t3].[Net Price] AS [t3_Net Price],
            ([t3].[Quantity] * [t3].[Net Price]) AS [a0]
        FROM (
            [Data].[Sales] AS [t3]
                LEFT JOIN [dbo].[Product] AS [t2] ON ([t3].[ProductKey] = [t2].[ProductKey])
            )
        ) AS [t0]
    GROUP BY [t2_Brand]
    ) AS [MainTable]
WHERE (NOT (([a0] IS NULL)))
```

The execution time of the SQL query is around 1.5 seconds.

Total	SE CPU		Line	Subclass	Duration	CPU	Par.	Rows	KB	Timeline
1,553 ms	1,546 ms		1	SQL	1,546	1,546	x1.0			
	x1.0									

FE	SE
9 ms	1,544 ms
0.6%	99.5%

SE Queries	SE Cache
1	0
	0.0%

	Total DQ
	1,546 ms

```
SELECT TOP (1000001) *
FROM (
    SELECT [t2_Brand],
        SUM([a0]) AS [a0]
    FROM (
        SELECT [t2].[Brand] AS [t2_Brand],
            [t3].[Quantity] AS [t3_Quantity],
            [t3].[Net Price] AS [t3_Net Price],
            ([t3].[Quantity] * [t3].[Net Price]) AS [a0]
        FROM (
```

However, if we change the datatype of *Sales[Net Price]* in Tabular to a Decimal Number, then the same query includes a CAST operation:

```
SELECT TOP (1000001) *
FROM (
    SELECT [t2_Brand],
        SUM([a0]) AS [a0]
    FROM (
        SELECT [t2].[Brand] AS [t2_Brand],
            [t3].[Quantity] AS [t3_Quantity],
            [t3].[Net Price] AS [t3_Net Price],
            ([t3].[Quantity] * [t3].[Net Price]) AS [a0]
        FROM (
            (
                SELECT [ProductKey],
                    [Quantity],
                    CAST([Net Price] AS FLOAT) AS [Net Price]
                FROM ([Data].[Sales]) AS [t3]
            ) AS [t3]
            LEFT JOIN [dbo].[Product] AS [t2] ON ([t3].[ProductKey] = [t2].[ProductKey])
        )
    ) AS [t0]
    GROUP BY [t2_Brand]
) AS [MainTable]
WHERE (NOT (([a0] IS NULL)))
```

The price to pay is extremely high. The query running in 1.5 seconds now runs in around 3 seconds.

Total	SE CPU		Line	Subclass	Duration	CPU	Par.	Rows	KB	Timeline
3,032 ms	3,028 ms									
	×1.0		1	SQL	3,028	3,028	×1.0			

FE	SE	
4 ms	3,028 ms	
0.1%	99.9%	

SE Queries SE Cache
1   0
           0.0%

Total DQ
3,028 ms

```
SELECT TOP (1000001) *
FROM (
  SELECT [t2_Brand],
    SUM([a0]) AS [a0]
  FROM (
    SELECT [t2].[Brand] AS [t2_Brand],
      [t3].[Quantity] AS [t3_Quantity],
      [t3].[Net Price] AS [t3_Net Price],
      ([t3].[Quantity] * [t3].[Net Price]) AS [a0]
    FROM (
```

A simple operation like CAST is fast. However, even a tiny number becomes important when the operation is executed billions of times. Moreover, the CAST operation makes the query more complex, making it harder for SQL Server to optimize it. While this is not the case in such a simple scenario, the resulting SQL query might be much more complicated in more complex queries.

Another critical aspect of data types is the allowed range of values. SQL Server offers many data types with similar characteristics but with different ranges of values. Speaking about integers, SQL Server offers four different data types: TINYINT, SMALLINT, INT, and BIGINT, using respectively 1, 2, 4, or 8 bytes. From a storage point of view, database administrators often choose the smallest type of integer to store all the possible values required for a column. This choice reduces the space the database uses, thus improving performance.

Tabular, on the other hand, uses only one type for integers: INT. Tabular integer values all use the maximum range, using 8 bytes, the largest range. The simplicity of Tabular comes from the fact that – in VertiPaq – most columns are hash-encoded, making the integer range less important for optimization purposes. Letting developers choose between different data types results in an unnecessary complication without tangible benefits.

The different way of handling value ranges also affects the aggregation of values. A column may contain values that can be stored – individually – in a SMALLINT, ranging from -32,768 to +32,767. However, when summing millions of rows, the sum of all the values likely exceeds the range. If this happens in a SQL query, it results in an overflow error.

For example, the *Quantity* column in *Sales* is of type INT, but a simple aggregation in SQL Server fails:

```
SELECT SUM ( [Quantity] ) FROM Data.Sales
```

The previous SQL query generates an error:

```
Msg 8115, Level 16, State 2, Line 1
Arithmetic overflow error converting expression to data type int.
```

For this reason, Tabular always casts columns to the largest data type, making SQL Server use BIGINT math calculations also on INT columns. For example, the following query generates an SQL query with a cast:

```
EVALUATE
SUMMARIZECOLUMNS (
    "Sales", SUM ( Sales[Quantity] )
)
```

The SQL code generated is the following:

```
SELECT SUM(CAST([t3].[Quantity] AS BIGINT)) AS [a0]
FROM ([Data].[Sales]) AS [t3]
```

The SQL query is executed in around 200 milliseconds.

Total	SE CPU		Line	Subclass	Duration	CPU	Par.	Rows	KB	Timeline
238 ms	235 ms									
	x1.0		1	SQL	235	235	x1.0			

FE	SE
3 ms	235 ms
1.3%	98.7%

SELECT SUM(CAST([t3].[Quantity] **AS BIGINT**)) **AS** [a0]
FROM ([Data].[Sales1]) **AS** [t3]

SE Queries	SE Cache
1	0
	0.0%

Total DQ
235 ms

The CAST operation is unnecessary if the *Quantity* column is already a BIGINT in SQL. To simulate this, we added a new column, *QuantityBigInt,* using a BIGINT datatype:

```
EVALUATE
SUMMARIZECOLUMNS (
    "Sales", SUM ( Sales[QuantityBigInt] )
)
```

The CAST operation is no longer present, and the query is much faster.

Total	SE CPU		Line	Subclass	Duration	CPU	Par.	Rows	KB	Timeline
31 ms	26 ms		1	SQL	27	26	x1.0			
	x1.0									

FE	SE
4 ms	27 ms
12.9%	87.1%

SELECT SUM([t3].[QuantityBigInt]) **AS** [a0]
FROM ([Data].[Sales1]) **AS** [t3]

SE Queries	SE Cache
1	0
	0.0%

Total DQ
27 ms

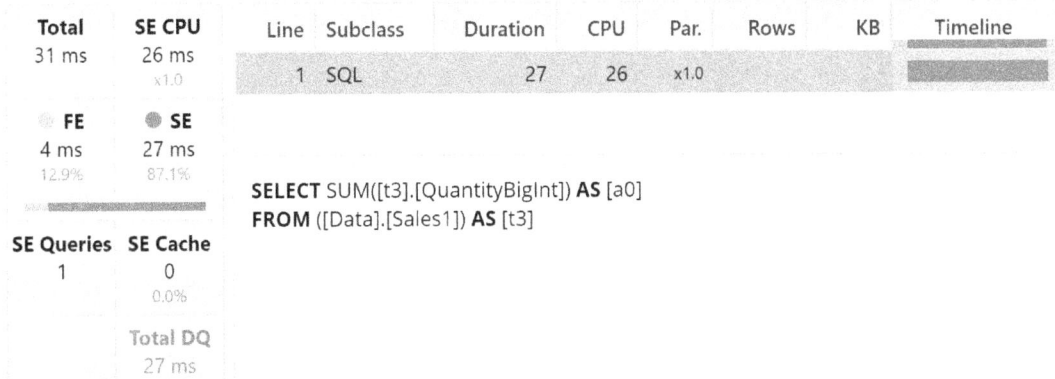

Developers should evaluate the benefits of storing the correct data type in SQL Server and the increased space used in the database. As usual, there are no golden rules: extensive testing is needed to find the correct balance for your specific scenario.

Do not use Power Query transformations

When using DirectQuery, there is a limit on the types of transformations that can be executed through Power Query. If the model uses DirectQuery, then the Query Folding feature must be active. In a Power Query transformation, the query folding is active if the entire transformation can be pushed to the server as a single SQL statement.

The rationale for the limitation is relatively straightforward. Every DAX query generates several SQL queries; these SQL queries cannot require the intervention of the Power Query M engine, or else performance would suffer.

From a more practical standpoint, we suggest avoiding any type of M transformation, including those that maintain query folding. Indeed, any Power Query transformation requires more complex SQL code that must be executed for every query. We have already demonstrated that a simple datatype cast operation has a very high cost; the same – if not worse – applies to any other transformation.

When using DirectQuery, the key to performance is simplicity. The best practice is to precompute all the columns of all the tables with the proper data type already set in SQL, materialize the content in a column store, and make it available to your Tabular model through a simple SELECT statement.

Optimizing relationships

Making sure the relationships in your model are optimized is of paramount importance in the design of the database. This section analyzes relationships in more detail, as well as how to ensure they are appropriately designed.

Choosing the best data type for relationships

When working with VertiPaq, the data type of a column does not really matter. Most columns are hash-encoded; therefore, the data type impacts only the dictionary size. Specifically for relationships, neither the data type nor the type of encoding has any measurable effect on the performance of the relationship.

SQL Server is different. In SQL Server, an integer is the best data type for a column involved in a relationship. Other data types may slow down the join operations.

We have created a new column in both *Customer* and *Sales* to demonstrate this fact. We used a GUID as an alternate primary key in *Customer* and added the same GUID in *Sales*. Then, we duplicated the relationship between *Customer* and *Sales*: the active relationship uses *Sales[CustomerKey]*, whereas the inactive relationship uses *Sales[CustomerGuidKey]*.

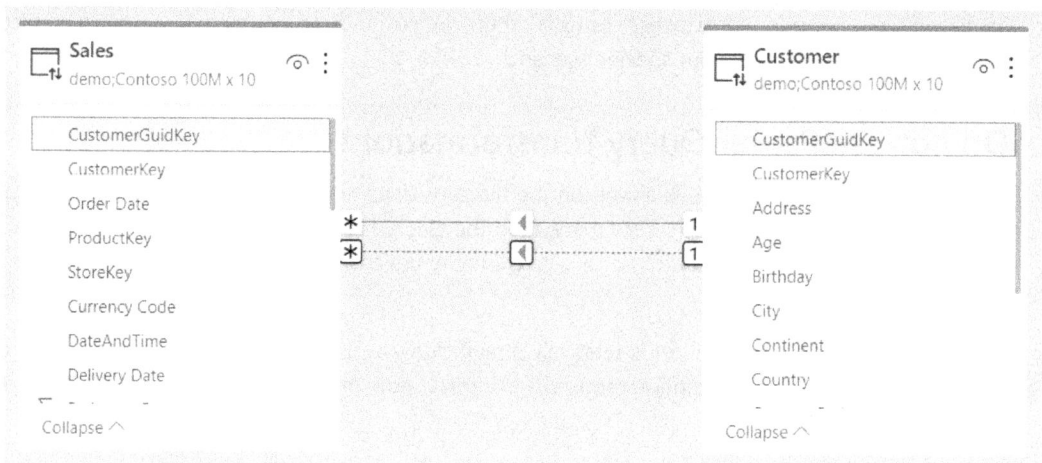

We tested the performance of both relationships by executing a simple aggregation of *Sales* by *Customer[Continent]*, activating first one relationship and then the other:

```
EVALUATE
SUMMARIZECOLUMNS (
    Customer[Continent],
    "Sales", [Sales Amount]
)
```

The first execution runs using the relationship between *Sales[CustomerKey]* and *Customer[CustomerKey]*, an integer column. The SQL code generated shows that the join between *Sales* and *Customer* uses the integer columns:

```
SELECT TOP (1000001) *
FROM (
    SELECT [t0_Continent],
        SUM([a0]) AS [a0]
    FROM (
        SELECT [t0].[Continent] AS [t0_Continent],
            [t3].[Quantity] AS [t3_Quantity],
            [t3].[Net Price] AS [t3_Net Price],
            ([t3].[Quantity] * [t3].[Net Price]) AS [a0]
        FROM (
            [Data].[Sales1] AS [t3]
                LEFT JOIN [dbo].[Customer] AS [t0]
                    ON ([t3].[CustomerKey] = [t0].[CustomerKey])
            )
        ) AS [t0]
    GROUP BY [t0_Continent]
    ) AS [MainTable]
WHERE (NOT (([a0] IS NULL)))
```

Performance-wise, the SQL query is relatively fast, running in around 3.5 seconds.

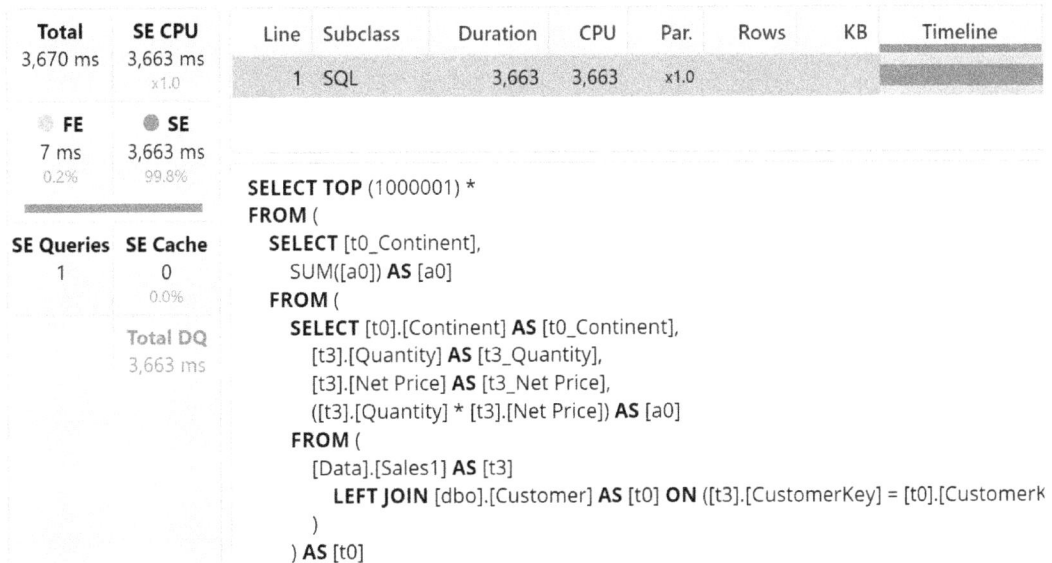

Total	SE CPU		Line	Subclass	Duration	CPU	Par.	Rows	KB	Timeline
3,670 ms	3,663 ms									
	x1.0		1	SQL	3,663	3,663	x1.0			

FE	SE
7 ms	3,663 ms
0.2%	99.8%

SE Queries	SE Cache
1	0
	0.0%

Total DQ
3,663 ms

```
SELECT TOP (1000001) *
FROM (
  SELECT [t0_Continent],
    SUM([a0]) AS [a0]
  FROM (
    SELECT [t0].[Continent] AS [t0_Continent],
      [t3].[Quantity] AS [t3_Quantity],
      [t3].[Net Price] AS [t3_Net Price],
      ([t3].[Quantity] * [t3].[Net Price]) AS [a0]
    FROM (
      [Data].[Sales1] AS [t3]
        LEFT JOIN [dbo].[Customer] AS [t0] ON ([t3].[CustomerKey] = [t0].[Customerk
      )
    ) AS [t0]
```

Suppose we deactivate the relationship using *Sales[CustomerKey]* and *Customer[CustomerKey]*, and activate the relationship based on the GUID. In that case, the SQL code shows that the join uses the GUID column:

```
SELECT TOP (1000001) *
FROM (
    SELECT [t0_Continent],
        SUM([a0]) AS [a0]
    FROM (
        SELECT [t0].[Continent] AS [t0_Continent],
            [t3].[Quantity] AS [t3_Quantity],
            [t3].[Net Price] AS [t3_Net Price],
            ([t3].[Quantity] * [t3].[Net Price]) AS [a0]
        FROM (
            [Data].[Sales1] AS [t3]
                LEFT JOIN [dbo].[Customer] AS [t0]
                    ON ([t3].[CustomerGuidKey] = [t0].[CustomerGuidKey])
        )
    ) AS [t0]
    GROUP BY [t0_Continent]
) AS [MainTable]
WHERE (NOT (([a0] IS NULL)))
```

The server timings show a substantial degradation in terms of performance.

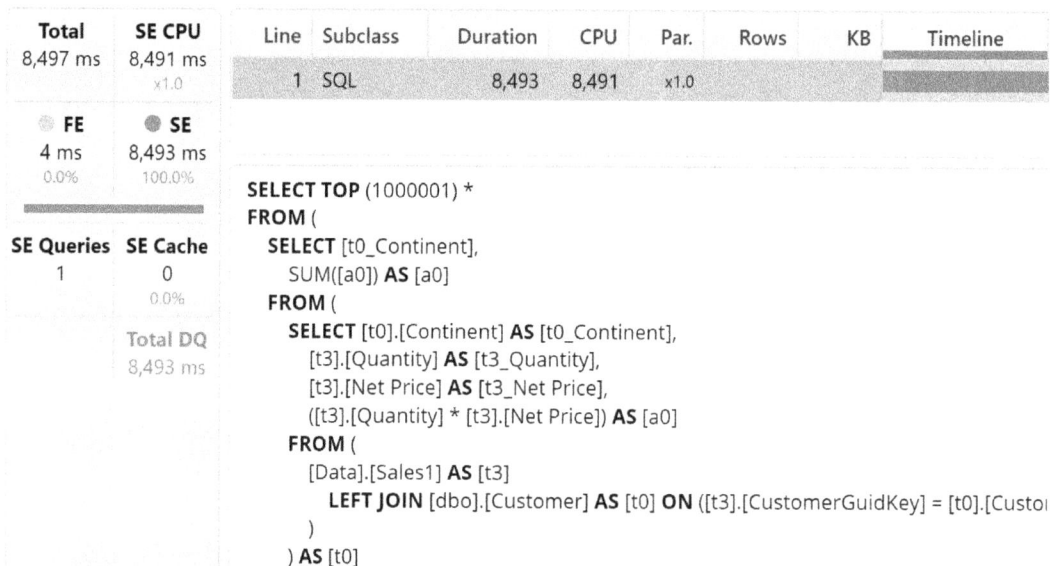

Total	SE CPU	Line	Subclass	Duration	CPU	Par.	Rows	KB	Timeline
8,497 ms	8,491 ms ×1.0	1	SQL	8,493	8,491	×1.0			

FE	SE
4 ms	8,493 ms
0.0%	100.0%

SE Queries	SE Cache
1	0
	0.0%

Total DQ
8,493 ms

```
SELECT TOP (1000001) *
FROM (
  SELECT [t0_Continent],
    SUM([a0]) AS [a0]
  FROM (
    SELECT [t0].[Continent] AS [t0_Continent],
      [t3].[Quantity] AS [t3_Quantity],
      [t3].[Net Price] AS [t3_Net Price],
      ([t3].[Quantity] * [t3].[Net Price]) AS [a0]
    FROM (
      [Data].[Sales1] AS [t3]
        LEFT JOIN [dbo].[Customer] AS [t0] ON ([t3].[CustomerGuidKey] = [t0].[Custo
      )
    ) AS [t0]
```

Be mindful that the performance penalty of the GUID in the relationship is enormous, as the query now runs in 8.5 seconds instead of around 3.5 seconds when we used the integer column for the relationship: the execution time has more than doubled. This additional cost is applied whenever a query needs to group *Sales* by any column in *Customer*.

Relying on referential integrity

In the previous chapter, we introduced the flag to control referential integrity in a relationship, to drive

Tabular to use INNER joins rather than OUTER joins. Depending on the model, the hardware running SQL, the architecture of the SQL database, and the data quality, you can obtain different performance levels using one of the two types of joins.

Be mindful that constantly activating the flag is not a best practice. We have noticed mixed results in different environments. Moreover, as we will see in the next chapter, activating the flag can benefit some queries, and yet it may slow down others. Therefore, we recommend extensive testing every single time before making any decisions.

Let us briefly recap the feature. You can enable the "Assume referential integrity" flag when editing a relationship.

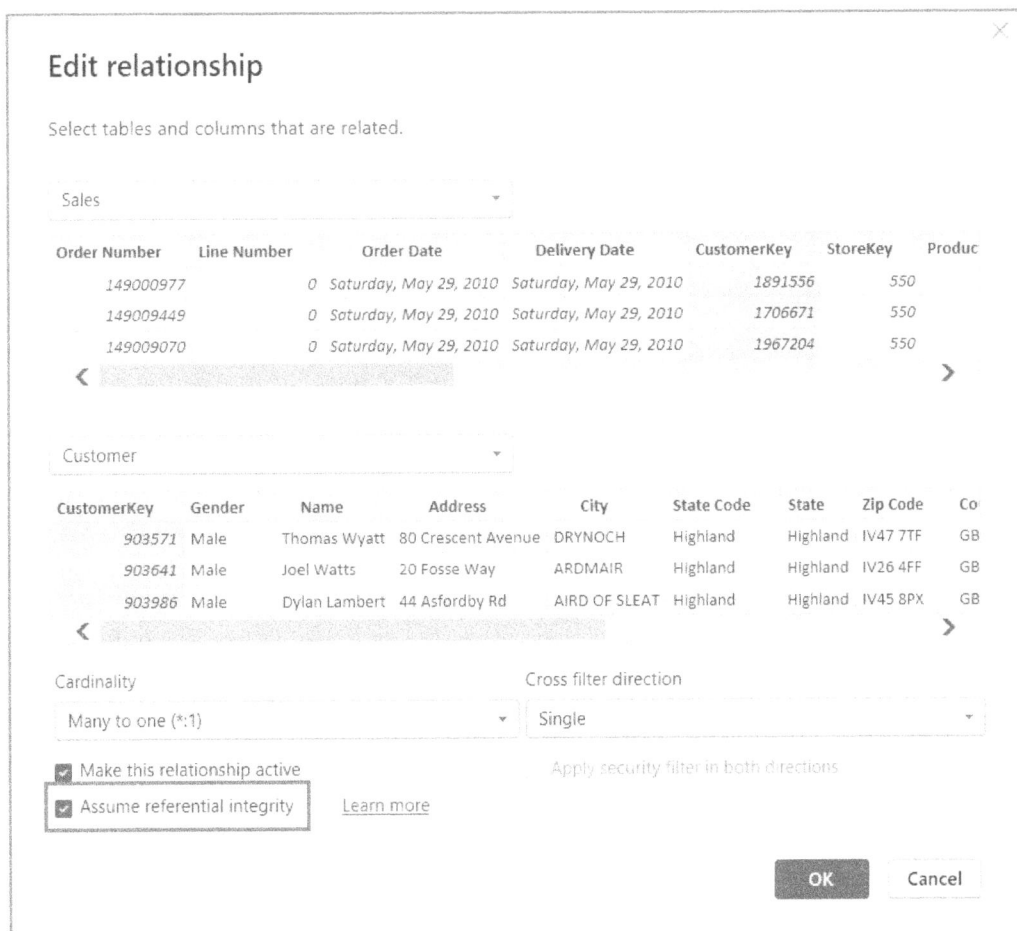

Tabular uses an INNER JOIN to query the model when the flag is enabled. When the flag is disabled, Tabular uses an OUTER JOIN, assuming the relationship may be invalid. The engine does not perform any runtime checks about the validity of the relationship. Consequently, the developer oversees the validation of the relationship.

A simple query like the following shows the difference:

```
EVALUATE
SUMMARIZECOLUMNS (
    Customer[Continent],
    "Sales", [Sales Amount]
)
```

When executed, the DAX query produces a single SQL query:

```
SELECT TOP (1000001) *
FROM (
    SELECT [t0_Continent],
        SUM([a0]) AS [a0]
    FROM (
        SELECT [t0].[Continent] AS [t0_Continent],
            [t3].[Quantity] AS [t3_Quantity],
            [t3].[Net Price] AS [t3_Net Price],
            ([t3].[Quantity] * [t3].[Net Price]) AS [a0]
        FROM (
            [Data].[Sales] AS [t3]
                INNER JOIN [dbo].[Customer] AS [t0]
                    ON ([t3].[CustomerKey] = [t0].[CustomerKey])
        )
        ) AS [t0]
    GROUP BY [t0_Continent]
    ) AS [MainTable]
WHERE (NOT (([a0] IS NULL)))
```

DirectQuery implements the JOIN between *Sales* and *Customer* with an INNER JOIN rather than an OUTER join. Executing the query with the referential integrity flag set (therefore with an INNER JOIN) shows 5.6 seconds of SE CPU.

Total	SE CPU	Line	Subclass	Duration	CPU	Par.	Rows	KB	Timeline
5,651 ms	5,647 ms x1.0	1	SQL	5,647	5,647	x1.0			

FE	SE
4 ms	5,647 ms
0.1%	99.9%

SE Queries	SE Cache
1	0
	0.0%

	Total DQ
	5,647 ms

```
SELECT TOP (1000001) *
FROM (
    SELECT [t0_Continent],
        SUM([a0]) AS [a0]
    FROM (
        SELECT [t0].[Continent] AS [t0_Continent],
            [t3].[Quantity] AS [t3_Quantity],
            [t3].[Net Price] AS [t3_Net Price],
            ([t3].[Quantity] * [t3].[Net Price]) AS [a0]
```

If we clear the flag, the same DAX query generates a different SQL code using a LEFT JOIN:

```
SELECT TOP (1000001) *
FROM (
    SELECT [t0_Continent],
        SUM([a0]) AS [a0]
    FROM (
        SELECT [t0].[Continent] AS [t0_Continent],
            [t3].[Quantity] AS [t3_Quantity],
            [t3].[Net Price] AS [t3_Net Price],
            ([t3].[Quantity] * [t3].[Net Price]) AS [a0]
        FROM (
            [Data].[Sales] AS [t3]
                LEFT JOIN [dbo].[Customer] AS [t0]
                    ON ([t3].[CustomerKey] = [t0].[CustomerKey])
            )
        ) AS [t0]
    GROUP BY [t0_Continent]
    ) AS [MainTable]
WHERE (NOT (([a0] IS NULL)))
```

Performance-wise, this query runs in around 5.1 seconds.

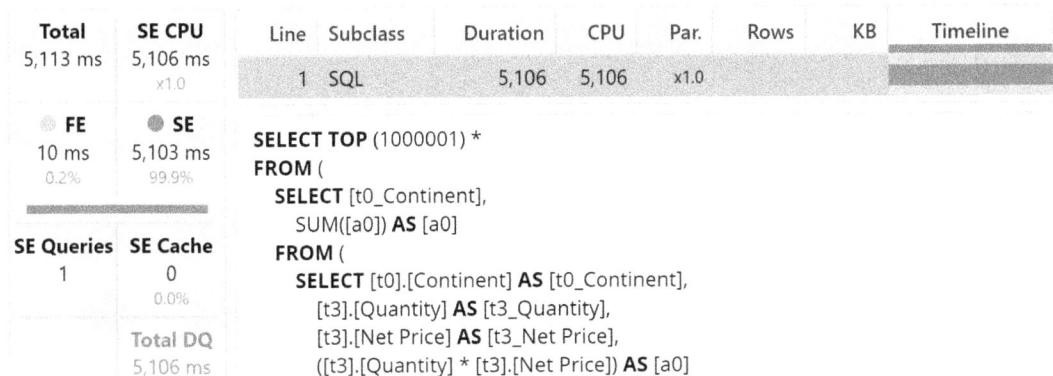

Total	SE CPU	Line	Subclass	Duration	CPU	Par.	Rows	KB	Timeline
5,113 ms	5,106 ms								
	×1.0	1	SQL	5,106	5,106	×1.0			

FE	SE
10 ms	5,103 ms
0.2%	99.9%

SE Queries	SE Cache
1	0
	0.0%
	Total DQ
	5,106 ms

```
SELECT TOP (1000001) *
FROM (
    SELECT [t0_Continent],
        SUM([a0]) AS [a0]
    FROM (
        SELECT [t0].[Continent] AS [t0_Continent],
            [t3].[Quantity] AS [t3_Quantity],
            [t3].[Net Price] AS [t3_Net Price],
            ([t3].[Quantity] * [t3].[Net Price]) AS [a0]
```

In this first example, it looks like the LEFT JOIN is faster. Indeed, the *Sales* table uses a columnstore, where left joins are typically slightly faster than inner joins. However, as we said in the introduction, the difference in performance needs to be carefully measured because the benefits of INNER JOIN, if any, depend on multiple factors.

From the SQL Server point of view, left joins are usually slightly better if data is stored using a columnstore. In a regular rowstore, inner joins might perform better on smaller databases, whereas left joins may still be faster on large databases. Do not take these rules as definitive ones. The number of cores, the speed of disks, the CPU architecture, and the number of rows in the relationships are just a few of the many factors that affect the performance of an SQL join operation.

However, SQL is just one of the factors to consider. The other, even more relevant, is DAX. When a relationship is invalid, Tabular adds a blank row to the one-side of the relationship to accommodate invalid rows. VertiPaq handles the blank row smoothly, whereas SQL Server does not. Consequently, the executed SQL queries – when the blank row is expected – are much more complex. In the next chapter, we analyze one of these scenarios. In this section, we are mainly interested in analyzing the SQL Server performance.

To provide more details, we created two test databases: in both scenarios, we created a copy of both *Sales* and *Customer* using heaps. Then, we created two indexes to cover the test query:

```
SELECT Sales.*
INTO Data.Sales1
FROM Data.Sales WITH ( TABLOCK )

GO

SELECT Customer.*
INTO Data.Customer1
FROM Data.Customer WITH ( TABLOCK )
GO

CREATE CLUSTERED INDEX CustomerIndex ON Data.Customer1 ( CustomerKey )
GO

CREATE NONCLUSTERED INDEX SalesIndex ON [Data].[Sales1] (Quantity, [Net Price],
[CustomerKey] )

GO
```

Finally, we executed the test queries with both INNER and LEFT joins in two databases – one with 2.4B rows, and one with 1.8M rows:

```
SET STATISTICS TIME ON
GO
SELECT TOP (1000001) *
FROM (
    SELECT [t0_Continent],
        SUM( [a0] ) AS [a0]
    FROM (
        SELECT [t0].[Continent] AS [t0_Continent],
            [t3].[Quantity] AS [t3_Quantity],
            [t3].[Net Price] AS [t3_Net Price],
            ([t3].[Quantity] * [t3].[Net Price]) AS [a0]
        FROM (
            [Data].[Sales1] AS [t3]
                LEFT JOIN [Data].[Customer1] AS [t0]
                    ON ( [t3].[CustomerKey] = [t0].[CustomerKey] )
            )
        ) AS [t0]
    GROUP BY [t0_Continent]
    ) AS [MainTable]
WHERE (NOT (([a0] IS NULL)))
```

Here are the results we gathered by using three different sizes of databases joining the rowstore version of Sales and Customer. The execution time is in milliseconds.

Database	LEFT JOIN	INNER JOIN
Contoso 100M x 10	14,484	17,346
Contoso 100M	13,200	9,233
Contoso 10M	689	653

As you see, it looks like INNER JOIN runs slower on large databases, whereas INNER JOIN wins on smaller databases. Given the many factors contributing to the difference, there is no golden rule. However, a wise Tabular developer must measure the performance of different queries with different databases to decide how to set the flag.

Using COMBINEVALUES to implement multi-column relationships

In the VertiPaq chapters, we discussed currency conversion, and tested different solutions to compute the currency conversion for each transaction date. For example, we considered a relationship between *Currency Exchange* and *Sales* based on the source currency and the order date. This solution requires creating a new column containing the concatenation of the order date and the source currency because Tabular only supports relationships based on a single column. This solution is not a good option in Vertipaq because of its high memory cost and processing time.

The same solution is more interesting in DirectQuery. Because DirectQuery does not materialize calculated columns, calculated columns thus do not increase the model size. However, developers should use COMBINEVALUES rather than string operators to concatenate multiple columns in calculated columns used in a relationship. The reason is that COMBINEVALUES allows Tabular to use a JOIN with the various columns used in COMBINEVALUES rather than a JOIN on a single calculated column with the concatenated string. Indeed, SQL supports JOIN operators with multiple columns, producing better performance than performing a join with a single concatenated string.

To demonstrate this, we create two calculated columns in *Sales* and *Currency Exchange*:

```
-----------------------------------------------------
-- Calculated column in 'Currency Exchange' table
-----------------------------------------------------
CurrencyDate =
'Currency Exchange'[FromCurrency] & "-"
    & 'Currency Exchange'[ToCurrency] & "-"
    & 'Currency Exchange'[Date]


-------------------------------------------
-- Calculated column in Sales table
-------------------------------------------
CurrencyDate = Sales[Currency Code] & "-USD-" & Sales[Order Date]
```

Once the two columns are in place, we link the two tables based on a regular one-to-many relationship.

Finally, we execute the following DAX query to compute the sales amount in the original currency:

```
EVALUATE
SUMMARIZECOLUMNS (
    Sales[Currency Code],
    "Original Currency",
        SUMX (
            Sales,
            Sales[Quantity] * Sales[Net Price] / RELATED ( 'Currency Exchange'[Exchange] )
        )
)
```

The code traverses the relationship based on the calculated columns. As we know, DirectQuery does not materialize calculated columns. Therefore, the corresponding SQL query contains the definition of the calculated columns in subqueries:

```
SELECT TOP (1000001) *
FROM (
    SELECT [t3_Currency Code],
        SUM([a0]) AS [a0]
    FROM (
        SELECT [t3].[Quantity] AS [t3_Quantity],
            [t3].[Net Price] AS [t3_Net Price],
            [t3].[Currency Code] AS [t3_Currency Code],
            [t5].[Exchange] AS [t5_Exchange],
            (([t3].[Quantity] * [t3].[Net Price]) / COALESCE(CAST([t5].[Exchange] AS MONEY),
0)) AS
            [a0]
        FROM (
            (
                SELECT [t3].[Quantity] AS [Quantity],
                    [t3].[Net Price] AS [Net Price],
                    [t3].[Currency Code] AS [Currency Code],
                    (
                        COALESCE(RTRIM([t3].[Currency Code]), '') + (N'-USD-' +
                        COALESCE(CAST([t3].[Order Date] AS VARCHAR(4000)), '')
                        )
                    ) AS [CurrencyDate]
                FROM ([Data].[Sales]) AS [t3]
                ) AS [t3]
                LEFT JOIN (
                SELECT [t5].[Exchange] AS [Exchange],
                    (
                        COALESCE(RTRIM([t5].[FromCurrency]), '') + (
                        N'-' + (
                            COALESCE(RTRIM([t5].[ToCurrency]), '') +
                            (N'-' + COALESCE(CAST([t5].[Date] AS VARCHAR(4000)), '')
                            )
                        )
                        )
                    ) AS [CurrencyDate]
                FROM ([dbo].[Currency Exchange]) AS [t5]
                ) AS [t5] ON ([t3].[CurrencyDate] = [t5].[CurrencyDate])
            )
        ) AS [t0]
    GROUP BY [t3_Currency Code]
    ) AS [MainTable]
WHERE (NOT (([a0] IS NULL)))
```

Unfortunately, the query is very slow. The issue is not the calculation of the columns inside the SELECT statements. The problem is the join based on the calculated columns between *t3* and *t5*. As we can see, the query runs in around 26 seconds.

Total	SE CPU		Line	Subclass	Duration	CPU	Par.	Rows	KB	Timeline
26,334 ms	26,327 ms		1	SQL	26,330	26,327	x1.0			
	x1.0									

FE	SE
4 ms	26,330 ms
0.0%	100.0%

SE Queries	SE Cache
1	0
	0.0%

Total DQ
26,330 ms

```
SELECT TOP (1000001) *
FROM (
    SELECT [t3_Currency Code],
      SUM([a0]) AS [a0]
    FROM (
        SELECT [t3].[Quantity] AS [t3_Quantity],
          [t3].[Net Price] AS [t3_Net Price],
          [t3].[Currency Code] AS [t3_Currency Code],
          [t5].[Exchange] AS [t5_Exchange],
```

We used a calculated column to create the relationship between the two tables. The calculated column is nothing but a string concatenation of three other columns. Building the relationship between *Sales* and *Currency Exchange* using the existing columns would have been better if we had the option. However, this is not possible in Tabular; you should modify the SQL data source to enable that scenario. By using a complex expression in the join condition, the SQL Server engine must compute the expression for each row before executing the join, which makes the execution very expensive.

To let the engine run the query using a join on multiple columns without expressions in the join condition, we must create the calculated column using COMBINEVALUES. COMBINEVALUES creates a calculated column with the same content as the column using string concatenation. The difference is that when a relationship references the column, COMBINEVALUES can join the tables using the parameters of COMBINEVALUES rather than the result of the calculated column expression.

However, the optimization provided by COMBINEVALUES only kicks in if all its arguments are model columns. If one of the arguments is an expression, the optimization is disabled. It is precisely for this reason that our first trial will not work.

We change the definition of the columns by using COMBINEVALUES:

```
----------------------------------------------------
-- Calculated column in 'Currency Exchange' table
----------------------------------------------------
CurrencyDate =
COMBINEVALUES (
    "-",
    'Currency Exchange'[FromCurrency],
    'Currency Exchange'[ToCurrency],
    'Currency Exchange'[Date]
)


-------------------------------------
-- Calculated column in Sales table
-------------------------------------
CurrencyDate = COMBINEVALUES ( "-", Sales[Currency Code], "USD", Sales[Order Date] )
```

If we execute our test query again, it runs slower than the previous test (28 seconds instead of 26) because the join still references the calculated column expression. Here are the server timings.

Total	SE CPU	Line	Subclass	Duration	CPU	Par.	Rows	KB	Timeline
28,123 ms	28,107 ms								
	x1.0	1	SQL	28,107	28,107	x1.0			

FE	SE
16 ms	28,107 ms
0.1%	99.9%

SE Queries	SE Cache
1	0
	0.0%

	Total DQ
	28,107 ms

```
SELECT TOP (1000001) *
FROM (
  SELECT [t3_Currency Code],
    SUM([a0]) AS [a0]
  FROM (
    SELECT [t3].[Quantity] AS [t3_Quantity],
      [t3].[Net Price] AS [t3_Net Price],
      [t3].[Currency Code] AS [t3_Currency Code],
      [t5].[Exchange] AS [t5_Exchange],
```

The SQL code executed for this first test of COMBINEVALUES is the following:

```
SELECT TOP (1000001) *
FROM (
    SELECT [t3_Currency Code],
        SUM([a0]) AS [a0]
    FROM (
        SELECT [t3].[Quantity] AS [t3_Quantity],
            [t3].[Net Price] AS [t3_Net Price],
            [t3].[Currency Code] AS [t3_Currency Code],
            [t5].[Exchange] AS [t5_Exchange],
            (([t3].[Quantity] * [t3].[Net Price])
                / COALESCE(CAST([t5].[Exchange] AS MONEY), 0)) AS [a0]
        FROM (
            (
                SELECT [t3].[Quantity] AS [Quantity],
                    [t3].[Net Price] AS [Net Price],
                    [t3].[Currency Code] AS [Currency Code],
                    (
                        COALESCE(RTRIM([t3].[Currency Code]), '') + (
                            N'-' + (N'USD' + (N'-' +
                            COALESCE(CAST([t3].[Order Date] AS VARCHAR(4000)), ''))
                                )
                            )
                    ) AS [CurrencyDate]
                FROM ([Data].[Sales]) AS [t3]
            ) AS [t3]
```

```
                    LEFT JOIN (
                    SELECT [t5].[Exchange] AS [Exchange],
                        (
                            COALESCE(RTRIM([t5].[FromCurrency]), '') + (
                                N'-' + (
                                    COALESCE(RTRIM([t5].[ToCurrency]), '') +
                                    (N'-' + COALESCE(CAST([t5].[Date] AS VARCHAR(4000)), '')
                                    )
                                )
                            )
                        ) AS [CurrencyDate]
                    FROM ([dbo].[Currency Exchange]) AS [t5]
                    ) AS [t5] ON ([t3].[CurrencyDate] = [t5].[CurrencyDate])
                )
            ) AS [t0]


        GROUP BY [t3_Currency Code]
        ) AS [MainTable]
    WHERE (NOT (([a0] IS NULL)))
```

COMBINEVALUES does not trigger the expected optimization because one of the arguments is a constant string. COMBINEVALUES requires all arguments to be column references to perform its optimization. There are two possible solutions: the first is to create a new table for the currency conversion that only includes USD as the target currency. By doing so, the source currency and the date together act as a table, and we can use COMBINEVALUES with only two columns – we thus avoid the constant value of USD. However, this requires changing the model and adding a table to obtain better performance in a measure.

A better option is to overcome the limitation of COMBINEVALUES by creating another calculated column containing a constant value. Remember that calculated columns do not use memory in DirectQuery, which computes them on the fly as part of the query. Despite this usually being a disadvantage, it is an excellent option in this specific scenario because it lets us use COMBINEVALUES with model columns only.

We create a new calculated column USD containing the constant value "USD":

```
----------------------------------------
-- Calculated column in Sales table
----------------------------------------
USD = "USD"
```

Then, we change the definition of the calculated column in *Sales*:

```
--------------------------------------
-- Calculated column in Sales table
--------------------------------------
CurrencyDate =
COMBINEVALUES (
    "-",
    Sales[Currency Code],
    Sales[USD],
    Sales[Order Date]
)
```

Now, all the arguments of COMBINEVALUES are columns. This simple modification produces a different SQL query:

```
SELECT TOP (1000001) *
FROM (
    SELECT [t3_Currency Code],
        SUM([a0]) AS [a0]
    FROM (
        SELECT [t3].[Quantity] AS [t3_Quantity],
            [t3].[Net Price] AS [t3_Net Price],
            [t3].[Currency Code] AS [t3_Currency Code],
            [t5].[Exchange] AS [t5_Exchange],
            (([t3].[Quantity] * [t3].[Net Price])
                / COALESCE(CAST([t5].[Exchange] AS MONEY), 0)) AS [a0]
        FROM (
            (
                SELECT [t3_Order Date] AS [Order Date],
                    [t3_Quantity] AS [Quantity],
                    [t3_Net Price] AS [Net Price],
                    [t3_Currency Code] AS [Currency Code],
                    (
                        COALESCE(RTRIM([t3_Currency Code]), '') + (
                            N'-' + (
                                COALESCE([c66], '') +
                                (N'-' + COALESCE(CAST([t3_Order Date] AS VARCHAR(4000)), '')
                                )
                            )
                        )
                    ) AS [CurrencyDate],
                    [c66] AS [USD]
                FROM (
                    SELECT [t3].[Order Date] AS [t3_Order Date],
                        [t3].[Quantity] AS [t3_Quantity],
                        [t3].[Net Price] AS [t3_Net Price],
                        [t3].[Currency Code] AS [t3_Currency Code],
                        N'USD' AS [c66]
                    FROM ([Data].[Sales]) AS [t3]
                    ) AS [t3]
                ) AS [t3]
```

```
            LEFT JOIN (
            SELECT [t5].[Date] AS [Date],
                [t5].[FromCurrency] AS [FromCurrency],
                [t5].[ToCurrency] AS [ToCurrency],
                [t5].[Exchange] AS [Exchange],
                (
                    COALESCE(RTRIM([t5].[FromCurrency]), '') + (
                        N'-' + (
                            COALESCE(RTRIM([t5].[ToCurrency]), '') +
                            (N'-' + COALESCE(CAST([t5].[Date] AS VARCHAR(4000)), '')
                            )
                        )
                    )
                ) AS [CurrencyDate]
            FROM ([dbo].[Currency Exchange]) AS [t5]
            ) AS [t5] ON (
                ([t3].[Currency Code] = [t5].[FromCurrency])
                AND ([t3].[USD] = [t5].[ToCurrency])
                AND ([t3].[Order Date] = [t5].[Date])
                )
            )
        ) AS [t0]
    GROUP BY [t3_Currency Code]
    ) AS [MainTable]
WHERE (NOT (([a0] IS NULL)))
```

The join between *t3* and *t5* now uses multiple model columns instead of the calculated column expression. The boost in terms of performance is impressive: the query runs in only four seconds instead of the 26-28 seconds of the previous tests.

Total	SE CPU	Line	Subclass	Duration	CPU	Par.	Rows	KB	Timeline
4,184 ms	4,176 ms								
	x1.0	1	SQL	4,176	4,176	x1.0			

FE	SE
9 ms	4,175 ms
0.2%	99.8%

SE Queries	SE Cache
1	0
	0.0%

	Total DQ
	4,176 ms

```
SELECT TOP (1000001) *
FROM (
    SELECT [t3_Currency Code],
        SUM([a0]) AS [a0]
    FROM (
        SELECT [t3].[Quantity] AS [t3_Quantity],
            [t3].[Net Price] AS [t3_Net Price],
            [t3].[Currency Code] AS [t3_Currency Code],
            [t5].[Exchange] AS [t5_Exchange],
```

As you have seen in this example, the key to performance in DirectQuery is to drive the engine into using efficient SQL code. COMBINEVALUES is explicitly designed for this scenario and is worth using.

Using aggregations

To avoid scanning large fact tables to aggregate values, developers can create aggregated tables to obtain faster calculations thanks to a reduced table granularity. Aggregations can be either data source tables (like SQL Server) or VertiPaq tables. For them to work, aggregations require a correct configuration.

We cannot cover all the details about aggregations in this section. While it is true that they are an important tool for DAX developers using DirectQuery, we do not have the space to cover all the technical details about their implementation. However, we point out the most interesting aspects of aggregations so that interested readers may dive deeper into the topic and master aggregations. Moreover, some non-trivial techniques are worth describing, like using calculated columns to use aggregations over complex calculations.

Introducing aggregations

We introduce aggregations with an example. Let us pretend our report includes a very frequently executed query that computes the sum of *Sales[Quantity]* grouped by *Customer[Continent]*, *Customer[Country]*, *Date[Year]*, and some user-defined attributes in *Product*. An example of such query is the following:

```
EVALUATE
    SUMMARIZECOLUMNS (
        'Date'[Year],
        'Product'[Brand],
        Customer[Continent],
        Customer[Country],
        "Quantity", SUM ( Sales[Quantity] )
    )
```

The query scans *Sales* and traverses three relationships: one with *Customer*, one with *Date*, and one with *Product*:

```
SELECT TOP (1000001) *
FROM (
    SELECT [t0].[Country] AS [t0_Country],
        [t0].[Continent] AS [t0_Continent],
        [t1].[Year] AS [t1_Year],
        [t2].[Brand] AS [t2_Brand],
        SUM(CAST([t3].[Quantity] AS BIGINT)) AS [a0]
    FROM (
        (
            (
                [Data].[Sales] AS [t3]
                    LEFT JOIN [dbo].[Customer] AS [t0]
                        ON ([t3].[CustomerKey] = [t0].[CustomerKey])
            )
            LEFT JOIN [dbo].[Date] AS [t1] ON ([t3].[Order Date] = [t1].[Date])
        )
        LEFT JOIN [dbo].[Product] AS [t2] ON ([t3].[ProductKey] = [t2].[ProductKey])
    )
    GROUP BY [t0].[Country],
        [t0].[Continent],
        [t1].[Year],
        [t2].[Brand]
) AS [MainTable]
WHERE (NOT (([a0] IS NULL)))
```

The query runs in around 3.5 seconds.

Total	SE CPU	Line	Subclass	Duration	CPU	Par.	Rows	KB	Timeline
3,453 ms	3,439 ms x1.0	2	SQL	3,440	3,439	x1.0			

FE	SE
13 ms	3,440 ms
0.4%	99.6%

SE Queries	SE Cache
1	0
	0.0%

Total DQ
3,440 ms

```
SELECT TOP (1000001) *
FROM (
    SELECT [t0].[Country] AS [t0_Country],
        [t0].[Continent] AS [t0_Continent],
        [t1].[Year] AS [t1_Year],
        [t2].[Brand] AS [t2_Brand],
        SUM(CAST([t3].[Quantity] AS BIGINT)) AS [a0]
    FROM (
        (
```

If you think about the amount of work required to scan 1.4 billion rows in *Sales*, traverse the relationships, and perform the math, performance is quite impressive here. However, if the query is executed regularly, precomputing most values would be better to reduce the number of rows scanned. An aggregation is a more compact version of the same data as the original table, with reduced granularity and some precomputed columns.

An aggregation can be created in the SQL Server database or as a VertiPaq table. We will first create it as a table in SQL Server and later transform it into a VertiPaq structure.

Note   Because the aggregation should speed up calculations, it does not make sense to create it as a view. Indeed, if we create an aggregation based on an SQL view, it would be executed for every query scanning the original table. However, the view makes sense when the goal is to create the aggregation as a VertiPaq object: a single execution of the view happens during data refresh and never again at query time.

We create the *Data.AggregatedSales* table in SQL Server with the following code:

```sql
SELECT
    [Date].[Year],
    [Date].[Year Month],
    [Date].[Year Month Number],
    ProductKey,
    Customer.CountryFull AS Country,
    Customer.Continent,
    SUM ( [Quantity] ) AS SumOfQuantity,
    SUM ( [Quantity] * [Net Price] ) AS SumOfAggLineAmount,
    COUNT ( [Quantity] ) AS CountOfQuantity
INTO Data.AggregatedSales
FROM
    Data.Sales WITH ( TABLOCK )
    INNER JOIN Data.Date WITH ( TABLOCK )
        ON [Order Date] = [Date]
    INNER JOIN Data.Customer WITH ( TABLOCK )
        ON Customer.CustomerKey = Sales.CustomerKey


GROUP BY
    ProductKey,
    [Date].[Year],
    [Date].[Year Month],
    [Date].[Year Month Number],
    Customer.CountryFull,
    Customer.Continent
GO
CREATE CLUSTERED COLUMNSTORE INDEX [IDX_Clustered] ON Data.AggregatedSales
    WITH (DROP_EXISTING = OFF, COMPRESSION_DELAY = 0)
GO
```

The aggregation materializes some of the columns from *Date* and *Customer*, the *ProductKey*, the *Sales[Quantity]* total (Sum) and count, and the *Sales[Quantity] * Sales[Net Price]* total (Sum). Once we link the table in the model, we still need to tell Tabular the meaning of the columns. The developer who created the *AggregatedSales* table knows that the *Year* column corresponds to the *Date[Year]* column in Tabular; however, Tabular does not know about this relationship. We provide this information to Tabular through the Design Aggregation feature of Power BI Desktop.

Manage aggregations

Aggregations accelerate query performance to unlock big-data sets. Learn more

Aggregation table   Precedence ⓘ

AggregatedSales   ⌄   0

AGGREGATION COLUMN	SUMMARIZATION	DETAIL TABLE	DETAIL COLUMN	
Continent	GroupBy ▾	Customer ▾	Continent ▾	🗑
Country	GroupBy ▾	Customer ▾	Country ▾	🗑
ProductKey	GroupBy ▾	Product ▾	ProductKey ▾	🗑
SumOfQuantity	Sum ▾	Sales ▾	Quantity ▾	🗑
Year	GroupBy ▾	Date ▾	Year ▾	🗑

This table will be hidden if aggregations are set because aggregation tables must be hidden.

Apply all   Cancel

Some columns, like *Continent* and *Country*, are GroupBy columns, meaning they summarize the original table. You map group-by columns to the model columns they represent. On the other hand, *SumOfQuantity* is a Sum column, meaning that its value represents the sum of the model column to which it is associated.

The aggregation contains *ProductKey*, and we use this column to build a relationship with the *Product* table.

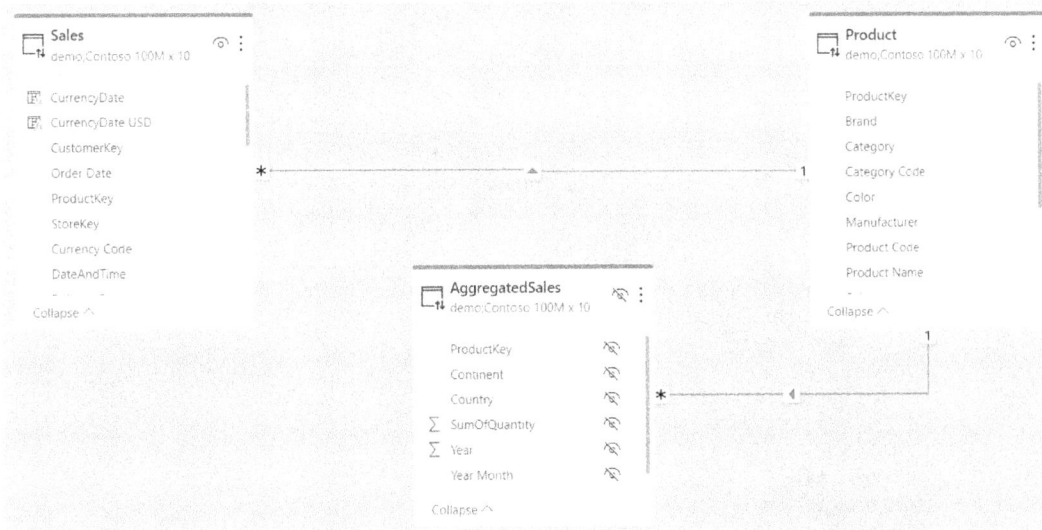

Once the information about the aggregation is defined, Tabular automatically uses the relationship if the DAX query groups by columns that are part of the aggregation itself. These include the *Country* and *Continent* columns of *Customer*, *Year* and *Year Month* columns of *Date*, and all the columns of *Product* (because of the relationship in place between the *AggregatedSales* aggregation and *Product*).

If we execute the same DAX query with the aggregation in place again, we notice a new event, **RewriteAttempted**.

Total	SE CPU	Line	Subclass	Duration	CPU	Par.	Rows	KB	Timeline
117 ms	104 ms	1	RewriteAttempted	0					
	×1.0	2	SQL	104	104	×1.0			
FE	SE								
13 ms	104 ms								
11.1%	88.9%								

Match Result:
  ✓ matchFound

SE Queries	SE Cache
1	0
	0.0%

Original Table:
  Sales

Total DQ
104 ms

Mapped To:
  AggregatedSales

Tabular replaces the original table (*Sales*) with the aggregation (*AggregatedSales*) and executes the SQL query by using the aggregation instead of the original table:

```
SELECT TOP (1000001) *
FROM (
    SELECT [t7_Country],
        [t7_Continent],
        [t7_Year],
        [t2_Brand],
        SUM(CAST([t7_SumOfQuantity] AS BIGINT)) AS [a0]
    FROM (
        SELECT [t7].[Country] AS [t7_Country],
            [t7].[Continent] AS [t7_Continent],
            [t7].[Year] AS [t7_Year],
            [t2].[Brand] AS [t2_Brand],
            [t7].[SumOfQuantity] AS [t7_SumOfQuantity]
        FROM (
            [Data].[AggregatedSales] AS [t7]
                LEFT JOIN [dbo].[Product] AS [t2] ON ([t7].[ProductKey] = [t2].[ProductKey])
            )
        ) AS [t0]
    GROUP BY [t7_Country],
        [t7_Continent],
        [t7_Year],
        [t2_Brand]
    ) AS [MainTable]
WHERE (NOT (([a0] IS NULL)))
```

The query only has one relationship to traverse (the one with *Product*) and runs much faster: only 104 milliseconds compared with 3,439 without the aggregation.

Tabular can use columns included in the aggregation for both grouping and filtering. For example, the following DAX query uses *Product[Color]* for both grouping and filtering. The SQL query is still entirely executed by utilizing the aggregation:

```
EVALUATE
    SUMMARIZECOLUMNS (
        'Date'[Year],
        'Product'[Color],
        Customer[Continent],
        Customer[Country],
        TREATAS ( { "Red", "Blue", "White" }, 'Product'[Color] ),
        "Quantity", SUM ( Sales[Quantity] )
    )
```

As a result of the filter on *Product[Color]*, the SQL code includes the WHERE condition over *Product*:

```
SELECT TOP (1000001) *
FROM (
    SELECT [t7_Country],
        [t7_Continent],
        [t7_Year],
        [t2_Color],
        SUM(CAST([t7_SumOfQuantity] AS BIGINT)) AS [a0]
    FROM (
        SELECT [t7].[Country] AS [t7_Country],
            [t7].[Continent] AS [t7_Continent],
            [t7].[Year] AS [t7_Year],
            [t2].[Color] AS [t2_Color],
            [t7].[SumOfQuantity] AS [t7_SumOfQuantity]
        FROM (
            [Data].[AggregatedSales] AS [t7]
                LEFT JOIN [dbo].[Product] AS [t2] ON ([t7].[ProductKey] = [t2].[ProductKey])
            )
        ) AS [t0]
    WHERE (
            ( [t2_Color] IN (N'Red', N'Blue', N'White' ) )
            )
    GROUP BY [t7_Country],
        [t7_Continent],
        [t7_Year],
        [t2_Color]
    ) AS [MainTable]
WHERE (NOT (([a0] IS NULL)))
```

Performance-wise, the query is very fast, running in less than 50 milliseconds.

If the DAX query references columns not included in the aggregation, the storage engine request specifies a regular DirectQuery query. For example, a filter on the *Customer[Gender]* column requires a scan of *Sales*, as the aggregation includes neither *Customer[Gender]* nor *CustomerKey*:

```
EVALUATE
    SUMMARIZECOLUMNS (
        'Date'[Year],
        'Product'[Color],
        Customer[Continent],
        Customer[Country],
        TREATAS ( { "Red", "Blue", "White" }, 'Product'[Color] ),
        TREATAS ( { "Male" }, Customer[Gender] ),
        "Quantity", SUM ( Sales[Quantity] )
    )
```

As we can see in server timings, the rewrite operation fails.

Total	SE CPU		Line	Subclass	Duration	CPU	Par.	Rows	KB	Timeline
1,101 ms	1,084 ms		1	RewriteAttempted	0					
	x1.0									
❄ FE	● SE		2	SQL	1,084	1,084	x1.0			
17 ms	1,084 ms									
1.5%	98.5%									

Match Result:
  ✗ attemptFailed

SE Queries	SE Cache
1	0
	0.0%

Original Table:
  Sales

Total DQ
1,084 ms

Mapped To:

The SQL Server code includes a scan of *Sales*:

```
SELECT TOP (1000001) *
FROM (
    SELECT [t0].[Country] AS [t0_Country],
        [t0].[Continent] AS [t0_Continent],
        [t1].[Year] AS [t1_Year],
        [t2].[Color] AS [t2_Color],
        SUM(CAST([t3].[Quantity] AS BIGINT)) AS [a0]
    FROM (
        (
            (
                [Data].[Sales] AS [t3]
                    LEFT JOIN [dbo].[Customer] AS [t0]
                        ON ([t3].[CustomerKey] = [t0].[CustomerKey])
            )
            LEFT JOIN [dbo].[Date] AS [t1] ON ([t3].[Order Date] = [t1].[Date])
        )
        LEFT JOIN [dbo].[Product] AS [t2] ON ([t3].[ProductKey] = [t2].[ProductKey])
    )
    WHERE (
        ([t0].[Gender] = N'Male')
        AND (
            ( [t2_Color] IN (N'Red', N'Blue', N'White' ) )
        )
    )
    GROUP BY [t0].[Country],
        [t0].[Continent],
        [t1].[Year],
        [t2].[Color]
) AS [MainTable]
WHERE (NOT (([a0] IS NULL)))
```

The rewrite operation takes place at the storage engine level. In a single DAX query, you might have some storage engine queries that use the aggregation and other storage engine queries that hit *Sales*.

Introducing VertiPaq aggregation and Dual storage mode

The aggregation we designed in the previous section is a DirectQuery aggregation. Aggregations can produce better results when stored in VertiPaq because you obtain the VertiPaq performance whenever the query hits the aggregation.

However, changing the storage mode of an aggregation is not enough to obtain the best performance. Developers should pay extra attention to the storage mode of any table related to the aggregation. In our example, the *AggregatedSales* aggregation has a relationship with *Product*.

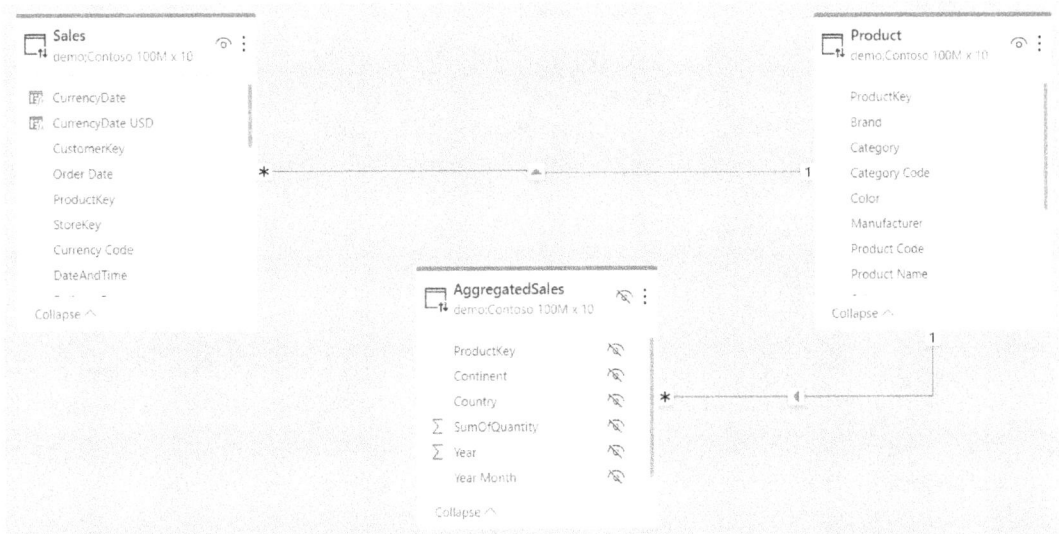

If *AggregatedSales* were a VertiPaq table, performing a JOIN at the storage engine level between *Product* and *AggregatedSales* would be impossible. If two different storage engines handled the two tables, there would be no way to execute a single query that joins the two tables. The storage mode of a table can be one of three: VertiPaq (also known as Import mode), DirectQuery, or Dual. We already know about both VertiPaq and DirectQuery. A Dual table can work with two storage engines: its content is copied in the VertiPaq storage engine, but it can also read the data through DirectQuery. Consequently, a dual table can be part of both SQL and xmSQL queries.

When we change the storage mode of the aggregation to VertiPaq, Power BI warns about the requirement to update related tables to Dual storage mode. In our example, the only table that must be switched to Dual storage mode is *Product*.

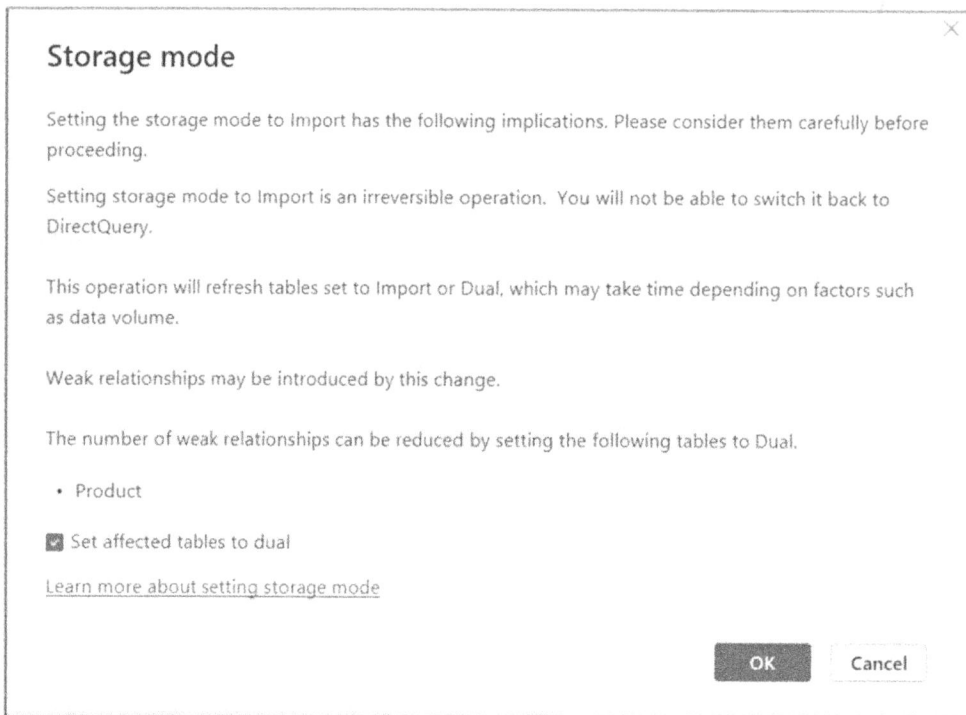

Storage mode

Setting the storage mode to Import has the following implications. Please consider them carefully before proceeding.

Setting storage mode to Import is an irreversible operation. You will not be able to switch it back to DirectQuery.

This operation will refresh tables set to Import or Dual, which may take time depending on factors such as data volume.

Weak relationships may be introduced by this change.

The number of weak relationships can be reduced by setting the following tables to Dual.

- Product

☑ Set affected tables to dual

Learn more about setting storage mode

OK   Cancel

After the update, the diagram shows the three storage modes of *Sales* (DirectQuery), *Product* (Dual), and *AggregatedSales* (Import/VertiPaq).

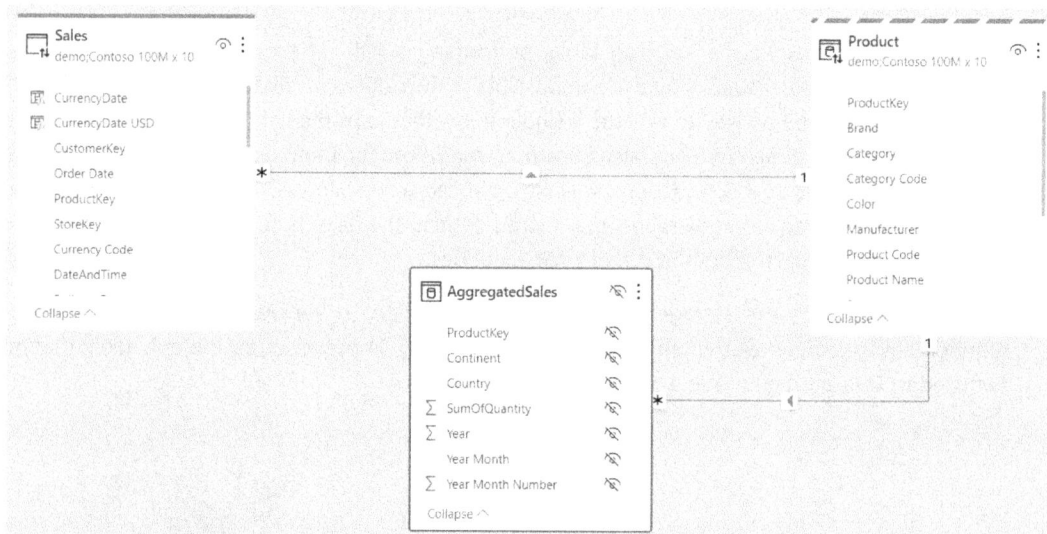

With the table in VertiPaq mode, running a DAX query that hits the aggregation takes place entirely inside the VertiPaq engine:

```
EVALUATE
SUMMARIZECOLUMNS (
    'Date'[Year],
    'Product'[Color],
    Customer[Continent],
    Customer[Country],
    "Quantity", SUM ( Sales[Quantity] )
)
```

The server timings pane shows a significant improvement in terms of speed.

Total	SE CPU	Line	Subclass	Duration	CPU	Par.	Rows	KB	Timeline
11 ms	0 ms x0.0	1	RewriteAttempted	0					
		3	Scan	4	0		17,556	275	

FE	SE
7 ms	4 ms
63.6%	36.4%

SE Queries	SE Cache
1	0
	0.0%

Total DQ
0 ms

SET DC_KIND="AUTO";
SELECT
  'AggregatedSales'[Country],
  'AggregatedSales'[Continent],
  'AggregatedSales'[Year],
  'Product'[Color],
  SUM ('AggregatedSales'[SumOfQuantity])
FROM 'AggregatedSales'
  LEFT OUTER JOIN 'Product'
    ON 'AggregatedSales'[ProductKey]='Product'[ProductKey];

The xmSQL storage engine query shows that the join between *AggregatedSales* (which is now a VertiPaq table) and *Product* (which is Dual) happens inside the VertiPaq storage engine:

```
SELECT
    'AggregatedSales'[Country],
    'AggregatedSales'[Continent],
    'AggregatedSales'[Year],
    'Product'[Color],
    SUM ( 'AggregatedSales'[SumOfQuantity] )
FROM 'AggregatedSales'
    LEFT OUTER JOIN 'Product'
        ON 'AggregatedSales'[ProductKey]='Product'[ProductKey];
```

If a model contains an aggregation in VertiPaq mode, but the related tables are not in Dual mode, the engine only partially uses the aggregation. To demonstrate this, we performed the transition of the aggregation to VertiPaq mode, keeping *Product* in DirectQuery mode.

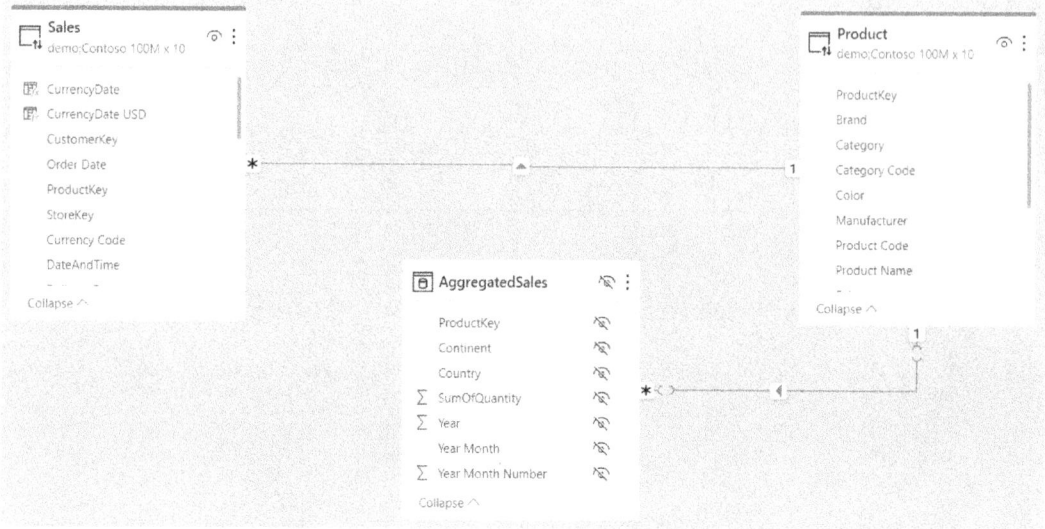

If we execute that same previous query that groups by *Product[Color]*, the engine does not use the aggregation.

Total	SE CPU		Line	Subclass	Duration	CPU	Par.	Rows	KB	Timeline
3,430 ms	3,413 ms		1	RewriteAttempted	0					
	x1.0									
● **FE**	● **SE**		2	SQL	3,413	3,413	x1.0			
17 ms	3,413 ms									
0.5%	99.5%									

SE Queries | **SE Cache**
1 | 0
| 0.0%

Total DQ
3,413 ms

Match Result:
  ✗ attemptFailed

Original Table:
  Sales

Mapped To:

The engine does not use the *AggregatedSales* aggregation because the query involves columns in *Product*, which requires traversing the relationship. Because *AggregatedSales* and *Product* are stored in two different data islands, the relationship between the two tables is limited. This prevents the aggregation from being used.

If we remove the reference to *Product* in the query, the engine goes back to using the aggregation:

```
EVALUATE
SUMMARIZECOLUMNS (
    'Date'[Year],
    Customer[Continent],
    Customer[Country],
    "Quantity", SUM ( Sales[Quantity] )
)
```

The rewrite operation does happen this time, and the storage engine query is executed in VertiPaq.

Total	SE CPU	Line	Subclass	Duration	CPU	Par.	Rows	KB	Timeline
7 ms	0 ms x0.0	1	RewriteAttempted	0					
		3	Scan	3	0		924	15	

FE	SE
4 ms	3 ms
57.1%	42.9%

SE Queries	SE Cache
1	0
	0.0%

Total DQ
0 ms

Match Result:
  ✓ matchFound

Original Table:
  Sales

Mapped To:
  AggregatedSales

As a rule, related tables should be in Dual mode when an aggregation table is in VertiPaq mode to obtain the best performance.

Designing aggregations for simple calculations

When developers define an aggregation, a column is either a group-by column or an aggregation. The list of aggregations available is limited: you can define an aggregation to be COUNT, MAX, MIN, SUM, or COUNT OF ROWS. Any calculation requiring a different type of aggregation that cannot be expressed with basic (supported) aggregations cannot leverage aggregations. This limitation is not a real issue because the list of aggregation types covers the most used aggregation functions. However, fancy aggregation functions like PRODUCT are not covered.

For example, the following query uses the *Sales[Quantity]* column with three different calculations involving aggregation functions:

```
EVALUATE
SUMMARIZECOLUMNS (
    'Date'[Year],
    Customer[Continent],
    Customer[Country],
    "Sum of Quantity", SUM ( Sales[Quantity] ),
    "Average of Quantity", AVERAGE ( Sales[Quantity] ),
    "Quantity if large",
        IF (
            SUM ( Sales[Quantity] ) >= 10E6,
            SUM ( Sales[Quantity] )
        )
)
```

Aggregations can solve *Sum of Quantity*, whereas *Average of Quantity* does not seem covered by the aggregations available. However, the AVERAGE function is computed by summing a column and dividing the sum by the count of that column. The engine uses the aggregation if the aggregation includes SUM and COUNT of *Sales[Quantity]*. The *Quantity if large* calculation includes an IF statement. However, the storage engine query only computes the sum of *Sales[Quantity]*, whereas the formula engine executes the IF function.

The entire DAX query is resolved through two storage engine requests, both covered by the aggregation with xmSQL statements.

Total	SE CPU	Line	Subclass	Duration	CPU	Par.	Rows	KB	Timeline
11 ms	0 ms x0.0	1	RewriteAttempted	0					
FE 4 ms 36.4%	SE 7 ms 63.6%	3	Scan	4	0		924	29	
		4	RewriteAttempted	0					
		6	Scan	3	0		924	15	
SE Queries 2	SE Cache 0 0.0%								
	Total DQ 0 ms	Match Result: ✓ matchFound							

The first xmSQL statement retrieves the sum of *Sales[Quantity]*, whereas the second xmSQL query contains a filter for the rows in *AggregatedSales* where the IF condition is true. Here is the first xmSQL query:

```
SELECT
    'AggregatedSales'[Country],
    'AggregatedSales'[Continent],
    'AggregatedSales'[Year],
    SUM ( 'AggregatedSales'[SumOfQuantity] ),
    SUM ( 'AggregatedSales'[SumOfQuantity] ),
    SUM ( 'AggregatedSales'[CountOfQuantity] )
FROM 'AggregatedSales';
```

And here is the second xmSQL query that retrieves the sum of *Sales[Quantity]* for a selection of rows:

```
SELECT
    'AggregatedSales'[Country],
    'AggregatedSales'[Continent],
    'AggregatedSales'[Year],
    SUM ( 'AggregatedSales'[SumOfQuantity] )
FROM 'AggregatedSales'
WHERE
    ( 'AggregatedSales'[Year], 'AggregatedSales'[Continent], 'AggregatedSales'[Country] ) IN { ( 2013, 'Europe', 'Netherlands' ) , (
2017, 'Europe', 'France' ) , ( 2017, 'North America', 'United States' ) , ( 2011, 'Europe', 'United Kingdom' ) , ( 2019, 'Europe', 'France'
) , ( 2019, 'North America', 'United States' ) , ( 2014, 'Australia', 'Australia' ) , ( 2012, 'Europe', 'Germany' ) , ( 2012, 'North America',
'Canada' ) , ( 2017, 'Europe', 'Netherlands' ) ..[71 total tuples, not all displayed]};
```

As we know from the previous chapters, using variables or IF.EAGER reduces the number of storage engine queries, further improving performance:

```
EVALUATE
SUMMARIZECOLUMNS (
    'Date'[Year],
    Customer[Continent],
    Customer[Country],
    "Sum of Quantity", SUM ( Sales[Quantity] ),
    "Average of quantity", AVERAGE ( Sales[Quantity] ),
    "Quantity if large",
        IF.EAGER (
            SUM ( Sales[Quantity] ) >= 10E6,
            SUM ( Sales[Quantity] )
        )
)
```

This last DAX query produces a single xmSQL query.

Total	SE CPU		Line	Subclass	Duration	CPU	Par.	Rows	KB	Timeline
7 ms	0 ms									
	x0.0		1	RewriteAttempted	0					
FE	SE		3	Scan	4	0		924	29	
3 ms	4 ms									
42.9%	57.1%									

SE Queries	SE Cache
1	0
	0.0%

Total DQ
0 ms

Remember to write the DAX code so the optimizer can determine whether the aggregation can solve the query. As soon as the expression is not a simple aggregation of a column, the optimizer does not use the aggregation. For example, the following code iterates over *Sales* and computes an expression that is equivalent to *Sales[Quantity]*, but it includes a multiplication by 1:

```
EVALUATE
SUMMARIZECOLUMNS (
    'Date'[Year],
    Customer[Continent],
    Customer[Country],
    "Sum of Quantity", SUMX ( Sales, Sales[Quantity] * 1 )
)
```

Running the query shows no attempt to use the aggregation.

Total	SE CPU		Line	Subclass	Duration	CPU	Par.	Rows	KB	Timeline
2,515 ms	2,509 ms		1	SQL	2,510	2,509	x1.0			
	x1.0									

FE	SE
5 ms	2,510 ms
0.2%	99.8%

SE Queries	SE Cache
1	0
	0.0%

Total DQ
2,510 ms

```
SELECT TOP (1000001) *
FROM (
    SELECT [t0_Country],
        [t0_Continent],
        [t1_Year],
        SUM([a0]) AS [a0]
    FROM (
        SELECT [t0].[Country] AS [t0_Country],
```

Looking into the SQL code, you can spot the multiplication executed by SQL:

```
SELECT TOP (1000001) *
FROM (
    SELECT [t0_Country],
        [t0_Continent],
        [t1_Year],
        SUM([a0]) AS [a0]
    FROM (
        SELECT [t0].[Country] AS [t0_Country],
            [t0].[Continent] AS [t0_Continent],
            [t1].[Year] AS [t1_Year],
            [t3].[Quantity] AS [t3_Quantity],
            ([t3].[Quantity] * 1) AS [a0]
        FROM (
            (
                [Data].[Sales] AS [t3]
                    LEFT JOIN [dbo].[Customer] AS [t0]
                        ON ([t3].[CustomerKey] = [t0].[CustomerKey])
            )
                LEFT JOIN [dbo].[Date] AS [t1] ON ([t3].[Order Date] = [t1].[Date])
        )
    ) AS [t0]
    GROUP BY [t0_Country],
        [t0_Continent],
        [t1_Year]
) AS [MainTable]
WHERE (NOT (([a0] IS NULL)))
```

You can use a calculated column to aggregate more complex expressions, as shown in the following section.

Designing aggregations for row-level calculations

Based on what we have learned in the previous section, the following query cannot benefit from aggregations because it is aggregating an expression that includes a multiplication:

```
EVALUATE
SUMMARIZECOLUMNS (
    'Date'[Year],
    Customer[Continent],
    Customer[Country],
    "Sum of Quantity", SUMX ( Sales, Sales[Quantity] * Sales[Net Price] )
)
```

Indeed, running the query shows that the SQL code includes the multiplication operation. The engine cannot use the aggregation because it is not a SUM of a column. Tabular does not even try to rewrite the query, and it produces the following SQL code:

```
SELECT TOP (1000001) *
FROM (
    SELECT [t0_Country],
        [t0_Continent],
        [t1_Year],
        SUM([a0]) AS [a0]
    FROM (
        SELECT [t0].[Country] AS [t0_Country],
            [t0].[Continent] AS [t0_Continent],
            [t1].[Year] AS [t1_Year],
            [t3].[Quantity] AS [t3_Quantity],
            [t3].[Net Price] AS [t3_Net Price],
            ([t3].[Quantity] * [t3].[Net Price]) AS [a0]
        FROM (
            (
                [Data].[Sales] AS [t3]
                    LEFT JOIN [dbo].[Customer] AS [t0]
                        ON ([t3].[CustomerKey] = [t0].[CustomerKey])
                )
                LEFT JOIN [dbo].[Date] AS [t1] ON ([t3].[Order Date] = [t1].[Date])
            )
        ) AS [t0]
    GROUP BY [t0_Country],
        [t0_Continent],
        [t1_Year]
    ) AS [MainTable]
WHERE (NOT (([a0] IS NULL)))
```

Complex measures performing elaborate calculations cannot benefit from aggregations. However, scenarios like the one we are showing are common: the measure aggregates an expression computed on a row-by-row basis. In these scenarios, developers can take advantage of aggregations by using calculated columns.

A calculated column in DirectQuery does not use memory; it is computed on the fly during the query execution. Therefore, we can express the same calculation using a calculated column and a simple sum, and then extend the aggregation to include aggregated values for the calculated column.

So first, we create a calculated column in the *Sales* table:

```
----------------------------------------
-- Calculated column in Sales table
----------------------------------------
Agg line amount = Sales[Quantity] * Sales[Net Price]
```

Then, we modify the query using a more straightforward expression, with SUM of the newly-created column:

```
EVALUATE
SUMMARIZECOLUMNS (
    'Date'[Year],
    Customer[Continent],
    Customer[Country],
    "Sum of Quantity", SUM ( Sales[Agg line amount] )
)
```

Running the query shows that Tabular tries to rewrite the query to use the aggregation. The rewrite operation fails because there are no suitable columns in the aggregation to satisfy what the query needs. However, the simple fact that it is trying is a sign that we are moving in the right direction.

Total	SE CPU	Line	Subclass	Duration	CPU	Par.	Rows	KB	Timeline
2,740 ms	2,729 ms	1	RewriteAtter	0					
	x1.0	2	SQL	2,730	2,729	x1.0			

FE	SE
10 ms	2,730 ms
0.4%	99.6%

SE Queries	SE Cache
1	0
	0.0%

Total DQ
2,730 ms

Match Result:
  ✗ attemptFailed

Original Table:
  Sales

Mapped To:

Now that the *Agg line amount* calculated column is in place, we need to update the aggregation by adding a column (*SumOfAggLineAmount*) that serves our purpose.

Manage aggregations

Aggregations accelerate query performance to unlock big-data sets. Learn more

Aggregation table
AggregatedSales ⌄

Precedence ⓘ
0

Continent	GroupBy ▾	Customer ▾	Continent ▾	🗑
CountOfQuantity	Count ▾	Sales ▾	Quantity ▾	🗑
Country	GroupBy ▾	Customer ▾	Country ▾	🗑
ProductKey	GroupBy ▾	Product ▾	ProductKey ▾	🗑
SumOfAggLineAmount	Sum ▾	Sales ▾	Agg line amount ▾	🗑
SumOfQuantity	Sum ▾	Sales ▾	Quantity ▾	🗑

This table will be hidden if aggregations are set because aggregation tables must be hidden.

Apply all   Cancel

Running the same query with the aggregation in place now shows that the rewrite attempt has succeeded.

Total	SE CPU		Line	Subclass	Duration	CPU	Par.	Rows	KB	Timeline
23 ms	0 ms									
	x0.0		1	RewriteAtter	0					
FE	SE		3	Scan	15	0		924	15	
10 ms	13 ms									
43.5%	65.2%									

SE Queries	SE Cache
1	0
	0.0%

Total DQ
0 ms

Match Result:
 ✓ matchFound

Original Table:
 Sales

Mapped To:
 AggregatedSales

An xmSQL query solves the DAX query:

```
SELECT
    'AggregatedSales'[Country],
    'AggregatedSales'[Continent],
    'AggregatedSales'[Year],
    SUM ( PFCAST ( 'AggregatedSales'[SumOfAggLineAmount] AS INT ) )
FROM 'AggregatedSales';
```

This technique lets you benefit from aggregations when your model includes measures that are simple aggregations of complex formulas evaluated on a row-by-row basis. Remember that the additional calculated column does not increase the model size because calculated columns in DirectQuery are not stored in the model. This simple example further demonstrates that a data model must be optimized based on the storage engine used by Tabular. This calculated column makes total sense for DirectQuery; however it would not be a good option in VertiPaq.

Designing aggregations for distinct counts

Among the different aggregations available for aggregations, DISTINCTCOUNT is noticeably missing. However, aggregations can be extremely useful in computing distinct counts. The key to making Tabular use an aggregation to solve distinct counts is to add the required column as a group-by column.

As an example, consider the following query:

```
EVALUATE
SUMMARIZECOLUMNS (
    'Date'[Year],
    Product[Brand],
    "Sum of Quantity", SUM ( Sales[Quantity] )
)
```

We know that the query is going to hit the aggregation because:

- *AggregatedSales[Year]* is a group-by column aliasing *Date[Year]*;

- *AggregatedSales[ProductKey]* has a relationship with *Product*, enabling the group-by with any *Product* attributes like *Product[Brand]*.

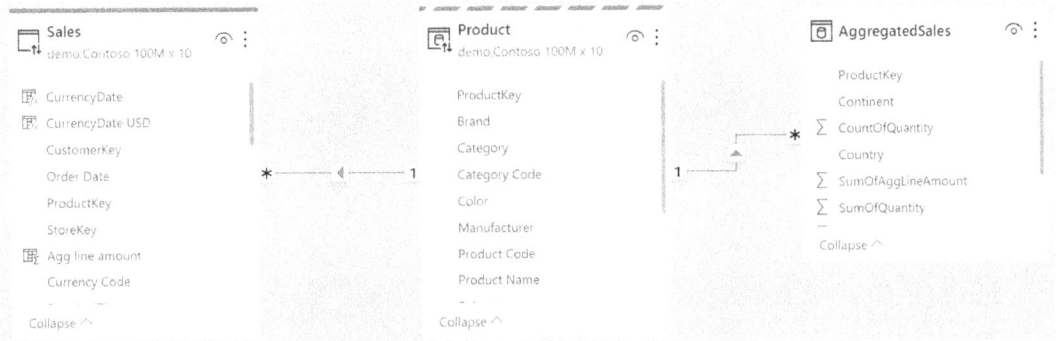

It is worth noting that *AggregatedSales[ProductKey]* does not have to be a GROUPBY column.

Manage aggregations

Aggregations accelerate query performance to unlock big-data sets. Learn more

Aggregation table | Precedence ⓘ
AggregatedSales ▾ | 0

AGGREGATION COLUMN	SUMMARIZATION	DETAIL TABLE	DETAIL COLUMN	
Continent	GroupBy ▾	Customer ▾	Continent ▾	🗑
CountOfQuantity	Count ▾	Sales ▾	Quantity ▾	🗑
Country	GroupBy ▾	Customer ▾	Country ▾	🗑
ProductKey	Select Summarization... ▾	▾	▾	🗑
SumOfAggLineAmount	Sum ▾	Sales ▾	Agg line amount ▾	🗑

Apply all   Cancel

The relationship between *Product* and *AggregatedSales* triggers the aggregation use whenever the DAX code groups by any of the *Product* attributes. Indeed, the engine executes the DAX query by using the *AggregatedSales* table.

Total	SE CPU		Line	Subclass	Duration	CPU	Par.	Rows	KB	Timeline
7 ms	0 ms		1	RewriteAtter	0					
	x0.0									
FE	SE		3	Scan	2	0		924	15	
5 ms	2 ms									
71.4%	28.6%									

Match Result:
  ✓ matchFound

SE Queries	SE Cache
1	0
	0.0%

Total DQ
0 ms

Original Table:
  Sales

Mapped To:
  AggregatedSales

However, the engine does not use the aggregation if the query executes a DISTINCTCOUNT of *Sales[ProductKey]*:

```
EVALUATE
SUMMARIZECOLUMNS (
    'Date'[Year],
    Product[Brand],
    "Number of products", DISTINCTCOUNT ( Sales[ProductKey] )
)
```

Indeed, the rewrite attempt fails when executing the last DAX query.

Total	SE CPU		Line	Subclass	Duration	CPU	Par.	Rows	KB	Timeline
11,001 ms	10,990 ms		1	RewriteAtter	0					
	x1.0									
FE	SE		2	SQL	10,990	10,990	x1.0			
11 ms	10,990 ms									
0.1%	99.9%									

SELECT TOP (1000001) [t0].[Country] **AS** [t0_Country],
  [t0].[Continent] **AS** [t0_Continent],
  [t1].[Year] **AS** [t1_Year],
  (
    COUNT_BIG(**DISTINCT** [t3].[ProductKey]) + MAX(**CASE**
      WHEN [t3].[ProductKey] **IS NULL**
      THEN 1
    ELSE 0

SE Queries	SE Cache
1	0
	0.0%

Total DQ
10,990 ms

The query runs in around 11 seconds because it is SQL Server that executes it. The *AggregatedSales[ProductKey]* must be specified as a group-by column for *Sales[ProductKey]* to use the *AggregatedSales* aggregation.

By providing this information, Tabular optimizes distinct counts too by executing the query using the *AggregatedSales* table.

Total	SE CPU	Line	Subclass	Duration	CPU	Par.	Rows	KB	Timeline
107 ms	125 ms	1	RewriteAtter	0					
	x1.3	5	Scan	97	125	x1.3	88	2	

FE	SE
10 ms	97 ms
9.3%	90.7%

SE Queries	SE Cache
1	0
	0.0%

Total DQ
0 ms

```
SET DC_KIND="AUTO";
SELECT
    'AggregatedSales'[Country],
    'AggregatedSales'[Continent],
    'AggregatedSales'[Year],
    DCOUNT ( 'AggregatedSales'[ProductKey] )
FROM 'AggregatedSales';
```

When an aggregation includes a relationship key, it is a good practice to both create the relationship with the dimension and set the columns as a group-by column in the fact table. That way, both distinct counts and aggregations grouping by the dimension make a smooth job of attributing the work.

Aggregations are not VertiPaq aliases of DirectQuery tables

One crucial detail to remember about aggregations is that they are what they are: aggregations. The engine uses aggregations only when they contain group-by-columns and aggregated values. It would be tempting to use aggregations to store the most used columns of a table in VertiPaq, and leave the less frequently-used columns in DirectQuery to save space in the model. Unfortunately, this is not a real option. While it is true that most of the columns are in VertiPaq, therefore very fast to access, the way Tabular implements aggregations renders this technique almost useless.

Let us show this with an example. The largest column in the fact table of the Contoso database is *Sales[Order Number]*. Due to its large cardinality, the column puts tremendous memory pressure on the model. Moreover, most queries do not use *Sales[Order Number]*. Some users may want to drill down to the individual order level to produce detailed reports, but most of the queries aggregate values from *Sales* without including *Sales[Order Number]*. A tempting idea is to create a VertiPaq aggregation containing all the *Sales* columns except for *Sales[Order Number]*. The resulting table would be relatively small and could compute any query not involving *Sales[Order Number]*.

We created a VertiPaq table called *Sales Vp* (where Vp stands for VertiPaq) that includes all the rows and columns in *Sales* except *Sales[Order Number]*. Afterwards, we created a set of relationships with the dimensions, changing their storage mode to Dual so Tabular can use the dimensions in both DirectQuery and VertiPaq.

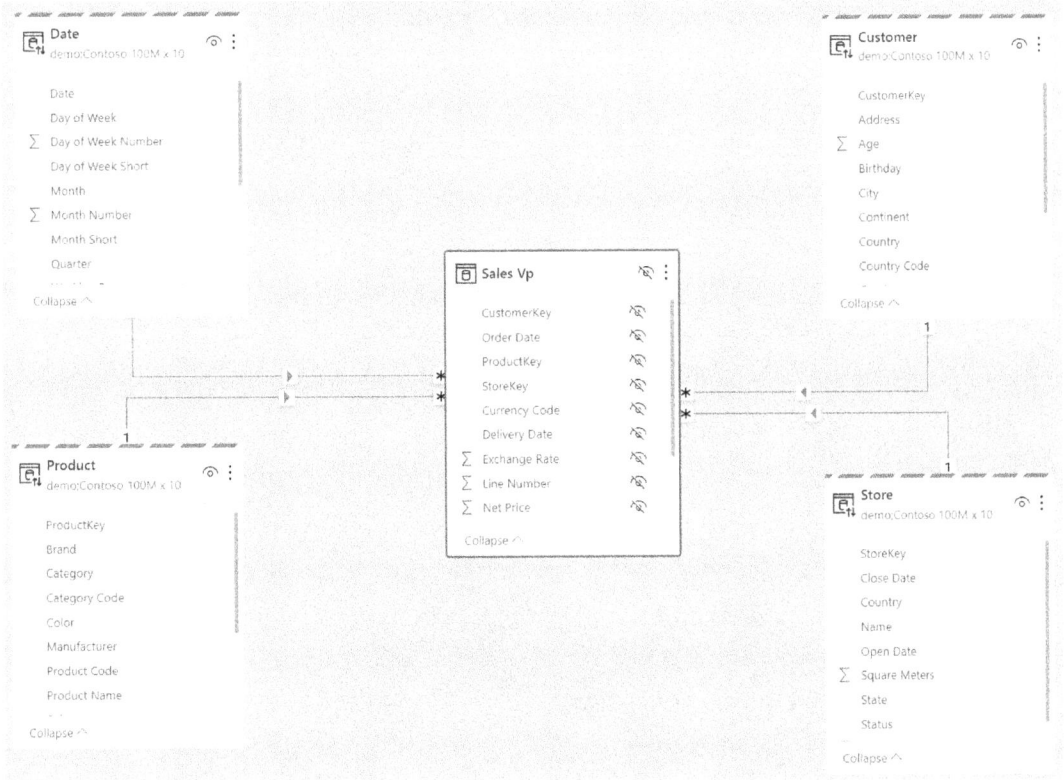

Next, we defined the role of columns in *Sales Vp*, setting all the columns in the aggregation as groupby columns of the corresponding column in *Sales*.

In defining the role of columns, we also set the numeric columns as group-by columns: *Unit Cost,*

Quantity, and *Unit Price* are group-by columns of their corresponding columns in *Sales*.

Finally, we need a column aggregating the number of rows of *Sales*. This column is necessary to force the use of aggregations, as shown at the end of this section.

After we set the aggregation, we test the following DAX query:

```
EVALUATE
SUMMARIZECOLUMNS (
    'Date'[Year],
    Customer[Continent],
    Customer[Country],
    "Sales", SUMX ( Sales, Sales[Quantity] * Sales[Net Price] )
)
```

The query uses only columns that are present in the aggregation. Consequently, we hope that VertiPaq can resolve the entire query. However, things are different. When we execute the query, we notice that Tabular does not even try to rewrite the query to execute it in VertiPaq mode.

Total	SE CPU		Line	Subclass	Duration	CPU	Par.	Rows	KB	Timeline
2,738 ms	2,730 ms		1	SQL	2,730	2,730	x1.0			
	x1.0									

FE	SE
8 ms	2,730 ms
0.3%	99.7%

SE Queries	SE Cache
1	0
	0.0%

Total DQ
2,730 ms

```
SELECT TOP (1000001) *
FROM (
    SELECT [t0_Country],
        [t0_Continent],
        [t1_Year],
        SUM([a0]) AS [a0]
    FROM (
        SELECT [t0].[Country] AS [t0_Country],
            [t0].[Continent] AS [t0_Continent],
```

The RewriteAttempt event is entirely missing. Tabular tries to rewrite a DirectQuery query exclusively when the aggregation works with a single column. To force the use of the aggregation, we should define the *LineAmount* calculated column. However, that column would use a considerable amount of memory because of its cardinality, thus destroying the advantage we were hoping for when we decided to create the aggregation in the first place.

We could rewrite the DAX code to force the use of *Sales[Quantity]* and *Sales[Net Price]* as group-by columns. The following DAX query uses the aggregation, but it is so poorly written that performance is just horrible:

```
EVALUATE
SUMMARIZECOLUMNS (
    'Date'[Year],
    Customer[Continent],
    Customer[Country],
    "Sales",
        SUMX (
            SUMMARIZE ( Sales, Sales[Quantity], Sales[Net Price] ),
            Sales[Quantity] * Sales[Net Price] * CALCULATE ( COUNTROWS ( Sales ) )
        )
)
```

This time, the rewrite attempt is present and successful. However, the query took 23 seconds to run.

Total	SE CPU	Line	Subclass	Duration	CPU	Par.	Rows	KB	Timeline
23,170 ms	145,406 ms	1	RewriteAtter	0					
	x7.9	3	Scan	18,490	145,406	x7.9	7,105,089	83,263	
FE	**SE**								
4,680 ms	18,490 ms								
20.2%	79.8%								

SE Queries	SE Cache
1	0
	0.0%

Total DQ
0 ms

Match Result:
✓ matchFound

Original Table:
Sales

Mapped To:
Sales Vp

The issue in performance is the excessive materialization caused by the xmSQL query to VertiPaq:

```
SELECT
    'Customer'[Country],
    'Customer'[Continent],
    'Date'[Year],
    'Sales Vp'[Quantity],
    'Sales Vp'[Net Price],
    SUM ( 'Sales Vp'[Rows] )
FROM 'Sales Vp'
    LEFT OUTER JOIN 'Customer'
        ON 'Sales Vp'[CustomerKey]='Customer'[CustomerKey]
    LEFT OUTER JOIN 'Date'
        ON 'Sales Vp'[Order Date]='Date'[Date];
```

The aggregation of the multiplication between *Sales[Quantity]* and *Sales[Net Price]* does not happen inside VertiPaq. The xmSQL query materializes a data cache containing 7 million rows, later iterated by the formula engine to compute the result.

Using a column as a group-by column to force Tabular to use VertiPaq aggregations instead of querying the underlying DirectQuery table does not lead to good performance. It only makes the DAX code much more intricate, creating issues for maintenance and optimization.

Manually activating aggregations in DAX

As shown in the previous section, aggregations cannot be aliases of the original DirectQuery table. Aggregations are designed to store the pre-aggregated value of a column. Their use is limited to scenarios where the DAX optimizer can rewrite an SQL query using VertiPaq.

However, it is possible to manually handle aliases of tables by intercepting the presence of specific filters and directing the calculation over the best table: either VertiPaq or DirectQuery. With the very same architecture as the one we used in the previous section, we can force the use of the aggregation by checking whether the *Sales[Order Number]* column is filtered. If no explicit filters exist on the column, then the entire calculation can be executed by scanning the aggregation. Otherwise, we must direct the calculation to the DirectQuery table.

The following measure shows the technique:

```
DEFINE
    MEASURE Sales[Sales Amount] =
        IF (
            ISFILTERED ( Sales[Order Number] ),
            SUMX ( Sales, Sales[Quantity] * Sales[Net Price] ),
            SUMX ( 'Sales Vp', 'Sales Vp'[Quantity] * 'Sales Vp'[Net Price] )
        )

EVALUATE
SUMMARIZECOLUMNS (
    'Date'[Year],
    Customer[Continent],
    Customer[Country],
    "Sales", [Sales Amount]
)
```

The Tabular engine usually evaluates ISFILTERED statically before the execution starts, as in this query. Consequently, the execution plan does not evaluate the expression in the false condition. When executed, the query generates a single xmSQL query.

Total	SE CPU	Line	Subclass	Duration	CPU	Par.	Rows	KB	Timeline
538 ms	4,438 ms x8.5	2	Scan	521	4,438	x8.5	924	15	

FE	SE
17 ms	521 ms
3.2%	96.8%

SE Queries	SE Cache
1	0
	0.0%

Total DQ
0 ms

```
SET DC_KIND="AUTO";
WITH
    $Expr0 := ( PFCAST ( 'Sales VP'[Quantity] AS INT ) * PFCAST ( 'Sales VP'[Net Price] AS
SELECT
    'Customer'[Country],
    'Customer'[Continent],
    'Date'[Year],
```

The xmSQL query uses only *Sales Vp*:

```
WITH
    $Expr0 := ( PFCAST ( 'Sales VP'[Quantity] AS INT ) * PFCAST ( 'Sales VP'[Net Price] AS INT ) )
SELECT
    'Customer'[Country],
    'Customer'[Continent],
    'Date'[Year],
    SUM ( @$Expr0 )
FROM 'Sales VP'
    LEFT OUTER JOIN 'Customer'
        ON 'Sales VP'[CustomerKey]='Customer'[CustomerKey]
    LEFT OUTER JOIN 'Date'
        ON 'Sales VP'[Order Date]='Date'[Date];
```

As soon as there is a filter over *Sales[Order Number]*, or a grouping by *Sales[Order Number]*, the same measure scans the *Sales* table in DirectQuery:

```
DEFINE
    MEASURE Sales[Sales Amount] =
        IF (
            ISFILTERED ( Sales[Order Number] ),
            SUMX ( Sales, Sales[Quantity] * Sales[Net Price] ),
            SUMX ( 'Sales Vp', 'Sales Vp'[Quantity] * 'Sales Vp'[Net Price] )
        )

EVALUATE
SUMMARIZECOLUMNS (
    'Date'[Year],
    Customer[Continent],
    Customer[Country],
    Sales[Order Number],
    TREATAS ( { 1213156 }, Customer[CustomerKey] ),
    "Sales", [Sales Amount]
)
```

The execution of the DAX query generates a SQL query using the DirectQuery storage engine.

Total	SE CPU	Line	Subclass	Duration	CPU	Par.	Rows	KB	Timeline
9,753 ms	9,744 ms x1.0	1	SQL	9,744	9,744	x1.0			

FE	SE
10 ms	9,743 ms
0.1%	99.9%

SE Queries	SE Cache
1	0
	0.0%

```
SELECT TOP (1000001) *
FROM (
    SELECT [t0_Country],
        [t0_Continent],
        [t1_Year],
        [t3_Order Number],
        SUM([a0]) AS [a0]
```

It is helpful to note that the pruning of the query plan happens even in the presence of variables or of the IF.EAGER function. The following code uses both IF.EAGER and variables, and yet the pruning still occurs correctly:

```
DEFINE
    MEASURE Sales[Sales Amount] =
        VAR SalesVP = SUMX ( 'Sales Vp', 'Sales Vp'[Quantity] * 'Sales Vp'[Net Price] )
        VAR SalesDQ = SUMX ( Sales, Sales[Quantity] * Sales[Net Price] )
        RETURN
        IF.EAGER (
            ISFILTERED ( Sales[Order Number] ), SalesDq, SalesVp
        )

EVALUATE
SUMMARIZECOLUMNS (
    'Date'[Year],
    Customer[Continent],
    Customer[Country],
    "Sales", [Sales Amount]
)
```

Another interesting aspect of this type of optimization is that it will work even when users drill down a Power BI matrix partially. For example, the following visual is expanded at the *Year*, *Continent*, and *Country* level; therefore, we know it will be computed out of *Sales Vp*.

Year	Sales Amount
⊟ **2010**	**37,995,287,577.26**
⊟ **Australia**	**1,894,030,094.32**
Australia	1,894,030,094.32
⊟ **Europe**	**14,132,025,559.14**
France	944,094,042.28
Germany	3,113,774,570.56
Italy	2,013,553,021.18
Netherlands	1,060,401,662.23
United Kingdom	7,000,202,262.89
⊞ **North America**	**21,969,231,923.80**
⊞ **2011**	**67,835,749,272.36**
⊞ **2012**	**79,803,170,199.92**

Expanding the Australia continent to the Order Number level requires computing the matrix out of *Sales* and querying the DirectQuery structure. However, DAX uses DirectQuery to compute only Australia and uses VertiPaq for all the remaining levels. We obtain the following report.

Year	Sales Amount
⊟ **2010**	**37,995,287,577.26**
⊟ **Australia**	**1,894,030,094.32**
⊟ **Australia**	**1,894,030,094.32**
138000024	2,326.43
138000058	24,771.80
138000097	12,720.77
138000105	19,954.37
138000108	19,855.36
138000109	32,305.15
138000120	16,348.61
138000171	467.98
138000179	9,666.39

The query being executed (slightly simplified for readability) is the following:

```
DEFINE
    VAR __DM3FilterTable = TREATAS ( {2010}, 'Date'[Year] )

    VAR __DM5FilterTable =
        TREATAS (
            { (2010, "Australia"), (2010, "Europe") },
            'Date'[Year],
            'Customer'[Continent]
        )

    VAR __DM7FilterTable =
        TREATAS (
            {(2010, "Australia", "Australia")},
            'Date'[Year],
            'Customer'[Continent],
            'Customer'[Country]
        )
```

```
EVALUATE
SUMMARIZECOLUMNS (
    ROLLUPADDISSUBTOTAL (
        'Date'[Year], "IsGrandTotalRowTotal",
        'Customer'[Continent], "IsDM1Total",
            NONVISUAL (__DM3FilterTable),
        'Customer'[Country], "IsDM3Total",
            NONVISUAL (__DM3FilterTable),
            NONVISUAL (__DM5FilterTable),
        'Sales'[Order Number], "IsDM5Total",
            NONVISUAL (__DM3FilterTable),
            NONVISUAL (__DM5FilterTable),
            NONVISUAL (__DM7FilterTable)
    ),
    "Sales_Amount", 'Sales'[Sales Amount]
)
```

There are four subtotal levels in the visual, reflected in four levels in the query, generating four queries. Of the four, only one (the order number level) requires hitting the DirectQuery storage. The first three queries are xmSQL:

```
WITH
    $Expr0 := ( PFCAST ( 'Sales ( Vp )'[Quantity] AS INT ) * PFCAST ( 'Sales ( Vp )'[Net Price] AS INT ) )
SELECT
    'Customer'[Country],
    'Customer'[Continent],
    SUM ( @$Expr0 )
FROM 'Sales ( Vp )'
    LEFT OUTER JOIN 'Customer'
        ON 'Sales ( Vp )'[CustomerKey]='Customer'[CustomerKey]
    LEFT OUTER JOIN 'Date'
        ON 'Sales ( Vp )'[Order Date]='Date'[Date]
WHERE
    'Customer'[Continent] IN ( 'Europe', 'Australia' ) VAND
    'Date'[Year] = 2010 VAND
    ( 'Date'[Year], 'Customer'[Continent] ) IN { ( 2010, 'Australia' ) , ( 2010, 'Europe' ) };


WITH
    $Expr0 := ( PFCAST ( 'Sales ( Vp )'[Quantity] AS INT ) * PFCAST ( 'Sales ( Vp )'[Net Price] AS INT ) )
SELECT
    'Customer'[Continent],
    SUM ( @$Expr0 )
FROM 'Sales ( Vp )'
    LEFT OUTER JOIN 'Customer'
        ON 'Sales ( Vp )'[CustomerKey]='Customer'[CustomerKey]
    LEFT OUTER JOIN 'Date'
        ON 'Sales ( Vp )'[Order Date]='Date'[Date]
WHERE
    'Date'[Year] = 2010;
```

```
WITH
    $Expr0 := ( PFCAST ( 'Sales ( Vp ) '[Quantity] AS INT ) * PFCAST ( 'Sales ( Vp ) '[Net Price] AS INT ) )
SELECT
    'Date'[Year],
    SUM ( @$Expr0 )
FROM 'Sales ( Vp ) '
    LEFT OUTER JOIN 'Date'
        ON 'Sales ( Vp ) '[Order Date]='Date'[Date];
```

The three queries include filters for the levels where the order number is not required. The only query
that hits DirectQuery is the following;

```
SELECT TOP (1000001) *
FROM (
    SELECT [t3_Order Number],
        SUM([a0]) AS [a0]
    FROM (
        SELECT [t0].[Country] AS [t0_Country],
            [t0].[Continent] AS [t0_Continent],
            [t1].[Year] AS [t1_Year],
            [t3].[Order Number] AS [t3_Order Number],
            [t3].[Quantity] AS [t3_Quantity],
            [t3].[Net Price] AS [t3_Net Price],
            ([t3].[Quantity] * [t3].[Net Price]) AS [a0]
        FROM (
            (
                [Data].[Sales] AS [t3]
                    LEFT JOIN [dbo].[Customer] AS [t0]
                        ON ([t3].[CustomerKey] = [t0].[CustomerKey])
            )
                LEFT JOIN [dbo].[Date] AS [t1] ON ([t3].[Order Date] = [t1].[Date])
        )
    ) AS [t0]
    WHERE (
        (
            ([t0_Country] = N'Australia')
            AND ([t0_Continent] = N'Australia')
        )
        AND (
            ([t1_Year] = 2010)
            AND (
                (
                    ([t1_Year] = 2010)
                    AND ([t0_Continent] = N'Australia')
                )
                OR (
                    ([t1_Year] = 2010)
                    AND ([t0_Continent] = N'Europe')
                )
            )
        )
    )
```

```
      GROUP BY [t3_Order Number]
   ) AS [MainTable]
WHERE (NOT (([a0] IS NULL)))
```

Hence, the pruning of the measure has removed all the unnecessary scans of the DirectQuery table, resulting in optimal performance.

Using automatic aggregations

You can enable automatic aggregations if your model uses Power BI Premium (capacity or per-user). When using automatic aggregations, the service uses AI to analyze the query log and automatically build aggregations to speed up the most frequent queries.

Automatic aggregations use the very same technology as user-defined aggregations. Consequently, all the limitations discussed in the previous sections still apply. The most relevant difference is that developers do not need to fine-tune aggregations as the service creates and maintains them.

Of course, this comes with pros and cons. On the one hand, it is a fire-and-forget feature. Once enabled, Power BI creates, updates, and deletes automatic aggregations without human interaction. On the other hand, developers lose control over the aggregations created; therefore, they need to trust the automatic system.

You can use automatic aggregations in conjunction with manual aggregations. The Power BI service tags automatic aggregations as system aggregations. The automatic aggregations management only considers system aggregations, leaving manual aggregations as they are.

Using hybrid tables

A table in a Tabular model can contain multiple VertiPaq partitions and – optionally – one DirectQuery partition. A table containing partitions with different storage modes is called a **hybrid table**. Hybrid tables are a premium feature, available only in Power BI Premium (capacity or per-user). Hybrid tables are helpful in scenarios where you need real-time data but want to avoid using DirectQuery for the entire table, or when you are dealing with a very large model and do not want to import the entire database into memory.

In the first scenario, you have a VertiPaq table containing sales transactions, and then you add a DirectQuery partition for the latest transactions (the last day or week). Whenever DAX needs to scan *Sales*, it executes two queries: one on VertiPaq for the historical data and one on DirectQuery for the latest data.

The second scenario does not involve real-time requirements. You might have a massive database with 10 years of data that would require too much memory if loaded in VertiPaq. If that is the case, you can create a historical partition in DirectQuery to hold most of the data and a smaller partition in VertiPaq containing the latest rows. For example, the previous 9 years remain in SQL Server, whereas VertiPaq stores the last year. Users are likely more interested in the latest sales. Therefore, they experience outstanding performance when querying the freshest data and slightly lower performance when querying historical data.

The first scenario (latest data in DirectQuery, historical data in VertiPaq) can be handled with the Power BI user interface when implementing incremental refresh. The second scenario requires developers to use an external tool like Tabular Editor to manually set the partitions. In this book, we are interested in the hybrid tables technology, its strengths, and its weaknesses, rather than in the user interface and the ways to create hybrid tables. Therefore, we analyze the second scenario (which is a bit more complex to set up) in depth to describe the technology of hybrid tables. We briefly introduce the user interface available for the incremental refresh at the end of the section.

Introducing hybrid tables

Hybrid tables require multiple partitions: one in DirectQuery and one or more in VertiPaq. There can be only one DirectQuery partition, while there is no limit regarding the number of VertiPaq partitions. In our example, we create only two partitions: one in VertiPaq with 9 years worth of data and one in DirectQuery for the last year. Moreover, all tables linked to *Sales* must be in Dual mode. Indeed, when filtering *Sales* by any *Product* attribute, two different storage engines manage that job: VertiPaq and DirectQuery. Therefore, Tabular must be able to use both engines for any table that can filter *Sales*.

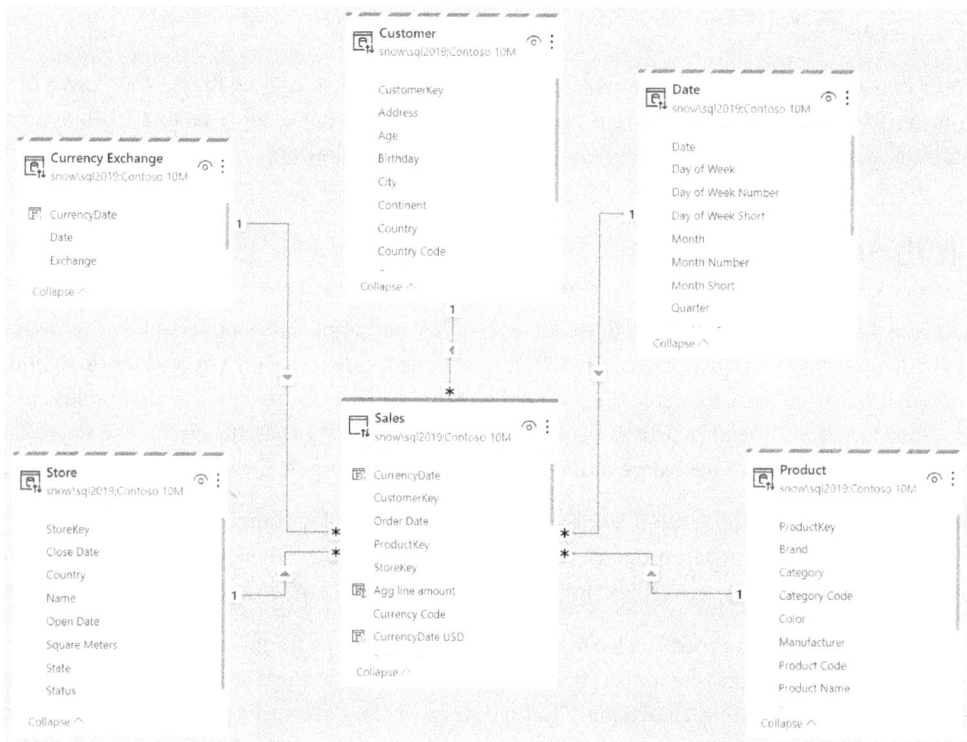

At the time of writing, Power BI Desktop does not support tables with multiple partitions. Therefore, we start by creating the model with *Sales* in DirectQuery mode. The partition contains a filter on *Sales[OrderDate]* to show only years before 2020. We then deploy the model on the Power BI Service and create the VertiPaq partition for 2020 using Tabular Editor. Once the model is ready, we perform our tests and evaluate performance.

The *Sales* table contains two partitions.

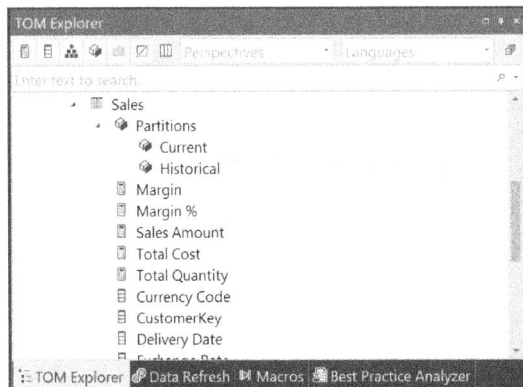

The two partitions share the same M code, except for the filter: *Current* contains dates after December 31st, 2019, whereas *Historical* contains the previous dates. *Historical* is a DirectQuery partition, whereas *Current* is VertiPaq:

```
Let
    Source = Sql.Databases("SNOW\SQL2019"),
    #"Contoso 10M" = Source{[Name="Contoso 10M"]}[Data],
    dbo_Sales = #"Contoso 10M"{[Schema="Data",Item="Sales"]}[Data],
    #"Filtered Rows" = Table.SelectRows(dbo_Sales, each [Order Date] <= #date(2019, 12, 31))
in
    #"Filtered Rows"
```

A simple DAX query computing the sales amount sliced by year creates two storage engine queries:

```
EVALUATE
SUMMARIZECOLUMNS ( 'Date'[Year], "Sales", [Sales Amount] )
ORDER BY 'Date'[Year]
```

Tabular retrieves years before 2020 from SQL Server and 2020 onwards from VertiPaq. Here are the server timings.

		Line	Subclass	Duration	CPU	Par.	Rows	KB	Timeline
Total 391 ms	**SE CPU** 204 ms x1.0	1	SQL	188	188	x1.0			
		3	Scan	17	16	x0.9	14	1	
FE 186 ms 47.6%	**SE** 205 ms 52.4%								

SELECT TOP (1000001) *
FROM (
  SELECT [t1_Year],
    SUM([a0]) **AS** [a0]
  FROM (
    SELECT [t1].[Year] **AS** [t1_Year],
      [t3].[Quantity] **AS** [t3_Quantity],
      [t3].[Net Price] **AS** [t3_Net Price],

SE Queries	**SE Cache**
2	0 0.0%
	Total DQ 188 ms

We dig deeper and see that Tabular executes one SQL query:

```
SELECT TOP (1000001) *
FROM (
    SELECT [t1_Year],
        SUM([a0]) AS [a0]
    FROM (
        SELECT [t1].[Year] AS [t1_Year],
            [t3].[Quantity] AS [t3_Quantity],
            [t3].[Net Price] AS [t3_Net Price],
            ([t3].[Quantity] * [t3].[Net Price]) AS [a0]
        FROM (
            (
                SELECT [_].[Order Number],
                    [_].[Line Number],
                    [_].[Order Date],
                    [_].[Delivery Date],
                    [_].[CustomerKey],
                    [_].[StoreKey],
                    [_].[ProductKey],
                    [_].[Quantity],
                    [_].[Unit Price],
                    [_].[Net Price],
                    [_].[Unit Cost],
                    [_].[Currency Code],
                    [_].[Exchange Rate]
                FROM [Data].[Sales] AS [_]
                WHERE [_].[Order Date] <= convert(DATE, '2019-12-31')
                ) AS [t3]
                LEFT JOIN [dbo].[Date] AS [t1] ON ([t3].[Order Date] = [t1].[Date])
            )
        ) AS [t0]
    GROUP BY [t1_Year]
    ) AS [MainTable]
WHERE (NOT (([a0] IS NULL)))
```

Please note that the SQL code includes no filter over the year. Tabular does not even know the difference between the two partitions. We, as developers, know that the SQL partition contains older data. From a Tabular point of view, the *Historical* partition is just a partition like any other. Similarly, the xmSQL code does not include any filter:

```
WITH
    $Expr0 := ( PFCAST ( 'Sales'[Quantity] AS INT ) * PFCAST ( 'Sales'[Net Price] AS INT ) )
SELECT
    'Date'[Year],
    SUM ( @$Expr0 )
FROM 'Sales'
    LEFT OUTER JOIN 'Date'
        ON 'Sales'[Order Date]='Date'[Date];
```

We are stressing the fact that filters are missing because this is one of the critical points of hybrid tables: the Tabular engine does not know the content of the partitions. Therefore, it cannot perform partition pruning – unless you use the **DataCoverageDefinition** partition property described later. Any query scanning *Sales* always results in two storage engine queries: one to DirectQuery and one to VertiPaq.

Indeed, if we change the query to scan only 2020 – which we know exists only in the VertiPaq partition – we still have the execution of two different queries:

```
EVALUATE
SUMMARIZECOLUMNS (
    'Date'[Year],
    TREATAS ( { 2020 }, 'Date'[Year] ),
    "Sales", [Sales Amount]
)
ORDER BY 'Date'[Year]
```

The server timings pane shows the two storage engine queries.

Total	SE CPU		Line	Subclass	Duration	CPU	Par.	Rows	KB	Timeline
250 ms	63 ms		1	SQL	63	63	x1.0			
	x1.0		3	Scan	0	0		1	1	

FE	SE
187 ms	63 ms
74.8%	25.2%

SE Queries	SE Cache
2	0
	0.0%

Total DQ
63 ms

This time, the SQL query does not return any value because the condition over the year conflicts with the condition over the date:

```
SELECT SUM([a0]) AS [a0]
FROM (
    SELECT [t1].[Year] AS [t1_Year],
        [t3].[Quantity] AS [t3_Quantity],
        [t3].[Net Price] AS [t3_Net Price],
        ([t3].[Quantity] * [t3].[Net Price]) AS [a0]
    FROM (
        (
            SELECT [_].[Order Number],
                [_].[Line Number],
                [_].[Order Date],
                [_].[Delivery Date],
                [_].[CustomerKey],
                [_].[StoreKey],
                [_].[ProductKey],
                [_].[Quantity],
                [_].[Unit Price],
                [_].[Net Price],
                [_].[Unit Cost],
                [_].[Currency Code],
                [_].[Exchange Rate]


            FROM [Data].[Sales] AS [_]
            WHERE [_].[Order Date] <= convert(DATE, '2019-12-31')
            ) AS [t3]
            LEFT JOIN [dbo].[Date] AS [t1] ON ([t3].[Order Date] = [t1].[Date])
        )
    ) AS [t0]
WHERE ([t1_Year] = 2020)
```

Tabular cannot prune the partition because the filter is on *Date[Year]*, while the condition in the SQL code generated for the partition filters *Sales[Order Date]*. However, filtering *Sales[Order Date]* in DAX does not produce any benefit. The engine still sends a SQL query because Tabular does not even try to perform partition pruning:

```
EVALUATE
SUMMARIZECOLUMNS (
    'Date'[Year],
    FILTER (
        ALL ( 'Sales'[Order Date] ),
        Sales[Order Date] >= DATE ( 2020, 1, 1 )
    ),
    "Sales", [Sales Amount]
)
ORDER BY 'Date'[Year]
```

Here are the server timings, where you can easily spot the two queries executed.

Total	SE CPU	Line	Subclass	Duration	CPU	Par.	Rows	KB	Timeline
580 ms	79 ms	1	SQL	63	63	x1.0			
	x1.0	3	Scan	17	16	x0.9	14	1	
FE	**SE**								
500 ms	80 ms								
86.2%	13.8%								

SE Queries	SE Cache
2	0
	0.0%

Total DQ
63 ms

```
SELECT TOP (1000001) *
FROM (
    SELECT [t1_Year],
        SUM([a0]) AS [a0]
    FROM (
        SELECT [t1].[Year] AS [t1_Year],
            [t3].[Order Date] AS [t3_Order Date],
```

Now, the SQL query applies the filter on the *Sales[Order Date]* column filtered in the partition:

```
SELECT TOP (1000001) *
FROM (
    SELECT [t1_Year], SUM([a0]) AS [a0]
    FROM (
        SELECT [t1].[Year] AS [t1_Year],
            [t3].[Order Date] AS [t3_Order Date],
            [t3].[Quantity] AS [t3_Quantity],
            [t3].[Net Price] AS [t3_Net Price],
            ([t3].[Quantity] * [t3].[Net Price]) AS [a0]
        FROM (
            (
                SELECT [_].[Order Number],
                    [_].[Line Number],
                    [_].[Order Date],
                    [_].[Delivery Date],
                    [_].[CustomerKey],
                    [_].[StoreKey],
                    [_].[ProductKey],
                    [_].[Quantity],
                    [_].[Unit Price],
                    [_].[Net Price],
                    [_].[Unit Cost],
                    [_].[Currency Code],
                    [_].[Exchange Rate]
                FROM [Data].[Sales] AS [_]
                WHERE [_].[Order Date] <= convert(DATE, '2019-12-31')
                ) AS [t3]
                LEFT JOIN [dbo].[Date] AS [t1] ON ([t3].[Order Date] = [t1].[Date])
            )
        ) AS [t0]
    WHERE ([t3_Order Date] >= CAST('20200101 00:00:00' AS DATETIME))
    GROUP BY [t1_Year]
    ) AS [MainTable]
WHERE (NOT (([a0] IS NULL)))
```

Despite Tabular not performing partition pruning, SQL Server is smart enough to spot that executing the query is pointless if the filter is on the column being used in the partition filter, *Sales[Order Date]*. Let us compare the execution plans of the previous SQL query and of this last one. The following is the query plan of the query that filters *Date[Year]*.

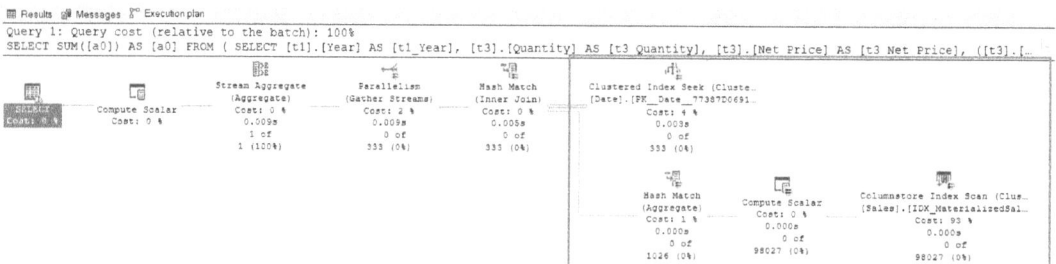

The highlighted section includes an Index Seek over *Date* (at the top) to retrieve the values of *Date[Date]* satisfying the condition over *Date[Year]*. The list of dates obtained is then used to filter the scan of *Sales* (at the bottom). The execution of the code is extremely fast; still, it requires some effort from the point of view of SQL Server.

The query where the filter is placed on *Sales[Order Date]* shows a very different query plan.

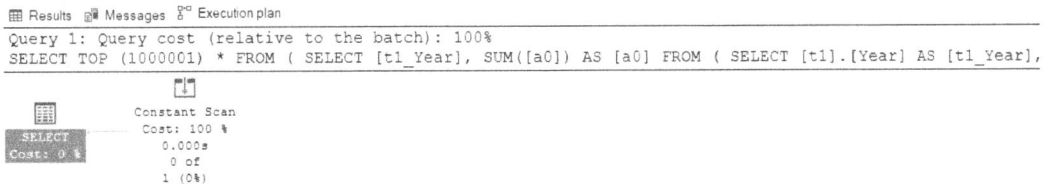

```
⊞ Results  ⊞ Messages  ⁿ Execution plan
Query 1: Query cost (relative to the batch): 100%
SELECT TOP (1000001) * FROM ( SELECT [t1_Year], SUM([a0]) AS [a0] FROM ( SELECT [t1].[Year] AS [t1_Year],
```

```
                          ╔═╗
                          ║↑║
                          ╚═╝
                     Constant Scan
 ⊞                    Cost: 100 %
 SELECT ───────────     0.000s
 Cost: 0 %               0 of
                         1 (0%)
```

SQL Server did not even try to execute the query. Because the two conditions over *Sales[Order Date]* are conflicting, SQL Server does not execute any code and returns an empty table.

Still, the SQL query must be executed; therefore, Tabular pays the price of connecting to SQL, sending the query, and retrieving the result. Depending on the configuration, the execution time can be short or long. However, our tests did not show a significant impact on performance, despite the fact that we configured the environment to run through a gateway that increases latency in communication.

Limitations of hybrid tables

When working with hybrid tables, developers must deal with an important limitation: hybrid tables cannot contain calculated columns. You get an error if you try to add a calculated column to an already-defined hybrid table, or to convert a table with calculated columns into a hybrid table.

Remember that calculated columns on large fact tables are the wrong choice when working with VertiPaq. However, calculated columns are useful when using DirectQuery. They are useful to create aggregations, to simplify complex calculations, and to use COMBINEVALUES to build multi-column relationships optimized for SQL. Therefore, calculated columns in DirectQuery are helpful and are typically considered part of the architecture. However, you cannot use calculated columns and hybrid tables simultaneously.

This is quite a substantial limitation in terms of modeling capabilities. This limitation makes the relevance of hybrid tables limited to certain situations. Developers cannot build a complete solution based on hybrid tables, as the limitation would be hard to deal with. However, you can consider hybrid tables as an option in the architecture design in specific scenarios, such as when you need real-time or when the memory pressure of the entire table in VertiPaq is too heavy.

As a possible alternative to hybrid tables, you can build two tables: one with the VertiPaq part and one with the DirectQuery part. The results of the two tables can be mixed and controlled through measures. This solution works well, except for distinct counts and other non-additive calculations that either cannot be computed or result in too complex a DAX code, as discussed in the following section.

Reducing partition queries with DataCoverageDefinition

In February 2024 – during the final publishing process of this book – Microsoft introduced a property that can remove superfluous SQL queries for partitions that do not contain relevant data based on the new **DataCoverageDefinition** property, which specify a DAX logical condition that must be true to send the query to the external data source.

You must run a "Process Recalc" after modifying the DataCoverageDefinition property in order to make the change effective. Read more about this property and its limitations on Microsoft documentation: https://tinyurl.com/data-coverage-definition.

Hybrid tables and distinct counts

Hybrid tables show a peculiar behavior when computing distinct counts. Indeed, because the data resides in different partitions handled by two different storage engines, there are no ways to compute a distinct count separately and then aggregate the partial results later.

Consider the following query:

```
EVALUATE
SUMMARIZECOLUMNS (
    Customer[Country],
    "# Products", DISTINCTCOUNT ( Sales[ProductKey] )
)
```

DirectQuery handles nine years of data, and one year is in VertiPaq. The distinct count of *Sales[ProductKey]* cannot be computed separately and then aggregated because the query groups by *Customer[Country]*. Tabular must retrieve the *Customer[Country]* and *Sales[ProductKey]* pairs from both data sources, merge the results, and then compute the distinct count in the formula engine.

Total	SE CPU		Line	Subclass	Duration	CPU	Par.	Rows	KB	Timeline
453 ms	203 ms									
	x1.0		1	SQL	187	187	x1.0			
FE	**SE**		3	Scan	16	16	x1.0	27,720	217	
253 ms	200 ms									
55.8%	44.8%									

SE Queries	SE Cache
2	0
	0.0%

Total DQ
187 ms

The SQL query does not contain any distinct count. It just retrieves the pairs of *Country* and *ProductKey*:

```sql
SELECT TOP (1000001) [t0].[Country],
    [t3].[ProductKey]
FROM (
    (
        SELECT [_].[Order Number],
            [_].[Line Number],
            [_].[Order Date],
            [_].[Delivery Date],
            [_].[CustomerKey],
            [_].[StoreKey],
            [_].[ProductKey],
            [_].[Quantity],
            [_].[Unit Price],
            [_].[Net Price],
            [_].[Unit Cost],
            [_].[Currency Code],
            [_].[Exchange Rate]
        FROM [Data].[Sales] AS [_]
        WHERE [_].[Order Date] <= convert(DATE, '2019-12-31')
        ) AS [t3]
        LEFT JOIN [dbo].[Customer] AS [t0] ON ([t3].[CustomerKey] = [t0].[CustomerKey])
    )
GROUP BY [t0].[Country],
    [t3].[ProductKey]
```

The xmSQL code has a similar structure:

```
SELECT
    'Customer'[Country],
    'Sales'[ProductKey]
FROM 'Sales'
    LEFT OUTER JOIN 'Customer'
        ON 'Sales'[CustomerKey]='Customer'[CustomerKey];
```

The formula engine scans and joins the two datacaches computing the distinct count. The internal storage engine queries are not a simple distinct count, and the resulting datacaches can be much larger than the DAX output. Adding too many group-by columns to the query results in an error:

```
EVALUATE
SUMMARIZECOLUMNS (
    Customer[Country],
    'Date'[Date],
    "# Products", DISTINCTCOUNT ( Sales[ProductKey] )
)
```

Executing the query raises the error that the DirectQuery request returns more than 1M rows.

The resultset of a query to external data source has exceeded the maximum allowed size of '1000000' rows.

Technical Details:
RootActivityId: 4fd4812e-54f8-41da-8c2e-66e51d904ee7
Date (UTC): 8/23/2023 1:31:37 PM

Total	SE CPU		Line	Subclass	Duration	CPU	Par.	Rows	KB	Timeline
7,393 ms	125 ms									
	x1.0		1	SQL	80	78	x1.0			
FE	**SE**		3	Scan	47	47	x1.0	218,540	854	
7,266 ms	127 ms									
98.3%	1.7%									

SELECT TOP (1000001) [t0].[Country],
  [t1].[Date],
  [t3].[ProductKey]
FROM (
  (
    (
      SELECT [_].[Order Number],
      [ ] [Line Number]

SE Queries	SE Cache
2	0
	0.0%

Total DQ
80 ms

Because of the large materialization required to complete the calculation in the formula engine, hybrid tables should not use non-additive measures such as distinct counts, to avoid performance issues.

Creating hybrid tables with incremental refresh

As mentioned in the introduction to hybrid tables, it is possible to create hybrid tables in an automated way when you configure an incremental refresh for a table. Setting an incremental refresh requires creating two Power Query parameters (*RangeStart*, *RangeEnd*) to filter the loaded data and then publishing the model on the service to activate the incremental refresh.

Among different options, the dialog box offers you the possibility to **Get the latest data in real time with DirectQuery**.

Incremental refresh and real-time data

Refresh large tables faster with incremental refresh. Plus, get the latest data in real time with DirectQuery (Premium only). Learn more

ⓘ These settings will apply when you publish the dataset to the Power BI service. Once you do that, you won't be able to download it back to Power BI Desktop. Learn more

1. Select table

Sales	⌄

2. Set import and refresh ranges

🔘 Incrementally refresh this table

Archive data starting [Enter value..] [Select value ⌄] before refresh date

Incrementally refresh data starting [Enter value..] [Select value ⌄] before refresh date

3. Choose optional settings

☑ Get the latest data in real time with DirectQuery (Premium only) Learn more

☑ Only refresh complete periods Learn more

☐ Detect data changes Learn more

4. Review and apply

	Archived		Incremental Refresh	Real-time
	Archival Start Date		Incremental Start Date	Refresh date

Apply   Cancel

Enabling this option automates the creation of an additional partition to hold the data after the latest refresh. Despite the feature being straightforward to activate, it is essential to note that all the limitations and the details we have outlined still apply.

Consequently, developers should consider this feature a convenient way to create the additional DirectQuery partition, but then they should also check that the feature does not disrupt the entire model.

Hybrid tables come with strengths and weaknesses, as with any other technology. They increase the number of options available to handle real-time and large model requirements using VertiPaq and DirectQuery in the same model. However, developers must evaluate the existing limitations before using hybrid tables in production.

Conclusions

The architecture of DirectQuery is very different compared to VertiPaq. Designing a SQL Server database optimized for DirectQuery requires making different decisions about multiple aspects. Using DirectQuery requires a profound knowledge of SQL and a specific design of tables, indexes, and views to fulfill the requirements of the Tabular formula engine. Moreover, to obtain the best performance, it is necessary to alter the DirectQuery data source (like the SQL Server database) considering the specific requirements of your model. Altering views, creating materialized views, indexes, calculated columns, or changing the datatype of columns are just some of the many changes required on your SQL Server database to boost performance.

Remember that DirectQuery should not be the default option for a Tabular model. Using VertiPaq provides straightforward access to top performance, whereas using DirectQuery requires much more work to obtain performance that is still inferior and not comparable to VertiPaq.

However, if DirectQuery is a requirement, then this chapter provided you with some starting points from where to optimize your model. In the next chapter, we cover a similar topic, but the focus is on what to do differently from the DAX point of view.

Optimizations examples for DirectQuery

We have mentioned on several occasions that optimizing DAX for DirectQuery differs from optimizing DAX for VertiPaq. Some optimization techniques are similar, whereas others are different because of the diverse architecture of SQL Server and VertiPaq, which also drives variations in how the storage engines collaborate with the formula engine.

In this chapter, we analyze some of the optimizations that we have already demonstrated in VertiPaq. The goal is to show that the optimal version of VertiPaq is not the same as DirectQuery. We do not repeat the description we already provided for VertiPaq. We take for granted that the reader has already studied the same patterns in VertiPaq so that we can focus on the differences.

Moreover, we avoid showing examples where the difference would not be relevant. We chose examples that reveal important differences between VertiPaq and DirectQuery.

Optimizing LASTDATE calculations

Standard time intelligence calculations are a challenge in both DirectQuery and VertiPaq. However, some limitations are more substantial in DirectQuery than in VertiPaq. Let us examine a simple calculation with LASTDATE. The following query retrieves the last price for each product:

```
EVALUATE
SUMMARIZECOLUMNS (
    'Product'[Product Name],
    "Last price",
        CALCULATE (
            AVERAGE ( Sales[Net Price] ),
            LASTDATE ( Sales[Order Date] )
        )
)
ORDER BY 'Product'[Product Name]
```

The same query runs quite slowly in VertiPaq, but it executes smoothly. First, the storage engine materializes a datacache containing all combinations of *Product[Product Name]* and *Sales[Order Date]*. Then, the formula engine retrieves the last date for each product and executes a second storage engine query to retrieve the average *Net Price* on that date.

Unfortunately, the query does not execute on DirectQuery because the resulting datacache exceeds 1M rows. In its simplicity, this query involving LASTDATE is not an option.

When optimizing VertiPaq, we tested a different version to reduce the size of the datacaches. This second query uses ADDCOLUMNS to compute the max order date per product, and then executes a second scan of *Sales* to compute the average *Net Price*:

```
EVALUATE
SUMMARIZECOLUMNS (
    'Product'[Product Name],
    "Last price",
        VAR ProdsAndDates =
            TREATAS (
                ADDCOLUMNS (
                    ALLSELECTED ( 'Product'[Product Name] ),
                    "@LastDate", CALCULATE ( MAX ( Sales[Order Date] ) )
                ),
                'Product'[Product Name],
                Sales[Order Date]
            )
        VAR Result =
            CALCULATE ( AVERAGE ( Sales[Net Price] ), KEEPFILTERS ( ProdsAndDates ) )
        RETURN
            Result
)
ORDER BY 'Product'[Product Name]
```

Having reduced the size of the datacaches, this version of the code runs successfully, even though it is slow (around 11 seconds).

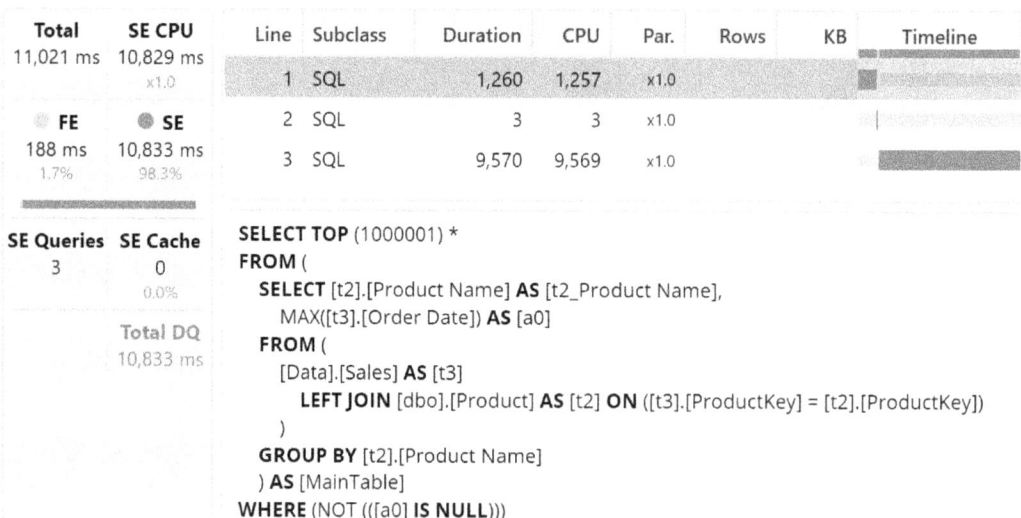

Total	SE CPU		Line	Subclass	Duration	CPU	Par.	Rows	KB	Timeline
11,021 ms	10,829 ms									
	x1.0		1	SQL	1,260	1,257	x1.0			
FE	**SE**		2	SQL	3	3	x1.0			
188 ms	10,833 ms		3	SQL	9,570	9,569	x1.0			
1.7%	98.3%									

SE Queries	SE Cache
3	0
	0.0%

Total DQ
10,833 ms

SELECT TOP (1000001) *
FROM (
    SELECT [t2].[Product Name] **AS** [t2_Product Name],
        MAX([t3].[Order Date]) **AS** [a0]
    FROM (
        [Data].[Sales] **AS** [t3]
            LEFT JOIN [dbo].[Product] **AS** [t2] **ON** ([t3].[ProductKey] = [t2].[ProductKey])
)
    GROUP BY [t2].[Product Name]
) **AS** [MainTable]
WHERE (NOT (([a0] **IS NULL**)))

The DirectQuery storage engine executes three SQL queries. The first one retrieves the maximum *Order*

Date by *Product Name*:

```
SELECT TOP (1000001) *
FROM (
    SELECT [t2].[Product Name] AS [t2_Product Name],
        MAX([t3].[Order Date]) AS [a0]
    FROM (
        [Data].[Sales] AS [t3]
            LEFT JOIN [dbo].[Product] AS [t2] ON ([t3].[ProductKey] = [t2].[ProductKey])
        )
    GROUP BY [t2].[Product Name]
    ) AS [MainTable]
WHERE (NOT (([a0] IS NULL)))
```

The second query is straightforward, as it only retrieves the product names:

```
SELECT TOP (1000001) [t2].[Product Name]
FROM ([dbo].[Product]) AS [t2]
GROUP BY [t2].[Product Name]
```

The third and most expensive query computes the average *Net Price*. It contains a giant UNION of multiple SELECT statements to create the proper filter of products and dates. Among the many rows, the one highlighted contains SELECT NULL for all the columns. For now, it is just relevant to observe its existence; the reason will become clear later:

```
SELECT TOP (1000001) [basetable0].[t2_Product Name],
    SUM([a0]) AS [a0], COUNT_BIG([a1]) AS [a1]
FROM (
    (
        SELECT [t2].[Product Name] AS [t2_Product Name],
            [t3].[Order Date] AS [t3_Order Date],
            [t3].[Net Price] AS [a0], [t3].[Net Price] AS [a1]
        FROM (
            [Data].[Sales] AS [t3]
                LEFT JOIN [dbo].[Product] AS [t2] ON ([t3].[ProductKey] = [t2].[ProductKey])
            )
    ) AS [basetable0]
    INNER JOIN (
    (SELECT N'A. Datum Advanced Digital Camera M300 Azure' AS [t2_Product Name],
     CAST('20200303 00:00:00' AS DATETIME) AS [t3_Order Date])
    UNION ALL (SELECT N'A. Datum Advanced Digital Camera M300 Black'
                        AS [t2_Product Name],
               CAST('20200303 00:00:00' AS DATETIME) AS [t3_Order Date])
    UNION ALL (SELECT N'A. Datum Advanced Digital Camera M300 Green'
                        AS [t2_Product Name],
               CAST('20200303 00:00:00' AS DATETIME) AS [t3_Order Date])
```

```
-- There are thousands of rows with the same structure, omitted in the text

        UNION ALL (SELECT N'WWI Wireless Transmitter and Bluetooth Headphones X250 White'
                         AS [t2_Product Name],
                   CAST('20200303 00:00:00' AS DATETIME) AS [t3_Order Date])
        UNION ALL (SELECT NULL AS [t2_Product Name], NULL AS [t3_Order Date])
        ) AS [semijoin1] ON (
            (
                [semijoin1].[t2_Product Name] = [basetable0].[t2_Product Name]
                OR [semijoin1].[t2_Product Name] IS NULL
                AND [basetable0].[t2_Product Name] IS NULL
                )
            AND (
                [semijoin1].[t3_Order Date] = [basetable0].[t3_Order Date]
                OR [semijoin1].[t3_Order Date] IS NULL
                AND [basetable0].[t3_Order Date] IS NULL
                )
            )
        )
GROUP BY [basetable0].[t2_Product Name]
```

The algorithm is relatively simple and precisely depicts what DAX expresses: a first SQL query retrieves the set of products and last dates, the second SQL query retrieves the list of product names, and the third SQL query retrieves – for each product name – the sum of *Sales[Net Price]* and the number of rows, which are the base ingredients to compute the average.

The query consists of several thousands of SQL code lines because the filter is expressed as a set of UNION ALL statements with constant values. This large textual filter is the effect of the formula engine retrieving the values to filter to pass them back as a filter to the SQL engine. The way DirectQuery and Tabular communicate is through SQL code. However, it would be misleading to consider the query length as the problem. The query is very long, but we need one more test to discover why it is so slow.

When analyzing the VertiPaq optimization, we have shown that the following, third version of the DAX code ran at a similar speed. It turns out that – using DirectQuery – this version is much faster:

```
EVALUATE
SUMMARIZECOLUMNS (
    'Product'[Product Name],
    "Last price",
        CALCULATE (
            VAR LastOrderDate =
                MAX ( Sales[Order Date] )
            VAR Result =
                CALCULATE ( AVERAGE ( Sales[Net Price] ), Sales[Order Date] = LastOrderDate
)
            RETURN
                Result
        )
)
ORDER BY 'Product'[Product Name]
```

When executed, it runs in two seconds instead of 11.

Total	SE CPU	Line	Subclass	Duration	CPU	Par.	Rows	KB	Timeline
2,330 ms	2,127 ms	1	SQL	4	4	x1.0			
	x1.0	2	SQL	1,242	1,242	x1.0			
FE	SE	3	SQL	93	92	x1.0			
201 ms	2,129 ms	4	SQL	790	789	x1.0			
8.6%	91.4%								

SE Queries SE Cache
4   0
       0.0%

Total DQ
2,129 ms

This time, there are four storage engine queries. The first one retrieves the product names:

```
SELECT TOP (1000001) [t2].[Product Name]
FROM ([dbo].[Product]) AS [t2]
GROUP BY [t2].[Product Name]
```

The second query retrieves the pairs of product name and last order date:

```
SELECT TOP (1000001) *
FROM (
    SELECT [t2].[Product Name] AS [t2_Product Name],
        MAX([t3].[Order Date]) AS [a0]
    FROM (
        [Data].[Sales] AS [t3]
            LEFT JOIN [dbo].[Product] AS [t2] ON ([t3].[ProductKey] = [t2].[ProductKey])
        )
    GROUP BY [t2].[Product Name]
    ) AS [MainTable]
WHERE (NOT (([a0] IS NULL)))
```

So far, the SQL code is very close to the one generated for the previous DAX query. There is a third SQL query, which retrieves the values of *Order Date*:

```
SELECT TOP (1000001) [t3].[Order Date]
FROM ([Data].[Sales]) AS [t3]
GROUP BY [t3].[Order Date]
```

The last SQL query text is long – as was the last SQL request for the previous DAX query – but this time it executes much faster:

```
SELECT TOP (1000001) [basetable0].[t2_Product Name],
    SUM([a0]) AS [a0],
    COUNT_BIG([a1]) AS [a1]
FROM (
    (
        SELECT [t2].[Product Name] AS [t2_Product Name],
            [t3].[Order Date] AS [t3_Order Date],
            [t3].[Net Price] AS [a0],
            [t3].[Net Price] AS [a1]
        FROM (
            [Data].[Sales] AS [t3]
                LEFT JOIN [dbo].[Product] AS [t2] ON ([t3].[ProductKey] = [t2].[ProductKey])
            )
        ) AS [basetable0]
        INNER JOIN (
        (SELECT N'A. Datum Advanced Digital Camera M300 Azure' AS [t2_Product Name],
        CAST('20200303 00:00:00' AS DATETIME) AS [t3_Order Date])
        UNION ALL (SELECT N'A. Datum Advanced Digital Camera M300 Black'
                        AS [t2_Product Name],
                    CAST('20200303 00:00:00' AS DATETIME) AS [t3_Order Date])
        UNION ALL (SELECT N'A. Datum Advanced Digital Camera M300 Green'
                        AS [t2_Product Name],
                    CAST('20200303 00:00:00' AS DATETIME) AS [t3_Order Date])

-- There are thousands of rows with the same structure, omitted in the text


        UNION ALL (SELECT N'WWI Wireless Transmitter and Bluetooth Headphones X250 White'
                        AS [t2_Product Name],
                    CAST('20200303 00:00:00' AS DATETIME) AS [t3_Order Date])
        ) AS [semijoin1] ON (
            ([semijoin1].[t2_Product Name] = [basetable0].[t2_Product Name])
            AND ([semijoin1].[t3_Order Date] = [basetable0].[t3_Order Date])
            )
    )
GROUP BY [basetable0].[t2_Product Name]
```

There are two differences between the previous version and this one. First, the row we had highlighted in the previous version (SELECT NULL) is absent. Second, the join condition is more straightforward, as it does not have to handle NULL.

To double-check our findings, we can execute both queries in SQL Server Management Studio. It turns out that the difference in speed is entirely because of the row containing NULL, which is present (and highlighted) in the previous example, yet absent here.

Tabular needs special handling for NULL because – in the model – the relationships between *Sales* and *Products* and between *Sales* and *Date* are not flagged with **Assume referential integrity**. Because of this, DAX assumes that the relationship might be invalid, thus generating slower SQL code.

If we set both relationships to assume referential integrity, then the two DAX queries run at similar speed. The first – important – takeaway of this demo is that assuming referential integrity in a relationship has two effects: first, the join between tables uses an INNER join rather than an OUTER join, as we have seen in previous examples. Second, the engine produces faster code if it can assume that a relationship is valid because it does not have to handle the case where the blank row appears for an invalid relationship.

Once we have a clear understanding of the effect of a potentially invalid relationship, we can author a last version of the query which restores great performance by using DISTINCT rather than ALLSELECTED to retrieve the product names:

```
EVALUATE
SUMMARIZECOLUMNS (
    'Product'[Product Name],
    "Last price",
        VAR ProdsAndDates =
            TREATAS (
                CALCULATETABLE (
                    ADDCOLUMNS (
                        DISTINCT ( 'Product'[Product Name] ),
                        "@LastDate", CALCULATE ( MAX ( Sales[Order Date] ) )
                    ),
                    ALLSELECTED ()
                ),
                'Product'[Product Name],
                Sales[Order Date]
            )
        VAR Result =
            CALCULATE ( AVERAGE ( Sales[Net Price] ), KEEPFILTERS ( ProdsAndDates ) )
        RETURN
            Result
)
ORDER BY 'Product'[Product Name]
```

This version of the query is very fast, even though the structure of the SQL queries is the same as before. The only noticeable difference is in the last one, which does not include NULL handling.

Total	SE CPU	Line	Subclass	Duration	CPU	Par.	Rows	KB	Timeline
2,387 ms	2,154 ms								
	x1.0	1	SQL	3	3	x1.0			
FE	SE	2	SQL	1,367	1,367	x1.0			
230 ms	2,157 ms	3	SQL	787	784	x1.0			
9.6%	90.4%								

SE Queries	SE Cache
3	0
	0.0%

Total DQ
2,157 ms

As demonstrated in this demo, optimizing DirectQuery requires a different perspective. Not only do developers need to work with DAX code, but they also need to check the SQL code to understand why a DAX query is slow. As always, the more you know about the internals of the engines, the better you can optimize DAX and data models.

Optimizing division by checking for zeroes

Another interesting example we have already shown in the VertiPaq section is about protecting from division by zero. The following query computes the number of transactions where the margin is greater than 200%:

```
EVALUATE
SUMMARIZECOLUMNS (
    'Product'[Brand],
    "Sales with large margin",
        COUNTROWS (
            FILTER (
                Sales,
                Sales[Net Price] / Sales[Unit Cost] >= 2
            )
        )
)
```

The DAX query runs in around nine seconds.

Total	SE CPU	Line	Subclass	Duration	CPU	Par.	Rows	KB	Timeline
8,942 ms	8,931 ms	1	SQL	8,931	8,931	x1.0			
	x1.0								

FE	**SE**
11 ms	8,931 ms
0.1%	99.9%

SE Queries	SE Cache
1	0
	0.0%

Total DQ
8,931 ms

```
    COUNT_BIG(*) AS [a0]
FROM (
    [Data].[Sales] AS [t3]
        LEFT JOIN [dbo].[Product] AS [t2] ON ([t3].[ProductKey] = [t2].[ProductKey])
)
```

There is only one SQL query, which is a direct translation of DAX:

```
SELECT TOP (1000001) [t2].[Brand] AS [t2_Brand],
    COUNT_BIG(*) AS [a0]
FROM (
    [Data].[Sales] AS [t3]
        LEFT JOIN [dbo].[Product] AS [t2] ON ([t3].[ProductKey] = [t2].[ProductKey])
)
WHERE (COALESCE(([t3].[Net Price] / COALESCE(CAST([t3].[Unit Cost] AS FLOAT), 0)), 0) >= 2.)
GROUP BY [t2].[Brand]
```

The only drawback of this code is that it is not protected in case *Sales[Unit Cost]* is blank or zero. If so, the division raises a "division by zero" error.

When optimizing VertiPaq, we have seen that adding an IF statement inside the iteration is not a brilliant idea. The reason is that – in VertiPaq – IF in the iterator requires a callback to the formula engine, resulting in low performance. However, this is not going to be the case in DirectQuery. Let us examine the following DAX code:

```
EVALUATE
SUMMARIZECOLUMNS (
    'Product'[Brand],
    "Sales with large margin",
        COUNTROWS (
            FILTER (
                Sales,
                IF (
                    Sales[Unit Cost] <> 0,
                    Sales[Net Price] / Sales[Unit Cost] >= 2
                )
            )
        )
)
```

It consumes a similar amount of time as the previous query.

Total	SE CPU		Line	Subclass	Duration	CPU	Par.	Rows	KB	Timeline
9,683 ms	9,677 ms		1	SQL	9,677	9,677	x1.0			
	x1.0									

FE	SE
6 ms	9,677 ms
0.1%	99.9%

SE Queries	SE Cache
1	0
	0.0%

	Total DQ
	9.677 ms

```
SELECT TOP (1000001) [t2].[Brand] AS [t2_Brand],
    COUNT_BIG(*) AS [a0]
FROM (
    [Data].[Sales] AS [t3]
        LEFT JOIN [dbo].[Product] AS [t2] ON ([t3].[ProductKey] = [t2].[ProductKey])
    )
WHERE (
    (
        CASE
```

Inspecting the SQL query shows that there is no need for a callback, as SQL is excellent in expressing the complexity of an IF statement:

```
SELECT TOP (1000001) [t2].[Brand] AS [t2_Brand],
    COUNT_BIG(*) AS [a0]
FROM (
    [Data].[Sales] AS [t3]
        LEFT JOIN [dbo].[Product] AS [t2] ON ([t3].[ProductKey] = [t2].[ProductKey])
    )
WHERE (
    (
        CASE
            WHEN (
                NOT (([t3].[Unit Cost] IS NULL))
                AND ([t3].[Unit Cost] <> CAST(N'0' AS MONEY))
            )

            THEN
                CAST( CASE
                    WHEN (
                        COALESCE(
                         ([t3].[Net Price] / COALESCE(CAST([t3].[Unit Cost] AS FLOAT), 0) ),
                         0
                        ) >= 2.
                    )
                    THEN 1
                    ELSE 0
                    END AS BIT
                )
            ELSE 0
        END
    ) <> 0
    )
GROUP BY [t2].[Brand]
```

Despite looking verbose because it is auto generated, the SQL code embeds the logic of the IF function and runs fine.

In VertiPaq, using DIVIDE rather than IF provides better performance. In DirectQuery, DIVIDE forces a different SQL query, resulting in lower performance. The following DAX query uses the DIVIDE function:

```
EVALUATE
SUMMARIZECOLUMNS (
    'Product'[Brand],
    "Sales with large margin",
        COUNTROWS (
            FILTER (
                Sales,
                DIVIDE ( Sales[Net Price], Sales[Unit Cost] ) >= 2
            )
        )
)
```

The query runs in more than 19 seconds.

Total	SE CPU	Line	Subclass	Duration	CPU	Par.	Rows	KB	Timeline
19,133 ms	19,122 ms	1	SQL	19,122	19,122	x1.0			
	x1.0								

FE	**SE**
13 ms	19,120 ms
0.1%	99.9%

SE Queries	**SE Cache**
1	0
	0.0%

Total DQ
19,122 ms

```
SELECT TOP (1000001) [t2].[Brand] AS [t2_Brand],
    COUNT_BIG(*) AS [a0]
FROM (
    [Data].[Sales] AS [t3]
        LEFT JOIN [dbo].[Product] AS [t2] ON ([t3].[ProductKey] = [t2].[ProductKey])
    )
WHERE (
    COALESCE((
        SELECT CASE
```

Inspecting the SQL code shows that the translation of DIVIDE requires more operations from the SQL point of view compared to the IF translation:

```
SELECT TOP (1000001) [t2].[Brand] AS [t2_Brand],
    COUNT_BIG(*) AS [a0]
FROM (
    [Data].[Sales] AS [t3]
        LEFT JOIN [dbo].[Product] AS [t2] ON ([t3].[ProductKey] = [t2].[ProductKey])
    )
WHERE (
        COALESCE((
                SELECT CASE
                        WHEN Op1 IS NULL
                            THEN NULL
                        ELSE CASE
                                WHEN Op2 IS NULL
                                    OR Op2 = 0
                                    THEN Op3
                                ELSE Op1 / Op2
                                END
                        END
                FROM (
                    SELECT [t3].[Net Price] AS Op1,
                        CAST([t3].[Unit Cost] AS FLOAT) AS Op2,
                        NULL AS Op3
                    ) AS AuxTable
                ), 0) >= 2.
    )
GROUP BY [t2].[Brand]
```

This is just another example where optimizing DAX for DirectQuery or VertiPaq requires a different approach. With VertiPaq, DIVIDE shows better performance compared with IF. The opposite happens with DirectQuery: IF is better than DIVIDE, at least in this simple example. We will never stop repeating that extensive testing is required before making any decision.

In VertiPaq, we also considered using IFERROR rather than IF. Unfortunately, it turns out that IFERROR requires a large materialization, exceeding the limit of 1M rows:

```
EVALUATE
SUMMARIZECOLUMNS (
    'Product'[Brand],
    "Sales with large margin",
        COUNTROWS (
            FILTER (
                Sales,
                IFERROR ( Sales[Net Price] / Sales[Unit Cost], BLANK () ) > 2
            )
        )
)
```

This DAX query does not run. Indeed, the SQL query tries to materialize a large amount of data, and the entire DAX query aborts when one SQL query exceeds 1M rows. IFERROR is such a peculiar function that it is not worth further testing. The most likely cause of the excessive materialization is that error handling needs to happen in the formula engine, producing excessive materialization.

The good news is that both VertiPaq and DirectQuery provide the best performance when using CALCULATE to remove zeroes upfront:

```
EVALUATE
SUMMARIZECOLUMNS (
    'Product'[Brand],
    "Sales with large margin",
        CALCULATE (
            COUNTROWS (
                FILTER (
                    Sales,
                    Sales[Net Price] / Sales[Unit Cost] > 2
                )
            ),
            Sales[Unit Cost] <> 0
        )
)
```

This DAX query runs very fast in around 6.5 seconds.

Total	SE CPU	Line	Subclass	Duration	CPU	Par.	Rows	KB	Timeline
6,570 ms	6,559 ms								
	x1.0	1	SQL	6,560	6,559	x1.0			

FE	SE
10 ms	6,560 ms
0.2%	99.8%

SE Queries	SE Cache
1	0
	0.0%

Total DQ
6,560 ms

```
SELECT TOP (1000001) [t2].[Brand] AS [t2_Brand],
    COUNT_BIG(*) AS [a0]
FROM (
    [Data].[Sales] AS [t3]
        LEFT JOIN [dbo].[Product] AS [t2] ON ([t3].[ProductKey] = [t2].[ProductKey])
    )
WHERE (
    (COALESCE(([t3].[Net Price] / CAST([t3].[Unit Cost] AS FLOAT)), 0) > 2.)
        AND ([t3].[Unit Cost] <> CAST(N'0' AS MONEY))
    )
GROUP BY [t2].[Brand]
```

The SQL code is more straightforward, as it does not contain inner calculations but only two filters:

```
SELECT TOP (1000001) [t2].[Brand] AS [t2_Brand],
    COUNT_BIG(*) AS [a0]
FROM (
    [Data].[Sales] AS [t3]
        LEFT JOIN [dbo].[Product] AS [t2] ON ([t3].[ProductKey] = [t2].[ProductKey])
    )
WHERE (
        (COALESCE(([t3].[Net Price] / CAST([t3].[Unit Cost] AS FLOAT)), 0) > 2.)
        AND ([t3].[Unit Cost] <> CAST(N'0' AS MONEY))
        )
GROUP BY [t2].[Brand]
```

For the sake of covering all the bases, we report that using an inner filter in DAX without CALCULATE performs at the same speed and uses the very same SQL query – even though CALCULATE is a preferred approach for flexibility:

```
EVALUATE
SUMMARIZECOLUMNS (
    'Product'[Brand],
    "Sales with large margin",
        COUNTROWS (
            FILTER (
                FILTER (
                    Sales,
                    Sales[Unit Cost] <> 0
                ),
                Sales[Net Price] / Sales[Unit Cost] > 2
            )
        )
    )
)
```

The takeaway here is that both VertiPaq and DirectQuery work better if data is filtered upfront. It does not matter that we used an iterator like FILTER in the last piece of DAX code. FILTER can produce a simple WHERE condition in both SQL and xmSQL. However, there are scenarios where we cannot use a simple FILTER. In that case, DirectQuery provides the best performance by using IF inside the iteration, whereas the DIVIDE function is the way to go in VertiPaq.

Optimizing time intelligence calculations

Calculations that use the DAX time intelligence functions mostly retrieve data at the day level, performing the required aggregations in the formula engine. By avoiding time intelligence DAX functions, you can force DAX to produce more optimized queries for your specific calculations.

DirectQuery and VertiPaq require the same patterns to optimize time intelligence calculations, even though the reasons are different. In VertiPaq, we try to stay away from DAX time intelligence functions to avoid large materialization at the day level. With SQL, materialization does not always happen because Tabular tries to push the grouping down to SQL. Still, time intelligence calculations often result in complex queries, and it is better to avoid the complexity by using simpler DAX code.

As an example, let us analyze a DAX query that for each month computes the growth in sales compared with the same month in the previous year:

```
DEFINE
    MEASURE Sales[Sales PY] =
            CALCULATE ( [Sales Amount], SAMEPERIODLASTYEAR ( 'Date'[Date] ) )
EVALUATE
SUMMARIZECOLUMNS (
    'Date'[Year Month],
    'Date'[Year Month Number],
    "Sales Growth %", DIVIDE ( [Sales Amount] - [Sales PY], [Sales PY] )
)
ORDER BY 'Date'[Year Month Number]
```

The query runs in around 3.2 seconds.

Total	SE CPU	Line	Subclass	Duration	CPU	Par.	Rows	KB	Timeline
3,197 ms	2,853 ms								
	x1.0	1	SQL	0	0				
● FE	● SE	2	SQL	0	0				
343 ms	2,854 ms	3	SQL	1,340	1,339	x1.0			
10.7%	89.3%	4	SQL	1,514	1,514	x1.0			
SE Queries	SE Cache								
4	0								
	0.0%								
	Total DQ								
	2,854 ms								

Most of the work happens inside SQL Server, even though the formula engine carries on some of the activities and consuming 10% of the overall execution time.

The first two SQL queries are trivial, as they only gather the dates and the relationship between dates and months. The first query returns the list of dates:

```
SELECT TOP (1000001) [t1].[Date]
FROM ([dbo].[Date]) AS [t1]
GROUP BY [t1].[Date]
```

This second query retrieves the relationship between dates and months because

SAMEPERIODLASTYEAR works at the date level. Therefore, the formula engine retrieves the dates present in the *Date* table for each month to shift them to the previous year:

```
SELECT TOP (1000001) [t1].[Date],
    [t1].[Year Month],
    [t1].[Year Month Number]
FROM ([dbo].[Date]) AS [t1]
GROUP BY [t1].[Date],
    [t1].[Year Month],
    [t1].[Year Month Number]
```

The third query retrieves sales at the date level. The original query is 3,679 lines long. We show just an excerpt:

```
SELECT TOP (1000001) *
FROM (
    SELECT [semijoin1].[c20],
        [semijoin1].[c22],
        SUM([a0]) AS [a0]
    FROM (
        (
            SELECT [t1_Date],
                [a0]
            FROM (
                SELECT [t1].[Date] AS [t1_Date],
                    [t3].[Quantity] AS [t3_Quantity],
                    [t3].[Net Price] AS [t3_Net Price],
                    ([t3].[Quantity] * [t3].[Net Price]) AS [a0]
                FROM (
                    [Data].[Sales] AS [t3]
                        LEFT JOIN [dbo].[Date] AS [t1] ON ([t3].[Order Date] = [t1].[Date])
                    )
                ) AS [t0]
            ) AS [basetable0]
        INNER JOIN (
        (SELECT N'January 2011' AS [c20], 24133 AS [c22],
                CAST('20100101 00:00:00' AS DATETIME) AS [t1_Date])
        UNION ALL (SELECT N'January 2011' AS [c20], 24133 AS [c22],
                    CAST('20100102 00:00:00' AS DATETIME) AS [t1_Date])
        UNION ALL (SELECT N'January 2011' AS [c20], 24133 AS [c22],
                    CAST('20100103 00:00:00' AS DATETIME) AS [t1_Date])
    ...
```

```
              UNION ALL (SELECT N'December 2020' AS [c20], 24252 AS [c22],
                             CAST('20191230 00:00:00' AS DATETIME) AS [t1_Date])
              UNION ALL (SELECT N'December 2020' AS [c20], 24252 AS [c22],
                             CAST('20191231 00:00:00' AS DATETIME) AS [t1_Date])
              ) AS [semijoin1] ON (([semijoin1].[t1_Date] = [basetable0].[t1_Date]))
          )
      GROUP BY [semijoin1].[c20],
          [semijoin1].[c22]
      ) AS [MainTable]
  WHERE (NOT (([a0] IS NULL)))
```

Despite being verbose, the query is relatively simple: it retrieves the sales amount grouped by month with a filter on the date that contains 9 years. Interestingly, the filter includes the group by columns for the current year, but the dates are in the previous year. If you focus on the first SELECT that filters the entire query, the values are January 2011 for the month name, 24133 for the month number, and January 1st, 2010 for the date. In other words, when the grouping happens for January 2011, the dates aggregated are in January 2010.

This detail is essential. It means that the grouping operation happens inside SQL. SQL must materialize an internal structure containing the sales amount by date, but it groups data at the month level and returns a small datacache containing only the result.

The last SQL query computes the sales amount at the month level:

```
SELECT TOP (1000001) *
FROM (
    SELECT [t1_Year Month],
        [t1_Year Month Number],
        SUM([a0]) AS [a0]
    FROM (
        SELECT [t1].[Year Month] AS [t1_Year Month],
            [t1].[Year Month Number] AS [t1_Year Month Number],
            [t3].[Quantity] AS [t3_Quantity],
            [t3].[Net Price] AS [t3_Net Price],
            ([t3].[Quantity] * [t3].[Net Price]) AS [a0]
        FROM (
            [Data].[Sales] AS [t3]
                LEFT JOIN [dbo].[Date] AS [t1] ON ([t3].[Order Date] = [t1].[Date])
            )
        ) AS [t0]
    GROUP BY [t1_Year Month],
        [t1_Year Month Number]
    ) AS [MainTable]
WHERE (NOT (([a0] IS NULL)))
```

As you see, the pattern in the communication between the storage engine and the formula engine is different from the one in VertiPaq. VertiPaq materializes data at the day level and groups by month in the formula engine, whereas DirectQuery groups data by month in the storage engine. However, the SQL query retrieving values from the previous year is quite complex.

We can perform in DirectQuery the same optimization applied to VertiPaq by using the *Date[Year Month Number]* mathematical properties to compute the sales in the previous year by just subtracting 12 from the current month:

```
DEFINE
    MEASURE Sales[Sales PY] =
        VAR CurrentMonth =
            MAX ( 'Date'[Year Month Number] )
        RETURN
            CALCULATE (
                [Sales Amount],
                REMOVEFILTERS ( 'Date' ),
                'Date'[Year Month Number] = CurrentMonth - 12
            )

EVALUATE
SUMMARIZECOLUMNS (
    'Date'[Year Month],
    'Date'[Year Month Number],
    "Sales Growth %", DIVIDE ( [Sales Amount] - [Sales PY], [Sales PY] )
)
ORDER BY 'Date'[Year Month Number]
```

This query lowers the execution time from 3.2 seconds to less than 2 seconds.

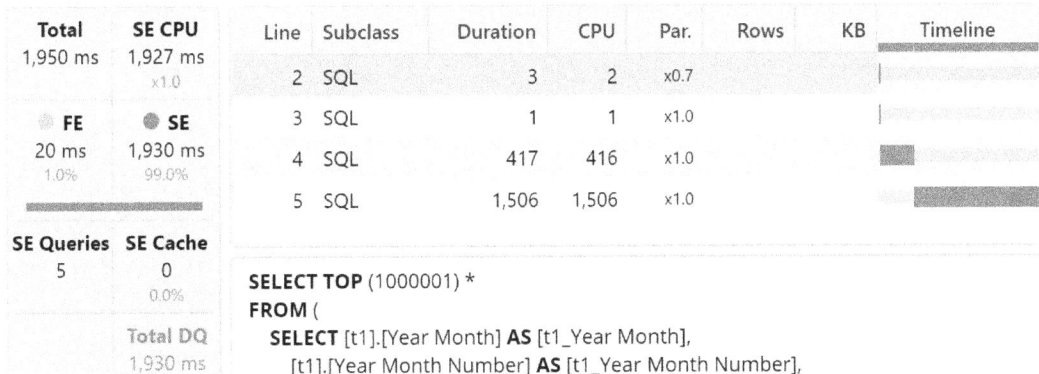

Total	SE CPU		Line	Subclass	Duration	CPU	Par.	Rows	KB	Timeline
1,950 ms	1,927 ms		2	SQL	3	2	x0.7			
	x1.0		3	SQL	1	1	x1.0			
FE	SE		4	SQL	417	416	x1.0			
20 ms	1,930 ms		5	SQL	1,506	1,506	x1.0			
1.0%	99.0%									

SE Queries	SE Cache
5	0
	0.0%

Total DQ
1,930 ms

SELECT TOP (1000001) *
FROM (
    SELECT [t1].[Year Month] **AS** [t1_Year Month],
        [t1].[Year Month Number] **AS** [t1_Year Month Number],

The first two SQL queries retrieve the basic columns from *Date*, and their execution time is irrelevant. This is the first one:

```
SELECT TOP (1000001) *
FROM (
    SELECT [t1].[Year Month] AS [t1_Year Month],
        [t1].[Year Month Number] AS [t1_Year Month Number],
        MAX([t1].[Year Month Number]) AS [a0]
    FROM ([dbo].[Date]) AS [t1]
    GROUP BY [t1].[Year Month],
        [t1].[Year Month Number]
    ) AS [MainTable]
WHERE (NOT (([a0] IS NULL)))
```

And this is the second SQL query:

```
SELECT TOP (1000001) [t1].[Year Month Number]
FROM ([dbo].[Date]) AS [t1]
GROUP BY [t1].[Year Month Number]
```

The third SQL query is much shorter than the equivalent for the previous DAX query:

```
SELECT TOP (1000001) *
FROM (
    SELECT [t1_Year Month Number],
        SUM([a0]) AS [a0]
    FROM (
        SELECT [t1].[Year Month Number] AS [t1_Year Month Number],
            [t3].[Quantity] AS [t3_Quantity],
            [t3].[Net Price] AS [t3_Net Price],
            ([t3].[Quantity] * [t3].[Net Price]) AS [a0]
        FROM (
            [Data].[Sales] AS [t3]
                LEFT JOIN [dbo].[Date] AS [t1] ON ([t3].[Order Date] = [t1].[Date])
            )
        ) AS [t0]
    WHERE (
        (
            [t1_Year Month Number] IN (
                24128, 24168,
...
                24173, 24215
                )
            )
        )
    GROUP BY [t1_Year Month Number]
    ) AS [MainTable]
WHERE (NOT (([a0] IS NULL)))
```

The WHERE condition is more straightforward, as it involves a single column. Moreover, the grouping naturally happens inside SQL more simply than in the previous example. This results in a faster execution time that accounts for most of the time saved.

The last query retrieves the sales amount by year month, and it is very similar to the corresponding query for the previous DAX query:

```
SELECT TOP (1000001) *
FROM (
    SELECT [t1_Year Month],
        [t1_Year Month Number],
        SUM([a0]) AS [a0]
    FROM (
        SELECT [t1].[Year Month] AS [t1_Year Month],
            [t1].[Year Month Number] AS [t1_Year Month Number],
            [t3].[Quantity] AS [t3_Quantity],
            [t3].[Net Price] AS [t3_Net Price],
            ([t3].[Quantity] * [t3].[Net Price]) AS [a0]
        FROM (
            [Data].[Sales] AS [t3]
                LEFT JOIN [dbo].[Date] AS [t1] ON ([t3].[Order Date] = [t1].[Date])
            )
        ) AS [t0]
    GROUP BY [t1_Year Month],
        [t1_Year Month Number]
    ) AS [MainTable]
WHERE (NOT (([a0] IS NULL)))
```

Using regular, optimized DAX code rather than DAX time intelligence functions, we executed simpler SQL code that saved a considerable amount of time. The formula engine time also became irrelevant – 20 milliseconds against 343 when using SAMEPERIODLASTYEAR.

Before we move on from this topic, it is essential to note that the optimization of DAX time intelligence functions that reduces the size of the datacache to the month level does not always kick in. SAMEPERIODLASTYEAR and DATEADD benefit from this optimization: with these functions, the DirectQuery engine groups data at the time granularity required by the DAX query. Other DAX functions like DATESBETWEEN and DATESYTD, or more complex DAX queries, still require data to be returned to the formula engine at the day level.

As an example, look at the following DAX query. It implements the behavior of SAMEPERIODLASTYEAR through several variables and a DATESBETWEEN. Despite being functionally equivalent to the version with SAMEPERIODLASTYEAR, it requires data at the day level sent from the DirectQuery storage engine:

```
DEFINE
    MEASURE Sales[Sales PY] =
        VAR LastDay = MAX ( 'Date'[Date] )
        VAR EndSPLY = EOMONTH ( LastDay, -12 )
        VAR StartSPLY = EOMONTH ( LastDay, -13 ) + 1
        RETURN
            CALCULATE ( [Sales Amount], DATESBETWEEN ( 'Date'[Date], StartSPLY, EndSPLY ) )

EVALUATE
SUMMARIZECOLUMNS (
    'Date'[Year Month],
    'Date'[Year Month Number],
    "Sales Growth %", DIVIDE ( [Sales Amount] - [Sales PY], [Sales PY] )
)
ORDER BY 'Date'[Year Month Number]
```

It is not worth analyzing the entire query. The critical part is the code that retrieves information for the sales in the previous year, which is the following SQL query:

```
SELECT TOP (1000001) *
FROM (
    SELECT [t1_Date],
        SUM([a0]) AS [a0]
    FROM (
        SELECT [t1].[Date] AS [t1_Date],
            [t3].[Quantity] AS [t3_Quantity],
            [t3].[Net Price] AS [t3_Net Price],
            ([t3].[Quantity] * [t3].[Net Price]) AS [a0]
        FROM (
            [Data].[Sales] AS [t3]
                LEFT JOIN [dbo].[Date] AS [t1] ON ([t3].[Order Date] = [t1].[Date])
            )
        ) AS [t0]
    WHERE (
            (
                [t1_Date] IN (
                    CAST('20120812 00:00:00' AS DATETIME),
                    CAST('20171219 00:00:00' AS DATETIME),


                    CAST('20120922 00:00:00' AS DATETIME),
                    CAST('20201203 00:00:00' AS DATETIME)
                    )
                )
            )
    GROUP BY [t1_Date]
    ) AS [MainTable]
WHERE (NOT (([a0] IS NULL)))
```

The SQL query groups by *Date;* this increases the size of the datacache exchanged between SQL Server and the formula engine, consequently putting more pressure on the formula engine. As with any optimization pattern, the DAX engine can evolve, so testing on your specific version of Tabular is required before making any assumption.

When seeking for optimal performance, DAX time intelligence functions should be avoided and, whenever possible, replaced with more basic code that can be controlled, seeking for the optimal query plan.

Computing distinct counts

In the VertiPaq section, we analyzed different ways to compute distinct counts. Specifically, one of the comparisons was between using DISTINCTCOUNT and SUMX (DISTINCT (), 1). The former pushes the calculation down to the storage engine, whereas the latter performs the calculation in the formula engine after a potentially significant materialization. However, there are multiple scenarios where using SUMX over DISTINCT provides better performance in VertiPaq.

Unfortunately, when using DirectQuery, large materializations are not an option. Therefore, the technique based on SUMX over DISTINCT is – in most scenarios – not applicable. A simple DAX query like the following does not run:

```
EVALUATE
SUMMARIZECOLUMNS (
    'Date'[Date],
    Customer[Country],
    'Product'[Color],
    "# Products", SUMX ( DISTINCT ( Sales[ProductKey] ), 1 )
)
```

The problem is that the query needs to materialize all the combinations of *Date, Country, Color,* and *ProductKey*. Tabular tries to materialize the existing combinations with the following SQL query:

```
SELECT TOP (1000001)
    [t0].[Country],
    [t1].[Date],
    [t2].[Color],
    [t3].[ProductKey]
FROM (
    (
        (
            [Data].[Sales] AS [t3]
                INNER JOIN [dbo].[Customer] AS [t0]
                    ON ([t3].[CustomerKey] = [t0].[CustomerKey])
        )
        LEFT JOIN [dbo].[Date] AS [t1] ON ([t3].[Order Date] = [t1].[Date])
    )
    LEFT JOIN [dbo].[Product] AS [t2] ON ([t3].[ProductKey] = [t2].[ProductKey])
)
GROUP BY [t0].[Country],
    [t1].[Date],
    [t2].[Color],
    [t3].[ProductKey]
```

Because the SQL query returns more than 1M rows, the execution of the DAX query does not complete and an error is raised. Therefore, the optimization of using SUMX over DISTINCT instead of DISTINCTCOUNT is not a viable option in DirectQuery. It would work with small models – although on small models, DISTINCTCOUNT works just fine and no optimization is required.

Regarding regular DISTINCTCOUNT, an important note is about blank values. Any column may contain BLANK values in Tabular. In SQL, blanks correspond to NULL values, and SQL counting functions do not count NULL values. However, DAX considers BLANK a value like any other and counts it for DISTINCTCOUNT. Therefore, whenever there is a DISTINCTCOUNT, it is translated into more complex SQL code with a price to pay for its execution. For example, the following simple query generates a complex piece of SQL code:

```
EVALUATE
SUMMARIZECOLUMNS (
    'Product'[Brand],
    "# Products",  DISTINCTCOUNT ( Sales[ProductKey] )
)
```

This DAX query runs in around two seconds.

Total	SE CPU		Line	Subclass	Duration	CPU	Par.	Rows	KB	Timeline
1,977 ms	1,972 ms									
	×1.0		1	SQL	1,973	1,972	×1.0			

FE	SE
4 ms	1,973 ms
0.2%	99.8%

SE Queries	SE Cache
1	0
	0.0%

Total DQ
1,973 ms

```
SELECT TOP (1000001) [t2].[Brand] AS [t2_Brand],
    (
        COUNT_BIG(DISTINCT [t3].[ProductKey]) + MAX(CASE
            WHEN [t3].[ProductKey] IS NULL
                THEN 1
            ELSE 0
            END)
        ) AS [a0]
```

The SQL code generated contains not only the COUNT_BIG function to perform the distinct count but also an expression to consider NULL values:

```
SELECT TOP (1000001) [t2].[Brand] AS [t2_Brand],
    (
        COUNT_BIG(DISTINCT [t3].[ProductKey]) + MAX(CASE
                WHEN [t3].[ProductKey] IS NULL
                    THEN 1
                ELSE 0
                END)
        ) AS [a0]
FROM (
    [Data].[Sales] AS [t3]
        LEFT JOIN [dbo].[Product] AS [t2] ON ([t3].[ProductKey] = [t2].[ProductKey])
    )
GROUP BY [t2].[Brand]
```

Although not complex, the expression comes at an unnecessary price in some scenarios. If you know in advance that blanks are not an issue because they are not present or they should not be counted, then DISTINCTCOUNTNOBLANK provides better performance:

```
EVALUATE
SUMMARIZECOLUMNS (
    'Product'[Brand],
    "# Products",  DISTINCTCOUNTNOBLANK ( Sales[ProductKey] )
)
```

Because DISTINCTCOUNTNOBLANK ignores blanks, the SQL code generated is more straightforward and faster.

		Line	Subclass	Duration	CPU	Par.	Rows	KB	Timeline
Total 1,207 ms	**SE CPU** 1,200 ms x1.0	1	SQL	1,200	1,200	x1.0			

FE 7 ms 0.6%	**SE** 1,200 ms 99.4%

SE Queries 1	**SE Cache** 0 0.0%

Total DQ
1,200 ms

```
SELECT TOP (1000001) [t2].[Brand] AS [t2_Brand],
    COUNT_BIG(DISTINCT [t3].[ProductKey]) AS [a0]
FROM (
    [Data].[Sales] AS [t3]
        LEFT JOIN [dbo].[Product] AS [t2] ON ([t3].[ProductKey] = [t2].[ProductKey])
    )
GROUP BY [t2].[Brand]
```

This time, the SQL code does not have to handle NULLs:

```
SELECT TOP (1000001) [t2].[Brand] AS [t2_Brand],
    COUNT_BIG(DISTINCT [t3].[ProductKey]) AS [a0]
FROM (
    [Data].[Sales] AS [t3]
        LEFT JOIN [dbo].[Product] AS [t2] ON ([t3].[ProductKey] = [t2].[ProductKey])
    )
GROUP BY [t2].[Brand]
```

The benefit of using DISTINCTCOUNTNOBLANK depends on the DirectQuery data source. Using a regular column store in SQL Server, we have seen that the benefit depends on the cardinality of the column. The larger the column, the lower the benefit. For example, when using *DISTINCTCOUNT (Sales[CustomerKey])* the same query runs in 10.2 seconds with DISTINCTCOUNT and 9.2 seconds using DISTINCTCOUNTNOBLANK. In contrast, the advantage is irrelevant when using *Sales[Order Number]* with a very large cardinality. However, we noticed a consistent benefit in every query; therefore, using DISTINCTCOUNTNOBLANK rather than DISTINCTCOUNT is a good option whenever possible.

Another relevant difference between VertiPaq and DirectQuery is when handling queries involving distinct counts and complex filters. For example, consider the following DAX query:

```
EVALUATE
SUMMARIZECOLUMNS (
    'Date'[Year Month Number],
    TREATAS ( { 2010 }, 'Date'[Year] ),
    "# Products",
        CALCULATE (
            DISTINCTCOUNTNOBLANK ( Sales[ProductKey] ),
            DATESYTD ( 'Date'[Date] )
        )
)
```

In VertiPaq, this DAX query would trigger many storage engine queries – at least 12, one for each month – because the formula engine cannot retrieve data at a higher granularity (the month number, in this scenario) and then aggregate the values by itself. However, because SQL is more expressive than xmSQL in VertiPaq, the same DAX query requires a smaller number of SQL queries in DirectQuery.

Total	SE CPU	Line	Subclass	Duration	CPU	Par.	Rows	KB	Timeline
1,883 ms	1,721 ms								
	x1.0	1	SQL	1	1	x1.0			
FE	SE	2	SQL	2	2	x1.0			
162 ms	1,721 ms	3	SQL	1	1	x1.0			
8.6%	91.4%	4	SQL	1,717	1,717	x1.0			

SE Queries	SE Cache
4	0
	0.0%

Total DQ
1,721 ms

SELECT TOP (1000001) [semijoin1].[c22],
    COUNT_BIG(**DISTINCT** [a0]) **AS** [a0]
FROM (

Indeed, the query includes a join with a static table containing the relationship between each month number and the dates that create the YTD of that month:

```
SELECT TOP (1000001) [semijoin1].[c22],
    COUNT_BIG(DISTINCT [a0]) AS [a0]
FROM (
    (
        SELECT [t1].[Date] AS [t1_Date],
            [t3].[ProductKey] AS [a0]
        FROM (
            [Data].[Sales] AS [t3]
                LEFT JOIN [dbo].[Date] AS [t1] ON ([t3].[Order Date] = [t1].[Date])
            )
        ) AS [basetable0]
        INNER JOIN (
        (SELECT 24121 AS [c22], CAST('20100101 00:00:00' AS DATETIME) AS [t1_Date])
        UNION ALL (SELECT 24121 AS [c22], CAST('20100102 00:00:00' AS DATETIME) AS [t1_Date])
        UNION ALL (SELECT 24121 AS [c22], CAST('20100103 00:00:00' AS DATETIME) AS [t1_Date])
...
        UNION ALL (SELECT 24132 AS [c22], CAST('20101230 00:00:00' AS DATETIME) AS [t1_Date])
        UNION ALL (SELECT 24132 AS [c22], CAST('20101231 00:00:00' AS DATETIME) AS [t1_Date])
        ) AS [semijoin1] ON (([semijoin1].[t1_Date] = [basetable0].[t1_Date]))
    )
GROUP BY [semijoin1].[c22]
```

Despite being very long (the query contains 2,379 lines for a single year), this single SQL query is more efficient than running 12 shorter SQL queries.

Conclusions

As you have seen, optimizing DirectQuery requires paying attention to different aspects. DirectQuery is very different from VertiPaq. Searching for the best DAX formulation for VertiPaq and DirectQuery is the same in many scenarios. However, there are several situations where the optimal DAX code for VertiPaq is not the best for DirectQuery.

Moreover, optimizing DirectQuery requires an excellent knowledge of the underlying relational database (like SQL Server) and the option of changing the data source content to execute the queries sent by the formula engine in the best possible way; for example, SQL Server can use indexes, statistics, materialized views, column store, and much more. This step is somewhat missing in VertiPaq because the changes developers can perform on the VertiPaq database are minimal.

Section 5
COMPOSITE MODELS

Understanding composite models

Composite models were previously named *"DirectQuery for Power BI datasets and Azure Analysis Services"*. The long name had its time and is no longer being used. The feature is now known as "composite models". Which is good, as the old name was long and complex to remember. However, despite being long and complex, it provided a good description of the technology: a composite model uses DirectQuery technology over another Tabular model.

A composite model mixes a local VertiPaq model, using VertiPaq, with a remote database whose storage engine is still VertiPaq. However, viewing a composite model as another storage engine would be a mistake. Indeed, because the remote model is a full-fledged Tabular model, the integration between the remote model and the local model goes much further than simple data access. In a composite model, the local model extends the remote model and can use all the tables, measures, and relationships defined in the remote model.

A composite model is a special case of a complex model. In a composite model there is a VertiPaq continent with one data island that is a DirectQuery connection to a remote Analysis Services model. Any other combination of storage engines is a complex model, and we will talk about these complex models later.

Understanding the interactions between the local and the remote models is important because they are paramount to building efficient composite models.

Introducing composite models

A composite model links two entities: the local and remote models. The local model is a regular VertiPaq database. The remote model is a model published on a Tabular database and linked to the local model rather than copied into the model. The remote data resides in the remote model: no data is copied from the remote model into the local model; same as what happens with DirectQuery over SQL. Local data, on the other hand, is stored in the local VertiPaq database.

There can be one local VertiPaq database and one or more remote Tabular data islands. We call the VertiPaq database the **VertiPaq Continent** and the Tabular islands **Data Islands**.

In this section we cover the most common scenario of composite models with one VertiPaq continent and just one more data island, using Tabular as the storage engine. Any model containing more than one data island is a complex model, and we will cover them in the next chapters. Therefore, because we only have two data models, we reference the VertiPaq continent as the **local model** and the Tabular data island as the **remote model**.

Be mindful that a composite model requires a local VertiPaq database, even though it may be an empty VertiPaq database. For example, you might think about a model containing only a DirectQuery island and a connection to a remote Tabular engine. Despite looking like it only contains two islands (DirectQuery and Tabular), it actually has three islands: DirectQuery, VertiPaq, and Tabular. Therefore, it is already a complex model. A composite model, in our definition, contains only one VertiPaq database and one connection to Tabular.

In a composite model, local data is stored in the local VertiPaq database. Therefore, model developers have full modeling capabilities on the local model. However, they also have the option to make changes to the remote model, or to merge the local and the remote model together, performing operations like:

- Creating new calculated columns on remote tables.
- Creating relationships between local and remote tables.
- Adding measure and calculation groups that work on local and remote tables.

The peculiarity of composite models is that the storage engine is a full-fledged Tabular engine that can understand and execute DAX code. Therefore, the formula engine can rely on a storage engine that is able to evaluate any DAX expression. The queries that the formula engine sends to the storage engine are neither SQL nor xmSQL: they are DAX queries.

When you create a composite model, tables and measures of the remote model are linked to local entities. In other words, Tabular creates a table and a measure in the local model for each table and measure in the remote model. This way, it is possible to rename tables, columns, and measures. For example, a composite model linked to Contoso contains new measures whose code is just a reference to the remote model:

```
-----------------------------------------
-- Measure in Sales table
-----------------------------------------
Sales Amount =
EXTERNALMEASURE ( "Sales Amount", CURRENCY, "DirectQuery to AS - Contoso 10M (Remote)" )
```

EXTERNALMEASURE is a special DAX function that invokes a measure stored in a remote model. The execution of the measure is entrusted to the remote model. The first argument is the measure name, the second argument is the result data type, and the third argument is the name of a shared expression that links to the remote model.

In a similar way, the local model includes tables that are linked to the original tables in the remote model. Model authors can change some of their properties – like the name – to avoid any ambiguity. However, no data is copied from the remote model to the local model.

Understanding wholesale and retail calculations

If a query only uses data stored in the remote model, then its execution can be pushed entirely to the remote Tabular database. In a similar way, a query that only works on local data can be entirely executed in the local VertiPaq server. In these scenarios, the engine performs **wholesale calculations**. A wholesale calculation is the evaluation of a query that can be entirely executed by one server, without accessing data that is stored in a separate server.

If a query mixes both data in the local model and data in the remote model, then the local formula engine needs to execute xmSQL code on the local model, then DAX code on the remote model, and finally merge the results properly to produce the result. In this second scenario we talk about **retail calculations**.

It is important to note a detail. When working with DirectQuery, some calculations need to be performed in the formula engine, despite the data being stored in SQL. This is because SQL does not have the full power of DAX. There are DAX functions requiring the intervention of the formula engine, just because they cannot be expressed in SQL. With composite models this is never the case. The storage engine can execute any DAX function, being itself a DAX engine. Therefore, if it can access the data, any calculation can be pushed down to the remote engine.

However, the remote engine cannot access local data; at the same time, the local engine cannot directly access remote data. Therefore, if a query mixes both local and remote data, then this data needs to be moved between the servers. The amount of data that is transferred depends on the complexity of the query, and if the number of rows exceeds one million, developers may encounter the same issues they have with DirectQuery over SQL: an error because the number of rows exceeds the maximum number of rows allowed for a DirectQuery result.

Optimizing composite models requires a good understanding of which part of the query is going to be executed remotely, which part is being executed locally, and the type of communication that must happen between the formula engine and the remote Tabular engine.

Let us elaborate on the topic with some examples. We created a composite model that is linked to Contoso 10M published on Power BI, and we added a local calculated table, containing some correction factors by year:

```
-------------------------------------
-- Calculated table CorrectionFactor
-------------------------------------
CorrectionFactor =
SELECTCOLUMNS (
    ALLNOBLANKROW ( 'Date'[Year] ),
    "Year", 'Date'[Year],
    "Correction Factor", ( 'Date'[Year] - 2000 ) / 10
)
```

The table content is not relevant, we use it for testing purposes only. The idea is to use the correction factor as a multiplier for the sales amount.

Year	Correction Factor
2,010	1.00
2,011	1.10
2,012	1.20
2,013	1.30
2,014	1.40
2,015	1.50

If we execute a query that only requires data stored in the remote model, this is going to be pushed entirely down to the remote DAX engine:

```
EVALUATE
SUMMARIZECOLUMNS (
    'Product'[Brand],
    "Sales", [Sales Amount]
)
```

Running the query shows a DAX subclass event.

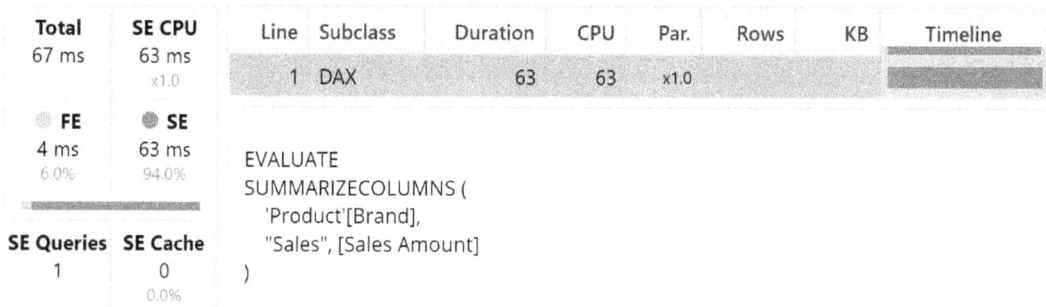

Total	SE CPU	Line	Subclass	Duration	CPU	Par.	Rows	KB	Timeline
67 ms	63 ms ×1.0	1	DAX	63	63	×1.0			

FE	SE
4 ms	63 ms
6.0%	94.0%

```
EVALUATE
SUMMARIZECOLUMNS (
    'Product'[Brand],
    "Sales", [Sales Amount]
)
```

SE Queries	SE Cache
1	0
	0.0%

This is a very simple example of a wholesale execution. The query only requires remote data, therefore it can be executed by the remote engine. In a similar way, a query running only on the local engine is wholesale:

```
EVALUATE
FILTER (
    CorrectionFactor,
    CorrectionFactor[Correction Factor] >= 1.5
)
```

This last query only uses the *CorrectionFactor* table, which is stored in the local VertiPaq storage. Therefore, its execution requires only one xmSQL query.

Total	SE CPU		Line	Subclass	Duration	CPU	Par.	Rows	KB	Timeline
4 ms	0 ms									
	x0.0		2	Scan	3	0		2,744	22	

FE	SE
1 ms	3 ms
25.0%	75.0%

SE Queries	SE Cache
1	0
	0.0%

Total DQ

```
SET DC_KIND="AUTO";
SELECT
    'CorrectionFactor'[RowNumber],
    'CorrectionFactor'[Correction Factor],
    'CorrectionFactor'[Year]
FROM 'CorrectionFactor'
WHERE
    ( PFCASTCOALESCE ( 'CorrectionFactor'[Correction Factor] AS REAL ) >= COALESCE
```

However, the point of creating composite models is to use both local and remote data. The next query computes and adjusts *Sales Amount* for each year with the correction factor stored locally:

```
EVALUATE
SUMMARIZECOLUMNS (
    'Product'[Brand],
    "Sales",
        VAR SalesByYear =
            SELECTCOLUMNS (
                VALUES ( 'Date'[Year] ),
                "@Year", 'Date'[Year] + 0,
                "@Sales Amount", [Sales Amount]
            )
        VAR Corrections =
            SELECTCOLUMNS (
                CorrectionFactor,
                "@Year", CorrectionFactor[Year] + 0,
                "@Correction Factor", CorrectionFactor[Correction Factor]
            )
        VAR SalesWithFactor =
            NATURALINNERJOIN ( SalesByYear, Corrections )
        VAR Result =
            SUMX ( SalesWithFactor, [@Sales Amount] * [@Correction Factor] )
        RETURN
            Result
)
```

We need to add zero to *@Year* in SELECTCOLUMNS to remove the data lineage of the year and make it possible to use NATURALINNERJOIN.

This query requires three execution steps:

- Retrieve the *SalesByYear* table from the remote server.

- Compute the *Corrections* table in the local VertiPaq model.

- Join the two tables by using the local formula engine, and then sum the results.

The query execution shows four storage engine (SE) queries being executed.

Total	SE CPU	Line	Subclass	Duration	CPU	Par.	Rows	KB	Timeline
590 ms	576 ms	1	DAX	443	442	x1.0			
	x1.0	3	Scan	1	0		2,744	22	
FE	SE	4	DAX	70	69	x1.0			
11 ms	579 ms	5	DAX	65	65	x1.0			
1.9%	98.1%								

SE Queries	SE Cache
4	0
	0.0%

	Total DQ
	578 ms

Three SE queries are DAX queries sent to the remote model. One is a VertiPaq scan executed locally. Let us analyze them deeper. The first DAX query computes the *SalesByYear* variable:

```
DEFINE
    VAR _Var0 = VALUES ( 'Product'[Brand] )
    VAR _Var1 = VALUES ( 'Date'[Year] )
EVALUATE
GROUPCROSSAPPLYTABLE (
    'Product'[Brand],
    _Var0,
    _Var1,
    "L1",
    GROUPCROSSAPPLY (
        'Date'[Year],
        KEEPFILTERS ( _Var1 ),
        "__Agg0", [Sales Amount]
    )
)
```

The DAX code uses GROUPCROSSAPPLYTABLE and GROUPCROSSAPPLY. We will dive deeper into these functions later in this chapter. For now, it suffices to know that GROUPCROSSAPPLY is close to SUMMARIZECOLUMNS: it performs a group-by and can compute new columns based on DAX expressions.

The resulting datacache contains *Brand*, *Year*, and *Sales Amount* in the *_Agg0* column.

Brand	Year	__Agg0
Contoso	2,010	50,992,471.92
Contoso	2,011	85,302,298.25
Contoso	2,012	95,479,837.47
Contoso	2,013	146,588,317.53
Contoso	2,014	186,419,114.68
Contoso	2,015	153,263,542.82

The second is an xmSQL query executed over the local VertiPaq engine that retrieves the *CorrectionFactor* table:

```
SELECT
    'CorrectionFactor'[RowNumber],
    'CorrectionFactor'[Correction Factor],
    'CorrectionFactor'[Year]
FROM 'CorrectionFactor';
```

The last two DAX queries are sent to the remote server with the sole purpose of retrieving years and brands, as required by SUMMARIZECOLUMNS and VALUES:

```
EVALUATE
SUMMARIZE (
    VALUES ( 'Date' ),
    'Date'[Year]
)

EVALUATE
SUMMARIZE (
    VALUES ( 'Product' ),
    'Product'[Brand]
)
```

The last operations in the original DAX query (NATURALINNERJOIN and SUMX) are executed inside the local formula engine.

Thus, we analyzed a DAX query that contains code executed by the local server, code executed by the remote server, and operations executed by the local formula engine to merge the partial results computed by the two storage engines.

The datacache returned by the remote engine should not exceed the maximum number of rows configured in the server. For example, if we change the granularity of the query grouping by *Product Code* and *City*, we can exceed the 1M rows limit:

```
EVALUATE
SUMMARIZECOLUMNS (
    'Product'[Product Code],
    Customer[City],
    "Sales",
        VAR SalesByYear =
            SELECTCOLUMNS (
                VALUES ( 'Date'[Year] ),
                "@Year", 'Date'[Year] + 0,
                "@Sales Amount", [Sales Amount]
            )
        VAR Corrections =
            SELECTCOLUMNS (
                CorrectionFactor,
                "@Year", CorrectionFactor[Year] + 0,
                "@Correction Factor", CorrectionFactor[Correction Factor]
            )
        VAR SalesWithFactor =
            NATURALINNERJOIN ( SalesByYear, Corrections )
        VAR Result =
            SUMX ( SalesWithFactor, [@Sales Amount] * [@Correction Factor] )
        RETURN
            Result
)
```

The execution of the DAX query produces nothing but an error.

The resultset of a query to external data source has exceeded the maximum allowed size of '1000000' rows.

Total	SE CPU		Line	Subclass	Duration	CPU	Par.	Rows	KB	Timeline
55,625 ms	50,880 ms		1	DAX	50,880	50,880	x1.0			
	x1.0									

FE	SE
4,745 ms	50,880 ms
8.5%	91.5%

SE Queries	SE Cache
1	0
	0.0%

The DAX code executed by the storage engine contains the three group-by columns:

```
DEFINE
    VAR _Var0 = VALUES ( 'Product'[Product Code] )
    VAR _Var1 = VALUES ( 'Customer'[City] )
    VAR _Var2 = VALUES ( 'Date'[Year] )
EVALUATE
GROUPCROSSAPPLYTABLE (
    'Product'[Product Code],
    'Customer'[City],
    _Var0,
    _Var1,
    _Var2,
    "L1",
    GROUPCROSSAPPLY (
        'Date'[Year],
        KEEPFILTERS ( _Var2 ),
        "__Agg0", [Sales Amount]
    )
)
```

The result provided by the storage engine contains the three columns and the sales amount.

Product Code	City	Year	__Agg0
0505018	Spokane Valley	2,018	9.99
0505015	Chicago	2,018	1,096.92
0505009	Columbus	2,018	142.02
0501067	Matthews	2,018	9.99
0602014	San Antonio	2,018	415.50
0505018	Indianapolis	2,018	303.90
0505018	Atlanta	2,018	373.23

However, the resulting datacache would contain 8,201,734 rows, which exceeds the limit and throws the error.

Most of the queries in composite models are retail. Indeed, the purpose of creating composite models is to enhance an existing model with tables, relationships, calculation groups, and measures that merge information gathered from the remote server with new data structures created on the local database.

Despite most queries being retail, the best performance is obtained by executing wholesale code. Whenever the two storage engines need to communicate, performance is at risk. We will elaborate further on this, as reducing the size of data structures passed back and forth between the two engines is the core of composite model optimization.

Calculated tables

Calculated tables can be created in composite models. A calculated table can be retail (as opposed to calculated columns, which must be wholesale) and its result is stored as part of the local VertiPaq model.

Calculated tables are processed during the refresh of the local model. They are a powerful tool for DAX optimizations because a wise use of calculated tables can overcome some of the limitations of composite models, as we will see in the next chapters.

Calculated columns

When using a composite model, developers can create calculated columns on both the local VertiPaq continent and remote tables as well. Calculated columns in the local model are just regular VertiPaq calculated columns.

Calculated columns created on remote tables are different: they are not materialized; they are computed on-the-fly using query calculated columns, much like is the case with DirectQuery over SQL. Consequently, calculated columns on remote tables must use expressions that can be computed wholesale. Retail calculated columns on the remote model are not supported.

Moreover, there are some differences in the way circular dependencies are detected. For example, despite a table having a primary key, the dependency on the CALCULATE context transition is always considered over all the table columns, making it necessary to write more verbose calculations. For example, the following calculated column clusters the products in two categories based on their sales compared with the average of all products:

```
--------------------------------------
-- Calculated column in Product table
--------------------------------------
Product Level =
VAR AverageSales =
    AVERAGEX (
        'Product',
        CALCULATE ( [Sales Amount], ALLEXCEPT ( 'Product', 'Product'[ProductKey] ) )
    )
VAR ProductSales =
    CALCULATE (
        [Sales Amount],
        ALLEXCEPT ( 'Product', 'Product'[ProductKey] )
    )
VAR Result = IF ( ProductSales >= AverageSales, "Top Seller", "Regular Seller" )
RETURN Result
```

In order to compute the sales amount for a product, we must use ALLEXCEPT in both *AverageSales* and *ProductSales* calculations to clearly state the dependency on *Product[ProductKey]* only. If we were to remove ALLEXCEPT, the *Product Level* calculated column would fail because of a circular dependency.

Despite being quite complex, the code is wholesale, because it uses only remote data. Therefore, you can create the calculated column.

When used in a query, the column is translated into a query calculated column. The following query returns the sales amount of the products by *Product Level*:

```
EVALUATE
SUMMARIZECOLUMNS (
    'Product'[Product Level],
    "Sales", [Sales Amount]
)
```

The result shows that grouping works just fine.

Product Level	Sales
Regular Seller	2,168,052,321.40
Top Seller	8,121,527,123.40

The DAX query is translated into a more complex DAX query sent to the remote server:

```
DEFINE
    COLUMN 'Product'[ASDQ_Product Level] =
        VAR ASDQ_AverageSales =
            AVERAGEX (
                'Product',
                CALCULATE ( [Sales Amount], ALLEXCEPT ( 'Product', 'Product'[ProductKey] ) )
            )
        VAR ASDQ_ProductSales =
            CALCULATE (
                [Sales Amount],
                ALLEXCEPT ( 'Product', 'Product'[ProductKey] )
            )
        VAR ASDQ_Result =
            IF ( ASDQ_ProductSales >= ASDQ_AverageSales, "Top Seller", "Regular Seller" )
        RETURN
            ASDQ_Result

EVALUATE
SUMMARIZECOLUMNS (
    'Product'[ASDQ_Product Level],
    "Sales", [Sales Amount]
)
```

The *Product[Product Level]* column is translated into *Product[ASDQ Product Level]*, which is defined as a calculated column in the query. Because the calculated column is evaluated by the remote server, it being wholesale is a requirement.

Apart from the wholesale requirement, calculated columns in composite models can be used to build relationships between tables and they behave exactly like regular calculated columns. However, from the performance point of view, it is important to note that these calculated columns are not persisted, and their evaluation happens for each query.

Tracing remote queries

As was the case with DirectQuery, the Server Timings pane does not report statistics about the queries executed by the remote server. Any storage engine DAX query reports just the elapsed time, without information about parallelism, storage engine CPU, and returned row count information.

For example, running the query we used in the previous example produces little information:

```
EVALUATE
SUMMARIZECOLUMNS (
    'Product'[Product Level],
    "Sales", [Sales Amount]
)
```

When it is executed, DAX Studio does not report full statistics, like the number of rows (blank) or the parallelism (always 1), despite the storage engine query being DAX.

Total	SE CPU	Line	Subclass	Duration	CPU	Par.	Rows	KB	Timeline
948 ms	943 ms								
	x1.0	1	DAX	943	943	x1.0			

FE	SE
5 ms	943 ms
0.5%	99.5%

```
Define
COLUMN 'Product'[ASDQ_Product Level] = VAR ASDQ_AverageSales = AVERAGEX ( Proc
[ProductKey] ) ) )
VAR ASDQ_ProductSales = CALCULATE ( [Sales Amount], ALLEXCEPT ( Product, Product
VAR ASDQ_Result = IF ( ASDQ_ProductSales >= ASDQ_AverageSales, "Top Seller", "Regu
RETURN
    ASDQ_Result

EVALUATE
SUMMARIZECOLUMNS (
    'Product'[ASDQ_Product Level],
    "Sales", [Sales Amount]
)
```

SE Queries	SE Cache
1	0
	0.0%

Total DQ
943 ms

The total execution time of 943 milliseconds is the same value as the storage engine CPU, showing a parallelism of 1.0. Also, the number of rows is missing, making it a bit harder to evaluate the performance of a query in a composite model.

However, it is possible to connect directly to the remote server and execute the storage engine query on the remote server to investigate it further. You must use the XMLA endpoint to connect DAX Studio to the remote dataset. The DAX query to execute is the following:

```
DEFINE
    COLUMN 'Product'[ASDQ_Product Level] =
        VAR ASDQ_AverageSales =
            AVERAGEX (
                'Product',
                CALCULATE (
                    [Sales Amount],
                    ALLEXCEPT ( 'Product', 'Product'[ProductKey] )
                )
            )
        VAR ASDQ_ProductSales =
            CALCULATE (
                [Sales Amount],
                ALLEXCEPT ( 'Product', 'Product'[ProductKey] )
            )
        VAR ASDQ_Result =
            IF ( ASDQ_ProductSales >= ASDQ_AverageSales, "Top Seller", "Regular Seller" )
        RETURN
            ASDQ_Result

EVALUATE
SUMMARIZECOLUMNS (
    'Product'[ASDQ_Product Level],
    "Sales", [Sales Amount]
)
```

When executed on the remote server with server timings enabled, we get better insights about the execution flow.

Total	SE CPU		Line	Subclass	Duration	CPU	Par.	Rows	KB	Timeline
703 ms	6,172 ms		2	Scan	17	156	x9.2	2,520	60	
	x8.9		4	Scan	17	16	x0.9	1	1	
FE	SE		6	Scan	657	6,000	x9.1	2	1	
13 ms	690 ms									
1.8%	98.3%									

SE Queries	SE Cache
3	0
	0.0%

	Total DQ
	0 ms

The execution time of 703 milliseconds corresponds to 6,172 milliseconds of storage engine CPU, with a degree of parallelism of 8.9. Moreover, there are three xmSQL queries being executed.

At this stage, it is not relevant to further analyze the execution on the remote server. Indeed, optimizing the code further would require additional considerations. In this example, the remote server is a VertiPaq model, but it might well be the case that the remote server is a DirectQuery model, or maybe another composite model that is linked to a second remote server.

From the point of view of the local model, the remote server is a black box. However, when optimizing composite models, model authors should always consider the architecture of both the local and the remote databases. This is because it might be the case that the reason why a specific query is slow is not in the local architecture, but rather in some issues on the remote server.

Understanding relationships between tables

When you work with a composite model, you can also create relationships between local and remote tables. Creating relationships between remote tables is not supported because that would change the architecture of the remote model, and it would be impossible for wholesale code to run without it knowing about the new relationships created in the composite model – we are not considering complex models now, so we are referencing remote tables in the same data island. Relationships between local tables are nothing but regular relationships. The most interesting type of relationship is between a local and a remote table. Because the local table is stored in the VertiPaq continent, and remote tables are in their own data island, any relationship between a local and a remote table is a limited relationship.

The Tabular engine applies cross-island relationships in composite models by using dedicated functions for composite models, like GROUPCROSSAPPLY and GROUPCROSSAPPLYTABLE, which obtain the filter transfer of a relationship using DAX code in the query. The best way to understand how they work is to create a relationship and then perform the analysis of the DAX code produced.

As an example, we created a relationship between the *CorrectionFactor* table and *Date*, as a cross-island relationship based on the year.

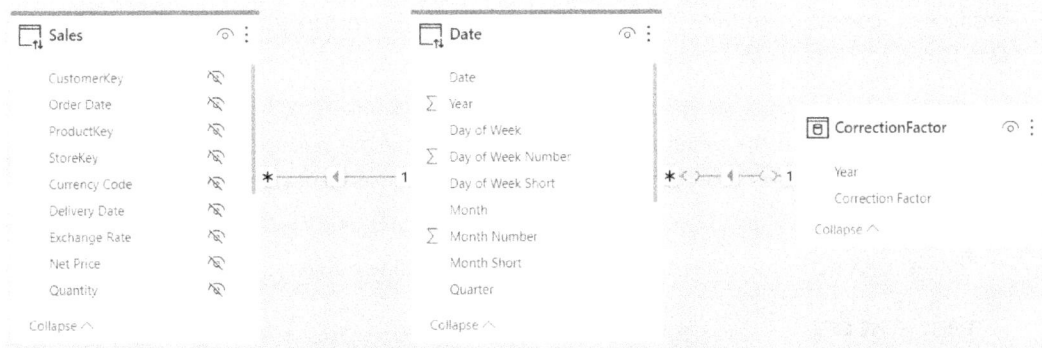

Because a cross-island relationship is limited, we cannot use RELATED, as no table expansion is happening. Therefore, the following code throws an error:

```
EVALUATE
SUMMARIZECOLUMNS (
    'Product'[Brand],
    "Sales",
        SUMX (
            Sales,
            Sales[Quantity] * Sales[Net Price]
                * RELATED ( CorrectionFactor[Correction Factor] )
        )
)
```

The error thrown is the following:

```
The column 'CorrectionFactor[Correction Factor]' either doesn't exist or doesn't have a
relationship to any table available in the current context.
```

However, it is possible to author the *Sales* calculation by relying on regular filter context propagation:

```
EVALUATE
SUMMARIZECOLUMNS (
    'Product'[Brand],
    "Sales",
        SUMX (
            CorrectionFactor,
            [Sales Amount] * CorrectionFactor[Correction Factor]
        )
)
```

When *Sales Amount* is evaluated, the row context from the iteration over a local table (*CorrectionFactor*) produces a context transition. Therefore, the filter from *CorrectionFactor* is moved to *Sales* through *Date[Year]*, which connects *CorrectionFactor* to *Date*.

We must understand how the engine moves the filter from the local model to the remote model. Please be mindful that the remote model has no clue about the very existence of the *CorrectionFactor* table. *CorrectionFactor* is a table stored in the local model. Consequently, the remote model cannot access its content.

The last DAX query internally executes three storage engine queries.

Total	SE CPU		Line	Subclass	Duration	CPU	Par.	Rows	KB	Timeline
117 ms	108 ms									
	×1.0		2	Scan	0	0		2,744	22	
FE	SE		4	Scan	0	0			14	1
7 ms	110 ms		5	DAX	110	108	×1.0			
6.0%	94.0%									

SE Queries	SE Cache
3	0
	0.0%

	Total DQ
	110 ms

The first two Scan lines are xmSQL queries over the local VertiPaq model, whereas the third is a DAX query executed on the remote model.

The first xmSQL query retrieves the content of *CorrectionFactor*, as its column values will later be sent to the remote server:

```
SELECT
    'CorrectionFactor'[RowNumber],
    'CorrectionFactor'[Correction Factor],
    'CorrectionFactor'[Year]
FROM 'CorrectionFactor';
```

The second xmSQL query retrieves the values of the *Year* column from the *CorrectionFactor* table, whose internal name is still reported as *Table*:

```
SELECT
    'CorrectionFactor'[Year]
FROM 'CorrectionFactor';
```

The third and most interesting query is the DAX storage engine query:

```
DEFINE
    TABLE _T76 =
        UNION (
            SELECTCOLUMNS ( _Var1, "Value", [Value] ),
            SELECTCOLUMNS ( _Var2, "Value", [Value1] )
        )
    VAR _Var0 =
        VALUES ( 'Product'[Brand] )
    VAR _Var1 = { 3, 4, 5, 6, 7, 8, 9, 10, 11, 12, 13 }
    VAR _Var2 = {
        ( 3, 2010 ),
        ( 4, 2011 ),
        ( 5, 2012 ),
        ( 6, 2013 ),
        ( 7, 2014 ),
        ( 8, 2015 ),
        ( 9, 2016 ),
        ( 10, 2017 ),
        ( 11, 2018 ),
        ( 12, 2019 ),
        ( 13, 2020 )
    }

EVALUATE
GROUPCROSSAPPLYTABLE (
    'Product'[Brand],
    _T76[Value],
    _Var0,
    NONFILTER ( TREATAS ( _Var1, _T76[Value] ) ),
    "L1",
        GROUPCROSSAPPLY (
            TREATAS ( DEPENDON ( _Var2, EARLIER ( _T76[Value], 1 ) ), 'Date'[Year] ),
            "__Agg0", [Sales Amount]
        )
)
```

Understanding this query is very relevant because it is the first time that we see how a filter is moved between the two servers. Let us start by recapping the algorithm we need to execute.

The local server groups data by rows in *CorrectionFactor* because of the SUMX iteration. During SUMX iteration, there is a context transition to compute the *Sales Amount* value for each row in *CorrectionFactor*, which is linked to *Date* through the *Year* column. *CorrectionFactor[Year]* filters *Date[Year]*, which in turn filters *Sales*.

Consequently, the formula engine retrieves the value of *Sales Amount* grouped by year (the granularity of the relationship between *CorrectionFactor* and *Date*). Then, it uses the correct year value for the iterated row in *CorrectionFactor*.

As model authors, we know there is a 1:1 correspondence between years and rows in *CorrectionFactor*. However, the engine cannot make this assumption. It groups *Sales Amount* by *CorrectionFactor* row number, despite the grouping in *Date* being at the year level.

The engine needs a variable (_Var2) to store the relationship between the year (granularity at which the remote engine can perform the grouping) and the row number in *CorrectionFactor*. The _Var1 variable contains the possible values of the row number: it is helpful if the *CorrectionFactor* table contains blanks in the *Year* column. The union of _Var1 and _Var2 contains all the possible values of the row number in the _T76 table. _T76 must be a table rather than a variable because its lineage is about to be used by DEPENDON later.

_Var2 contains the association between row number and year; _Var1 contains the row numbers, and _T76 contains – again – all the row numbers, but with data lineage. These variables are used by GROUPCROSSAPPLYTABLE, which groups by *Brand* and _T76[Value], which corresponds to the *CorrectionFactor* row number.

The real magic happens in GROUPCROSSAPPLY to evaluate **L1**. The innermost GROUPCROSSAPPLY places a filter on *Date[Year]* during the calculation of *Sales Amount* using DEPENDON. DEPENDON uses _Var2, which contains the association between row number and year and the current value of _T76[Value] (the current row number); eventually, DEPENDON returns the year associated with the row number. TREATAS changes the lineage of the *Year* column to filter *Date[Year]* so that *Sales Amount* is computed for the year associated with the year of the current row.

By using variables and DEPENDON, the query groups by row number, whereas the filtering happens by year thanks to a variable that stores the association between row numbers and years and a combination of GROUPCROSSAPPLY functions.

Because of the implementation of cross-island relationships, there is no significant difference in composite models among one-to-many, many-to-many, and one-to-one relationships. However, after seeing the details, it is possible to start figuring out why performance may be an issue.

To enforce a relationship, the local engine sends the content of the local tables to the remote server through variables. For small tables, this is not an issue. Large tables with more than a few thousand rows start to be an issue because the DAX code is long, and processing takes time.

It is not unusual to witness remote storage engine queries with hundreds of thousands of rows because they need to share large tables in a single query. Luckily, with some care, it is most often possible to write DAX code that reduces these verbose queries to the minimum required. However, this is an entirely new skill to add to your DAX optimizer toolbelt.

Understanding special DAX functions for composite models

Some special DAX functions are heavily used in DAX storage engine queries made by composite models. These functions are rarely used in generic measures for two very good reasons. First, these functions are not documented; their test was limited to the scope of automatically-generated queries for composite models but are not general-purpose functions. Second, these specific functions aim to let a filter context be serialized and only sent to the remote server.

The lack of support and proper documentation means that we can only share high-level details about the functions because they may change at any point in time, and the description of their behavior is based on our observations rather than on official documentation.

We strongly recommend our readers do not use these functions in measures. As we said, the functions have been designed specifically for composite models and have not been tested as general-purpose functions.

Understanding GROUPCROSSAPPLY and GROUPCROSSAPPLYTABLE

First, despite the similar naming technique, the difference between GROUPCROSSAPPLY and GROUPCROSSAPPLYTABLE is not the same as the difference between CALCULATE and CALCULATETABLE. CALCULATE returns a scalar, whereas CALCULATETABLE returns a table: in that case, the difference is in the function output. With GROUPCROSSAPPLY, both functions return a table. The difference is in how the new columns are added to the output. GROUPCROSSAPPLY adds columns one by one, similarly to how ADDCOLUMNS works, whereas GROUPCROSSAPPLYTABLE adds all the table columns, similarly to the behavior of GENERATE.

Both GROUPCROSSAPPLY and GROUPCROSSAPPLYTABLE use the same set of arguments: first, the set of group-by columns; second, the tables that need to be grouped; and finally, the columns to add to the output. The order of the argument is different when compared with SUMMARIZE, SUMMARIZECOLUMNS, or other DAX functions – which can be confusing, at least in the beginning.

The easiest way to think about these functions is to consider them like SUMMARIZECOLUMNS. Indeed, their behavior is quite similar. As an example, let us look at a query we used earlier:

```
DEFINE
    VAR _Var0 = VALUES ( 'Product'[Brand] )
    VAR _Var1 = VALUES ( 'Date'[Year] )
EVALUATE
GROUPCROSSAPPLYTABLE (
    'Product'[Brand],
    _Var0,
    _Var1,
    "L1",
    GROUPCROSSAPPLY (
        'Date'[Year],
        KEEPFILTERS ( _Var1 ),
        "__Agg0", [Sales Amount]
    )
)
```

The output contains three columns.

Brand	Year	__Agg0
Contoso	2,010	50,992,471.92
Contoso	2,011	85,302,298.25
Contoso	2,012	95,479,837.47
Contoso	2,013	146,588,317.53
Contoso	2,014	186,419,114.68
Contoso	2,015	153,263,542.82

Despite the query adding a new set of columns with the name *L1*, the name *L1* does not appear in the output because GROUPCROSSAPPLYTABLE uses the entire table returned by GROUPCROSSAPPLY, merging it with the original table, like what GENERATE does. Therefore, the *L1* name provided in the query is useless, even though it is syntactically required.

The order of arguments in GROUPCROSSAPPLYTABLE is unusual. The first set of arguments (*Product[Brand]* and *Date[Year]*) are the group-by columns. The two following arguments are the source tables, stored in the _Var0 and _Var1 variables. GROUPCROSSAPPLYTABLE cross-joins _Var0 and _Var1 and groups the result by *Product[Brand]* and *Date[Year]*.

For each row of the cross-join result, GROUPCROSSAPPLYTABLE evaluates the expression of *L1*. *L1* returns a table containing _Agg0, which is *Sales Amount* grouped by *Year*.

Because you can use GROUPCROSSAPPLYTABLE with multiple group-by columns, an alternative way to express the same query is the following:

```
DEFINE
    VAR _Var0 = VALUES ( 'Product'[Brand] )
    VAR _Var1 = VALUES ( 'Date'[Year] )
EVALUATE
GROUPCROSSAPPLY (
    'Product'[Brand],
    'Date'[Year],
    _Var0,
    _Var1,
    "__Agg0", [Sales Amount]
)
```

You can mark table arguments with several modifiers: NONVISUAL, NONFILTER, and ALWAYSAPPLY. These modifiers are purely for the remote model query generation: they affect how the function handles the table expression in the filter context. For example, NONFILTER creates a table that does not participate in the filter context.

Understanding DEPENDON

DEPENDON is a table function that returns the rows of a table, given a set of keys. The columns with the keys must be the first columns in the source table. DEPENDON returns all the rows matching the keys provided, including all the columns except the keys.

An example is helpful to understand this. The following query defines a variable (*Customers*) with four rows containing *Key*, *Name*, and *Country*. Then, it defines a table (*CustomerList*) containing only the keys (1, 2, 3). DEPENDON returns the columns from *Customers* matching the keys in the *CustomerList* table:

```
DEFINE
    VAR Customers =
        SELECTCOLUMNS (
            {
                ( 1, "Alberto", "Italy" ),
                ( 2, "Daniele", "Italy" ),
                ( 2, "Marco", "USA" ),
                ( 3, "Claire", "France" )
            },
            "Key", [Value1],
            "Name", [Value2],
            "Country", [Value3]
        )
    TABLE CustomerList = { 1, 2, 3 }

EVALUATE
GENERATE (
    CustomerList,
    DEPENDON ( Customers, CustomerList[Value] )
)
ORDER BY [Value], [Name]
```

Because *Customers* contains the value 2 twice, and the matching occurs based only on the key, the result contains four rows.

Value	Name	Country
1	Alberto	Italy
2	Daniele	Italy
2	Marco	USA
3	Claire	France

If we use the value 2 twice in *CustomerList*, and we remove the value 3, we execute the following code:

```
DEFINE
    VAR Customers =
        SELECTCOLUMNS (
            {
                ( 1, "Alberto", "Italy" ),
                ( 2, "Daniele", "Italy" ),
                ( 2, "Marco", "USA" ),
                ( 3, "Claire", "France" )
            },
            "Key", [Value1],
            "Name", [Value2],
            "Country", [Value3]
        )
    TABLE CustomerList = { 1, 2, 2 }

EVALUATE
GENERATE (
    CustomerList,
    DEPENDON ( Customers, CustomerList[Value] )
)
ORDER BY [Value], [Name]
```

The result has five rows duplicating those with value 2 in the *Key* column, because the matching only shows the values that exist in both *Customers* and *CustomerList*. Moreover, the result does not include the row with 3 in the *Key* column because it is missing in *CustomerList*.

Value	Name	Country
1	Alberto	Italy
2	Daniele	Italy
2	Daniele	Italy
2	Marco	USA
2	Marco	USA

In other words, DEPENDON is like an inner join between the two tables that uses the columns specified in the second and following arguments to specify the join condition. Indeed, DEPENDON can match multiple columns. The following query returns only three rows because the matching now occurs by *Key* and *Name*:

```
DEFINE
    VAR Customers =
        SELECTCOLUMNS (
            {
                ( 1, "Alberto", "Italy" ),
                ( 2, "Daniele", "Italy" ),
                ( 2, "Marco", "USA" ),
                ( 3, "Claire", "France" )
            },
            "Key", [Value1],
            "Name", [Value2],
            "Country", [Value3]
        )
    TABLE CustomerList =
        SELECTCOLUMNS ( Customers, [Key], [Name] )

EVALUATE
GENERATE (
    CustomerList,
    DEPENDON ( Customers, CustomerList[Key], CustomerList[Name] )
)
ORDER BY [Key], [Name]
```

The result contains four rows, without duplicating any data.

Key	Name	Country
1	Alberto	Italy
2	Daniele	Italy
2	Marco	USA
3	Claire	France

The main use of DEPENDON is to track dependencies between columns stored in a variable, as we have seen in previous queries.

There may be some common patterns for DEPENDON, like in the following example that retrieves customer names given the code:

```
DEFINE
    VAR CustomerList = { 1212507, 1204911 }
EVALUATE
GENERATE (
    CustomerList,
    DEPENDON (
        SELECTCOLUMNS ( Customer, Customer[CustomerKey], Customer[Name] ),
        [Value]
    )
)
```

The result contains the pairs of *CustomerKey* and *Name*.

Value	Name
1,212,507	Antonio Nichols
1,204,911	Chad Walker

As we said earlier, it is better to avoid using these DAX functions directly in your code until they are at least documented and officially supported.

Splitting calculations between wholesale and retail

The very purpose of a composite model is to merge both wholesale and retail calculations in the same query. For example, one may want to create a budgeting system where the budget is local, while *Sales* and all the relevant dimensions are remote. The following is the diagram of the composite model with the *Budget* table.

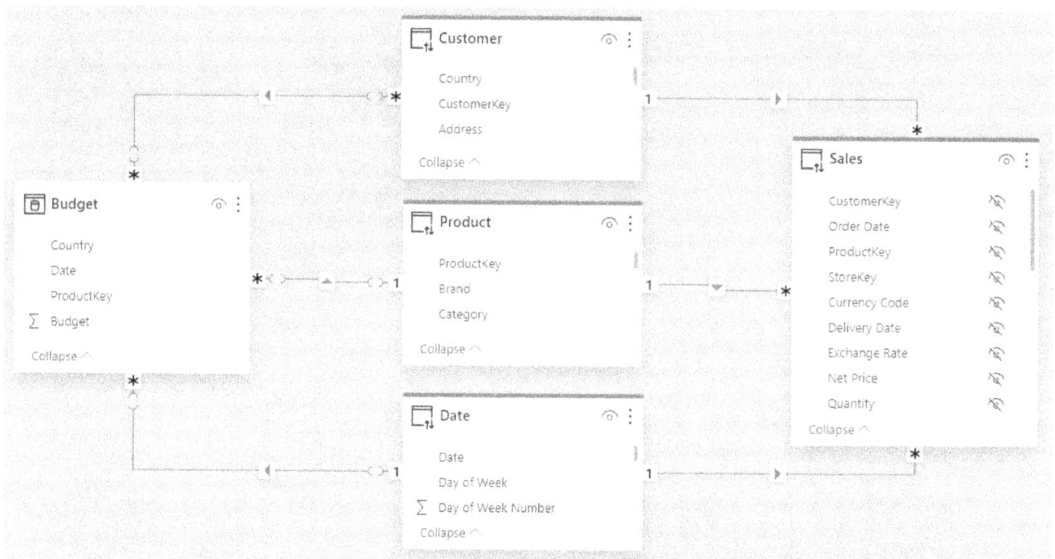

When running a query, the query plan is very different depending on whether the query is wholesale or retail. Let us analyze a few examples. The first query we consider is the following:

```
EVALUATE
SUMMARIZECOLUMNS (
    'Product'[Brand],
    "Sales", [Sales Amount]
)
```

Sales Amount is a measure in the remote model, so the query is wholesale. Executing the query shows a single DAX storage engine query that is equivalent to the original query and internally uses SUMMARIZECOLUMNS.

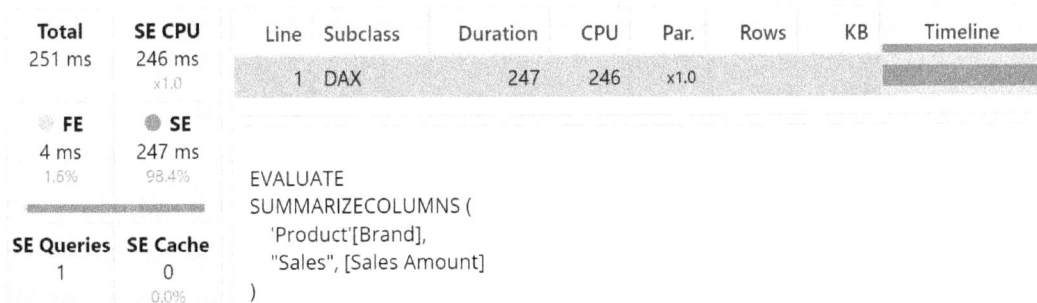

Total	SE CPU		Line	Subclass	Duration	CPU	Par.	Rows	KB	Timeline
251 ms	246 ms									
	x1.0		1	DAX	247	246	x1.0			

FE	SE
4 ms	247 ms
1.6%	98.4%

```
EVALUATE
SUMMARIZECOLUMNS (
    'Product'[Brand],
    "Sales", [Sales Amount]
)
```

SE Queries	SE Cache
1	0
	0.0%

In this scenario, the execution time is optimal because there is no overhead. The composite model shows the same speed as a regular VertiPaq model. However, if the same query includes calculations that scan the local model, then the pattern is different. For example, the following DAX query computes *Budget* by brand and produces two storage engine queries:

```
EVALUATE
SUMMARIZECOLUMNS (
    'Product'[Brand],
    "Budget", [Budget Amount]
)
```

The local engine retrieves the association between *Product[ProductKey]* and *Product[Brand]* from the remote model to move the filter between *Product* and *Budget*. Therefore, we now observe two storage engine queries.

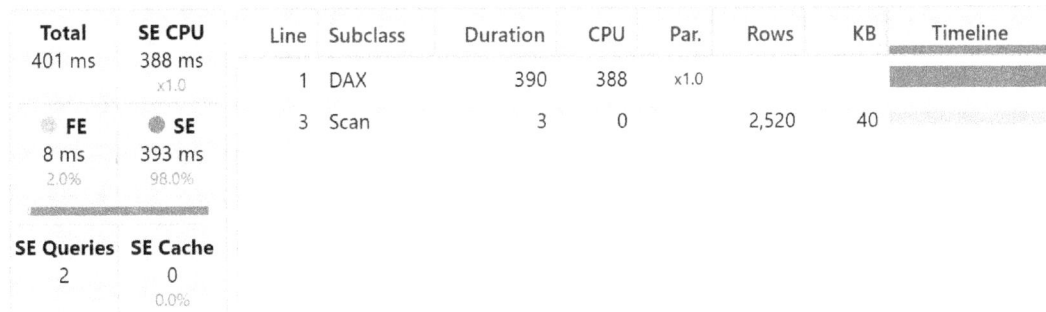

Total	SE CPU		Line	Subclass	Duration	CPU	Par.	Rows	KB	Timeline
401 ms	388 ms									
	x1.0		1	DAX	390	388	x1.0			
FE	SE		3	Scan	3	0		2,520	40	
8 ms	393 ms									
2.0%	98.0%									

SE Queries	SE Cache
2	0
	0.0%

The first is a DAX query sent to the remote engine:

```
DEFINE
    VAR _Var0 = VALUES ( 'Product'[Brand] )
EVALUATE
GROUPCROSSAPPLYTABLE (
    'Product'[Brand],
    _Var0,
    "L1",
    SUMMARIZE (
        VALUES ( 'Product' ),
        'Product'[ProductKey]
    )
)
```

The result includes all the combinations of *Product[Brand]* and *Product[ProductKey]*. This list is used to group *Budget* by *Product[ProductKey]* in the following storage engine query, leaving the task of grouping by *Brand* to the formula engine, which uses the result gathered in this first datacache.

The following storage engine query is a regular xmSQL query that retrieves the budget amount by *Budget[ProductKey]*, only for the product keys that were previously retrieved by the first DAX storage engine query:

```
SELECT
    'Budget'[ProductKey],
    SUM ( 'Budget'[Budget] )
FROM 'Budget'
WHERE
    'Budget'[ProductKey] IN ( 2174, 1620, 1869, 385, 178, 2080, 1763, 1288, 2476, 1383..[2,517 total values, not all displayed] ) ;
```

It is interesting to observe what happens if – in the same query – we execute the calculation of both *Sales Amount* and *Budget Amount*:

```
EVALUATE
SUMMARIZECOLUMNS (
    'Product'[Brand],
    "Sales", [Sales Amount],
    "Budget", [Budget Amount]
)
```

The code execution produces three storage engine queries. However, the interesting part is that the calculation of *Sales Amount* is now different.

Total	SE CPU		Line	Subclass	Duration	CPU	Par.	Rows	KB	Timeline
190 ms	172 ms									
	x1.0		1	DAX	64	64	x1.0			
FE	SE		2	DAX	108	108	x1.0			
15 ms	175 ms		4	Scan	3	0		2,520	40	
7.9%	92.1%									

SE Queries	SE Cache
3	0
	0.0%

The second and third storage engine queries are identical to the two storage engine queries in the previous example: they compute *Budget Amount* after having computed the relationship between *Product[Brand]* and *Product[ProductKey]*. However, here the first storage engine query computes *Sales Amount* by *Brand*, this time with a different DAX query:

```
DEFINE
    VAR _Var0 = VALUES ( 'Product'[Brand] )
EVALUATE
GROUPCROSSAPPLY (
    'Product'[Brand],
    _Var0,
    "__Agg0", [Sales Amount]
)
```

This DAX storage engine query uses GROUPCROSSAPPLY instead of SUMMARIZECOLUMNS, as it did in our first example when we requested only *Sales Amount*. The reason for this is that the engine identified that the same query requires both wholesale and retail queries. Therefore, it used the composite model technique. Performance-wise, the difference is not relevant in this example. However, we should always consider that the composite model technique requires moving filters back and forth between the servers, which might generate less optimal performance in other scenarios.

When a query includes both wholesale and retail code, the engine executes queries using the composite model method. The analysis of wholesale versus retail occurs at the measure level. One measure can be wholesale, whereas another one can be retail. Tabular chooses the optimal execution plan for each measure.

It is of paramount importance to recognize that the analysis occurs at the measure level. Code written outside of a measure can result in inferior performance. Let us see this with an example.

The following query sums both *Sales Amount* and *Budget Amount* in the same column:

```
EVALUATE
SUMMARIZECOLUMNS (
    'Product'[Brand],
    "Combined Amount", [Sales Amount] + [Budget Amount]
)
```

Sales Amount is wholesale and *Budget Amount* is local. The engine uses the same composite model technique as the previous DAX query. This technique computes both sub-expressions and then the local engine sums them together.

Total	SE CPU		Line	Subclass	Duration	CPU	Par.	Rows	KB	Timeline
897 ms	879 ms		1	DAX	760	760	x1.0			
	x1.0		2	DAX	120	119	x1.0			
FE	**SE**		4	Scan	3	0		2,520	40	
14 ms	883 ms									
1.6%	98.4%									

SE Queries	SE Cache
3	0
	0.0%

	Total DQ
	880 ms

So far, the three storage engine queries executed are identical to the ones in the previous query. However if instead of using the measures, we expand their internal code in the query, things are very different:

```
EVALUATE
SUMMARIZECOLUMNS (
    'Product'[Brand],
    "Combined Amount",
        SUMX ( Sales, Sales[Quantity] * Sales[Net Price] )
      + SUMX ( Budget, Budget[Budget] )
)
```

Now, the analysis of wholesale versus retail can no longer rely on measures. Because it results in being retail, the entire expression is analyzed and executed using the composite model technique. Despite the sub-expression corresponding to *Sales Amount* being wholesale, Tabular does not recognize it. Consequently, it tries to retrieve all the quantity and net price combinations from *Sales* to perform the multiplication in the local formula engine. In our model, this triggers an error of exceeding the maximum allowed number of rows in a datacache.

The resultset of a query to external data source has exceeded the maximum allowed size of '1000000' rows.

		Line	Subclass	Duration	CPU	Par.	Rows	KB	Timeline
Total	**SE CPU**								
44,338 ms	36,526 ms	1	DAX	117	116	x1.0			
	x1.0								
		3	Scan	3	0		2,520	40	
FE	**SE**								
7,808 ms	36,530 ms	4	DAX	36,410	36,410	x1.0			
17.6%	82.4%								

SE Queries	**SE Cache**
3	0
	0.0%

Total DQ
36,527 ms

DEFINE
VAR Var0 = VALUES('Product'[Brand])

The query that triggered the error is the following one:

```
DEFINE
    VAR _Var0 = VALUES ( 'Product'[Brand] )
EVALUATE
GROUPCROSSAPPLYTABLE (
    'Product'[Brand],
    _Var0,
    "L1",
    SELECTCOLUMNS (
        'Sales',
        "__RN", BLANK (),
        "'Sales'[Quantity]", 'Sales'[Quantity],
        "'Sales'[Net Price]", 'Sales'[Net Price],
        "'Product'[Brand]", RELATED ( 'Product'[Brand] )
    )
)
```

The innermost SELECTCOLUMNS function retrieves the entire *Sales* table to perform the grouping by *Brand* in the local formula engine. This request triggers an error in our scenario, as *Sales* contains several million rows. However, the query would still be very inefficient on a smaller model because of this large materialization.

Be mindful that this behavior is observed only when the entire expression is retail. If the entire expression is wholesale, then it is not necessary to use measures because the entire formula can be executed on the server:

```
EVALUATE
SUMMARIZECOLUMNS (
    'Product'[Brand],
    "Sales Amount",
        SUMX ( Sales, Sales[Quantity] * Sales[Net Price] )
)
```

Once analyzed, the code results in being wholesale;   it is sent to the remote engine as is, with a single DAX storage engine query.

Total	SE CPU	Line	Subclass	Duration	CPU	Par.	Rows	KB	Timeline
73 ms	68 ms	1	DAX	68	68	x1.0			
	x1.0								

FE	SE
6 ms	67 ms
8.2%	93.2%

SE Queries	SE Cache
1	0
	0.0%

	Total DQ
	68 ms

```
EVALUATE
SUMMARIZECOLUMNS (
    'Product'[Brand],
    "Sales Amount",
        SUMX ( Sales, Sales[Quantity] * Sales[Net Price] )
)
```

A wise DAX developer working with composite models should pay extra attention to defining a well-designed set of measures to help the Tabular engine find the optimal way to execute a query. Splitting the measures between retail and wholesale is an excellent way to obtain good performance.

Conclusions

Optimizing composite models requires all the skills gained through the VertiPaq optimization sections. In addition, there is the added complexity of communication between the local and the remote engines.

In the next chapter, we introduce several optimization examples focused on reducing the communication between the two engines.

Composite models optimization examples

As outlined in the previous chapter, composite models have some limitations for calculated columns, which must be wholesale. The main challenge in optimizing composite models is to reduce the communication needs between the local and remote servers. However, reducing communication might come at a cost, and you should carefully evaluate any change.

This chapter shows examples of composite models and the considerations needed to make them run faster.

Static segmentation

Static segmentation is a common scenario and one of the best fits for composite models. We want to categorize the products based on their sales volume according to the *Product Segment* configuration table.

Segment	MinValue	MaxValue
Low Sales	0	100,000
Medium Sales	100,000	1,000,000
High Sales	1,000,000	99,999,999,999

If we were to work on a regular model, we would use the solution provided at https://www.daxpatterns.com/. Unfortunately, this is not an option here because the canonical solution requires creating a calculated column in *Product,* which retrieves the segment name from the *Product Segment* table and applies a suitable filter based on the sales of the current product. The following is a possible implementation that would not work in our scenario:

```
-----------------------------------------
-- Calculated column in Product table
-----------------------------------------
Segment =
VAR ProductSales = [Sales Amount]
VAR Segments =
    FILTER (
        'Product Segment',
        AND (
            'Product Segment'[MinValue] <= ProductSales,
            'Product Segment'[MaxValue] > ProductSales
        )
    )

VAR Result =
    IF (
        COUNTROWS ( Segments ) = 1,
        MAXX ( Segments, 'Product Segment'[Segment] )
    )
RETURN
    Result
```

This calculated column cannot be created in a composite model because it would need to access the local table. Therefore, its evaluation would not be wholesale. In a calculated column, retail code is not an option.

One possible solution is to avoid the configuration table and embed the boundaries of the segments directly in the code by using a simple SWITCH function. This solution would work fine, but it is not desirable as it is not data-driven.

A viable solution is to create a lookup table containing the different values of *Sales Amount* categorized based on the configuration table. Then, we can build a relationship between the configuration table and the *Product* table, using a calculated column in *Product* to hold the sales amount of the product itself.

We start by creating a calculated column in *Product*:

```
-----------------------------------------
-- Calculated column in Product table
-----------------------------------------
Product Sales = [Sales Amount]
```

Please note that the calculated column is not materialized. However, we can use it to write a calculated table that categorizes the values of *Product Sales* based on the segments defined in *Product Segment*:

```
----------------------------------------
-- Calculated table 'Sales Segmented'
----------------------------------------
Sales Segmented =
GENERATE (
    ALLNOBLANKROW ( Product[Product Sales] ),
    FILTER (
        'Product Segment',
        AND (
            'Product Segment'[MinValue] <= Product[Product Sales],
            'Product Segment'[MaxValue] > Product[Product Sales]
        )
    )
)
```

We used GENERATE to bring all the segment columns in the *Sales Segmented* table to sort the segment name by minimum value. This way, we obtain a sensible sorting order instead of the default alphabetical sorting.

Once the calculated table and column are in place, we can build a relationship with *Product*.

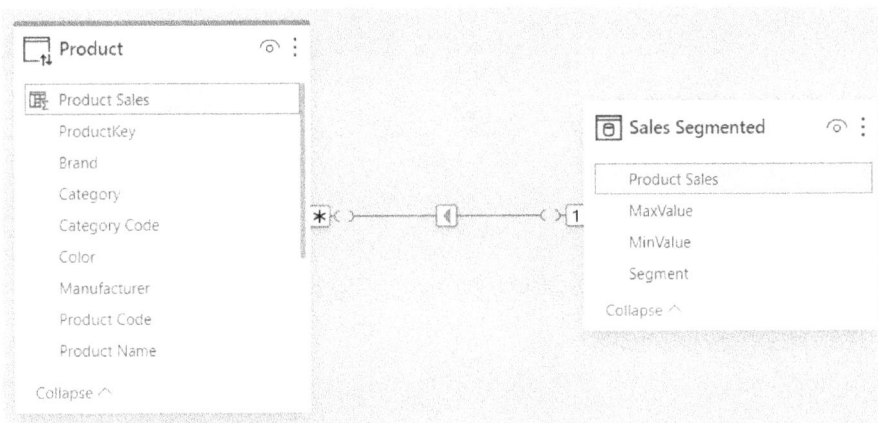

Before moving further, it is helpful to stop for a minute and appreciate the hidden complexity of this solution: we created a calculated column in *Product*, used it to create a VertiPaq table in the local model, and we are eventually building a relationship between the calculated table and the calculated column. If you consider that the calculated column is not materialized, you can probably appreciate how complex handling such a scenario is. Nonetheless, Tabular composite models handle this complexity in a straightforward fashion.

Sales Segmented is entirely data-driven and can be used to slice the *Product* table to obtain the reports we desire.

Segment	Sales Amount
Low Sales	10,931,997.90
Medium Sales	449,973,791.95
High Sales	9,828,673,654.94
Total	**10,289,579,444.80**

Now that the model works, we can discuss performance. The calculated table is not an issue, as the data refresh computes it. However, the relationship between the *Sales Segmented* calculated table and *Product* is based on a calculated column, which we know is not being materialized. Let us look at the DAX query that populates the matrix shown above. Once cleaned up, it looks like this:

```
--
--   Query executed on the local model
--
EVALUATE
SUMMARIZECOLUMNS (
    ROLLUPADDISSUBTOTAL (
        ROLLUPGROUP ( 'Sales Segmented'[Segment], 'Sales Segmented'[MinValue] ),
        "IsGrandTotalRowTotal"
    ),
    "Sales_Amount", 'Sales'[Sales Amount]
)
ORDER BY
    [IsGrandTotalRowTotal] DESC,
    'Sales Segmented'[MinValue],
    'Sales Segmented'[Segment]
```

As innocent as it may seem, this query hides the fact that the relationship between *Sales Segmented* and *Product* is based on the *Product Sales* calculated column. The *Sales Segmented* and *Product* tables are local and remote, respectively.

The Server Timings pane shows five different queries.

Total	SE CPU	Line	Subclass	Duration	CPU	Par.	Rows	KB	Timeline
1,293 ms	1,350 ms	1	DAX	94	94	x1.0			
	x1 1	2	DAX	247	246	x1.0			
FE ⚠	SE	4	Scan	0	0		36	1	
36 ms	1,257 ms	6	Scan	0	0		2,517	10	
2.8%	97.2%	7	DAX	1,010	1,010	x1.0			
SE Queries	SE Cache								
5	0								
	0.0%								
	Total DQ								
	1,351 ms								

The first DAX storage engine query computes the total:

```
--
--  Query executed on the remote model
--
EVALUATE
GROUPCROSSAPPLY(
    "__Agg0", [Sales Amount]
)
```

The second DAX storage engine query is interesting. It retrieves the value of the *Product Sales* calculated column for each product:

```
--
--  Query executed on the remote model
--
DEFINE
    VAR _Var0 =
        SUMMARIZE (
            VALUES ( 'Product' ),
            'Product'[ProductKey],
            'Product'[Product Code],
            'Product'[Product Name],
            'Product'[Manufacturer],
            'Product'[Brand],
            'Product'[Color],
            'Product'[Weight Unit Measure],
            'Product'[Weight],
            'Product'[Unit Cost],
            'Product'[Unit Price],
            'Product'[Subcategory Code],
            'Product'[Subcategory],
            'Product'[Category Code],
            'Product'[Category]
        )
```

```
EVALUATE
GROUPCROSSAPPLY (
    'Product'[ProductKey],
    'Product'[Product Code],
    'Product'[Product Name],
    'Product'[Manufacturer],
    'Product'[Brand],
    'Product'[Color],
    'Product'[Weight Unit Measure],
    'Product'[Weight],
    'Product'[Unit Cost],
    'Product'[Unit Price],
    'Product'[Subcategory Code],
    'Product'[Subcategory],
    'Product'[Category Code],
    'Product'[Category],
    _Var0,
    "__Agg0", [Sales Amount]
)
```

It is interesting to note that despite being fast, the query materializes the entire *Product* table. The reason is that – when we defined the calculated column – we used the context transition to compute sales by product. The semantics of the context transition require placing a filter on every column of the table; it would be better to filter only the key column. We will further discuss this query later, searching for a way to make it faster. For now, it is enough to note that this is a fast query with a potentially large datacache.

The following two xmSQL queries to the local VertiPaq storage engine retrieve values from the *Sales Segmented* table:

```
--
-- xmSQL queries executed on the local model
--

SELECT
    'Sales Segmented'[Segment],
    'Sales Segmented'[MinValue]
FROM 'Sales Segmented';

SELECT
    'Sales Segmented'[Segment],
    'Sales Segmented'[MinValue],
    'Sales Segmented'[Product Sales]
FROM 'Sales Segmented';
```

The core of the execution is in the last DAX storage engine query, which is 2,548 lines long. Here is an excerpt:

```
--
-- DAX DirectQuery query executed on the remote model
--
DEFINE
    TABLE _T79 =
        UNION (
            SELECTCOLUMNS ( _Var0, "Value", [Value1] ),
            SELECTCOLUMNS ( _Var1, "Value", [Value1] )
        )
    TABLE _T80 =
        UNION (
            SELECTCOLUMNS ( _Var0, "Value", [Value2] ),
            SELECTCOLUMNS ( _Var1, "Value", [Value2] )
        )
    COLUMN 'Product'[ASDQ_Product Sales] = [Sales Amount]
    VAR _Var0 = { ( 3, 3 ), ( 4, 4 ), ( 5, 5 ) }
    VAR _Var1 =
        {
            ( 5, 5, CURRENCY ( 12025669160 / 10000.0 ) ),
            ( 5, 5, CURRENCY ( 11487307260 / 10000.0 ) ),
            ( 5, 5, CURRENCY ( 11883382740 / 10000.0 ) ),
            ( 5, 5, CURRENCY ( 11781714080 / 10000.0 ) ),
            ( 5, 5, CURRENCY ( 12207109470 / 10000.0 ) ),
            ( 5, 5, CURRENCY ( 11688620450 / 10000.0 ) ),

            -- ...  around 2,000 more rows, removed from this list

            ( 3, 3, CURRENCY ( 978528135 / 10000.0 ) ),
            ( 3, 3, CURRENCY ( 694757700 / 10000.0 ) )
        }


EVALUATE
GROUPCROSSAPPLYTABLE (
    _T79[Value],
    _T80[Value],
    NONFILTER ( TREATAS ( _Var0, _T79[Value], _T80[Value] ) ),
    "L1",
        GROUPCROSSAPPLY (
            TREATAS (
                DEPENDON ( _Var1, EARLIER ( _T79[Value], 1 ), EARLIER ( _T80[Value], 1 ) ),
                'Product'[ASDQ_Product Sales]
            ),
            "__Agg0", [Sales Amount]
        )
)
```

The query structure is close to what we analyzed in the previous chapter. The *ASDQ_Product Sales* query column corresponds to the *Product Sales* calculated column. The *_Var1* variable holding the relationship between *Product* and *Sales Segmented* is based on a table containing around 2,000 rows: *Sales Segmented*. Even though the query is not extremely slow, it is already challenging. Once formatted, the query is 2,224 rows long. On the other hand, the datacache returned is tiny: it contains only three rows.

2,000 rows of DAX code for a relationship over a composite model is quite borderline: not huge, but at the same time, not small enough. If we need to optimize the model, we see a possible path: we must reduce the relationship size.

In this specific scenario, it is helpful to note that the boundaries of the configuration table are a multiple of 100,000. The first range is between zero and 100,000. All the other values are multiples of 100,000. There is no need to build the *Sales Segmented* table with every possible value for *Sales Amount*. We can use multiples of 100,000 to create both the *Sales Segmented* calculated table and the *Product Sales* calculated column:

```
-----------------------------------------
-- Calculated column in Product table
-----------------------------------------
Product Sales = INT ( [Sales Amount] / 1E5 )
```

The following is the code of the new version of *Sales Segmented*:

```
-----------------------------------------
-- Calculated table 'Sales Segmented'
-----------------------------------------
Sales Segmented =
VAR Multiplier = 1E5
RETURN
GENERATE (
    ALLNOBLANKROW ( Product[Product Sales] ),
    FILTER (
        'Product Segment',
        AND (
            'Product Segment'[MinValue] <= Product[Product Sales] * Multiplier,
            'Product Segment'[MaxValue] > Product[Product Sales] * Multiplier
        )
    )
)
```

This small change reduces the size of the *Sales Segmented* table from over 2,000 rows to 224 rows. Consequently, the query that was previously requiring more than 2,000 rows becomes smaller:

```
--
--  DAX DirectQuery query executed on the remote model
--
DEFINE
    TABLE _T79 =
        UNION (
            SELECTCOLUMNS ( _Var0, "Value", [Value1] ),
            SELECTCOLUMNS ( _Var1, "Value", [Value1] )
        )
    TABLE _T80 =
        UNION (
            SELECTCOLUMNS ( _Var0, "Value", [Value2] ),
            SELECTCOLUMNS ( _Var1, "Value", [Value2] )
        )
    COLUMN 'Product'[ASDQ_Product Sales] =
        INT ( [Sales Amount] / 100000 )
    VAR _Var0 = { ( 3, 3 ), ( 4, 4 ), ( 5, 5 ) }
    VAR _Var1 =
        {
            ( 5, 5, CURRENCY ( 130000 / 10000.0 ) ),
            ( 5, 5, CURRENCY ( 120000 / 10000.0 ) ),
            --
            --    Total of 225 rows
            --
            ( 4, 4, CURRENCY ( 100000 / 10000.0 ) ),
            ( 4, 4, CURRENCY ( 50000 / 10000.0 ) ),
            ( 4, 4, CURRENCY ( 20000 / 10000.0 ) )
        }


EVALUATE
GROUPCROSSAPPLYTABLE (
    _T79[Value],
    _T80[Value],
    NONFILTER ( TREATAS ( _Var0, _T79[Value], _T80[Value] ) ),
    "L1",
        GROUPCROSSAPPLY (
            TREATAS (
                DEPENDON ( _Var1, EARLIER ( _T79[Value], 1 ), EARLIER ( _T80[Value], 1 ) ),
                'Product'[ASDQ_Product Sales]
            ),
            "__Agg0", [Sales Amount]
        )
)
```

Despite the query being smaller, the gain in performance in this specific scenario is irrelevant. Executing the query shows that the timing is basically the same, if not worse.

Total	SE CPU	Line	Subclass	Duration	CPU	Par.	Rows	KB	Timeline
1,387 ms	1,414 ms	1	DAX	63	62	x1.0			
	x1.0	2	DAX	267	265	x1.0			
FE ⚠	**SE**	4	Scan	3	0		36	1	
30 ms	1,357 ms	6	Scan	1	0		8,172	64	
2.2%	97.8%								
		7	DAX	1,087	1,087	x1.0			
SE Queries	**SE Cache**								
5	0								

```
DEFINE
TABLE _T79 = UNION(SELECTCOLUMNS(_Var0, "Value", [Value1]),SELECTCOLUMNS(_Va
TABLE _T80 = UNION(SELECTCOLUMNS(_Var0, "Value", [Value2]),SELECTCOLUMNS(_Va
```

Total DQ 1,417 ms

The slower performance is because the change in the calculated column introduced the INT function in the DAX code, thus requiring a callback to the formula engine. We can double-check this by executing the DAX storage engine query directly on the **remote** model.

Total	SE CPU	Line	Subclass	Duration	CPU	Par.	Rows	KB	Timeline
563 ms	1,140 ms	2	Scan	16	31	x1.9	2,520	40	
	x2.2	4	Scan	517	1,109	x2.1	77	1	
FE	**SE**								
33 ms	530 ms								
5.9%	94.7%								

```
SET DC_KIND="AUTO";
WITH
    $Expr0 := ( PFCAST ( 'Sales'[Quantity] AS INT ) * PFCAST ( 'Sales'[Net Price] AS INT ) )
SELECT
    COLUMN ( ASDATAID ( [EncodeCallback ( INT ( [Sales Amount] / 1E5 ) ) ] ( PFDATAI
    SUM ( @$Expr0 )
FROM 'Sales'
```

SE Queries 2 **SE Cache** 0 0.0%

Total DQ 0 ms

The remote query requires a callback to evaluate the INT function. It is helpful to look at the two xmSQL queries executed by the remote server to better understand the behavior.

The first xmSQL query retrieves the values of *Sales Amount* by *ProductKey*. The remote formula engine caches the values of the calculated column:

```
WITH
    $Expr0 := ( PFCAST ( 'Sales'[Quantity] AS INT ) * PFCAST ( 'Sales'[Net Price] AS INT ) )
SELECT
    'Product'[ProductKey],
    SUM ( @$Expr0 )
FROM 'Sales'
    LEFT OUTER JOIN 'Product'
        ON 'Sales'[ProductKey]='Product'[ProductKey];
```

The INT function call is absent because the formula engine cannot execute it. The second query performs the grouping based on the calculated column, and here we find the INT callback:

```
WITH
    $Expr0 := ( PFCAST ( 'Sales'[Quantity] AS INT ) * PFCAST ( 'Sales'[Net Price] AS INT ) )
SELECT
    COLUMN ( ASDATAID ( [EncodeCallback ( INT ( [Sales Amount] / 1E5 ) ) ] ( PFDATAID ( 'Product'[ProductKey] ) ) ) ),
    SUM ( @$Expr0 )
FROM 'Sales'
    LEFT OUTER JOIN 'Product'
        ON 'Sales'[ProductKey]='Product'[ProductKey]
WHERE
    COLUMN ( ASDATAID ( [EncodeCallback ( INT ( [Sales Amount] / 1E5 ) ) ] ( PFDATAID ( 'Product'[ProductKey] ) ) ) )
        IN ( 14, 55, 96, 137, 178, 219, 28, 69, 110, 151..[224 total values, not all displayed] ) ;
```

The same DAX storage engine query executed on the previous version of *Sales Amount* without the INT function shows a close behavior, even though there is a noticeable difference.

Total	SE CPU	Line	Subclass	Duration	CPU	Par.	Rows	KB	Timeline
500 ms	391 ms	2	Scan	17	16	x0.9	2,520	40	
	x2.1								
FE	SE	4	Scan	172	375	x2.2	0	1	
313 ms	187 ms								
62.6%	37.8%								

```
SET DC_KIND="AUTO";
WITH
    $Expr0 := ( PFCAST ( 'Sales'[Quantity] AS INT ) * PFCAST ( 'Sales'[Net Price] AS INT ) )
SELECT
    COLUMN ( ASDATAID ( [EncodeCallback ( SUMX ( Sales, Sales[Quantity] * Sales[Net
( 'Product'[ProductKey] ) ) ) ),
    SUM ( @$Expr0 )
```

SE Queries	SE Cache
2	0
	0.0%

Total DQ
0 ms

The callback is still present, but it does not include any reference to the INT function; indeed, the storage engine resolves the calculated column autonomously. Consequently, the remote formula engine finds the value of the calculated column directly in the datacache without requiring further calculations, resulting in a better execution time.

You might notice that the timings of the queries are different when seen from the local or remote models. The execution of DAX storage engine queries on the remote model provides more insights on the number of rows and the parallelism, and it shows a faster execution.

The time measured on the local model represents the total execution time, including the time required to send the query and retrieve the data; that time is removed when the query is executed on the remote model.

Attention to these details is essential to better understand other possible optimization opportunities and their actual effects. Let us see this with a further example.

When we executed the first DAX query of this example, a DAX storage engine query had to retrieve the value of *Sales Amount* by materializing the entire product table. Indeed, the code of the *Product Sales* calculated column is now:

```
-----------------------------------------
-- Calculated column in Product table
-----------------------------------------
Product Sales = INT ( [Sales Amount] / 1E5 )
```

The code of this calculated column relies on context transition. To execute the context transition, DAX must filter all the columns in the table. Tabular includes an optimization that is triggered when a table contains a primary key. In that scenario, Tabular can assume that a filter on the primary key of the table provides the same result as filtering all the columns, because filtering the primary key is enough to guarantee the uniqueness of the results. However, the same optimization is not triggered if Tabular works with remote tables.

A good way to ensure that the filter takes place only on the primary key is to author *Product Sales* using CALCULATE and explicitly stating that the calculation depends only on the primary key:

```
-----------------------------------------
-- Calculated column in Product table
-----------------------------------------
Product Sales =
CALCULATE (
    INT ( [Sales Amount] / 1E5 ),
    ALLEXCEPT ( 'Product', 'Product'[ProductKey] )
)
```

This change in the calculated column definition simplifies the execution of the second DAX storage engine query, making it somewhat faster.

Total	SE CPU	Line	Subclass	Duration	CPU	Par.	Rows	KB	Timeline
1,293 ms	1,336 ms								
	x1.0	1	DAX	60	60	x1.0			
FE	SE	2	DAX	103	103	x1.0			
12 ms	1,281 ms	4	Scan	1	0		36	1	
0.9%	99.1%								
		6	Scan	0	0		8,172	64	
SE Queries	SE Cache	7	DAX	1,177	1,173	x1.0			
5	0								
	0.0%								

Total DQ
1,340 ms

```
DEFINE
VAR _Var0 = VALUES('Product'[ProductKey])
EVALUATE
GROUPCROSSAPPLY(
    'Product'[ProductKey],
    _Var0,
    "__Agg0", [Sales Amount]
)
```

This time, GROUPCROSSAPPLY does not group all the columns in *Product* but only uses *Product[ProductKey]*, resulting in a smaller datacache and a faster execution. It is now running in 103 milliseconds, against the 267 milliseconds required in the previous version. However, the benefit gained in the second storage engine query is lost on the last one, which is now slower. Indeed, the last query includes the definition of the calculated column, which now contains CALCULATE and ALLEXCEPT:

```
DEFINE
...
    COLUMN 'Product'[ASDQ_Product Sales] =
        CALCULATE (
            INT ( [Sales Amount] / 1E5 ),
            ALLEXCEPT ( 'Product', 'Product'[ProductKey] )
        )
...
```

The increased complexity of the calculated column has a profound, negative effect on performance. This impact can be appreciated only by running the last DAX storage engine query on the remote server.

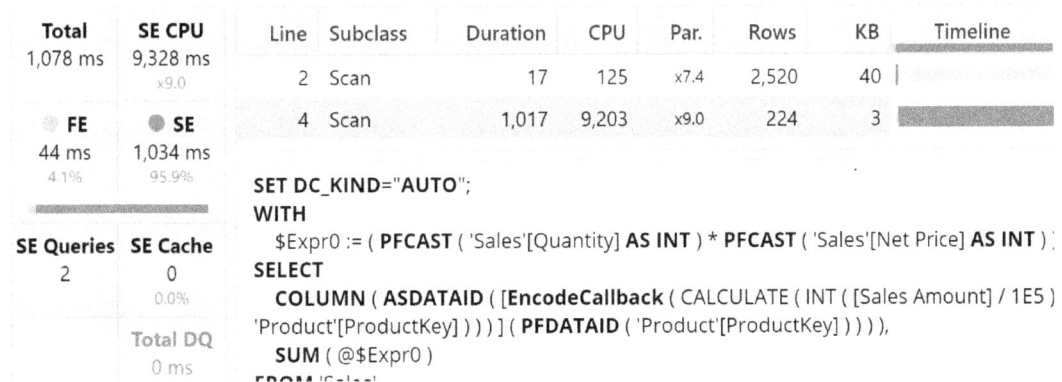

Total	SE CPU	Line	Subclass	Duration	CPU	Par.	Rows	KB	Timeline
1,078 ms	9,328 ms								
	x9.0	2	Scan	17	125	x7.4	2,520	40	
FE	SE	4	Scan	1,017	9,203	x9.0	224	3	
44 ms	1,034 ms								
4.1%	95.9%								

```
SET DC_KIND="AUTO";
WITH
    $Expr0 := ( PFCAST ( 'Sales'[Quantity] AS INT ) * PFCAST ( 'Sales'[Net Price] AS INT ) )
SELECT
    COLUMN ( ASDATAID ( [EncodeCallback ( CALCULATE ( INT ( [Sales Amount] / 1E5 )
'Product'[ProductKey] ) ) ) ] ( PFDATAID ( 'Product'[ProductKey] ) ) ) ),
    SUM ( @$Expr0 )
FROM 'Sales'
```

SE Queries	SE Cache
2	0
	0.0%

Total DQ
0 ms

Despite the total execution time being around the same as before, the remote SE CPU has now skyrocketed to 9,328 milliseconds. The total execution time is still good because of parallelism. However, the amount of resources the query uses is much more considerable than before.

It turns out that – in this specific scenario – none of our optimization techniques produce a good result. This is not a negative outcome at all. Knowing that your code is already the best possible is a critical piece of information. Moreover, the more you learn about the details of a piece of code, the more confident you are in deciding when and how to use a pattern.

For example, the information we collected led us to conclude that we can use a segmentation technique on small tables (less than 1M rows). On large tables, the query that retrieves the values of the calculated column cannot be executed because it would retrieve more than 1M rows, resulting in a runtime error. This information alone is worth the time spent investigating on the behavior of the engine.

Finally, the key to optimizing the model is to make a small change to the remote model. As you have seen in the various tests, the pivot point of the entire pattern is the *Product Sales* calculated column. If we could create the calculated column in the remote model, it would be materialized on the remote model, thus reducing the complexity of the entire solution. We created this column in the remote model as *Product Sales* and renamed it *Product Sales Remote* in the local model to run different tests side-by-side.

We get the following result by using the *Product Sales Remote* calculated column on the remote model.

Total	SE CPU	Line	Subclass	Duration	CPU	Par.	Rows	KB	Timeline
120 ms	171 ms								
	x1.5	2	Scan	0	0		36	1	
FE ⚠	● SE	4	Scan	0	0		224	1	
7 ms	113 ms	5	DAX	63	61	x1.0			
5.8%	94.2%	6	DAX	110	110	x1.0			
SE Queries	SE Cache								
4	0								
	0.0%								

The execution is much faster, and we also reduced the number of storage engine queries required. Namely, the most expensive query now missing is the one that retrieved all the possible values of the calculated column. This small change makes it possible to use this pattern on large tables, like in *Customer*.

Be mindful that when working with *Customer*, we need to handle a table with more than one million rows. Therefore, reducing the number of values of the calculated column is necessary, using the technique implemented for *Product*. When we did it on *Product*, we tried an optimization that did not work as expected. When dealing with *Customer*, it becomes a necessity.

We created the calculated column on the remote model:

```
----------------------------------------
-- Calculated column in Customer table
----------------------------------------
Customer Sales =
CALCULATE (
    INT ( [Sales Amount] / 100),
    ALLEXCEPT ( Customer, Customer[CustomerKey] )
)
```

Then, we created the *Sales Segmented Customer* calculated table on the local model:

```
-------------------------------------------------
-- Calculated table 'Sales Segmented Customer'
-------------------------------------------------
Sales Segmented Customer =
VAR Multiplier = 100
RETURN
GENERATE (
    ALLNOBLANKROW ( Customer[Customer Sales] ),
    FILTER (
        'Customer Segment',
        AND (
            'Customer Segment'[MinValue] <= Customer[Customer Sales] * Multiplier,
            'Customer Segment'[MaxValue] > Customer[Customer Sales] * Multiplier
        )
    )
)
```

After we create a many-to-one relationship between *Customer[Customer Sales]* and *'Sales Segmented Customer'[Customer Sales]*, we can finally execute a test query, similar to what we did with *Product*:

```
--
-- Query executed on the local model
--
EVALUATE
SUMMARIZECOLUMNS (
    ROLLUPADDISSUBTOTAL (
        ROLLUPGROUP (
            'Sales Segmented Customer'[Segment],
            'Sales Segmented Customer'[MinValue]
        ),
        "IsGrandTotalRowTotal"
    ),
    "Sales_Amount", 'Sales'[Sales Amount]
)


ORDER BY
    [IsGrandTotalRowTotal] DESC,
    'Sales Segmented Customer'[MinValue],
    'Sales Segmented Customer'[Segment]
```

The execution time is awesome: 1.8M customers are segmented in a matter of milliseconds.

Total	SE CPU	Line	Subclass	Duration	CPU	Par.	Rows	KB	Timeline
210 ms	263 ms	2	Scan	0	0		36	1	
	x1.3	4	Scan	0	0		748	3	
FE ⚠	● SE	5	DAX	64	64	x1.0			
10 ms	200 ms	6	DAX	199	199	x1.0			
4.8%	95.2%								

SE Queries	SE Cache
4	0
	0.0%

	Total DQ
	263 ms

The time spent optimizing *Product* paid off: we can now implement segmentation on large tables even though the solution requires a slight change to the remote model.

Budget and time intelligence calculations

We have repeatedly stressed that the main driver of composite model optimization is the reduction of communication between the local and the remote models. This communication is required to move a filter between the engines.

In this example, we analyze a scenario where the remote model contains *Sales*, and we extend the model with a *Budget* table containing the budget for 2020. The budget table is at the *Product*, *Country*, and *Month* granularity. The budget is in an Excel file imported into the local VertiPaq model.

Date	ProductKey	Country	Budget
11/01/20	1580	United States	69,377.45
01/01/20	1580	United States	91,191.60
02/01/20	1580	United States	93,430.66
10/01/20	1623	United States	74,810.40
11/01/20	1623	United States	56,440.68
01/01/20	1623	United States	99,599.45
03/01/20	1623	United States	35,854.68
11/01/20	1625	United States	60,240.77
12/01/20	1625	United States	107,529.00
01/01/20	1625	United States	101,342.69

The *Budget* table must have relationships to dimensions that are already present in the remote model.

All relationships are limited because they are cross-island. The relationships with *Date* and *Product* are one-to-many because the relationship corresponds to the primary key of those tables. The relationship with *Customer* is a many-to-many cardinality relationship because it connects the *Country* attribute, which is not unique in the *Customer* table.

It is interesting to perform a deep analysis of the execution of a query that computes values from the local *Budget* table when filters are applied to tables in the remote model. The following query computes the year-to-date budget for 2020 grouping by year, month, and country:

```
EVALUATE
SUMMARIZECOLUMNS (
    Customer[Country],
    'Date'[Year],
    'Date'[Month Number],
    TREATAS ( { 2020 }, 'Date'[Year] ),
    "Budget YTD",
        CALCULATE (
            [Budget Amount],
            DATESYTD ( 'Date'[Date] )
        )
)
ORDER BY
    [Country],
    [Year],
    [Month Number]
```

Before analyzing the storage engine queries, let us analyze a couple of details about what the query needs to perform:

- Grouping happens by columns on the remote model. However, the result is computed by scanning the *Budget* table, which is local. Therefore, Tabular must retrieve the values from the remote model and then use them to group and filter the local scan.

- The measure returned is the year-to-date of the budget. Consequently, Tabular defines the dates that construct the year-to-date of every month by scanning the remote *Date* table and then uses those dates to filter the local model.

- The *Budget Amount* measure computed is additive; therefore, the year-to-date calculation can be computed by either summing individual rows or performing multiple scans of the *Budget* table.

We expect to see some DAX queries to retrieve the values of countries, years, and months. Then, either the local or the remote engine should compute the year-to-date. Finally, we expect one or more scans of the local *Budget* table to compute the budget.

The Server Timings pane shows six different storage engine queries, of which only the last one is VertiPaq.

Total	SE CPU	Line	Subclass	Duration	CPU	Par.	Rows	KB	Timeline
537 ms	502 ms	1	DAX	72	72	x1.0			
	x1.0	2	DAX	107	105	x1.0			
FE	**SE**	3	DAX	63	62	x1.0			
30 ms	507 ms	4	DAX	97	97	x1.0			
5.6%	94.4%	5	DAX	167	166	x1.0			
		7	Scan	1	0		165	3	
SE Queries	**SE Cache**								
6	0								
	0.0%								
	Total DQ								
	506 ms								

The first storage engine query retrieves the values of *Customer[Country]* from the remote engine:

```
DEFINE
    VAR _Var0 = VALUES ( 'Customer'[Country] )
EVALUATE
GROUPCROSSAPPLYTABLE (
    'Customer'[Country],
    _Var0,
    "L1",
    SUMMARIZE (
        VALUES ( 'Customer' ),
        'Customer'[Country]
    )
)
```

The query seems complex just because it is computer-generated. What it does is quite simple: it returns the values of *Customer[Country]* in two columns, both named *Country*.

Country	Country
United States	United States
Australia	Australia
United Kingdom	United Kingdom
Germany	Germany
Canada	Canada
France	France
Netherlands	Netherlands
Italy	Italy

The second storage engine query retrieves all the *Date[Date]* values. Please note that – despite the filter for 2020 being part of the query – this DAX storage engine query always retrieves the complete list of dates. The local formula engine executes the YTD function. Therefore, the local formula engine needs all the dates in *Date* to resolve any time intelligence calculation:

```
EVALUATE
SUMMARIZE (
    VALUES ('Date'),
    'Date'[Date]
)
```

The third storage engine query retrieves the values of *Date[Year]* and *Date[Month Number]* for only 2020:

```
DEFINE
    VAR _Var0 = { 2020 }
EVALUATE
GROUPCROSSAPPLYTABLE (
    'Date'[Year],
    TREATAS (
        _Var0,
        'Date'[Year]
    ),
    "L1",
        SUMMARIZE (
            VALUES ( 'Date' ),
            'Date'[Month Number]
        )
)
```

The fourth DAX storage engine query maps the date axis of SUMMARIZECOLUMNS (year and month) to individual dates. Indeed, for time intelligence to work, the engine needs a selection of dates. It needs to know which dates compose each time period used as a group-by column:

```
DEFINE
    VAR _Var0 = { 2020 }
EVALUATE
GROUPCROSSAPPLYTABLE (
    'Date'[Year],
    'Date'[Month Number],
    ALLSELECTEDREMOVE (
        FILTERCLUSTER (
            'Date'[Year],
            'Date'[Month Number],
            TREATAS ( _Var0, 'Date'[Year] ),
            "",
            SUMMARIZE ( VALUES ( 'Date' ), 'Date'[Year], 'Date'[Month Number] )
        ),
        'Date'[Month Number]
    ),
    "L1", SUMMARIZE ( 'Date', 'Date'[Date] )
)
```

The result is straightforward: it contains 366 rows that let DAX know which dates are present for every month.

Year	Month Number	Date
2,020	2	02/27/2020
2,020	2	02/28/2020
2,020	2	02/29/2020
2,020	3	03/01/2020
2,020	3	03/02/2020
2,020	3	03/03/2020
2,020	3	03/04/2020

As you have seen, the first four storage queries do not compute year-to-date. Their task is only to prepare the environment in which the local formula engine maps each time period (year and month) to the set of dates, including the year-to-date. This preparation becomes clearer when we analyze the fifth query. The fifth storage engine query contains a variable that already defines the year-to-date grouping whose primary goal is to validate the calculation; this also implies that the year-to-date calculation happens in the local formula engine. The query is very long (more than three thousand rows); here is an excerpt:

```
DEFINE
    VAR _Var0 = { 2020 }
    VAR _Var1 = {
        ( 2020, 1, DT"2020-1-1" ),
        ( 2020, 1, DT"2020-1-2" ),

        ...

        ( 2020, 2, DT"2020-2-29" ),
        ( 2020, 3, DT"2020-1-1" ),
        ( 2020, 3, DT"2020-1-2" ),
        ( 2020, 3, DT"2020-1-3" ),
        ( 2020, 3, DT"2020-1-4" ),

        ...

        ( 2020, 12, DT"2020-12-31" )
    }
EVALUATE
GROUPCROSSAPPLYTABLE (
    'Date'[Year],
    'Date'[Month Number],
    NONFILTER (
        FILTERCLUSTER (
            'Date'[Year],
            'Date'[Month Number],
            TREATAS ( _Var0, 'Date'[Year] ),
            "",
            SUMMARIZE ( VALUES ( 'Date' ), 'Date'[Year], 'Date'[Month Number] )
        )
    ),
    "L1",
        GROUPCROSSAPPLYTABLE (
            TREATAS (
                DEPENDON (
                    _Var1,
                    EARLIER ( 'Date'[Year], 1 ),
                    EARLIER ( 'Date'[Month Number], 1 )
                ),
                'Date'[Date]
            ),
            "L2", SUMMARIZE ( VALUES ( 'Date' ), 'Date'[Date] )
        )
)
```

The _Var1 variable contains the relationship between year, month, and all the dates to compute the YTD of that specific year and month. If you compare the result of this last storage engine query with the previous one, you can note that – for March – the first of January is included in this output, whereas it was missing in the previous result.

Year	Month Number	Date
2,020	2	02/27/2020
2,020	2	02/28/2020
2,020	2	02/29/2020
2,020	3	01/01/2020
2,020	3	01/02/2020
2,020	3	01/03/2020
2,020	3	01/04/2020

So far, the first five storage engine queries did not compute any value from *Budget*. Their task is only to prepare a proper filter to compute the result from *Budget*. The last query – the only VertiPaq one – computes the actual values:

```
SET DC_KIND="AUTO";
SELECT
    'Budget'[Date],
    'Budget'[Country],
    SUM ( 'Budget'[Budget] )
FROM 'Budget'
WHERE
    'Budget'[Date] IN ( 44075.000000, 44136.000000, 43831.000000, 43862.000000, 44105.000000, 43891.000000,
44166.000000, 43922.000000, 43952.000000, 43983.000000..[12 total values, not all displayed] ) VAND
    'Budget'[Country] IN ( 'United States', 'United Kingdom', 'Canada', 'Italy', 'France', 'Germany', 'Netherlands', 'Australia' ) ;
```

Because the measure is additive, the formula engine scans the most granular results (at the day level), and then the formula engine computes the sum of the individual days. Because data in the budget is at the month level, there are only twelve values in the date filter.

It is worth noting that out of the 537 milliseconds of total execution time, one millisecond is the time required to scan *Budget*, the formula engine consumes 30 milliseconds, and the remaining time is communication between the servers to gather the axis of the queries.

An interesting optimization to reduce the communication needs is to perform the YTD function on a local date table rather than on the remote *Date* table. By doing this, we reduce the need to retrieve the lists of year-to-date from the remote engine, leaving the task to VertiPaq scans.

We create a new VertiPaq table named *Local Date* with this simple DAX expression:

```
----------------------------------
-- Calculated table 'Local Date'
----------------------------------
Local Date = ALLNOBLANKROW ( 'Date'[Date] )
```

Then, we create a relationship between the remote *Date* table and the VertiPaq *Local Date* table, linking *Budget* with the local date rather than directly with *Date*.

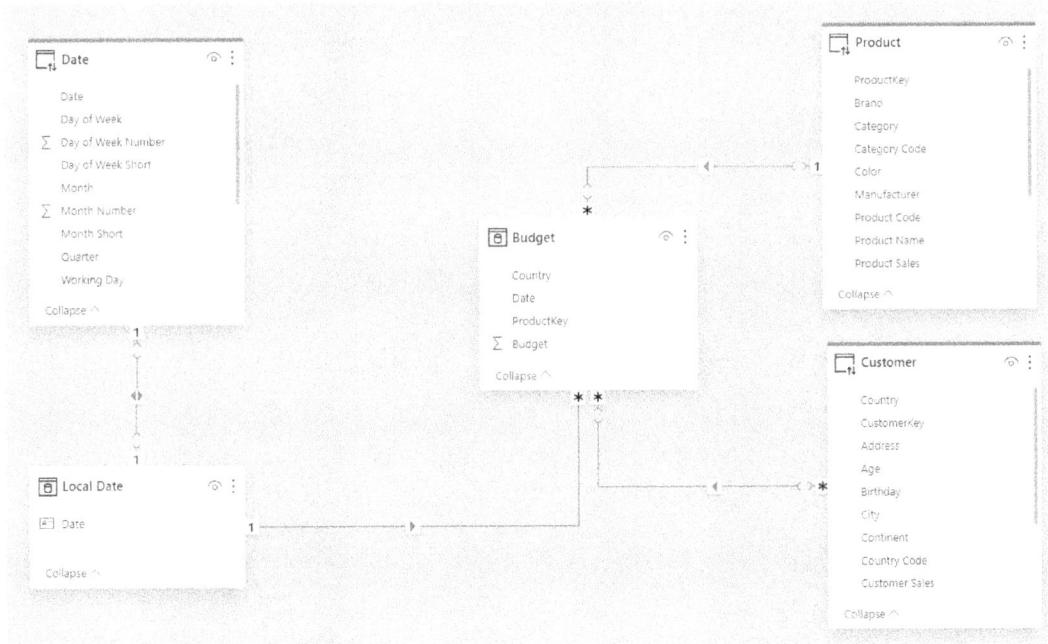

The idea is the following: the query still places the filter on *Date*. From there, the filter moves to *Local Date* and then to *Budget*. Therefore, the filter flow is the same as before, with an additional hop inside VertiPaq. We will use DATESYTD over *Local Date*, simultaneously removing any filter from *Date*.

The net effect of the calculation is the same. However, the hope is that most queries will hit VertiPaq, thus reducing the communication between the servers to a minimum. Here is the query with the updated measure:

```
EVALUATE
SUMMARIZECOLUMNS (
    Customer[Country],
    'Date'[Year],
    'Date'[Month Number],
    TREATAS ( { 2020 }, 'Date'[Year] ),
    "Budget YTD",
        CALCULATE (
            [Budget Amount],
            REMOVEFILTERS ( 'Date' ),
            DATESYTD ( 'Local Date'[Date] )
        )
)
ORDER BY
    [Country],
    [Year],
    [Month Number]
```

The Server Timings pane still shows six storage engine queries. This time, three are VertiPaq scan queries against only one in the previous model.

Total	SE CPU	Line	Subclass	Duration	CPU	Par.	Rows	KB	Timeline
250 ms	227 ms ×1.0	2	Scan	1	0		4,021	32	
FE 14 ms 5.6%	**SE** 236 ms 94.4%	3	DAX	63	63	×1.0			
		4	DAX	103	102	×1.0			
		6	Scan	3	0		4,021	32	
SE Queries 6	SE Cache 0 0.0%	7	DAX	63	62	×1.0			
		9	Scan	3	0		96	2	
	Total DQ 229 ms								

The query structure is very close to the previous version. However, some queries are faster this time because they hit VertiPaq rather than the remote model.

The first xmSQL storage engine query retrieves the dates from the *Local Dates* table:

```
SELECT
    'Local Date'[Date]
FROM 'Local Date';
```

This query runs in one millisecond, compared to 72 for the previous version.

The second storage engine query is the same as the third one in the previous version, consuming approximately the same amount of time:

```
DEFINE
    VAR _Var0 = { 2020 }
EVALUATE
GROUPCROSSAPPLYTABLE (
    'Date'[Year],
    TREATAS (
        _Var0,
        'Date'[Year]
    ),
    "L1",
        SUMMARIZE (
            VALUES ( 'Date' ),
            'Date'[Month Number]
        )
)
```

The third storage engine query is the same as the fourth one in the previous version, with a similar execution time:

```
DEFINE
    VAR _Var0 = { 2020 }
EVALUATE
GROUPCROSSAPPLYTABLE (
    'Date'[Year],
    'Date'[Month Number],
    ALLSELECTEDREMOVE (
        FILTERCLUSTER (
            'Date'[Year],
            'Date'[Month Number],
            TREATAS ( _Var0, 'Date'[Year] ),
            "",
            SUMMARIZE ( VALUES ( 'Date' ), 'Date'[Year], 'Date'[Month Number] )
        ),
        'Date'[Month Number]
    ),
    "L1", SUMMARIZE ( 'Date', 'Date'[Date] )
)
```

The following storage engine query retrieves the values of dates from *Local Dates* rather than from the remote *Date* table, again saving around 100 milliseconds:

```
SELECT
    'Local Date'[Date]
FROM 'Local Date'
WHERE
    'Local Date'[Date] IN ( 43963.000000, 43922.000000, 43840.000000, 44127.000000, 43881.000000, 44004.000000,
44045.000000, 44086.000000, 43977.000000, 43936.000000..[366 total values, not all displayed] ) ;
```

The fifth storage engine query retrieves the list of countries using the same technique used by the first storage engine query of the previous model:

```
DEFINE
    VAR _Var0 = VALUES ( 'Customer'[Country] )
EVALUATE
GROUPCROSSAPPLYTABLE (
    'Customer'[Country],
    _Var0,
    "L1",
    SUMMARIZE(
        VALUES ( 'Customer' ),
        'Customer'[Country]
    )
)
```

Finally, the last storage engine query is identical to the last DAX query of the previous model:

```
SELECT
    'Budget'[Country],
    'Local Date'[Date],
    SUM ( 'Budget'[Budget] )
FROM 'Budget'
    LEFT OUTER JOIN 'Local Date'
        ON 'Budget'[Date]='Local Date'[Date]
WHERE
    'Budget'[Country] IN ( 'United States', 'United Kingdom', 'Canada', 'Italy', 'France', 'Germany', 'Netherlands', 'Australia' )
VAND
    'Local Date'[Date] IN ( 43840.000000, 43881.000000, 43922.000000, 43963.000000, 44004.000000, 44045.000000,
44086.000000, 44127.000000, 43895.000000, 43936.000000..[366 total values, not all displayed] ) ;
```

As you can see, the YTD calculation still takes place in the local formula engine. However, because more datacaches used by the formula engine originated from VertiPaq rather than from the remote server, the communication between different servers is reduced, thus improving the execution speed.

As is often the case with optimizations, saving 2/300 milliseconds may very well not be worth the effort. However, there are two takeaways from this demo:

- Reducing the communication between servers requires creativity and unusual models. Developers can only think about these non-canonical solutions if they know the internals of the engine.

- Pushing calculations down to the local VertiPaq engine saves server communication time. The amount saved depends on many factors. In this example, we saved a bunch of milliseconds. The savings can be more significant on larger models or columns with a larger cardinality.

In most scenarios, this level of optimization is not necessary. After all, the original model runs just fine. However, for when the going gets tough, you now have more tools in your DAX optimizer toolbelt.

Dynamic ABC analysis

Another fascinating example of composite model optimization is the dynamic ABC analysis. ABC clusters products in three groups: A, B, and C. Group A contains products that contribute up to 70% of sales, B includes the next 20%, whereas class C includes products that generate only the remaining 10% of sales altogether. The pattern (and the code) is an extract from ABC classification at https://www.daxpatterns.com/abc-classification/. We only optimized it a bit to use window functions, a feature not available when the pattern was first released.

ABC can be either static or dynamic. For this example, we are focusing on dynamic ABC, because the formula is quite complex, and the optimization is rather interesting.

The goal is to obtain a report like the following.

ABC Class	Pct	ABC Sales Amount	# Products
A	70%	7,201,480,882.70	460
B	20%	2,057,341,358.12	577
C	10%	1,030,757,203.98	1,480
Total	**100%**	**10,289,579,444.80**	**2,517**

The local model contains a calculated table (*ABC Classes*) that defines the three classes:

```
-----------------------------------
-- Calculated table 'ABC Classes'
-----------------------------------
ABC Classes =
SELECTCOLUMNS (
    {
        ( "A",  0,   0.7 ),
        ( "B",  0.7, 0.9 ),
        ( "C",  0.9, 1.0 )
    },
    "ABC Class", [Value1],
    "Lower Boundary", [Value2],
    "Upper Boundary", [Value3]
)
```

Based on the *ABC Classes* table, the following *ABC Sales Amount* measure computes the *Sales Amount* for the selected class in *ABC Classes*:

```
--------------------------------------
-- Measure in Sales table
--------------------------------------
ABC Sales Amount =
VAR AllSales =
    CALCULATE ( [Sales Amount], ALLSELECTED ( 'Product' ) )
VAR PctByProduct =
    ADDCOLUMNS ( ALLSELECTED ( 'Product' ), "@ProdPct", [Sales Amount] / AllSales )
VAR CumulatedPctByProduct =
    ADDCOLUMNS (
        PctByProduct,
        "@CumulatedPct",
            SUMX (
                WINDOW ( 0, ABS, 0, REL, PctByProduct, ORDERBY ( [@ProdPct], DESC ) ),
                [@ProdPct]
            )
    )


VAR ProductsInClass =
    FILTER (
        CROSSJOIN ( CumulatedPctByProduct, 'ABC Classes' ),
        AND (
            [@CumulatedPct] > 'ABC Classes'[Lower Boundary],
            [@CumulatedPct] <= 'ABC Classes'[Upper Boundary]
        )
    )
VAR Result =
    CALCULATE ( [Sales Amount], KEEPFILTERS ( ProductsInClass ) )
RETURN
    Result
```

The measure is quite complex: for each product, it computes the percentage of sales of all the products that sell at least the same amount as the current product. Window functions are beneficial, but the code is not trivial.

In the code, there is a clear separation between what happens locally and what happens on the remote model. The only variable where we use local tables is *ProductsInClass*; all the remaining parts of the code are wholesale. However, the entire measure is retail and cannot be separated into different measures because the code of *ProductsInClass* depends on the other variables.

As a test query, we use a simple SUMMARIZECOLUMNS, enriched with a filter to better show the dynamic nature of the calculation:

```
EVALUATE
SUMMARIZECOLUMNS (
    'ABC Classes'[ABC Class],
    TREATAS ( { "Europe" }, Customer[Continent] ),
    "ABC Sales Amount", [ABC Sales Amount]
)
ORDER BY 'ABC Classes'[ABC Class]
```

The query runs in less than three seconds, and it requires six storage engine queries.

Total	SE CPU	Line	Subclass	Duration	CPU	Par.	Rows	KB	Timeline
3,050 ms	2,732 ms	1	DAX	62	62	x1.0			
	x1.0								
FE ⚠	● SE	3	Scan	3	0		6	1	
378 ms	2,672 ms	5	Scan	0	0		546	5	
12.4%	87.6%								
		6	DAX	259	259	x1.0			
SE Queries	SE Cache	7	DAX	960	960	x1.0			
6	0	8	DAX	1,451	1,451	x1.0			
	0.0%								

Most of the time is spent on the last two storage engine queries. Let us start analyzing all of them in detail.

The first query is a DAX storage engine query that retrieves *Sales Amount* in Europe. It is required to compute the value of the *SalesOfAll* variable:

```
DEFINE
    VAR _Var0 = { "Europe" }
EVALUATE
GROUPCROSSAPPLY (
    TREATAS ( _Var0, 'Customer'[Continent] ),
    "__Agg0", [Sales Amount]
)
```

The second and third storage engine queries are the only VertiPaq ones, and they are straightforward – they retrieve the values of the *ABC Classes* table:

```
SELECT
    'ABC Classes'[ABC Class]
FROM 'ABC Classes';


SELECT
    'ABC Classes'[ABC Class],
    'ABC Classes'[Lower Boundary],
    'ABC Classes'[Upper Boundary]
FROM 'ABC Classes';
```

The fourth storage engine query retrieves the entire *Product* table from the remote model:

```
EVALUATE
SELECTCOLUMNS (
    VALUES ( 'Product' ),
    "__RN", BLANK (),
    "'Product'[ProductKey]", 'Product'[ProductKey],
    "'Product'[Product Code]", 'Product'[Product Code],
    "'Product'[Product Name]", 'Product'[Product Name],
    "'Product'[Manufacturer]", 'Product'[Manufacturer],
    "'Product'[Brand]", 'Product'[Brand],
    "'Product'[Color]", 'Product'[Color],
    "'Product'[Weight Unit Measure]", 'Product'[Weight Unit Measure],
    "'Product'[Weight]", 'Product'[Weight],
    "'Product'[Unit Cost]", 'Product'[Unit Cost],
    "'Product'[Unit Price]", 'Product'[Unit Price],
    "'Product'[Subcategory Code]", 'Product'[Subcategory Code],
    "'Product'[Subcategory]", 'Product'[Subcategory],
    "'Product'[Category Code]", 'Product'[Category Code],
    "'Product'[Category]", 'Product'[Category],
    "'Product'[Product Sales]", 'Product'[Product Sales]
)
```

The entire *Product* table is necessary because – in the code – there are multiple references to *ALLSELECTED (Product)*, which is the entire table. The problem is not only that the table must be retrieved from the server: as we are about to see, the entire table is then passed back in the following two DAX storage engine queries as a filter.

The fifth storage engine query computes *Sales Amount* by product. However, because ADDCOLUMNS operates on *ALLSELECTED(Product)*, the entire *Product* table is saved in a variable, resulting in a query with 2,700 lines:

```
DEFINE
    VAR _Var0 = { "Europe" }
    VAR _Var1 =
        SUMMARIZE (
            VALUES ( 'Product' ),
            'Product'[ProductKey],
            'Product'[Product Code],
            'Product'[Product Name],
            'Product'[Manufacturer],
            'Product'[Brand],
            'Product'[Color],
            'Product'[Weight Unit Measure],
            'Product'[Weight],
            'Product'[Unit Cost],
            'Product'[Unit Price],
            'Product'[Subcategory Code],
            'Product'[Subcategory],
            'Product'[Category Code],
            'Product'[Category],
            'Product'[Product Sales]
        )
    VAR _Var2 =
        {
            ( 1707, "0702001", "MGS Dal of Honor Airborne M150", "Tailspin Toys", "Tailspin
Toys", "Silver", BLANK (), BLANK (), CURRENCY ( 322500 / 10000.0 ), CURRENCY ( 701300 /
10000.0 ), "0702", "Download Games", "07", "Games and Toys", CURRENCY ( 70000 / 10000.0 ) ),
            ( 1708, "0702002", "MGS Collector's M160", "Tailspin Toys", "Tailspin Toys",
"Black", BLANK (), BLANK (), CURRENCY ( 322500 / 10000.0 ), CURRENCY ( 701300 / 10000.0 ),
"0702", "Download Games", "07", "Games and Toys", CURRENCY ( 70000 / 10000.0 ) ),


            ...


            ( 2353, "0807006", "Contoso Air conditioner 6000BTU E0180 White", "Contoso,
Ltd", "Contoso", "White", "pounds", 8.8E1, CURRENCY ( 1019600 / 10000.0 ), CURRENCY (
1999900 / 10000.0 ), "0807", "Air Conditioners", "08", "Home Appliances", CURRENCY ( 50000 /
10000.0 ) ),
            ( 2354, "0807007", "Contoso Air conditioner 5200BTU E0100 White", "Contoso,
Ltd", "Contoso", "White", "pounds", 8.8E1, CURRENCY ( 560800 / 10000.0 ), CURRENCY ( 1099900
/ 10000.0 ), "0807", "Air Conditioners", "08", "Home Appliances", CURRENCY ( 30000 / 10000.0
) )
        }
```

```
EVALUATE
GROUPCROSSAPPLYTABLE (
    TREATAS ( _Var0, 'Customer'[Continent] ),
    _Var1,
    "L1",
    GROUPCROSSAPPLY (
        'Product'[ProductKey],
        'Product'[Product Code],
        'Product'[Product Name],
        'Product'[Manufacturer],
        'Product'[Brand],
        'Product'[Color],
        'Product'[Weight Unit Measure],
        'Product'[Weight],
        'Product'[Unit Cost],
        'Product'[Unit Price],
        'Product'[Subcategory Code],
        'Product'[Subcategory],
        'Product'[Category Code],
        'Product'[Category],
        'Product'[Product Sales],
        KEEPFILTERS (
            TREATAS (
                _Var2,
                'Product'[ProductKey],
                'Product'[Product Code],
                'Product'[Product Name],
                'Product'[Manufacturer],
                'Product'[Brand],
                'Product'[Color],
                'Product'[Weight Unit Measure],
                'Product'[Weight],
                'Product'[Unit Cost],
                'Product'[Unit Price],
                'Product'[Subcategory Code],
                'Product'[Subcategory],
                'Product'[Category Code],
                'Product'[Category],
                'Product'[Product Sales]
            )
        ),
        "__Agg0", [Sales Amount]
    )
)
```

Despite being lengthy, the query retrieves the entire *Product* table and the *Sales Amount* for each product, as required by the *PctByProduct* variable.

The last storage engine query is very interesting. It uses the previous result (the entire *Product* table plus *Sales Amount* for each product) along with a couple of variables that send the relevant content of *ABC Classes* to the remote server, so that the remote DAX engine can group the products by the corresponding classes.

The result of the last query is the following.

Value	__Agg0
5	326,236,158.35
3	2,280,940,575.77
4	653,754,739.78

Here is the code:

```
DEFINE
    TABLE _T71 =
        UNION (
            SELECTCOLUMNS ( _Var1, "Value", [Value] ),
            SELECTCOLUMNS ( _Var2, "Value", [Value1] )
        )
    VAR _Var0 = { "Europe" }
    VAR _Var1 = { 3, 4, 5 }
    VAR _Var2 =
        {
            ( 3, 1765, "0702059", "MGS Age of Empires Expansion: The Rise of Rome X900",
"Tailspin Toys", "Tailspin Toys", "Blue", BLANK (), BLANK (), CURRENCY ( 1983900 / 10000.0
), CURRENCY ( 5988000 / 10000.0 ), "0702", "Download Games", "07", "Games and Toys",
CURRENCY ( 600000 / 10000.0 ) ),
            ( 3, 416, "0303001", "Adventure Works Desktop PC2.33 XD233 Silver", "Adventure
Works", "Adventure Works", "Silver", "pounds", BLANK (), CURRENCY ( 3210500 / 10000.0 ),
CURRENCY ( 9690000 / 10000.0 ), "0303", "Desktops", "03", "Computers", CURRENCY ( 9320000 /
10000.0 ) ),
            ...
            ( 5, 2353, "0807006", "Contoso Air conditioner 6000BTU E0180 White", "Contoso,
Ltd", "Contoso", "White", "pounds", 8.8E1, CURRENCY ( 1019600 / 10000.0 ), CURRENCY (
1999900 / 10000.0 ), "0807", "Air Conditioners", "08", "Home Appliances", CURRENCY ( 50000 /
10000.0 ) ),
            ( 5, 2354, "0807007", "Contoso Air conditioner 5200BTU E0100 White", "Contoso,
Ltd", "Contoso", "White", "pounds", 8.8E1, CURRENCY ( 560800 / 10000.0 ), CURRENCY ( 1099900
/ 10000.0 ), "0807", "Air Conditioners", "08", "Home Appliances", CURRENCY ( 30000 / 10000.0
) )
        }
```

```
EVALUATE
GROUPCROSSAPPLYTABLE (
    _T71[Value],
    TREATAS ( _Var0, 'Customer'[Continent] ),
    NONFILTER ( TREATAS ( _Var1, _T71[Value] ) ),
    "L1",
        GROUPCROSSAPPLY (
            TREATAS (
                DEPENDON ( _Var2, EARLIER ( _T71[Value], 1 ) ),
                'Product'[ProductKey],
                'Product'[Product Code],
                'Product'[Product Name],
                'Product'[Manufacturer],
                'Product'[Brand],
                'Product'[Color],
                'Product'[Weight Unit Measure],
                'Product'[Weight],
                'Product'[Unit Cost],
                'Product'[Unit Price],
                'Product'[Subcategory Code],
                'Product'[Subcategory],
                'Product'[Category Code],
                'Product'[Category],
                'Product'[Product Sales]
            ),
            "__Agg0", [Sales Amount]
        )
)
```

The first column in _Var2_ is the cluster (A, B, or C) assigned to each product.

As you can see, there are no references to DAX window functions. The window functions are entirely executed in the formula engine. To summarize the algorithm, this is what happens:

- The local engine retrieves *Sales Amount* by product, the total *Sales Amount*, and the entire *Product* table.

- The local formula engine computes the percentages of each product, calculates the cumulative percentage of each product, and assigns the corresponding class to each product.

- The information computed so far is used to send a query to the remote engine to compute *Sales Amount* for the different groups of products.

The algorithm is a very nice implementation of our requirements. The only drawback is that the entire *Product* table needs to be passed back and forth between the engines, which slows down the query and makes the code hard to read and understand.

The line is clear: we must avoid using *ALLSELECTED(Product)* and replace it with a different DAX expression requiring less memory and obtaining the same behavior. Indeed, we can compute *ALLSELECTED(Product)* in a variable with a different expression. We must reference only the

Product[ProductKey] column. We can obtain the result by removing any filter from *Product* and using ALLSELECTED with no arguments:

```
--------------------------------------
-- Measure in Sales table
--------------------------------------
ABC Sales Amount v2 =
VAR AllSelectedProducts =
    CALCULATETABLE (
        VALUES ( Product[ProductKey] ),
        ALLSELECTED ( ),
        REMOVEFILTERS ( Product )
    )
VAR AllSales = CALCULATE ( [Sales Amount], AllSelectedProducts )
VAR PctByProduct = ADDCOLUMNS ( AllSelectedProducts, "@ProdPct", [Sales Amount] / AllSales )
VAR CumulatedPctByProduct =
    ADDCOLUMNS (
        PctByProduct,
        "@CumulatedPct",
            SUMX (
                WINDOW ( 0, ABS, 0, REL, PctByProduct, ORDERBY ( [@ProdPct], DESC ) ),
                [@ProdPct]
            )
    )
VAR ProductsInClass =
    FILTER (
        CROSSJOIN ( CumulatedPctByProduct, 'ABC Classes' ),
        AND (
            [@CumulatedPct] > 'ABC Classes'[Lower Boundary],
            [@CumulatedPct] <= 'ABC Classes'[Upper Boundary]
        )
    )
VAR Result = CALCULATE ( [Sales Amount], KEEPFILTERS ( ProductsInClass ) )
RETURN
    Result
```

Executing the code shows a very good improvement in terms of speed.

Total	SE CPU	Line	Subclass	Duration	CPU	Par.	Rows	KB	Timeline
533 ms	453 ms	1	DAX	107	107	x1.0			
	x1.2								
FE ⚠	SE	2	DAX	88	88	x1.0			
162 ms	371 ms	4	Scan	1	0		6	1	
30.4%	69.6%	6	Scan	3	0		546	5	
SE Queries	SE Cache	7	DAX	133	132	x1.0			
6	0	8	DAX	127	126	x1.0			
	0.0%								

There is no need to run through the different storage engine queries again. The structure of the queries is the same as before. The only difference is that the only column retrieved from the server and then passed back as a filter is now the *Product[ProductKey]* column, as shown by the first DAX query:

```
EVALUATE
SUMMARIZE (
    VALUES ( 'Product' ),
    'Product'[ProductKey]
)
```

In this example, the benefit of reducing the amount of data moved back and forth between the two engines paid off. The *Product* table is no longer moved back and forth with all the columns; it only keeps the *Product[ProductKey]* column. We reduced the execution time from three seconds to half a second, resulting in a more responsive report.

Understanding complex models

In learning how to optimize DAX, we started with VertiPaq models, where we learned about the storage engine, the formula engine, and all the details pertaining to the internals of VertiPaq.   Then, we changed the storage engine, and we learned about DirectQuery. Using DirectQuery, the optimization becomes more complex because of the power and complexity of relational databases like SQL Server. In the last chapters, we introduced and described composite models: the marriage between a remote Tabular model and a local model. It is time to put everything together and discuss complex models.

A complex model is any model that uses more than one storage engine, except for the unique case of composite models. Therefore, a model with one VertiPaq database and one DirectQuery connection is a complex model. In the same way, a model with one VertiPaq database, two DirectQuery islands, and connected with three different remote Tabular databases, is also a complex model.

Optimizing complex models requires a deep understanding of all the concepts we outlined in the previous chapters because in the end, a complex model is nothing but the union of multiple simpler models.

Complex models do not introduce additional theoretical aspects to what we have already analyzed in the previous chapters. This is why in this chapter, we aim to use practical examples rather than theoretical ones. We introduce concepts like the role of calculated columns, and then we immediately show an example where the difference between regular models and complex ones becomes relevant.

Understanding the role of the formula engine in complex models

At the beginning of their DAX optimization journey, model authors feel that the formula engine is the weak link in the chain. The formula engine is slow, and optimizing DAX means using the formula engine as little as possible.

The more you learn about the Tabular query architecture, the clearer it becomes that the formula engine is the orchestra director of any DAX query. Its role is to coordinate the work done by different storage engines and merge the partial results, performing the calculations that the storage engines could not complete. Indeed, the formula engine is the main engine of DAX. When the going gets tough and you start building complex architectures, the role of the formula engine becomes more relevant.

The main piece of information to keep in mind is that storage engines cannot communicate with each other. Whenever you need to mix information from different databases, it must be gathered in the formula engine first and then used for its purpose.

Let us see an example of this concept. The following model mixes two DirectQuery tables and four VertiPaq tables in the same semantic model. The presence of multiple storage engines makes the model a complex model.

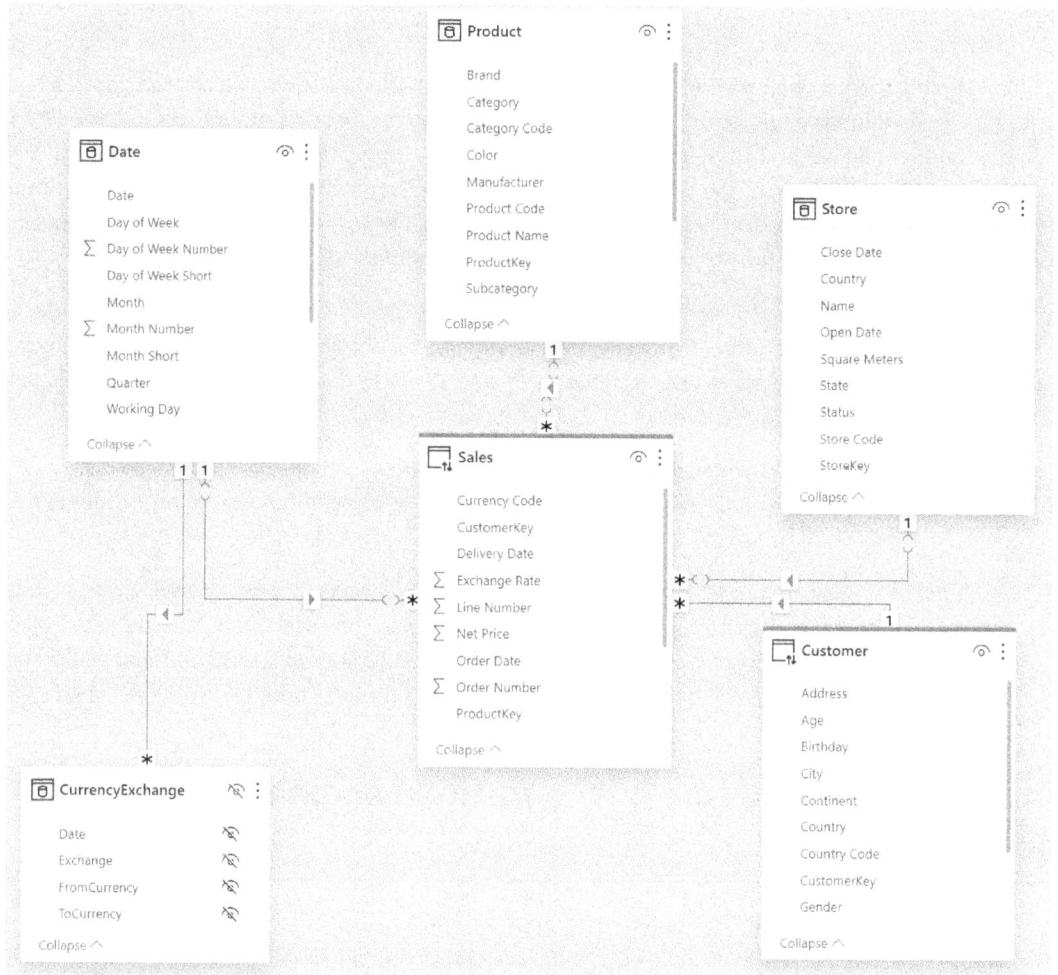

The rationale behind this architecture is that the large tables (*Customer* and *Sales*) are stored in DirectQuery, whereas the smaller tables are stored in VertiPaq mode. The resulting Power BI Desktop file is tiny because the larger tables are in external relational databases (SQL Server in this example).

A simple query that groups by continent and brand already requires some effort from the formula engine:

```
EVALUATE
SUMMARIZECOLUMNS (
    Customer[Continent],
    'Product'[Brand],
    "Sales", [Sales Amount]
)
```

Customer and *Sales* are in DirectQuery, while *Product* is in VertiPaq. Consequently, it is impossible to author an SQL query that groups by *Product[Brand]*: SQL does not even know about the existence of *Product*.

The relationship between *Product* and *Sales* is based on the *ProductKey* column. *ProductKey* has a much larger cardinality than *Brand*. However, executing an SQL query that groups *Sales* by *Product[Brand]* is impossible because *Product[Brand]* is not available in SQL. Tabular has two options: either it groups *Sales* by *Sales[ProductKey]* and generates a large datacache, or it sends the information about the association between *ProductKey* and *Brand* in the SQL query that computes *Sales Amount*.

Generating a large datacache is often the wrong choice. Be mindful that Tabular does not know the cardinality of columns stored in DirectQuery. In our specific scenario, it is not known how many values are present for the *Customer[Continent]* table. As humans, we know that *Customer[Continent]* is a small column. Tabular does not possess this information. If the engine chose to group by *Sales[CustomerKey]*, it would generate 2,517 rows per continent; if *Customer[Continent]* contained a few thousand values, the datacache would exceed the limit of 1M rows. Therefore, Tabular chose to reduce the size of the datacache.

Therefore, there is a first xmSQL query to retrieve the combinations of *ProductKey* and *Brand*. Next, this list of values is embedded in the SQL query sent to SQL Server so that it can perform the grouping by *Product[Brand]*.

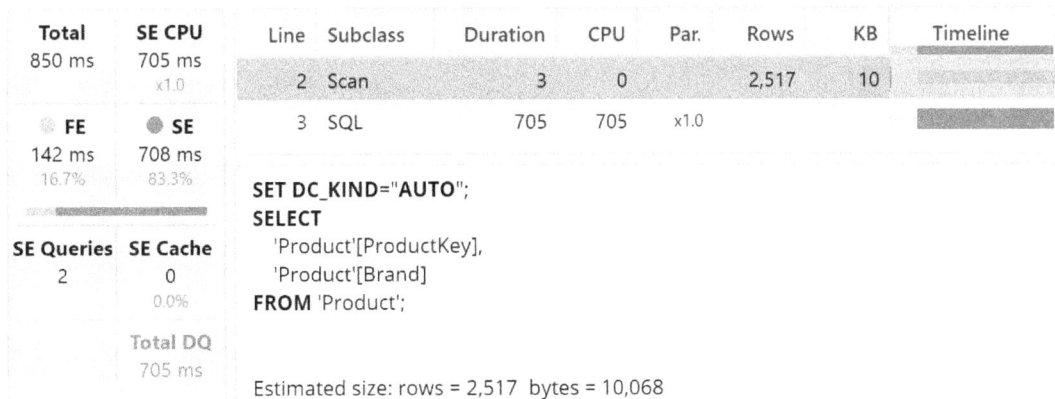

Total	SE CPU	Line	Subclass	Duration	CPU	Par.	Rows	KB	Timeline
850 ms	705 ms x1.0	2	Scan	3	0		2,517	10	
		3	SQL	705	705	x1.0			

FE	SE
142 ms	708 ms
16.7%	83.3%

```
SET DC_KIND="AUTO";
SELECT
  'Product'[ProductKey],
  'Product'[Brand]
FROM 'Product';
```

SE Queries	SE Cache
2	0
	0.0%

Total DQ
705 ms

Estimated size: rows = 2,517 bytes = 10,068

The first storage engine query retrieves the combinations of *ProductKey* and *Brand* from VertiPaq. The timeline shows the formula engine working after the first query for several milliseconds while it prepares the SQL query for DirectQuery. The second storage engine query is an SQL statement that contains around

2,500 lines in a gigantic UNION ALL to pass to SQL Server the result of the first xmSQL query:

```
SELECT TOP (1000001) *
FROM (
    SELECT [semijoin1].[c22],
        [basetable0].[t4_Continent],
        SUM([a0]) AS [a0]
    FROM (
        (
            SELECT [t3_ProductKey],
                [t4_Continent],
                [a0]
            FROM (
                SELECT [t3].[ProductKey] AS [t3_ProductKey],
                    [t3].[Quantity] AS [t3_Quantity],
                    [t3].[Net Price] AS [t3_Net Price],
                    [t4].[Continent] AS [t4_Continent],
                    ([t3].[Quantity] * [t3].[Net Price]) AS [a0]
                FROM (
                    [dbo].[Sales] AS [t3]
                        LEFT JOIN [dbo].[Customer] AS [t4]
                            ON ([t3].[CustomerKey] = [t4].[CustomerKey])
                )
                ) AS [t0]
            ) AS [basetable0]
        INNER JOIN (
            (SELECT 13 AS [c22], 1707 AS [t3_ProductKey])
            UNION ALL (SELECT 13 AS [c22], 1708 AS [t3_ProductKey])
            UNION ALL (SELECT 13 AS [c22], 1709 AS [t3_ProductKey])
--  2,500 lines (removed)
            UNION ALL (SELECT 3 AS [c22], 2353 AS [t3_ProductKey])
            UNION ALL (SELECT 3 AS [c22], 2354 AS [t3_ProductKey])
            ) AS [semijoin1]
        ON (([semijoin1].[t3_ProductKey] = [basetable0].[t3_ProductKey]))
    )
    GROUP BY [semijoin1].[c22],
        [basetable0].[t4_Continent]
    ) AS [MainTable]
WHERE (NOT (([a0] IS NULL)))
```

VertiPaq and SQL execute part of the query, but the real meaning of their work is known only to the formula engine, which orchestrates the queries to gather data from one engine and pass it down to the next.

As simple as this example is, it already shows the roles of the different engines in Tabular: the storage engines are responsible for scanning the data and retrieving values. The formula engine instructs the storage engines, retrieves their results, and combines them in the query output.

Each storage engine has strengths and weaknesses, a different query language, and several limitations. You can easily imagine that combining multiple data islands with multiple storage engines on different architectures leads to extremely high complexity.

The formula engine handles all this complexity, making it possible to build advanced model architectures. However, model authors must be very aware of the technology limitations. It would be easy to rely on something magical happening so that the query is somehow resolved, but developers cannot rely on a complex model as a black box that somehow produces the result. We must use all the knowledge gained so far to drive the model and the DAX code in the right direction.

Finally, before diving into the details, a warning: we cannot cover all possible types of complex models. Tabular gives developers much freedom regarding the number of data islands, the storage engines to use, and the types of calculations and relationships created in the model. Therefore, the number of models that developers can create is enormous. We focus on a small number of examples that – based on our experience – are the most likely to be created. When developing a complex model, you must perform the same reasoning we would do on our models, question each decision and measure performance at every step.

Calculated tables

As you may recall from the DirectQuery chapters, calculated tables are not an option when using DirectQuery. However, the limitation is that DirectQuery models have no storage where the calculated table can be hosted. In a complex model, this limitation is not present.

If you create a calculated table in a complex model, the calculated table is stored in VertiPaq, even in rare scenarios where the calculated table is the only VertiPaq table of the entire model. Indeed, when only DirectQuery data islands are present, the storage mode of the semantic model is DirectQuery by default. However, when you create a calculated table, the storage mode becomes *mixed,* and the calculated table is stored in the VertiPaq database.

Therefore, calculated tables are part of the modeling options in complex models. Developers must remember that the 1M row limit is present for DirectQuery islands. The formula executed for a calculated table must not generate more than 1M rows (or the limit set on the service). Otherwise, the data refresh generates a runtime error.

Calculated columns

Calculated columns may or may not be available depending on the data island a table belongs to. The following limitations are in place:

- **VertiPaq continent**: Calculated columns are available, and they are stored in the VertiPaq continent.

- **DirectQuery island**: Calculated columns can be created following the limitations of DirectQuery calculated columns. These calculated columns are computed at query time and not stored in the model.

- **Tabular remote island**: Calculated columns can be created, provided that the code of the calculated column is wholesale. Calculated columns are always computed at query time and not stored in the local model.

Calculated columns can be used to create relationships across data islands. You should always pay special attention when calculated columns are not persisted and used in a relationship because of the additional work required to compute their value. Moreover, the limitations on different data islands might make a solution harder, if not impossible, to solve.

Let us elaborate on this with an example. We want to solve the same static segmentation scenario we have seen with composite models. This time, we are facing a complex model with two DirectQuery islands and the VertiPaq continent.

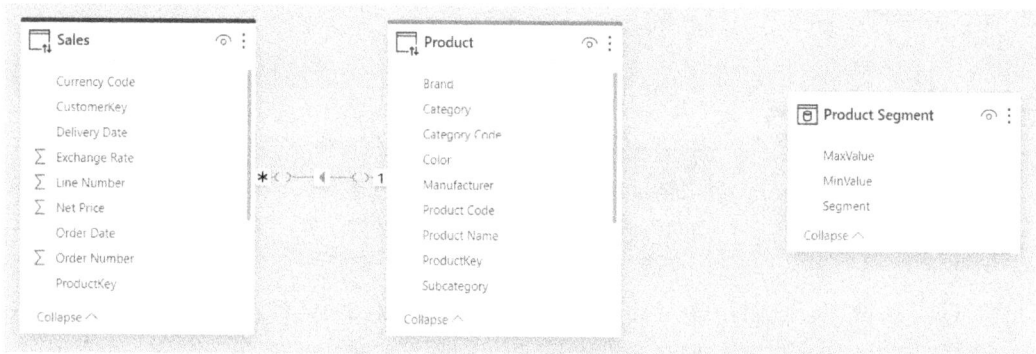

Sales is in a DirectQuery island, *Product* is in a different DirectQuery island, and the *Product Segment* table is stored as a calculated table in VertiPaq. The *Product Segment* configuration table contains three categories we want to use to cluster products based on *Sales Amount*.

Segment	MinValue	MaxValue
Low Sales	0	100,000
Medium Sales	100,000	1,000,000
High Sales	1,000,000	99,999,999,999

We have already solved this scenario both in VertiPaq and in composite models. In VertiPaq, we created a calculated column in *Product* with the product segment; it was a simple and efficient solution. With composite models, we had to create a calculated column in *Product* with the product sales, and a calculated table with the segment assigned to each value of *Sales Amount*.

With this complex model based on DirectQuery islands, neither previous solution is an option. Due to the limitations of DirectQuery, we cannot create a calculated column in *Product* with the sales amount because the calculated column would include the SUMX function, which is not allowed in DirectQuery calculated columns.

A limitation in one of the data islands prevents us from using one of the solutions we have already found. We must create a relationship between a VertiPaq table and a DirectQuery table based on a column we cannot create. The solution is quite creative and counterintuitive: since we cannot create the calculated column in DirectQuery, we create one calculated table in VertiPaq with the sole purpose of storing the calculated column:

```
-------------------------------------
-- Calculated table 'Product Sales'
-------------------------------------
Product Sales =
VAR ProductsAndSales =
    ADDCOLUMNS (
        ALLNOBLANKROW ( 'Product'[ProductKey] ),
        "Product Sales", CALCULATE ( [Sales Amount] )
    )
VAR ProductsAndSalesCategorized =
    ADDCOLUMNS (
        ProductsAndSales,
        "Segment",
        SELECTCOLUMNS (
            FILTER (
                'Product Segment',
                AND (
                    'Product Segment'[MinValue] < [Product Sales],
                    'Product Segment'[MaxValue] >= [Product Sales]
                )
            ),
            "Segment", 'Product Segment'[Segment]
        )
    )
RETURN
    ProductsAndSalesCategorized
```

The table contains the product key, the product sales, and the segment that product sales belongs to.

ProductKey	Product Sales	Segment
1	87,533.42	Low Sales
2	90,930.57	Low Sales
3	96,781.13	Low Sales
4	153,327.29	Medium Sales
5	147,846.03	Medium Sales
6	152,253.90	Medium Sales

We now have a new VertiPaq table, and we can use *ProductKey* to create a relationship between *Product* and *Product Sales* using a 1:1 relationship.

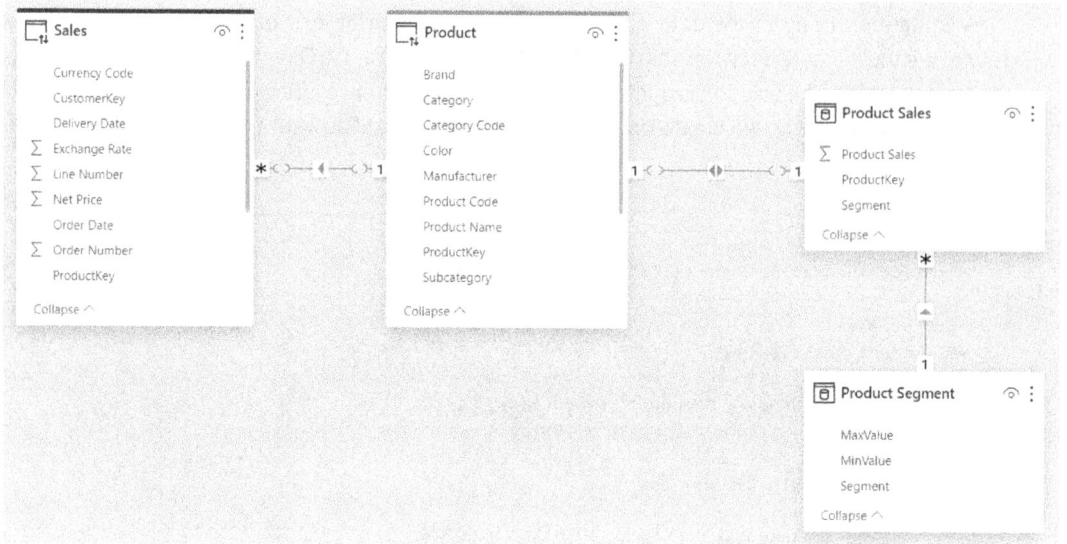

In this diagram, you can appreciate the power of complex models: two DirectQuery data islands and two tables in the VertiPaq continent, all linked as part of a single semantic model. We can now slice *Sales* by *Product Segment*, traversing a DirectQuery island during the process.

Let us quickly analyze the following query:

```
EVALUATE
SUMMARIZECOLUMNS (
    'Product Segment'[Segment],
    "Amount", [Sales Amount]
)
```

The DAX query execution requires three storage engine queries.

Total	SE CPU	Line	Subclass	Duration	CPU	Par.	Rows	KB	Timeline
1,218 ms	937 ms x1.0	2	Scan	3	0		15,120	119	
FE 274 ms 22.5%	**SE** 944 ms 77.5%	3	SQL	4	4	x1.0			
		4	SQL	937	933	x1.0			
SE Queries	SE Cache								
3	0 0.0%								
	Total DQ 941 ms								

Be mindful: the filter must be moved from *Product Segment* (in VertiPaq) down to the DirectQuery data island containing *Sales*. *Product* is in the middle of the relationship chain and stored in a different DirectQuery island.

The first storage engine query is in VertiPaq and retrieves the relationship between *Product Segment* and *Product Sales[Product Key]* from our newly-introduced calculated table:

```
SELECT
    'Product Sales'[ProductKey],
    'Product Segment'[Segment]
FROM 'Product Sales'
    LEFT OUTER JOIN 'Product Segment'
        ON 'Product Sales'[Segment]='Product Segment'[Segment];
```

The second storage engine query uses the result of the first to retrieve the association between *Product[ProductKey]* and the product segment:

```
SELECT TOP (1000001) [basetable0].[t0_ProductKey],
    [semijoin1].[c65]
FROM (
    (
        SELECT [t0].[ProductKey] AS [t0_ProductKey]
        FROM ([dbo].[Product]) AS [t0]
        GROUP BY [t0].[ProductKey]
        ) AS [basetable0]
        INNER JOIN (
        (SELECT 3 AS [c65], 1 AS [t0_ProductKey])
            UNION ALL (SELECT 3 AS [c65], 2 AS [t0_ProductKey])
            UNION ALL (SELECT 3 AS [c65], 3 AS [t0_ProductKey])
-- 2,500 lines (removed)
            UNION ALL (SELECT 5 AS [c65], 2513 AS [t0_ProductKey])
            UNION ALL (SELECT 5 AS [c65], 2514 AS [t0_ProductKey])
        ) AS [semijoin1] ON (([semijoin1].[t0_ProductKey] = [basetable0].[t0_ProductKey]))
    )
GROUP BY [basetable0].[t0_ProductKey],
    [semijoin1].[c65]
```

This intermediate step is needed to bring the filter down to *Sales*. Indeed, *Sales* can be filtered by *Product[ProductKey]* but not by *Product Sales[ProductKey]*. Despite the values of the two columns being the same, Tabular needs a generic algorithm, so it introduces this additional step.

After the execution of the second query, the engine is ready to bring the filter down to *Sales* in the other DirectQuery island by using the third storage engine query:

```
SELECT TOP (1000001) *
FROM (
    SELECT [semijoin1].[c65],
        SUM([a0]) AS [a0]
    FROM (
        (
            SELECT [t1_ProductKey],
                [a0]
            FROM (
                SELECT [t1].[ProductKey] AS [t1_ProductKey],
                    [t1].[Quantity] AS [t1_Quantity],
                    [t1].[Net Price] AS [t1_Net Price],
                    ([t1].[Quantity] * [t1].[Net Price]) AS [a0]
                FROM ([dbo].[Sales]) AS [t1]
            ) AS [t0]
        ) AS [basetable0]
        INNER JOIN (
        (SELECT 3 AS [c65], 1 AS [t1_ProductKey])
            UNION ALL (SELECT 3 AS [c65], 2 AS [t1_ProductKey])
            UNION ALL (SELECT 3 AS [c65], 3 AS [t1_ProductKey])
--  2,500 lines (removed)
            UNION ALL (SELECT 5 AS [c65], 2513 AS [t1_ProductKey])
            UNION ALL (SELECT 5 AS [c65], 2514 AS [t1_ProductKey])
        ) AS [semijoin1]
        ON (([semijoin1].[t1_ProductKey] = [basetable0].[t1_ProductKey]))
    )
    GROUP BY [semijoin1].[c65]
) AS [MainTable]
WHERE (NOT (([a0] IS NULL)))
```

This last SQL query retrieves the sales amount, directly grouped by product segment.

To simplify the work done by the Tabular engine in this scenario, we should apply a change to the model that – once we complete the analysis – appears obvious: why did we create the relationship between *Product Sales* and *Product*, when we could have created the relationship directly between *Product Sales* and *Sales*? By doing so, we could avoid one step. We create a new – inactive – relationship between *Product Sales* and *Sales*.

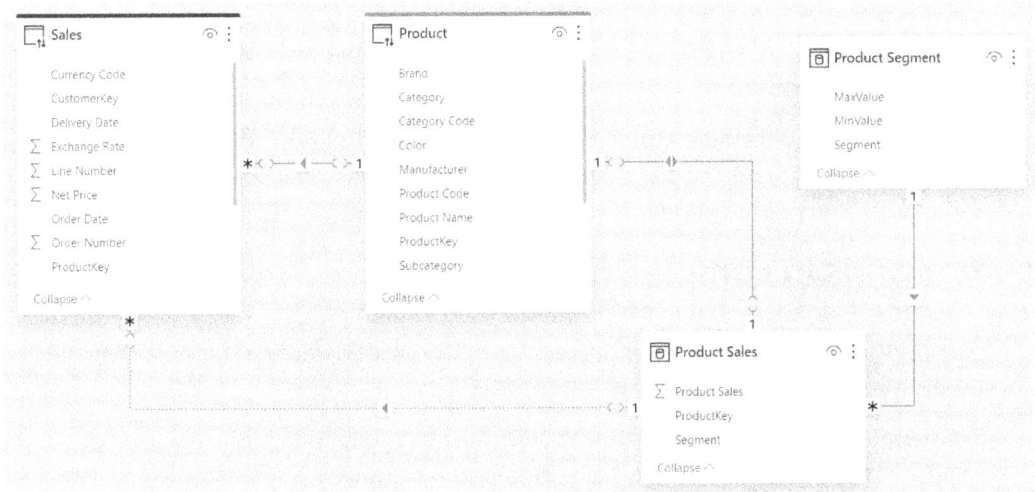

We must also change the query to use the new relationship:

```
EVALUATE
SUMMARIZECOLUMNS (
    'Product Segment'[Segment],
    "Amount",
        CALCULATE (
            [Sales Amount],
            USERELATIONSHIP ( 'Product Sales'[ProductKey], Sales[ProductKey] )
        )
)
```

Executing this query on the new model shows that only two storage engine queries are executed.

Total	SE CPU	Line	Subclass	Duration	CPU	Par.	Rows	KB	Timeline
1,083 ms	935 ms								
	x1.0	2	Scan	1	0		15,120	119	
FE	SE	3	SQL	935	935	x1.0			
147 ms	936 ms								
13.6%	86.4%								

SE Queries	SE Cache
2	0
	0.0%
	Total DQ
	935 ms

```
SET DC_KIND="AUTO";
SELECT
    'Product Sales'[ProductKey],
    'Product Segment'[Segment]
FROM 'Product Sales'
    LEFT OUTER JOIN 'Product Segment'
        ON 'Product Sales'[Segment]='Product Segment'[Segment];
```

The first storage engine query retrieves the product keys and uses them to filter *Sales* in the following query.

Performance-wise, there are no differences in this specific case because the higher cost of the query is the scan of *Sales* – we removed an inexpensive query in this case. However, you may find very different results in different scenarios.

This demo aimed to show how limitations on calculated columns affect the adoption of specific solutions and how complex models handle relationships between different islands.

Relationships in complex models

The purpose of a relationship is to move a filter between tables. In a complex model, there are two types of relationships: intra-island and cross-island.

In the previous chapters, we discussed and described intra-island relationships, both strong and limited. Regarding complex models, there is nothing new to add. A strong intra-island relationship in DirectQuery is translated into a JOIN clause in the SELECT statement; a limited intra-island relationship in DirectQuery is resolved through subqueries. In VertiPaq, the engine uses VertiPaq relationships for the former and batches for the latter.

Cross-island relationships are different. First, any cross-island relationship is limited by nature. Second, cross-island relationships always require the intervention of the formula engine. The formula engine materializes the filter by scanning one island. Then, it either pushes the filter to the other island by injecting it in the storage engine query, or resolves the filter by joining and filtering large datacaches in the formula engine itself. We have already seen several examples of this behavior in the previous sections of this chapter. Moreover, when learning about composite models, we already had to manage relationships between remote and local engines.

The first hard limitation of cross-island relationships is the cardinality of the relationship. The limit of 1M rows for the intermediate result set means that we cannot create a relationship between two tables if the column used for the relationship has more than 1M distinct values. Indeed, in that scenario, the engine needs to retrieve the list of values from one island to send to the storage engine of the other island. You cannot retrieve a filter like this if the list of values exceeds one million rows (by default).

You can change the maximum number of rows retrieved per query. You can change the **MaxIntermediateRowsetSize** setting in the local msmdsrv.ini file or by using an XMLA script in Power BI and Azure Analysis Services. However, the setting is global to the instance of Analysis Services. Raising the limit on all the databases in the instance (or workspace in Power BI) can lead to heavy queries being executed rather than aborted, potentially slowing down the performance for a larger number of users.

As an example, we used two DirectQuery islands: one includes *Customer* (1.8M rows), and the other contains *Sales* (10M rows).

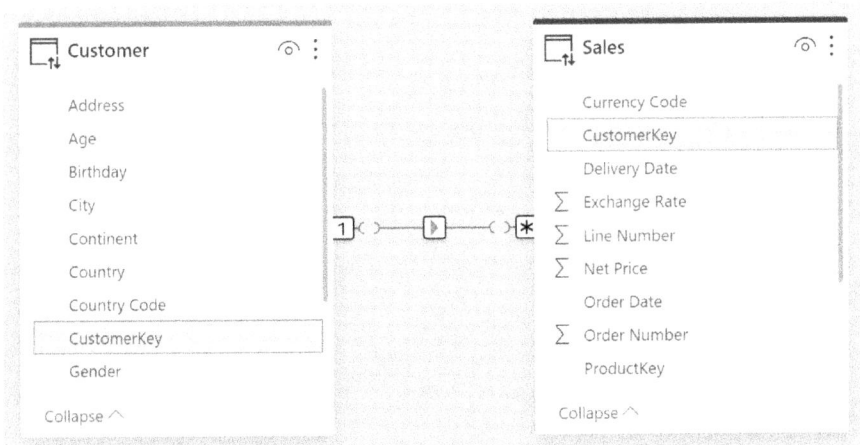

In this model, a simple query like the following fails:

```
EVALUATE
SUMMARIZECOLUMNS (
    Customer[Continent],
    "Amount", [Sales Amount]
)
```

Executing the query raises the error about the 1M row limit.

The resultset of a query to external data source has exceeded the maximum allowed size of '1000000' rows.

Total	SE CPU	Line	Subclass	Duration	CPU	Par.	Rows	KB	Timeline
2,607 ms	1 ms								
	x1.0	1	SQL	1	1	x1.0			

FE	SE
2,606 ms	1 ms
100.0%	0.0%

SE Queries	SE Cache
1	0
	0.0%

SELECT TOP (1000001) [t2].[CustomerKey],
   [t2].[Continent]
FROM ([dbo].[Customer]) **AS** [t2]
GROUP BY [t2].[CustomerKey],
   [t2].[Continent]

The first step in solving the query is to retrieve the association between customer keys and continents from *Customer*. The resulting dataset would contain 1.8M rows; therefore, the engine raises an error. If we were to add a filter to the query, the error would still be present:

```
EVALUATE
SUMMARIZECOLUMNS (
    Customer[Continent],
    TREATAS ( { "Male" }, Customer[Gender] ),
    "Amount", [Sales Amount]
)
```

Indeed, there are less than 1M rows in Customer who are male. However, this time the error is raised with the second query.

The resultset of a query to external data source has exceeded the maximum allowed size of '1000000' rows.

Total	SE CPU	Line	Subclass	Duration	CPU	Par.	Rows	KB	Timeline
5,580 ms	114 ms	1	SQL	1	1	x1.0			
	x1.0	2	SQL	113	113	x1.0			
FE	**SE**								
5,466 ms	114 ms								
98.0%	2.0%								

SE Queries	SE Cache
2	0
	0.0%

SELECT TOP (1000001) *
FROM (
    SELECT [t1_CustomerKey],
    SUM([a0]) **AS** [a0]
    FROM (

The first storage engine query correctly retrieves its datacache because there are fewer than 1M customers with the Male gender:

SELECT TOP (1000001) [t2].[CustomerKey],
        [t2].[Continent]
FROM ([dbo].[Customer]) **AS** [t2]
WHERE ([t2].[Gender] = N'Male')
GROUP BY [t2].[CustomerKey],
        [t2].[Continent]

However, the second storage engine query computes the sales amount by customer with no filters:

```
SELECT TOP (1000001) *
FROM (
    SELECT [t1_CustomerKey],
        SUM([a0]) AS [a0]
    FROM (
        SELECT [t1].[CustomerKey] AS [t1_CustomerKey],
            [t1].[Quantity] AS [t1_Quantity],
            [t1].[Net Price] AS [t1_Net Price],
            ([t1].[Quantity] * [t1].[Net Price]) AS [a0]
        FROM ([dbo].[Sales]) AS [t1]
        ) AS [t0]
    WHERE (1 = 1)
    GROUP BY [t1_CustomerKey]
    ) AS [MainTable]
WHERE (NOT (([a0] IS NULL)))
```

Although the first storage engine query retrieves less than 1M rows, the second query retrieves all the customer keys and their sales amount, still exceeding the 1M rows limit.

We can configure the MaxIntermediateRowsetSize to 2M – for example, by applying this change to the msmdsrv.ini of a local instance of Analysis Services.

```
<DAX>
    <DQ>
        <MaxIntermediateRowsetSize>2000000</MaxIntermediateRowsetSize>
        <SelectCartridgeUsingConnectionString>0</SelectCartridgeUsingConnectionString>
        <ConnectToDatasourceForCSDL>1</ConnectToDatasourceForCSDL>
        <PushInSelect>1</PushInSelect>
        <EnableDQCalcCol>1</EnableDQCalcCol>
    </DQ>
```

With the new setting for MaxIntermediateRowsetSize, the query runs smoothly, even though it is extremely slow.

Total	SE CPU	Line	Subclass	Duration	CPU	Par.	Rows	KB	Timeline
6,523 ms	113 ms x1.0	1	SQL	1	1	x1.0			
FE 6,410 ms 98.3%	SE 113 ms 1.7%	2	SQL	112	112	x1.0			

SE Queries	SE Cache
2	0 0.0%
	Total DQ 113 ms

```
SELECT TOP (2000001) *
FROM (
    SELECT [t1_CustomerKey],
        SUM([a0]) AS [a0]
    FROM (
        SELECT [t1].[CustomerKey] AS [t1_CustomerKey],
            [t1].[Quantity] AS [t1_Quantity],
            [t1].[Net Price] AS [t1_Net Price],
            ([t1].[Quantity] * [t1].[Net Price]) AS [a0]
```

The figure shows that the query spends most of its time inside the formula engine. Indeed, the formula engine merges two large datacaches (one with 1M rows, the other with 1.8M rows) to perform the grouping by continent.

Besides, it is important to note that the formula engine can aggregate the sales amount because the measure is additive. We can better see the issue with large dimensions by replacing *Sales Amount* with a DISTINCTCOUNT calculation:

```
EVALUATE
SUMMARIZECOLUMNS (
    Customer[Continent],
    TREATAS ( { "Male" }, Customer[Gender] ),
    "# Customers", DISTINCTCOUNT ( Sales[CustomerKey] )
)
```

This time, the formula engine cannot perform the aggregation by itself; it needs to push the calculation down to the storage engine because the distinct count is non-additive. Consequently, the list of customer keys and continents must be embedded in the query. The DAX query with DISTINCTCOUNT runs for more than 25 minutes.

Total	SE CPU	Line	Subclass	Duration	CPU	Par.	Rows	KB	Timeline
1,584,257 ms	17,529 ms	1	SQL	1	1	x1.0			
	x1.0	2	SQL	17,528	17,528	x1.0			

FE	**SE**
1,566,728 ms	17,529 ms
98.9%	1.1%

SELECT TOP (2000001) [t2].[CustomerKey],
    [t2].[Continent]
FROM ([dbo].[Customer]) **AS** [t2]
WHERE ([t2].[Gender] = N'Male')
GROUP BY [t2].[CustomerKey],
    [t2].[Continent]

SE Queries	**SE Cache**
2	0
	0.0%
	Total DQ
	17,529 ms

The first storage engine query (shown in the figure) retrieves the customer keys, as in the previous example. The second query contains more than 1M rows because of the gigantic UNION ALL present to embed the association between customer and continent in the query itself:

```
SELECT TOP (2000001) *
    [semijoin1].[c40],
    (COUNT_BIG(DISTINCT [a0]) + MAX(CASE WHEN [a0] IS NULL THEN 1 ELSE 0 END)) AS [a0]
FROM
(
    SELECT [t1].[CustomerKey] AS [c20], [t1].[CustomerKey] AS [a0]
    FROM Sales  AS [t1]
) AS [basetable0] (
(
    (SELECT 3 AS [c40],1279112 AS [c20] )   UNION ALL
    (SELECT 5 AS [c40],166945 AS [c20] )   UNION ALL
    (SELECT 5 AS [c40],166991 AS [c20] )   UNION ALL
    (SELECT 5 AS [c40],167122 AS [c20] )   UNION ALL

    . .

    . .
    (SELECT 3 AS [c40],1211409 AS [c20] )   UNION ALL

    . .

    . .
    (SELECT 3 AS [c40],399987 AS [c20] )   UNION ALL
    (SELECT 3 AS [c40],392899 AS [c20] )
) AS [semijoin1] on
    ([semijoin1].[c20] = [basetable0].[c20])
)
GROUP BY [semijoin1].[c40]
```

Increasing the MaxIntermediateRowsetSize parameter is an option but comes with critical side effects. Performance may be severely affected when a query requires materializing large datacaches or the transmission of large filters in the query itself.

When working with cross-island relationships in complex models, the critical factor is the reduction of the cardinality of the column used for the relationship. Reducing column cardinality was also important in VertiPaq, but it is even more critical in complex models.

Changing the cardinality of the relationship is not an easy task. It involves finding a suitable dimension with a smaller cardinality and modifying the original databases so that the key of the new dimension is available.

For example, a possible dimension that exposes the same columns used in *Customer* but lowers the cardinality of the relationship between *Customer* and *Sales* can be the following:

```
-----------------------------------------
-- Calculated table CustomerAttributes
-----------------------------------------
CustomerAttributes =
SUMMARIZECOLUMNS (
    Customer[Gender],
    Customer[State Code],
    Customer[State],
    Customer[Country Code],
    Customer[Country],
    Customer[Continent]
)
```

A developer can easily create this table in the VertiPaq continent by choosing the most used attributes. Linking the table with *Customer* is easy, as all the columns in the new dimension are already present in *Customer*. However, linking the new *CustomerAttributes* dimension with *Sales* is impossible because *Sales* only contains the *CustomerKey* column. Consequently, to build the complex model, it is necessary to update the *Sales* table and add the keys needed to link it with the *CustomerAttributes* table. Any attempt to link *CustomerAttributes* with *Sales[CustomerKey]* would fail.

Moreover, it is essential to note that using a dimension like *CustomerAttributes* would change the granularity of the relationship, limiting any more detailed analysis. However, reducing granularity is necessary, given the 1M row limitation.

If the SQL Server database used as a data source contains its copy of the *Customer* dimension, then a possible solution would be to import the *Customer* table from both data sources – the second one will be *CustomerSales* – and relate them through a many-to-many relationship with a single-direction filter going from *Customer* to *CustomerSales*.

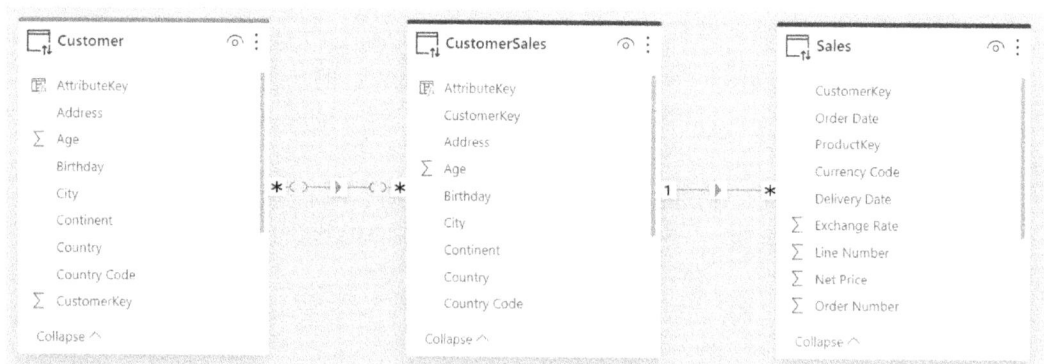

Customer	CustomerSales	Sales
AttributeKey	AttributeKey	CustomerKey
Address	CustomerKey	Order Date
Age	Address	ProductKey
Birthday	Age	Currency Code
City	Birthday	Delivery Date
Continent	City	Exchange Rate
Country	Continent	Line Number
Country Code	Country	Net Price
CustomerKey	Country Code	Order Number
Collapse ⌃	Collapse ⌃	Collapse ⌃

Customer and *CustomerSales* are the same table in two different data islands. These two tables are related through a column (*AttributeKey*) that defines the granularity of the relationship. *CustomerSales* and *Sales* are two tables in the same data island, and they are linked through *CustomerKey*. The code of *AttributeKey* in *Customer* is the following:

```
-----------------------------------------
-- Calculated column in Customer table
-----------------------------------------
AttributeKey =
COMBINEVALUES (
    ",",
    Customer[Gender],
    Customer[State Code],
    Customer[State],
    Customer[Country Code],
    Customer[Country],
    Customer[Continent]
)
```

The code of *AttributeKey* in *CustomerSales* is symmetric. The only difference is the table name of the concatenated columns:

```
-----------------------------------------
-- Calculated column in CustomerSales table
-----------------------------------------
AttributeKey =
COMBINEVALUES (
    ",",
    CustomerSales[Gender],
    CustomerSales[State Code],
    CustomerSales[State],
    CustomerSales[Country Code],
    CustomerSales[Country],
    CustomerSales[Continent]
)
```

The high-cardinality *CustomerKey* column is still present, but this time, it links two tables in the same data island (*CustomerSales* and *Sales*), so it is unnecessary to fetch its values and use them as a filter. The *CustomerSales* table is likely to be hidden, as it is only a technical table needed to let *Customer* filter *Sales* without using *CustomerKey*.

We can now execute the test query computing DISTINCTCOUNT:

```
EVALUATE
SUMMARIZECOLUMNS (
    Customer[Continent],
    TREATAS ( { "Male" }, Customer[Gender] ),
    "# Customers", DISTINCTCOUNT ( Sales[CustomerKey] )
)
```

The difference in terms of speed is amazing.

		Line	Subclass	Duration	CPU	Par.	Rows	KB	Timeline
Total 738 ms	**SE CPU** 686 ms ×1.0	1	SQL	141	141	×1.0			
		2	SQL	547	545	×1.0			
FE 50 ms 6.8%	**SE** 688 ms 93.2%								
SE Queries 2	**SE Cache** 0 0.0%								

The two queries still retrieve the keys for the relationship, but this time, their cardinality is smaller. The first storage engine query retrieves the *AttributeKey* values from *Customer*:

```
SELECT TOP (1000001) [t2].[State Code],
    [t2].[State],
    [t2].[Country Code],
    [t2].[Country],
    [t2].[Continent],
    [t2].[AttributeKey]
FROM (
    SELECT [t2].[Gender] AS [Gender],
        [t2].[State Code] AS [State Code],
        [t2].[State] AS [State],
        [t2].[Country Code] AS [Country Code],
        [t2].[Country] AS [Country],
        [t2].[Continent] AS [Continent],
        (
            COALESCE([t2].[Gender], '') + (
                N',' + (
                    COALESCE([t2].[State Code], '') + (
                        N',' + (
                            COALESCE([t2].[State], '') + (
                                N',' + (
                                    COALESCE([t2].[Country Code], '') + (
                                        N',' + (COALESCE([t2].[Country], '')
                                            + (N',' + COALESCE([t2].[Continent], '')))
                                    )
                                )
                            )
                        )
                    )
                )
            )
        ) AS [AttributeKey]
    FROM ([dbo].[Customer]) AS [t2]
    ) AS [t2]
WHERE ([t2].[Gender] = N'Male')
GROUP BY [t2].[State Code],
    [t2].[State],
    [t2].[Country Code],
    [t2].[Country],
```

```
        [t2].[Continent],
        [t2].[AttributeKey]
```

The second storage engine query filters the second *Customer* table (corresponding to the *CustomerSales* table that is in the same data island as *Sales*) with a filter embedded inside the SQL query:

```
SELECT TOP (1000001) [semijoin1].[c40],
    (
        COUNT_BIG(DISTINCT [a0]) + MAX(CASE
                WHEN [a0] IS NULL
                    THEN 1
                ELSE 0
                END)
        ) AS [a0]
FROM (
    (
        SELECT [t6].[Gender] AS [t6_Gender],
            [t6].[State Code] AS [t6_State Code],
            [t6].[State] AS [t6_State],
            [t6].[Country Code] AS [t6_Country Code],
            [t6].[Country] AS [t6_Country],
            [t6].[Continent] AS [t6_Continent],
            [t6].[AttributeKey] AS [t6_AttributeKey],
            [t1].[CustomerKey] AS [a0]
        FROM (
            [dbo].[Sales] AS [t1]
                LEFT JOIN (
                SELECT [t6].[CustomerKey] AS [CustomerKey],
                    [t6].[Gender] AS [Gender],
                    [t6].[State Code] AS [State Code],
                    [t6].[State] AS [State],
                    [t6].[Country Code] AS [Country Code],
                    [t6].[Country] AS [Country],
                    [t6].[Continent] AS [Continent],
                    (
                        COALESCE([t6].[Gender], '') + (
                            N',' + (
                                COALESCE([t6].[State Code], '') + (
                                    N',' + (
                                        COALESCE([t6].[State], '') + (
                                            N',' + (
                                                COALESCE([t6].[Country Code], '') + (
                                                    N',' + (
                                                        COALESCE([t6].[Country], '')
                                                    + (N',' + COALESCE([t6].[Continent], '')
                                                        )
                                                    )
                                                )
                                            )
                                        )
                                    )
                                )
                            )
                        )
                    )
```

```
                                )
                            )
                        ) AS [AttributeKey]
                FROM ([dbo].[Customer]) AS [t6]
                ) AS [t6] ON ([t1].[CustomerKey] = [t6].[CustomerKey])
            )
        ) AS [basetable0]
        INNER JOIN (
            (SELECT 3 AS [c40],
                    N'Male,Torbay,Torbay,GB,United Kingdom,Europe' AS [t6_AttributeKey])
            UNION ALL (SELECT 3 AS [c40],
                        N'Male,GR,Groningen,NL,Netherlands,Europe' AS [t6_AttributeKey])
            UNION ALL (SELECT 3 AS [c40],
                        N'Male,PI,Pisa,IT,Italy,Europe' AS [t6_AttributeKey])

--  skipping around 500 rows

            UNION ALL (SELECT 3 AS [c40], N'Male,Anglesey,Anglesey,GB,United Kingdom,Europe'
                            AS [t6_AttributeKey])
            UNION ALL (SELECT 3 AS [c40], N'Male,Armagh,Armagh,GB,United Kingdom,Europe'
                            AS [t6_AttributeKey])
        ) AS [semijoin1]
        ON ((([semijoin1].[t6_AttributeKey] = [basetable0].[t6_AttributeKey]))
    )
    GROUP BY [semijoin1].[c40]
```

In this example, we used a set of attributes to move the filter from one instance of *Customer* to a second one (renamed as *CustomerSales* in the model), which finally filters *Sales*.

Be mindful that changing the granularity of the relationship comes with limitations. You will get unexpected results if you apply filters on columns not supported by the granularity of the relationship – like *City*, for example.

Using SQL Server features to avoid multiple data islands

As we have seen in the previous sections, multiple data islands create issues in transferring filters from one table to another. Reducing the number of data islands mitigates the problem, and whenever possible, is a good option.

Depending on your data source, there may be opportunities to reduce the number of data islands. In our scenario, we are using Microsoft SQL Server, and there are a couple of techniques worth learning: linked server and multi-part queries.

If you load data from two databases on the same SQL Server instance, you can specify the database name as part of the table name if the same user can access both databases. You can reference different databases in Power BI by specifying a custom query rather than picking the table from a list.

For example, in the following figure, we reference the *Customer* table in the Contoso 100M database despite the connection being with Contoso 10M.

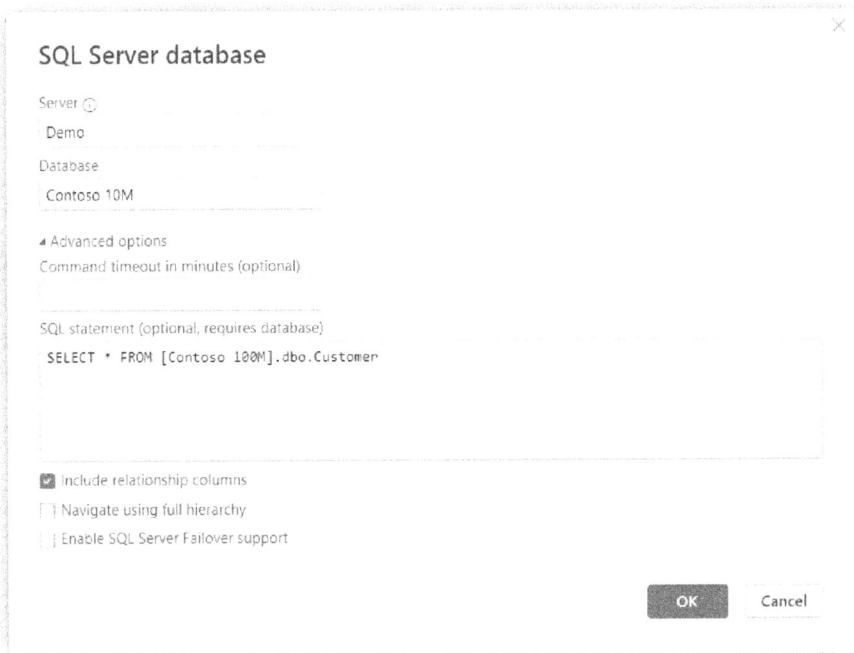

Using this syntax, the queries sent to the server include the database name as part of the table. Tabular will use regular joins between database tables, and SQL Server can apply all the internal optimization.

Indeed, the two tables appear as part of the same data island.

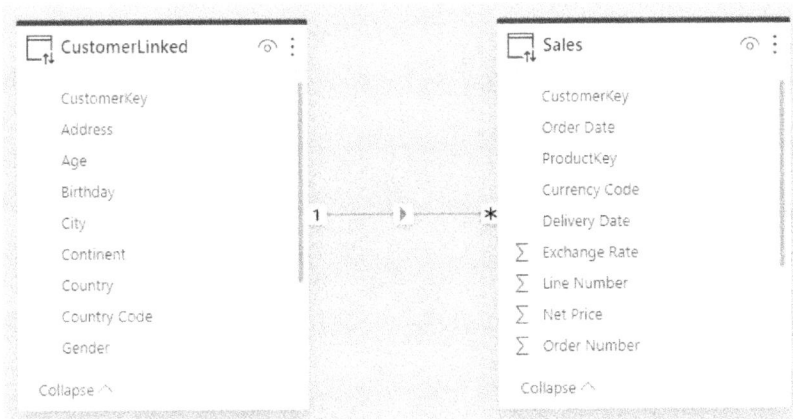

Executing a query similar to the ones we used in the previous section shows that – this time – the formula engine does not need to perform the join operation:

```
EVALUATE
SUMMARIZECOLUMNS (
    CustomerLinked[Continent],
    TREATAS ( { "Male" }, CustomerLinked[Gender] ),
    "Amount", [Sales Amount]
)
```

The entire DAX query is resolved with a single SQL query.

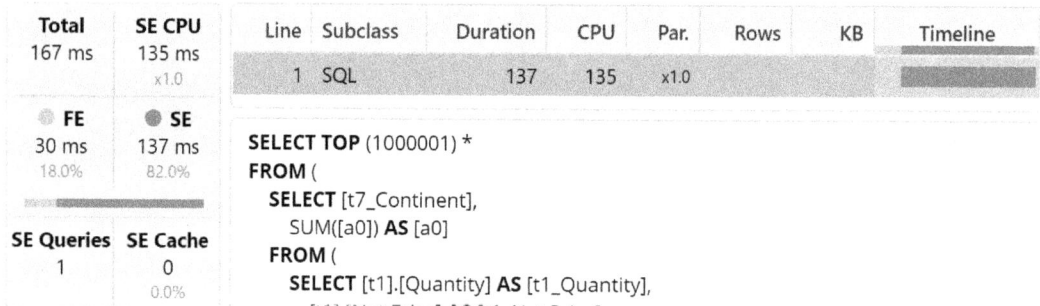

Total	SE CPU		Line	Subclass	Duration	CPU	Par.	Rows	KB	Timeline
167 ms	135 ms		1	SQL	137	135	x1.0			
	x1.0									

FE	SE
30 ms	137 ms
18.0%	82.0%

SE Queries	SE Cache
1	0
	0.0%

```
SELECT TOP (1000001) *
FROM (
    SELECT [t7_Continent],
        SUM([a0]) AS [a0]
    FROM (
        SELECT [t1].[Quantity] AS [t1_Quantity],
            [t1] [Net Price] AS [t1_Net Price]
```

The storage engine query code joins the two tables and includes the WHERE condition on *Gender*, thus producing the same aggregated result expected for the DAX query. Therefore, SQL Server is entirely in charge of the optimization of the query:

```
SELECT TOP (1000001) *
FROM (
    SELECT [t7_Continent],
        SUM([a0]) AS [a0]
    FROM (
        SELECT [t1].[Quantity] AS [t1_Quantity],
            [t1].[Net Price] AS [t1_Net Price],
            [t7].[Gender] AS [t7_Gender],
            [t7].[Continent] AS [t7_Continent],
            ([t1].[Quantity] * [t1].[Net Price]) AS [a0]
        FROM (
            [dbo].[Sales] AS [t1]
                LEFT JOIN (
                SELECT *
                FROM [Contoso 100M].dbo.Customer
                ) AS [t7] ON ([t1].[CustomerKey] = [t7].[CustomerKey])
            )
        ) AS [t0]
    WHERE ([t7_Gender] = N'Male')
    GROUP BY [t7_Continent]
    ) AS [MainTable]
WHERE (NOT (([a0] IS NULL)))
```

Because the same SQL Server manages the databases, the SQL optimizer performs a great job of producing a good query plan. Because the formula engine is no longer part of the equation, the limit of 1M rows in *Customer* is no longer an issue.

This technique produces excellent query plans in particular scenarios where multiple databases are hosted on the same server. SQL Server also provides a feature to connect multiple servers in the same SQL query called **linked servers**. However, linked servers do not produce the same optimal query plans.

When using a linked server, the SQL Server optimizer can no longer push where conditions and joins to the remote server. Therefore, it needs to retrieve the entire *Customer* table from the remote server and then perform the join locally, using a technique close to the one used by the formula engine.

Indeed, performance becomes much worse by executing the same query, this time using a linked server to connect to *Customer*.

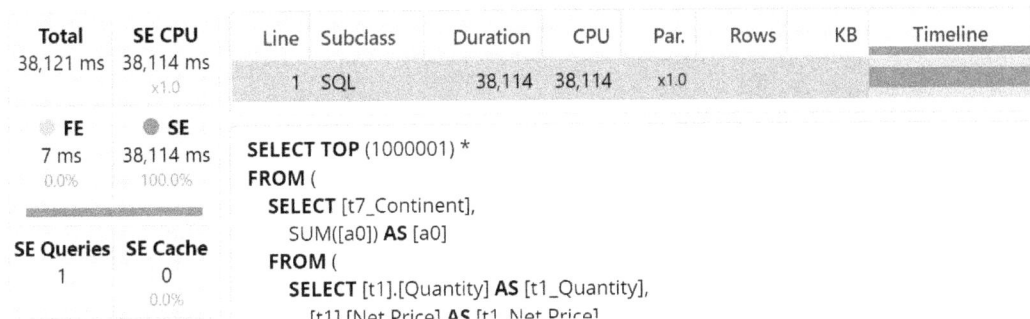

Total	SE CPU		Line	Subclass	Duration	CPU	Par.	Rows	KB	Timeline
38,121 ms	38,114 ms		1	SQL	38,114	38,114	x1.0			
	x1.0									

FE	SE
7 ms	38,114 ms
0.0%	100.0%

SE Queries	SE Cache
1	0
	0.0%

```
SELECT TOP (1000001) *
FROM (
    SELECT [t7_Continent],
        SUM([a0]) AS [a0]
    FROM (
        SELECT [t1].[Quantity] AS [t1_Quantity],
        [t1].[Net Price] AS [t1_Net Price]
```

The only difference is that now, the *Customer* table must be fetched from a remote server:

```
SELECT TOP (1000001) *
FROM (
    SELECT [t7_Continent],
        SUM([a0]) AS [a0]
    FROM (
        SELECT [t1].[Quantity] AS [t1_Quantity],
            [t1].[Net Price] AS [t1_Net Price],
            [t7].[Gender] AS [t7_Gender],
            [t7].[Continent] AS [t7_Continent],
            ([t1].[Quantity] * [t1].[Net Price]) AS [a0]
        FROM (
            [dbo].[Sales] AS [t1]
                LEFT JOIN (
                SELECT *
                FROM [LinkedServer].[Contoso 100M].dbo.Customer
                ) AS [t7] ON ([t1].[CustomerKey] = [t7].[CustomerKey])
        )
        ) AS [t0]
    WHERE ([t7_Gender] = N'Male')
    GROUP BY [t7_Continent]
    ) AS [MainTable]
WHERE (NOT (([a0] IS NULL)))
```

Depending on the architecture you are working with, you might use SQL Server features to make Power BI believe that there is a single data island, even for different databases. If you use other relational databases, you can rely on their available features to obtain a similar goal.

Using VertiPaq to snapshot expensive DirectQuery queries

Complex models can be helpful in several scenarios. In this example, we analyze and optimize one pattern by leveraging a complex model. In the VertiPaq section, we analyzed the Open Orders scenario among the many patterns, which requires computing how many orders are open in a given time frame.

The starting point is a pure DirectQuery model.

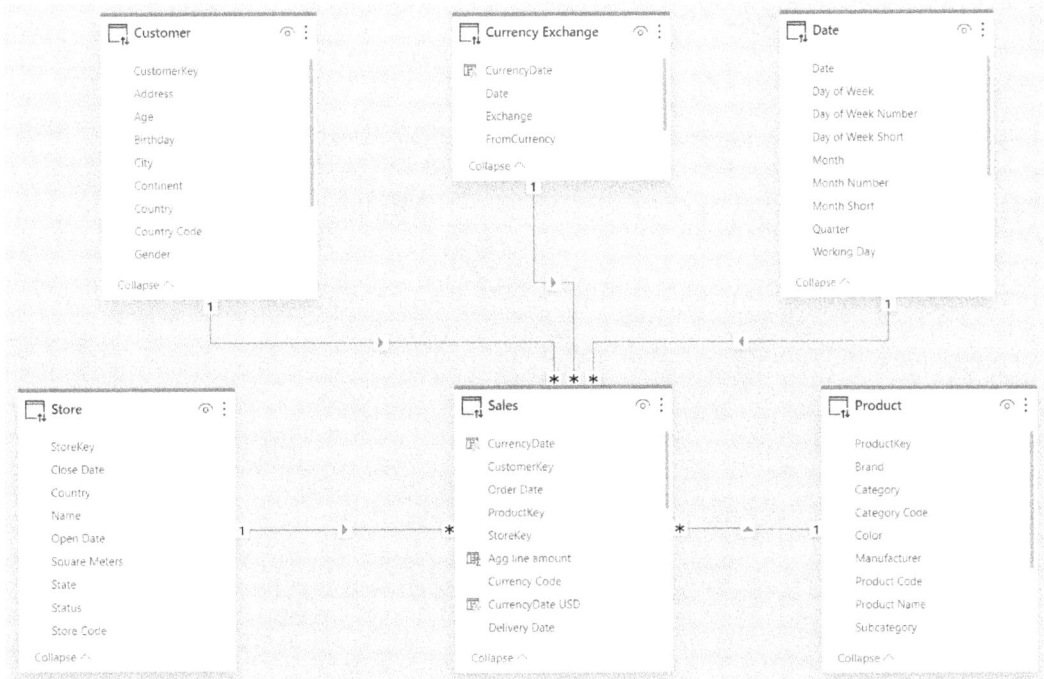

The original query is the following:

```
EVALUATE
SUMMARIZECOLUMNS (
    'Date'[Year],
    'Date'[Month Number],
    "# Open Orders",
        VAR MinDate =
            MIN ( 'Date'[Date] )
        VAR MaxDate =
            MAX ( 'Date'[Date] )
        VAR Result =
            CALCULATE (
                DISTINCTCOUNT( Sales[Order Number] ),
                Sales[Order Date] <= MaxDate,
                Sales[Delivery Date] >= MinDate,
                REMOVEFILTERS ( 'Date' )
            )
        RETURN
            Result
)
```

The output contains the number of orders handled each month.

Year ↑	Month Number ↑	# Open Orders
2,010	5	120,535
2,010	6	273,220
2,010	7	261,037
2,010	8	268,582
2,010	9	302,935
2,010	10	310,868
2,010	11	306,881
2,010	12	518,987
2,011	1	411,376

Because DISTINCTCOUNT is non-additive, the calculation is quite heavy. If we were to run this code on a DirectQuery model, using a model with 200M rows in *Sales*, the result would be depressing, to state it mildly.

Total	SE CPU		Line	Subclass	Duration	CPU	Par.	Rows	KB	Timeline
1,443,736 ms	1,145,641 ms		1	SQL	3	3	x1.0			
	x1.0		2	SQL	123	123	x1.0			
FE	**SE**		3	SQL	3	1	x0.3			
298,092 ms	1,145,644 ms		4	SQL	118	118	x1.0			
20.6%	79.4%		5	SQL	1,145,397	1,145,396	x1.0			
SE Queries	**SE Cache**									
5	0									
	0.0%									

The DAX query runs for 24 minutes. The first four SQL storage engine queries are not a big issue. The first one retrieves the first and last date by year and month:

```
SELECT TOP (1000001) *
FROM (
    SELECT [t1].[Year] AS [t1_Year],
        [t1].[Month Number] AS [t1_Month Number],
        MAX([t1].[Date]) AS [a0],
        MIN([t1].[Date]) AS [a1]
    FROM ([dbo].[Date]) AS [t1]
    GROUP BY [t1].[Year],
        [t1].[Month Number]
    ) AS [MainTable]
WHERE (
        NOT (([a0] IS NULL))
        OR NOT (([a1] IS NULL))
        )
```

The second SQL storage engine query collects the values of the order dates:

```
SELECT TOP (1000001) [t3].[Order Date]
FROM ([Data].[Sales]) AS [t3]
GROUP BY [t3].[Order Date]
```

The third SQL storage engine query retrieves the combinations of year and month:

```
SELECT TOP (1000001) [t1].[Year],
    [t1].[Month Number]
FROM ([dbo].[Date]) AS [t1]
GROUP BY [t1].[Year],
    [t1].[Month Number]
```

And the fourth SQL storage engine query collects the values of *Delivery Date*:

```
SELECT TOP (1000001) [t3].[Delivery Date]
FROM ([Data].[Sales]) AS [t3]
GROUP BY [t3].[Delivery Date]
```

After four SQL queries, the engine has only collected base information. The formula engine then uses this information to build a monster query that produces the actual result. The query is 446,867 lines long; here is an excerpt:

```
SELECT TOP (1000001) [semijoin2].[c16],
    [semijoin2].[c25],
    COUNT_BIG(DISTINCT [a0]) AS [a0]
FROM (
    (
        (
            SELECT [t3].[Order Date] AS [t3_Order Date],
                [t3].[Delivery Date] AS [t3_Delivery Date],
                [t3].[Order Number] AS [a0]
            FROM ([Data].[Sales]) AS [t3]
        ) AS [basetable0]
        INNER JOIN (
            (SELECT 2019 AS [c16], 12 AS [c25],
                    CAST('20200125 00:00:00' AS DATETIME) AS [t3_Delivery Date])
            UNION ALL (SELECT 2019 AS [c16], 12 AS [c25],
                    CAST('20191219 00:00:00' AS DATETIME) AS [t3_Delivery Date])
            UNION ALL (SELECT 2019 AS [c16], 12 AS [c25],
                    CAST('20200105 00:00:00' AS DATETIME) AS [t3_Delivery Date])
-- … skipping thousands of rows
```

```
                UNION ALL (SELECT 2019 AS [c16], 12 AS [c25],
                           CAST('20110822 00:00:00' AS DATETIME) AS [t3_Order Date])
                UNION ALL (SELECT 2019 AS [c16], 12 AS [c25],
                           CAST('20101026 00:00:00' AS DATETIME) AS [t3_Order Date])
        ) AS [semijoin2] ON (
            ([semijoin2].[t3_Order Date] = [basetable0].[t3_Order Date])
            AND (
                [semijoin2].[c16] = [semijoin1].[c16]
                OR [semijoin2].[c16] IS NULL
                AND [semijoin1].[c16] IS NULL
                )
            AND (
                [semijoin2].[c25] = [semijoin1].[c25]
                OR [semijoin2].[c25] IS NULL
                AND [semijoin1].[c25] IS NULL
                )
            )
        )
    )
GROUP BY [semijoin2].[c16],
    [semijoin2].[c25]
```

There is not much space for optimization here. The engine chooses a path to generate the code that minimizes the number of queries executed. It cannot rely on relationships, because the measure does not use any.

Building a complex model to speed up the query is very smart in a scenario like this. Following the same path we used when optimizing VertiPaq, we could create a calculated table stored in VertiPaq that contains the data at the order granularity. The table must be created in SQL, because it includes more than 1M rows, and using DAX would be impossible for the materialization limit. We want to be able to slice by *Customer* and *Store*, so we use this SQL query to create the snapshot table:

```
SELECT
    [Order Number],
    [CustomerKey],
    [StoreKey],
    MIN ( [Order Date] ) AS [Order Date],
    MAX ( [Delivery Date] ) AS [Delivery Date]
FROM
    Data.Sales
GROUP BY [Order Number], [CustomerKey], [StoreKey]
```

We do not want to materialize the table in SQL, as it serves a specific purpose (that is, optimizing a calculation in Power BI). Therefore, we use VertiPaq to store the result of the SQL query, transforming the model from DirectQuery into a complex model.

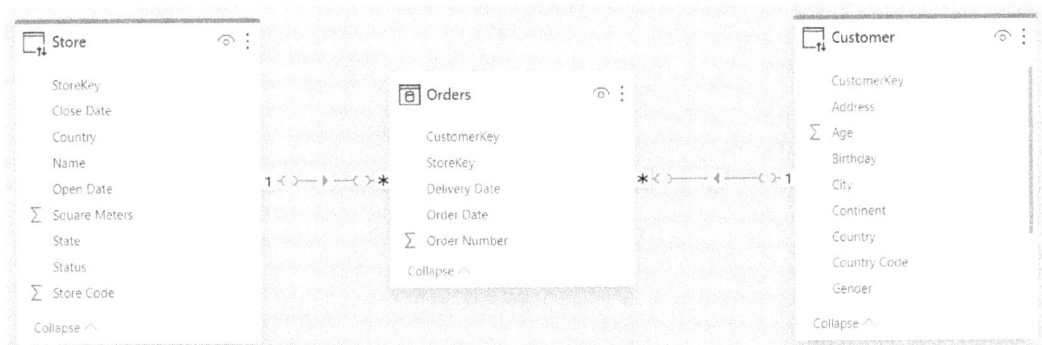

You might notice that we did not create any relationship with *Date*. The reason is that the query we want to optimize does not use the relationship with *Date* – it actually removes its effect through REMOVEFILTERS –therefore, the relationship would be useless.

We modify the original DAX query to take advantage of the new Orders table, still returning the required result. Indeed, we can use COUNTROWS on *Orders* instead of DISTINCTCOUNT on *Sales[Order Number]*:

```
EVALUATE
SUMMARIZECOLUMNS (
    'Date'[Year],
    'Date'[Month Number],
    "# Open Orders",
        VAR MinDate =
            MIN ( 'Date'[Date] )
        VAR MaxDate =
            MAX ( 'Date'[Date] )
        VAR Result =
            CALCULATE (
                COUNTROWS ( Orders ),
                Orders[Order Date] <= MaxDate,
                Orders[Delivery Date] >= MinDate,
                REMOVEFILTERS ( 'Date' )
            )
        RETURN
            Result
)
```

Running the query produces a much better result.

Total	SE CPU	Line	Subclass	Duration	CPU	Par.	Rows	KB	Timeline
550 ms	1,707 ms x12.6	1	SQL	3	2	x0.7			
		3	Scan	13	219	x16.8	3,284	26	
FE 414 ms 75.3%	SE 136 ms 24.7%	4	SQL	3	2	x0.7			
		6	Scan	14	0		3,392	27	
SE Queries 5	SE Cache 0 0.0%	8	Scan	103	1,484	x14.4	44,656	524	

The structure of the queries is the same as before. The queries retrieving *Orders[Order Date]* and *Orders[Delivery Date]* are now xmSQL queries, as is the final one, which is way faster. This is the code of the last xmSQL query:

```
SELECT
    'Orders'[Order Date],
    'Orders'[Delivery Date],
    COUNT ( )
FROM 'Orders'
WHERE
    'Orders'[Order Date] IN ( 43762.000000, 40424.000000, 40718.000000, 42988.000000, 41024.000000, 43014.000000,
41536.000000, 43694.000000, 43072.000000, 42673.000000..[3,281 total values, not all displayed] ) VAND
    'Orders'[Delivery Date] IN ( 40957.000000, 42038.000000, 43261.000000, 40844.000000, 42325.000000, 42343.000000,
40376.000000, 40501.000000, 40430.000000, 42658.000000..[3,389 total values, not all displayed] ) ;
```

However, the work has not been done yet. We still have several optimization steps to perform and a minor problem to solve.

Having added a VertiPaq table, the model now contains a VertiPaq continent, and we need to evaluate the amount of RAM we are using to obtain the boost in performance. A quick analysis of the VertiPaq storage in DAX Studio shows the following consumption for the *Orders* table.

Name	Cardinality	Total Size ↓	Data	Dictionary	Hier Size
▲ **Orders**	**94,094,678**	**4,559,057,092**	**735,871,688**	**3,055,429,2...**	**767,756,112**
Order Number	94,094,678	4,017,754,832	250,931,144	3,014,066,248	752,757,440
CustomerKey	1,868,084	306,902,904	250,931,144	41,027,072	14,944,688
Delivery Date	3,389	127,941,708	127,747,160	167,428	27,120
Order Date	3,281	106,349,856	106,157,840	165,760	26,256
StoreKey	74	96,136	92,880	2,648	608

The *Orders* table uses 4.5 gigabytes of RAM to hold 94M rows. The *Order Number* column uses most of the table space. Reducing the table size seems like an interesting goal.

It turns out that we do not need the *Order Number* column at all. The query is counting the number of rows, and it is not performing any distinct count. Therefore, we can remove the column entirely without affecting the performance of the query, but it will save a large amount of memory. Also, removing the attribute hierarchies from all the table columns is a good option. The result is the following.

Name	Cardinality	Total Size ↓	Data	Dictionary	Hier Size
⊿ **Orders**	**94,094,678**	**526,303,588**	**484,940,544**	**41,363,044**	**0**
CustomerKey	1,868,084	291,958,216	250,931,144	41,027,072	0
Delivery Date	3,389	127,914,588	127,747,160	167,428	0
Order Date	3,281	106,323,600	106,157,840	165,760	0
StoreKey	74	95,528	92,880	2,648	0

The test query works fine. However, the careful reader might notice that we are storing the *Orders[CustomerKey]* column with a cardinality of more than 1M values, and we are using the column for a relationship. This is going to generate an error as soon as we try to slice by any attribute of Customer, like with the following DAX query:

```
EVALUATE
SUMMARIZECOLUMNS (
    Customer[Continent],
    'Date'[Year],
    "# Open Orders",
        VAR MinDate =
            MIN ( 'Date'[Date] )
        VAR MaxDate =
            MAX ( 'Date'[Date] )
        VAR Result =
            CALCULATE (
                COUNTROWS ( Orders ),
                Orders[Order Date] <= MaxDate,
                Orders[Delivery Date] >= MinDate,
                REMOVEFILTERS ( 'Date' )
            )
        RETURN
            Result
)
ORDER BY [Continent], [Year]
```

Indeed, the result is an error.

The resultset of a query to external data source has exceeded the maximum allowed size of '1000000' rows.

Total	SE CPU	Line	Subclass	Duration	CPU	Par.	Rows	KB	Timeline
2,592 ms	70 ms	1	SQL	3	3	x1.0			
	x1.4	3	Scan	21	31	x1.5	3,284	26	
FE	SE	4	SQL	3	2	x0.7			
2,542 ms	50 ms								
98.1%	1.9%	6	Scan	20	31	x1.6	3,392	27	
		7	SQL	3	3	x1.0			
SE Queries	SE Cache								
5	0								
	0.0%								

Total DQ
9 ms

```
SELECT TOP (1000001) [t0].[CustomerKey],
    [t0].[Continent]
FROM ([dbo].[Customer]) AS [t0]
GROUP BY [t0].[CustomerKey],
    [t0].[Continent]
```

If we want to maintain the capability of slicing by customer attributes, the simplest and most effective way of obtaining the goal is to define the *Customer* table storage as Dual.

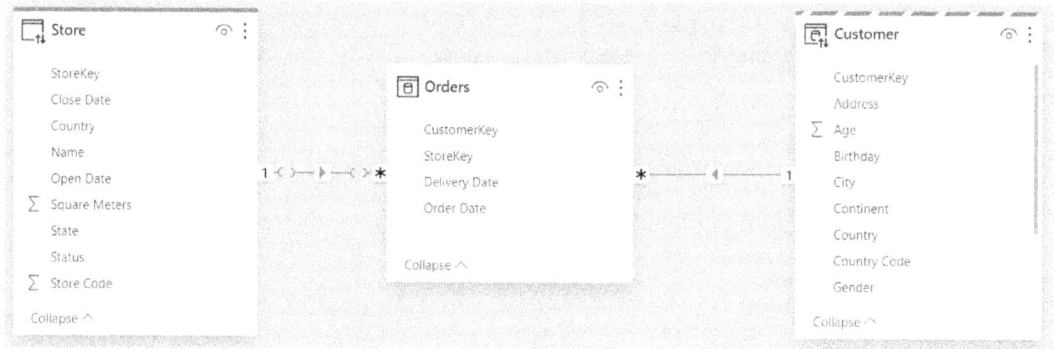

By storing the *Customer* table in the VertiPaq continent, the relationship between *Orders* and *Customer* is a regular VertiPaq relationship, and the limit of 1M rows is no longer present. Our test query runs fine, mixing SQL and xmSQL code to produce the result.

Total	SE CPU	Line	Subclass	Duration	CPU	Par.	Rows	KB	Timeline
373 ms	2,488 ms	1	SQL	2	2	x1.0			
	x10.5	3	Scan	12	234	x19.5	3,284	26	
FE	SE	4	SQL	3	2	x0.7			
135 ms	238 ms								
36.2%	63.8%	6	Scan	13	0		3,392	27	
		8	Scan	207	2,250	x10.9	120,170	1,409	
SE Queries	SE Cache								
6	0	10	Scan	1	0		6	1	
	0.0%								

A final look at the metrics of the database is useful to get a picture of the RAM used to speed up the query.

Name	Cardinality	Total Size ↓	Data	Dictionary	Hier Size
⊿ **Orders**	**94,094,678**	**531,285,156**	**484,940,544**	**41,363,044**	**0**
CustomerKey	1,868,084	291,958,216	250,931,144	41,027,072	0
Delivery Date	3,389	127,914,588	127,747,160	167,428	0
Order Date	3,281	106,323,600	106,157,840	165,760	0
StoreKey	74	95,528	92,880	2,648	0
⊿ **Customer**	**1,868,084**	**265,474,072**	**26,110,360**	**201,948,752**	**37,414,960**
Address	1,109,554	83,032,400	4,981,688	69,174,264	8,876,448
Name	1,224,584	77,805,232	4,981,688	63,026,856	9,796,688
CustomerKey	1,868,084	60,953,448	4,981,688	41,027,072	14,944,688
Zip Code	374,548	23,478,720	2,762,320	17,720,000	2,996,400
City	74,311	7,109,456	2,730,312	3,784,648	594,496
Birthday	24,493	4,742,636	3,736,304	810,380	195,952
Age	67	1,443,772	1,441,632	1,596	544
State	616	1,298,840	223,232	1,070,664	4,944
State Code	571	1,298,056	223,232	1,070,248	4,576
Gender	2	1,113,456	47,728	1,065,696	32
Country Code	8	1,065,960	136	1,065,744	80
Country	8	1,065,960	136	1,065,744	80
Continent	3	1,065,872	136	1,065,704	32

We might save some of the 37Mb used for the hierarchies by removing attribute hierarchies from *Customer* columns like *CustomerKey* and *Zip Code* if they are not displayed in the reports.

Conclusions

Complex models are the most challenging among the various types of semantic models. To properly optimize a complex model, you must use all the knowledge about the simpler semantic models and then merge all the information together in order to apply effective solutions.

A complex model inherits all the limitations and drawbacks of its components. However, on the bright side, a complex model can display great performance with a limited impact on RAM. A good Tabular model author should know all the internals of the simpler models and how the formula engine coordinates the different storage engines to author complex models efficiently.

Alberto Ferrari and **Marco Russo** co-founded SQLBI, where they publish frequent articles about DAX and other Microsoft tools.

They are regular speakers at major international conferences such as Microsoft Fabric Conference and SQLBits. Both currently teach, consult, and mentor on Microsoft Business Intelligence technologies.

www.sqlbi.com

Latest books

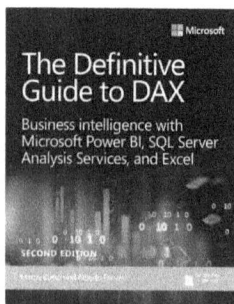

The Definitive Guide to DAX, Second Edition

Microsoft Press

DAX Patterns, Second Edition

SQLBI